THE DEMOCRATIC EXPERIMENT

THE DEMOCRATIC EXPERIMENT

NEW DIRECTIONS IN AMERICAN POLITICAL HISTORY

Edited by

MEG JACOBS

WILLIAM J. NOVAK

JULIAN E. ZELIZER

PRINCETON UNIVERSITY PRESS

PRINCETON AND OXFORD

Copyright 2003 by Princeton University Press
Published by Princeton University Press, 41 William Street, Princeton, New Jersey 08540
In the United Kingdom: Princeton University Press, 3 Market Place,
Woodstock, Oxfordshire OX20 1SY
All Rights Reserved

Library of Congress Cataloging-in-Publication Data

The democratic experiment : new directions in American political history.
Edited by Meg Jacobs, William J. Novak, and Julian E. Zelizer
p. cm.
Includes bibliographical references and index
ISBN 0-691-11376-9 (alk. paper) — ISBN 0-691-11377-7 (pbk. : alk. paper)
1. United States—Politics and government—Historiography. 2. United States—Politics
and government. 3. Political culture—United States—History. 4. Democracy—United
States—History. 5. Federal government—United States—History. I. Jacobs, Meg,
1969– II. Novak, William J., 1961– III. Zelizer, Julian E.

E183.D46 2003
320.973—dc21   2002192499

British Library Cataloging-in-Publication Data is available

This book has been composed in Sabon
Printed on acid-free paper. ∞
www.pupress.princeton.edu
Printed in the United States of America
10 9 8 7 6 5 4 3 2 1

To Abigail Helen and Sophia Miriam

CONTENTS

CONTRIBUTORS

Brian Balogh is Associate Professor of History at the University of Virginia and codirector of the American Political Development Program at the Miller Center of Public Affairs. He is the author of *Chain Reaction: Expert Debate and Public Participation in American Nuclear Power* (1991) and is completing two works about the rise of big government: *Before the State: Reconciling Public and Private in Nineteenth-Century America* (to be published by Cambridge University Press) and "*Building a Modern State: Gifford Pinchot and the Tangled Roots of Modern Administration in the United States.*"

Sven Beckert is Dunwalke Associate Professor at Harvard University, where he teaches nineteenth-century United States history. He is the author of *The Monied Metropolis: New York City and the Consolidation of the American Bourgeoisie* (2001). Beckert wrote the essay in this volume while being a fellow at the Center for Scholars and Writers in New York City. Currently, he is at work on a book on the global connections fostered by nineteenth-century capitalism, *The Empire of Cotton: A Global History*, to be published by Alfred A. Knopf.

Rebecca Edwards is Associate Professor of History at Vassar College and the author of *Angels in the Machinery: Gender in American Party Politics from the Civil War to the Progressive Era* (1997). She is working on a narrative history of the late-nineteenth-century United States and a biography of Populist orator Mary Elizabeth Lease.

Joanne B. Freeman is Professor of History at Yale University and author of *Affairs of Honor: National Politics in the New Republic* (2001), and *Alexander Hamilton: Writings* (2001). Her next book will explore the culture of Congress in antebellum America.

Meg Jacobs is Assistant Professor of History at MIT. She is completing a book, *Pocketbook Politics in Twentieth-Century America*, to be published with Princeton University Press. She has published articles in the *Journal of American History* and *International Labor and Working-Class History*. Her next book will explore the political economy of postwar America.

Richard R. John is Associate Professor of History at the University of Chicago at Illinois. He is the author of *Spreading the News: The American Postal System from Franklin to Morse* (1995). He is currently writing

Making Connections: Inventing American Telecommunications, 1839–1919, which will be published by Harvard University Press. He was the Lloyd Lewis Fellow at the Newberry Library in 2002–2003 and the co-winner of the 2002 Harold F. Williamson Prize from the Business History Conference.

Ira Katznelson is Ruggles Professor of Political Science and History at Columbia University. His books include *Black Men, White Cities* (1973), *City Trenches* (1981), *Schooling for All* (1985, coauthored with Margaret Weir), *Marxism and the City* (1992), *Liberalism's Crooked Circle* (1996), and *Desolation and Enlightenment: Political Knowledge after Total War, Totalitarianism, and the Holocaust* (2003).

James T. Kloppenberg is Professor of History at Harvard University. He is the author of *Uncertain Victory: Social Democracy and Progressivism in European and American Thought, 1870–1920* (1986), awarded the Merle Curti Prize by the Organization of American Historians; and *The Virtues of Liberalism* (1998); and is coeditor, with Richard Wightman Fox, of *A Companion to American Thought* (1995). Current projects include a history of democracy in Europe and America and a study of history and critical theory.

Matthew D. Lassiter is Assistant Professor of History at the University of Michigan, specializing in the political, social, and metropolitan history of the twentieth-century United States. He is the coeditor of *The Moderates' Dilemma: Massive Resistance to School Desegregation in Virginia* (1998) and the author of *The Silent Majority: Suburban Politics in the Sunbelt South*, which will be published by Princeton University Press.

William J. Novak is Associate Professor of History at the University of Chicago and Research Fellow at the American Bar Foundation. He is the author of *The People's Welfare: Law and Regulation in Nineteenth-Century America* (1996).

Thomas J. Sugrue is Bicentennial Class of 1940 Professor of History and Sociology at the University of Pennsylvania. His publications include *The Origins of the Urban Crisis* (1996), winner of the Bancroft Prize and several other awards; *W.E.B. DuBois, Race, and the City* (with Michael B. Katz, 1998); and more than twenty-five articles on topics such as liberalism, urban history, race relations, affirmative action, labor, and public policy. He is currently finishing a book on the history of civil rights politics in the urban north and writing a history of America in the twentieth century.

Michael Vorenberg is Assistant Professor of History at Brown University. He is the author of *Final Freedom: The Civil War, the Abolition of Slavery, and the Thirteenth Amendment* (2001), and he is currently working on a book about the impact of the Civil War on American notions of citizenship.

Michael Willrich is Assistant Professor of History at Brandeis University. A former journalist, Willrich writes about the history of American law and society. He has just published his first book, *City of Courts: Socializing Justice in Progressive Era Chicago* (2003). His articles have appeared in the *Journal of American History*, *Law and History Review*, and the *Journal of Urban History*.

Julian E. Zelizer is Associate Professor of Public Policy, Public Administration and Political Science at the State University of New York at Albany. He is the author of *Taxing America: Wilbur D. Mills, Congress, and the State, 1945–1975* (1998), which was awarded the 1998 D. B. Hardeman Prize and the 2000 Ellis Hawley Prize. Zelizer, who has authored numerous articles and book chapters on American political history, is currently completing a history of congressional reform since 1945, which will be published with Cambridge University Press, and editing *The Reader's Companion to the American Congress*, which will be published with Houghton Mifflin. Zelizer is a coeditor of the Politics and Society in Twentieth-Century America book series of Princeton University Press. His writing has also appeared in the *New York Times*, *Los Angeles Times*, and *Albany Times Union*. Zelizer received his Ph.D. in history from the Johns Hopkins University.

ACKNOWLEDGMENTS

All books rely on the help of many individuals and organizations, and that is especially the case with an edited collection like this. This volume grew out of two conferences held at MIT in September 2000 and May 2001. We would like to thank MIT's Provost Fund, Dean's Fund, and History Faculty for their generous funding of those conferences. The Center for Comparative Legal History at the University of Chicago also provided additional support. We would like to thank all the contributors for making this a rewarding collaborative experience and for working hard on their many drafts. Elizabeth Sanders, David King, Jim Morone, and Sid Milkis read and commented on the essays, and for that we are thankful. Nelson Lichtenstein and Gary Gerstle provided helpful feedback on the volume's introduction. All of the readers' reports for this volume were extremely constructive. We want to thank especially Jim Kloppenberg and Ira Katznelson for their integral involvement from beginning to end. We are also deeply grateful to Brigitta van Rheinberg at Princeton University Press for her enthusiasm and support of this project. We would also like to thank William Hively for his great work as our copyeditor. Finally, the book is dedicated to Meg's daughter Abigail and Julian's daughter Sophia, both of whom were born during the course of this project. They are our proudest accomplishments.

THE DEMOCRATIC EXPERIMENT

Chapter One

THE DEMOCRATIC EXPERIMENT

NEW DIRECTIONS IN AMERICAN POLITICAL HISTORY

MEG JACOBS AND JULIAN E. ZELIZER

W E ARE NOW in a moment when American political history is flourishing. The contributors in this volume, who are all part of this exciting revitalization of the field, focus on two central questions. The first concerns the relationship of citizens to the government in a context where suspicion of a powerful state has been the overriding theme of American political culture. The second addresses the continually evolving mechanisms of democratic participation. As this volume shows, democracy in America has come alive in political contests over these two issues. Most modern democratic polities have confronted the need to legitimate the exercise of political authority, but that fact poses particular problems in the United States, where a fear of centralized power has left a distinctive mark on American political culture and institutional arrangements. From the beginning, Americans have fought protracted struggles over the exercise of strong central state authority. Given the institutional and cultural manifestations of antistatism, constructing a strong federal government was never easy. At the same time, the basic questions of who would be granted representation and how remained up for grabs. Despite the fact that America is the oldest democracy in the world, the means and extent of participation have never been settled. Although the founders articulated clear ideas about what representative government should be, the forms political power would take were constantly contested and transformed. The mechanisms linking enfranchised citizens to political leaders and the right to representation remained fluid. In essays that go from the founding through the late twentieth century, the authors offer a fresh historical examination of the political problems posed by democratic government and their complex resolutions.

Antistatism has operated as a powerful force in the history of American democracy. Having a long Anglo-American tradition, antistatism became concrete and institutionalized in the United States in battles over slavery, the rise of industrialized capitalism, and the centralizing and standardizing impulses of the Progressive–New Deal moment. As these essays explore, its multiple manifestations include the endurance of fragmented and locally based political institutions, a devotion to rigid constitutionalism, a reliance on political patronage over bureaucratic administration, the fear of interest groups corrupting politicians, a hostility to federal taxation, and more. Antistatism derives its strength in part because it has taken on so many different forms. Yet this book is not a tale about how a multifaceted antistatism prevented the growth of the federal government in America. Rather, many of the authors show how antistatism shaped the structure of the federal government in particular ways. The result was not simply a state that was weak by European standards, although this was one effect in many areas of public life, but a state that commanded significant political strength in numerous policy domains and one that substantially influenced American life. Furthermore, the authors suggest that the American state did not develop in a linear fashion. This is not a story of a nation that starts with no federal government and ends the twentieth century with a strong federal government. Rather, the pattern of state growth in America was one of fits and starts.

The authors also explore the changing meaning and mechanisms of representative government. The essays consider the relationship of political elites to the voting public, the political and voluntary institutions through which Americans gained their political standing, and mediating institutions that connected citizens to elected officials. Voluntary associations, political parties, interest groups, and other institutionalized forms of political representation have helped government actors enlarge the government that antistatism kept small. Throughout, fundamental questions of citizenship have served as an animating force of American democracy.

By exploring how struggles over the role of the central state and the character of representative democracy shaped public life, the work in this volume reveals a revitalization of American political history well under way with exciting possibilities for the future. The essays examine pivotal moments and manifestations of the challenge to translate democratic preferences into public policy. In tackling central questions about the American democratic experiment, the contributors all strive to integrate institutions, culture, and society into fresh accounts of the nation's political past, starting with the founding. As historians, we focus on specific times and places and ground our analysis in narratives. Influenced by two new approaches to political history that have arisen since the 1960s—the new institutionalism as well as social and cultural political history (which we label sociocultural political history)—we take seriously the interplay between specific contingent factors and large structural forces. Integrating an institutional analysis with the study of social groups, we document the precise and changing relationships between state and society that have profoundly influenced democratic politics for over two hundred years.

Reconceiving American Political History

In the last three decades, scholars working across disciplinary boundaries and subfields have developed exciting new approaches to studying America's public life, polity, and the exercise of political power.[1] Despite the professional decline of political history since the 1960s,[2] warnings about the intellectual death of the field were, in retrospect, greatly exaggerated. Historians, along with colleagues in political science, economics, and sociology, fundamentally reconceptualized American political history. This section focuses on the emergence of two important methodological approaches to political history—the new institutionalism (which is composed of the subfields of the organizational synthesis, policy history, and American Political Development) and sociocultural political history—to understand the value of each and the opportunities created by bringing them together.

In the turbulent 1960s, a generation of scholars developed a stinging critique of political history as it had been practiced. Amid struggles over civil rights and Vietnam, the New Left criticized the liberal view of American history, which saw little of the social conflict that beset European nations. The liberal view—a depiction of a shared ideological consensus that revolved around individualism and property rights—left little room to account for ongoing battles over race relations and social class. Political historians, the new generation said, had falsely presented a handful of political elites, particularly presidents, as embodiments of a progressive national experience. Moreover, the cycle of the presidential synthesis, in the minds of these critics, did not accurately capture the evolution of politics.[3] Younger historians, who came of age in an era when college students railed against President Lyndon Johnson and his fellow Democratic leaders, also doubted an older generation of progressive historians who believed that the expansion of the federal government had stemmed from a desire to serve "the people," resulting in their triumph over vested interests. They were convinced by a group of maverick historians in this decade who said that liberalism had been an ideology that serviced big corporations, which dominated twentieth-century government despite its democratic rhetoric.[4] Those critiques led to two seemingly divergent responses. Within the historical discipline, a social and cultural history revolution took place that pushed scholars to broaden their canvas to emphasize the study of American history from the "bottom up" and at the local level, turning to questions such as class formation, gender relations, and cultural consciousness. At the same time, other scholars, in history and in political science, also broadened their inquiries, but rather than studying social groups, they looked at how institutional forces shaped and limited political development and public policy evolution.

Reacting against the liberal, president-centered history of midcentury, new institutionalists shifted their focus to the structure of American government and its impact on public policy.[5] Much of the scholarship started with the "organizational synthesis" in the 1960s and 1970s, an analysis that saw the emergence of large-scale national institutions, including the corporation, professions, and administrative state between 1880 and 1920 as the most significant development in modern American history. Seeking to understand American politics, scholars such as Samuel Hays, Ellis Hawley, Morton Keller, Robert Wiebe, Barry Karl, and Louis Galambos were more interested in the history of bureaucracies, commissions, and expert staffs than in presidents or cycles of reform.[6] For them, the central dividing line in American politics was not liberalism versus conservatism but, rather, what they saw as nineteenth-century localism and parochialism versus twentieth-century nationalization and efficiency. Consciously downplaying the differences between presidential administrations and personalities, their work emphasized the long-term structural shifts that shaped conditions within which all political actors operated. For instance, the organizational synthesis showed how much of the New Deal reflected policies and institutions that had been created well before the 1930s. Their research was rooted in the functionalist outlook that took its inspiration from Parsonian sociology and prevailed in the social sciences at the time.[7]

The organizational synthesis inspired policy historians to analyze contemporary political debates and to break free from president-centered narratives. Policy historians opened up the arena of politics to include the unwieldy world of policy experts, think tanks, lobbyists, academics, bureaucrats, staffers, and congressional committees that shaped the workings of government in Washington and state capitals. They were joined by those working in the new field of public history, whose earliest practitioners were deeply committed to tackling policy problems (in the 1980s and 1990s, the field would reorient itself around museums, historical tourist attractions, and computer technology). Based on a course that they taught at Harvard's Kennedy School of Government, Richard E. Neustadt and Ernest R. May published a widely popular book, used to teach policy and public administration students, that outlined the practical uses of historical analysis to policy makers.[8] Although policy historians never formed an association, through their journal, monographs, and conferences they created an innovative interpretation of political history that incorporated a broad range of actors.[9] In 1989, Donald Critchlow and Peri Arnold launched the *Journal of Policy History* as the main forum for this scholarship.

As a whole, public policy history presented several different types of arguments. Some scholars attempted to show how particular cultural assumptions were embedded in policies, others looked at lost alternatives from the past, and many hoped to provide historical correctives to assumptions and analogies that were used in contemporary debate.[10] In this subfield, it became clear that the history of policies revolved around the stages of the policy-making process (agenda setting, legislation, and implementation), which did not always fit neatly into the standard chronology of political history. In fact, policy scholars suggested that there were multiple histories taking place in politics simultaneously. Each domain had its own historical trajectory, even though the trajectories sometimes intersected.[11] Numerous social historians, moreover, contributed to policy history by studying how welfare and education policies impacted, and were shaped by, individuals who received or were denied benefits.[12] Before the start of the *Journal of Policy History*, some of the most original research in this subfield was published in the *Journal of Social History*.[13]

The organizational synthesis also created one of the foundations for another strand of the new institutionalism: American Political Development.[14] During the 1980s, a group of political scientists and sociologists brought historical institutionalism back into the study of politics. In contrast to the tradition of using historical case studies to prove broader analytic arguments, these political scientists argued that politics was a fundamentally historical process.[15] At a time when mainstream political science was moving toward presenting politics as a competition between rational actors who constantly re-created the political playing field—and as a response to previous models of political science that focused on Marxism, pluralism, crisis theory, and electoral realignment—American Political Development offered a compelling alternative to political scientists and sociologists working in different fields ranging from comparative politics to political theory. Scholars such as Theda Skocpol, Eldon Eisenach, Martin Shefter, Amy Bridges, Elizabeth Sanders, Stephen Skowronek, Ira Katznelson, and Richard Bensel argued that politics was profoundly historical and could not be understood otherwise. When these scholars focused on the problem of "American exceptionalism," meaning the reasons why America's welfare state seemed meager in comparison to European welfare states, the issue that animated most of the research in the 1980s and 1990s, their answers usually came back to institutions. Each historical period, they said, took place within preexisting institutional structures. As a result, politicians, activists, and organizations always operated within the institutional context that they inherited while newer institutions were layered on top of the old. In a book that helped shape the field, Stephen Skowronek revealed how Progressive Era reformers were forced to construct the modern administrative state over, rather than instead of, the nineteenth-century state of courts and parties.[16] Acknowledging the significance of "bounded change,"[17] this scholarship stressed the influence of path dependence whereby state builders were constrained by policies and institutions that had been put into place during earlier eras. In contrast to interpretations that stressed the power of big business or the weakness of working-class consciousness, practitioners of American Political Development created a "polity-centered" approach that claimed that the most important constraints on state building involved factors such as federalism, the separation of power, and the underdeveloped bureaucratic capacity of American government.[18]

In looking at institutional settings, American Political Development portrayed state builders as having their own autonomous agendas and interests, rather than as individuals who responded only to external social and economic pressure.[19] There were many important analytic concepts that this subfield introduced beyond the claim that institutions mattered. For instance, they used the term "policy feedback" to explain how new policies reconfigured politics. In a landmark work, Theda Skocpol argued that the corruption of Civil War pensions in the nineteenth century caused social insurance reformers in the Progressive and New Deal eras to avoid similar programs that depended on general revenue.[20] Other scholars looked at how the structure of the legislative process played a pivotal role in racial politics, since it gave southern legislators disproportionate influence during critical moments of state building, enabling them to protect existing patterns of race relations.[21] This literature, along with the organizational synthesis, triggered several political scientists and historians to look again at the early republic and antebellum periods to show how national political institutions were extremely important in an era that they felt their colleagues had erroneously considered stateless.[22] Historians such as Alan Brinkley who were interested in the fate of the New Deal order and the welfare state recognized that they could not ignore classic questions of statecraft.[23] To advance the subfield of American Political Development, the founders of this group launched a journal, *Studies in American Political Development*, and a section in the American Political Science Association.

While institutional political history looked to structures of governance, sociocultural political history explored social movements and political culture from a nonelite perspective.[24] Earlier generations of historians had acknowledged that forces representing the "people" were important to shaping politics, but they had focused their attention on political elites. In contrast, sociocultural political history devoted its archival analysis to political life outside of the White House and beyond Capitol Hill. They rejected the classic arguments of Louis Hartz, who had proclaimed in the 1950s that American political culture had been defined by a liberal consensus since the founding. Instead, they depicted a nation that was replete with bitter social and ideological conflict that bubbled up from the grass roots, where the basic terms of democracy were constantly contested. These historians followed the lead of the short-lived "new political history" in the 1970s, whose practitioners used quantitative techniques to determine what factors motivated voting behavior.[25] Although a bountiful literature emerged on the nineteenth-century party system that integrated voting behavior with political institutions, interest in the "new political history" significantly diminished over the next two decades, as social historians believed that electoral studies defined politics too narrowly.[26]

Covering many different themes and issues, sociocultural political history integrated nonelites into familiar narratives of the past. In a pathbreaking work, for example, Eric Foner's synthesis of Reconstruction recast the story by placing freed African-American citizens at the front and center of the battle to shape this macropolitical event.[27] Lawrence Goodwyn, casting aside Richard Hofstadter's portrait of the Populist movement as backward, marginal, and irrational, claimed these farmers as true democrats.[28] Labor historians, moreover, offered some of the most stimulating social histories of politics. In his study of labor in nineteenth-century New York City, Sean Wilentz showed how workers achieved a degree of class consciousness and were able to mobilize in electoral politics by drawing on the ideology of republicanism (rather than socialism) that dated back to the American Revolution.[29] David Montgomery traced the complex relationship between changes on the shop floor at the turn of the century and organized labor's unfolding involvement with the modern state and Democratic party.[30] Lizabeth Cohen synthesized popular culture, social history, unions, and political parties in explaining how workers made a New Deal.[31]

Whereas social historians looked at the historical influence of those who were outside formal positions of public authority, cultural historians examined the ideological assumptions and underlying rules that governed political behavior from government elites on down. Influenced by anthropologists such as Clifford Geertz and philosophers such as Thomas Kuhn, scholars of political culture tapped into a vigorous debate about the ideologies and discourses that had shaped American politics since the Revolution, one subject area where politics remained central in the historical profession.[32] Blending cultural, intellectual, social, and political history, the literature on political culture looked at how ideologies, languages, and symbols shaped all political actors in given historical periods.[33] An important effect of the work on political culture was to inspire many gender historians to reenter the debate over the political past. Moving beyond initial efforts to document women's exclusion from politics, gender historians used the concept of political culture to reveal how women were influential in all periods of American history. Paula Baker, for example, argued that there were two different political cultures in the United States before the 1920s, each of which revolved around distinct conceptions of gender. While women did not participate in male-centered party politics, Baker claimed that through voluntary associations, female reformers took the lead in social welfare activities and developed new forms of political participation that would later be absorbed by the modern state.[34] Linda Gordon, Eileen Boris, and Alice Kessler-Harris, in their studies on the welfare state between the Progressive Era and New Deal and World War II, demonstrated how gendered ideas of work and citizenship shaped domestic policy.[35]

Bringing together the new institutionalism and sociocultural political history offers today's historians methods for revisiting the study of politics while responding to the powerful criticisms that were raised about the field in the 1960s. In the 1980s and 1990s there was little collective sense that political history was vibrant, especially since practitioners of the new institutionalism and sociocultural political history often worked independently of one another. In large part, that sense reflected the professional status of the field rather than its intellectual vitality. Many scholars were constructing exciting approaches to political history even though the field seemed professionally defunct. The institutional approach helped scholars situate political elites within specific contexts rather than depicting them as embodiments of the nation. The new institutionalism revealed the complex institutional settings within which political elites operated and broadened the historical canvas beyond presidencies to include bureaucracies, legislators, staffers, experts, and policies. The institutional approach also forced historians to develop a more realistic understanding of the constraints that faced all politicians at any given moment in history rather than presenting a nation that could constantly be re-created with each election. Political change, it was now clear, often evolved in response to developments within the political realm and not just from external social pressures, as both older political and newer social historians had claimed. There was growing evidence that preceding institutional relationships structured political change. At the same time, the sociocultural approach pushed historians to integrate a history of social conflict into their analysis of politics and to incorporate nonelite groups into their narratives about political history. It enabled them to consider categories such as gender and race as well as factors such as symbols, ideology, and rhetoric. This collection combines institutional analysis with the study of social groups and culture, synthesizing the past two decades of scholarship into new understandings of American political history.

Toward New Directions

The authors in this collection examine key moments of transformations in American institutional arrangements and reigning political culture. In many instances, tensions within political institutions themselves, as much as demands from society, generated reform. Several essays examine how antistatism has expressed itself in several overlapping guises from localism and decentralization to a resistance to federal intervention and aversion to federal taxes. That belief, constructed and reconstructed, resulted in cultural ideologies and institutions that complicated efforts to rule at the national level. Other essays explore the evolution of mediating institutions and governing arrangements of representation to accommodate the various strains of American antistatism. In focusing on American politics, these essays explore the cultural and social bases of policy making and their interactions with the institutional structures of government. As a whole, they stress both structure and change in exploring the historical evolution of American democracy.

From the nation's founding, Americans have balanced antistatist sentiment with the need to endow a central government with legitimacy and authority. In her essay Joanne Freeman shows how, among a generation fearful of an overweening state, the personal reputation and honor of the nation's political elites stood in for elaborate bureaucracy and mass politics. As she puts it, "In a government lacking formal precedent and institutional traditions, reputation was the glue that held the polity together." That perhaps made sense in an age when much of politics transpired among a relatively small number of elites who had fashioned the national community. In the 1790s the French Revolution forced the new nation to face a series of crises that would at once challenge the reigning political culture and foster institutional innovations. Soon after George Washington famously counseled against entangling alliances in his Farewell Address, the public found itself divided over France. There ensued a heated and often acrimonious debate in which each side slandered the other's views in newspapers. Given the heavy reliance on personal reputation in an era that preceded the acceptance of political parties, these attacks threatened the very future of the republic, and thus political leaders sought to stifle libelous attacks. By considering cultural factors in examining and decoding political events, Freeman explains why some of the Founding Fathers sought to undermine, through passage of the Sedition Act of 1798, the freedom of speech that many of them had just fought a revolution to obtain. As Freeman concludes, this crisis captures "a government of character striving to become a government of rules within its new constitutional framework."

As the nation grew beyond face-to-face conventions and communications among a handful of political elite, the polity expanded. Although most public power centered in local communities, there were several areas where central governing agencies emerged. One of the most important was the Post Office, through which news—a major vehicle for civic life—disseminated. The Post Office Act of 1792 had facilitated the expansion of the press, revealing how institutional changes shaped political developments. War in the early republic had a similar effect. The nineteenth-century state was not merely the modern administrative twentieth-century state writ small. The bureaucracy never approached the same complexity, the social welfare and regulatory system paled by comparison, there was not a substantial federal income tax system, and the federal government did not engage in the type of foreign military campaigns and domestic investigative activities that would characterize the twentieth century. Nonetheless, the eight thousand local offices of the Post Office did reach into all corners, linking together what was otherwise, as historian Robert Wiebe labeled it, a nation of island communities, and this network even created a growing sense of entitlement among many Americans that the government would provide more help with the domestic infrastructure. Yet, as Richard John argues, the threat of centralized power greatly concerned some Jacksonian-era Americans, particularly southerners who feared that government-assisted economic development would shift political and economic power toward nonslaveholding states. Those fears of a strong federal government led Jacksonians to embrace political parties as an antidote. As John suggests, the patronage of mass parties emerged as a way to place governmental positions under local political control. Thus this nascent state created the technical preconditions for the rise of the mass party, an institution that bound together governance and politics in a nineteenth-century spoils system of patronage.

In the nineteenth century, and in important ways in the twentieth as well, American political life largely revolved around the local rather than the national polity. The institutions and political customs of patronage, localized parties, and federalism conditioned the exercise of central authority. In fact, as William Novak argues, Americans invested so little stock in the authority of a central state that a national notion of citizenship, one that outlined rights and responsibilities, simply did not exist in the antebellum era. Put simply, Americans did not share a singular definition of themselves as citizens of a nation, but rather, they understood their political standing through participation in local associations. Alexis de Tocqueville famously characterized Americans as a nation of joiners and pointed to their rich tradition of voluntary associations as evidence of a vibrant democratic culture. As Novak explains, these organizations— from cemeteries to churches to corporations to cities—all received recognition as public entities under an elaborate system of common laws that outlined rules of membership. In these local bodies civic liberty and self-government came alive. Yet Novak is quick to point out that while Americans joined institutions for all aspects of life, their common laws of membership—their "rights and duties, privileges and penalties, and inclusions and exclusions"—were embedded in undemocratic hierarchies of status. Common-law relationships such as master-servant, guardian-ward, and parent-child constituted "a mode of governance—a method of distributing public power and regulating the allocation of personal rights and duties." Indeed, Novak claims that this system, of which slavery was of course a central part, collapsed when, in the absence of a national law of citizenship, common laws could not sufficiently govern the rights of masters, slaves, and freed blacks beyond local borders.

Most changes to America's governing framework in the nineteenth century occurred under the direction of local and state government officials and within the boundaries of constitutional law. Through the amendment process, the founders had crafted a mechanism to allow for institutional change, but Americans were reluctant to use it before the Civil War. As Michael Vorenberg explains in his essay, "an unchanging written Constitution held . . . the greatest promise of legitimizing the new nation" and providing a source of what he calls "protonationalism," albeit one defined more by its structure than its content. Unwillingness to amend the Constitution for purposes of social reform stood as a testament to the strength of constitutionalism. Given the centrality of the law to the polity and the propensity to legislate change, reform was both more difficult to enact and more powerful. When the Civil War broke the nation asunder however, that radical break enabled and indeed necessitated a fresh approach to the amendment process. Support of the Thirteenth Amendment to end slavery required not only a commitment to emancipation but also a broader rationale to justify amending the Constitution. The amending rationale the nation's politicians devised put into motion a new approach to governance when, a generation later amid rapid industrialization and urbanization, constitutional amendments would become yet another weapon in reformers' arsenals.

Following the Civil War, at a time when many aspects of politics seemed up for grabs, from suffrage to citizenship rights to notions of constitutionalism to the structure of government institutions, many citizens who had a vested interest in the status quo had much to fear.[36] At the local level, where the stakes were high and the interlocking processes of industrialization, urbanization, and immigration transformed the nation's cities, late-nineteenth-century localities spawned movements to limit democratic participation. As Sven Beckert's essay shows, the assimilation of immigrant newcomers into urban machine politics, even if not into the rest of American life, proved particularly problematic to an older governing elite who sought to restrict suffrage rights through constitutional reform. New York elites discovered, however, that it was difficult to take democratic rights away from citizens once they had them. Even though they failed, a shared set of ideological concerns encouraged northern elites to lend support to the Compromise of 1877, a deal that ended Reconstruction and undermined democracy in the South by preventing the full enfranchisement of African-Americans into the nation's representative system.

In the wake of Reconstruction, national politics began to shift attention away from the Civil War and toward the economy, largely as a response to the forces of industrialization that generated the dramatic upheavals of the Gilded Age. In the midst of rapid economic development, the ethnocultural regional loyalties that had been an important factor in partisan attachment throughout the century proved enduring. But questions of political economy were front and center during the Gilded Age, including the gold standard, the regulation of the marketplace, and the tariff.[37] Debates over the tariff, for instance, reflected different visions of economic growth and different regional economic interests that were shaping struggles over political economy. In this period, Republicans supported the tariff and other expansions of state power to promote prosperity and northern industrial power. In doing so, as Rebecca Edwards argues, they wrapped their programs in a particular domestic vision of the family-oriented male breadwinner. From fighting Mormonism to setting up the Freedmen's Bureau to supporting a high tariff, Republicans portrayed the use of expanded state authority as a campaign to uphold and protect the home. An elaborate system of Civil War pensions, articulated as a program to maintain stable domestic homes, built partisan loyalty and extended patronage from the local arena to the national. While there were multiple causes behind the enactment of federal legislation in these critical decades, the heavy reliance on domestic rhetoric shows how state builders brokered the new world through familiar traditions and social norms. Such policies not only appropriated the rhetoric of domestic ideology but also envisioned an expanded federal presence in the most intimate aspects of family life.

But there was no direct progression toward a modern administrative state. Nineteenth-century party politics, premised on patronage and services in exchange for votes, mobilized citizens for individual benefits but not in support of a bigger or radically different kind of state. Many historians and political scientists, such as Morton Keller and Stephen Skowronek, have documented the political and institutional obstacles to crafting a powerful administrative state.[38] In addition to the parties, most conventional narratives have presented the courts as a major roadblock to state development. While the Civil War may have freed the amendment process from the constraints of constitutionalism, the higher courts by and large hewed to a strict interpretation, proving resistant to an expansion of governmental authority. Local courts, especially the pervasive justice-of-the-peace system, were tied to partisan power. That system, where citizens and noncitizens alike felt public authority most readily, again demonstrates the interlocking web of local politics and governance. In an important finding, Michael Willrich demonstrates how Progressive Era urban courts abolished their justice-of-the-peace systems, replacing them with professionalized municipal courts signaling a halfway step to a modern state. Rather than simply clearing the way for new administrative agencies that, as of yet, had little political or constitutional standing, these municipal courts themselves became new administrative tribunals. In the process, they inscribed their own cultural assumptions about breadwinner domesticity into social policy. As local judicial institutions, this "court-based social governance" avoided the specter of a large and impersonal bureaucracy and thereby gained legitimacy.

While progressive reformers crafted new administrative mechanisms at the local level, politicians looked for new means to capture votes of ever broadening and diverse populations. The challenge of how to connect citizens and government was key as older nineteenth-century partisan loyalties had less hold and as government assumed greater administrative responsibilities. As Brian Balogh explores in his examination of Herbert Hoover's 1928 presidential campaign, interest groups became the twentieth-century version of the political party. Balogh shows that the turn to interest groups was not simply a functionalist response but rather a creative political adaptation that linked constituencies to administrative agencies and also organized electoral campaigns. The targeted style of identifying interest groups took its cue from the emergence of a consumer economy that segmented populations not by old categories of region, ethnicity, or party but by income, occupation, and gender. Whereas political parties of the nineteenth century limited the expansion of administrative and bureaucratic government, the interest groups of the twentieth century accommodated that kind of governmental growth by mobilizing citizens in support of particular public policies.

As much as politicians reconfigured constituencies and bound them together into electoral majorities, citizens at the grassroots level influenced state building from the bottom up. Politicians paid close attention to average voters as they crafted public policies and electoral appeals. Challenging the conventional wisdom that consumers remained politically insignificant until the 1970s, Meg Jacobs shows how they were pivotal during the Great Depression as they joined organized labor in pressuring Democrats into building programs that would ensure a federally enforced decent standard of living. Yet the grassroots pressure from consumers that strengthened state building during the New Deal and World War II was not easy to control. Many consumers turned against the state by the 1950s and 1960s. Estrangement between organized labor and the unorganized middle classes produced and prefigured a broader split between an increasingly insulated constellation of interest groups and a mass public ever more hostile to the state.

Perhaps the clearest manifestation of antistate sentiment found expression in broad opposition to taxes. As Julian Zelizer points out, only in times of emergency have politicians been able to raise direct and visible taxes with relative ease. Resistance to taxation at the federal and even local level dates as far back as the early republic.[39] Progressive Era state building preceded the federal income tax as the New Deal preceded the mass income tax. Those realities shaped how politicians built the state with citizens paying for earned benefits like Social Security and Medicare through earmarked contributions. World War II enabled the institutionalization of a mass income tax but did not guarantee popular support for ever increasing rates. High taxes could erode postwar expectations of abundance and increased living standards. Moreover, antitax populism remained strong especially as Cold War fears of totalitarian regimes reinforced an American aversion to centralized power. By looking at antitax sentiment, Zelizer reminds us that support for governmental programs does not automatically generate support for a fiscal state. While the federal government has grown, it has faced limits in large part by the resistance to pay for it. State builders overcame voters' resistance but only by continuing to link taxes to specific benefits, as the success of Medicare demonstrated. Given the limits to additional public spending, Americans constructed a private welfare state that at times undercut support for increased governmental services.

American ambivalence about a strong central state meant that powerful local institutions shaped and structured federal power. Indeed, since the Progressive Era, local governments continued to expand and centralize their administrative and regulatory capacities in no small part to facilitate new federal programs under their control. Here local public officials gave meaning and expression to expanded federal power, in the process themselves becoming more bureaucratized. While we know much about the creation of the New Deal, we know far less about how these programs reconfigured local politics, or how their distribution was determined and administered locally. Thomas Sugrue shows how President Johnson's Great Society programs, particularly the War on Poverty, which envisioned the creation of new community organizations outside local machines, faced constraints as had the New Deal. The Supreme Court, after a short burst of federal-empowering decisions, shifted much authority back toward the states in crucial policy areas such as redistricting and school integration. Sugrue explains that local administration enabled racial and class biases to influence the delivery of state largesse.

Nowhere did antistate, localist sentiment emerge more strongly than in the growing suburbs of postwar America. According to Matthew Lassiter, suburban middle-class voters developed an ideology revolving around property rights, individualism, and limited government, even though the suburbs themselves had been shaped by federal programs such as tax credits for home owners and the GI Bill. Inadvertently, government programs gave rise to a constituency that opposed further government intervention. This suburban ideology became a primary obstacle to Great Society programs that aimed at ameliorating racism. Democrats and Republicans vied for these suburban middle-class voters in an era when stable political majorities proved elusive. Suburban ideological views ensured that federal programs to tackle racism would not advance.

Since the founding, practical questions of democratic governance have forced Americans to negotiate between antistatism (in both institutions and culture) and the need to rule. Today Americans have a large central state but one that accommodates antistatism. When central administration grew, local governments did not wither away, and the institutional mechanisms and cultural legacy of popular participation remained. Moreover, the means of attaching citizens to the state have continuously evolved. In exploring that process, the authors range in the degree to which they emphasize questions of political legitimacy, notions of the public, and the structure of governmental institutions, but these issues are embedded in all the pieces. In their sweeping conclusions, James Kloppenberg and Ira Katznelson argue for the promise of a new political history.[40] By drawing on new insights about public policy, political institutions, social movements, and political culture, as Kloppenberg and Katznelson point out, today's generation of historians stands poised to integrate and capitalize on the new institutionalism and sociocultural history. Collectively, these essays demonstrate the exciting potential for applying social and cultural approaches to politics and conversely analyzing the institutional setting for political battles.

NOTES

1. Mark H. Leff, "Revisioning U.S. Political History," *American Historical Review* 100 (1995): 829–53. Steven M. Gillon, "The Future of Political History," *Journal of Policy History* 9 (1997): 240–55; Joel H. Silbey, "The State of American Political History at the Millennium: The Nineteenth Century as a Test Case," *Journal of Policy History* 11 (1999): 1–30.

2. William E. Leuchtenburg, "The Pertinence of Political History: Reflections on the Significance of the State in America," *Journal of American History* 73 (1986): 585–600.

3. They picked up on a critique raised several decades earlier in Thomas C. Cohcran, "The 'Presidential Synthesis' in American History, *American Historical Review* 53, (1948): 748–53.

4. Gabriel Kolko, *The Triumph of Conservatism* (Glencoe, Ill.: Free Press, 1963), and James Weinstein, *The Corporate Ideal in the Liberal State* (Boston:

Beacon Press, 1968). They were also influenced by the sociological work on social control by Frances Fox Piven and Richard A. Cloward, *Regulating the Poor: The Functions of Public Welfare* (New York: Pantheon Books, 1971).

5. Julian E. Zelizer, "Beyond the Presidential Synthesis: Reordering Political Time," in *A Companion to Post-1945 America*, ed. Jean-Christophe Agnew and Roy Rosenzweig (Oxford: Blackwell Publishers, 2002), 345–70. The boundaries between policy history and American Political Development have always been difficult to discern. Indeed, a large number of scholars consider themselves part of both fields. The primary difference, in the minds of some, has been that American Political Development pays closer attention to institutional structures and analytic models of political history while policy historians tend to produce more archivally based and textured accounts that revolve around the policies themselves.

6. Ellis Hawley, *The New Deal and the Problem of Monopoly* (Princeton, N.J.: Princeton University Press, 1966); Samuel P. Hays, *The Response to Industrialism, 1885–1914* (Chicago: University of Chicago Press, 1957); Robert H. Wiebe, *The Search for Order, 1877–1920* (New York: Hill and Wang, 1967); Louis Galambos, "The Emerging Organizational Synthesis in Modern American history," *Business History Review* 44 (1970): 279–90; Morton Keller, *Affairs of State: Public Life in Late-Nineteenth-Century America* (Cambridge, Mass.: Harvard University Press, 1977); Louis Galambos, "Technology, Political Economy, and Professionalization," *Business History Review* 57 (1983): 471–93; Barry Karl, *The Uneasy State: The United States from 1915 to 1945* (Chicago: University of Chicago Press, 1983).

7. Louis Galambos, "Parsonian Sociology and Post-Progressive History," *Social Science Quarterly* 50 (1969): 25–45. For critiques of this scholarship, see Brian Balogh, "Reorganizing the Organizational Synthesis: Federal-Professional Relations in Modern America," *Studies in American Political Development* 5 (1991): 119–72, and Richard R. John, "Governmental Institutions as Agents of Change: Rethinking American Political Development in the Early Republic, 1787–1835," *Studies in American Political Development* 11 (1997): 347–80.

8. Richard E. Neustadt and Ernest R. May, *Thinking in Time: The Uses of History for Decision Makers* (New York: Free Press, 1986).

9. For some key works, see James T. Patterson, *America's Struggle against Poverty, 1900–1980* (Cambridge, Mass.: Harvard University Press, 1981); Thomas K. McCraw, *Prophets of Regulation: Charles Francis Adams, Louis D. Brandeis, James M. Landis, and Alfred E. Kahn* (Cambridge, Mass.: Harvard University Press, 1984); Edward D. Berkowitz, *Disabled Policy: America's Programs for the Handicapped* (Cambridge: Cambridge University Press, 1987); Christopher L. Tomlins, *The State and the Unions: Labor Relations, Law, and the Organized Labor Movement in America, 1880–1960* (Cambridge: Cambridge University Press, 1985).

10. For a detailed history of this subfield, see Julian E. Zelizer's "Clio's Lost Tribe: Public Policy History since 1978," *Journal of Policy History* 12 (2000): 369–94, and Hugh Davis Graham, "The Stunted Career of Policy History: A Critique and an Agenda," *The Public Historian* 15 (1993): 15–37.

11. Recent work has started to look at the complex relationship between public policy and corporate benefits, often subsidized by the government and produced

by collective bargaining. Jacob Hacker, *The Divided American Welfare State: Public and Private Benefits* (Cambridge: Cambridge University Press, 2002); Michael B. Katz, *The Price of Citizenship: Redefining the American Welfare State* (New York: Metropolitan Books, 2001); Christopher Howard, *The Hidden Welfare State: Tax Expenditures and Social Policy in the United States* (Princeton, N.J.: Princeton University Press, 1997); Steven A. Sass, *The Promise of Private Pensions: The First Hundred Years* (Cambridge, Mass.: Harvard University Press, 1997); Beth Stevens, "Blurring the Boundaries: How the Federal Government Has Influenced Welfare Benefits in the Private Sector," in *The Politics of Social Policy in the United States*, ed., Margaret Weir, Ann Shola Orloff, and Theda Skocpol (Princeton, N.J.: Princeton University Press, 1988), 123–48.

12. Michael B. Katz, *The Irony of Early School Reform: Educational Innovation in Mid-Nineteenth Century America* (Cambridge, Mass.: Harvard University Press, 1968); Katz, *In the Shadow of the Poorhouse: A Social History of Welfare in America* (New York: Basic Books, 1986).

13. See, for example, W. Andrew Achenbaum, "American Medical History: Social History and Medical History"; Daniel Fox, "History and Health Policy"; James Reed, "Public Policy on Human Reproduction and the Historian," *Journal of Social History* 18 (1985): 343–64; 383–97.

14. For a discussion of origins, see Julian E. Zelizer, "Stephen Skowronek's *Building a New American State* and the Origins of American Political Development," *Social Science History*, forthcoming.

15. Paul Pierson and Theda Skocpol, "Historical Institutionalism in Contemporary Political Science," in *Political Science: State of the Discipline*, ed. Ira Katznelson and Helen V. Milner (New York and Washington D.C.: Norton and American Political Science Association, 2002), 693–721.

16. Stephen Skowronek, *Building a New American State: The Expansion of National Administrative Capacities, 1877–1920* (Cambridge: Cambridge University Press, 1982). Another crucial foundational book was Theda Skocpol, *States and Social Revolutions: A Comparative Analysis of France, Russia, and China* (New York: Cambridge University Press, 1979).

17. Paul Pierson, "Not Just What, but *When*: Timing and Sequence in Political Processes," *Studies in American Political Development* 14 (2000): 76.

18. Theda Skocpol, *Protecting Soldiers and Mothers: The Political Origins of Social Policy in the United States* (Cambridge, Mass.: The Belknap Press of Harvard University, 1992). The same institutional logic was used to explain political and policy retrenchment. Paul Pierson, for instance, found that American conservatives in the 1980s were not very successful at rolling back the federal government, since public policies had created active constituencies who resisted their attacks while the structure of American political institutions made it difficult to mobilize against existing programs. Paul Pierson, *Dismantling the Welfare State? Reagan, Thatcher, and the Politics of Retrenchment* (Cambridge: Cambridge University Press, 1994).

19. This concept was introduced in the following two pioneering works: Skocpol, *States and Social Revolutions*; Dietrich Rueschemeyer, Theda Skocpol, and Peter Evans, *Bringing the State Back In* (Cambridge: Cambridge University Press, 1985).

20. Skocpol, *Protecting Soldiers and Mothers*.

21. Robert C. Lieberman, *Shifting the Color Line: Race and the American Welfare State* (Cambridge, Mass.: Harvard University Press, 1998); Jill Quadagno, *The Color of Welfare: How Racism Undermined the War on Poverty* (New York: Oxford University Press, 1994).

22. Richard R. John, *Spreading the News: The American Postal System from Franklin to Morse* (Cambridge, Mass.: Harvard University Press, 1995); and "Governmental Institutions as Agents of Change: Rethinking American Political Development in the Early Republic, 1787–1835," *Studies in American Political Development* 11 (1997): 347–80; Colleen A. Dunlavy, *Politics and Industrialization: Early Railroads in the United States and Prussia* (Princeton, N.J.: Princeton University Press, 1994); Kenneth R. Bowling and Donald R. Kennon, eds., *The House and Senate in the 1790s: Petitioning, Lobbying, and Institutional Development* (Athens: Ohio University Press, 2002); John Lauritz Larson, *Internal Improvement: National Public Works and the Promise of Popular Government in the Early United States* (Chapel Hill: University of North Carolina Press, 2001).

23. Alan Brinkley, *The End of Reform: New Deal Liberalism in Recession and War* (New York: Knopf, 1995). For important works by other historians, see Steve Fraser and Gary Gerstle, eds. *The Rise and Fall of the New Deal Order: 1930–1980* (Princeton, N.J.: Princeton University Press, 1989).

24. The promise of this approach to political history has been touched on in Leff, "Revisioning U.S. Political History"; Gillon, "The Future of Political History."

25. Samuel P. Hays, "The Social Analysis of American Political History," *Political Science Quarterly* 80 (1965): 373–94; Paul Kleppner, *The Cross of Culture: A Social Analysis of Midwestern Politics* (New York: Free Press, 1970); Joel H. Silbey, Allan G. Bogue, and William H. Flanigan, eds., *The History of American Electoral Behavior* (Princeton, N.J.: Princeton University Press, 1978). For a synthesis of the history of voting, see Alexander Keyssar, *The Right to Vote: The Contested History of Democracy in the United States* (New York: Basic Books, 2000).

26. Michael F. Holt, *The Political Crisis of the 1850s* (New York: Wiley, 1978); Joel H. Silbey, *The Partisan Imperative: The Dynamics of American Politics before the Civil War* (New York: Oxford University Press, 1985); Mark E. Neely, *The Union Divided: Party Conflict in the Civil War North* (Cambridge, Mass.: Harvard University Press, 2002); Glenn C. Altschuler and Stuart M. Blumin, *Rude Republic: Americans and Their Politics in the Nineteenth Century* (Princeton, N.J.: Princeton University Press, 2000); Paula Baker, "The Midlife Crisis of the New Political History," *Journal of American History* 86 (1999): 158–66.

27. Eric Foner, *Reconstruction: America's Unfinished Revolution, 1863–1877* (New York: Harper and Row, 1988).

28. Lawrence Goodwyn, *The Democratic Promise: The Populist Moment in America* (New York: Oxford University Press, 1976); Richard Hofstadter, *The Age of Reform: From Bryan to F.D.R.* (New York: Vintage, 1955). For an analysis that builds on Goodwyn, see Steven Hahn, *Roots of Southern Populism: Yeoman Farmers and the Transformation of the Georgia Upcountry, 1850–1890* (New York: Oxford University Press, 1983).

29. Sean Wilentz, *Chants Democratic: New York City and the Rise of the American Working Class, 1788–1850* (New York: Oxford University Press, 1984).

30. David Montgomery, *The Fall of the House of Labor: The Workplace, the State, and American Labor Activism, 1865–1925* (Cambridge: Cambridge University Press, 1987).

31. Lizabeth Cohen, *Making a New Deal: Industrial Workers in Chicago, 1919–1939* (Cambridge: Cambridge University Press, 1990).

32. James T. Kloppenberg, "The Virtues of Liberalism: Christianity, Republicanism, and Ethics in Early American Political Discourse," in *The Virtues of Liberalism* (New York: Oxford University Press, 1998), 21–37; Joyce Appleby, *Capitalism and a New Social Order* (New York: New York University Press, 1984); Drew R. McCoy, *The Elusive Republic: Political Economy in Jeffersonian America* (Chapel Hill: University of North Carolina Press, 1980); J.G.A. Pocock, *The Machiavellian Moment: Florentine Political Thought and the Atlantic Republican Tradition* (Princeton, N.J.: Princeton University Press, 1975); Gordon S. Wood, *The Creation of the American Republic, 1776–1787* (Chapel Hill: University of North Carolina Press, 1969); Bernard Bailyn, *The Ideological Origins of the American Revolution* (Cambridge, Mass.: The Belknap Press of Harvard University Press, 1967).

33. Jean Baker, *Affairs of Party: The Political Culture of Northern Democrats in the Mid–Nineteenth Century* (Ithaca, N.Y.: Cornell University Press, 1983); Daniel Walker Howe, *The Political Culture of the American Whigs* (Chicago: University of Chicago Press, 1979).

34. Paula Baker, "The Domestication of Politics: Women and American Political Society, 1780–1920," *American Historical Review* 89 (1984): 620–47. Molly Ladd-Taylor, *Mother-Work: Women, Child Welfare, and the State, 1890–1930* (Urbana: University of Illinois Press, 1994); Robyn Muncy, *Creating a Female Dominion in American Reform, 1890–1935* (New York: Oxford University Press, 1991).

35. Linda Gordon, *Pitied but Not Entitled: Single Mothers and the History of Social Welfare* (New York: Free Press, 1994); Eileen Boris, *Home to Work: Motherhood and the Politics of Industrial Homework in the United States* (Cambridge: Cambridge University Press, 1994); Alice Kessler-Harris, *In Pursuit of Equity: Women, Men, and the Quest for Economic Citizenship in Twentieth-Century America* (New York: Oxford University Press, 2001).

36. Keyssar, *The Right to Vote*.

37. Richard Bensel, *The Political Economy of American Industrialization, 1877–1900* (Cambridge: Cambridge University Press, 2001).

38. Skowronek, *Building a New American State*; Keller, *Affairs of State*.

39. Robin L. Einhorn, "Slavery and the Politics of Taxation in the Early United States," *Studies in American Political Development* 14 (2000): 156–83; Robin L. Einhorn, *Property Rules: Political Economy in Chicago, 1833–1872* (Chicago: University of Chicago Press, 1991).

40. For an excellent volume that offers overviews of each era of American politics, see Byron E. Shafer and Anthony J. Badger, eds., *Contesting Democracy: Substance and Structure in American Political History, 1775–2000* (Lawrence: University Press of Kansas, 2001).

Chapter Two

EXPLAINING THE UNEXPLAINABLE

THE CULTURAL CONTEXT OF THE SEDITION ACT

JOANNE B. FREEMAN

D EMOCRACY WAS A PROBLEM in the early republic. Though we view it as the heart of the American political system, the founding generation had no such assumption. In fact, they equated pure democratic governance with civic disorder and popular unrest. In a democracy, the entire population took part in the process of governance; republican governance seemed far more practicable, instilling order through the process of representation. Although political partisans of different stripes would come to have different understandings of democratic politics over the course of the 1790s, all agreed that America was not a democracy. The real question at the heart of the period's politics was precisely how democratic a republic America should be.

Such doubts about democracy suggest the alien nature of the early national political world—a simple fact that is easily overlooked. When we look to the founding period for the roots of modern political behavior, we impose a modern sense of political order and security onto a politics with its own distinct logic and integrity. In reality, the American republic was remarkably undeveloped and unsteady in its first decades, a political experiment with an uncertain outcome. Invigorating as this spirit of political experimentation might have been, it was also disquieting. Americans were creating the first polity of its kind in the modern world, and they were keenly aware that anything could happen. The result was an ongoing climate of crisis.

Any number of questions remained unanswered. Foremost was the simple question of survival. With the stability and long-term practicability of such a polity untested, there was every likelihood that the republic would collapse—particularly given the new nation's vulnerability on the world stage. Foreign powers held sway over international trade, impressed American seamen virtually at will, and tolerated rather than respected American diplomats in their royal courts. Joined with the fragility of the new American nation, it is no wonder that every foreign crisis seemed capable of destroying the republic. Indeed, fears of disunion and civil war plagued the period's politics. Alexander Hamilton and James Madison, two of the driving forces behind the Constitution, went to their death with the Union's vulnerability on their mind. Both men wrote final pleas for its preservation on the eve of their demise, Madison composing a memorandum titled "Advice to My Country," and Hamilton writing one last letter on the night before his duel with Aaron Burr, urging a friend to fight against the "Dismemberment of our Empire." Virginian Henry Lee's offhand comment in a 1790 letter to James Madison is a blunt reminder of the tenuous nature of the national union: "If the government should continue to exist," he wrote in passing, evidence of a mindset that is difficult to recapture.[1]

Questions about the precise nature of republican governance only magnified such fears. Although the republic was grounded on public opinion—the voting public installed and removed officeholders as they saw fit—the mechanics of this process had yet to be determined. It was one thing to establish a nation governed by the popular will and quite another to grapple with a populace empowered. How politically involved should average citizens be on a daily basis? Should they confine their demands to the structured bounds of the electoral process?[2] If not, how much popular protest crossed the line into civil disorder and political anarchy? How was the public to make its opinions known? And how would these opinions affect the authority of national leaders and their ability to govern? There was a wide spectrum of opinions on the matter, and no way to determine the answer other than through contest, trial, and error. The struggle to balance republican ideals with democratic realities would remain one of the foremost challenges in America's ongoing political experiment.

Equally disconcerting were questions about the organization of the national political process. A republic was grounded on a common concern for the general good. Such was the very purpose of the national government; it provided a forum for clashing interests to forge shared policies aimed at the nation's welfare. Organized political factions thus posed a large threat, particularly on the national stage, where a nationwide clash between Federalists (largely New Englanders) and Republicans (largely southerners) seemed likely to destroy the infant republic. Although today's political parties form the heart of America's political system, providing a framework for the nuts and bolts of democratic politics, the founding generation considered them anathema to republican governance. An institutionalized national two-party system seemed to strike at the heart of the Constitution, renouncing the process of accommodation and compromise that fueled republican governance.[3]

Yet, increasingly in the 1790s, political developments seemed to generate such polarized combat. Within years of the government's launching, two opposing political alliances had formed: the Federalists and the Republicans. New Englanders and city dwellers tended to be attracted to the Federalist persuasion. Favoring a strong central government that could protect liberty, property, and civic order from the tumult of popular politics, Federalists distrusted mass popular politicking outside of elections; to Republicans, Federalists were dangerous, power-hungry monarchists determined to convert the new republic into an old-world monarchy. Republicans tended to be southerners, farmers, and, eventually, ambitious members of the lower ranks. In favor of a weaker national government and friendlier to popular politicking, Republicans seemed like wild demagogues to their Federalist foes, promoting themselves through popular appeals that encouraged mass public disorder. Inchoate and unorganized as they might be, these two ideological groupings seemed to constitute an enormous threat to the new government. To Federalists and Republicans alike, there was only one answer: their faction must unite temporarily to eliminate opponents bent on destroying constitutional order. Unintentionally forging a system of opposition even as they attempted to eradicate it, they virtually guaranteed an ongoing climate of crisis. Political ideals seemed inextricably at odds with the demands of the moment.

These nascent political alliances complicated matters even further, for although there were two umbrellas of thought labeled Federalism and Republicanism, individuals shifted their politics from one issue to the next depending on bonds of regionalism, friendship, and principle that did not necessarily coincide. Partisan loyalty was one factor among many that guided political choices. National politics was like a war without uniforms: it was often difficult to distinguish friends from foes, and impossible to predict what strange combinations of circumstances might alter a man's political loyalties or forge an alliance between former enemies.[4] Absolute assurance and group discipline were rare commodities, and the most partisan man could occasionally leap a divide. Much as we envision politics in the 1790s as a structured clash known as "the first party system," the reality was more complex. Manning Dauer's work shows this in graphic form. In tables depicting congressional voting records between 1796 and 1802, he divides congressmen into categories that include "Federalist," "Federalist-moderate," "Federalist . . . elected as Republican," "Republican," "Republican-moderate," and "Federalist but voting regularly Republican."[5]

In this heated climate framed in political ambiguities, politics was violently personal. Because even the most seemingly solid partisan could sway under the right circumstances, personal character and reputation were vital tools for determining a man's politics. A man of poor character could not be trusted, nor did he merit a position of political leadership. Character attacks were thus a core weapon of political combat. Dishonor a man, and you could destroy his political career; dishonor enough of your opponents, and you could topple their cause.

In fact, many considered personal character to be the very basis of national governance. Less than ten years old, the experimental new government had little authority. What little respect it did command was vested in the character and reputation of its officeholders. In a government lacking formal precedent and institutional traditions, reputation was the glue that held the polity together. The fragile new republic was a government of character striving to become a government of rules within its new constitutional framework. Thus, an attack on the character of a national leader was an attack on the foundations of government itself. The political significance of personal honor and reputation on the national stage had an enormous influence on the tone and style of political combat, shaping the structure of political discourse, defining the bounds of congressional debate, and even guiding legislation on occasion.[6]

Clearly, the early national political world differed from ours in profound ways. Seeming inevitabilities were nowhere on the horizon. Modern institutions of democratic governance were problems to be monitored and avoided. This climate of contingency and crisis is apparent only when we examine the politics of the period in its proper context—not only the proper political context (the chain of causes and effects that defined the politics of the moment) but also the proper cultural context (the assumptions and customs that shaped political life). A full understanding of the political past is impossible outside of this cultural framework.

Perhaps no single event of the period better demonstrates this idea than the 1798 Sedition Act. Faced with the looming threat of war with France, Congress took action by passing four acts collectively known as the Alien and Sedition Acts. Three of the acts concerned the definition and treatment of aliens residing in the United States, calling for their registration with their local governments and empowering the president to deport those deemed dangerous. The fourth act, "An act for the punishment of certain crimes against the United States," had two sections. The first declared that anyone who conspired against the government, encouraged insurrections, or impeded government operation was guilty of a high misdemeanor and subject to a fine and imprisonment. The second section concerned sedition, defined as "false, scandalous and malicious writing or writings against the government of the United States . . . with intent to defame" it or bring it into "contempt or disrepute" so as to excite "the hatred of the good people of the United States." Anyone guilty of printing, uttering, publishing, or encouraging the publication of such material was subject to a fine and imprisonment.[7]

Repressive, tyrannical, a seeming violation of the core principles of republican governance, the Sedition Act seems impossible to justify according to any logic other than screaming partisanship and an urgent desire to retain political power. And so scholars have tended to explain it, condemning it as the desperate act of a beleaguered faction making opportunistic use of a foreign crisis.[8] Using the threat of war with France as their justification, Federalists attempted to quash their Republican opposition by destroying their vehicles of the press. The well-deserved outcry against this despotic measure damned the Federalists in the public eye, ultimately destroying the cause of Federalism and helping to raise Thomas Jefferson to the presidency in 1801 in a "revolution" of public sentiment.[9]

Such is the traditional account of the Sedition Act and its consequences—an account that paints the Federalists as hopelessly backward-looking aristocratic tyrants attempting to stem a tide of political democratization and thus doomed to fail. The reality, however, is more complex. Studied in a cultural context, the Sedition Act was not simply an opportunistic partisan lunge for power—unquestionably partisan as it was. It was also a logical attempt to reconcile long-standing views of political leadership with the burgeoning power of the democratic multitude. If the masses lost respect for their political leaders, what would be the foundation of government? Were the personal reputations of national political leaders the ultimate source of political legitimacy and authority? And if so, did seditious attacks against national officeholders strike at the process of democratic representation itself? As we shall see, such questions were not resolved with the collapse of Federalism. Republicans and Federalists alike saw a fundamental problem with the unbounded freedom of democracy. Beneath all the partisan rhetoric about monarchy and demagoguery was a more basic struggle over the nature of leadership and citizenship in the increasingly democratic American republic.

THE CRISIS MENTALITY OF 1798

From a modern perspective, the Federalist attempt to suppress a free press is arguably the most gripping crisis of the 1790s, but national leaders immersed in the moment thought otherwise. Close study of their correspondence reveals that although there was a lively (though brief) congressional debate surrounding the Sedition Act, there was far more anxious hand-wringing about the tenor of foreign relations and their impact on the new nation's survival.[10] Indeed, from the 1793 "Citizen" Genêt Affair through Jefferson's ascension to the presidency (and beyond), foreign affairs dominated national politics. An infant republic struggling to prove itself among the nations of the world, the United States was a sovereign nation more in theory than practice on the world stage; as convinced as Americans were of their international importance as a political exemplar, they were, in fact, insignificant upstarts, a defenseless new polity that depended on foreign allies for economic prosperity and self-defense.

Most problematic of all were the ongoing hostilities between Great Britain and France. As British subjects, Americans became entangled in this generational conflict long before the Revolution; their wartime alliance with France guaranteed their involvement in this feud well into the nation's future. Throughout the 1790s, America walked a diplomatic tightrope between Britain and France, struggling to accommodate both without antagonizing either. It was a difficult path to follow, every gesture toward one nation sparking a reaction in the other.

Such diplomatic realities were bad enough. But in an unstable republic still determining its national character, foreign influence could shape the tone of governance. Whether British influence might allow the Federalists to restore monarchical forms and trappings as Republicans feared, or French influence might provide the popular unrest necessary for the Republicans to promote disorder, overturn the government, and seize control as Federalists feared, the result would be the same. "The chance of our *future* state is imprecise," declared Fisher Ames in 1798. "[A]ll our good men should join their best efforts to keep this system from sinking."[11]

The French Revolution only intensified the prevailing sense of crisis. Initially viewed as the first outgrowth of America's Revolution—the onset of a worldwide revolt against old-world tyranny and repression—it grew to become a bugbear of national politics, influencing the new nation in both thought and practice. Federalists grew to despise it as the epitome of anarchy, lawlessness, and social disorder, the very things that the new constitutional order was designed to avoid. Given the republic's raw youth, such disorder seemed ever on the horizon. Indeed, considering that Americans had seen two governments overthrown in the last twenty years during two revolutions (in America, then France), Federalists had good reason to fear. Far more encouraged by the liberty-loving spirit that fueled the French Revolution, Republicans encouraged popular expressions of support, further justifying Federalist fears of disorder (though even Republicans took a step back when the Revolution collapsed into a bloody reign of terror.)[12]

An ongoing series of intrusive French ministers only added to the problem. Sensing potential support both ideological and financial, they courted politicians and the public alike. The French have an "unvaried plan of controuling our affairs by means of our rabble," wrote Fisher Ames in 1795 (with true Federalist flair). Through a combination of promises and threats, they even seemed to be interfering with the presidential electoral process. Jefferson should be ashamed of allowing such influences to contribute to his electoral victory, chided Connecticut Federalist Oliver Wolcott, Jr., in 1796. Swiss-born Albert Gallatin, the leading Republican in the House, was equally suspect of foreign influence. "Mr. Gallatin leads in all measures," wrote Wolcott in 1796, "& it is neither unreasonable nor uncandid to believe that Mr. Gallatin is directed by foreign politicks & influence."[13]

Federalist counterattempts to ensure friendly relations with Great Britain spawned similar fears among Republicans. As Kentucky Republican John Breckenridge wrote in 1798, an alliance with Britain would be an

> event of all others the most impolitic & humiliating. . . . Impolitic, because she is already bankrupt in her [Government] & fortunes, & has been for a century past, in her principles; & if she has [not] set already, will ere long sink under the regenerating arm of the French republic: Humiliating because she holds in contempt the American name & character. The sounds of rebel & Traitor have scarcely left our ears, & still she arrogantly & vainly looks forward to the time when the American Public will again return to their Colonial dependence.[14]

To Breckenridge, an alliance with Britain would be a blow against national sovereignty, honor, and independence.

Such anxieties peaked in 1798, as the diplomatic balance almost tipped toward war with France. In response to America's 1795 Jay Treaty with Britain, France had begun to interfere aggressively with American shipping; in December 1796, the French added insult to injury by refusing to receive Charles Cotesworth Pinckney, America's minister to France. When the American delegation sent to settle the controversy was first neglected and then asked for a bribe to commence negotiations, President John Adams began to prepare the nation for war.[15]

In the face of French hostility, Republican friendliness with the French seemed all the more suspicious. French diplomats had seemingly inveigled their way into the electoral process. They had open supporters among the French-friendly Republicans. They had inspired widespread popular demonstrations of support, in direct violation of America's supposed neutrality toward France. And now they were flagrantly dishonoring the American nation. Outraged at this attack on America's national honor, people of all political stripes rallied behind the war effort, eager to redeem the American name through a show of force. Federalist leaders gloried in this display of support, but they kept their eyes on the Republicans as well, worried that France's insulting behavior was intended to dishonor, discredit, and ultimately overthrow the Federalist regime.

This was the atmosphere that spawned the 1798 Sedition Act. While unquestionably serving partisan goals, the act was also designed to protect national security during a time of crisis, as suggested by the wording of the bill's first draft in the Senate. The proposed act declared France the enemy of the United States and classified any aid or support as treason, to be punishable by death; it also specified as seditious any expressions justifying France's insulting treatment of the American nation. Only in revision was this phrasing removed, when the treason and sedition bill was revised into an act specifically regarding sedition, its most drastic measures edited out.[16]

THE CULTURAL LOGIC OF THE SEDITION ACT

So repugnant is the resultant bill to modern sensibilities that it is difficult to study its logic with any detachment. It is hard to imagine a justification for stifling political opposition or silencing the press. Yet Federalist officeholders passed the Sedition Act in the face of pending elections. They did not envision it as a transgression that would outrage the public and, indeed, saw gains in the congressional election of 1798–1799—as Federalist representative Robert Goodloe Harper pointed out during debate several years later.[17] In fact, some Federalists considered the Sedition Act a praiseworthy protective measure against attacks on the process of democratic representative governance.[18] Wrongheaded and partisan as their actions might have been, Federalists were influenced by a deeper cultural logic that deserves study.

Perhaps the most fundamental assumption underlying the Sedition Act is the importance of public opinion. Certainly, there were practical reasons to worry about public opinion in time of war. Without popular support, it would be impossible to rouse the financial support and manpower required for national defense. In a most direct way, the popular will would determine the direction of national politics; this was the very basis of the nation's constitutional framework. Thus the desperate struggle in 1798 to mold public thought. Supportive of popular display on principle and skilled at public appeals as a minority interest, the Republicans had the advantage in this contest.

Discomfited by the logic and reality of popular politicking, the Federalists were in a difficult spot. They knew the importance of courting the public in time of war. As former president George Washington put it in 1797,

> it is time the People should be thoroughly acquainted with the political situation of this country, and the causes which have produced it, that they may either give active & effectual support to those to whom they have entrusted the Administration of the government (if they approve the principles on which they have acted); or sanction the conduct of those opposers, who have endeavoured to bring about a change by embarrassing all its measures—not even short of foreign means.[19]

Federalist George Cabot agreed. "It is impossible to make the people feel or see distinctly that we have much more to fear from peace than war," he lamented, yearning for popular support of a call to war.[20]

But how to spread this message without stooping to what they perceived as demagoguery?[21] A formal declaration of war would rouse popular support, but such a declaration was slow to come. "I cannot but lament that the public sentiment receives no good impression from the legislature," complained Fisher Ames. Without strong legislative action, there would be no way to expunge "Jacobin" ideas from the public's "weak heads," for they certainly would not be swayed by "arguments from books they do not read and from men whose conversation & company they do not enjoy."[22] Here we see Federalists struggling to sway public opinion without violating their sense of political proprieties. What were the mechanics of appealing to the public? How could one gain popular support without stirring up unrest? Republicans were in the process of discovering one answer. Republican newspapers would prove wildly effective at reaching the public—and thus wildly dangerous to the Federalists, who viewed them as demagogic tools aimed at inspiring opposition to the Federalist regime and, for that reason, potentially dangerous in time of war.

As Ames suggested, not only did the Federalists need to inform the public of "the truth," but they needed to refute Republican lies in the process. As many Federalists recognized, this would be no easy task. "[F]or God's sake, let not falsehood circulate without disproof," urged Noah Webster.

> It certainly is degrading for the Govt to carry on Newspaper Controversy with its opposers; but our govt stands on *popular opinion*, & if that should fail to support it, it must fail to be supported. The friends of govt labor hard in the cause; but mere contradiction does no good or very little, especially if anonymous. . . . If it is supposed that the low credit of the papers which first publish such assertions, or of the party which circulates them, will prevent undue impressions being made, we shall discover the fallacy, when too late. Innumerable false assertions, often repeated, have passed uncontradicted, by govt, I think, improperly; & they have been the principal instruments of extending the opposition to an alarming degree. I go farther, & aver that no govt can be durable & quiet, under the licentiousness of the press that now disgraces our country. Jacobinism must prevail, unless more pains are taken to *keep public opinion correct.* This *can* be done, & I think it *ought* to be done.[23]

Webster's comment reveals the awkwardness of the Federalist position at this time of crisis. It was "degrading" for the government to engage in newspaper combat—the best means of swaying public opinion. In the end, it was President John Adams who solved this dilemma with a series of rousing responses to public addresses of support. "[A]ll men, whose opinions I know, are *unbounded* in their applause of the manly just spirited & *instructive* sentiments expressed by the President in his answer to the addresses," wrote George Cabot. The good effects of such efforts "cannot be overrated—they have excited right feelings everywhere & have silenced clamour."[24] The Federalists were successfully swaying public opinion, but largely from speeches delivered on high, in response to respectful public expressions of support. It was a temporary solution to a profound political problem.

Immediate military concerns demanded popular support, but there were deeper, more fundamental reasons to worry about the direction of public sentiment. Public opinion ruled in a republic, a political truism that had particular importance during a national crisis. All authority stemmed from the good opinion of the American populace, so without popular support of their efforts, Federalists and Republicans alike would fail. The flip side of this axiom was also true: open opposition to the national government could topple not only the current regime but the entire government. "Take away from a republic the confidence of the people," declared North Carolina Federalist James Iredell, "and the whole fabric crumbles to dust."[25] In this sense, open opposition to national officeholders was a blow at the very foundations of American governance, an antidemocratic swipe at both elected officials and the people who had elected them.[26]

In the long view of history, such fears seem like the paranoid imaginings of a theory-minded generation. But in fact there was little other than common commitment holding the national government in place. The experimental new government had little authority other than the respect due to a national constitutional consensus and the personal authority of its officeholders. Thus, an attack on the character of a national leader was an attack on the foundations of government itself.[27]

This logic is evident in Federalist thought before the crises of 1798. Years earlier, Federalists were bemoaning the impact of character attacks on national leaders. "[D]uring this [past] period what dangers have been experienced, & what inroads have been made upon characters; who except the President has not been assailed with success?" asked Oliver Wolcott in 1796.[28] Alexander Hamilton decried such methods when defending himself against a Republican attack in 1797. The "spirit of jacobinism" accomplished its nefarious aims through calumny, he charged. "It is essential to its success that the influence of men of upright principles, disposed and able to resist its enterprises, shall be at all events destroyed." Through "corroding whispers" aimed at savaging reputations, the Jacobins aimed to destroy public men and overthrow the government.[29]

Attacks on personal character could topple the republic by destroying faith in public officers. Such attacks could also drive men of merit out of office. Reputation was "of as much importance to nations, in proportion, as to individuals," Adams noted in one of his wartime addresses. "Honor is a higher interest than reputation. The man or the nation without attachment to reputation, or honor, is undone. What is animal life, or national existence, without either?"[30] Given the profound importance of reputation to political authority and personal identity, the manifold risks of leadership in a climate of criticism might very well drive a man from office. "Our wisest and best public officers have had their lives embittered, and have been driven from their stations by unceasing and malignant slander," argued United States district judge Alexander Addison to a grand jury in western Pennsylvania. Unwilling to surrender their "character, reputation, or . . . good name," men of merit would be loath to accept public office should Republican character assassination continue in its present vein.[31]

Of course, Federalists were not above character assassination if it accomplished their purposes. As Noah Webster explained,

> the friends of govt must be active & vigilant—they must lay aside that delicacy about characters which men of honor observe in ordinary cases—they must expose the *real characters public* & *private*, of the leaders of opposition . . . by disclosing facts & anecdotes of their past lives which will clearly illustrate their selfish views. A great portion of the substantial people of the Country stand neuter, as to the parties now prevailing. If their opinion is tested, it will ultimately decide for *truth*; but *facts* must be known, & so must *characters*.[32]

As suggested by Webster's plea, where personal reputation and political authority were so intertwined, a character attack was a powerful weapon. And where public men were so convinced that their opponents were bent on destroying the government, such attacks seemed justified.

Debate over the Sedition Act echoed this train of thought. As Connecticut representative John Allen put it, the act was designed to combat a "dangerous combination . . . to overturn and ruin the Government by publishing the most shameless falsehoods against the Representatives of the people of all denominations, that they are hostile to free Governments and genuine liberty, and of course to the welfare of this country."[33] To protect the republic, something had to be done. Representative Robert Goodloe Harper of South Carolina agreed, reminding the House of the power of words. In the same way that a man had freedom of action but could not attack another man's person or property, he had freedom of speech but could not attack another man's reputation. Respect for personal reputation was a fundamental right.

Harper's statement makes little sense in a modern context, and indeed so argues James Morton Smith, one of the foremost scholars of the Sedition Act. Harper "placed the spoken word on the same footing with the fatal finality of assassination and made shooting off at the mouth a crime equivalent to that of shooting off a gun in order to murder a person," critiques Smith. The Federalist "completely overlooked the fact that whatever damage is inflicted by physical action cannot be undone but only punished, while erroneous and even false views propagated by speech and the press can be rebutted by similar methods. Insults may be rectified by apology, and in the last resort, civil, and even criminal, libel suits can be instituted in the state courts."[34]

Such logic might hold true today, but it was far from true in Harper's time. To an eighteenth-century gentleman, a spoken word could indeed inflict damage "equivalent to that of shooting off a gun." Indeed, most political duels of the period resulted from just that—a spoken (or written) word. An apology might heal a wounded reputation, but if an insult had spread widely or done serious damage, a simple apology might not be enough. Depending on the nature of an insult, even a libel suit might offer little reparation. As Bostonian Thomas Selfridge reasoned upon being dishonored by a political rival, a libel suit would have accomplished little.

> A legal remedy, from its nature . . . could not be so promptly and efficaciously administered as the degree and kind of injury imperiously required. It would take two or three years to have an action decided; but few persons, comparatively, would ever know the result, and those few would be those only, who were conversant with the reporter's volume . . . and while the process was pending, his business would dwindle away, and the cause would be unknown or forgotten, and the permanency of the evil would remain unrelieved.[35]

Thus the relative frequency of political honor disputes. All men relied on their reputation for their livelihood, but politicians gambled their reputation in an exposed arena that threatened widespread personal dishonor.[36]

Such dishonor was particularly harmful during a national crisis. The government needed all the authority it could muster in its military preparations, both to defend its dignity before the arrogance of the French and to command the compliance of the populace in the event of war. By slashing at the honor and reputations of the national elite, seditious libel slashed at the credibility and authority of the government.[37] Thus the Sedition Act. As much as the Federalists hoped to seize the moment to quash their political rivals, they were also motivated by sincere fears about the risks of dishonoring national leaders during a time of crisis, as well as by concerns about preserving the process of representative governance. Repressive and wrongheaded as it was, the Sedition Act had an internal logic that can be understood only in the political and cultural context of its time.

THE CASE OF THOMAS COOPER

This deeper understanding of the Sedition Act casts its enforcement in a new light. Historians traditionally have depicted the fourteen sedition prosecutions under the act as a blind partisan attack on the opposition press. And indeed, there is much truth to this perspective. Federalists *were* eager to retain power, maintain order, and tend to the public good (as they understood it) by crushing the Francophile Republicans once and for all. Federalist senator Theodore Sedgwick best summed up this attitude in his response to the onset of French hostilities in early 1798. "It will afford a glorious opportunity to destroy faction," he declared. "Improve it."[38]

But subtleties of honor and reputation also played a role in the unfolding of events surrounding the Sedition Act's enforcement. In a sense, Federalists were institutionalizing the logic of personal character defense within the federal system. According to the dictates of the code of honor, only equals could duel, and affairs of honor between gentlemen were to be settled man-to-man. As James Madison put it in 1798 when condemning a man for referring an honor affair to a congressional investigation rather than avenging his name himself, no self-respecting "man of the sword" consigned such affairs to a committee.[39] Gentlemen were personally responsible for their words and actions, and if they crossed a line, they had to face the consequences.

Inferiors, however, were an entirely different matter. According to the code of honor, an inferior who insulted a gentleman's character was to be caned or whipped rather than challenged to a duel—as Republican congressman Matthew Lyon discovered when he insulted a colleague, Federalist Roger Griswold, during the heightened tensions of 1798. Dismissing Lyon as an inferior who did not merit a duel, Griswold violently caned the Republican on the floor of the House. Because the political elite largely viewed newspaper editors as their inferiors, many editors suffered a similar fate; a remarkable number were threatened or publicly thrashed. Politicians who were discomfited by such violent displays or who sought long-term punishment sometimes chose to sue an editor instead, hoping to drive him out of business through the infliction of heavy fines. Federalists used some of this same logic in their enforcement of the Sedition Act. Twelve of the fourteen prosecutions under the act involved printers, newspaper editors, or men of questionable status.[40]

The clearest exception to this rule was Thomas Cooper, a man of science and sometime lawyer who was the close personal friend of renowned clergyman and chemist Joseph Priestley.[41] Born in London in 1759 and educated at Oxford, he had immigrated to America in 1794 after a brief career as a radical political activist. Joining ranks with Priestley, he took up residence in western Pennsylvania, where the two men hoped to establish a settlement for English immigrants. Although they never acted on their plan, Priestley and Cooper remained in Northumberland County, where they occupied themselves with matters scientific and philosophical. Over time, they became politically active as well; it would be Cooper's partisan statements during his two-month editorship of the *Sunbury and Northumberland Gazette* that would ultimately bring him to trial.[42]

Studying Cooper's prosecution and the circumstances surrounding it reveals the importance of examining the Sedition Act in its proper cultural context, for both his alleged sin and his legal defense were shaped by the ethic of honor. Ironically, his sufferings began when he resigned as editor of the *Sunbury and Northumberland Gazette*, returning the paper to its original editor, who had taken a leave of absence to publish a book.[43] Although Cooper declared his Republican sympathies throughout his term as editor, he announced them with particular vigor on June 29 in his last issue. Imagining himself the president of the United States, he outlined the policies that he would pursue if he intended to increase the power of the executive at the expense of the public good, summarizing (and thereby critiquing) Adams's policies in the process. If he were a power-hungry executive, he explained, he would encroach on the power of state governments, expand federal courts, "suppress all political conversation" with libel and sedition laws, and arm the administration with a standing army and navy. Pleased with his work and seeking to spread its impact, Cooper published it in handbills as well, allegedly financed, in part, by Priestley. Roughly two weeks later, it was reprinted in the Philadelphia *Aurora*, the nation's most powerful Republican organ.[44]

Cooper's efforts had their desired effect, discomfiting local Federalists enough to complain to Charles Hall, a Sunbury Federalist whom Adams had made an agent to assist in arbitration of American and British debts. As attested by Hall, several "friends of Government" confessed themselves "hurt at the circumstances" and wanted to "see if any thing ought to be done."[45] Hall's choice of words is a reminder of the personal impact of partisan animus outside of the halls of Congress. What we might dismiss as mere political rhetoric was actually a personal attack on the authority and motives of Sunbury Federalists by a member of their own community—a man of repute who had gained further authority by the appearance of his essay in the Philadelphia press.

Enclosing a copy of Cooper's "seditious performance," Hall addressed a letter to the United States attorney for Pennsylvania, William Rawle, asking for his advice. Rawle's response of July 23 has not been found, but clearly he was taken by Hall's request, for he asked the Federalist for an affidavit from the proprietor of the *Gazette* attesting to the facts of the case as Hall had recounted them. Complying with Rawle's request on

August 1, Hall added fuel to the fire by informing him that within the last two weeks, Cooper had published a pamphlet containing all of his inflammatory newspaper essays—and it was selling fast. To Hall, whether or not Cooper's "cautiously worded" essay contained a "direct palpable charge," it aimed "directly at the President" and endeavored "to traduce & villify the prevailing party in Congress & the laws they had made." Something had to be done.[46]

So eager was Hall to silence Cooper that he alerted Secretary of State Timothy Pickering as well. Obsequiously apologizing for taking Pickering's time, he denounced Cooper as a man of ambition and strong passions who doubtless hoped to rise to power on the coattails of his Republican cronies. To Hall, the damage to the public mind wrought by Cooper's essay had only one antidote—a firm refutation—and Hall considered himself just the man to write it. Enclosing the first portion of a lengthy essay, he asked Pickering to place it in a Philadelphia paper if it merited the effort. It was a savvy move on Hall's part, for not only might he refute Cooper's lies, but he could boost his own personal authority and reputation in the process.[47]

Apparently, Pickering was as taken with Cooper's alleged sedition as Rawle was, for shortly after receiving Hall's letter, he issued an enthusiastic response, informing President Adams as well. In his letter to Hall, Pickering praised Hall's essay and promised to get it published, even suggesting that Hall circulate it in handbills along the path traveled by Cooper's publication, offering to reimburse him for his efforts. Even so, Pickering anticipated that it would be difficult to repair the damage, for lies could be spread with a few words, while "many columns" would be "necessary to expose the misrepresentations and falsehoods: and many readers" would be "too indolent" to read them. Cooper's actions were no doubt due to the ambitions for power and office that he shared with "the mass of seditious, turbulent democrats." No government "which human wisdom could devise" would content such men "unless they were placed at its head." It was too bad that Cooper had become an American citizen, Pickering concluded, for he could have been deported under the Alien Law. He could only hope that Rawle would prosecute Cooper and Priestley besides. Pickering's letter to Adams included much the same sentiments.[48]

Pickering's assumptions about Cooper's motives reveal much about his understanding of partisan opposition; like Hall, he attributed Cooper's efforts to personal ambition and little else. To both Pickering and Hall, it was impossible to imagine that Cooper and his fellows had sincere grievances about national governance, for those in power thought that they themselves had unquestionably devoted themselves to the public good; to suggest otherwise was to question their motives and morals. As one statesman noted in 1791, "it is impossible to censure measures without condemning men."[49]

Pickering kept his promise, for Hall's lengthy response to Cooper's essay, signed "A True American," appeared in the Federalist *Gazette of the United States* on October 23.[50] Three days later, a far more personal attack on Cooper appeared in the Reading *Weekly Advertiser*. Was the Thomas Cooper who had attacked President Adams in the *Sunbury and Northumberland Gazette* the same Thomas Cooper who had unsuccessfully sought a government position from Adams two years past? asked the anonymous writer. Recounting Cooper's letter of application in great detail, as well as Priestley's accompanying letter of recommendation, the writer accused Cooper of attacking the president out of a sense of revenge. "Priestley and Cooper are both called upon to deny the above narrative," he concluded, for he was sure that the actual "letters themselves, would establish the accuracy of this anecdote, even to a syllable."[51]

This was a serious attack indeed. Not only did it malign Cooper's motives, but it exposed a private plea to public view. A request for office was demeaning enough without added exposure. Even worse, the essay's level of detail suggested that it had been written or supported by an insider with access to government files, giving it added credibility. And indeed, it virtually paraphrased the letter that Adams had sent to Pickering after hearing of Cooper's handbill.[52] Pickering had probably reframed Adams's words and staged the attack on Cooper's home ground, where it could do the most damage. Discrediting Cooper among people who knew him personally would destroy his influence at its source.

This was not the first time that Cooper's character had come under attack. Six years earlier, in 1792, Edmund Burke had denounced him in Parliament for his collusion with a French Jacobin club. Cooper's impassioned eighty-page response not only defended his actions and declared his principles but attacked Burke's character as well, charging him with making "obvious misrepresentations" and at least one "flagrant untruth"—essentially accusing him of lying, a serious charge. Burke chose not to respond, but Cooper had revealed himself to be an inflammatory combatant.[53] Remarkably, in 1792 as in 1799, Cooper's defense was deemed seditious, though in this earlier case he avoided charges by printing it in a pamphlet for elite readers rather than disseminating it in a newspaper for the masses.[54]

A quick-tempered man who vented his feelings with his pen, Cooper was not the man to allow this attack on his character to pass unnoticed. Indeed, its seeming authority virtually demanded a response, and in fact the writer had literally dared Cooper to step forward. So a week later he responded in a handbill that was soon reprinted in newspapers. "Yes; I am the Thomas Cooper alluded to," he defiantly declared. Denouncing the "malignant writer" of the challenge, he offered a detailed explanation of his request for office (oddly enough, he had been interested in Charles Hall's job), printing the two letters referred to in the *Weekly Advertiser* and denying any motive of revenge.

Nor had Cooper altered his political principles in requesting the job, he continued. He was no hypocrite. At the time of Cooper's application, Adams had just entered office and was still "in the infancy of political mistake." He had not yet revealed that he would deny offices to men of opposing politics. He had not yet "declared that 'a republican government may mean anything[,] . . . sanctioned the abolition of trial by jury in the alien law, or entrenched his public character behind the legal barriers of the sedition law." Nor was the nation yet saddled with the expense of a permanent navy, or threatened with the expense of a standing army. Had Adams revealed his true colors in August 1797, Cooper concluded, the president "would not have been troubled by any request" from Cooper.[55] This list of accusations ultimately led to Cooper's arrest.

Although the handbill outraged many, Cooper was not charged with seditious libel for another four months. Some scholars suggest that it was Cooper's actions in March 1800 that crossed the line. That month, *Aurora* editor William Duane, indicted under the Sedition Act, asked Republicans Alexander Dallas and Thomas Cooper to serve as legal counsel, but the two men refused, Cooper broadening his refusal into an attack on the Sedition Act as a gag law that threatened to turn citizens into subjects. Not surprisingly, the letter was printed in newspapers around the country—which was undoubtedly Cooper's intention.[56] Roughly two weeks later, on April 9, 1800, Cooper was arrested for seditious libel for his handbill of November 1799.[57]

Cooper's trial took place on April 19, and he served as his own counsel. Most of his efforts, like those of prosecuting attorney Rawle, focused on Cooper's intent and the nature of his charges, as was appropriate in a trial for seditious libel. Surrounding these arguments, however, was the logic and language of honor. For example, Cooper appealed to the jury by touching on their natural concern for their character and reputation. The judges and district attorney trying his case would doubtless be biased against him, Cooper argued, for they owed their offices to President Adams. But members of the jury, who had no ties to Adams, would doubtless remain unbiased, for they had "some character to support and some character to lose." They would abide by their sworn oaths of impartiality, Cooper argued, because to do otherwise would damage their reputation.[58]

Cooper again resorted to the logic of honor when explaining the motives behind his handbill. His remarks about Adams were no malicious attack, he argued. Adams had disclosed details that formed the basis of a "base and cowardly slander" that "dragged me . . . before the public in vindication of my moral and political character." His handbill was not voluntary, but rather an "involuntary publication" originating not from

> motives of turbulence and malice, but from self-defence; not from a desire of attacking the character of the President, but of vindicating my own. And in what way have I done this? My motives, my private character, my public character, were the object of falsehood and calumny, apparently founded on information of high authority. In reply, I give credit to the intentions of the President: I say nothing of his private character; and I attack only the tendency of measures notorious to the world.[59]

As recorded in Rawle's notes of Cooper's trial, Cooper felt that the president had "forced this pub[lication]" from him by being "the publisher of private letters."[60] The dictates of personal honor had compelled Cooper's publication. And unlike Adams, Cooper had attacked only Adams's public character and actions; it was Adams who had crossed the line by striking at a man's private character. Opportunistic as this argument may appear, it had a grain of truth, for Cooper had been insulted and challenged in the public prints by a man of some authority with ironclad evidence. Many a gentleman would have felt compelled to respond in the same way.[61]

The prosecution likewise deployed the logic of honor on their behalf, most notably in their attempt to prove Cooper's malicious motives. Unlike most people, Cooper had not concealed his name or hidden behind a pseudonym, Rawle argued.

> Being of the profession of the law, a man of education and literature, he availed himself of those advantages for the purpose of disseminating his dangerous productions in a remote part of the country where he had gained influence.[62]

By Rawle's logic, Cooper had deliberately deployed his high status and reputation to lend credibility to his charges—something of an unfair claim, for Cooper could not have vindicated himself without accepting the challenge of his attacker and defending himself under his own name.

Ultimately found guilty, Cooper suffered six months imprisonment and a $400 fine, decrying his fate in the newspapers throughout. Untamed by the experience, he left prison threatening to redeem his name with "personal chastisement," or in plainer terms a caning. As he explained in a letter to Caleb Wayne, the editor of the Federalist *Gazette of the United States*:

> I find your paper continues to make me an object of personal attack. Having been confined in Prison, it has not been in my power to repay insolence by personal chastisement, and on my coming out, I have been bound over to good behaviour for twelve months. . . . It is perfectly consistent with the cowardly

politics of your party to insult where you think you can do it with impunity . . . but if I continue to be the object of your abuse, I shall not forget to do myself justice, when I can do it without injury to my friends.[63]

Cooper may have been unable to redeem his name, but his friends and family were not. Within days, Cooper's friend Dr. James Reynolds, an Irish radical, redeemed Cooper's pledge by leading a group of "United Irishmen" to thrash Wayne; Cooper's son gave Federalist editor Andrew Brown similar treatment. Indeed, Federalist editors suffered heartily throughout the period, the editors of the Federalist *Gazette of the United States* being particular targets. In late 1798, Wayne's predecessor, John Ward Fenno, grappled with Republican *Aurora* editor Benjamin Franklin Bache in the street and was later assaulted outside of his house by a group of "United Irishmen." Roughly one month later, in January 1799, Reynolds challenged him to a duel. When Fenno refused the challenge, Reynolds posted him in a broadside denouncing him as a liar, scoundrel, and coward.[64] The Sedition Act gave Federalists a judicial cudgel to batter noxious editors; their minority status cutting them off from such power, Republicans defended their honor in other ways.

But Cooper was not done. Still smarting over his public humiliation, he decided to inflict a like wound on his opponents by attacking their leader, Alexander Hamilton. Just before the presidential election of 1800, Hamilton had responded to President Adams's ongoing hostility and insults by attacking him in a pamphlet titled *Letter . . . Concerning the Public Conduct and Character of John Adams, Esq.*, intending to push Federalist Charles Cotesworth Pinckney into the presidency and defend his own name in the process.[65] Enraged by Adams's behavior, Hamilton filled his pamphlet with violent abuse of Adams's public and private character. It was a shocking performance that did little for Hamilton's reputation. But despite the blatantly seditious nature of his publication, Hamilton escaped charges.[66] Cooper hoped to rectify matters. Released from prison in early October of 1800, by month's end he was in New York pursuing Hamilton on the Federalist's home ground. "The famous Thomas Cooper is in town" with Dr. Reynolds, noted the New York *Gazette*, "A precious pair!"[67]

Finding that Hamilton was in Albany, Cooper dispatched a letter informing him that he planned to bring him "before the public" by instituting against him "a prosecution under the detestable act of Congress, commonly known by the name of the 'Sedition Law,' in the hope of determining whether Republicanism is to be the victim of a law, which Aristocracy can break through with impunity." All Cooper needed was Hamilton's candid confession of authorship, which he felt sure Hamilton would supply out of respect for his own "character," for no gentleman who valued his reputation would lie or cavil. The ethic of honor would compel Hamilton to respond. Hamilton, however, entirely ignored Cooper's letter, not even deigning to reply; even worse, he broadcast his scorn by handing Cooper's unanswered letter to the Albany press. Publicly dishonored and unable to brook such contempt, Cooper published one more letter in December of 1800. He would let the matter drop, he explained, for the Federalists had been vanquished in the recent presidential election. Hamilton, however, had shown a complete "ignorance . . . of what was due to his own character, and to mine." He was "insensible . . . to the dictates of common politeness" and thus unworthy of Cooper's experiment. "No man has the character sufficient for the purpose, who from ignorance or irritation, from pride or peevishness, can put off the character of a gentleman." Hamilton was no gentleman, so his contempt was beneath notice. Hoping that he had salvaged his personal honor by slashing Hamilton's, Cooper finally laid the matter to rest.

Clearly, the entire Cooper case was threaded with the logic of honor. The power of status and reputation gave Cooper's initial attack some of its bite; the dictates of honor called Cooper into the open; the logic of honor was deployed during his trial; and the sting of dishonor prodded Cooper and his friends to redeem his name. Whether attacking their foes or defending themselves, Republicans and Federalists resorted to a deeper cultural logic that must be considered when exploring the significance and repercussions of the Sedition Act.

The Shared Language of Sedition

Republicans were not immune to this deeper logic.[68] As much as they condemned the tyrannical censorship of the Sedition Act, they understood the power of character attacks. It was the federal prosecution of such cases that troubled them, not the simple fact of prosecution itself. This became evident once they rose to power. Even as Republicans such as Virginian George Hay, James Monroe's son-in-law, denounced federal prosecution of seditious libel, they urged individual politicians to seek legal recourse in state courts against injuries to their "private character"—the "fame, the feelings, and the fortunes" of community leaders, as Pennsylvania governor Thomas McKean put it.[69] "The right of character is a sacred and valuable right, and is not forfeited by accepting a public employment," agreed New York Republican Tunis Wortman in a treatise on liberty of the press.[70]

The very symbol of Republicanism, President Thomas Jefferson, voiced similar sentiments, his distrust of the press growing ever stronger during eight years of Federalist abuse. By 1805, though he still disapproved of federal prosecution for libel, he advocated legal action against "the artillery of the press."[71] Two more years of Federalist abuse pushed him still further; in 1807, he supported the federal prosecution of four Connecticut Federalists who had attacked his character, measures, and administration, urging dismissal of the cases only when Federalists threatened to drag into court his youthful dalliance with the married Mrs. John Walker as a means of determining the "truth" about Jefferson's morality.[72] Massachusetts attorney general James Sullivan, a firm Republican, agreed with such prosecutions. Discussing the Sedition Act in an 1801 pamphlet, he attacked the Federalists for neglecting to secure the "confidence of the people" in its passage but upheld the general concept behind the act itself, arguing that federal common law included the right to punish seditious libel and that "Congress had an undoubted right to pass an act against seditious libels."[73] Like the Federalists before them, Republicans in power were struggling to accommodate political ideals with political realities.

It was not only the Republican leadership who made this shift. For example, shortly before the Connecticut Federalists were threatened with a trial, a group of Republican citizens sent Jefferson a statement about the situation in their state. "The opponents of the General Government" in Connecticut "have begun a systematic plan for the ruin of every Individual who holds an Office, or advocates the Government of the United States," they complained. Federalists had wrought a "general wreck of reputation" by launching a "systematic attack on character"—a sentiment echoing Federalist opinions of only a few years past.[74] For both Republicans and Federalists, in an age when character and status were the basis of personal and political authority, seditious libel was a real threat that demanded a response.

Indeed, this was the heart of the problem. As Pennsylvania representative Albert Gallatin pointed out during an 1801 debate of the Sedition Act (triggered by the imminent demise of the act as specified in its initial legislation),

> What . . . is meant by saying that the Government depends on public opinion? . . . It can only relate to the persons who administer the Government. It depends wholly on the public opinion, who shall administer the Government, but not whether there shall or shall not be a Government.[75]

"Public opinion" referred to the public's opinion of people in power; it could mean nothing else. Opposition to a measure was opposition to officeholders, and opposition to officeholders was an attack on their motives and character. In such a climate, neither Federalist nor Republican leaders could advocate absolute freedom of the press. Not until a later generation accepted the turbulent give-and-take of party politics would this change. Only then could politicians dismiss opposition as the impersonal, routine business of politics.

The Federalists may have pushed the Sedition Act through Congress with little thought about securing public confidence; they may have prosecuted Republican editors with particular zeal. But for all the Federalist discomfort with popular politicking and its implications, their Sedition Act was not simply an anomalous, tyrannical lunge for power. It was grounded in the culture of the time. Elite Federalist and Republican officeholders shared the same impulse to protect their character and reputation for the good of the political order. They saw the same link between their personal honor and the foundations of government.

This alien mentality is apparent only when viewing the Sedition Act in its proper cultural context, yet it is a vital part of the story of the nation's founding. It reminds us that democracy as we understand it was not a central tenet of American governance in the early republic. The democratization of American politics was an uneven, evolving process with dire stakes and an unknown outcome, shaped by cultural imperatives that have long since lost their power and meaning. Political realities and ideological assumptions were often at odds, raising serious concerns about the republic's survival. As Federalist Fisher Ames put it, "there is a want of accordance between our system and the state of our public opinion. THE GOVERNMENT IS REPUBLICAN; OPINION IS ESSENTIALLY DEMOCRATIC. . . . Either, events will raise public opinion high enough to support our government, or public opinion will pull down the government to its own level. They must equalize."[76] How democratic a republic should America be? Jefferson's presidential victory suggested that it should be more democratic than the Federalist reign of the 1790s, but the reality of this assertion had yet to be determined. Indeed, in many ways, this question is still up for debate—an ongoing process of change. Only by viewing this process in the proper political and cultural context can we grasp the full range of possibilities that confronted America in its earliest decades and beyond.

Notes

1. James Madison, "Advice to My Country," 1834, in Irving Brant, *James Madison: Commander in Chief, 1812–1836* (Indianapolis: Bobbs-Merrill, 1961), 530–31; Alexander Hamilton to Theodore Sedgwick, July 10, 1804, in *The Papers of Alexander Hamilton*, ed. Harold C. Syrett (New York: Columbia University Press, 1961–87), 26:309 (hereafter *Hamilton Papers*); Henry Lee to James Madison, April 3, 1790, *The Papers of James Madison*, ed. Robert Rutland, J.C.A. Stagg, et al., 17 vols. (Charlottesville: University Press of Virginia, 1962–), 13:136 (hereafter *Madison Papers*). On the crisis mentality of the period, see John Howe, "Republican Thought and the Political Violence of the 1790s," *American Quarterly* 19 (1967): 147–65; Marshall Smelser, "The Federalist Period as an Age of

Passion," *American Quarterly* 10 (1958): 391–419; Joanne B. Freeman, *Affairs of Honor: National Politics in the New Republic* (New Haven, Conn.: Yale University Press, 2001); Joanne B. Freeman, "The Election of 1800: A Study in the Logic of Political Change," *Yale Law Journal* 108 (June 1999): 1959–94; James Roger Sharp, *Politics in the Early Republic: The New Nation in Crisis* (New Haven, Conn.: Yale University Press, 1993), 1–8.

2. On the early national struggle toward the democratization of the American polity, see Gordon Wood, *The Radicalism of the American Revolution* (New York: Alfred A. Knopf, 1992). On elite sentiment toward democracy, see Wood, *Radicalism*, 240–43, 347–69; David Hackett Fischer, *The Revolution of American Conservatism: The Federalist Party in the Era of Jeffersonian Republicanism* (New York: Harper and Row, 1965).

3. On opposition to party development, see Richard Hofstadter, *The Idea of a Party System: The Rise of Legitimate Opposition in the United States* (Berkeley: University of California Press, 1969); Lance Banning, *The Jeffersonian Persuasion* (Ithaca, N.Y.: Cornell University Press, 1978); Richard Buel, Jr., *Securing the Revolution: Ideology in American Politics, 1789–1815* (Ithaca, N.Y.: Cornell University Press, 1972), 1–7.

4. It is important to note that state politics had a different dynamic. Locally, politicians could agree upon political priorities and principles far more readily than they could across regions; by 1800, local political parties were relatively organized, with statewide committees of correspondence and networks of influence. Because they posed little danger to the Union as a whole, such local organizations were far less threatening than their national equivalents, and far easier to institute and monitor among men who shared local interests. A host of scholarly studies of state politics bears this out. A sampling includes Harry Ammon, "The Formation of the Republican Party in Virginia, 1789–1796," *Journal of Southern History* 19 (August 1953): 283–310; Noble E. Cunningham, Jr., *The Jeffersonian Republicans: The Formation of Party Organization, 1789–1801* (Chapel Hill: University of North Carolina Press, 1957); Delbert H. Gilpatrick, *Jeffersonian Democracy of North Carolina, 1789–1816* (New York: Columbia University Press, 1931); Rudolph J. Pasler and Margaret C. Pasler, *The New Jersey Federalists* (Rutherford, N.J.: Fairleigh Dickinson University Press, 1975); Carl E. Prince, *New Jersey's Jeffersonian Republicans: The Genesis of an Early Party Machine* (Chapel Hill: University of North Carolina Press, 1967); Marx L. Fenzulli, Jr., *Maryland: The Federalist Years* (Rutherford, N.J.: Fairleigh Dickinson University Press, 1972); Lisle A. Rose, *Prologue to Democracy: The Federalists in the South, 1789–1800* (Lexington: University of Kentucky Press, 1968); Arthur Scherr, " 'The Republican Experiment,' and the Election of 1796 in Virginia," *West Virginia History* 37 (January 1976): 89–108; Harry M. Tinkcom, *The Republicans and Federalists in Pennsylvania, 1780–1801: A Study in National Stimulus and Local Response* (Harrisburg: Pennsylvania Historical and Museum Commission, 1950); Alfred F. Young, *The Democratic-Republicans of New York: The Origins, 1763–1797* (Chapel Hill: University of North Carolina Press, 1967); Norman L. Stamps, "Political Parties in Connecticut, 1789–1819," (Ph.D. dissertation, Yale University, 1950); Edmund B. Thomas, Jr., "Politics in the Land of Steady Habits:

Connecticut's First Political Party System, 1789–1820," (Ph.D. dissertation, Clark University, 1972).

5. Manning Dauer, *The Adams Federalists* (Baltimore: Johns Hopkins University Press, 1953), 267–74. Of course, between 1796 and 1802, there was some increase in partisan coherence, as Dauer's tables show.

6. On the political importance of personal character in the 1790s, see Freeman, *Affairs of Honor*, passim.

7. For the complete text of the acts, see James Morton Smith, *Freedom's Fetters: The Alien and Sedition Laws and American Civil Liberties* (Ithaca, N.Y.: Cornell University Press, 1956), 435–42. The acts were approved between June 18 and July 14, 1798.

8. See, for example, Leonard W. Levy, *Emergence of a Free Press* (New York: Oxford University Press, 1985), esp. 298–330. This attitude makes sense, given that the two major studies of the act—Levy's *Emergence of a Free Press*, initially published as *Legacy of Suppression: Freedom of Speech and Press in Early American History* (New York: Oxford University Press, 1960), and Smith, *Freedom's Fetters*—were written in the shadow of McCarthyism. On the Sedition Act, see also Jeffrey L. Pasley, *"The Tyranny of Printers": Newspaper Politics in the Early American Republic* (Charlottesville: University Press of Virginia, 2001), 105–31; Jeffrey A. Smith, *Printers and Press Freedom: The Ideology of Early American Journalism* (New York: Oxford University Press, 1998); Stanley Elkins and Eric McKitrick, *The Age of Federalism* (New York: Oxford University Press, 1993), 700–13; Norman L. Rosenberg, *Protecting the Best Men: An Interpretive History of the Law of Libel* (Chapel Hill: University of North Carolina Press, 1986), 79–100. Not surprisingly, new studies of early national political culture offer new insight into the logic of Federalist politics. See Barbara Oberg and Doron Ben-Atar, *Federalists Reconsidered* (Charlottesville: University Press of Virginia, 1998); Elkins and McKitrick, *The Age of Federalism*; Todd Estes, "Shaping the Politics of Public Opinion: Federalists and the Jay Treaty Debate," *Journal of the Early Republic* 20 (2000): 393–422.

9. Jefferson to John Dickinson, March 6, 1801, Thomas Jefferson Papers, Library of Congress.

10. Interestingly, Jefferson's final draft of the Kentucky Resolutions objects to the Sedition Act not on behalf of liberty of the press but as an unconstitutional display of federal power. In the Virginia Resolutions, on the other hand, Madison included a passage attesting to the importance of a free press. Though most elite politicians did not correspond extensively about the Sedition Act, it is important to note that there were popular and journalistic protests against it. See note 17 below.

11. Ames to Oliver Wolcott, Jr., April 22, 1798, Oliver Wolcott, Jr., Papers, Connecticut Historical Society.

12. On French-American relations, see Elkins and McKitrick, *Age of Federalism*, 301–73; Alexander DeConde, *The Quasi War: The Politics and Diplomacy of the Undeclared War with France, 1797–1801* (New York: Charles Scribner's Sons, 1966). On foreign relations generally, see Elkins and McKitrick, *Age of Federalism*, 375–449; Alexander DeConde, *Entangling Alliance: Politics and Diplomacy under George Washington* (Durham, N.C.: Duke University Press, 1958).

44 FREEMAN

13. Ames to Oliver Wolcott, Jr., September 2, 1795; Oliver Wolcott, Jr., to Oliver Wolcott, Sr., November 27, 1796; Oliver Wolcott, Jr. to Oliver Wolcott, Sr., April 18, 1796, Oliver Wolcott, Jr., Papers, Connecticut Historical Society.

14. Draft resolution, 1798, Breckenridge Family Papers, Library of Congress.

15. On the quasi war, see DeConde, *The Quasi War*; Elkins and McKitrick, *Age of Federalism*.

16. Smith, *Freedom's Fetters*, 108–10. The Federalists' other acts of the period—the Naturalization, Alien Friends, and Alien Enemies Acts—although blatantly partisan in their attempt to silence or deport largely Jeffersonian immigrants, were also spawned by a nativist impulse brought to flower by the foreign crises of the period.

17. January 21, 1801, *Annals of Congress*, 939. Federalists doubled their margin in the House, moving from 64 seats (versus 53 Republicans) in the Fifth Congress to 63 seats (versus 43 Republicans) in the Sixth Congress—but this tally is more complex than it first appears. In part, the election's timing complicates the matter; the Sedition Act was passed in July 1798, and congressional elections were held in various states between the spring of 1798 and the spring of 1799, raising questions about whether details about the act and its implications had yet trickled down to the masses. Further supporting this idea are the petitions against the act—some featuring impressive numbers of signatures—that began to appear in Congress in January 1800. The surge of support for the Federalists in the wake of the XYZ Affair probably influenced the elections as well. Also, it is important to note that although the Federalists were the victors in Congress, they lost the governorship of Pennsylvania and representation in the key states of Pennsylvania, New Jersey, and Maryland, as well as in southern legislatures, suggesting an equivocal response to Federalist policy, at best. Their main gains were in the South. John C. Miller, *The Federalist Era, 1789–1801* (New York: Harper and Row, 1963), 255; Sharp, *Politics in the Early Republic*, 223; Dauer, *Adams Federalists*, 233–34; Rose, *Prologue to Democracy*, 177; Cunningham, *Jeffersonian Republicans*, 133–35. For a sampling of popular and journalistic protests against the Sedition Act, see Donald H. Stewart, *The Opposition Press of the Federalist Period* (Albany: State University of New York Press, 1969), chap. 12.

18. See James P. Martin, "When Repression Is Democratic and Constitutional: The Federalist Theory of Representation and the Sedition Act of 1798," *University of Chicago Law Review* 66 (winter 1999): 117–82.

19. Washington to Oliver Wolcott, Jr., May 29, 1797, Oliver Wolcott, Jr., Papers, Connecticut Historical Society.

20. George Cabot to Oliver Wolcott, Jr., October 6, 1798, ibid.

21. In his study of Federalism in this period, David Hackett Fischer points out that there was a range of Federalist politicking, some men adapting better than others to the democratic demands of the moment. Fischer, *Revolution of American Conservatism*. See also Estes, "Shaping the Politics of Public Opinion."

22. Fisher Ames to Oliver Wolcott, Jr., March 24, 1797, Oliver Wolcott, Jr., Papers, Connecticut Historical Society.

23. Noah Webster to Oliver Wolcott, Jr., June 23, 1800, ibid.

24. George Cabot to Oliver Wolcott, Jr., June 9, 1798, ibid.

25. James Iredell [Grand Jury Charge at Philadelphia], April 1799, in Rosenberg, *Protecting the Best Men*, 84.

26. Martin, "When Repression Is Democratic," 127.

27. On the political importance of personal character in the 1790s, see Freeman, *Affairs of Honor.*

28. Oliver Wolcott, Jr., to William Heth, June 19, 1796, Oliver Wolcott, Jr., Papers, Connecticut Historical Society.

29. Alexander Hamilton, "Observations on Certain Documents Contained in No. V & VI of 'The History of the United States for the Year 1796,' In Which the Charge of Speculation Against Alexander Hamilton, Late Secretary of the Treasury, is Fully Refuted," (New York, 1797), *Hamilton Papers*, 21:238–39.

30. John Adams [Address to New Jersey College], 1798, in Smith, *Freedom's Fetters*, 99.

31. Alexander Addison, *Reports of Cases in the County Courts of the Fifth Circuit, and in the High Court of Errors and Appeals, of the State of Pennsylvania, and Charges to the Grand Juries of Those County Courts* [March sessions, 1797], in Pasley, *"Tyranny of Printers"*, 122. Addison was warning grand juries about the dangerous tendencies in libels against public officials as early as 1792. His comments about sedition to a 1798 grand jury were made into a pamphlet that was published around the country. Addison, *Liberty of Speech, and of the Press* (Washington, Pa., 1798). See also Rosenberg, *Protecting the Best Men*, 76–77.

32. Noah Webster to Oliver Wolcott, Jr., November 1, 1795, Oliver Wolcott, Jr., Papers, Connecticut Historical Society.

33. July 5, 1798, *Annals of Congress*, 2093–94. See also John Rutledge, Jr.'s defense of the Sedition Act, January 21, 1801, *Annals of Congress*, 933. On Federalist fears of the insurrectionary power of the press, see Pasley, *"Tyranny of Printers"*, 118–24.

34. Smith, *Freedom's Fetters*, 139.

35. Thomas O. Selfridge, *Trial of Thomas O. Selfridge, Attorney at Law . . . For Killing Charles Austin, on the Public Exchange, in Boston, August 4th, 1806* (Boston, 1806), 85–86.

36. On the logic and larger implications of honor disputes among early national politicians, see Freeman, *Affairs of Honor.*

37. Manning Dauer echoes this train of logic in *Adams Federalists*, 153. Elkins and McKitrick note the link between the Sedition Act and the unstable status of the political elite but make no connection between this instability and the instability of the political order. *Age of Federalism*, 713.

38. Sedgwick to unknown correspondent, March 7, 1798, Sedgwick Papers, Massachusetts Historical Society. Smith points out that there were also three indictments for sedition under the common law, two before the passage of the Sedition Act and one after. *Freedom's Fetters*, 185.

39. James Madison to Thomas Jefferson, ca. February 18, 1798, *Madison Papers*, 17:82.

40. Editor/printer victims included Benjamin Mayer and Conrad Fahnestock of the *Harrisburger Morgenrothe*; Vermont printer Judah P. Spooner; Thomas Adams of the Boston *Independent Chronicle*; William Duane of the Philadelphia *Aurora*; printer and pamphleteer James T. Callender; Anthony Haswell of the

Vermont Gazette; Charles Holt of the New London *Bee*; William Durrell of the *Mount Pleasant Register*; and editor Ann Greenleaf and foreman David Frothingham of the New York *Argus*. Matthew Lyon, a Vermont congressman of low repute, was also charged, as was David Brown, a common laborer and itinerant Republican public speaker, as well as frontier assemblyman Jedidiah Peck and lawyer Thomas Cooper (editor of the *Sunbury and Northumberland Gazette* for two months).

41. Jedidiah Peck, the other seeming exception, was a New York assemblyman and jack-of-all-trades in the frontier county of Otsego, a man of lower status than Cooper. See Alan Taylor, *William Cooper's Town* (New York: Alfred A. Knopf, 1995), 241–49.

42. On Cooper, see Dumas Malone, *The Public Life of Thomas Cooper, 1783–1839* (New Haven, Conn.: Yale University Press, 1926); Michael Durey, *Transatlantic Radicals and the Early American Republic* (Lawrence: University Press of Kansas, 1997), 24–25; Francis Wharton, *State Trials of the United States during the Administrations of Washington and Adams* (Philadelphia, 1849), 679–81; Smith, *Freedom's Fetters*, 307–8. On Cooper's trial, see Wharton, *State Trials*, 659–81; Smith, *Freedom's Fetters*, 307–33; *An Account of the Trial of Thomas Cooper of Northumberland on a Charge of Libel Against the President of the United States; Taken in Short Hand, with a Preface, Notes, and Appendix, by Thomas Cooper* (Philadelphia, John Bioren, printer, 1800).

43. Cooper edited the paper from April 20 to June 29, 1799, to allow the editor to prepare a book by Priestley for publication. Malone, *Public Life of Thomas Cooper*, 91.

44. Philadelphia *Aurora*, July 12, 1799; Charles Hall to William Rawle, July 18, 1799, Marion S. Carson Collection, Library of Congress. The essay was also reprinted in Cooper's collected *Political Essays*, which went through two editions between mid-1799 and February 1800. Thomas Cooper, *Political essays: originally inserted in the Northumberland Gazette,: with additions* (Northumberland Pa., printed by Andrew Kennedy, 1799). See also Smith, *Freedom's Fetters*, 308–9; Malone, *Public Life of Thomas Cooper*, 101–3.

45. Charles Hall to William Rawle, July 18, 1799, Marion S. Carson Collection, Library of Congress. Adams made the appointment in 1797. Smith, *Freedom's Fetters*, 309–10. Hall's letters to Rawle do not appear to have been previously discovered.

46. Charles Hall to William Rawle, August 1, 1799, Marion S. Carson Collection, Library of Congress.

47. Charles Hall to Timothy Pickering, July 26, 1799, Timothy Pickering Papers, Library of Congress.

48. Timothy Pickering to Charles Hall, August 1, 1799, ibid.; Timothy Pickering to John Adams, August 1, 1799, ibid.

49. William Plumer to Jeremiah Smith, December 10, 1791, William Plumer Papers, Library of Congress. See also Oliver Wolcott, Jr., to Oliver Wolcott, Sr., November 14, 1795, and Oliver Wolcott, Jr., to Oliver Wolcott, Sr., January [18??], 1794, Oliver Wolcott, Jr., Papers, Connecticut Historical Society.

50. Although there is no direct proof identifying Hall as "A True American," the little evidence that exists points in that direction. Based on Pickering's re-

sponse, Hall's essay was clearly lengthy, as is the essay by "A True American"; by Hall's own profession, his essay contained a section on Cooper's background, as does "A True American;" since Hall was still composing and editing his essay on August 1, a publication date of October 23 is quite logical, as is September 30 for the date on which the essay was completed. See also Smith, *Freedom's Fetters*, 312n10.

51. Reading *Weekly Advertiser*, October 26, 1799, in Wharton, *State Trials*, 660.

52. Adams to Pickering, August 13, 1799, Timothy Pickering Papers, Library of Congress.

53. On Cooper's clash with Burke, see Malone, *Public Life of Thomas Cooper*, 40–53.

54. Long after his clash with Burke, Cooper recalled that Attorney General Sir John Scott had warned him to publish his defense "in an octavo form, so as to confine it probably to that class of readers who may consider it coolly: so soon as it is published cheaply for dissemination among the populace, it will be my duty to prosecute." Malone, *Public Life of Thomas Cooper*, 53.

55. November 2, 1799, in Wharton, *State Trials*, 660–62. For a lengthy account of this exchange, and of Cooper's trial generally, see *An Account of the Trial of Thomas Cooper*.

56. On Cooper's involvement with Duane and its link with Cooper's arrest, see Smith, *Freedom's Fetters*, 315–16; Malone, *Public Life of Thomas Cooper*, 112–19. For Cooper's letter, see Philadelphia *Aurora*, March 27, 1800; *Philadelphia Gazette*, March 27, 1800.

57. This chain of events suggests a direct cause and response, but Rawle may have been simply waiting for the first session of the federal circuit court after Cooper's initial violation. Pickering's August 1799 letter urging Rawle to prosecute Cooper suggests as much.

58. Wharton, *State Trials*, 664.

59. Ibid., 666. See also ibid., 668.

60. Thomas Cooper, April 16, 1800, as quoted in William Rawle [Notes of Cooper's Trial], Marion S. Carson Collection, Library of Congress. Rawle's notes do not appear to have been previously discovered.

61. On the logic of "paper war" and the demands of self-defense, see Freeman, *Affairs of Honor*, chap. 3.

62. Wharton, *State Trials*, 662–63.

63. Thomas Cooper to C. P. Wayne, October 10, 1800, in *Gazette of the United States*, October 11, 1800.

64. Durey, *Transatlantic Radicals*, 254–55. Wayne succeeded John Ward Fenno as editor of the *Gazette of the United States* in 1800. Andrew Brown was also challenged to a duel by Republican John Richard McMahon in January 1799. There were many such attacks. Particularly notable are the attacks on Federalist editors William Cobbett, who was threatened by a group of Republicans in April 1797, and William Coleman, who was assaulted twice—in 1818 so viciously that he remained paralyzed from the waist down for the rest of his life. Republican editors received similar treatment. Bache was assaulted in 1797, as was William Duane in May 1799; attacked by a group of Federalist soldiers, Duane offered to

meet any one of them in a duel but was refused. Joseph Gales was assaulted during this period, James Lyon was threatened, and in December 1802, James Callender was caned. Durey, *Transatlantic Radicals*, 254–55; Smith, *Freedom's Fetters*, 285; Michael Durey, *"With the Hammer of Truth": James Thomson Callender and America's Early National Heroes* (Charlottesville: University Press of Virginia, 1990), 164–65; Fischer, *Revolution of American Conservatism*, 186.

65. Hamilton to Oliver Wolcott, Jr., August 3, 1800, *Hamilton Papers*, 25:54–55. Adams had declared Hamilton the head of "a British faction." For Adams's comments, see Timothy Phelps to Oliver Wolcott, Jr., July 15, 1800, Wolcott to Chauncey Goodrich, July 20, 1800, George Cabot to Wolcott, July 20, 1800, Benjamin Goodhue to Wolcott, July 30, 1800, Fisher Ames to Wolcott, August 3, 1800, Wolcott to Ames, August 10, 1800, Goodrich to Wolcott, August 26, 1800, in George Gibbs, *Memoirs of the Administrations of Washington and John Adams*, 2 vols. (New York: William Van Norden, printer, 1846), 2:380, 382, 383, 395, 400–2, 411–12.

66. Pennsylvania representative Albert Gallatin raised this fact during an 1801 discussion of the Sedition Act, charging that it demonstrated the partisan nature of the act and its enforcement. Massachusetts Federalist Harrison Gray Otis responded by noting that no one had interfered with the efforts of "a certain Northumbrian apostle of liberty" to bring charges against Hamilton, yet nothing had come of it. January 22, 1801, *Annals of Congress*, 958. On the influence of Hamilton's pamphlet on his reputation, see Freeman, *Affairs of Honor*, 119.

67. Quoted in Philadelpha *Gazette*, November 1, 1800, in Dumas Malone, "The Threatened Prosecution of Alexander Hamilton under the Sedition Act by Thomas Cooper," *American Historical Review* 29 (October 1923): 76–81, quote at 77. Other than Malone's article, scholarly studies have almost entirely overlooked the incident; it is mentioned in Smith, *Freedom's Fetters*, 405n; and Stewart, *Opposition Press*, 481.

68. See also Jeffrey L. Pasley, " 'Artful and Designing Men': Political Professionalism in the Early American Republic, 1775–1820" (Ph.D. dissertation, Harvard University, 1993), 457–74.

69. George Hay, *An Essay on the Liberty of the Press, Shewing that the Requisition of Security for Good Behavior from Libellers is Perfectly Compatible with the Constitution and Laws of Virginia* (Richmond, 1803), 41–45, in Rosenberg, *Protecting the Best Men*, 106; *Journal of the Senate of the Commonwealth of Pennsylvania* (Philadelphia, 1807), 13–14, in ibid., 106–7. Hay originally published his pamphlet in 1799. In the second edition, hoping to prevent last-minute slanders from corrupting the electoral process, he added a recommendation that justices of the peace should impose bonds for good behavior upon accused libelers—including newspaper editors—effectively silencing them before their trial. McKean agreed, proposing such a measure in 1806, as did New York Republicans in 1803. In ibid., 106–7, 299n15. See also generally, in ibid., 89–99, 105–6; Levy, *Emergence of a Free Press*, 304–8. As Rosenberg points out, James Madison and St. George Tucker had similar views about the political importance of personal character. *Protecting the Best Men*, 93–94.

70. Tunis Wortman, *A Treatise Concerning Political Inquiry and the Liberty of the Press* (New York, 1800), in Rosenberg, *Protecting the Best Men*, 93–94.

71. Thomas Jefferson, Second Inaugural Address, March 4, 1805, in *Jefferson: Writings*, ed. Merrill D. Peterson (New York: Library of America, 1984), 521–22. For a positive spin on Jefferson's evolving policy concerning the press, see Dumas Malone, *Jefferson the President: Second Term, 1805–1809* (Boston: Little Brown, 1974), 371–91. Nerone emphasizes a clash between Jefferson's view of the press in theory and in practice. John Nerone, *Violence against the Press: Policing the Public Sphere in U.S. History* (New York: Oxford University Press, 1994), 58. For a far darker view, see Leonard Levy, *Jefferson and Civil Liberties: The Darker Side* (Chicago: Elephant, 1963).

72. The four suits were against Barzillai Hudson and George Goodwin, publishers of the *Connecticut Courant*, who had criticized Jefferson's secret appropriation of funds to aid negotiations in western Florida; Thomas Collier, editor of the *Litchfield Monitor*, who had attacked Jefferson's official conduct; ministerial candidate Thaddeus Osgood, who had delivered a sermon denouncing Jefferson as "a base, traitorous infidel, debaucher and liar"; and Reverend Azel Backus, whose sermon had condemned Jefferson as "a liar, whoremaster, debaucher, drunkard, gambler," and infidel. Malone, *Jefferson the President*, 377–78. Even the Jefferson-friendly Malone acknowledges (372) that the Connecticut libel cases, "more perhaps than anything else that happened during his presidency, would appear to cast a shadow on his title as a conservator of human rights," and violate Jeffersonian principles as well.

73. [James Sullivan], *A Dissertation Upon the Constitutional Freedom of the Press in the United States of America* (1801), in Pasley, " 'Artful and Designing Men,' " 461, and Levy, *Emergence of a Free Press*, 334. Pasley suggests that Republicans wavered in their sedition prosecutions, aware that their actions were at odds with their political creed. " 'Artful and Designing Men,' " 467.

74. Thomas Seymour and six citizens to Thomas Jefferson, December 20, 1806, in Malone, *Jefferson the President*, 380–81.

75. January 22, 1801, *Annals of Congress*, 952.

76. Ames to Oliver Wolcott, Jr., January 12, 1800, in Gibbs, *Memoirs of the Administrations of Washington and John Adams*, 2:319.

Chapter Three

AFFAIRS OF OFFICE

THE EXECUTIVE DEPARTMENTS, THE ELECTION OF 1828,

AND THE MAKING OF THE DEMOCRATIC PARTY

RICHARD R. JOHN

SHORTLY AFTER THE INAUGURATION in March 1829 of Andrew Jackson as the seventh president of the United States, the influential Unitarian clergyman William Ellery Channing questioned the rationale for broadening the mandate of the government over which Jackson presided. The Constitution had established a national market, the federal courts had brokered disputes that might otherwise turn violent, and the Post Office Department had created a "chain of sympathies" that transformed the far-flung states into "one great neighborhood."[1] Why should legislators undertake new initiatives that might imperil the "actual beneficent influence" that these governmental institutions were *already* exerting?[2] High tariffs impeded "unrestricted commerce"—the "most important means of diffusing through the world knowledge, arts, comforts, civilization, religion, and liberty."[3] Federal public works raised constitutional questions of "no small difficulty" that would almost certainly embroil Congress in "endless and ever-multiplying intrigues" and become a "fountain of bitterness and discord."[4] "In our republic," Channing concluded, "the aim of Congress should be to stamp its legislation with all possible simplicity, and to abstain from measures, which, by their complication, obscurity, and uncertainty, must distract the public mind, and throw it into agitation and angry controversy."[5] As a people, we want "no new excitement": "Our danger is from overaction, from impatient and selfish enterprise, from feverish energy, from too rapid growth, rather than from stagnation and lethargy."[6]

Channing's remarks highlight two axioms of American politics that Jackson's contemporaries took for granted but which present-day commentators sometimes forget. By 1829, the central government had already become a leading actor on the national stage, and any broadening of its mandate was likely to prove contentious and might even put the Union at risk. In this way, Channing provides a frame of reference for this essay, which explores the relationship between state building and party formation in the period between the Missouri crisis of 1819–1821 and the abolitionist mails controversy of 1835.

This essay contends that the rise of the federal executive departments in the decades *preceding* Jackson's victory in the election of 1828 was a necessary precondition for the emergence of the Democratic party in the months immediately *following* Jackson's inauguration. It further contends that the political orbit around which Jackson's Democratic party revolved had been subtly yet fundamentally reoriented by the Missouri crisis of 1819–1821.

The federal executive departments were organized in the first federal Congress (1789–1793) in accordance with principles outlined in the federal Constitution. The most important were the Treasury Department, the State Department, the War Department, and the Post Office Department. Their rise during the next four decades was slow yet steady. As they grew larger and more geographically extensive, they assumed new responsibilities, increased their organizational capabilities, and acquired a considerable measure of bureaucratic autonomy—which, by the 1820s, tempted ambitious department heads eager to advance their political careers.

The Democratic party received its initial impetus from the heterogeneous political coalition that backed Andrew Jackson in the election of 1824. The coalition failed when, in a controversial decision, the House of Representatives rejected Jackson in favor of John Quincy Adams, even though Jackson had received more votes from both the electoral college and the electorate. It triumphed in 1828 when Jackson defeated Adams in the electoral college. In the months immediately following Jackson's inauguration, the coalition became transformed into the Democratic party, the lineal ancestor of the Democratic party of today.[7] The Democratic party was a genuinely new kind of institution, making its emergence an unusual event and, as such, one that invites explanation. It was, as is often noted, the world's first *mass* party, in the sense that it was a self-perpetuating organization that mobilized a large and diverse electorate on a regular basis in order to win elections and shape public policy. In addition, it was the first political party in the United States to unreservedly champion democracy. For each of these reasons, its origins have long intrigued students of American public life. From whence did it come? What best explains its emergence during the opening months of Jackson's administration, a half century *after* the adoption of the federal Constitution?

Recent scholarship on the making of the Democratic party traces its origins to a constellation of disruptive economic changes—often termed the "market revolution"—that triggered the Panic of 1819.[8] Jacksonians and

Democrats are supposed to have opposed market expansion; National Republicans and Whigs to have embraced it. Proponents of this view typically examine party formation from the standpoint of the electorate rather than party leaders, and dismiss the central government as little more than the arena within which the struggle over market expansion was waged. To clinch their argument, they highlight social divisions within the electorate that postdated the establishment of the Democratic party. Few demonstrate how these divisions explain the initial organization of the party in the months following Jackson's inauguration, or why party leaders made government corruption rather than market expansion the focus of Jackson's 1828 election campaign. This is not altogether surprising, since the favored methodology of these historians—the analysis of aggregate data using behavioral assumptions—is unsuited to the analysis of specific events.

One limitation of the "market revolution" thesis is the tendency of its proponents to exaggerate the aversion of ordinary Americans to market expansion. "The pleasing rhetoric of Jackson's moralizing fables notwithstanding," as one critic has aptly remarked, "Americans demanded the market revolution long before they understood it. . . ."[9] There is, in short, little reason to assume that hostility to market expansion hastened the Jacksonian ascendancy—or, for that matter, that the "revolution" that swept Andrew Jackson into the White House in 1828 originated with the people rather than with the politicians. On the contrary, as Robert V. Remini contended almost a half century ago, this "revolution" moved in "one direction only—from the top down."[10]

Just as scholars have exaggerated the economic traditionalism of the Democratic party, so, too, they have overstated its administrative modernity. Some three decades ago, historian Lynn L. Marshall and political scientist Matthew Crenson credited the Jacksonians with introducing to the central government the routinized administrative procedures that have come to be known as bureaucracy.[11] For Marshall, bureaucracy was a solution to economic inefficiency; for Crenson, a response to social disorder. Both regarded it as a Jacksonian legacy and hailed Jackson's postmaster general, Amos Kendall, as its guiding spirit.[12]

The Marshall-Crenson thesis neatly inverted the older view, originated by Jackson's contemporaries and endorsed by subsequent commentators for almost a century, that the Jacksonians *weakened* the administrative capacity of the central government by dismantling a preexisting bureaucracy and instituting a "spoils system" that replaced meritorious administrators with party hacks. For Marshall and Crenson, partisan maneuvering had the opposite effect of encouraging administrative reform. Or, as one enthusiastic proponent of their thesis put it: "Spoils bred bureaucracy."[13]

The Marshall-Crenson thesis has long been endorsed by political scientists interested in probing the origins of the modern American state.[14] Yet it rests on a slim empirical base. Several of the bureaucratic precedents that the Jacksonians had supposedly invented had, in fact, originated in the eighteenth century and had been significantly refined by a previous generation of public administrators that included Treasury Secretary William H. Crawford, Secretary of War John C. Calhoun, and Postmaster General John McLean. Once in office, the Jacksonians did little to modernize the administrative apparatus. If anything, their often clumsy directives made the administration of the executive departments even more burdensome and complex.[15]

Symptomatic of the problems with the Marshall-Crenson thesis is its treatment of the deliberate reorganizations of the executive departments that took place during Jackson's presidency—the "first practical test," Marshall gushed, of "innovative techniques of large-scale rational organization on a peculiarly American model."[16] A case in point was the reorganization of the Post Office Department that followed the enactment of the Post Office Act of 1836. Both Marshall and Crenson attributed this legislation to Kendall and hailed it as the quintessential Jacksonian administrative reform. In fact, however, the Post Office Act of 1836 originated with neither the Jacksonians nor the executive. Rather, it was a congressional response to a humiliating postal finance scandal that haunted the Jacksonians during Jackson's second term. It was pushed through Congress not by Kendall but, rather, by a bipartisan coalition headed by anti-Jacksonian Whigs. For a time, Jacksonian party leaders actually opposed its enactment in the fear that public exposure of their administrative shortcomings might hurt them at the polls.[17]

Marshall and Crenson's erroneous contention that the origins of the federal bureaucracy did not emerge until the 1830s—a half century *after* the adoption of the Constitution—is emblematic of an even more basic mischaracterization of the early American state. It has long been a cliché to dismiss the central government in the early republic as a "midget institution in a giant land."[18] The early American state, as political scientist Stephen Skowronek has declared in a widely influential formulation, was a "state of courts and parties," an "innocuous reflection" of the wider society in which executive departments were unimportant and a "sense of statelessness" was a hallmark of American political culture.[19]

The origins of this "courts and parties" school are complex.[20] Its persistence owes more than a little to the continuing influence of the disparaging—and indeed almost comic—portrait of the early Washington political establishment that political scientist James Sterling Young limned in his prizewinning *Washington Community*.[21] In this behaviorist tour de force, first published in 1966, Young attributed congressional voting patterns in the period between 1800 and 1828 less to party loyalty, public demand, or considerations of public policy than to the highly localized, and largely idiosyncratic, alliances that legislators forged in Capitol Hill boarding-houses. Not until the Jacksonians established the mass party, Young concluded, would public figures devise effective ways to link the government and the governed.[22]

For over three decades, Young's *Washington Community* has beguiled historians and political scientists with its methodological novelty, artful argumentation, and literary charm. Unfortunately, as numerous critics have demonstrated, it is neither a full nor an accurate guide to the main-springs of national politics during the early republic. Young underesti-mated the organizational capabilities of the executive departments, ne-glected policy issues, and discounted discrete events, such as the Missouri crisis (which is not even listed in the index).[23] In addition, he exaggerated the insulation of the citizenry from the central government in the period preceding the advent of the mass party. In particular, he ignored the many intermediary institutions that, long before 1828, linked the central govern-ment and the wider world. Of these, the most notable included the petition process, the newspaper press, the postal system, and nationally oriented voluntary associations. Most devastatingly, Young embellished his argu-ment with suggestive snippets from primary documents that he sometimes took out of context and that often rested, as critics have politely observed, on a "highly imaginative" reading of the evidence.[24] In short, the continu-ing popularity of *Washington Community* as a foundational text for stu-dents of American political development says more about the mistaken yet seductive and enduring appeal of a simple and uncomplicated past than it does about national politics in a formative age.

The remainder of this essay explores the relationship between the federal executive departments and the Democratic party. It builds on the insight, derived from political scientists and historical sociologists, that political events can have political origins and governmental institutions can be agents of change. In so doing, it challenges the common assumption that political events are, in some fundamental sense, the product of deeper or underlying social circumstances that originate outside of the political realm.[25]

Since arguments about the early American state are often misconstrued, it may be helpful to begin with a pair of disclaimers. It is not my intention to contend that, in the early republic, the American state was synonymous with the central government (let alone the executive departments). In this period—as today—the American state (or polity) consisted of a variety of institutions that included the states and localities as well as federalism and the common law. It is, similarly, not my intention to downplay the differences between the executive departments in the early republic and the administrative apparatus that has emerged since the Progressive Era. Much could be learned by tracing the continuities and discontinuities between, say, the War Department in the 1820s under John C. Calhoun and the Commerce Department in the 1920s under Herbert Hoover. Yet it would be anachronistic to treat the former as a microcosm of the latter—or, more broadly, to view nineteenth-century governmental institutions through a twentieth-century lens. This essay contends, on the contrary, that the origins of the Democratic party are best understood in relation to the rise of the executive departments in the period *preceding* the election of 1828.

Political commentators in the early republic took it for granted that the central government was an important institution and that the broadening of its mandate could threaten vested interests. Some, like Channing, opposed a broadened mandate; others, like John Quincy Adams, endorsed it. Few denied that the central government was an influential agent of change.

The ubiquity of this mental outlook owed much to the continuing influence in the early republic of certain habits of mind that had been influential in the late eighteenth century among the founders of the American republic. Known today as the "whig," "classical republican," or "country party" tradition, this mind-set had been popularized in seventeenth-century England by writers opposed to the consolidation of the English state and the establishment of the Bank of England. Among its tenets were the presumptions that political parties were evil, that economic conditions were a product of political fiat, and that the manipulation of government patronage for partisan ends was the essence of corruption.[26] Paradoxically, some of the same historians who treat this mind-set with the utmost seriousness when it found expression during the revolutionary era dismiss it as anachronistic and even paranoid when it was revived in the early republic. This was true even though, by almost any measure, the central government in the 1820s was more powerful—in the sense of commanding more resources, controlling more patronage, and reaching farther into the hinterland—than the imperial state in British North America had been in the period prior to 1775. The cultural repertoire of the early republic—like that of any epoch—was limited, and antistatism was one of its defining motifs. The specter of governmental consolidation, declared French traveler Alexis de Tocqueville in his *Democracy in America*—in reflecting on a trip to the United States that he had taken between 1831 and 1832—was the "one great fear" that haunted public figures throughout the

United States.[27] Tocqueville dismissed this fear as overblown, citing the diversity of the American people; for Channing, it was precisely this diversity that was cause for concern.

The Democratic party emerged in a political universe that had changed radically since the founders of the American republic drafted the federal constitution in 1787. The founders' political economy had focused resolutely on Europe. With the end of the Napoleonic wars in 1815, a new generation of statesmen reoriented the American political economy toward the vast North American interior. To facilitate the expansion of the home market, legislators promulgated an ambitious legislative agenda that would later become known as the "American System." Among its principal elements were a new national bank, a protective tariff, the orderly settlement of public lands, and the construction of public works. Beginning in 1816, much of this agenda was enacted. Legislative landmarks included the rechartering of the Bank of the United States in 1816; the tariffs of 1816, 1824, and 1828; the Land Act of 1820; and the General Survey Act of 1824. Its primary judicial expression was the affirmation of the constitutionality of the Bank of the United States by Chief Justice John Marshall in *M'Culloch v. Maryland* (1819).

Among the public figures to promote this ambitious agenda were Henry Clay, John Quincy Adams, and John McLean. John C. Calhoun also supported it early on, only to shift his position in response to changing conditions in South Carolina. For these "National Republicans," as they would come to be known, the founders' bold experiment in republican government was open-ended, and the central government a progressive, developmental force.[28]

The implementation of this developmental agenda ensured the continuing elaboration of the federal executive departments, which had been growing steadily since the 1790s.[29] In the United States, no less than in France, Germany, or Great Britain, big government *preceded* big business. By 1828, over 10,000 people staffed the myriad post offices, land offices, and customhouses that were scattered throughout the country. An additional 12,000 served in the military, half in the navy and marines and half in the army, stationed mostly in the West. The size and geographical reach of this administrative apparatus far exceeded that of any other institution in the country. No private enterprise could match the organizational capabilities of the Post Office Department, the Treasury Department, or the War Department. The Post Office Department alone had eight thousand offices, making it not only the largest public agency in the United States but also one of the largest, most administratively complex, and most geographically far-flung organizations in the world.

As the executive departments grew larger and more complex, ordinary Americans ratcheted up their expectations with regard to the kinds of benefits that they wished them to provide. In the realms of communications and transportation, popular demand for new and improved facilities was steady and insistent. Beginning in the 1790s, individuals throughout the United States successfully petitioned Congress to extend the postal network throughout the trans-Appalachian hinterland.[30] Before long, many came to regard mail delivery as a fundamental right, or what we would today call an entitlement. Most postal petitioners requested merely that Congress increase the number of routes upon which the mail was transmitted; only occasionally, and in special circumstances, did they *also* demand that the central government improve the roads over which the mail was conveyed. By the 1820s, this began to change. For many, it now seemed but a matter of time before the citizenry would compel Congress to bring the transportation infrastructure up to the level that the postal network had already attained.

The General Survey Act of 1824 was a legislative response to this popular demand. By creating a Board of Engineers to oversee the design of future public works, it validated the growing popular presumption that the central government had a mandate to construct a national system of roads and canals. In so doing, it paralleled the Post Office Act of 1792, which had established an analogous precedent for the elaboration of the republic's postal network. Following the enactment of the General Survey Act, popular expectations with respect to the kind of public works projects that the central government ought to undertake soared.[31] Between 1824 and 1828, ninety public works projects received federal funding—including the Chesapeake and Ohio Canal—inaugurating an internal improvements boom that would continue well into the Jackson administration.

Talent gravitates to power, and, in the 1820s, the executive departments became nurseries for presidential aspirants. John McLean used his position as head of the Post Office Department to catapult himself from almost total obscurity into a perennial presidential contender. In the election of 1824, three of the five principal candidates—Adams, Calhoun, and William H. Crawford—were department heads, while a fourth, Henry Clay, would soon be appointed secretary of state. Political insiders took it for granted that Crawford, as treasury secretary, was manipulating the four years law—which mandated the reappointment of the principal treasury officers every four years—to build a political machine. Should Crawford win in 1824, it was publicly announced that he would sweep the offices, encouraging speculation about appointments to positions from which the incumbents had yet to be displaced.[32] Calhoun, similarly, was assumed to be stealthily building a vast public works empire in the Department of War, to which the Board of Engineers had been attached.

In addition, Calhoun was quietly elaborating plans for the relocation of the remaining eastern tribes to the west of the Mississippi—laying the groundwork for the enactment, during Jackson's presidency, of the Indian Removal Act.

The alleged maladministration of the executive departments was a leading issue in the 1824 presidential campaign. Calhounites accused Crawford of official malfeasance, while Jacksonians attacked the federal bureaucracy as corrupt. For Jackson stalwart John Eaton, author of the anonymous *Letters of Wyoming*, Jackson's *lack* of executive experience became his most valuable asset—since it ensured that he, alone among the candidates, had never manipulated executive patronage to advance his career.[33] For the first time in the history of the republic, a presidential aspirant was portrayed as a virtuous outsider determined to take on the Washington establishment.

The growing prominence of department heads in national politics helps to explain why numerous contemporaries, as well as many historians, have characterized the executive branch under James Monroe and John Quincy Adams as weak. Whether or not the presidents in this period were weak is a debatable point; there can be no question, however, that the department heads were strong. The postmaster general, the treasury secretary, and the secretary of war each enjoyed an impressive measure of bureaucratic autonomy, due, in large part, to their uncontested authority over the patronage that their departments disbursed. Predictably, they grew accustomed to negotiating directly with power brokers within Congress and the states, raising the specter of corruption and occasioning frequent embarrassment for Monroe and Adams.[34]

The executive departments played an equally conspicuous role in the 1828 presidential campaign. The 1828 election was by far the most expensive to have been waged in the United States up to that point in time. Though it is impossible to know for certain, it probably cost around $1 million to elect Jackson president. This expense was borne primarily *not* by Jackson's supporters but, rather, by the Post Office Department through various hidden subsidies that postal patrons paid on their mail.[35] Of these subsidies, the most important was the franking privilege, which granted certain public officers—including postmasters—the privilege to send an unlimited number of pamphlets, newspapers, and letters through the mail.

The Jackson campaign was coordinated from Washington, D.C., by Duff Green, a Missouri-based entrepreneur who in 1826 had secured the editorship of the Washington-based *United States Telegraph*. Green used the *Telegraph* to coordinate a far-flung media blitz that embraced a galaxy of strategically located Jacksonian newspapers. Had postal facilities remained as limited as they had been in 1800, it would have been technically impossible to mount such an elaborate campaign. In the absence of the franking privilege, it would have been prohibitively expensive.

Green recognized in the supposed maladministration of the executive departments a compelling campaign issue, and freely elaborated in the *Telegraph* on themes that Eaton had raised in his *Letters of Wyoming*. In editorial after editorial, Green lambasted the "corruption" that executive patronage had supposedly fostered and trumpeted the need for "retrenchment and reform." No issue preoccupied Green more than Adams's appointment of Clay as Adams's secretary of state soon after Clay had secured Adams the vote of the Kentucky delegation during the 1824 presidential election—an outcome Green derided, in the best tradition of eighteenth-century English opposition writer James Burgh, as a "corrupt bargain." Adams, Green contended, had rewarded Clay with a lucrative office in an executive department in return for Clay's support in securing Adams's election.

In a certain sense, Green's anticorruptionism marked a shift in the Jacksonians' appeal. As recently as 1821, Jackson himself had denounced the "*mania* for retrenchment," while, as a Tennessee senator between 1823 and 1825, he had supported a protective tariff and federal public works.[36] Yet Green's verbal assault reflected far more than merely his outrage at Adams's appointment of Clay. Eaton's *Letters of Wyoming*, after all, had been published before the House vote that decided the election of 1824. Rather, Green built upon, and exploited, the pervasive anxiety about the evils of governmental consolidation that Tocqueville had reflected upon in his *Democracy*. The rise of the executive departments—declared Jacksonian stalwart Thomas Hart Benton, in a congressional report on executive patronage that he authored in 1826—"completely falsified" James Madison's celebrated contention in *Federalist* 45 and 46 (1788) that the central government would never acquire the resources to challenge the prerogative of the states. Should Congress fail to enact remedial legislation, Benton warned, the central government would soon dominate the states as effectively as if they were "so many provinces of one vast empire."[37] Benton greatly exaggerated the impending demise of states' rights; yet his report documented the extent to which the rise of the executive departments had rendered anticorruptionism plausible. The growing popular demand for public works had an analogous effect. Had Adams not appointed Clay as his secretary of state, Green would have had little trouble inventing some other "corrupt bargain" with which to taunt the Adamsites and embolden the Jackson campaign.

Green's editorial stance helped bridge the ideological divide between Jackson's early supporters, most of whom hailed from the West, and the many southerners who had initially backed Crawford in 1824, but who eventually swung around to Jackson following Crawford's defeat. For westerners intent on rapid commercial development, anticorruptionism cast the central government as an impediment to the release of entrepreneurial energy. For southerners fearful that the central government might imperil the institution of slavery, it provided reassurance that a Jackson administration would champion no new government initiatives that might put their interests at risk.

The rise of the executive departments might in other circumstances have benefited the Adams campaign. After all, Adams, as president, had—at least in theory—control over the patronage that his department heads disbursed. In practice, however, Adams refused to interfere with his department heads' autonomy, depriving himself of a resource that might well have strengthened his campaign. Adams went so far as to retain John McLean as his postmaster general, even though McLean was widely presumed (correctly) to have been surreptitiously dispensing postal patronage in order to hasten Adams's defeat—and, or so McLean hoped, boost McLean's own presidential aspirations. "Patronage is a sacred trust," McLean sanctimoniously lectured Massachusetts Adamsite Edward Everett, in rebuffing Everett's efforts to appoint Adams's supporters to office: "It was never designed for the personal gratification of the individual holding it." Should political supporters be rewarded with official preferment, the "struggle for office" would be perpetual and "thus would perish, perhaps forever, the best hope of man."[38] Everett saw matters differently. President Adams, Everett observed, made the "experiment" of appointing public officers with "exclusive regard to merit," and "what has been the reward"? A "most furious opposition, rallied on the charge of corrupt distribution of office, and the open or secret hostility of three-fourths of the officeholders in the Union."[39] In Great Britain, Everett elaborated, there existed a multitude of options for ambitious men seeking public renown, including the military and the peerage. In the United States, in contrast, there was nothing but public office. As a consequence, Everett explained, the lure of official preferment was virtually irresistible: "Office here is family, rank, hereditary fortune, in short everything out of the range of private life. This links its possession with innate principles of our nation; and truly incredible are the efforts men are willing to make, the humiliation they will endure, to get it."[40]

For Green, the promise of official preferment was a tempting reward to dangle before the party workers who coordinated the Jackson campaign. Ironically, the very practices that Green attacked as corrupt gave him a compelling incentive with which to tantalize his supporters. By lambasting the Adams administration for its manipulation of executive patronage, Green established a plausible rationale for a general sweep of the executive departments. Indeed, it was largely for this reason that party workers found anticorruptionism so compelling. From their perspective, it held out the promise of a rich harvest in offices and contracts should Jackson prevail. And who could have a better claim on these perquisites than the men who had engineered Adams's defeat?

Jackson's critics agreed. The "mass" of *all* the political parties of the day, Everett perceptively observed shortly before the election, was held together *not* by principle—as political parties had been in the 1790s, when the Federalists battled the Republicans—but, rather, by the "hope of office, and its honors and emoluments."[41] Should Jackson publicly proclaim, Everett wryly predicted, that, if victorious, he would dismiss none of his political antagonists and appoint no one on account of his political support, this would "cost him every vote out of Tennessee."[42]

For sensitive observers such as Channing, the brazenness of the scramble for office was appalling. The selection of a president, Channing warned, though a "comparatively inferior concern"—in relation to, for example, to the deliberations of Congress—had become so all-consuming that the quadrennial campaigns for the "Executive Department" had come to pose the single greatest immediate threat to the Union. It would be better, Channing concluded, to choose the president by lot, rather than to "repeat the degrading struggle through which we have recently passed."[43]

Jackson's victory paved the way for the establishment of the Democratic party as a self-perpetuating organization. To set the stage for the much heralded purge, Green publicly announced in the *Telegraph* that Jackson would "reward his friends and punish his enemies."[44] In the "distribution of the federal patronage"—Green explained to one Jackson supporter, shortly before Jackson's inauguration—"General Jackson will have much in his power. He can enrich and strengthen his party by a transfer of the lucrative offices into sound hands."[45] With other Jackson supporters, Green was more forthright. "How is your postmaster?" Green queried a campaign worker shortly before Jackson's inauguration: "Can't I serve you there? Or can't I obtain for you a mail contract? Let me hear from you fully on these points. . . . I am now in a position where I can serve my friends. . . ."[46]

In response to Green's call, hundreds of would-be-officeholders descended on Washington. Little wonder that Jackson's inauguration turned into a near riot. The principal attendees were not sturdy backwoodsmen drawn to the capital to witness the "first people's inaugural," as generations of historians have naively assumed.[47] Rather, they were expectant officeholders ravenous for spoils.[48]

The partisan dismissals that began shortly after Jackson's inauguration were a genuinely new development in American politics. Long before 1829, partisan dismissals had become familiar features of electoral politics in the Middle Atlantic states—and, in particular, in New York and Pennsylvania. Yet nothing even remotely like the purge that Green had prefigured in the *Telegraph* had ever before taken place in Washington, D.C.[49] For the first time in American history, public figures throughout the country observed the workings of patronage politics as they had come to be practiced in Albany and Harrisburg. For many, including some of Jackson's oldest supporters, it was an appalling spectacle, and one that would dominate popular perceptions of Jackson's administration for one hundred years. The revulsion at the Jacksonians' conduct was particularly widespread in the South, where northern patronage practices remained unknown. Writing in 1861, Jackson biographer James Parton articulated the shared consensus. Even if all of Jackson's other executive decisions had been commendable, Parton concluded, his acquiescence in the partisan dismissal of meritorious public officers would still render his administration deplorable.[50] Only after civil service reform had supplanted the "spoils system," as the Jacksonian patronage policy would come to be known, would historians fix the spotlight on other features of Jackson's administration, such as Jackson's support for Indian removal or his war on the bank.[51]

Among the first officeholders to be displaced was McLean. Since McLean had covertly backed Jackson's election, he might seem like an unlikely victim of a partisan sweep. Yet Jacksonian party leaders had no intention of permitting him to retain control over a department that controlled such an abundance of contracts and jobs. After all, McLean had been a leading proponent of the public trust doctrine and had no desire to preside over a partisan turnout of his staff. Jackson neatly resolved what might otherwise have become his first cabinet crisis by appointing him to a vacant seat on the Supreme Court—somewhat to McLean's chagrin, since he had hoped he might become head of the War Department, with all of the power and patronage that it controlled. Once McLean was out of the way—and the weak-willed William Barry installed as his successor—the purge of the Post Office Department could proceed, just as Green had intended.

The significance of the partisan dismissals is easily overlooked. Consider the changes in the Post Office Department, the source of the vast majority of federal jobs. During the eight years of Jackson's presidency, postal administrators dismissed 13 percent of the postmasters in the country. This percentage was not markedly different from that of previous administrations—and, in fact, it has often been interpreted as proof that the Jacksonians merely followed time-honored precedent. In fact, this percentage reveals little. Most postmasterships paid little and, thus, were not considered patronage plums.

If one breaks down the postal dismissals by region and level of compensation, a more revealing pattern emerges. During the first year of Jackson's presidency, postal administrators dismissed 38 percent of all the postmasters holding offices worth more than $300 in New England and the Middle Atlantic states, and 33 percent in the Northwest. In the South Atlantic, in contrast, they dismissed only slightly more than 2 percent of the postmasters who fell into this category.[52]

This pattern cannot be explained as a response to the economic inefficiency of the incumbents (*pace* Marshall) or the social disorder of the region in which the dismissals occurred (*pace* Crenson). Many took place in New England, a region much admired for the high quality of its mail service and little prone to social disorder. Rather, it was a product of the deliberate party-building strategy of Jacksonian party leaders such as Green. The Jacksonians' political base was in the South and West; by rewarding supporters in the North and East, party leaders built a national party. "The aristocracy will retreat to New England and entrench themselves behind local patronage," Green confided to a Jackson supporter shortly before Jackson's inauguration: "Our policy then is obvious. We must carry the war into the enemies' camp and break down the force of their patronage by the influence of our principles and the aid of the federal patronage."[53]

While party leaders sometimes claimed that the partisan dismissals had democratized the civil government, in fact, they displayed scant animus against officeholders of high social standing. Displacing incumbents was far less important than rewarding supporters.[54] Had party leaders had some other kind of perquisite at their disposal, they might well have settled their debts in some other way and left the administrative apparatus intact. To expose the hidden logic of the Jacksonians' strategy, follow the money. Many of the most lucrative public offices went to men who had invested heavily in Jackson's election campaign.[55]

Party leaders rationalized their patronage policy by invoking the time-honored doctrine of rotation in office, which Jackson announced in his first annual message in December 1829. Rotation in office had long been urged by political theorists as a precaution against the evils that might ensue should ambitious and grasping men monopolize the most powerful and prestigious public offices such as the presidency. The Jacksonians' innovation was to extend the doctrine to almost every office in the government, including thousands of minor positions—such as village postmasterships—that involved little administrative discretion. Rotation superseded—and, in large measure, overturned—the public trust doctrine that McLean had articulated during his tenure as postmaster general. McLean's public trust doctrine had established the presumption that officeholders had the right to remain in office *unless* they had been guilty of a dereliction of duty. Rotation in office nullified this presumption.[56]

In no sense was rotation in office a core Jacksonian belief. It had never been broached during the 1824 campaign and was not openly discussed until after Jackson's inauguration—even by party insiders.[57] Jackson himself does not appear to have alluded to it in writing until several months following his inauguration, when he observed in a private memorandum book that it would "perpetuate our liberty."[58] Only slowly and haltingly would it acquire a prominent place in the political lexicon. Indeed, it would hardly be an exaggeration to suggest that rotation in office has received more approving commentary from twentieth-century historians than it did in Jackson's own day. In the years immediately following Jackson's inauguration, for example, Jackson's congressional supporters only rarely invoked rotation to justify the staffing changes that Jackson's administrators oversaw. And almost never did they echo the blunt yet honest assessment of New York senator William L. Marcy, who in 1832 asserted that the new administration had a right to appoint supporters to office, since "to the victor belongs the spoils."[59] Most continued to maintain— sometimes with little effort to conceal their blatant hypocrisy—that the public trust doctrine remained intact, and that every dismissed office-holder was guilty of some kind of dereliction of duty. This was true even though everyone familiar with the specifics of the appointment process understood that the only impropriety with which the vast majority of ex-officeholders could justly stand accused was the possession of an office coveted by party leaders as a reward for party workers. Jackson himself repeated this outrageous canard in a private letter to a longtime supporter as late as 1832, in which he dared an opposition editor to name a single public officer whom his administration had dismissed who had "not been swindling the government or was not a defaulter."[60]

Opposition to rotation was by no means confined to administration critics. It sparked sharp dissent from within Jackson's cabinet and among some of Jackson's most loyal supporters. Rotation was also unpopular among the influential Washington society matrons who in previous administrations had worked diligently behind the scenes to match promising young men with suitable government berths.[61] Few doubted that the new doctrine was anything more than a thinly veiled rationalization for the bestowal of lucrative offices upon campaign workers. In the political vocabulary of the day, this was not reform but corruption—the same charge that the Jacksonians had leveled against the Adamsites during the preceding campaign.

Notwithstanding its unpopularity, rotation in office gave party leaders the necessary incentives to transform the Jacksonian coalition into the Democratic party. The partisan dismissals helped the Jacksonians pay their campaign debts; rotation in office changed the rules of the game. The significance of this shift was independent of, and can in no sense be conflated with, the percentage of officeholders whom the Jacksonians dismissed. By creating a *mechanism* for the periodic replacement of a substantial fraction of the civil government, rotation established the material basis for the mass party as a self-perpetuating organization—a new institution that, along with the voluntary association, was one of the most notable institutional innovations of the age. Prior to 1829, when a national public figure referred to the spoils of office, he typically had in mind the benefits that legislators bestowed upon their constituents.[62] Following Jackson's' victory, the spoils would increasingly come to refer merely to the perquisites that party leaders lavished on campaign workers. Rather than something to fight for, the spoils became, as it were, something to fight with.[63]

Grafted by party leaders onto a preexisting administrative apparatus, Jackson's Democratic party grew in fertile soil. In less than a decade, the Post Office Department had been transformed from the central administrative apparatus of the early American state into the wellspring of the mass party. In the process, it helped underwrite the distinctive electioneering style that would dominate presidential politics in the United States for the next eighty years.

President Jackson is often credited with strengthening the presidency by establishing a direct relationship with the American people and by declaring, in his nullification proclamation, that secession was treason and the Union perpetual.[64]

Jackson may have strengthened the presidency, yet his administration significantly weakened the organizational capabilities of the central government. This was largely by design. The main thrust of Jackson's administration was to reduce, whenever possible, the role of government in American life.[65] By blocking internal improvements, endorsing tariff reduction, disbanding the Board of Engineers, vetoing a major land bill, and opposing the rechartering of the Bank of the United States, Jackson affirmed his faith in an antidevelopmental, states' right agenda quite different from the prodevelopmental, nationally oriented agenda of Adams and Clay. Though Jackson is acclaimed a nationalist, in fact, he relied on states' rights principles even during the nullification controversy, when he deployed one variant of states' rights to challenge a competing variant promulgated by the nullifiers of South Carolina.[66] Jackson's opposition to the bank was, similarly, less economic than political, and rooted in the traditional English "country party" fear that bank officials might deploy the patronage at their disposal to subvert the regime—or, what was for Jackson the same thing, to underwrite the election campaign of his opponents.[67] Even Jackson's notorious struggles with his cabinet over Peggy Eaton and over the removal of the bank deposits had the effect—as may well have been their intent—of curtailing the bureaucratic autonomy of his department heads and undermining the relationships they had forged with local notables in the capital and the states.[68]

Jackson's endorsement of the rapid and inexpensive disbursement of the public lands also had an antidevelopmental rationale. By hastening the privatization of the public domain, Jackson discouraged the accumulation of a surplus in the treasury that might provide the occasion for new federal initiatives that could threaten vested interests. Indian removal, the major legislative achievement of Jackson's first term, may have been dependent on the army for its enforcement, yet it greatly increased the stock of cheap land and, thus, decreased the likelihood that the sale of the public domain would become a source of general revenue. Tariff reduction had an analogous logic, as did Jackson's determination to eliminate the federal debt, a goal he briefly attained in 1835. If the Treasury Department's coffers were bare, ambitious congressmen would lack the resources to embark on expansive new programs that might challenge the status quo.

Rotation in office was consistent with this antidevelopmental agenda. By lowering the prestige of public office and forestalling the emergence of administrative expertise, it limited the ability of the executive departments to perform the tasks they had been assigned. Jacksonian appointees were almost always less qualified than the men they had supplanted and often became embroiled in scandal and graft. In every public agency that historians have scrutinized—the Post Office Department, the General Land Office, the military armory at Harper's Ferry, and the Army Corps of Engineers—the Jacksonians' administrative record fluctuated between the undistinguished and the abysmal.[69] Not until the twentieth century would the executive departments regain the prestige that they had attained in the years immediately preceding Jackson's election.

Early in Jackson's administration, Amos Kendall hailed Jackson's party for championing "simple, virtuous, and efficient government" and the abandonment of "all pretensions to power" that would "necessarily create collisions with the states."[70] On the eve of the election of 1832, administration critic Alexander H. Everett offered up a rather less flattering assessment. By undermining federal prerogatives, defying the Supreme Court, and denying legislators "all their most important powers," the Jacksonians had attempted to "bring back the present Constitution to the imbecility of the Old Confederation."[71]

Jacksonian antidevelopmentalism provides insight into the political ethos that historians term "Jacksonian Democracy." To the extent that the Jacksonians can be said to have had a guiding vision, it was reactionary—

they strove, that is, to restore the balance of power between the central government and the states that the rise of the executive departments had upset. Their project, as one historian sagely observed almost half a century ago in reflecting upon Jackson's assault on the bank, was essentially a "dismantling operation."[72]

Yet it was ultimately impossible for the Jacksonians to restore the republic to the days of its youth. For the Jacksonians were also heirs to the new political realities that had emerged following the Missouri crisis. They sought, in short, not only to parry the heightened expectations with which ordinary Americans looked to the central government, but also to diffuse the multiple dangers that the slavery issue posed.[73]

The Jacksonians fully endorsed the post-Missouri consensus—sustained by nonslaveholders and slaveholders alike—that it was imperative to keep the slavery issue off the national political agenda. In the 1790s, it had been relatively easy to maintain this conspiracy of silence: the government was new and its mandate amorphous. The antislavery petition effort of Pennsylvania Quakers in 1790 may well have sparked an acrimonious congressional debate, yet the petitioners' appeals were swiftly rejected, and the controversy was soon forgotten.[74] By the 1810s, the slavery issue had become considerably more complex and less easily disposed of. During the Missouri crisis, some northern legislators went so far as to propose the imposition of restrictions on slavery as a condition for Missouri statehood, a direct assault on slaveholder prerogatives that sparked a firestorm of opposition among political insiders in the slaveholding states. And by the 1820s, the national legislative agenda was crowded with ambitious proposals to purchase slaves and relocate free blacks—proposals that were rendered increasingly plausible by the steadily growing organizational capabilities of the executive departments. No one doubted that the Treasury Department possessed the requisite administrative machinery to collect enormous sums of money from tariffs on imported goods—or, for that matter, that the War Department commanded the necessary resources to remove entire Indian tribes to the west of the Mississippi. What, then, was to prevent an executive department from relocating free blacks outside of the country, or even undertaking a general slave emancipation?

For slaveholders and their allies, such questions were profoundly unsettling. Ever since the adoption of the Constitution, slaveholders had exercised a disproportionate influence in national politics. Slaveholders were the major beneficiaries of the three-fifths clause, which augmented the political power of the slaveholding states. And in 1820, they secured a major congressional victory when they converted a slim restrictionist majority into a small antirestrictionist majority in order to secure the admission of Missouri as a slave state.[75]

Shifting demographics, however, rendered the future uncertain. During the revolutionary era, many statesmen had echoed James Madison's well-known prediction that slaveholders would retain control of the levers of power following the adoption of the Constitution, since the population of the slaveholding states would increase faster than the population of the nonslaveholding states. By the 1820s, few doubted that Madison's prediction was wrong. As the nonslaveholding states surpassed the slaveholding states in population, slaveholders recognized that they had best unite to prevent Congress from enacting legislation that might endanger prerogatives they had long taken for granted—including the right to own slaves.[76]

Jacksonians understood the slaveholders' predicament. To articulate it, they recast in a popular idiom the antidevelopmental argument long espoused by the "Old Republicans"—a small yet purposeful group of southern and, indeed, mostly Virginian statesmen, writers, and editors who had held aloft the mantle of Thomas Jefferson and the Republican party of the 1790s. Often dismissed as hopeless reactionaries during the presidencies of Thomas Jefferson and James Madison, the Old Republicans enjoyed a revival beginning in 1818, when they jousted with "National Republicans" over the merits of an extensive program of federal public works.[77] This revival stemmed primarily from the growing realization among slaveholders that the rise of the executive departments had rendered their gloomy warnings about the dangers of governmental consolidation less a paranoid fantasy than a realistic fear.

Old Republicans exerted a major influence upon the 1828 election campaign and, eventually, the Democratic party. Few, to be sure, had supported Jackson's presidential aspirations early on; indeed, most supported Crawford rather than Jackson in the election of 1824. Yet with Jackson's controversial defeat, many concluded—if often begrudgingly—that Jackson was a superior alternative to Adams in 1828.

Old Republicans provided Jackson not only with votes but also with an intellectual rationale for his campaign.[78] In particular, they made explicit the implicit threat that slaveholders had always believed a strong central government posed to the institution of slavery. Even before the Missouri crisis, North Carolina congressman Nathaniel Macon had warned that any augmentation in the mandate of the central government could foster certain kinds of civic engagement that might challenge slaveholder prerogatives. Macon found especially troubling the recent establishment of nationally oriented voluntary associations such as the American Colonization Society (1816). Should legislators "stretch" the Constitution by authorizing the construction of public works, Macon warned in a private letter to a political ally, these voluntary associations—animated as they were by a "character and spirit of perseverance, bordering on enthusiasm"—would undoubtedly "push them to try the question of emancipation."[79] During the congressional debate that preceded the enactment of the General Survey Act, Virginia congressman John Randolph gave public expression to Macon's private concern. Should Congress enact this bill, Randolph warned, it could "emancipate every slave in the United States—and with stronger color of reason than they can exercise the power now contended for."[80]

The relationship between a broadened government mandate and antislavery was often oblique. No responsible public figure seriously contemplated attacking slavery directly within the states. Yet few doubted, as the Missouri crisis had revealed, that slavery *was* vulnerable on the margins. And here lay the danger. Should Congress enact a major new legislative initiative—such as a national system of public works—it risked not only stretching the Constitution, as Macon had feared, but also, and no less ominously, strengthening antislavery sentiment in the North and the West. This was because—or so both champions and critics of a broadened government mandate assumed—government-sponsored economic development would encourage alternatives to slave-based agriculture that would increase economic opportunities for free labor.[81] Equally troubling were the various proposals to relocate free blacks outside of the country and to compensate slaveholders for the emancipation of their slaves. If enacted, such proposals would almost certainly undermine popular support for slavery in the border states—where the institution was weak—and build popular support for its conditional termination in the rest of the country.[82]

Few legislative initiatives sparked more concern than the linkage of a compensated slave emancipation with a public land sale. Land-for-slave swaps had been debated in Congress as early as 1790 and were extensively discussed during the Missouri crisis.[83] "For one," declared Illinois congressman Daniel P. Cook in February 1820, "I am prepared to devote every inch of the public soil west of the Mississippi, if so much shall be necessary, to the redemption of our country from this fatal, this deplorable evil."[84] The issue reemerged five years later, on the eve of Adams's inauguration, when New York senator Rufus King proposed that under certain circumstances the revenue from all future land sales be "inviolably applied" to the emancipation of slaves and the relocation of free blacks outside of the United States.[85] In 1832, Clay included in a land bill the proviso that Congress designate revenue generated by land sales for the relocation of free blacks outside of the country.

Legislative proposals to rid the United States of its black population are understandably unpalatable to present-day sensibilities, inflected, as they were, by the pervasive racism of the age. Yet they were the only administrative response to the slavery issue that stood the slightest chance of enactment. Had Congress opposed the relocation of free blacks, it could never have considered the question of emancipation, since all proposals to end slavery were vulnerable to the unanswerable objection that they might leave former slaves in close physical proximity to their former enslavers.[86]

No Jacksonian was more forthright in his analysis of the political implications of the slavery issue than Duff Green. In the final months of the 1828 campaign, Green privately warned several correspondents of the perilous consequences for the Union should a North-West political alliance agitate the slavery issue to consolidate its power.[87] "The antislave party in the North is dying away," Green wrote reassuringly to a Kentuckian a few months before the election, and a Jackson-Calhoun victory would "put it to sleep for twenty years": "Upon this subject I know more than I can prudently communicate by paper." It has been "part of my business"—Green boasted, in reference to the slavery issue—to "prevent the agitation of that question." Green's sensitivity on this score led him to oppose the substitution of DeWitt Clinton for Calhoun as Jackson's running mate. Clinton, as a nonslaveholder, might have been expected to appease antislavery voters in the North and, thus, help forestall the emergence of a North-West antislavery party. Yet Green opposed him anyway. "The very reasons which induce you as a slaveholder to support Mr. Clinton," Green explained to the Kentuckian, "prompt me as a slaveholder to oppose him." The only way to "keep down" the "antislave party" in the United States was to identify it with the antiwar Federalist party of 1812, which Clinton had led.[88]

Characteristic of Green's prosouthern, proslavery orientation was his eagerness to run two slaveholders—Jackson and Calhoun—on the same presidential ticket, an event unique in American political history, and one that could conceivably have inflamed disunionist sentiment in the North. "Some object to the nomination of Mr. Calhoun because he is from the south and a slaveholding state," Green conceded. Yet this was "so much the better": "Now is the time to crush the demon of disunion—roll the chariot wheels of Jackson's popularity over it, and it will be ages before it can again raise its head in our land."[89]

Green's candor on the slavery issue spoke directly to the new political realities that had grown out of the Missouri crisis. Green never doubted that Congress lacked the constitutional authority to regulate slavery within the states. Indeed, Green himself had forcefully argued this position as a delegate to the Missouri constitutional convention in 1820—and had publicly declared that liberty—including, presumably, the liberty to own slaves—was for him dearer than the privilege of remaining within the Union.[90] Green recognized that, at least for the moment, the antislavery movement was weak and divided. Yet he was deeply troubled by the determination of northerners to make restrictions on slavery a condition for Missouri statehood—and with good reason. Restriction, after all, raised the specter that at some future juncture the central government might take even more direct steps to restrict slaveholder prerogatives— including those of Missouri slaveholders such as Green himself. And for Green, this was the crux of the matter. The very malleability of govern- mental institutions made it impossible to know for certain whether some antislavery scheme might someday succeed. In an age in which the central government was steadily broadening its mandate, the executive depart- ments were becoming increasingly powerful and autonomous, and volun- tary associations were fast emerging as effective vehicles of popular mobi- lization—and in the absence of stable political parties to direct and diffuse popular dissent—every presidential election became a referendum, not only on a particular candidate or on a specific policy agenda, but on the future of the Union.[91]

Green's apprehensions concerning possible future assaults on slave- holder prerogatives were subtly reinforced by his personal familiarity with antislavery activists. Green was related by marriage to Daniel P. Cook, the Kentucky-born Illinois congressman who had forcefully attacked slavery during the Missouri crisis. And Cook, as it happens, was an ardent ad- mirer of John Quincy Adams—and, apparently, something of an Adams protégé. In the critical state-by-state House vote that gave Adams the pres- idency, Cook, as the sole Illinois congressman, cast the state's vote for Adams. Several years earlier, during the Illinois statehood debate, Cook, as an Illinois newspaper editor, had urged the admission of Illinois as a free state—a controversial position that angered Illinois slaveholders, in- cluding Green's own brother-in-law, and one that Illinois slaveholders tried to overturn as late as 1824. And in the fall of 1817, as the slavery issue was beginning to emerge as a national issue, Cook published in a Washington newspaper two remarkable open letters on the topic.[92] In these letters, Cook lambasted slaveholders as lazy and tyrannical, com- pared rebellious slaves to the patriots of the American War of Indepen- dence, and urged President Monroe to endorse legislation to hasten the abolition of slavery throughout the United States. Should future legislators emulate Cook's antislavery fervor, Green had little doubt that slaveholders would find themselves struggling to protect their prerogatives from a North-West antislavery alliance. Almost sixty years later, Green reprinted a substantial excerpt from the second of Cook's letters in his memoir, with the bold—and highly distorted—claim that their initial publication in 1817 marked the beginnings of the "antislavery conspiracy" to build a northern antislavery party. To combat this conspiracy, Green declared, had been the goal of his political career, and the primary impetus behind his endorsement of Andrew Jackson in the election of 1828.[93]

Green's preoccupation with the slavery issue during the 1828 campaign was highly atypical, at least within Jackson's inner circle. Neither Kendall nor Francis P. Blair—nor even Jackson himself—gave the issue more than passing attention. In large measure, this was because they did not have to. With the exception of borderland outposts like Missouri and Illinois, the ramparts of slavery were so well defended that the Jacksonians could focus their attention on issues that were less potentially divisive. The paucity of references by Jacksonian party leaders to slavery—even in personal correspondence—during a political campaign notorious for its raucous vulgarity has often been cited to demonstrate the unimportance of the issue to the Jackson campaign.[94] From Green's vantage point—shaped, as it had been, by his personal familiarity with the precariousness of slavery in Missouri and Illinois—the submergence of the slavery issue was, on the contrary, a tribute to his success at preventing it from *once again* commanding attention on the national stage.[95]

Green's Jacksonianism was unabashedly opportunistic. A Calhounite at heart, he abandoned Jackson shortly after the election; by 1830, he was endorsing public positions that Jackson opposed. In the 1840 election, Green backed the Whigs, and, in 1861, he cast his lot with the Confederacy, running iron mills in Alabama and Tennessee during the Civil War. In 1828, however, these events lay in the future. In the final, frenzied months of the 1828 election campaign, it was Green—the prime editorial spokesman for the Jackson campaign—who rallied the faithful with the promise of preferment. In many ways, this made Green the most representative Jacksonian of them all.[96]

Almost half a century ago, British political scientist S. E. Finer underscored the administrative achievements of the central government in the United States in the period preceding the Jacksonian ascendancy. "On the eve of Jackson's election," Finer wrote, "the United States administrative system was a going concern, steadily expanding its services and progressively adapting its organization to the new burdens." As a student of British public administration—which, in the early nineteenth century, remained a patronage engine for the well connected and the well to do—Finer was in an excellent position to acknowledge this notably American achievement.[97]

This essay has contended that the rise of the executive departments in the 1820s was a necessary—though not sufficient—precondition for the establishment of the Democratic party. Institutions beget institutions; nowhere was this truism more aptly illustrated than by the changes set in motion with Jackson's victory in the election of 1828. The Jacksonian coalition was midwife to the party the executive departments spawned. Jackson's Democratic party championed a legislative agenda that grew directly out of the determination of party leaders—such as Duff Green—to keep the slavery issue off the national political agenda. In pursuit of this goal, the Jackson administration supported policies that weakened the organizational capabilities of the central government and protected the vested interests of the slaveholders who dominated its party's political base.

The Jacksonian ascendancy—and, with it, the flowering of "Jacksonian Democracy"—is best understood as a problem neither of classes, nor even of regions, but of entitlements. In the years preceding the election of 1828, ordinary Americans presumed themselves entitled to an ever increasing array of government benefits. In response to this popular movement, Jacksonian Democracy was born. Here, then, was one of the most curious ironies of the age: the first national political party to call itself democratic was programmatically committed to limiting the role of the government in American life.

The influence of the Jacksonians on the democratization of American politics is easily exaggerated. White male suffrage antedated the Jacksonian ascendancy, as did the advent of an avowedly egalitarian and often populistic style of electioneering.[98] Long before the making of the Democratic party, and long after it as well, voluntary associations, often in conjunction with third parties and reform movements, popularized causes far more progressive than anything even the most radical Democratic party leader would have found politically possible to sustain.[99] To dismiss such impulses as peripheral to the "partisan imperative" of two-party competition makes sense only if one assumes a priori that the mass party was the logical fulfillment of the promise of democracy. Even rotation in office—the most avowedly democratic of the Jacksonians' innovations—did little to increase the access of previously underrepresented groups to public office.[100] In addition, by institutionalizing what has aptly been called an "alienating grammar of corruption," it might well have discouraged civic engagement. [101] It may, in short, be time to reconsider whether rotation ought to be regarded as a core element of the democratic creed.

The Jacksonians may have succeeded in limiting the role of the government in American life, yet they failed to keep the slavery issue off the national political agenda. The abolitionist mails controversy in 1835 dashed their hopes. When the leaders of the American Anti-Slavery Society used the facilities of the Post Office Department to agitate the slavery issue in the slaveholding states, they sparked a swift and hostile reaction not only from slaveholders but also from Postmaster General Kendall and President Jackson. Almost immediately, antiabolitionist mobs sprang into action in the North as well as the South, with the covert endorsement of prominent Jacksonians, including Vice President Martin Van Buren. Jackson himself proposed sweeping antiabolitionist legislation, which, though unsuccessful, fueled the growing suspicion of radical abolitionists that the central government had become the pliant tool of a grasping slaveholding cabal. No longer would the postal system remain the nation-building institution that Channing had proclaimed it to be as recently as 1829. Henceforth, it would exacerbate the long-smoldering conflict over slavery that would continue without interruption from 1835 until the Civil War.[102]

Jackson's strident antiabolitionism is a pointed reminder of the troubling legacy of the antidevelopmental agenda that his administration endorsed. In the absence of outside coercion, it is unrealistic to assume that a full-scale slave emancipation could have succeeded in the nineteenth-century United States. Peaceful emancipations required the intervention of a central government, as in the British West Indies; violent emancipations followed slave rebellions, as in Haiti.[103] The voluntary, state-sponsored emancipation upon which so many statesmen of Jefferson's generation invested such high hopes—including, albeit fitfully, Jefferson himself—was doomed to fail.

It is impossible to know if the developmental agenda of Adams and Clay might, under different circumstances, have ended slavery peacefully within the United States. Indeed, it is entirely conceivable that slaveholder dominance in national politics was so formidable that *any* deliberate augmentation in the mandate of the central government would, alternatively, have hastened the nationalization of slavery—just as Abraham Lincoln would come in the 1850s to fear. Yet there can be little doubt that—just as Duff Green had intended—the antidevelopmental agenda of Andrew Jackson and Amos Kendall left slaveholder prerogatives intact. By weakening the organizational capabilities of the central government—the only institution that could have peacefully orchestrated a slave emancipation—Jackson's Democratic party made the perpetuation of the Union contingent on the suppression of antislavery, and the agitation of the slavery issue a prelude to civil war.

NOTES

For suggestions and advice, I am grateful to Richard H. Brown, Tom Coens, Patricia Conley, Daniel Feller, Robert P. Forbes, Meg Jacobs, John Lauritz Larson, Michael Perman, John Reda, Robert V. Remini, W. J. Rorabaugh, and Julian Zelizer.

1. William E. Channing, "The Union," in *The Works of William E. Channing* (Boston: George G. Channing, 1849), 1:353. This essay was originally published in May 1829 in the *Christian Examiner*. All references are to the 1849 edition.

2. Ibid., 351.

3. Ibid., 350.

4. Ibid., 351.

5. Ibid., 345.

6. Ibid., 353.

7. In its early years, the Democratic party had no agreed-upon name. As late as the presidential campaign of 1832, it was known officially as the "Republican" party even though, as far back as 1824, it had also been called the "Democratic Republican" party and also, occasionally, the "Democratic" party. Samuel Rhea Gammon, *The Presidential Election of 1832* (Baltimore: Johns Hopkins University Press, 1922), 162. Only after the organization of the Whig party in 1834 would it become customary for Jacksonian party leaders to call their party "Democratic" or, more simply, the "Democracy."

8. The role of the "market revolution" in the making of the Democratic party is explored in Harry L. Watson, *Liberty and Power: The Politics of Jacksonian America* (New York: Hill and Wang, 1990), and Charles Sellers, *The Market Revolution: Jacksonian America, 1815–1846* (New York: Oxford University Press, 1991). See also Harry L. Watson, "The Ambiguous Legacy of Jacksonian Democracy," in Peter B. Kovler, ed., *Democrats and the American Idea: A Bicentennial Reappraisal* (Washington, D.C.: Center for National Policy Press, 1992), 29–75. For an incisive critique, see William E. Gienapp, "The Myth of Class in Jacksonian America," *Journal of Policy History* 6 (1994): 232–59.

9. John Lauritz Larson, *Internal Improvement: Public Works and the Promise of Popular Government in the Early United States* (Chapel Hill: University of North Carolina Press, 2001), 224.

10. Robert V. Remini, *The Election of Andrew Jackson* (Philadelphia and New York: J. B. Lippincott Co., 1963), 87.

11. Lynn L. Marshall, "The Strange Stillbirth of the Whig Party," *American Historical Review* 72 (1967): 445–68; Matthew A. Crenson, *The Federal Machine: Beginnings of Bureaucracy in Jacksonian America* (Baltimore: Johns Hopkins University Press, 1975). Marshall and Crenson both drew on the "organizational synthesis," a new approach to American history in the 1960s, which took as its primary focus the development of large-scale institutions, including government bureaucracies.

12. Marshall and Crenson's highly laudatory assessment of Kendall's administrative achievements built on the earlier work of political scientist Leonard D. White, whose *Jacksonians* (1954) credited Kendall with a "Postal Renaissance." For a more detailed discussion of White's treatment of the Jacksonians, see Richard R. John, "Leonard D. White and the Invention of American Administrative History," *Reviews in American History* 24 (1996): 344–60.

Why White lavished such praise on Kendall's tenure as postmaster general is an interesting question. According to a colleague, White found "immense pleasures" in discovering creative public servants—especially if, like White, they had graduated from Dartmouth. Dartmouth, as it happens, was also Kendall's alma mater. John M. Gaus, "Leonard Dupee White, 1891–1958," *Public Administration Review* 18 (1958): 235.

The proof text for White's admiring portrait of Kendall was Kendall's *Autobiography*, which Kendall's son-in-law, William Stickney, completed following Kendall's death. Nineteenth-century historians, familiar with Kendall's enviable gifts as a partisan polemicist, used Kendall's memoir sparingly. Their twentieth-century successors have been less cautious. A case in point was Kendall's account of the

Post Office Act of 1836. In his memoir, Kendall credited himself with being the primary inspiration for its enactment—a remarkable claim for a department head, and one that, by marginalizing Congress, ignoring the Whigs, and downplaying the Jacksonians' own administrative shortcomings, has misled scholars for almost fifty years.

13. Michael Nelson, "A Short, Ironic History of American National Bureaucracy," *Journal of Politics* 44 (1982): 760.

14. Ibid., 761–62; James A. Morone, *The Democratic Wish: Popular Participation and the Limits of American Government* (New York: Basic Books, 1990), 87–94; Martin Shefter, *Political Parties and the State: The American Historical Experience* (Princeton, N.J.: Princeton University Press, 1994), 67–68.

See also Joel D. Schwartz, ed., "Liberty, Democracy, and the Origins of American Bureaucracy," in *Harvard Law Review* 97 (1984): 825–28. Schwartz's essay critiqued William E. Nelson's *Roots of American Bureaucracy* (1982), one of the few post-Crenson studies of early American bureaucracy that did *not* endorse Crenson's revisionism. Predictably, Schwartz faulted Nelson for his supposed shortcoming.

15. Richard R. John, *Spreading the News: The American Postal System from Franklin to Morse* (Cambridge, Mass.: Harvard University Press, 1995), 242–48.

16. Marshall, "Strange Stillbirth," 468.

17. Washington *Globe*, March 26, 1836. See also John, *Spreading the News*, 242–52, and Edward Pessen, review of *Federal Machine*, in *Journal of Southern History* 41 (1975): 553–54. Pessen characterized Crenson's analysis of the administrative reorganizations that took place during Jackson's administration as "not simply a monocausal explanation of a complex historical phenomenon but in a sense a giant whitewash of some of the Jacksonian politicians, whose own misdeeds 'triggered' a clamor for reform" (554). See also Pessen, *Jacksonian America: Society, Personality, and Politics,* rev. ed. (Urbana: University of Illinois Press, 1985), 362.

18. John M. Murrin, "The Great Inversion, or Court versus Country: A Comparison of the Revolution Settlements in England (1688–1721) and America (1776–1816)," in *Three British Revolutions: 1641, 1688, 1776*, ed. J.G.A. Pocock (Princeton, N.J.: Princeton University Press, 1980), 425.

19. Stephen Skowronek, *Building a New American State: The Expansion of National Administrative Capacities, 1877–1920* (Cambridge: Cambridge University Press, 1982), 19, 23.

20. For a more extended critique of the "courts and parties" tradition, see Richard R. John, "Governmental Institutions as Agents of Change: Rethinking American Political Development in the Early Republic, 1787–1835," *Studies in American Political Development* 11 (1997): 347–80.

21. James Sterling Young, *The Washington Community, 1800–1828* (New York: Columbia University Press, 1966). For a recent tribute to Young's book by an eminent political scientist (who termed it "excellent"), see Ira Katznelson, "Flexible Capacity: The Military and Early American Statebuilding," in *Shaped by War and Trade: International Influences on American Political Development*, ed. Katznelson and Martin Shefter (Princeton, N.J.: Princeton University Press, 2002), 107n29.

22. Young, *Washington Community*, xi.

23. Characteristic of Young's underestimation of the importance of the central government in the early republic was his erroneous assumption that, in this period, the Post Office Department transmitted little besides personal correspondence. In fact, the Post Office Department also conveyed a large volume of public information—including newspapers, magazines, and government documents. Ibid., 31–32.

24. Allan G. Bogue and Mark Paul Marlaine, "Of Mess and Men: The Boardinghouse and Congressional Voting, 1821–1842," *American Journal of Political Science* 19 (1975): 226. See also Marion Nelson Winship, "The 'Practicable Sphere' of a Republic: Western Ways of Connecting to Congress," in *The House and Senate in the 1790s: Petitioning, Lobbying, and Institutional Development*, ed. Kenneth R. Bowling and Donald R. Kennon (Miami, Ohio: Ohio University Press, 2002), 145, and Noble E. Cunningham, Jr., *The Process of Government under Jefferson* (Princeton, N.J.: Princeton University Press, 1978), 210, 286, 303. "There is no evidence in the records of the petitioning process of the Jeffersonian era"—Cunningham observed, in a pointed rejoinder to Young—"to suggest a feeling that the national government was distant and unapproachable" (303).

25. For a related discussion, see two valuable review essays by Ronald P. Formisano: "State Development in the Early Republic: Substance and Structure, 1780–1840," in *Contesting Democracy: Substance and Structure in American Political History, 1775–2000*, ed. Byron E. Shafer and Anthony J. Badger (Lawrence: University Press of Kansas, 2001), 7–35, and "The Concept of Political Culture," *Journal of Interdisciplinary History* 31 (2001): 393–426.

26. The continuing influence of English opposition thought in the early republic is the subject of a large historical literature. See, for example, Daniel Walker Howe, *The Political Culture of the American Whigs* (Chicago: University of Chicago Press, 1979); Jean H. Baker, *Affairs of Party: The Political Culture of Northern Democrats in the Mid–Nineteenth Century* (Ithaca, N.Y.: Cornell University Press, 1983), chap. 4; Robert V. Remini, *Andrew Jackson and the Course of American Freedom, 1822–1832* (New York: Harper and Row, 1981); Major L. Wilson, "The 'Country' versus the 'Court': A Republican Consensus and Party Debate in the Bank War," *Journal of the Early Republic* 15 (1995): 619–47; Major L. Wilson, "Republicanism and the Idea of Party in the Jacksonian Period," *Journal of the Early Republic* 8 (1988): 419–42; and Richard B. Latner, "Preserving 'The Natural Equality of Rank and Influence': Liberalism, Republicanism, and Equality of Condition in Jacksonian Politics," in *The Culture of the Market: Historical Essays*, ed. Thomas L. Haskell and Richard F. Teichtraeber, III (Cambridge: Cambridge University Press, 1993), 189–230.

27. Alexis de Tocqueville, *Democracy in America*, ed. Harvey C. Mansfield and Delba Winthrop (Chicago: University of Chicago Press, 2000), 368. According to one Tocqueville scholar, Tocqueville's underestimation of the role of the central government in American public life was the "basic error" in his discussion of the nature and future of the American federation. James T. Schleifer, *The Making of Tocqueville's Democracy in America* (Chapel Hill: University of North Carolina Press, 1980), 111.

28. For an authoritative survey of the public policy debates of the early republic, see Merrill D. Peterson, *The Great Triumvirate: Webster, Clay, and Calhoun* (New York: Oxford University Press, 1987). Peterson traces the National Republicans' legislative agenda to the Madisonian wing of the Jeffersonian Republican party and, thus, considers it fitting that it was sometimes termed the "Madisonian platform." This ideological genealogy is worth underscoring, since commentators often assume—mistakenly—that the American System was little more than a warmed-over version of the Federalist political program of the 1790s. See also Howe, *Political Culture of the American Whigs*, 49, 90–91, and Larson, *Internal Improvement*, 160. See also Michael J. Lacey, "Federalism and National Planning: The Nineteenth-Century Legacy," in *The American Planning Tradition: Culture and Policy*, ed. Robert Fishman (Washington, D.C.: Woodrow Wilson Center Press, 2000), 89–111.

29. Prior to 1788, the new republic could hardly be said to possess a central administrative apparatus at all. The outstanding exception was the Continental Army. Interestingly, several of the most influential proponents of a stronger central government (including George Washington, Alexander Hamilton, and John Marshall) had been army officers, while several of the leading critics of the new regime (including Thomas Jefferson and James Madison) had never served in the military. On the legacy of this military heritage—and its often intentional neglect—see Charles Royster, *A Revolutionary People at War: The Continental Army and American Character* (Chapel Hill: University of North Carolina Press, 1979), chap. 8, and Joseph J. Ellis, *Founding Brothers: The Revolutionary Generation* (New York: Alfred A. Knopf, 2000), esp. 154–55.

30. Richard R. John and Christopher J. Young, "Rites of Passage: Postal Petitioning as a Tool of Governance in the Age of Federalism," in Bowling and Kennon, *House and Senate in the 1790s*, 100–38.

31. Larson, *Internal Improvement*, 173.

32. Everett to McLean, August 18, 1828, in "Use of Patronage in Elections," ed. Worthington C. Ford, *Proceedings of the Massachusetts Historical Society*, 3d ser. (1908), 1:374 (hereafter *Proceedings*).

33. M. J. Heale, *The Presidential Quest: Candidates and Images in American Political Culture, 1787–1852* (London: Longman, 1982), 57–61.

34. Anticorruptionist rhetoric so dominated public discourse during the Monroe and Adams administrations that Robert V. Remini has dubbed the period between 1816 and 1828 the "Era of Corruption." Remini's novel periodization highlights the *perception* among public figures in the 1810s and 1820s that the executive departments were becoming larger and more autonomous and, thus, more prone to corruption. Yet he conflates perception and reality when he hails Jackson with heading the "first reform movement in American political history." Remini, *Andrew Jackson and the Course of American Freedom*, 13–15, 99.

35. Robert V. Remini, "Election of 1828," in *The Coming to Power: Critical Presidential Elections in American History*, ed. Arthur M. Schlesinger, Jr. (New York: Chelsea House, 1981), 75.

36. Andrew Jackson to James Monroe, February 11, 1821, in *The Papers of Andrew Jackson, 1821–1824*, ed. Harold D. Moser, et al. (Knoxville: University of Tennessee Press, 1996), 5:10. I am grateful to Tom Coens for this reference.

37. Thomas Hart Benton, *Report of the Select Committee on Executive Patronage*, 19th Cong., 1st sess., 1826, S. Doc. 88 (serial 128), 11.

38. McLean to Everett, August 8, 1828, in *Proceedings*, 366, 367.

39. Everett to McLean, August 1, 1828, in *Proceedings*, 362.

40. Everett to McLean, August 18, 1828, in *Proceedings*, 376.

41. Everett to McLean, August 1, 1828, in *Proceedings*, 361.

42. Everett to McLean, August 18, 1828, in *Proceedings*, 376.

43. Channing, "The Union," 358, 355, 359.

44. *United States Telegraph*, November 3, 11, and 18, 1828.

45. Green to C. P. Van Ness, December 28, 1828, Green letterbook, August 1827–April 1830, Green Papers, Library of Congress, Washington, D.C.

46. Green to Benjamin F. Edwards, December 17, 1828, Green letterbook, Green Papers.

47. Remini, *Andrew Jackson and the Course of American Freedom*, chap. 9. See also Remini, "The Democratic Party in the Jacksonian Era," in Kovler, *Democrats and the American Idea*, 38, and Jeffrey B. Morris and Richard B. Morris, eds., *Encyclopedia of American History*, 7th ed. (New York: Harper/Collins, 1996), 188.

48. John, *Spreading the News*, chap. 6, esp. 210–14.

49. Following Thomas Jefferson's victory in the election of 1800, there is no evidence that *any* government clerk complained about having been discriminated against on political grounds. Cunningham, *Process of Government*, 180.

50. James Parton, *Life and Times of Andrew Jackson* (New York: Mason Brothers, 1861), 3: 691–92. Robert V. Remini has discounted Parton's preoccupation with Jackson's patronage policy as "practically pathological." Remini, *Andrew Jackson and the Course of American Democracy, 1833–1845* (New York: Harper and Row, 1984), 600n26. In fact, Parton's critique was rarely contested and widely shared. Indeed, prior to the twentieth century, the phrase "Jacksonian Democracy" was often used to refer *not* to a broad social movement but, rather, to a narrowly based—and patronage-obsessed—political party sometimes called *the* "Jacksonian Democracy." Richard J. Moss, "Jacksonian Democracy: A Note on the Origins and Growth of the Term," *Tennessee Historical Quarterly* 34 (1975): 145–53.

51. On the Jacksonians as spoilsmen, see William F. Mugleton, "Andrew Jackson and the Spoils System: An Historiographical Survey," *Mid-America* 59 (1977): 117–25, and Frank Freidel, "Jackson's Political Removals as Seen by Historians," *Historian* 2 (1939): 41–52. For a recent reevaluation, see John, *Spreading the News*, chap. 6 and esp. 334–35n117. Still useful, despite its pronounced anti-Whig bias, is Charles Sellers, "Andrew Jackson versus the Historians," *Mississippi Valley Historical Review* 44 (1958): 615–34.

52. John, *Spreading the News*, 221–36.

53. Green to U. Updike, February 1, 1829, Green letterbook, Green Papers.

54. For a different interpretation, see Shefter, *Political Parties and the State*, 66–68.

55. John, *Spreading the News*, chap. 6, esp. 220–21.

56. For a different account of the origins of rotation in office, see Robert V. Remini, *The Legacy of Andrew Jackson: Essays on Democracy, Indian Removal,*

and Slavery (Baton Rouge: Louisiana State University Press, 1988), 30–31. Jackson, Remini contended, supported rotation not merely to "terminate a corruption he believed had long festered within the executive branch" but also to "establish the democratic doctrine that in a free country no one has a special privilege or right to control or run the nation" (30–31). See also Remini, *The Revolutionary Age of Andrew Jackson* (New York: Harper and Row, 1976), chap. 5 ("Who Shall Hold Office?").

57. Robert P. Hay, "The Case for Andrew Jackson in 1824: Eaton's *Wyoming Letters,*" *Tennessee Historical Quarterly* 29 (1970): 145.

58. Private memorandum book, cited in Remini, *Andrew Jackson and the Course of American Freedom*, 183.

59. Even Remini conceded that Marcy's attempt to excuse Jackson's patronage policy was a "colossal blunder" that gave Jackson's opponents a "telling quotation with which to bludgeon the administration during the election campaign." Robert V. Remini, *Henry Clay: Statesman for the Union* (New York: W. W. Norton and Co., 1991), 384. See also Remini, *Andrew Jackson and the Course of American Freedom*, 185.

60. Jackson to William B. Lewis, August 18, 1832, cited in Remini, *Andrew Jackson and the Course of American Freedom*, 379.

61. Catherine Allgor, *Parlor Politics: In Which the Ladies of Washington Help Build a City and a Government* (Charlottesville: University Press of Virginia, 2000), chaps. 3, 5.

62. See, for example, Larson, *Internal Improvement*, chap. 5 ("Spoiling Internal Improvements").

63. The indispensability of material incentives to the making of the mass party provides a new perspective on the influential thesis—originated by political scientist Theodore Lowi and popularized by historian Richard L. McCormick—that, in the nineteenth century, American politics had a distributional cast. Following the Jacksonian ascendancy, the primary beneficiary of political largesse was often, and sometimes exclusively, not the electorate, but the party. The preoccupation of nineteenth-century politicians with the judicious disbursement of patronage to party supporters will be evident to anyone who has read through their correspondence. Many politicians regarded it as one of their most important—and challenging—tasks.

64. Robert V. Remini, *Andrew Jackson and the Bank War: A Study in the Growth of Presidential Power* (New York: W. W. Norton and Co., 1967); Kenneth M. Stampp, "The Concept of a Perpetual Union," in *The Imperiled Union: Essays on the Background of the Civil War* (New York: Oxford University Press, 1980), esp. 33–35.

65. Remini, *Andrew Jackson and the Course of American Freedom*, esp. 29, 116.

66. Richard E. Ellis, *The Union at Risk: Jacksonian Democracy, States' Rights, and the Nullification Crisis* (New York: Oxford University Press, 1987). The nullification crisis, Ellis concluded, was "not simply, and perhaps not even mainly, a struggle between the proponents of nationalism and states' rights. In a very fundamental way, it also involved a struggle between advocates of different kinds of states' rights thought" (178).

67. Remini, *Andrew Jackson and the Bank War*, 44.

68. Shefter, *Political Parties and the State*, 66–68.

69. John, *Spreading the News*, chap. 6; Malcolm Rohrbough, *The Land Office Business: The Settlement and Administration of American Public Lands, 1789–1837* (New York: Oxford University Press, 1968), chap. 12; Merritt Roe Smith, *Harpers Ferry and the New Technology: The Challenge of Change* (Ithaca, N.Y.: Cornell University Press, 1977), chap. 9; Todd Shallat, *Structures in the Stream: Water, Science, and the Rise of the U.S. Army Corps of Engineers* (Austin: University of Texas Press, 1994), chap. 5; Forest G. Hill, *Roads, Rails, and Waterways: The Army Engineers and Early Transportation* (Norman: University of Oklahoma Press, 1957), chap. 3. In complementary ways, each of these studies challenges Remini's assertion that the central government was better administered under Jackson than it had been under Monroe and Adams. Remini, *Andrew Jackson and the Course of American Democracy*, 245.

70. Kendall to Francis P. Blair, April 25, 1830, cited in Richard B. Latner, *The Presidency of Andrew Jackson: White House Politics, 1829–1837* (Athens: University of Georgia Press, 1979), 58.

71. Alexander H. Everett, *The Conduct of the Administration* (Boston: Stimpson and Clapp, 1832), 76. The "insane man-worship" of Jackson's supporters, Everett added, had *strengthened* the presidency—and, in different circumstances, would "justly excite the most serious alarm for the permanence of our institutions."

72. Marvin Meyers, *The Jacksonian Persuasion: Politics and Belief* (Stanford, Calif.: Stanford University Press, 1957), 29.

73. Richard H. Brown, "The Missouri Crisis, Slavery, and the Politics of Jacksonianism," *South Atlantic Quarterly* 65 (1966): 55–72; Leonard L. Richards, "The Jacksonians and Slavery," in *Antislavery Reconsidered: New Perspectives on the Abolitionists*, ed. Lewis Perry and Michael Fellman (Baton Rouge: Louisiana State University Press, 1979), 99–118; William J. Cooper, Jr., *Liberty and Slavery: Southern Politics to 1860* (New York: Alfred A. Knopf, 1983), chap. 8.

74. Ellis, *Founding Brothers*, chap. 3.

75. Robert Pierce Forbes, "Slavery and the Meaning of America, 1819–1833," Ph. D. dissertation, Yale University, 1994, chaps. 4–5. See also Don E. Fehrenbacher, *The South and Three Sectional Crises* (Baton Rouge: Louisiana State University Press, 1980), 17–23.

76. Leonard L. Richards, *The Slave Power: The Free North and Southern Domination, 1780–1860* (Baton Rouge: Louisiana State University Press, 2000), 101–6. See also Robin L. Einhorn, "Species of Property: The American Property-Tax Uniformity Clauses Reconsidered," *Journal of Economic History* 61 (2001): 1–34, and Einhorn, "Slavery and the Politics of Taxation in the Early United States," *Studies in American Political Development* 14 (2000): 156–83.

77. Larson, *Internal Improvement*, 126–35.

78. Norman K. Risjord, *The Old Republicans: Southern Conservatism in the Age of Jefferson* (New York: Columbia University Press, 1965), chap. 9; Remini, *Andrew Jackson and the Course of American Freedom*, esp. 29, 31, 116; Remini, *Legacy of Andrew Jackson*, 9.

79. Macon to Bartlett Yancey, March 8, 1818, in Kemp P. Battle, ed., "Letters of Nathaniel Macon," in *James Sprunt Historical Monographs*, no. 2 (Chapel Hill: University of North Carolina, 1900), 48–49. "The states having no slaves," Macon added, "may not feel as strongly as the states having slaves about stretching the Constitution, because no such interest is to be touched by it" (49). Macon's assumption that broadening the mandate of the central government would foster social activism anticipated the contention of historical sociologist Theda Skocpol that the expansion in the administrative capacity of the state could *encourage* civic engagement. Theda Skocpol, "The Tocqueville Problem: Civic Engagement in American Democracy," *Social Science History* 21 (1997): 455–79.

80. Cited in Larson, *Internal Improvement*, 143.

81. That public works spending would create conditions favorable to free labor may not seem self-evident today. Yet it was taken for granted in the early republic by public figures as otherwise diverse as George Washington, John Quincy Adams, and Thomas Dew. Samuel Flagg Bemis, *John Quincy Adams and the Union* (New York: Alfred A. Knopf, 1956), 60–63; Alison Goodyear Freehling, *Drift toward Dissolution: The Virginia Slavery Debate of 1831–1832* (Baton Rouge: Louisiana State University Press, 1982), 202–8.

82. William W. Freehling, *The Reintegration of American History: Slavery and the Civil War* (New York: Oxford University Press, 1994), chap. 9.

83. Betty L. Fladeland, "Compensated Emancipation: A Rejected Alternative," *Journal of Southern History* 42 (May 1976): 169–86.

84. *Annals of Congress*, February 4, 1820, 1109.

85. *Register of Debates*, February 18, 1825, 623; Fladeland, "Compensated Emancipation," 176.

86. Freehling, *Reintegration of American History*, chap. 7; Ellis, *Founding Brothers*, 106–8.

87. David Wayne Moore, "Duff Green and the South, 1824–35" (Ph.D. dissertation, Miami University, Miami, Ohio 1983). The slavery issue, Moore concluded, was "particularly important" in explaining Green's devotion to Jackson. Throughout the campaign, Green remained "haunted" by the fear that the more populous north would "unite in a sectional party hostile to the South's 'peculiar institution'" (18). See also Michael D. Goldhaber, "The Tragedy of Classical Republicanism: Duff Green and the *United States Telegraph*, 1826–1837" (B.A. thesis, Harvard University, 1990).

88. Green to Worden Pope, January 4, 1828, Green letterbook, Green Papers.

89. Green to William Snowden, November 16, 1827, Green letterbook, Green Papers.

90. Fletcher M. Green, "Duff Green," in *Dictionary of American Biography*, ed. Allen Johnson and Dumas Malone (New York: Charles Scribner's Sons, 1931), 7: 540.

91. For a related discussion, see Michael F. Holt, "Change and Continuity in the Party Period: The Substance and Structure of American Politics, 1835–1885," in Shafer and Badger, *Contesting Democracy*, 106. Holt's essay includes a compelling critique of the "party period" synthesis of nineteenth-century American political history that had been developed most fully by Joel H. Silbey and Richard L. McCormick. One of the most important things "structuring politics" in the mid–

nineteenth century, Holt suggestively observes, was the belief among political actors that partisan loyalties among voters and leaders might "imminently be displaced" and, thus, that the *entire* political system was "malleable, mutable, and open to change and reorganization" (106). Holt intended this generalization to apply to the half century *after* 1835, when two-party competition was entrenched; it applies even more forcefully to the two decades *preceding* 1835, when it was not.

92. [Daniel P. Cook], "To James Monroe, President of the United States of America," *National Register*, 13 and 20 September 1817; Duff Green, *Facts and Suggestions, Biographical, Historical, Financial, and Political* (New York: Richardson and Co., 1866), 32.

"We were favored by Heaven in our revolutionary struggle," Cook declared in his second letter, "and believing ourselves injured, we even appealed to the Divinity to aid and assist us—we were fighting for our *natural* rights; those rights which we believed the God of Nature intended '*all*' should '*equally*' enjoy. To that appeal the Heavens bowed propitiously. . . . With this recent example of the justice of Heaven before us; can we, with any well-founded hope of escaping a similar visitation of divine justice, expect to go on, inflicting more unwarrantable oppressions upon others than were inflicted upon us? No! The ways of Heaven are alike, are unalterable, and for us they will not swerve from their ordered course. . . . "

93. Green, *Facts and Suggestions*, 28, 30–33. The goal of this conspiracy, Green declared, was not to free the slaves but to enslave the "white man" by the "centralization of a corrupt, irresponsible power in the federal government, in open violation of the fundamental principles of the Constitution" (34).

94. John M. McFaul, "Expediency vs. Morality: Jacksonian Politics and Slavery," *Journal of American History* 62 (1975): 24–27; Latner, *Presidency of Andrew Jackson*, 207–12; Remini, *Legacy of Andrew Jackson*, 86.

95. For the more traditional view, see Remini, *Legacy of Andrew Jackson*, chap. 3, and Latner, *Presidency of Andrew Jackson*, 207–12. Remini faulted Richard H. Brown for exaggerating the role of the slavery issue in the Jacksonians' ascendancy and claimed that Brown had been misled by the self-serving retrospective pronouncements of John Quincy Adams. Latner contended that the slavery issue had little influence on Jackson's supporters from the western border states, the "primary inspiration," in his view, for the program of the Democratic party (208). Neither devoted much attention to Green, even though he was the primary editorial spokesman for the Jacksonian party during the 1828 campaign and hailed from the border state of Missouri.

96. The absence of a full-scale scholarly biography of Green is a major gap in the literature on nineteenth-century American politics, political economy, and proslavery thought.

97. S. E. Finer, "Patronage and the Public Service: Jeffersonian Bureaucracy and the British Tradition," *Public Administration* 30 (1952): 329–60, quotation on 330. Finer based his characterization of American administrative developments on the first two volumes of Leonard D. White's history of American public administration: *The Federalists* (1948) and *The Jeffersonians* (1951).

98. Andrew W. Robertson, " 'Look on This Picture . . . and on This!' Nationalism, Localism, and Partisan Images of Otherness in the United States, 1787–

1820," *American Historical Review* 106 (2001): 1263–80; David Waldstreicher, *In the Midst of Perpetual Fetes: The Making of American Nationalism, 1776–1820* (Chapel Hill: University of North Carolina Press, 1997); Jeffrey A. Pasley, *'The Tyranny of Printers': Newspaper Politics in the Early American Republic* (Charlottesville: University Press of Virginia, 2001).

99. Mark Voss-Hubbard, "The 'Third Party Tradition' Reconsidered: Third Parties and American Public Life, 1830–1900," *Journal of American History* 86 (1999): 121–50.

100. Remini, *Andrew Jackson and the Course of American Freedom*, 249–50.

101. Glenn C. Altschuler and Stuart M. Blumin, "Limits of Political Engagement in Antebellum America: A New Look at the Golden Age of Participatory Democracy," *Journal of American History* 84 (1997): 884. For a book-length elaboration, see Glenn C. Altschuler and Stuart M. Blumin, *Rude Republic: Americans and Their Politics in the Nineteenth Century* (Princeton, N.J.: Princeton University Press, 2000). While Altschuler and Blumin may well understate the civic engagement of ordinary Americans, they persuasively highlight the persistence of popular hostility toward the mass party and the patronage practices that sustained it. For a parallel assessment, see Mark E. Neely, Jr., *The Union Divided: Party Conflict in the Civil War North* (Cambridge, Mass.: Harvard University Press, 2002). Neely challenges the presumption—originated by twentieth-century behaviorist social science, and popularized among historians by Joel H. Silbey and Richard L. McCormick—that a "party system" propelled by a "partisan imperative" *existed* in the mid–nineteenth century (187). Neely further contends that the patronage practices that sustained the mass parties should not be conflated with a program of "management development or equal opportunity": "Patronage did not cultivate future candidates for public office, and it did not study or attempt to improve government administration. No other part of the two-party system more merited the criticism that parties put self before commonwealth" (192).

102. John, *Spreading the News*, chap. 7.

103. Robert P. Forbes, "Slavery and the Evangelical Enlightenment," in *Religion and the Antebellum Debate over Slavery*, ed. John P. McGivigan and Mitchell Snay (Athens: University of Georgia Press, 1998), 70. "Slaveholders," Forbes observes, "were unanimous in viewing the strong federal government created by the Constitution as the principal potential threat to slavery" (77). This perception had implications not only for the Jacksonian ascendancy but also for Jefferson's victory in the election of 1800. By "dismantling the detested apparatus of the Federalist state and replacing it with the hands-off Jeffersonian government," Jefferson's victory "neutralized the one institution in the United States capable of implementing effective measures against slavery" (82).

Chapter Four

THE LEGAL TRANSFORMATION OF CITIZENSHIP
IN NINETEENTH-CENTURY AMERICA

WILLIAM J. NOVAK

We must not thrust our modern "State-concept" upon the
reluctant material.
—*Frederic William Maitland*

A S HISTORIANS SEARCH for ways to reintroduce "the political"
back into American history, one interpretive possibility that cannot be overlooked is the idea of citizenship. The concept of citizenship is in the midst of an extraordinary theoretical revival.[1] For good
reasons. First, citizenship has the potential to integrate social and political
history. Citizenship directs attention precisely to that point where bottom-
up constructions of rights consciousness and political participation meet
the top-down policies and formal laws of legislatures, courts, and administrative agencies.[2] Second, citizenship deals directly with what has become a preeminent social and political question in our time—inclusion
and exclusion based on identity. Third, citizenship brings the state back
in, focusing attention on the claims and obligations of the rights-bearing
subject in distinctly modern nation-states. Fourth, citizenship brings democracy back in, illuminating issues of civic participation and the construction of civil society.[3] Fifth (taking a cue from T. H. Marshall's influential discussion "Citizenship and Social Class"), the citizenship
framework can expansively incorporate three different kinds of rights—
civil, political, and socioeconomic—integrating in a single developmental
story the early emergence of property and contract, nineteenth-century
struggles over suffrage, and the rise of twentieth-century social welfare
states.[4] Finally, the language of citizenship transfers smoothly to the discussion of transnational politics in an increasingly global, multicultural
world. Citizenship thus has much to recommend to American political
historians.

But the so-called citizenship debates bring one potential hazard to a
discussion of American politics (particularly nineteenth-century American
politics), and that is the danger of anachronism. For most recent discussions of American citizenship have been framed by the thoroughly modern

and constitutional perspective generated by contemporary civil rights movements. The social movements of the 1960s, the Civil Rights Act of 1964, and the Voting Rights Act of 1965 are the reference points for an understanding of what is at stake in modern citizenship and rights debates. The central issues involve the relationship of the individual and the central nation-state, the constitutional guarantees of private rights and public participation, and perhaps most important, the political exclusion of and discrimination against certain "discrete and insular minorities."[5] The issues are familiar, because for the most part they are the way we currently understand and debate the constitutional consequences of citizenship at the opening of the twenty-first century. Modern definitions of citizenship emphasize union, universality, and unilinear development. The citizen is the unified legal subject of a modern nation-state, thereby entitled to make rights claims upon that state. This modern idea of citizenship brings a presumption of universality and uniformity in the allocation of rights and duties—*all* citizens are entitled to the same bundle of state protections and privileges qua national citizens. All other local statuses, social memberships, and public and private personalities are rendered subordinate to this supreme equalizing political and juridical identity of the national citizen. A clear aspirational teleology drives the modern citizenship framework as more and more encompassing forms of individual rights claims— from political to economic to civil and social rights—are seen as natural and irresistible motors of historical change and social progress.

The danger for American political history is that this modern understanding of citizenship and statecraft will be read back into reluctant historical material as scholars search for the roots of present political aspirations and ailments. Rogers Smith, for example, has recently used just such a modern and constitutional conception of citizenship to boldly resynthesize the whole of American history from the American Revolution forward. In contrast to the old syntheses of Alexis de Tocqueville and Louis Hartz (which he claims emphasized a consistent liberal-democratic egalitarianism in the American political past), Smith argues that "through most of U.S. history, lawmakers pervasively and unapologetically structured U.S. citizenship in terms of illiberal and undemocratic racial, ethnic, and gender hierarchies."[6] Smith's understanding of the structure and stakes of American citizenship is thoroughly contemporary. He posits a unitary body of rules called "citizenship laws"—laws consciously "crafted by political elites" assigning "political identities . . . on the basis of such ascribed characteristics as race, gender, and the usually unaltered nationality and religion into which people were born." Smith finds such laws in the form of federal statutes and federal court decisions, which he argues constitute a consistent and coherent national law of constitutional identity governing the universe of rights claims that citizens can or cannot make on the polity.[7]

Linda Kerber similarly locates in the concept of citizenship a synthetic structure for making sense of much of American women's history.[8] Kerber's synthesis is more attuned than Smith's to the centrality of duties (as well as rights) to early American conceptions of citizenship, and Kerber is especially sensitive to the peculiar legal understandings and particular historical contexts of early American struggles over citizenship. Indeed, a central theme of her study is the strange persistence of the common law of coverture in mediating and controlling women's citizenship in America. But Kerber too explicitly argues for the applicability of a modern citizenship framework to the legal and political struggles of the past: "Modern citizenship was created as part of the new political order courageously constructed in the era of the American Revolution. Reaching back to the Greeks and reinventing what they discovered, the founding generation produced a new and reciprocal relationship between state and citizen."[9] For both Kerber and Smith, the legal category of citizenship operated for most of American history much as it does today—as the principal constitutional arbiter of important social, cultural, and economic conflicts over political participation, civil rights, and group privilege.

This essay is an attempt to question that assumption—to challenge the straightforward applicability of a modern conception of citizenship to nineteenth-century American understandings of individual rights, public power, and democratic governance. Was citizenship an important part of nineteenth-century law? Was nineteenth-century American citizenship a primary constitutional marker of access, status, privilege, and obligation? Did citizenship operate in the nineteenth century as a controlling opening legal concept prefiguring other subordinate rights and duties? Was inclusion and exclusion in nineteenth-century American public life primarily an issue of citizenship? If not, when did it become so? Is there an important story of *change over time* in the emergence of citizenship law as an important part of American political and socioeconomic development? These are the kinds of questions that need to be addressed before rushing to citizenship as an all-encompassing framework for synthesis in American history.

THE PROBLEM OF NINETEENTH-CENTURY CITIZENSHIP

Some rather obvious difficulties confront the idea of citizenship as a central ordering principle of early American politics and law. For one thing, early-nineteenth-century Americans were in the midst of self-consciously constituting a new governmental regime in which they wrote endlessly about first principles of American government and constitutionalism—from formal charters, declarations, and constitutions to the extensive commentaries of Federalists and Anti-Federalists to an extraordinary legal and political treatise tradition illuminating almost every corner of American private and public law. And yet the fact of the matter is that before *Dred Scott* and the Civil War, citizenship simply did not figure as a particularly significant part of that eminent discussion of American public law. From the beginning, in fact, the idea of citizenship was tossed about rather loosely—even in formal constitutional documents—as if the legal ramifications of precisely demarcating who was or was not a "citizen" were not in and of themselves determinative of much substance. In the Articles of Confederation, Article 4 was the important founding statement regarding the privileges and immunities of "citizens." But the language of that flawed charter was classically elusive: "The free inhabitants of each of these states, paupers, vagabonds, and fugitives from Justice excepted, shall be entitled to all privileges and immunities of free citizens in the several states; and the people of each state . . . shall enjoy therein all the privileges of trade and commerce, subject to the same duties, impositions, and restrictions, as the inhabitants thereof respectively." As James Madison noted in *Federalist* 42, "There is a confusion of language here which is remarkable." Not only did Article 4 establish a national tradition of deference to the states on the substantive content of citizenship, but the loose interchangeability of the terms "free inhabitants" and "free citizens," and of "people" and "inhabitants," opened the peculiar possibility that aliens (but "free inhabitants") of one state might be entitled to the privileges of citizens (thus being effectively "naturalized") in another. This carelessly ambiguous language of the Articles of Confederation provides an early clue that citizenship was not contemplated as the primary test of freedom and unfreedom in early America.[10]

Despite its added rigor and its role in establishing the new nation, the United States Constitution also did not overtly rely on citizenship to ground its elaborate structure of governmental powers and limitations. Along with the power to establish uniform bankruptcy laws, Congress was granted the authority to establish a uniform law of naturalization. Citizenship was cited three times as a prerequisite for federal office, including the requirement that the president of the United States be a "natural born citizen." And diversity of state citizenship became a constitutional cornerstone for the jurisdiction of federal courts. But after such official and jurisdictional stipulations, discussion of citizenship was once again relegated to the same essential (but this time more precise) delineation of state comity—the idea in Article 4, Section 2, that "citizens of each state shall be entitled to all privileges and immunities of citizens in the several states." Though Alexander Hamilton would detect in this clause "the basis of the Union" as opposed to confederation, the Constitution provided no formal definition of citizenship, no listing of the privileges and immunities of citizens, nor even an express description of the relationship between national and state citizenship.[11] All that could be immediately derived from the privileges and immunities clause was that citizens of different states should not be made aliens to one another—that is, that out-of-state citizens were entitled to all the citizenship[12] protections of in-state citizens. In the whole voluminous debate over the Constitution, the substantive topic of citizenship per se rarely arose. Indeed the use of the word "citizen" occurred most frequently as a title (as in "A Citizen of Philadelphia" by Pelatiah Webster), as a reference to Roman governance, and as a simple antonym for the officeholder.[13] As late as 1875, Chief Justice Morrison Waite argued in *Minor v. Happersett* that the word "citizen" in the Articles of Confederation and in the Constitution of the United States was simply a republican synonym for the earlier terms "subject" and "inhabitant"—"conveying the idea of membership of a nation, and nothing more."[14] As Alexander Bickel concluded more recently, "The concept of citizenship play[ed] only the most minimal role in the American constitutional scheme. . . . The original Constitution . . . held itself out as bound by certain standards of conduct in its relations with people and persons, not with some legal construct called citizen."[15]

In the extraordinary legal treatises that dominated early American political and constitutional discourse, the idea of citizenship fared little better. Though William Blackstone famously devoted the first book of his *Commentaries on the Laws of England* (1765–1769) to the "Rights of Persons," the concept of citizenship was not predominant. Blackstone talked briefly of "the people" in contradistinction to "the magistrates" and divided the people into the categories "aliens, denizens, or natives." It was the "natural-born subject" ("born within the dominions of the crown of England"), not the national citizen, that was the focus of Blackstone's inquiry, involving not a discussion of individual *right* but of political jurisdiction and the *duty* of ligeance: "Allegiance is the tie, or *ligamen*, which binds the subject to the king, in return for that protection which the king affords the subject."[16] Blackstone's discussion followed closely the logic of Edward Coke's often-cited argument in *Calvin's Case*.[17] Not modern citizenship rights but traditional concerns of land, inheritance, jurisdiction, subjectship, and *dominium* were the main features of this discussion, as captured by its roots in the subjects' oath of allegiance: "To be true and faithful to the king and his heirs, and truth and faith to bear of life and limb and terrene honour, and not to know or hear of any ill or damage intended him, without defending him therefrom." As Matthew Hale remarked about this early modern statement of the allegiance of governed to governor: "It was short and plain, not entangled with long or intricate clauses or declarations, and yet [was] comprehensive of the whole duty from the subject to his sovereign."[18]

St. George Tucker's 1803 American edition of Blackstone added little of substance to this discussion of citizenship, but for a short excursus on the constitutional comity clause.[19] And most nineteenth-century American treatise writers followed suit. In Joseph Story's influential *Commentaries on the Constitution of the United States* (1851), the "privileges of citizens" was the topic of a very short chapter 40, where it shared space with a comparative discussion of fugitives and slaves.[20] Thomas Cooley's *Constitutional Limitations* (1868), as intent as Cooley was on finding constitutional protections for individual rights, found little need for a substantive discussion of citizenship.[21] The two leading general political commentaries of the nineteenth century, Francis Lieber's *Civil Liberty and Self-Government* and Alexis de Tocqueville's *Democracy in America*, similarly made no analytical or organizational use of the concept of citizenship in their discussions of government, liberty, and democracy. Even James Bryce's sweeping late-nineteenth-century survey, *The American Commonwealth* (1881), devoted but three pages to an elaboration of "Citizenship of the United States."[22] No wonder that as late as 1873 in the first United States Supreme Court decision to interpret the Fourteenth Amendment, Justice Miller could argue that the "privileges and immunities of citizens of the United States"—the rights of "the citizen of this great country"—involved things like the right "to come to the seat of government," to have "free access to its seaports," to "demand the care and protection of the Federal government . . . when on the high seas," and to "peaceably assemble and petition."[23] Without underestimating the importance of this group of privileges, it seems that one must look beyond national citizenship to understand the substantive rights and duties, privileges and penalties, and inclusions and exclusions involved in early American public life.

But if the first problem with citizenship in nineteenth-century America is simply that early American legal and political commentators did not talk much about its positive attributes (that citizenship was an important category in early-nineteenth-century American political thought and that it was missed by Tocqueville, Lieber, Bryce, *and* Theodore Woolsey seems almost inconceivable), is it possible that the significance of citizenship was present in the negative, that is, in discussions of the rights and duties, privileges and disabilities of noncitizens? Nineteenth-century commentators did spend time sorting through the legal status of aliens, especially after postrevolutionary controversies involving the property of loyalists and later the passage of the Alien and Sedition Acts. But even those discussions of the liabilities of not being a citizen in early America—the most elaborate of which was in James Kent's *Commentaries on American Law*

(1826)—suggest more about the relative insignificance of nineteenth-century citizenship. Like Blackstone, Chancellor Kent turned to the topic of the rights and duties of "Aliens and Natives" after (and distinguished from) his lecture on "the absolute rights of individuals." There Kent enumerated a series of real disabilities affecting noncitizens.[24] Aliens were unable "to have a stable freehold interest in land,[25] or to hold any civil office, or vote at elections, or take any active share in the administration of the government." While these disabilities were serious, one will note immediately that most of them also applied to most citizens in the nineteenth-century United States, especially women and free blacks. Citizenship or the question of native versus alien was certainly not the only determinant of political participation. Moreover, many of these particular disabilities of alienage could be overridden by special or general state statute. The lack of stable freehold interest in land, for example, was virtually removed by state statutes allowing aliens to take, hold, and transmit real property, upon taking an oath of residency in a state with an intention to reside in the United States and to eventually become a naturalized citizen.[26] Rights in movable property were not even an issue, as aliens were "capable of acquiring, holding, and transmitting movable property, in like manner as our own citizens, and they can bring suits for the recovery and protection of that property." As Kent also noted, "Even alien enemies, resident in the country, may sue and be sued as in time of peace; for protection to their persons and property is due, and implied from the permission to them to remain." The duties of resident aliens remained basically the same as those of citizens: "They owe a local allegiance, and are equally bound with natives to obey all general laws for the maintenance of peace and the preservation of order, . . . and if they are guilty of any illegal act, or involved in disputes with our citizens, or with each other, they are amenable to the ordinary tribunals of the country." Aliens could be enrolled in state militias, and they could be held to the same duties, assessments, and taxes as state citizens. In short, the linkage that many contemporary scholars want to draw between rights and citizenship in an effort to establish the fundamental constitutional category that marks the free and the unfree is fraught with difficulties in the case of nineteenth-century American public law. Louis Henkin is but the most recent commentator to highlight that difficulty by pointing to the obvious but troubling fact that the provisions of the first ten amendments to the United States Constitution—the great charter of American rights and liberties—were enjoyed by noncitizens as well as citizens.[27]

In addition to the nonbarking dogs of formal legal and political discourse concerning citizenship and alienage, a third problem with the application of a modern citizenship framework to nineteenth-century American public law is the peculiar way in which citizenship was discussed when it was in fact brought up. The frequent constitutional references to citizenship as primarily a matter for individual states and for national comity suggest the difficulty of applying modern assumptions about union, universality, and uniformity to nineteenth-century American law and statecraft. Whereas modern citizenship involves a single, formal, and undifferentiated legal status—membership in a central nation-state—that confers universal and internal transjurisdictional rights upon its holders, nineteenth-century American governance was precisely about differentiation, jurisdictional autonomy, and local control. Federalism—the dominant feature of early American governance—wreaked havoc on the substantive articulation of a coherent conception of national citizenship rights. As the United States Constitution made clear, most privileges and immunities were products of state citizenship rather than national citizenship. And as a national matter, the exact nature of those overarching privileges and immunities was left unspecified. In *Connor v. Elliott* (1856), the United States Supreme Court explicitly refused to describe and define such privileges and immunities generally, preferring a slow, case-by-case elaboration. The furthest national authorities were prepared to go was to suggest through the comity doctrine that citizens of different states should not be deemed aliens to one another, that is, that they were entitled to the same general protections as other state citizens. As the contentious course of nineteenth-century American federalism made clear, however, comity did not prevent states from discriminating and extending to their own resident citizens certain exclusive privileges and rights not available to outsiders. In the classic example of *Corfield v. Coryell* (1823), Justice Bushrod Washington upheld a New Jersey statute that granted the right to take oysters from state waters solely to New Jersey residents.[28] Similarly, the privileges and immunities clause was held not to apply to certain contracts and corporations (giving rise to the important field of "foreign," i.e., out-of-state, corporation law).[29] Thus even at the level of state constitutional law, the American law of rights and duties, privileges and immunities remained profoundly disparate and diverse—a law of multiple jurisdictions. As Chancellor Kent noted, "The privileges thus conferred are local and necessarily territorial in their nature. The laws and usages of one state cannot be permitted to prescribe qualifications for citizens, to be claimed and exercised in other states, in contravention to their local polity." But even the multiplicity of state constitutional law does not quite capture how segmented the American polity remained in the nineteenth century. As will be seen momentarily, below the level of state statutes and constitutional conventions, most American individual rights and obligations remained the products of local governments and courts elaborating highly differentiated common-law rules of status, membership, and association.[30] This federal, local, and common-law nature of nineteenth-century American governance makes applying a universal, uniform, and constitutional conception of citizenship problematic indeed.

The final problem confronting a citizenship framework for nineteenth-century American public law is the assumption of unidirectional development. In contrast to the teleological story of unfolding rights of ever higher forms of citizenship, the discussions of Blackstone, Story, Kent, and Cooley seem to suggest that citizenship was simply not present as a significant part of antebellum public law. We know, however, that by the time of the Civil War and the passage of the Reconstruction amendments, citizenship emerged as perhaps the defining category of modern American constitutionalism. Thus, rather than forcing reluctant nineteenth-century material to conform to our modern ideas about citizenship, the treatise evidence suggests that we might be better off trying to interrogate and historicize the very idea of citizenship. That is, rather than reducing nineteenth-century American law to a Western template of progressive rights development, we might instead try to historically account for the relative absence of citizenship concerns in the early nineteenth century followed by the sudden emergence of citizenship in the constitutional crises surrounding the Civil War and its aftermath. Instead of simply applying the weighted evolutionary chronology of T. H. Marshall and his progeny, we might begin to investigate a story of legal transformation and historical change over time.

That is the objective of the rest of this essay—to read history forward rather than backward—to account for the absence and subsequent rise of American citizenship. For though citizenship was a problematic concept in the early nineteenth century, issues of privileges and immunities, rights and powers, and inclusion and exclusion were extremely important parts of early American legal and political life. If the idea of citizenship did not provide the main legal framework for understanding and resolving conflicts over those issues, what did? Part 2, the next section of this essay, attempts an answer to that question in the form of a highly differentiated common law of status and membership. Part 3, the last section, then introduces the story of change over time. For clearly at some point in the nineteenth century, the language of constitutional citizenship became increasingly central. This section attempts to map at least the beginnings of that story of transformation and constitutionalization. Some aspects of that story are very familiar, for example, the *Dred Scott* case, the Fourteenth Amendment, the *Slaughter-House Cases*. But my hope is that these historical commonplaces take on some new significance through a clearer portrait of what came before, of what was legally and politically at stake, and of what exactly changed. For the story of nineteenth-century American citizenship was not simply another episode in the linear evolution of citizenship in the West; it involved a particular American story of legal change and constitutional transformation. It entailed the emergence of a new kind of state and jurisprudence and the historical invention of a new juridical subject—the creation of the rights-bearing citizen in modern America.

THE COMMON LAW OF STATUS AND MEMBERSHIP

The integrated legal status of the rights-bearing citizen was not born free in America as the natural outgrowth of Lockean-liberal political philosophy and the original founding of a constitutional nation-state in 1787. That story is as overly simple as it is conveniently popular. Rather, American citizenship was manufactured through the fierce political conflicts and complex legal contests of nineteenth-century history. Though contemporary theorists like to approach citizenship as a simple on-off test of modern liberty (a unified, universal, and unidirectional marker of the line between freedom and unfreedom, rights and servitudes, inclusion and exclusion), a very different, nonconstitutional understanding of citizenship pervaded nineteenth-century American legal thought and political practice. That understanding began not with a top-down constitutional enumeration of the rights and responsibilities of citizens of a new nation-state, but with a bottom-up common-law tradition in which citizenship was considered but the last form of membership in a continuum of public jurisdictions and civil associations. Nineteenth-century jurists and commentators approached the question of citizenship not as a singular, all-important political question but as simply another place for the elaboration of common-law rules governing varying forms of human association and public jurisdiction, from the law of agency, partnership, and contract to the laws governing membership in voluntary associations, churches, unions, and corporations to the laws governing participation in towns, municipalities, and political parties. The common law of status and membership in such associations formed a dense and variegated legal history in which questions of private rights, public responsibilities, and issues of inclusion (and entry) and exclusion (and exit) were constantly debated and decided. That common law of status and membership forms an important legal backdrop to understanding the emergence of modern citizenship as a salient political issue in United States history.

One place to start to unpack this unwieldy notion of a common law of membership is with the law of personal status. For despite Henry Maine's premise about the modern shift from status to contract, personal status remained an important barometer of legal rights and obligations in nineteenth-century America.[31] As discussed above, both William Blackstone and James Kent began their comprehensive commentaries on English and American law with separate books on the rights of persons. But Blackstone's and Kent's delineations of such "rights of persons" were rather peculiar. Both began with a brief, abstract testament to the "absolute" rights of individuals in an "unconnected" or "natural" state. But the vast majority of each of their tracts was devoted to articulating the rights and duties of persons as "members of society"—persons as they stood in "civil and domestic" relation to one another.[32] Here the abstract individual of natural-law thinking gave way to the real person enmeshed in an intricate web of civil, social, economic, and political relations and activities. Here rights and duties were not determined by abstract reflection on the state of nature but through the elaboration of a great hierarchy of very specific and highly differentiated legal statuses. In this vast hierarchy, the status of citizen, native, alien, or denizen was merely one status (and hardly the principal one) designating one subset of particular rights and duties. A person's actual bundle of total privileges and immunities was dependent not upon a single determination of whether one was a citizen but upon a whole host of differentiated positions, offices, jurisdictions, and civic identities. The line between freedom and unfreedom in this early Anglo-American legal regime of status was crooked, ambulant, and highly particularized, dependent upon each individual's personal pattern of residence, jurisdiction, office, job, service, organization, association, family position, age, gender, race, and capacity.

Blackstone's hierarchy was indicative of just how far this common law of personal status diverged from the integrated and equalizing conception of modern rights of citizens. Blackstone first divided the rights and duties of persons (in society as opposed to a state of nature) into public and private—the governors and the governed, the magistrates and the people. For it mattered significantly to a person's bundle of rights and duties whether one was an officer or not, whether one was a member of Parliament, the king, a member of the royal family, a councillor, or a subordinate magistrate. A multitude of very particular rights and duties and important powers and obligations (e.g., the king's prerogative) were assigned by the common law by virtue of the legal status of officer: sheriff, coroner, justice of the peace, constable, surveyor, overseer of the poor. Next Blackstone divided the people into clergy and laity with similar status and rights differentiation. The laity were then divided into civil, military, and maritime persons. The civil state included nobility and commonalty: nobleman, knight, gentleman, and peasant. Blackstone completed his survey of the rights of persons with his classic listing of the important hierarchical legal statuses of private relations (household and economic): master and servant, husband and wife, parent and child, and guardian and ward. And he closed with an important discussion of the rights and duties of artificial persons in the guise of corporations.

While many of Blackstone's legal statuses did not apply to the republican governments of the newly formed United States, Chancellor Kent made clear the continued predominance of the importance of hierarchical legal statuses to the distribution of American rights and duties. Kent organized his understanding of the legal "rights of persons" around the same Blackstonian status relationships: husband and wife, parent and child, guardian and ward, master and servant, infants, and corporations. Though it would take a long treatise to fully elaborate the particular rights and duties attending these various legal statuses, one can get an idea of the severe differentiation of this hierarchical system by contemplating just some of the privileges of masters (service) or parents (discipline) and some of the disabilities of wives (coverture) or servants (bondage). The legal status of slave, Kent's first subdivision of servants, rendered one virtually rightless. In Kent's words:

> In contemplation of their laws, slaves are considered in some respects . . . as things or property, rather than persons, and are vendible as personal estate. They cannot take property by descent or purchase, and all they find, and all they hold, belongs to the master. They cannot make lawful contracts, and they are deprived of civil rights. They are assets in the hands of executors, for the payment of debts, and cannot be emancipated by will or otherwise, to the prejudice of creditors.

In contrast, the legal status of a corporation as an artificial person brought such extraordinary privileges as the right

1. to have perpetual succession;
2. to sue and be sued, and to grant and to receive by their corporate name;
3. to purchase and hold lands and chattels;
4. to have a common seal;
5. to make bylaws for the government of the corporation;
6. to remove members.

In striking contrast to the theorists searching for a uniform conception of citizenship rights that determined personal status in early America, Kent seems to be suggesting that the relationship worked the other way around—that legal status was the principal determiner of early American rights and duties.[33]

That also seems to be the overwhelming conclusion of a burgeoning social history literature on nineteenth-century American culture and society. The sociolegal histories of scholars such as Christopher Tomlins on labor, Ariela Gross and Thomas Morris on slavery, Hendrik Hartog and Nancy Cott on marriage, Michael Grossberg on the family, and Michael Katz on the poor law all reinforce the degree to which Kent's primary legal statuses—master and servant, husband and wife, parent and child, guardian and ward—remained the most important markers of individual possibility and penalty in nineteenth-century America, irrespective of formal citizenship concerns.[34] Slaves were not citizens in antebellum states. But before *Dred Scott*, their servitude did not flow from the fact that they were not citizens but from their legal status as slaves under an extreme derivation of the common law of master and servant. Most married women were considered citizens before the Civil War, but that did not stop the imposition of a host of civil, political, and economic disabilities through the common law of coverture. Some Native Americans did enjoy certain legal rights in some early American jurisdictions despite the problematic nature of their citizenship claims. And as Chancellor Kent hinted, aliens—whom one would expect to be the most unambiguously unfree if citizenship were the reigning factor in the allocation of legal and political privileges and immunities—frequently exercised far more rights and powers (sometimes including the right to vote) than citizens of lesser social status. Citizenship still primarily determined jurisdiction and subjectness in early American law; status filled in most substantive determinations of rights and duties.

Of course, the general hierarchies of the laws of personal status are a fairly well known aspect of early Anglo-American law (though often still ignored in favor of the brief natural rights forays of Locke, Blackstone, and Kent). But within the law of personal status lurks a less well known but important area of law that I call the common law of membership. The law of the great legal statuses described by Blackstone and Kent was fundamentally about membership. They were describing the relational rights and duties of persons as members of society, and they subdivided those rights and duties according to membership in the subordinate organizational components of that society: membership in Parliament, a household, a family, or a corporation. But beyond these largest official organizations and household relations, early American common law continued to dole out legal privileges and immunities in accordance with a person's membership in a vast array of supplementary associations and affiliations.

When Frederic William Maitland went searching for the historical roots of English law and liberties, he passed quickly by some popular sources: Magna Charta, the Petition of Right, the Habeas Corpus Act. Instead he began a series of detailed investigations into the law of primary associations and jurisdictions of English political life: the county, the hundred, the vill, the manor, the township, the borough, the trust, the corporation.[35] He found the myriad laws regarding the organization, membership, and internal self-governance of those associational entities to be far more significant to the everyday legal privileges and obligations of persons than the abstract declarations of great charters and bills of rights. That law of associations penetrated deeply into every corner of social relations. Maitland indicated the range of such a law of fellowship by potentially including within its bounds such a diverse range of institutions and organizations as "religious houses, mendicant orders, non-conforming bodies, a presbyterian system, universities old and new, the village community which Germanists revealed to us, the manor in its growth and decay, the township, the New England town, the counties and hundreds, the chartered boroughs, the gild in all its manifold varieties, the inns of court, the merchant adventurers, the militant 'companies' of English condottieri who returning home help to make the word 'company' popular among us, the trading companies, the companies that become colonies, the companies that make war, the friendly societies, the trade unions, the clubs, the group that meets at Lloyd's Coffee-house, the group that becomes the Stock Exchange, and so on even to the one-man-company, the Standard Oil Trust, and the South Australian statutes for communistic villages." Maitland hinted, following the example of Otto von Gierke's *Das Deutsche Genossenschaftsrecht*, that the various laws governing these multiple bodies and associations were more central to medieval and early modern European conceptions of rights than abstract ideas about modern citizenship.[36]

In the early-nineteenth-century United States, a similarly differentiated law of fellowship and association predominated in which a key index of personal rights and duties was membership in particular communities, associations, and corporations. Alexis de Tocqueville drew attention to the pivotal role of associations in early American society as early as the 1830s: "Americans of all ages, all stations in life, and all types of disposition are forever forming associations. . . . In every case, at the head of any new undertaking, where in France you would find the government or in England some territorial magnate, in the United States you are sure to find an association."[37] But Tocqueville and many later commentators erred in viewing such associations as primarily a civil society alternative to organized statecraft. In fact, early American associationalism was a mode of governance—a method of distributing public power and regulating the allocation of personal rights and duties. Membership in and exclusion from a range of differentiated self-governing associations determined one's bundle of privileges, obligations, and immunities much more than the abstract and underdeveloped constitutional category of national citizenship.[38]

The first thing to note about early American associations was their distinctly public rather than private character. Associations embodied an early American strategy of political development that eagerly delegated to subsidiary jurisdictions tasks that in the twentieth century would be seen as within the special purview of the central nation-state. One quick indicator of the public quality of early American associations was their formal creation and regulation by state governments. Like early American corporations generally, a vast range of political, economic, and social organizations were formally chartered and incorporated by state authorities, giving them a decidedly public cast, granting them special governing authority, and making them susceptible to public control.[39] Between 1777 and 1857, for example, the state of New York passed hundreds of special statutes recognizing and incorporating associations organized under at least forty separate descriptive titles, among which were the following:

1. Academies
2. Agricultural societies
3. Aqueduct associations
4. Banks
5. Bridge companies
6. Canal companies
7. Cemeterie
8. Charitable and religious societies
9. Churches
10. Cities
11. Colleges and universities
12. Dams
13. Dock companies
14. Ferry companies
15. Fire companies
16. Fishing and fisheries
17. Gas-light companies
18. Highways
19. Horticultural societies
20. Hydraulic works
21. Insurance companies
22. Land companies
23. Libraries
24. Literary institutions
25. Manufacturing corporations
26. Mechanics
27. Medical societies
28. Mining companies
29. Navigation companies
30. Railroad companies
31. Roads
32. Schools
33. School districts
34. Scientific societies
35. Telegraph companiess
36. Towns
37. Turnpike companies
38. Villages
39. Water companies
40. Whaling companies

New York's listing (quite typical for the period)[40] reflected an important aspect of early American associationalism: the ease with which officials merged the great range of associations from formal political entities (cities, towns, and villages) to public utilities (fire companies and highway, canal, and bridge companies) to eleemosynary institutions (schools, academies, and colleges and universities) to private corporations (banks, insurance companies, land companies, and mining companies) to more voluntary associations (charitable and religious societies and mechanic associations). While twentieth-century jurists would attempt to categorically separate these organizations as public versus private, political versus economic, civil versus social, antebellum theorists were fond of thinking of the whole of society and government as linked by a continuous chain of such self-governing associations joining formal government institutions to economic corporations to social organizations to household relations. As Francis Lieber explained in the dominant political text of the time, civil liberty and self-government in America were the product of the exercise of power through local self-governing associations—"a vast system of institutions, whose number supports the whole, as the many pillars support the rotunda of our capital."[41]

Next to its publicness, the second important aspect of nineteenth-century American associationalism was its regulatory character. Self-government through associations involved the extensive delegation of public regulatory authority to such subsidiary institutions and organizations. Of course, the clearest example of the delegation of public power to regulate members came in the case of those associations that functioned as actual civil subdivisions of the state, such as municipal corporations, towns, counties, and villages. Nineteenth-century state governments did not hesitate to delegate extraordinary police, taxing, and eminent-domain powers to local governing bodies. While incorporating the town of Salisbury, for example, the North Carolina legislature carefully enumerated the powers of town officers, including the power (a) to *acquire property* for public squares, markets, and buildings; (b) to *tax* real estate, polls, dogs, cellars, merchants, auctioneers, retailers, billiard tables, ten pin alleys, drays, hotels, brokers, insurance companies, lecturers, photographs, lawyers and physicians, officers and agents, vehicles, watches, pianos, pistols and knives, merchants, carriages, playing cards, barber shops, saloons, lumber yards, mills and machine shops, tan yards, brick yards, apothecaries, express companies, stage players, etcetera; and (c) to generally pass *police regulations* for the health, safety, and welfare of its members, for example, "rules and regulations concerning the firing of fire-arms within the said Town; the pace and speed at which horses may be ridden and driven through the streets of said Town; the arrangement of stovepipes in buildings; . . . the manner in which powder and other explosive and inflammable substances may be kept; . . . the manner in which dogs and goats may be kept; . . . to cause all lots, cellars, privies, stables, and other places of like character to be visited and examined by the Town Constables . . . and to prohibit all trades or occupations, which are nuisances, from being carried on in said Town."[42]

Such wide delegations of open-ended regulatory powers to local governmental authorities were a staple of nineteenth-century governance.[43] What is perhaps more surprising is the extent to which such delegations of power to some extent also accompanied the establishment of all other economic and social associations. As Kent made clear, the very acts of incorporation for societies of all sorts (e.g., "civil, religious, and eleemosynary") created "one single, artificial, and fictitious being" subsisting as a "body politic" endowed with special "powers, rights, and capacities." Blackstone elaborated that when persons were "consolidated and united into a corporation . . . as one person, they have one will; . . . this one will may establish rules and orders for the regulation of the whole, which are a sort of municipal laws of this little republic; or rules and statutes may be prescribed to it at its creation." Consequently, states chartered the range of American associations with discrete powers, often grouped into six categories: (i) to have perpetual succession, and the power of electing members in place of those removed by death or otherwise; (ii) to sue and be sued, and to grant and to receive, by their corporate name; (iii) to purchase and hold lands and chattels; (iv) to have a common seal; (v) to have the power of a motion, or removal of members; and most important (vi) to make bylaws for the government of the association or corporation.[44] Transportation companies received public grants of land, rights-of-way, and powers of eminent domain. But even noneconomic societies such as scientific societies, literary associations, and social clubs (incorporated as well as unincorporated) received the power to draft constitutions and pass bylaws regulating officers, membership, dues, profits, penalties, personal conduct, and all facets of group activity, from the consumption of liquor to the removal of offenders.

The effect of this decentralized regime of political, economic, and social self-governance and lawmaking via subsidiary associations was to make the issue of a person's actual bundle of rights and duties the product of a very complicated and varied tally of the rules, regulations, and bylaws of the host of differentiated associations to which one belonged, from family and church to union and corporation to city and county to state and nation. Whereas a modern conception of national citizenship usually entails a notion of top-down primary membership in the federal polity, which trumps all subordinate memberships and uniformly regulates the general rights and duties of all citizens no matter what their secondary associations, early American rights and duties flowed from the bottom up, hinging on the particular regulations and policies of a panoply of secondary jurisdictions and institutional affiliations. Constitutional rights of citizenship did not trump or limit the power of these majoritarian organizations. On the contrary, full membership in some of these self-governing associations was the key determinant of the substantive rights of many antebellum Americans. Nowhere was that clearer than in the power of associations to exclude some from membership and consequently from rights.

A classic early example of the powers of local associations to deny persons rights by excluding them from membership was the administration of the poor law in Massachusetts and Maine. Drawing on Elizabethan precedent, the Massachusetts system linked a claim of the poor to public relief, support, and decent burial to a person's settlement—or membership—in a particular town. And while American law later developed a presumption of membership in quasi corporations such as cities, towns, parishes, and school districts constituted by residence alone (i.e., irrespective of the desires of the person or the corporation),[45] early Massachusetts and Maine developed a whole series of legal measures to limit that settlement. Towns in Massachusetts and Maine (as well as in New York, Rhode Island, and other states) put into practice elaborate systems of permissions, warnings, forced removals, port prohibitions, and time, property, age, and status requirements to limit membership and thus limit the rights of the poor and the duties of public relief.[46] Neither state nor national citizenship trumped the power of these local associations to police their membership and determine rights of mobility, association, and support. Indeed, town overseers of the poor were sometimes empowered themselves as quasicorporations with vast discretionary power over the "rights" of poor citizens. In Maine, any two overseers in any town had authority to commit to the workhouse "all persons of able body to work and not having estate or means otherwise to maintain themselves, who refuse or neglect so to do; live a dissolute vagrant life, and exercise no ordinary calling or lawful business, sufficient to gain an honest livelihood." When Adeline G. Nott complained that Portland's summary practice of rounding up the poor violated her natural right to a trial and hearing before a judge, Maine's Supreme Court defended the town's "parental" right to have her "removed from temptation, and compelled to cultivate habits of industry, to be again restored to society, as a useful member, as soon as may be." The local police regulation of persons by self-governing communities recognized few modern limitations based on claims of citizenship, constitution, or due process of law.[47]

But beyond such ubiquitous particular associational practices of exclusion and regulation, the common law of status and membership entailed an entirely different way of looking at the problem of the rights of persons (whether citizens or aliens). The extensive tradition of local and associational police regulation in antebellum America involved a great deference to the self-governing and self-determining powers of local organizations to police their members without great regard for modern constitutional protections of individual rights. Indeed, Akhil Amar has recently argued that before the Civil War, rights in America were understood as collective, positive, and relative rather than individual, negative, and absolute. The Bill of Rights was understood primarily as protecting majorities—protecting the people's right to self-govern in a federated republic—as opposed to the modern interpretation of such rights as liberal bulwarks protecting minority citizens from majoritarian coercions.[48] The common law of membership reflected that very different understanding of rights—public and political rights based on inclusion and participation in local, self-governing jurisdictions. Nowhere is that alternative vision more clear than in the paradigmatic case of *People v. Hall*.[49]

People v. Hall was decided in the California Supreme Court in 1854, and in many ways it captured the exclusionary and political force of rights under the common law of membership—a regime that dominated American law to the Civil War but that was transformed with the reconstruction of national citizenship in the Fourteenth Amendment. The appellate case originated in a simple murder trial in which George W. Hall, a free white citizen of California, was convicted upon the testimony of several Chinese witnesses. Hall claimed that as a white man he was legally protected against such Chinese testimony and offered in his defense two separate California statutes governing civil and criminal procedure. While neither statute explicitly mentioned Chinese testimony, the civil procedure law provided that "no Indian or Negro" should be allowed to be a witness in any action in which a "White person" was a party; and the criminal statute held that "no Black or Mulatto person, or Indian" should be allowed to give evidence for or against a "white man." Hall argued that a prohibition on Chinese testimony was implicit in those other racial categories—Indian, Negro, Black, and Mulatto—against which California whites were protected.

The first thing to notice about the *Hall* case is that it was not originally framed in terms of citizenship rights. The California civil and criminal procedure statutes were not framed in terms of protecting citizens from noncitizen testimony but in terms of protecting all whites (whether citizens or not) from all Indian, Negro, Black, and Mulatto witnesses (no matter what their claims to citizenship). Though they frequently overlapped, racial status not juristic citizenship was the key determinant of inclusion and exclusion—of membership. But as Chief Justice Murray began to interpret those statutes and evaluate Hall's rights claims, issues of citizenship as membership in a self-governing body politic began to seep into the discussion. Murray's argument came in two parts. First he engaged in a curious but revealing bit of statutory construction in which he took judicial notice of past ethnographic knowledge in concluding that, taking the European perspective of Columbus, the name of Indian had long been used to "designate, not alone the North American Indian, but the whole of the Mongolian race." Accordingly, the terms Indian, Negro, Black, and Mulatto in the procedural statutes should be understood not in their specific but in their generic sense as each signifying "the opposite of 'white.'" The obvious intent of the California legislature in Murray's interpretation was to adopt "the most comprehensive terms to embrace every known class or shade of color, as the apparent design was to protect the white person from the influence of all testimony other than that of persons of the same caste." Chinese testimony was thus included within the statutory ban, as "the use of these terms must, by every sound rule of construction, exclude every one who is not of white blood."[50]

The second part of Murray's stunning argument attempted to justify this exclusion in terms of George W. Hall's rights. It is here that Murray introduced the language of rights and citizen, but in a way that reflected the distinctiveness of antebellum conceptions of self-governance and membership. In a decisive paragraph, Murray argued that "the evident intention of the Act was to throw around the citizen a protection for life and property, which could only be secured by removing him above the corrupting influences of the degraded castes." What is interesting about this paragraph is, first, that Hall was referred to here as a generic "citizen"—a member of the imagined body politic—not because he was legally a citizen of California or of the United States, but because of his racial status as white (i.e., white noncitizens were included within the same statutory protections).[51] But even more significant was the particular meaning of the fundamental rights of "life and property" that Murray saw himself protecting. For clearly Murray did not have in mind here the modern constitutional understanding of such rights as individual, egalitarian, and negative—protecting private individuals equally and absolutely against the coercions of overreaching majorities. To the contrary, like poor-law administration, Murray's conception of rights was distinctly inegalitarian—exclusive—delimiting the boundaries of the imagined self-governing body politic and protecting the majority against the public participation and individual claims of minority individuals. It was precisely the lack of a strong negative constitutional rights tradition and the open-ended plenary power of self-governing states, localities, and associations that caused Murray to worry so much about policing the membership of the body politic. As he put it, "The same rule which would admit [the Chinese] to testify, would admit them to all the equal rights of citizenship, and we might soon see them at the polls, in the jury box, upon the bench, and in our legislative halls."[52] Even as Murray moved toward the legal vocabulary of citizenship, he remained fully within the public language of the common law of status and membership. Rights of citizens were not individual trumps protecting private minorities against the community; rather rights were public and political, protecting the extensive powers and procedures of self-governing communities against all threatening nonmembers.

The exclusions of the New England poor law and California criminal procedure were just two examples of the way in which the common law of status and membership operated in early-nineteenth-century America. What mattered most in this regime was not the formal constitutional designation of whether one was a citizen or not. In many ways, citizenship still functioned as it did in Blackstone or *Calvin's Case* as an issue of subjectness or jurisdiction. It was not the principal determinant of rights and duties in antebellum law. What did determine the substantive rights and duties of early Americans was, first, personal legal status—office, property, household position, race, gender, infirmity, and age. Such status markers raised significant hurdles to one's membership in the imagined body politic (and the privileges and immunities entailed therein), regardless of one's official citizenship. The second determinant of such substantive rights and duties was membership in the host of subsidiary associations that constituted the early American polity, society, and economy. The multitude of particular bylaws and police regulations of such associations affected real rights and duties in innumerable ways. Despite isolated pockets of dissent and disagreement, the common-law regime of status and membership dominated American legal life throughout the early nineteenth century. It was displaced only through the midcentury struggle over slavery and civil war, with dramatic consequences for the meaning of rights and duties, inclusion and exclusion in modern American history.

THE MAKING OF MODERN CITIZENSHIP

The legal worldview captured in the cases of Adeline G. Nott and George W. Hall began to constitutionally unravel after the Civil War. In 1876 the Maine Supreme Court declared Portland's pauper law unconstitutional—in violation of the newly minted Fourteenth Amendment to the United States Constitution. As Justice Walton put it, "That article declares that no state shall deprive any person of life, liberty, or property, without due process of law; . . . it needs no argument to prove that an *ex parte* determination of two overseers of the poor is not such a process." Moreover, Walton reflected on the larger ramifications of a legal and racial world that prohibited slavery, servitude, and their badges and incidences: "If white men and women may be thus summarily disposed of at the north, of course black ones may be disposed of in the same way at the south; and thus the very evil which it was particularly the object of the fourteenth amendment to eradicate will still exist."[53] Similarly, in *People v. Washington* (1869), the California Supreme Court acknowledged the transformative effect of the Thirteenth Amendment and the Civil Rights Act of 1866 by declaring "null and void" the (now explicit statutory) prohibition on Chinese testimony regarding whites. Of course, there were limits to this constitutional reconstruction of the civil, political, and social rights of citizens. The ground for decision in *Washington*, after all, was that the law which prohibited Chinese testimony against a white person, yet would "allow them to testify against a black person in a similar case, would discriminate against the personal liberty of the latter."[54] And the United States Supreme Court rollback of the promise of Fourteenth Amendment citizenship rights, from the *Slaughter-House Cases* to the *Civil Rights Cases* to *Plessy v. Ferguson*, is a staple of public law historiography. Nonetheless, the Civil War and Reconstruction unmistakably put into motion the modern constitutional process of redefining fundamental rights and duties in America as attributes of a general and single national citizenship rather than the local agglomeration of particular common-law statuses and multiple associational memberships. It is important to at least outline the historical roots of this still ongoing constitutional rights revolution.

As noted above, the substance of the antebellum conception of rights was primarily reflected in the everyday common law of status and membership. But it did receive some constitutional expression as well. In 1895, Harvard Law School's James Bradley Thayer began to reconsolidate the substance of American constitutional law in his influential casebooks. After an introductory part 1 in which Thayer took up formative issues of constitution making, departments of government, and jurisdiction of the United States, he began part 2 with a chapter titled "Citizenship. – Fundamental Civil and Political Rights. – The Later Amendments to the Constitution of the United States." There Thayer started his discussion of the emergence of citizenship rights in the United States with Chief Justice John Marshall's opinion in the case of *Barron v. Baltimore* (1833).[55]

Barron v. Baltimore was a constitutional case that nicely captured the substance of the common law of membership, local police regulation, and the limits of constitutionally protected individual rights before the Civil War. In *Barron*, Marshall upheld the public works powers of the city of Baltimore to regulate harbors and streets for the health of the community even though they diverted water from Barron's wharf, leaving it inaccessible to vessels. Barron made a fundamental rights claim, arguing that the liberty of the citizen was protected against such governmental intervention by the Fifth Amendment to the federal constitution prohibiting "the taking of private property for public use, without just compensation." Despite his nationalism and his concern for rights of property and contract, John Marshall made short order of such national rights claims in antebellum constitutional law. "The Constitution was ordained and established by the people of the United States for themselves, for their own government, and not for the government of the individual states," he argued. Consequently, the Fifth Amendment's rights guarantees applied "solely as a limitation on the exercise of power by the government of the United States, and [was] not applicable to the legislation of the States." Marshall's opinion made clear the power of dual federalism and divided, residual sovereignty in early American constitutionalism—that is, the degree to which local and state authorities retained plenary powers in their respective jurisdictions without regard to rights claims based on national citizenship. Here even the explicit constitutional limitations of the Bill of Rights were interpreted as applying only to the powers of the federal government and not to the open-ended policing powers of the individual states and localities. *Barron v. Baltimore* thus nicely represented the degree to which early nineteenth-century jurists did not see the United States Constitution as primarily a guarantor of national individual rights. After all, this was a document that explicitly enumerated only three prohibitions that applied to both state *and* federal governments: passing bills of attainder, enforcing ex post facto laws, and granting titles of nobility.[56]

Barron v. Baltimore also reflected the jurisdictional, divided, and bottom-up nature of discussions of early American sovereignty, citizenship, and rights. This was a world that substantively separated the spheres of national and state and local governmental power and that understood national citizenship as dependent upon local determinations of status and rights. As early-nineteenth-century treatise writers concluded, the best the national constitutional system could do in protecting the privileges and immunities of citizens was the promotion of state comity—the fuzzy Articles of Confederation idea that "in a given state, every citizen of every other state shall have the same privileges and immunities—that is, the same rights—which the citizens of that State possess."[57] And even when those privileges and immunities were given their most expansive substantive definition, they still did not prevent states from discriminating against out-of-state citizens of the United States. As Justice Washington put it in *Corfield v. Coryell*, "We cannot accede to the proposition [that] the citizens of the several States are permitted to participate in all the rights which belong exclusively to the citizens of any other particular State, merely upon the ground that they are enjoyed by those citizens; much less, that in regulating the common property of the citizens of such State, the legislature is bound to extend to the citizens of all other States the same advantages as are secured to their own citizens."[58] Such was the decentralized, divided, and discriminating world of early American citizenship law.

And as long as the primary controversies between states and localities involved the poor law, wharf lines, fisheries, and occasional commercial conflicts, this federated, decentralized, and regulated conception of members' rights proved workable. Where it exploded, of course, was in its attempt to manage the interstate problem of slavery. As Paul Finkelman and others have shown in convincing detail, the effort to fit the extreme and radically opposed status and rights understandings involved in different states' treatment of free blacks and slaves into the established jurisprudence on comity and privileges and immunities tore the system apart. From *Somerset v. Stewart* to the *Dred Scott* case, the lack of a national law of citizenship rights created crisis after crisis in the adjudication of the rights of masters, slaves, and free blacks as they moved beyond the boundaries of their local jurisdictions and memberships. Moreover the harshness of slave law and the restrictions imposed on antislavery activities provided a constitutional lesson on the dangers of majoritarianism and local discrimination and the potential benefits of a more individual and absolute conception of certain fundamental rights.[59]

Dred Scott became the flash point for legal-constitutional concern about the state of citizenship law in the United States. Justice Nelson, who began authoring the first "opinion of the court," found perhaps the least controversial grounds for decision by attempting to fix Scott's legal status via traditional principles of comity. Scott (a Missouri slave) was not freed by virtue of his residence in free Illinois, Nelson argued, because of the force of state sovereignty in this federated republic. Citing Joseph Story's *Conflicts of Laws*, Nelson argued that each state had exclusive sovereignty over all persons within its jurisdiction. Consequently, upon Scott's return to Missouri, "her laws affect and bind all property and persons residing within it. It may regulate the manner and circumstances under which property is held, and the condition, capacity, and state, of all persons therein." So too with Scott's sojourn to the Wisconsin Territory. Citing Roger Taney's opinion in *Strader v. Graham*, Nelson again deferred to the local jurisdiction. As "every state has an undoubted right to determine the status or domestic condition of the persons domiciled within its territory," the laws of Congress in the territories carried no force within the boundaries of Missouri.[60] While Nelson's opinion was not welcomed by abolitionists, it remained fully within the decentralized, dual-sovereignty world of antebellum jurisprudence, where membership, domicile, and residence in a particular jurisdiction determined most rights and duties outside of any overarching national constitutional imperatives.

It was precisely Roger Taney's attempt to solve the problem of slavery by establishing such national constitutional imperatives in a proslavery direction that ironically paved the way for the reconstruction of American constitutionalism around new antislavery imperatives. Taney's heavy-handed and absolutist elimination of all American blacks, free as well as slave, from any past or future claim to national citizenship and the new substantive constitutional protection he offered the individual property rights of masters in slaves through his expansive interpretation of the due process clause of the Fifth Amendment now threatened the self-governing powers of free states to protect their own citizens and inhabitants. It was just such a concern that caused Lincoln to famously worry in his "house divided" speech: "We shall all lie down pleasantly dreaming that the people of Missouri are on the verge of making their State free, and we shall awake to the reality instead that the Supreme Court has made Illinois a slave State."[61]

The Fourteenth Amendment to the United States Constitution was a direct repudiation of *Dred Scott*, marking a sea change in American constitutionalism. Indeed, it is impossible to overstate its significance in reshaping the legal-political landscape of the United States. The Fourteenth Amendment remade the American state, and that process of re-creation began with a redefinition of national citizenship and the rights entailed therein. In direct opposition to *Dred Scott*'s attempt to limit the citizenship status of all blacks (free as well as slave) and to limit national citizenship rights to those rights emanating from individual or prospective states, the Fourteenth Amendment opened with a bold declaration of national membership: "All persons born or naturalized in the United States, and subject to the jurisdiction thereof, are citizens of the United States, and of the State wherein they reside." In contradistinction to the common law of status and membership and states' rights, the opening clause of the Fourteenth Amendment established one supreme membership in the body politic of the United States that stood above all others. And as the amendment went on to make clear, this was a national citizenship status of consequence. This was a national citizenship accompanied by constitutional protections against lesser jurisdictions. The second clause of the amendment spelled out the content of these new rights: "No state shall make or enforce any law which shall abridge the privileges and immunities of citizens of the United States; nor shall any State deprive any person of life, liberty, or property, without due process of law; nor deny to any person within its jurisdiction the equal protection of the laws." Quite significantly, the fifth section of the amendment gave the national legislature authority to enforce it through appropriate legislation. Though the constitutional effect of these important clauses would be the subject of the next hundred years of rights debate in the United States, what was clear from the beginning was the establishment of a new preeminent legal status in national citizenship, a distinct shift in public power to the national government at the expense of the states and lesser jurisdictions, and a new cross-jurisdictional concern with the privileges and immunities and due process and equal protection rights of individuals.

Of course, the actions of the Reconstruction Congress and the drafting of the Reconstruction amendments are enormously complex historical and legal topics that have yielded a prodigious secondary literature.[62] For the limited purposes of this essay, two things are worth highlighting about the drafting of the Fourteenth Amendment. First is the degree to which the creation of national citizenship rights made clear to the drafters and debaters the lack of a clear delineation of such rights in antebellum public law. In 1862, Attorney General Edward Bates circulated a frustrated opinion on the question of national citizenship rights:

> I have often been pained by the fruitless search in our law books and the records of our courts for a clear and satisfactory definition of the phrase citizen of the United States. . . . Eighty years of practical enjoyment of the [rights of national] citizenship, under the Constitution, have not sufficed to teach us wither the exact meaning of the word or the constituent elements of the thing we prize so highly.

The distinguished legal-constitutional skills of Horace Binney and Francis Lieber were similarly tested when they were charged by Republican congressmen in 1866 with exploring the meaning of "citizen." As Binney complained to Lieber, "The word citizen or citizens is found ten times at least in the Constitution of the United States, and no definition of it is given anywhere."[63] It was precisely this ambiguity in American citizenship law that created the conditions for *Dred Scott* and that had to be corrected through explicit constitutional amendment.

The framers of that constitutional revolution were quite clear on the magnitude of the transformation in state power and individual right precipitated by that amendment. As Joseph Story wrote to Francis Lieber upon Leiber's draft of proposed amendments, this "puts the State upon its true foundation: a society for the establishment and administration of general justice, —justice to all, equal and fixed, recognizing individual rights and not imparting them." It recognizes "the important truth—in a republican government, the fundamental truth—that the minority have indisputable and inalienable rights; that the majority are not every thing and the minority nothing; that the people may not do what they please, but that their power is limited to what is just to all composing society."[64] Charles Sumner went even further on the implications of this new constitutional charter of fundamental citizenship rights:

> Within the sphere of their influence no person can be *created*, no person can be *born*, with civil or political privileges not enjoyed equally by all his fellow-citizens; nor can any institution be established recognizing distinction of birth. Here is the great charter of every human being drawing vital breath upon this soil, whatever may be his condition and whoever may be his parents. He may be poor, weak, humble, or black, —he may be of Caucasian, Jewish, Indian, or

Ethiopian race, —he may be of French, German, English, or Irish extraction; but before the Constitution all these distinctions disappear. . . . He is a MAN, the equal of all his fellow-men. He is one of the children of the State, which, like an impartial parent, regards all of its offspring with an equal care. . . . The State, imitating the divine justice, is no respecter of persons.[65]

Sumner's meditation marked a new and modern understanding of citizenship in the United States: one that bound a new national "State" to its individual citizens without regard to distinction, through the creation and protection of civil rights.

Of course, Sumner's revolutionary vision of the Fourteenth Amendment's re-creation of American citizenship remained not fully realized even a century later. In many ways, the postwar amendments only started an elaborate and still ongoing process of drawing constitutional lines, determining which rights in particular were rights of citizens of the United States guaranteed by the national government and which were still susceptible to local, state, and associational regulation and discrimination. That process included much of the next century's constitutional jurisprudence involving the distinctions between civil, political, social, and economic rights; between the privileges and immunities, due process, and equal protection clauses of the Fourteenth Amendment; and between the particular amendments of the Bill of Rights incorporated within Fourteenth Amendment protection. That extended and contentious debate was prefigured in the first effort of the United States Supreme Court to interpret the legacy of constitutional reconstruction in the *Slaughter-House Cases*. There John Campbell argued for the radical constitutional consequences of a world in which state slave law was not a possibility. "How [was] the case now?" he provocatively asked. "The Constitution by declaring that every member in the empire is its citizen, every member within its jurisdiction derives his state and condition from its authority, and at the same time stating to those States, that this citizen of ours must not be disturbed in his life, liberty, or property, brings the Government into immediate contact with every person, and gives every person a claim upon its protection." But when the state of Louisiana rejoined with a long list of the local police regulations that would be called into question with such a radical reconstruction of individual rights, Justice Miller was forced to consider skeptically, "Was it the purpose of the fourteenth amendment, by the simple declaration that no State should make or enforce any law which shall abridge the privileges and immunities of citizens of the United States, to transfer the security and protection of all civil rights . . . from the States to the Federal government?" Miller answered his own question with a classically narrow interpretation of the privileges and immunities of citizens of the United States.[66]

Still, despite the slow and contentious pace of actual constitutional and political change in post–Civil War America, the Fourteenth Amendment transformed the parameters of debate fundamentally. Despite the contested and ultimately limited content of the rights to be attributed to citizens of the United States, no one debated that that was the fundamental question. Indeed, most of American public law after the Civil War came to be rewritten in terms of the rights of citizens of the national government and the federal powers that would guarantee those rights. The constitutional rights of United States citizenship became the organizing principle of American public law, displacing the differentiated common law of status and membership as the main determiner of rights and duties in American life. As early as 1875, Theophilus Parsons attempted somewhat unsuccessfully to synthesize American public law around this new ideal in *The Political, Personal, and Property Rights of a Citizen of the United States*.[67] For the next 125 years, the unfinished project of American public law remained the project of integrating the manifold memberships and statuses of early American common law into the single, comprehensive constitutional right of national citizenship.

NOTES

1. For a sampling, see the essays in Will Kymlicka and Wayne Norman, eds., *Citizenship in Diverse Societies* (New York: Oxford University Press, 2000); Gershon Shafir, ed., *The Citizenship Debates: A Reader* (Minneapolis: University of Minnesota Press, 1998).

2. For the best example of just how bifurcated such approaches can be, see the constitutional bicentennial issue of the *Journal of American History*, where the first half of the volume offers traditional discussions of formal doctrine and institutions while the second half focuses on social histories of rights discourse. David Thelen, ed., *The Constitution in American Life* (Ithaca, N.Y.: Cornell University Press, 1988).

3. See, for example, Robert D. Putnam, *Bowling Alone: The Collapse and Revival of American Community* (New York: Simon and Schuster, 2000); Theda Skocpol and Morris P. Fiorina, eds., *Civic Engagement in American Democracy* (Washington, D.C.: Brookings Institution Press, 1999).

4. T. H. Marshall, "Citizenship and Social Class," in *Citizenship and Social Class*, ed. Tom Bottomore (London: Pluto Press, 1992), 3–51.

5. *United States v. Carolene Products*, 304 U.S. 144 (1938), 152. The famous footnote number 4 to Justice Stone's decision in *Carolene* is sometimes regarded as the great charter of modern constitutional rights jurisprudence. See Owen Fiss, "The Supreme Court, 1978 Term—Foreword: The Forms of Justice," *Harvard Law Review* 93 (1979): 1–58; Robert Cover, "The Origins of Judicial Activism in the Protection of Minorities," *Yale Law Journal* 91 (1982): 1287–1316.

6. Rogers M. Smith, *Civic Ideals: Conflicting Visions of Citizenship in U.S. History* (New Haven, Conn.: Yale University Press, 1997), 1.

7. Ibid., 3, 4, 6.

8. Linda K. Kerber, *No Constitutional Right to Be Ladies: Women and the Obligations of Citizenship* (New York: Hill and Wang: 1998).

9. Ibid., xx.

10. Articles of Confederation, Art. 4. In *Federalist* 42, James Madison, defending the establishment of a uniform rule of naturalization, argued that a perfectly plausible construction of this statement of citizenship is that "free inhabitants" of one state must be extended all the privileges of "free citizens" of another, that is, "to greater privileges than they may be entitled to in their own State." Madison even surmised that this clause left open the possibility whereby "the very improper power would still be retained by each State, of naturalizing aliens in every other State . . . and thus the law of one State, be preposterously rendered paramount to the law of another, within the jurisdiction of the other." James Madison, *Federalist* 42, "On the Powers of the Federal Government: Relations with Foreign Nations, and other Provisions of Article I, Section 8," in Bernard Bailyn, ed., *The Debate on the Constitution*, 2 vols. (New York: Library of America, 1993), 2: 64–70, 68–69. Joseph Story concurred with Madison's analysis in his discussion "Privileges of Citizens—Fugitives—Slaves" in his *Commentaries on the Constitution of the United States*, 4th ed., 2 vols. (1851; Boston: Little Brown and Company, 1873), 2: 558–59.

11. United States Constitution, Art. 1, Sec. 8; Art. 2, Sec. 1; Art. 4, Sec. 2; Alexander Hamilton, *Federalist* 80, "On the Bounds and Jurisdiction of the Federal Courts," in Bailyn, *Debate*, 2: 479.

12. This was an important qualification. For nineteenth-century American state law remained replete with discriminating provisions against out-of-staters. As Justice Stephen Field argued in *Paul v. Virginia*, 75 U.S. 168 (1869): "The privileges and immunities secured to citizens of each State in the several States by the provision in question are those privileges and immunities which are common to the citizens in the latter State, under their constitution and laws, by *virtue of their being citizens*" (emphasis added).

13. Bailyn, *Debate*, 1:142, 176, 441.

14. *Minor v. Happersett*, 88 U.S. 162 (1874), 165–66. Waite defined this "membership" in distinctly traditional terms: "The very idea of a political community, such as a nation is, implies an association of persons for the promotion of their general welfare. Each one of the persons associated becomes a member of the nation formed by the association. He owes it allegiance and is entitled to its protection. Allegiance and protection are, in this connection, reciprocal obligations. The one is compensation for the other; allegiance for protection and protection for allegiance. For convenience it has been found necessary to give a name to this membership." As articulated below, Waite's understanding of citizenship remains very much in the tradition of Blackstone's definition of subject and ligeance and the common law of status and membership.

15. Alexander M. Bickel, *The Morality of Consent* (New Haven, Conn.: Yale University Press, 1975), 33.

16. William Blackstone, *Commentaries on the Laws of England: A Facsimile of the First Edition of 1765–1769*, 4 vols. (Chicago: Chicago University Press, 1979), 1:354–55.

17. *Calvin's Case*, 7 Co. Rep. 4 (1608).

18. Hale quoted in Blackstone, *Commentaries*, 1:355–56.

19. St. George Tucker, *Blackstone's Commentaries: With Notes of Reference to the Constitution and Laws of the Federal Government of the United States and of the Commonwealth of Virginia*, 5 vols. (Philadelphia, 1803), 1:365–66.

20. Story, *Commentaries*, 2:558–66.

21. The exception again is a short and equivocal section on state privileges and immunities. Thomas M. Cooley, *A Treatise on the Constitutional Limitations* (Boston: Little Brown and Company, 1868), 15–16.

22. Francis Lieber, *On Civil Liberty and Self-Government*, 3d ed. rev. (Philadelphia: J. B. Lippincott Co., 1891); Alexis de Tocqueville, *Democracy in America*, ed. J. P. Mayer, (New York: Harper and Row, 1969). James Bryce, *The American Commonwealth*, 2d ed. rev., 2 vols. (1888; London: MacMillan and Company, 1891), 1:406, 681; 2:95. Though he built his political science directly upon a "doctrine of rights," Theodore Woolsey similarly ignored the category of citizenship. Theodore D. Woolsey, *Political Science or the State Theoretically and Practically Considered*, 2 vols. (New York: Scribner, Armstrong and Co., 1878).

23. *Slaughter-House Cases*, 83 U.S. 36 (1873), 78–79.

24. James Kent, *Commentaries on American Law*, 4 vols. (1826; Boston: Little, Brown and Co., 1873), 2:65. All subsequent quotations are from this edition of Kent's *Commentaries*, where one gets the added benefit of Oliver Wendell Holmes, Jr.'s, late-nineteenth-century annotations.

25. As Kent elaborated, "An alien cannot acquire a title to real property by descent. . . . The alien has no inheritable blood through which a title can be deduced. If an alien purchase land, or if land be devised to him, the general rule is, that in these cases he may take and hold, until an inquest of office has been had; but upon his death, the land would instantly and of necessity (as the freehold cannot be kept in abeyance), without any inquest of office, escheat and vest in the state, because he is incompetent to transmit by hereditary descent." Thus, "Though an alien may purchase land, or take it by devise, yet he is exposed to the danger of being devested of the fee, and of having his lands forfeited to the state, upon an inquest of office found. His title will be good against every person but the state, and if he dies before any such proceeding be had, we have seen that the inheritance cannot descend, but escheates of course." Ibid., 2:53–54, 62. As noted below, this disability regarding real property was substantially removed by subsequent state statutes.

26. The legislature of the State of New York, for example, passed over 2,660 special statutes between 1777 and 1857 authorizing aliens to purchase and hold real estate in New York. See *General Index of the Laws of the State of New York, 1777–1857* (Albany, 1859), 30–72.

27. Ibid., 63–64. Louis Henkin, "'Selective Incorporation' in the Fourteenth Amendment," *Yale Law Journal* 73 (1963): 74.

28. *Connor v. Elliott*, 18 How. 591 (U.S., 1856). Justice Washington in *Corfield v. Coryell* went furthest in attempting to substantively define privileges and

immunities of citizens of a state that could not be abridged by other states: "What are the privileges and immunities of the several States? We feel no hesitation in confining these expressions to those privileges and immunities which are in their nature *fundamental*; which belong to the citizens of all free governments; and which have, at all times, been enjoyed by the citizens of the several States which compose this Union, from the time of their becoming free, independent, and sovereign. What those fundamental principles are it would perhaps be more tedious than difficult to enumerate. They may, however, be all comprehended under the following general heads: Protection by the government, the enjoyment of life and liberty, with the right to acquire and possess property of every kind, and to pursue and obtain happiness and safety, subject nevertheless to such restraints as the government may justly prescribe for the general good of the whole. The right of a citizen of one State to pass through or reside in any other State, for the purposes of trade, agriculture, professional pursuits, or otherwise, to claim the benefit of the writ of *habeas corpus*; to institute and maintain actions of every kind in the courts of the State; to take, hold, and dispose of property, either real or personal; and an exemption from higher taxes or impositions than are paid by citizens of the other State, may be mentioned as some of the particular privileges and immunities of citizens which are clearly embraced by the general description of privileges deemed to be fundamental; to which may be added the elective franchise as regulated and established by the laws or constitution of the State in which it is to be exercised. These, and many others might be mentioned, are, strictly speaking, privileges and immunities, and the enjoyment of them by the citizens of each State in every other State was manifestly calculated (to use the expressions of the preamble of the corresponding provision in the old articles of confederation) 'the better to secure and perpetuate mutual friendship and intercourse among the people of the different States of the Union.' " *Corfield v. Coryell*, 6 Fed. Cas. 546 (U.S.C.C. N.J., 1823), 551–52. Also see *Lemmon v. People*, 20 N.Y. 562 (1860).

29. See *Warren Manuf. Co. v. Aetna Ins. Co.*, 2 Paine 501; *Paul v. Virginia*, 8 Wall. 180. For further elaboration of these distinctions and discriminations, see the case list that Thomas Cooley appended to Joseph Story's discussion of privileges and immunities: *Butler v. Farnsworth*, 4 Wash. C.C. 101; *State v. Medbury*, 3 R.I. 138; *Murray v. McCarthy*, 3 Munf. 393; *Lemmon v. People*, 20 N.Y. 562; *Campbell v. Morris*, 3 H & McH. 554; *Abott v. Bayley*, 6 Pick. 92; *Amy v. Smith*, 1 Lit. 326; *Crandall v. State*, 10 Conn. 340; *Commonwealth v. Towles*, 5 Leigh 743; *Haney v. Marshall*, 9 Md. 194; *Ward v. State*, 31 Md. 279; *Slaughter v. Commonwealth*, 13 Grat. 767; *People v. Coleman*, 4 Cal. 46; *People v. Imlay*, 20 Barb. 68; *Fire Dept. v. Noble*, 3 E. D. Smith 441; *Fire Dept. v. Helfenstein*, 16 Wisc. 136; *People v. Thurber*, 13 Ill. 554; *Ducat v. Chicago*, 48 Ill. 172; *Pheonix Ins. Co. v. Commonwealth*, 5 Bush 68; *Downham v. Alexandria Council*, 10 Wall. 173; *Liverpool Ins. Co. v. Mass.*, 10 Wall. 567; *Ward v. State of Maryland*, 12 Wall. 418.

30. Kent, *Commentaries*, 2:71. See, supra, Section 2.

31. Henry Maine, *Ancient Law* (1861; New York: E. P. Dutton and Co., 1931).

32. Blackstone, *Commentaries*, 1:119, 142; Kent, *Commentaries*, 2:1.

33. Kent, *Commentaries*, 2:253, 277–78.

34. Christopher Tomlins, *Law, Labor, and Ideology in the Early American Republic* (New York: Cambridge University Press, 1993); Robert J. Steinfeld, *The Invention of Free Labor: The Employment Relation in English and American Law and Culture, 1350–1870* (Chapel Hill: University of North Carolina Press, 1991); Ariela J. Gross, *Double Character: Slavery and Mastery in the Antebellum Southern Courtroom* (Princeton, N.J.: Princeton University Press, 2000); Thomas D. Morris, *Southern Slavery and the Law, 1619–1860* (Chapel Hill: University of North Carolina Press, 1996); Kerber, *No Constitutional Right*; Hendrik Hartog, *Man and Wife in America: A History* (Cambridge, Mass.: Harvard University Press, 2000); Nancy F. Cott, *Public Vows: A History of Marriage and the Nation* (Cambridge: Harvard University Press, 2000); Michael Grossberg, *Governing the Hearth: Law and Family in Nineteenth-Century America* (Chapel Hill: University of North Carolina Press, 1985); Michael B. Katz, *In the Shadow of the Poorhouse: A Social History of Welfare in America* (New York: Basic Books, 1986).

35. Maitland also focused on the law of personal status ("the sorts and conditions of men"): the king, the earls and barons, the knights, the unfree, the religious, the clergy, aliens, the Jews, outlaws, excommunicates, women, and lepers, lunatics, and idiots. Frederick Pollock and Frederic William Maitland, *The History of English Law before the Time of Edward I*, 2d ed., 2 vols. (1899; Washington, D.C.: Lawyers' Literary Club, 1959); Frederic William Maitland, *Township and Borough* (Cambridge: Cambridge University Press, 1898); H. D. Hazeltine, G. Lapsley, and P. H. Winfield, eds. *Maitland: Selected Essays* (Cambridge: Cambridge University Press, 1936).

36. Frederic William Maitland, "Translator's Introduction," in Otto Gierke, *Political Theories of the Middle Age*, trans. Maitland (1900; Boston: Beacon Press, 1958), vii–xlv, xxvii.

37. Tocqueville, *Democracy in America*, 513.

38. For a fuller explication of this theme, see William J. Novak, "The American Law of Association: The Legal-Political Construction of Civil Society," *Studies in American Political Development* 15 (2001): 163–88.

39. The public and quasi-public nature of early American business corporations is now a staple of the legal-historical literature. See James Willard Hurst, *The Legitimacy of the Business Corporation in the Law of the United States, 1780–1970* (Charlottesville: University Press of Virginia, 1970); Joseph S. Davis, *Essays in the Earlier History of American Corporations*, 2 vols. (Cambridge, Mass.: Harvard University Press, 1917); and William J. Novak, *The People's Welfare: Law and Regulation in Nineteenth-Century America* (Chapel Hill: University of North Carolina Press, 1996), 105–11.

40. *General Index of the Laws of the State of New York*. See also *Resolves and Private Laws of the State of Connecticut, 1789–1865*, 5 vols. (New Haven, 1837–1871); *Private Laws of the State of Illinois, 1851, 1853, 1855*, 3 vols., (Springfield, 1851–1855); *Private and Special Laws of the State of Maine, 1820–1839*, 4 vols. (Portland, 1828).

41. Francis Lieber, *On Civil Liberty and Self-Government*, 3rd ed. rev. (1853; Philadelphia, 1891), 300. Like Maitland, Lieber compiled a list exemplary of the range of such subsidiary institutions past and present, good and bad, expedient and unwise, human and divine: a bank, Parliament, a court of justice, the bar, the

church, the mail, a state, the Lord's Supper, a university, the Inquisition, property, the sabbath, the feudal system, the Roman triumph, the "Hindoo" castes, the bill of exchange, the French Institute, our presidency, the New York tract society, the Areopagus, the Olympic Games, an insurance company, the janizaries, the English common law, the episcopate, the tribunate, the captainship of a fishing fleet, the crown, the German book trade, the Goldsmiths' Company, our Senate, our representatives, our Congress, our state legislatures, courts of conciliation, the justiceship of the peace, the priesthood, a confederacy, the patent, the copyright, hospitals for lunatics, estates, the East India Company (301–2).

42. "An Act to Consolidate and Amend the Several Acts Relating to the Incorporation of the Town of Salisbury," chap. 73, *Private Laws of the State of North Carolina Passed by the General Assembly at Its Session 1868–69* (Raleigh, N.C., 1869), 203–8.

43. See, for example, John F. Dillon, *Treatise on the Law of Municipal Corporations* (Chicago: James Cockcroft and Co., 1872); Ernst Freund, *The Police Power: Public Policy and Constitutional Rights* (Chicago: Callaghan and Co., 1904); and Novak, *People's Welfare*.

44. Kent, *Commentaries*, 2:267–315; Blackstone, *Commentaries*, 1:455–73.

45. See, for example, the discussion of membership and citizenship in Charles Fisk Beach, Jr., *Commentaries on the Law of Public Corporations Including Municipal Corporations and Political or Governmental Corporations of Every Class*, 2 vols. (Indianapolis: Bowen-Merrill Co., 1893), 1:133–35.

46. For some excellent discussions, see Michael B. Katz, *The Undeserving Poor: From the War on Poverty to the War on Welfare* (New York: Pantheon, 1989), 12–15; Douglas L. Jones, "The Transformation of the Law of Poverty in Eighteenth-Century Massachusetts," in *Law in Colonial Massachusetts, 1630–1800*, ed. Daniel R. Coquillette (Boston: Colonial Society of Massachusetts, 1984), 153–90; Gerald L. Neuman, *Strangers to the Constitution: Immigrants, Borders, and Fundamental Law* (Princeton, N.J.: Princeton University Press, 1996), 23–29; and Kunal M. Parker, "Citizenship, Poverty, and Territory: The Legal Construction of Immigrants in Antebellum Massachusetts," *Law and History Review* 19 (2001): 583–643.

47. *Laws of Maine* (1821), c. 124, s. 6 and 7; *Nott's Case*, 11 Me. 208 (1834), 211. For similar examples of the judicial defense of local discretionary power over members not subject to constitutional scrutiny with respect to citizenship, see *Portland v. Bangor*, 42 Me. 403 (1856), and *Shafer v. Mumma*, 17 Md. 331 (1861).

48. Akhil Reed Amar, *The Bill of Rights* (New Haven, Conn.: Yale University Press, 1998).

49. *People v. Hall*, 4 Cal. 399 (1854).

50. *People v. Hall*, 402–3.

51. Similarly, Murray referred to the problems of naturalization for the Chinese under the U.S. statute limiting naturalization to "free white citizens," citing Chancellor Kent's dictum that "it is a matter of doubt whether, under this provision, any of the tawny races of Asia can be admitted to citizenship." But Murray used this reference not to suggest that rights follow citizenship status but to bolster his interpretive case that the Chinese should be included in all other nonwhite

racial designations, that is, Indian, Negro, Black, and Mulatto. Ibid., 403–4; Kent, *Commentaries*, 2:72.

52. *People v. Hall*, 404.

53. *Portland v. Bangor*, 65 Me. 120 (1876), 121. In an earlier case, Justice Rice of Maine had explicitly compared the conditions of poor law and slave law: "Pauperism works most important changes in the condition of the citizen. Through its influence, he is deprived of the elective franchise, and of the control of his own person. The pauper may be transported from town to town, and place to place against his will; he loses the control of his family; his children may be taken from him without his consent; he may himself be sent to the work-house, or made the subject of a five years contract, without being personally consulted. In short the adjudged pauper is subordinated to the will of others, and reduced to a condition but little removed from that of chattel slavery, and until recently, by the statute of 1847, c. 12, like the slave, was liable to be sold upon the block of the auctioneer for service or support." *Portland v. Bangor*, 42 Me. 403 (1856), 411.

54. *People v. Washington*, 36 Cal. 658 (1869), 671, 666. Indeed, in *People v. Brady*, 40 Cal. 198 (1870), the California court retreated further from the limited equalitarian sentiments of *Washington*, upholding California's Chinese testimonial exclusion law in the face of the newly adopted Fourteenth Amendment. The equalitarian black-white sentiment expressed by the California Supreme Court in *Washington* expanded into a distinctly national vision of citizenship rights protected by explicit federal constitutional and statutory provision. These new rights were purchased at the expense of the Chinese aliens, who emerged in *Brady* as the "class" distinctly excluded from the constitutional protections of national citizenship. That new citizenship claims could have a distinctly exclusionary force should come as no surprise after Roger Taney's argument in the *Dred Scott* Case. For further discussion of testimonial exclusion in California, see J.A.C. Grant, "Testimonial Exclusion Because of Race: A Chapter in the History of Intolerance in California," in *Chinese Immigrants and American Law*, ed. Charles McClain (New York: Garland, 1994), 82–91.

55. James Bradley Thayer, *Cases on Constitutional Law*, 2 vols. (Cambridge, Mass.: Charles W. Sever, 1895), 1:449.

56. *Barron v. Baltimore*, 32 U.S. 243 (1833), 250–51. For an excellent discussion of this limitation, see Amar, *Bill of Rights*, 128.

57. This interpretation of the privileges and immunities clause comes from *Lemmon v. People*, 20 N.Y. 562 (1860).

58. *Corfield v. Coryell*, 546, 552.

59. Paul Finkelman, *An Imperfect Union: Slavery, Federalism, and Comity* (Chapel Hill: University of North Carolina Press, 1981). See also William M. Wiecek, *The Sources of Antislavery Constitutionalism in America, 1760–1848* (Ithaca, N.Y.: Cornell University Press, 1977); Paul Finkelman, *Dred Scott v. Sandford: A Brief History with Documents* (New York: Bedford Books, 1997).

60. *Dred Scott v. Sandford*, 19 How. 393 (1857), 482.

61. Roy P. Basler, ed., *Collected Works of Lincoln* (New Brunswick, N.J.: Rutgers University Press, 1953–1990), 2:467.

62. See, for example, Harold Hyman, ed., *The Radical Republicans and Reconstruction, 1861–1870* (New York: Bobbs-Merrill, 1967); Harold Hyman, *A More Perfect Union: The Impact of the Civil War and Reconstruction on the Constitution* (Boston: Houghton Mifflin, 1975); William Nelson, *The Fourteenth Amendment: From Political Principle to Judicial Doctrine* (Cambridge, Mass.: Harvard University Press, 1988); Eric Foner, *Reconstruction: America's Unfinished Revolution, 1863–1877* (New York: Harper and Row, 1988); Michael Vorenberg, *Final Freedom: The Civil War, the Abolition of Slavery, and the Thirteenth Amendment* (New York: Cambridge University Press, 2001).

63. U.S. Attorney General, *Opinions*, 10, 383. Quoted in Harold M. Hyman and William M. Wiecek, *Equal Justice under Law: Constitutional Development, 1835–1875* (New York: Harper and Row, 1982), 411–12. Binney quoted in Michael Vorenberg, "Legal Theory and Practical Politics: Francis Lieber and the Republicans," manuscript in author's possession. I am indebted to Vorenberg for bringing this material to my attention. As late as 1910, W. W. Willoughby continued the tradition of eminent public law scholars being surprised by the *lack* of discussion of citizenship before the Civil War: "Prior to the argument of the Dred Scott case there was surprisingly little discussion of [the relationship of these two citizenships, state and national]." W. W. Willoughby, *The Constitutional Law of the United States*, 2 vols. (New York: Baker, Voorhis and Co., 1910), 1:260.

64. *Life and Letters of Justice Story*, 2:278; Story, *Commentaries*, 3:42. Lieber's originally proposed new constitutional amendments appear in an 1865 pamphlet, *Amendments of the Constitution Submitted to the Consideration of the American People*, in Francis Lieber, *Miscellaneous Writings*, 3 vols. (Philadelphia: J. B. Lippincott and Co., 1881), 2:137–79. Lieber's "Amendment G" read: "The free inhabitants of each of the states, territories, districts, or places within the limits of the United States, either born free within the same or born in slavery within the same and since made or declared free, and all other inhabitants who are duly naturalized according to the laws of the United States, shall be deemed citizens of the United States, and without any exception of color, race, or origin, shall be entitled to the privileges of citizens, as well in courts of jurisdiction as elsewhere."

65. Charles Sumner, "Equality Before the Law," in *Speeches*, 2:341.

66. *Slaughter-House Cases*, 21 L. Ed. 395, 83 U.S. 26 (1873), 399–400, 77.

67. Theophilus Parsons, *The Political, Personal, and Property Rights of a Citizen of the United States: How to Exercise and How to Preserve Them* (Cincinnati: National Publishing Co., 1875).

Chapter Five

BRINGING THE CONSTITUTION BACK IN

AMENDMENT, INNOVATION, AND POPULAR DEMOCRACY

DURING THE CIVIL WAR ERA

Michael Vorenberg

READING THE CONSTITUTION is like skimming an American history textbook—albeit a dated one. The original body of the Constitution and the first ten amendments, the Bill of Rights, give a sense of the causes and resolution of the American Revolution, and each successive amendment reveals the country at a moment of evolution, ostensibly toward the "more perfect union" described by President Abraham Lincoln in the Gettysburg Address of 1863. This feature of the Constitution—its potential to serve as a road map of the country's imagined march toward perfection—is perhaps the reason that, of all the genres of historical writing, constitutional history is most susceptible to whiggishness, to a tendency to see American political development as generally moving toward some higher form of democracy. Obviously, the tendency is to be resisted. Like all the best political history, constitutional history must avoid simplistic explanation and instead highlight the peculiar collision of people, trends, and ideologies that led to unpredictable developments, and it must avoid allowing political assumptions of the present to shade the telling of the past.

An especially dangerous pitfall involves the study of constitutional amendments. Too often, Americans assume that each amendment represented an inevitable development in the country's past, an obvious step in bringing the nation's written charter into line with its actual conditions. Implicit in the assumption are two misguided premises: first, that the creation of constitutional amendments was the result less of contingent, unforeseeable events than of overpowering popular ideology; and second, that Americans, from the founding to the present, generally regarded amending the Constitution not only as legitimate but as the best and most effective means of achieving a national reform.

Take, for example, the Reconstruction amendments. Historians rightly see the Civil War and Reconstruction as a watershed moment in constitutional history, a time when an unprecedented number of amendments were proposed and three were adopted: the thirteenth, which abolished slavery; the fourteenth, which prohibited states from denying people "due process" and "equal protection" and defined citizenship (or at least attempted to); and the fifteenth, which prohibited the states and nation from denying the vote on the basis of "race, color, or previous condition of servitude." Historians—again, rightly—acknowledge the amendments as crucial in transforming African-Americans from members of an inferior legal class (either slaves or free people with few rights) to full citizens and in transforming the United States from a loose confederation of states to a cohesive nation. The racial and state-building dimensions of the Reconstruction amendments are the most interesting to historians as well as to legal scholars, not least of all because of present-day concerns about racial equality and federalism. Yet, the focus on these two dimensions can flatten out the complexity of this moment of constitutional creativity, the way that contingent, now forgotten phenomena and actions secured the amendments' adoption.

Also, in viewing the Reconstruction amendments as obvious, necessary steps that had to be taken as a result of the Civil War, we too easily lose sight of the fact that most Americans in the mid–nineteenth century were not accustomed to using the amendment method as a means of reform, and many of them resisted the amendment method as ill-conceived if not illegitimate. Between the adoption of the Bill of Rights and the beginning of the Civil War, the number of amendments proposed to Congress during any four-year period was as low as ten or as high as fifty. The entire decade of the 1850s saw only twenty-two proposals. But during the four-year period of the Civil War there were nearly two hundred proposals, and in almost every year after the war and before the turn of the century the number of proposals was in double digits. Not since the making of the Bill of Rights had the United States witnessed such a surge of proposed constitutional amendments.[1]

The quality of the proposed amendments was as remarkable as the quantity. These were not simply measures restraining the federal government, like the first ten amendments—the Bill of Rights—or making adjustments in the operation of government, like the eleventh, which limited federal jurisdiction so as not to include suits against states, or the twelfth, which revised the electoral college system because of flaws exposed in the deadlocked presidential election of 1800. The amendments proposed during the Civil War, by contrast, were far more sweeping, and they empowered, rather than restrained, the federal government. These were some of the first measures proposing to use the Constitution to accomplish major social reforms, such as the abolition of slavery, the regulation of marriage (by abolishing polygamy), and the prohibition of the consumption of alcohol.

Reformers during the Civil War came to see the Constitution as a potential tool for social change. That was a major shift from the antebellum era, when reformers tended to seek change at the state level because of an assumption, often unstated but nonetheless powerful, that the Constitution could not be (or even should not be) interpreted or amended to achieve change nationally. Abolitionists, who were the best-known reformers of the antebellum era, were particularly dubious of the Constitution's potential to aid their cause. A few radical abolitionists argued that the Constitution was an antislavery document that empowered Congress to abolish slavery nationally, but most thought that it was either entirely or partly proslavery. The skepticism of antislavery activists was buttressed by federal legislative acts and judicial decisions that upheld or strengthened laws requiring the return of fugitive slaves to their owners. Although the Republican party, which emerged in the 1850s, gave unprecedented political power to the antislavery movement, most party members acquiesced to fugitive slave laws and contended that the Constitution empowered Congress to prohibit slavery only in the federal territories and the District of Columbia, not in the southern states. The Civil War shifted the landscape of politics and reform. It drove proslavery southerners out of the Union government, making the adoption of an antislavery Constitution politically possible. The war also opened people's minds to innovative methods of interpreting or expanding the Constitution. These conditions enabled the rise to prominence and influence of reformers who had been outside of the abolition movement or marginalized within it during the antebellum period. The reformers were less a cohesive unit than an amalgam of small groups united only by the insight, so far rarely contemplated, that the best means of abolishing slavery was by constitutional amendment. Their ranks included radical abolitionists, foreign-born critics of the American Constitution, and Democrats newly convinced that the Union could not endure with slavery intact. At this unprecedented constitutional moment, they led abolitionists, Republicans, and ultimately most Americans in a new direction—toward a belief that social change is best effected by a constitutional amendment.

Historians tend to see the Civil War less as a transforming moment of creative constitutionalism than as a national crisis during which the Constitution was a crucial stabilizing, conservative force. Much has changed in the historiography of Civil War constitutionalism, but the older literature as well as more recent interpretations, including those by political scientists and sociologists, share a view of the Civil War as a time of convulsion contained by the norms of constitutional thought and behavior. If the country took a step toward becoming a national state during the Civil War, it was a limited step at best, argue most historians. They concede that the Reconstruction amendments were significant and perhaps the most tangible results of the war, but they stress the limited, short-term impact of the measures because of poor enforcement and eviscerating judicial interpretations. The measurable constitutional change produced by the war was indeed limited. The postbellum era witnessed the persistence of localism over nationalism, the resistance to extensive national bureaucracies, and the continuing belief in state governments rather than the federal government as the primary guardians of individual rights.[2]

Yet, simultaneously, the war sparked or accelerated meaningful, even revolutionary movements toward a modern nation-state, movements sometimes so subtle that their effects were not fully felt until the late nineteenth century. A few legal scholars have made much—perhaps too much—of the Civil War era as a transformative period during which the Constitution was employed in constructive state building.[3]

Even these scholars, however, rarely acknowledge what was perhaps the most revolutionary constitutional change wrought by the war: the awakening of public awareness that the Constitution, specifically through its amending device, could be an instrument of reform. As historians have noted, the subject of the amending power received the greatest attention during the Progressive Era, but it was during the Civil War that the discussion really began. The people's ultimate acceptance of the legitimacy and efficacy of far-reaching constitutional amendments paved the way for future amendments. The path toward modernization and centralization would be smoothed rather than blocked by the Constitution.[4]

Prior to the Civil War, most Americans thought of the federal Constitution as static and the amending device as a means to preserve that stasis. The idea of an amendable Constitution was deeply rooted in the Anglo-American legal tradition, so it was no surprise that the document contained an article, Article 5, that provided for revision. But the procedural burdens in Article 5 ensured that the Constitution could not be whimsically revised or rewritten. Like most of the framers of the Constitution, James Madison approved of the article, for he saw popular democracy as a potential threat to the republic and worried that if the people could too easily change the Constitution, the new nation might dissolve. As he put it in *Federalist* 49, frequent amendments might endanger the new nation, for they would "disturb the public tranquility by interesting too strongly the public passions" and "deprive the government of that veneration which time bestows on every thing."[5] Madison was more cynical than his friend

Thomas Jefferson, who had more faith in popular democracy and looked more favorably on the prospect of frequent amendments to the Constitution. Jefferson went so far as to suggest a revision of the Constitution with every new generation.[6]

Jefferson's thinking helped pave the way for the Bill of Rights, but ultimately it was Madison's view that came to dominate both elite and popular constitutional thought during the early nineteenth century. Between the adoption of the Twelfth Amendment in 1804 and the beginning of the secession crisis in 1860, only about four hundred constitutional amendments were proposed in Congress, roughly the same number that we might expect to appear today in a single presidential term. Only one amendment was passed by Congress during this period, a measure banning titles of nobility that was aimed at foreign-born dignitaries during the War of 1812, but it did not receive the necessary votes from the states for ratification. Outside of Congress, calls for constitutional amendments were equally rare during the five decades leading up to the Civil War. Occasionally during this period, a reformer would make a futile effort to secure an amendment that regulated personal behavior—such measures included an amendment banning dueling and one providing for a national plan of poor relief—but almost all of the proposed amendments dealt instead with the procedure of governance. The most commonly proposed amendments sought to tinker with the electoral college system so that no section of the country would have too much say in who was elected president. Another favorite was an amendment prohibiting presidential candidates from holding federal office. That measure had received strong support from the presidential candidate Andrew Jackson, who feared that candidates serving in Congress would use their office to gain an unfair advantage in the election. Once elected to the presidency, Jackson would often praise the amending device as a method of increasing federal power more appropriate than congressional action. Like President James Madison, who had declared that an amendment was needed to expand legislative power before Congress could pass the "bonus bill" for internal improvements, Andrew Jackson told Congress that it could not pass measures for internal improvements or national banks without a constitutional amendment enlarging congressional power.[7]

In the antebellum era, Americans generally regarded the amending device not as a means of securing new rights or outlawing old evils but rather as a means of preserving the federalist structure of the nation and curbing the powers of any single governing branch. Under this regime, the constitutional order experienced both stability and evolution: while the text of the federal Constitution remained unchanged, judicial review and revision or rewriting of state constitutions adapted law to circumstance. By 1860, if not earlier, the process had left its mark on governance.

Judicial review, even of federal laws, was an accepted practice, even if particular judicial decisions, such as *Dred Scott* in 1857, were unpopular with certain groups. Meanwhile, most Americans had grown accustomed to frequent changes in *state* constitutions. All of the state constitutions were frequently amended in the period between 1790 and 1860, and quite a few were rewritten completely by popular conventions. Such changes both revealed and perpetuated the belief that state constitutions lacked the iconic power of the unchanging federal Constitution. In contrast to Americans' reverence for the federal Constitution as it was, which helped to preserve a Constitution unchanged since 1804, their assumption that the alteration of state constitutions was not radical but rather a necessity helped lead to the creation of state constitutions that were often complex and absurdly long—little more than patchwork statute books. Indeed, perhaps Americans' assumption of an unchanging federal Constitution, combined with the procedural difficulty of amending that document, led them to seek textual change only in state constitutions, all of which contained provisions for revision and redrafting that were less burdensome than similar provisions in the federal Constitution. Partly as a result of these established patterns of constitutional behavior in the antebellum era, people voiced their concerns and expressed their opinions through the established channels of party politics and state-level constitutional reform rather than through conventions assembled to propose or consider changes to the national Constitution. The Constitution was viewed more as an instrument maintaining discipline, or the rule of law, than as an instrument promoting democratic processes that would lead to significant social reforms. Conflict over the meaning of the Constitution took place, to be sure, and led to significant developments in constitutional law. But that development took place within the confines of a consensus that the text of the charter should remain static. Even onetime Anti-Federalists determined to restrain federal power turned their efforts slowly away from creating formal amendments and toward strengthening the power of the states, especially through a more sharply articulated "compact theory" of states' rights.[8]

For example, in the most famous antebellum clash over states' rights, the nullification crisis of 1828–1833, few of those involved sought to use the amendment method to achieve their goals. With the exception of a few petitions from southern state legislatures, never debated, that sought a national convention to craft an amendment clarifying the powers of the federal and state governments, pronullification and antinullification proposals took the standard form of state or national resolutions or statutes that did not mention an amendment to the federal convention. John C. Calhoun, the driving force behind nullification in South Carolina, did suggest that the federal amendment process might be involved in his proposed Nullification system, but it is telling that he saw the creation of a new amendment as the *last* resort. He assumed that state and federal lawmakers could arrive at agreements outside of the prescribed amendment method.[9]

Even the many antebellum reformers who sought to cure social ills did not look to the amendment method. Instead, they either rejected political and legal remedies altogether, or they looked to statutes and judicial decisions. Between the adoption of the Constitution and the outbreak of Civil War, Congress considered no proposals for constitutional amendments on the subjects of temperance, women's marital and political rights, or the observance of the Sabbath. And with only a few exceptions—most notably, a set of measures proposed by John Quincy Adams during the gag rule crisis of 1836–1844—abolition never appeared before Congress in the form of a constitutional amendment in the period after the abolition of slave importation in 1808.[10] Outside of Congress, in private meetings or pamphlets and petitions, abolitionists almost never proposed amendments.[11]

In general, antislavery activists during the antebellum era adopted one of three stances toward the Constitution, none of which inclined toward amending the document. "Radical constitutionalists" such as Lysander Spooner and Amos A. Phelps argued that the Constitution was antislavery and thus authorized all congressional emancipation legislation. For them, an antislavery amendment was at best redundant and at worst a sign that the original Constitution was proslavery.[12] A second approach was taken by the followers of the well-known abolitionist William Lloyd Garrison, who argued that the Constitution was proslavery, a position that might have led naturally to proposals for antislavery amendments (indeed, Garrison himself considered such measures in the early 1830s) but led instead to a belief that the whole Constitution was corrupt and beyond repair.[13] Finally, the Free-Soil approach to the Constitution, which was ultimately adopted by the Republican party, took the middle course of reading the Constitution as authorizing slavery where it already existed but restricting its expansion so that it would ultimately expire.[14] Republicans' near religious devotion to the idea of an original constitutional compromise supporting slavery made it unlikely that they would overturn that compromise with a constitutional amendment.[15] They believed in constitutional growth, but they looked to legislative and judicial action instead of the amending power as the mechanism for that growth.

Look at the Republicans' reaction in 1857 to *Dred Scott*. That Supreme Court decision helped to solidify the Republicans and divide the Democrats, but it also revealed shared, underlying attitudes of both parties toward amending the Constitution. Republicans detested the majority opinion, written by Chief Justice Roger Taney, which denied the slave Dred Scott his freedom, refused consideration of African-Americans as national or state citizens, and ruled unconstitutional the Missouri Compromise, which had prohibited slavery in northern federal territories. Today, politicians and reformers faced with a distasteful Supreme Court decision turn almost instinctively to a proposal for a constitutional amendment to override the court's move, even if there is no likelihood of the amendment's adoption. But Republicans in the wake of *Dred Scott* seem never to have considered such an option. Abraham Lincoln, a former United States congressman from Illinois who planned to run for the Senate in 1858, sought remedy not in the form of an antislavery amendment but in the Supreme Court's future overruling of its decision.[16]

One of the few people who did seem to have considered the amendment remedy was Taney, whose majority opinion suggested that antislavery measures such as the prohibition of slavery in federal territories required a constitutional amendment; Taney even seemed to assume that this was the ultimate ploy of the Republicans.[17] As one of the founders of a Democratic party that preferred formalistic legal alternatives—codification of laws by popular assembly over traditional, elitist common law, and constitutional revisions over excessive legislative discretion—Taney assumed that the natural strategy of an antislavery party would be to propose an abolition amendment.[18] Proslavery southerners shared Taney's suspicions. When secession began on the heels of Republican electoral victory in 1860, a number of southerners predicted that the incoming Lincoln administration would abolish slavery by constitutional amendment.[19] Despite such dire warnings, Lincoln and the Republicans would not arrive at this strategy until they had fought more than two years of war.

Why did antislavery activists, along with other reformers, ignore the amending process? Garrisonians ignored it because they saw the Constitution as not worth preserving. Others ignored it because the channels of reform politics had opened along alternative paths—most commonly state-level reform. Also, in this so-called party era of politics, the competitiveness of the parties made it unlikely that any amendment could receive the supermajorities needed in Congress and in the states for adoption. In most antebellum elections, even at the local level, the strength of the major parties was almost equal. Rare was the election when more than 10 percent of the popular vote divided the major parties.[20] The balance of the parties everywhere, but especially in Congress, meant that a single party faced an impossible challenge if it wanted to push through a constitutional amendment, which required the support of two-thirds of Congress and three-quarters of the state ratifying conventions. Yet, the impossibility of achieving a measure rarely stops reformers in their tracks, and it is difficult to believe that the political situation alone was responsible for reformers' failure to take up the amendment method.

More likely, reformers simply could not overcome the commitment that they shared with most Americans to an unchanging written Constitution. In the absence of any meaningful collective identity, most Americans in this very young republic, reformers included, found in the unchanging written Constitution and a reverence for the framers a much needed source of "protonationalism," that feeling described by E. J. Hobsbawm of "the consciousness of belonging or having belonged to a lasting political identity."[21]

No other country could boast a written Constitution that was so permanent—a fact that Americans dwelt on at great length during the antebellum period. This pride blinded most Americans to the fact that constitutional veneration existed elsewhere, but in forms not viable in their own country. In Great Britain, the search for a written constitution, which had engaged so many Whigs in the seventeenth and eighteenth centuries, had given way to a national consensus that the unwritten constitution, formed by centuries of institutional growth and a shared tradition of individual rights rooted in the Magna Carta, was far superior to the Americans' written Constitution, which the historian Thomas Macaulay called "all sail and no anchor."[22] The English varied in the way they understood their constitutional history but nonetheless spoke in what James Epstein terms the same "constitutional idiom."[23] Germans likewise were prone to be skeptical of a written constitution, especially after the failure of the 1848 Frankfurt Constitution to create a unified Germany. Most preferred to follow Hegel's lead in regarding a constitution as an unwritten, unfolding spirit of the state infused with the people's unity of psychic and political purpose.[24] Americans had available to them neither England's centuries-old tradition nor Germany's long-brewing, unifying *Geist*; an unchanging written Constitution held for them the greatest promise of legitimizing the new nation. As a young, aspiring politician in Illinois in 1838, Abraham Lincoln declared the Constitution the bedrock of the country's "political religion."[25] Americans were quick to contrast the permanence of their written Constitution with the precarious or elusive constitutions of other countries. Theophilus Parsons, an eminent legal scholar at Harvard Law School, went so far as to say that "a Constitution is, in fact, an American invention," whereas the British had no "real" constitution because theirs could be changed by whim of the legislature.[26] Little wonder, then, that some of the most creative proposals for amending the American Constitution during the Civil War would come not from native-born Americans but from European immigrants.

The clearest manifestation of Americans' desire to preserve their constitutional text came during the secession crisis of 1860–1861—ironically, in the form of a surge of proposed amendments. Rather than seeking to reform the Constitution, these amendments sought to freeze it, to give constitutional legitimacy to principles or procedures that would establish a permanent balance of power between proslavery and free-labor interests. There were precedents to this strategy, most notably Senator John C. Calhoun's proposed amendment of 1850 making a dual executive—one president from the North, one from the South.[27] But never had the nation witnessed so many such proposals. Between the time of South Carolina's secession in December 1860 and Lincoln's inauguration in March 1861, Congress considered roughly 150 proposed amendments, all of which offered some protection to slavery. Not only national leaders but ordinary citizens pondered revisions. A Rochester man wrote to his local paper that the key doctrines of the *Dred Scott* decision should be written into the Constitution.[28] A Baltimore resident thought that the South could be appeased by an amendment prohibiting the succession of two northern presidents.[29] As Americans searched for an immutable compromise, they turned naturally to some sort of deal that could be added to the Constitution and thus become as permanent as that document. The reason to support a compromise amendment, wrote Illinois senator Stephen A. Douglas, the leader of the Democratic party, was that it could take "the slavery question out of Congress forever . . . and gives assurance of permanent peace."[30]

Ultimately, Congress passed only one amendment: the "Corwin amendment," an "unamendable" amendment prohibiting congressional interference with slavery in the states where it existed.[31] Harold Hyman sees this amendment as yet another "measure of how low secession had brought the constitutional ethics of many Americans," but Americans of the time did not see it in such negative terms; rather, they saw the amendment as a positive sign of their commitment to an unchanging Union and Constitution.[32] And for some, even this minor alteration of text was too much. Schuyler Colfax, the future Speaker of the House of Representatives, worried that the measure flouted the principle of "the Constitution as our fathers made it."[33] William Dennison, a future member of Lincoln's cabinet, preferred that the compromise take the form not of an amendment but of an "ordinance," which "would preserve to the Constitution the sanctity with which it is now regarded . . . [whereas] any direct amendment would dispel this hallowed charm and only lead to such future amendments as would destroy it altogether."[34] By the time of the passage of the Corwin amendment, if not before, the desire to protect slavery where it existed had become nearly as crucial a component of American political culture as the desire to keep the text of the Constitution unchanged. Indeed, the idea of the permanence of slavery where it was and the idea of the permanence of the Constitution as it was had become almost hopelessly entangled. Not only the criticism of slavery but also the mere absence of protection for it seemed to be an assault upon the

Constitution, and every move toward reforming the Constitution, real or imagined, seemed tantamount to an attack on slavery. The Constitution itself had become enslaved, its text fixed in subservience to the institution that represented the greatest threat to the Union.

Once the conflict over slavery had shattered the Union, three sets of circumstances prepared the ground for the monumental shift in the way that Americans regarded the Constitution and constitutional amendments. First, and perhaps most important, almost all the congressmen of the seceded states left their seats and returned home, leaving lawmaking in the Union to northerners and border-state Unionists. A majority of the remaining congressmen were Republicans. Indeed, the Thirty-Seventh Congress, which convened from the summer of 1861 to the spring of 1863, had the necessary number of antislavery congressmen to secure passage of an antislavery amendment. As it turned out, this Congress considered no amendments that immediately abolished slavery. Nonetheless, the departure of the southerners played an important role by removing the potential objection to an antislavery amendment that it was certain to fail. Second, politics in the Union in general and in Congress in particular was plagued by unprecedented uncertainty and chaos. Republicans were a young party. Party members had almost no experience in governing, and they had difficulty establishing patterns of lawmaking in part because of the high turnover rate (the average tenure of a congressman during this period was three years). Meaningful blocs would take years to form.[35] Meanwhile, the Democrats had been left rudderless by the death of Senator Stephen Douglas during the summer of 1861. Rampant factionalism between and within the propeace and prowar wings of the party would plague the Democratic party throughout the war.[36] This turbulent climate, made even more chaotic by the unpredictability of the war, made it increasingly likely that an old style of constitutional politics might give way to something new. Third, the failure of the Constitution "as it is" to hold the Union together opened people's minds to the possibility that the document was inadequate and needed to be improved.[37] Lincoln gave voice to these feelings when he called for a "new birth of freedom" at Gettysburg in late 1863. Neither Lincoln nor the proclaimers of the Constitution's inadequacy embraced the amendment method early on, but their critique made it more likely that people would regard the amending device as a legitimate means of achieving a major reform.

These circumstances—the departure of southern lawmakers for the Confederacy, the chaos of politics, and the critique of the Constitution as it was—were but the necessary preconditions for a regime change in constitutional politics. Despite these developments, constitutional politics operated as before during the first two years of the war. No significant constitutional amendments were proposed inside or outside of Congress. The only major proposals during this period came from Lincoln in his annual message to Congress of December 1862. His amendments would have protected slavery where it existed until at least 1900, compensated owners for slaves freed by the action of the war, and provided funds to colonize freed people abroad. These measures, which really sought to protect slavery rather than to destroy it, were never debated in Congress.[38]

Even after Lincoln signed the final Emancipation Proclamation on January 1, 1863, Americans did not seize upon the amending method as the preferred way of making abolition universal, permanent, and constitutionally secure. The amendment was never a predictable sequel to the Emancipation Proclamation.[39] Most Democrats hoped that Lincoln would retract his proclamation or that, if he refused, he would be replaced in the 1864 election by someone who would. Meanwhile, Republicans in 1863 proposed just about every plan for making abolition universal and permanent *except* an antislavery constitutional amendment. Republican proposals instead entailed passing emancipation statutes for the seceded states or urging if not forcing those states to write new, proemancipation constitutions. Until late 1863, only a few proposals for antislavery amendments had been put forward—not by mainstream party politicians but mainly by radical, foreign-born reformers who were not burdened by the illusion that amending the Constitution necessarily jeopardized American democracy. The Polish-born abolitionist Ernestine L. Rose, for example, urged an antislavery amendment in 1863 on the basis that "a good constitution is a very good thing; but even the best of constitutions need sometimes to be amended and improved."[40] At about the same time, Karl Heinzen, a veteran of the 1848 German revolution, pressed for a constitutional amendment that secured not only emancipation but equal rights for African-Americans.[41] That call was echoed by a group of radical German-Americans in Cleveland, who asked for "a revision of the Constitution in the spirit of the Declaration of Independence."[42]

How, then, did the idea of amending the Constitution to abolish slavery enter the political mainstream? The answer reveals much about the contingent quality of political development not only during the Civil War but in all eras. The ground had been prepared, but what opened a new channel of constitutional politics was an unlikely alliance between two normally antagonistic groups. The first was less a cohesive group than a loose network of grassroots abolitionist organizations spearheaded by the Women's Loyal National League. Composed mostly of northeastern middle-class white women, the league had a healthy blend of old-line abolitionists and suffragists, such as the league leaders Elizabeth Cady Stanton and Susan B. Anthony, as well as younger, equally dynamic activists and orators, such as the mesmerizing Anna Elizabeth Dickinson. Early in 1863, the league began to petition the federal government to broaden the scope of the Emancipation Proclamation so that all slaves would be free. These early petitions did not call for a constitutional amendment abolishing slavery. That strategy may have reflected the traditional preference for a static constitutional text felt by most reformers as well as most Americans in the antebellum era. Just as likely, the absence of a call for an abolition amendment by the league reflected the strategy of "nonspecific" petitioning especially common among antebellum female reformers. "Nonspecific" petitioning, the call for a particular cause without a recommended piece of legislation, allowed women to take their traditional role as moral agents without treading on the traditional role of men as the actual lawmakers. For some women, "nonspecific" petitioning was also a subtle protest, a means of highlighting their exclusion from formal lawmaking by refusing to invoke an actual measure.[43]

The second group to pave the way for the antislavery amendment was a small, unorganized array of Democrats, almost all of whom despised reformers such as those who belonged to the Women's Loyal National League. For the most part, these Democrats had been marginalized by the main factions of the party during the Civil War. The two most prominent groups among them were midwestern Germans, many of them from the St. Louis area, who were fiercely pro-Union and usually pro-Lincoln, and upstate New Yorkers who resented the power of New York City Democrats and objected to their frequent harsh blasts against Lincoln and to their occasional friendly words for the South. Uniting all of these Democrats was the belief that slavery had divided the Union and thus had to be abolished, combined with the traditional Democratic position that the Constitution granted no powers to Congress beyond those that were explicit. Their narrow reading of the Constitution made them dubious of the legality of Lincoln's Emancipation Proclamation and the various Republican plans for permanent abolition. If abolition were to be achieved constitutionally, they declared, it had to be made explicit; there had to be an antislavery constitutional amendment. Some of them genuinely wanted to see such an amendment adopted. Others had strictly political motives: they hoped to form a third party, a combination of Democrats and Republicans in favor of the antislavery amendment, which would split the Republican party and hand the 1864 election to the main body of Democrats. That strategy materialized in the creation of the "Radical Democrats," an odd mix of abolitionists and antislavery Democrats who met in Cleveland, Ohio, in May 1864 and nominated John C. Frémont for president on a platform that included an abolition amendment. Regardless of their motives, these Democrats helped to publicize the amendment in their newspapers and local political meetings. Eventually, the leaders of the Women's Loyal National League embraced the amendment method as the surest "safeguard" against slavery.[44]

Only after grassroots abolitionist groups and proamendment Democrats began to tout the amendment, sometimes in tandem and sometimes independently, did Republicans join—and eventually lead—the movement for an antislavery amendment. Congressional Republicans were divided over the concrete details of reconstruction, but they had been awakened by the proposals of non-Republicans to the wisdom of pushing for an amendment that assured the death of slavery, regardless of which specific plan of restoration prevailed. By mid-February 1864, the Senate Judiciary Committee, which was dominated by Republicans, had framed the final version of the amendment by revising a version proposed by a Democrat, Senator John Henderson of Missouri. In April, the Senate passed the amendment, but in July, the House failed to carry it. Just before the House vote, Lincoln finally endorsed the amendment, mainly because he wanted to steal some of the thunder of the Radical Democrats. Lincoln thus helped to transform a proposal initially sponsored by grassroots abolitionists and antislavery Democrats into a Republican policy.[45]

An unforeseeable, concerted effort among strange bedfellows had been the triggering event that had set the antislavery amendment on the road to becoming a national issue. The changed circumstances brought on by the war had made the product of this unlikely alliance stand some chance of success. But the ultimate change in constitutional politics could not have taken place without contingency—the creation of this unlikely alliance. The eventual result of these unforeseeable circumstances was not only the creation of the Thirteenth Amendment but the beginning of a peeling away of Americans' adherence to an unchanging constitutional text. Once proposals for an antislavery amendment began to circulate and gain publicity, reformers of all stripes awakened to the possibility of using the amendment method to achieve their goals, and they newly crafted their reforms into the shape of proposed amendments to the Constitution. The immediate origins of the Thirteenth Amendment offer a lesson for all constitutional history: the course of politics that leads to constitutional change is set not only by established paths or changed circumstances brought on by a crisis such as a war; it is set as well by contingent factors such as unforeseen alliances that carve new channels into the prepared ground.

The sudden national attention to the proposed antislavery amendment in 1864 made Americans aware as never before about the possibility of using the Constitution as a vehicle of reform. Once Lincoln had joined congressional Republicans and antislavery Democrats in backing the abolition amendment, a wide array of politicians, legal theorists, and popular writers for the first time began to think about other sorts of amendments that might suit the Constitution well. The proposals were not necessarily new, but the *form* of the proposals—constitutional amendments—was. One proposed amendment declared the indisputable supremacy of God, while another prohibited polygamy, which Republicans had long before declared, along with slavery, one of the "twin relics of barbarism."[46] Some amendments, including one on the platform of the Radical Democrats, even guaranteed equal rights for African-Americans.[47] These equal-rights amendments circulating outside of Congress anticipated by more than a year similar measures that would be proposed in Congress in 1865 and ultimately take shape in the Fourteenth Amendment.

Of course, the opening of the floodgates for a wide stream of proposed amendments did not wash away entirely Americans' desire to see the constitutional text preserved inviolate. Opponents of the antislavery amendment in particular argued that the new measure was illegitimate, that it destroyed the Constitution by annulling one of the original agreements made by the framers. Such reasoning sounds odd to us today, for we have long been accustomed to frequent proposals for constitutional amendments. But the argument was nonetheless heartfelt, a passionate belief born from antebellum political culture that the nation could not withstand such a significant revision to the Constitution, one that seemed more far-reaching than the first twelve amendments because it went against most of the framers' wishes, whereas the first twelve amendments had received the approval of most of the framers during their lifetime. John V. L. Pruyn, a Democratic congressman from New York, privately struggled for days with the question of the Constitution's amendability, finally declaring that "the right to amend is not a right to *extend and enlarge* the powers granted under the Constitution" but rather a right merely to fix small, technical problems of governance that the framers had not anticipated.[48] Pruyn's objection was clearly more than mere partisan posturing, for his concern was voiced even by some of his political opponents. The *New York Times* and the *Chicago Tribune*, both Republican papers, initially advised against any alteration of the Constitution's text.[49] And during the final debate on what became the Thirteenth Amendment, Representative George S. Boutwell of Massachusetts, one of the more radical Republicans in the House, declared that there were limits on the amending power (the Constitution could not be amended to create a monarchy, for example), though he did not think that the abolition amendment reached beyond those limits.[50]

The tenacity of some Americans to preserve the constitutional text as it was forced the supporters of the antislavery amendment to develop and articulate an explicit defense of an unlimited amending power. The absence of a strong tradition of proposed amendments in the antebellum period meant that this defense had to be constructed wholly anew. In other words, although political culture had begun to shift in a way that made Americans more comfortable with the idea of amendments as vehicles of major reform, no one had yet explained publicly and explicitly why this new use of the amending power was legitimate and beneficial. Proamendment Democrats in Congress such as Senators Reverdy Johnson of Maryland and John Henderson of Missouri were among the first to champion the advantages of an unlimited amending power.[51] But it was Samuel "Sunset" Cox of Ohio, a Democrat who ultimately voted against the amendment, who proved to be most persuasive. "This power of unlimited amendment is an element of democracy . . . ," Cox declared. "Why should we of the nineteenth century tie up the hands of the twentieth?"[52] The justification offered by Republicans could be equally eloquent. In his defense of an unlimited amending power, William "Pig Iron" Kelley, a Republican congressman from Pennsylvania, even departed from the reverence traditionally shown to the Constitution's framers: they "were good men and were wise in their day and generation, but all wisdom did not die with them, and we are expiating in blood and agony and death and bereavement one of their errors . . . the toleration and perpetuation of human slavery."[53] Such powerful, public pronouncements made manifest what had so far been latent: the radical shift in American political culture to a belief in the constitutional text as something to be perfected rather than preserved. Fittingly, a generation later, Kelley's daughter Florence would play a crucial role in moving political culture even further toward the acceptance of the Constitution as a living, evolving document that should facilitate rather than restrain reform. Her program of sociological jurisprudence helped convince elite jurists as well as ordinary Americans that constitutional law must adapt to respond to society's needs.

During the debate over the antislavery amendment, some of the most persuasive and well-publicized arguments in favor of an unlimited amending power were made outside of Congress—and by writers born outside of the United States. In his pamphlet of proposed constitutional amendments, the German-born Francis Lieber included a long introduction defending a broad amendment power on the basis that, as he put it, "the framers were *not* inspired."[54] E. L. Godkin, who had been born in Ireland and would later help to found *The Nation*, praised amendments as the cure for "Constitution worship," an ailment suffered by Americans who saw the Constitution as "a final result, which required no modification, and to which coming generations would have to adapt themselves, not it to them."[55] Perhaps because these writers had grown up outside of a culture that exalted the permanence of the written Constitution, they found it easier than most to see the wisdom of amending the document.

By February 1865, after Congress had adopted the resolution for the Thirteenth Amendment and sent it to the states for ratification, almost all Americans were ready to pronounce their newfound joy at the discovery that the Constitution was a living document that could be amended to respond to society's needs. William Lloyd Garrison, who had once denounced the Constitution as a "covenant with death," now proclaimed that an amendment could make it a "covenant with life."[56] A pseudonymous contributor to the *Cincinnati Gazette* captured this dramatic shift when he wrote, "the 'Constitution as it is' is too good for traitors to enjoy or treason to overturn, but the guilt and the woes of a destiny unfulfilled await the people if they long not and labor not for the Constitution *as it ought to be*. . . . The work of the fathers was done to little purpose if it has not made the children wiser than they—better able than they out of motive to bring movement, out of power to evoke progress, out of boundless capabilities to evoke glorious results. . . . *The Constitution was made so well that we can make it better.*"[57]

Perhaps the most sophisticated defense of the amending power—and surely the most modern—came from Gerrit Smith, an abolitionist and radical constitutionalist who had once criticized the antislavery amendment as an unseemly appendage to a Constitution that was already antislavery. By early 1865, he had changed his mind. He now believed that there were two Constitutions—one "literal," the antislavery document created by the framers, and one "historical," the "cunning and wicked substitution" invented by proslavery interests. This latter Constitution was a fiction so powerful that it could be unwritten only by rewriting the "literal" text of the Constitution.[58] Smith's was a new sort of argument, one rooted in a larger intellectual trend away from the idea that the United States was created as perfect and must strive to preserve that original state and toward the idea that the country was not fully evolved, that it was at the whim of historical forces that had the capacity though not necessarily the interest to move the country closer to perfection.[59] Radical constitutionalists such as Smith usually had held to the first of these ideas, and they had argued accordingly that the original Constitution was adequate if not ideal and that the antislavery reading they were giving to the document would ultimately win the day.[60] In breaking ranks with his fellow radical constitutionalists and taking seriously the role of history in constitutional development, Smith helped open the floodgates for future amendments that would change the Constitution to accommodate historical developments.

Smith lived to see the fulfillment of his vision. Before he died, the country adopted not only the Thirteenth Amendment abolishing slavery but the Fourteenth Amendment granting African-Americans civil rights and the Fifteenth Amendment granting them voting rights. These measures, which have rightly been criticized for not going far enough to solidify the nation and to secure full legal and political equality for all Americans, were nonetheless the fulfillment of Smith's radical vision, for they revealed that Americans had newly accepted the amendment method as one of the ideal means of improving a Constitution they viewed as inadequate. During the early years of the Civil War, Americans faced with the possibility that the Constitution was inadequate had offered a number of remedies *except* the one most obvious today—a constitutional amendment. Some had argued for the temporary suspension of the Constitution during wartime. Others, most notably Sidney George Fisher, a Pennsylvania jurist and pamphlet writer, argued that the federal government should slowly begin to take on new powers not prohibited by the Constitution. As he wrote in 1862, the American Constitution should evolve as the English constitution had, not by new amendments but by new usage. "New forms [amendments] are not easily invented," Fisher wrote, "even when necessary, to serve a growing and advancing people."[61] In the last years of the war, defenders of a broad amending power drew from Fisher's notion of an evolving Constitution but reshaped it to champion formal amendments as the ideal means of perfecting the Constitution.

This shift in favor of constitutional amendments was a crucial moment in the emergence of the idea of a living, evolving Constitution, and it was also an impetus for the creation of constitutional law as an academic discipline. A scientific approach would be needed to determine *how* to perfect the Constitution, to determine what sort of constitutional development should be achieved by amendments rather than judicial and legislative decisions.[62]

Americans' new fondness for constitutional amendments also gave a boost to their faith in popular democracy. Although some writers during Reconstruction as well as in recent years have argued that the Reconstruction amendments circumvented proper constitutional procedures—for example, that the federal government forced the southern states to ratify the Fourteenth Amendment—most Americans of the time, certainly those in the North, saw the amendments as legitimate and were persuaded by their adoption that further proposed amendments might meet with success. The cumbersome amendment method, which James Madison originally had seen as a potential brake on popular initiatives to alter the Constitution, had come to be seen as a vital tool of popular democracy. Although forty years would pass after the adoption of the Fifteenth Amendment before the nation adopted a new amendment, the number of *proposed* constitutional amendments exploded during the postwar era. "Amendment fever," as some modern critics have described the phenomenon, had broken out. Americans would not become fully cognizant of the disease until the Progressive Era, when critics would point out that social reforms had become difficult to achieve in large part because they were usually framed in the form of constitutional amendments that stood little chance of adoption. The rediscovery of the amending device was one of the lasting innovations of the Civil War era. It helped expand the role of the written Constitution from a repository of national identity to a motor driving the formation of the modern nation-state.[63]

NOTES

1. See John R. Vile, *Encyclopedia of Constitutional Amendments, Proposed Amendments, and Amending Issues, 1789–1995* (Santa Barbara, Calif.: ABC-CLIO, 1996), 362–80. The author wishes to thank his fellow contributors for their comments on this essay and to express special gratitude to Meg Jacobs for her extensive, helpful editorial suggestions.

2. For early histories of constitutional development during the Civil War, see the relevant essays in William Archibald Dunning, *Essays on the Civil War and Reconstruction*, rev. ed. (1897; New York: Macmillan, 1904), and James G. Randall, *Constitutional Problems under Lincoln*, rev. ed. (1926; Urbana: University of Illinois Press, 1951). For more recent interpretations, see Harold M. Hyman, *A More Perfect Union: The Impact of the Civil War and Reconstruction on the Constitution* (New York: Alfred A. Knopf, 1973); Hyman and William M. Wiecek, *Equal Justice under Law: Constitutional Development, 1835–1875* (New York: Harper and Row, 1982); Herman Belz, *Abraham Lincoln, Constitutionalism, and Equal Rights in the Civil War Era* (New York: Fordham University Press, 1998); Belz, *Emancipation and Equal Rights: Politics and Constitutionalism during the War* (New York: W. W. Norton, 1978); Belz, *A New Birth of Freedom: The Republican Party and Freedmen's Rights, 1861 to 1866* (Westport, Conn.: Greenwood Press, 1976); Belz, *Reconstructing the Union: Theory and Policy during the Civil War* (Ithaca, N.Y.: Cornell University Press, 1969); Michael Les Benedict, *A Compromise of Principle: Congressional Republicans and Reconstruction, 1863–1869* (New York: W. W. Norton, 1974); Phillip Shaw Paludan, *A Covenant with Death: The Constitution, Law, and Equality in the Civil War Era* (Urbana: University of Illinois Press, 1975); Mark E. Neely, Jr., *The Fate of Liberty: Abraham Lincoln and Civil Liberties* (New York: Oxford University Press, 1991); Neely, *Southern Rights: Political Prisoners and the Myth of Confederate Constitutionalism* (Charlottesville: University Press of Virginia, 1999) (in the contrasting account of civil liberties offered in the two books by Neely, it is the Confederate rather than the Union government that appears innovative and aggressive); Eric Foner, *Reconstruction: America's Unfinished Revolution, 1863–1877* (New York: Harper and Row, 1988). For a full review of the historical literature on the Constitution during the Civil War and Reconstruction, see Michael Les Benedict, "A Constitutional Crisis," in *Writing the Civil War: The Quest to Understand*, ed. James M. McPherson and William J. Cooper, Jr. (Columbia: University of South Carolina Press, 1998), 154–73. Political scientists and sociologists who stress the way that constitutionalism limited the scope and duration of

state expansion include Richard Franklin Bensel, *Yankee Leviathan: The Origins of Central State Authority in America, 1859–1877* (New York: Cambridge University Press, 1990); Theda Skocpol, *Protecting Soldiers and Mothers: The Political Origins of Social Policy in the United States* (Cambridge, Mass.: Harvard University Press, 1992), esp. 68; and Stephen Skowronek, *Building a New American State: The Expansion of National Administrative Capacities, 1877–1920* (New York: Cambridge University Press, 1982), esp. 30, 290–92. On the history of constitutional amendments, see David E. Kyvig, *Explicit and Authentic Acts: Amending the U.S. Constitution, 1776–1995* (Lawrence: University Press of Kansas, 1996); Richard B. Bernstein with Jerome Agel, *Amending America: If We Love the Constitution So Much, Why Do We Keep Trying to Change It?* (New York: Times Books, 1993); and John R. Vile, *The Constitutional Amending Process in American Political Thought* (New York: Praeger, 1992).

3.   Robert J. Kaczorowski, "To Begin the Nation Anew: Congress, Citizenship, and Civil Rights after the Civil War," *American Historical Review* 92 (February 1987): 45–68; Akhil Reed Amar, "Forty Acres and a Mule: A Republican Theory of Minimal Entitlements," *Harvard Journal of Law and Public Policy* 13 (winter 1990): 37–43; Amar, "Remember the Thirteenth," *Constitutional Commentary* 10 (summer 1993): 403–8; Bruce Ackerman, *We the People*, vol. 2, *Transformations* (Cambridge, Mass.: Harvard University Press, 1998), 99–252. Like Ackerman, Amar is interested in the question of the relationship between formal rules of amendment and governmental activism; see, for example, Amar, "Philadelphia Revisited: Amending the Constitution outside Article V," *University of Chicago Law Review* 55 (fall 1988): 1043–1104. Some historians have criticized these legal scholars for painting too rosy a picture of progressive constitutional development during the Civil War and Reconstruction. For example, Kaczorowski's belief in the revolutionary quality of Reconstruction-era civil rights legislation is not shared by leading historians in the field such as Michael Les Benedict and Herman Belz; see Benedict, "Preserving the Constitution: The Conservative Basis of 'Radical Reconstruction,' " *Journal of American History* 61 (June 1974): 65–90, and Belz, "The Constitution and Reconstruction," in *The Facts of Reconstruction: Essays in Honor of John Hope Franklin*, ed. Eric Anderson and Alfred A. Moss, Jr. (Baton Rouge: Louisiana State University Press, 1991), 189–217. The legal scholar Earl M. Maltz also challenges Kaczorowski's thesis; see Maltz, *Civil Rights, the Constitution, and Congress, 1863–1869* (Lawrence: University Press of Kansas, 1990). Ackerman's treatment of the Civil War and Reconstruction has similarly been questioned by historians; see, for example, Eric Foner, "The Strange Career of the Reconstruction Amendments," *Yale Law Journal* 108 (June 1999): 2003–10.

4.   On the Progressive Era as the crucial period in which notions of a "living" Constitution began to flourish, see Howard Gillman, "The Collapse of Constitutional Originalism and the Rise of the Notion of the 'Living Constitution' in the Course of American State-Building," *Studies in American Political Development* 11 (fall 1997): 191–247. While this essay concurs with Gillman's argument about the importance of a "living" Constitution in the state-building process, it differs from his approach by examining formal amendments (and proposals for formal amendments) instead of judicial decisions. Adam Winkler adopts a similar ap-

proach to mine but locates the emergence of notions of a living Constitution in the women's suffrage movement after the Civil War, whereas I locate it in the antislavery movement during the war. See Winkler, "A Revolution Too Soon: Woman Suffragists and the 'Living Constitution,' " *New York University Law Review* 76 (November 2001): 1456–1526. In describing how amendments can make the Constitution an "agent of change," and thus an instrument in state building, I draw on the notion of institutions as agents of change described in Richard R. John, "Governmental Institutions as Agents of Change: Rethinking American Political Development in the Early Republic," *Studies in American Political Development* 11 (fall 1997): 347–80.

5. Clinton Rossiter, ed., *The Federalist Papers* (New York: New American Library, 1961), 314. See Sanford Levinson, "Veneration and Constitutional Change: James Madison Confronts the Possibility of Constitutional Amendment," *Texas Tech Law Review* 21 (1990): 2443–61, and Philip A. Hamburger, "The Constitution's Accommodation of Social Change," *University of Michigan Law Review* 88 (1989): 239–327, esp. 241.

6. See Jefferson to Madison, September 6, 1789, in *The Portable Thomas Jefferson*, ed. Merrill D. Peterson (New York: Penguin Books, 1975), 449.

7. See Vile, *Encyclopedia of Constitutional Amendments*. For the pre-1900 period, see also Herman Ames, *The Proposed Amendments to the Constitution of the United States during the First Century of Its History* (1896; New York: Burt Franklin, 1970). For Madison's approach to the bonus bill, see Kyvig, *Explicit and Authentic Acts*, 131.

8. Stephen M. Griffin, *American Constitutionalism: From Theory to Politics* (Princeton, N.J.: Princeton University Press, 1996), 26–46; Michael Kammen, *A Machine That Would Go of Itself: The Constitution in American Culture* (1986; New York: Vintage Books, 1987), 29–39. The use of "consensus" here derives from Kammen's phrase describing constitutional contests as "conflict within consensus" (29). On state constitutions, see Laura J. Scalia, *America's Jeffersonian Experiment: Remaking State Constitutions, 1820–1850* (DeKalb: Northern Illinois University Press, 1999), and Alan G. Tarr, *Understanding State Constitutions* (Princeton, N.J.: Princeton University Press, 1998). On the fate of the Anti-Federalists in the early 1800s, see Saul Cornell, *The Other Founders: Anti-Federalism and the Dissenting Tradition in America, 1788–1828* (Chapel Hill: University of North Carolina Press, 1999), 221–45.

9. On the political and constitutional positions of Calhoun and others involved in the nullification debate, see Lacy K. Ford, "Inventing the Concurrent Majority: Madison, Calhoun, and the Problem of Majoritarianism in American Political Thought, *Journal of Southern History* 60 (February 1994): 19–58, and Richard E. Ellis, *The Union at Risk: Jacksonian Democracy, States' Rights, and the Nullification Crisis* (New York: Oxford University Press, 1987).

10. Adams's amendments, proposed in February 1839, declared free all children born of slaves after 1842; prohibited the admission of future slave states; and abolished slavery and the slave trade in the District of Columbia after 1845. Congress did not debate the measures. See Ames, *Proposed Amendments*, 193, 349; William Lee Miller, *Arguing about Slavery: The Great Battle in the United States Congress* (New York: Alfred A. Knopf, 1996), 353–54; and William W.

Freehling, *The Road to Disunion: Secessionists at Bay, 1776–1854* (New York: Oxford University Press, 1990), 343–44. An exception to the trend described here is the issue of colonization of free blacks. In 1832, Congress considered two proposals, one from a Virginia congressman and another from the Maryland legislature, for amendments to allow for federal spending on colonization. Congress did not seriously consider either proposal. The proposed colonization amendment was revived by Senator Stephen A. Douglas in 1860–1861 and then by President Lincoln in his annual message of 1862. See Ames, *Proposed Amendments*, 206–7.

11. Two exceptions were proposals by David L. Child and Henry B. Stanton, both of whom briefly toyed with the possibility of using an antislavery amendment to build popular support for their cause. See Child, *The Despotism of Freedom* (Boston: Young Men's Anti-Slavery Association, 1833), 25, and Stanton, speech of May 7, 1839, cited in William M. Wiecek, *The Sources of Antislavery Constitutionalism in America, 1760–1848* (Ithaca, N.Y.: Cornell University Press, 1977), 256.

12. Wiecek, *Sources of Antislavery Constitutionalism*, 259–63; Amos A. Phelps, *Lectures on Slavery and its Remedy* (Boston: New-England Anti-Slavery Society, 1834), 192–96.

13. Louis S. Gerteis, *Morality and Utility in American Antislavery Reform* (Chapel Hill: University of North Carolina Press, 1987), 48–51. For an example of William Lloyd Garrison's early contemplation of constitutional approaches to abolition, including antislavery amendments, see Garrison to Thomas Shipley, December 17, 1835, in *The Letters of William Lloyd Garrison*, ed. Walter M. Merrill, vol. 1, *I Will Be Heard! 1822–1835* (Cambridge, Mass.: Harvard University Press, 1971), 584.

14. Eric Foner, *Free Soil, Free Labor, Free Men: The Ideology of the Republican Party before the Civil War* (New York: Oxford University Press, 1970), 73–102; Wiecek, *Sources of Antislavery Constitutionalism*, 191–93, 216–20.

15. See Peter B. Knupfer, *The Union As It Is: Constitutional Unionism and Sectional Compromise, 1787–1861* (Chapel Hill: University of North Carolina Press, 1991), esp. 55.

16. Roy P. Basler, ed., and Marion Dolores Pratt and Lloyd A. Dunlap, asst. eds., *The Collected Works of Abraham Lincoln* (New Brunswick, N.J.: Rutgers University Press, 1953–1955), 2:401 (hereafter *CW*).

17. *Dred Scott v. John F. A. Sandford, United States Reports*, 19 Howard (October 1857), 426.

18. On the Democrats' preference for formalism, see Michael F. Holt, *The Political Crisis of the 1850s* (1978; New York: W. W. Norton, 1983), 106–9; Perry Miller, *The Life of the Mind in America: From the Revolution to the Civil War* (New York: Harcourt, Brace and World, 1965), chap. 7; and Hyman and Wiecek, *Equal Justice under Law*, 3–5 (which describes the role of Rhode Island's "Dorr Rebellion" of the 1840s in establishing the Democrats' preference for state constitutional revision over legislative discretion).

19. See, for example, speech of Henry L. Benning, November 19, 1860, in William W. Freehling and Craig M. Simpson, eds., *Secession Debated: Georgia's Showdown in 1860* (New York: Oxford University Press, 1992), 119.

20. Joel H. Silbey, *The American Political Nation, 1838–1893* (Stanford, Calif.: Stanford University Press, 1991).

21. E. J. Hobsbawm, *Nations and Nationalism since 1780: Programme, Myth, Reality,* 2d ed. (New York: Cambridge University Press, 1992), 46, 73.

22. Kammen, *A Machine That Would Go of Itself,* 159–61; J. W. Burrow, *A Liberal Descent: Victorian Historians and the English Past* (New York: Cambridge University Press, 1981), 100–08. The earlier English fascination with the possibility of discovering a written constitution is detailed in J.G.A. Pocock, *The Ancient Constitution and the Feudal Law* (New York: Cambridge University Press, 1957).

23. James Epstein, *Radical Expression: Political Language, Ritual, and Symbol in England, 1790–1850* (New York: Oxford University Press, 1994). See also James Vernon, "Narrating the Constitution: The Discourse of the 'Real' and the Fantasies of Nineteenth-Century Constitutional History," in *Re-reading the Constitution: New Narratives in the Political History of England's Long Nineteenth Century,* ed. Vernon (New York: Cambridge University Press, 1996), 204–29.

24. Hegel's ideas on constitutions are given their fullest expression in *The Philosophy of Right.* See Eric Weil, *Hegel and the State,* trans. Mark A. Cohen (Baltimore: John Hopkins University Press, 1998), 56–72.

25. *CW,* 1:112.

26. Kammen, *A Machine That Would Go of Itself,* 158–59.

27. Bernstein, *Amending America,* 80–81; Ames, *Proposed Amendments,* 103–4.

28. *Rochester Democrat and American,* December 29, 1860, p. 2.

29. Neilson Poe to Thurlow Weed, December 19, 1860, Thurlow Weed Papers, Rush Rhees Library, University of Rochester, Rochester, N.Y.

30. Stephen A. Douglas to Charles H. Lanphier, December 25, 1860, Charles Lanphier MSS, Illinois State Historical Library, Springfield.

31. R. Alton Lee, "The Corwin Amendment in the Secession Crisis," *Ohio Historical Quarterly* 70 (January 1961): 1–26. The amendment was ultimately ratified by the Maryland and Ohio legislatures and by an Illinois convention.

32. Hyman, *A More Perfect Union,* 41. For a more sophisticated and balanced assessment of the amendment's constitutionality, see Mark E. Brandon, "The 'Original' Thirteenth Amendment and the Limits to Formal Constitutional Change," in *Responding to Imperfection: The Theory and Practice of Constitutional Amendment,* ed. Sanford Levinson (Princeton, N.J.: Princeton University Press, 1995), 215–36.

33. Schuyler Colfax to Orville Hickman Browning, January 13, 1861, Orville Hickman Browning Papers, Illinois State Historical Library, Springfield.

34. William Dennison to Francis P. Blair, Sr., February 20, 1861, Blair Family Papers, Manuscripts Division, Library of Congress.

35. Allan G. Bogue, *The Congressman's Civil War* (Cambridge: Cambridge University Press, 1989).

36. Joel H. Silbey, *A Respectable Minority: The Democratic Party in the Civil War Era, 1860–1868* (New York: W. W. Norton, 1977).

37. Kammen, *A Machine That Would Go of Itself,* 110–12; Hyman, *A More Perfect Union,* 99–140.

38. *CW,* 5:529–30.

39. See Michael Vorenberg, *Final Freedom: The Civil War, Abolition, and the Thirteenth Amendment* (Cambridge: Cambridge University Press, 2001), 36–60.

40. Elizabeth Cady Stanton, Susan B. Anthony, and Matilda Joslyn Gage, *History of Woman Suffrage,* 6 vols. (1889–1894; New York: Arno and the New York Times, 1969), 2:75.

41. James M. McPherson, *The Struggle for Equality: Abolitionists and the Negro in the Civil War and Reconstruction* (Princeton, N.J.: Princeton University Press, 1964), 260–62.

42. Washington, D.C., *Daily National Intelligencer,* October 29, 1863, p. 3.

43. Rebecca Edwards, *Angels in the Machinery: Gender in American Party Politics from the Civil War to the Progressive Era* (New York: Oxford University Press, 1997), 21–35; Wendy Hamand Venet, *Neither Ballots nor Bullets: Women Abolitionists and the Civil War* (Charlottesville: University Press of Virginia, 1991), 109–22; Mary P. Ryan, *Women in Public: Between Banners and Ballots, 1825–1880* (Baltimore: Johns Hopkins University Press, 1990), 141–55; Stanton et al., *History of Woman Suffrage,* 2:50–89; P. J. Staudenraus, "The Popular Origins of the Thirteenth Amendment," *Mid-America* 50 (April 1968): 108–15. On female petitioning, see Julie Roy Jeffrey, *The Great Silent Army of Abolitionism: Ordinary Women in the Antislavery Movement* (Chapel Hill: University of North Carolina Press, 1998), 86–93, 214–17; Nancy Isenberg, *Sex and Citizenship in Antebellum America* (Chapel Hill: University of North Carolina Press, 1998), 64–69; Susan Marie Zaeske, "Petitioning, Antislavery, and the Emergence of Women's Political Consciousness" (Ph.D. dissertation, University of Wisconsin, 1997), esp. 339–47; Deborah Bingham Van Broekhoven, " 'Let Your Names Be Enrolled': Method and Ideology in Women's Antislavery Petitioning," in *The Abolitionist Sisterhood: Women's Political Culture in Antebellum America,* ed. Jean Fagan Yellin and John C. Van Horne (Ithaca, N.Y.: Cornell University Press, 1994), 179–99.

44. Susan B. Anthony to Charles Sumner, March 1, 1864, Charles Sumner Papers, Houghton Library, Harvard University, Cambridge, Mass.

45. This sequence is described in Vorenberg, *Final Freedom,* 115–27.

46. Record Group 233 (House of Representatives), boxes HR 37A-G7.2 and HR 37A-G7.3, National Archives. For an exchange between Lincoln and a group of clergymen who proposed an amendment declaring God's supremacy, see Washington, D.C., *Daily National Intelligencer,* February 24, 1864, p. 3. For antipolygamy amendments, see Gerrit Smith to Charles Sumner, December 5, 1864, in Gerrit Smith, *Speeches and Letters of Gerrit Smith,* vol. 2 (New York: American News Company, 1865), 2:59, and resolution of Mr. Tripp, January 23, 1865, *Journal of the House of Representatives of Ohio for 1865,* 90–91. Also see Sarah Barringer Gordon, "The 'Twin Relic of Barbarism': A Legal History of Antipolygamy in Nineteenth-Century America" (Ph.D. dissertation, Princeton University, 1995).

47. Edward McPherson, *The Political History of the United States of America during the Great Rebellion* (1865; New York: Da Capo Press, 1972), 411–12; William F. Zornow, "The Cleveland Convention, 1864, and the Radical Democrats," *Mid-America* 36 (January 1954): 39–53; "G.M.," "The War and its Issues," Washington, D.C., *Daily National Intelligencer,* June 18, 1864, p. 2; Fran-

cis Lieber, "Proposed Amendments to the Constitution," in *Miscellaneous Writings*, vol. 2, *Contributions to Political Science* (Philadelphia: J. B. Lippincott and Co., 1881), 2:177–79. Lieber's proposed amendments, though published in 1865, were drafted and privately circulated in mid-1864. See Lieber to Henry W. Halleck, March 10, 1864, Lieber to Charles Sumner, March 5, 1864, and various notes in the folder titled "Proposed Amendments of the Constitution," folder LI 168, Francis Lieber Papers, Huntington Library, San Marino, Calif.

48. *Congressional Globe*, 38th Cong., 1st sess. (June 14, 1864), pt. 4, 2940. See John V. L. Pruyn, Washington Journal, June 14, 1864, New York State Library, Albany; Pruyn to Manton M. Marble, June 15, 1864, Manton M. Marble Papers, Manuscript Division, Library of Congress.

49. *New York Times*, February 11, 1864, p. 4, and February 13, 1864, p. 6; *Chicago Tribune*, February 17, 1864, p. 2.

50. *Congressional Globe*, 38th Cong., 2d sess. (January 11, 1865), pt. 1, 222.

51. Ibid., 38th Cong., 1st sess. (April 5, 1864), pt. 2, 1423 (Johnson); (April 7, 1864), pt. 2, 1460 (Henderson).

52. Ibid. (January 12, 1865), pt. 1, 241, 239.

53. Ibid. (June 15, 1864), pt. 4, 2983.

54. Francis Lieber, undated memorandum, folder LI 168, Lieber Papers, Huntington Library; see Lieber, "Proposed Amendments to the Constitution" in *Miscellaneous Writings*, 2:139–77.

55. E. L. Godkin, "The Constitution, and its Defects," *North American Review* 99 (July 1864): 117–18. See Godkin to Charles Eliot Norton, October 12, 1864, Charles Eliot Norton Papers, Houghton Library, Harvard University.

56. *Liberator*, February 10, 1865, p. 2.

57. "Jomil," "Constitution Worship and National Progress," *Cincinnati Gazette*, February 4, 1865, p. 1.

58. Gerrit Smith to Charles Sumner, December 5, 1864, in Smith, *Speeches and Letters*, 2:57. For Smith's earlier position on amendments, see Smith, "To My Neighbors," February 24, 1864, in Smith, *Speeches and Letters*, 2:5. Smith's reasoning anticipated modern arguments in favor of respectable legal fictions; see, for example, Aviam Soifer, "Reviewing Legal Fictions," *Georgia Law Review* 20 (summer 1986): 871–915.

59. On early American ideas about the need to stay true to the original Constitution, see Jack N. Rakove, *Original Meanings: Politics and Ideas in the Making of the Constitution* (New York: Alfred A. Knopf, 1996), 339–65. On the emergence of American ideas about the nature of historical forces in mid- and late-nineteenth-century America, see Dorothy Ross, "Historical Consciousness in Nineteenth-Century America," *American Historical Review* 89 (October 1984): 919. On the impact of this new mode of thought on constitutional doctrine, see Paul W. Kahn, *Legitimacy and History: Self-Government in American Constitutional Theory* (New Haven, Conn.: Yale University Press, 1992), 65–73.

60. For an example of this sort of argument, see the pamphlet of William Howard Day quoted in Donald G. Nieman, *Promises to Keep: African-Americans and the Constitutional Order, 1776 to the Present* (New York: Oxford University Press, 1990), 32.

61. Sidney George Fisher, *The Trial of the Constitution* (Philadelphia: J. B. Lippincott, 1862), 360.

62. The pressure for a scientific approach to constitutional law that I describe here worked in tandem with a pressure in the same direction that emerged in response to the country moving from a state controlled by localism and common-law regulation to a modern liberal state controlled by a desire to protect private enterprise from centralization and national authority. See William J. Novak, *The People's Welfare: Law and Regulation in Nineteenth-Century America* (Chapel Hill: University of North Carolina Press, 1996), 235–48.

63. The desire to preserve the Constitution as it was originally framed never did fully disappear. For example, some expressed this desire during the debates over the Fourteenth Amendment; see William E. Nelson, *The Fourteenth Amendment: From Political Principle to Judicial Doctrine* (Cambridge, Mass.: Harvard University Press, 1988), 95–96. Arguments for implied limits to the amending power can still be found today, though the arguments tend to take a different, more sophisticated form than they did in the nineteenth century. For a review of the recent debates over the "amendability" of the Constitution, see Kyvig, *Explicit and Authentic Acts*, 461–87, and Sanford Levinson, "Introduction: Imperfection and Amendability," in *Responding to Imperfection*, ed. Levinson, 3–11. One of the modern critics of the phenomenon of frequent proposed amendments is Kathleen Sullivan, who coined the term "amendment fever." See Sullivan, "Constitutional Constancy: Why Congress Should Cure Itself of Amendment Fever," *Cardozo Law Review* 17 (January 1996): 691–704. She develops her argument more fully in Alan Brinkley, Nelson W. Polsby, and Kathleen M. Sullivan, *The New Federalist Papers: Essays in Defense of the Constitution* (New York: W. W. Norton, 1997). For Progressive Era reconsiderations of the advantages and disadvantages of the amendment procedure, see Kyvig, *Explicit and Authentic Acts*, 191–93.

Chapter Six

DEMOCRACY IN THE AGE OF CAPITAL

CONTESTING SUFFRAGE RIGHTS IN GILDED AGE NEW YORK

Sven Beckert

O N APRIL 7, 1877, a crowd of New York merchants, industrialists, bankers, and elite professionals marched into Chickering
Hall at Fifth Avenue and Eighteenth Street in Manhattan for a
meeting of "taxpayers." Despite their historic distaste for collective mobilizations, they assembled on this spring day to discuss a weighty issue: a
proposed amendment to the constitution of the state of New York that
set out to limit universal male suffrage in municipal elections. This remarkably antidemocratic amendment, unveiled only four weeks earlier,
promised to consolidate significant areas of municipal government in a
newly created Board of Finance. Property owners would elect the board,
in effect excluding about half of the city's voters. "The real object for
which this meeting was called was to assail the principle of universal suffrage," the *Labor Standard* commented with genuine alarm.[1]

Antidemocratic proposals were not uncommon in the polarized world
of urban politics in the Gilded Age United States. Yet, in an unusual show
of unity and political mobilization, upper-class New Yorkers gave this
radical measure unprecedented political support: this first meeting alone,
as the *New York Times* reported, was "a notable demonstration of the
solid wealth and respectability of the Metropolis."[2] Peter Cooper, Joseph
Seligman, Levi P. Morton, Royal Phelps, Josiah Macy, Amos R. Eno,
H. B. Claflin, and John B. Cornell, among many others, cheered on the
speakers who argued that the proposed constitutional amendment would
"separate . . . us at once from that continual change of persons which
makes anything like permanent and useful administration utterly impossible."[3] Before this warm audience, one speaker summed up the evening's
sentiment by declaring that the idea that "a mere majority should direct
how the public expenses . . . should be regulated [was] preposterous."[4]
Energized by such blunt talk, bourgeois New Yorkers seized upon this
chance to increase their control over the city, a city that, in their eyes,
had become dangerously unruly. They confronted, however, an equally
agitated opposition of mostly working-class and lower-middle-class New

Yorkers who sided with labor leader Leander Thompson's judgment that the amendment represented a "direct stab . . . [at] the Institutions of free government."[5] The battle lines were drawn.

Though the amendment eventually foundered, the effort to pass it was a crucial moment in nineteenth-century politics. The breadth and depth of upper-class New Yorkers' hostility toward popular suffrage, a central, indeed defining, feature of democracy, was remarkable and sharply discordant with cherished notions about the rise of American democracy. Historians for some time have documented the eclipse of democracy in the racial and class conflicts of the "New South," have understood that Gilded Age reformers embraced antidemocratic ideas, and have argued that the last three decades of the nineteenth century saw a general retreat from the expansive notions of democracy that had flourished during the Civil War years. Historians have also told the story of the amendment itself, either as an attempt by "reform intellectuals" to fight corrupt political machines, as an early awkward draft in the long-term crafting of more rational forms of municipal administration, or, most persuasively, as part of the story of the "decline of popular politics" during the Gilded Age and Progressive Era.[6] However, we still lack an account that links these reform discourses to a powerful political movement and to a social group that carried them into the political arena.[7]

Indeed, to be fully understood, the amendment needs to be seen as a decisive moment in the emergence of a self-conscious bourgeoisie.[8] It was so in two distinct manners. First, the struggle for passage of the amendment brought merchants, manufacturers, bankers, and elite professionals together in unprecedented ways. For this group of capital-owning New Yorkers, whose economic interests were often centrifugal, who embraced diverse religious beliefs, and who originated from all over the world, such an articulation of shared identities and collective political mobilization was a dramatic departure. Second, the prominence of the movement itself resulted directly from the unity of its upper-class supporters. Yet despite these important links, historians have not examined the manner in which democratic assumptions became contested among northern economic elites in the last third of the nineteenth century and how the retreat from expansive notions of democracy was the specific result of upper-class political mobilizations.[9] We thus lack a persuasive explanation of how and why upper-class New Yorkers of the 1870s worked with uncharacteristic fervor and unity on a full-scale redefinition of the meaning and content of democracy.

This moment in the annals of American democracy has partly been obscured by whiggish and teleological views of history that have either implicitly or explicitly presented economic development as a sufficient condition for the rise of liberal democracy. In an American context, historians have narrated the history of the United States as a continuous unfolding of its democratic promise. More general accounts, informed by modernization theory or some strands of Marxism, have emphasized a universal correlation between the rise of capitalism, the bourgeoisie, and liberal democracy. Though their arguments differ, prominent thinkers ranging from Vladimir I. Lenin to Seymour Martin Lipset and Barrington Moore have all argued that it was the "bourgeois revolutions" that forged capitalist social relations and, eventually, liberal democracy—that is, societies characterized by universal male suffrage along with the rule of law, the functional separation of the state from civil society, and citizenship rights that cannot be violated by the state, such as freedom of speech and assembly.[10] Many of these accounts have placed the bourgeoisie center stage and presented it as the social class that carried the banner of democracy. As Moore concisely put it, "No bourgeois, no democracy."[11] During the Cold War, such statements found their way deep into popular political discourse. Indeed, to argue that capitalism begets democracy and democracy capitalism has become nearly a platitude, a relationship taken as so unexceptional as to make the two virtual synonyms. And no national history seemed to illustrate this promise better than that of the United States.

A commitment to American exceptionalism further obscured the complex career of democracy in the United States: Seymour Martin Lipset, for example, has contended that American exceptionalism is rooted in liberal notions of freedom and equality, notions that cut across time as well as social classes.[12] Such a vision of United States history, by emphasizing ideological uniformity, also precludes notions of the emergence of a "bourgeois class passion."[13] And even social historians, who fundamentally disagreed with exceptionalist interpretations of United States history and have uncovered in detail the "class passions" of workers, southern slaveholders, and yeomen farmers, left those of the northern upper class, including that of New York, largely unexamined and refrained from interrogating their relationship to democracy.[14]

Studying the bourgeoisie without such preconceptions reveals a class with no preordained beliefs, capable of powerful collective action and in a profound state of alarm by the 1870s. Indeed, the battle over New York's constitutional amendment was the high point of a broader disenchantment with democracy that spread among New York's upper class in the last three decades of the nineteenth century. The elite weekly *The Nation* argued as early as 1871 that a democratic city government was a "ridiculous anachronism," as "[t]he vast horde of persons who swarm here to pick up a living, and who now vote away all . . . property . . . should have nothing to do with the management of municipal affairs."[15] And this was hardly an unusually radical position. Bourgeois reformers organized in the Citizens' Association also found that "it is not safe to place the laws in the hands of the classes against which they are principally to be enforced."[16] Alarm spread quickly among upper-class New Yorkers during the Gilded Age that the universal enfranchisement of white men, let alone African-Americans in the South and women throughout the nation, would bankrupt the republic and would end in barbarism. While the institutional axis of democracy—the rule of law, the freedom of assembly and speech, among others—did not come under attack, the participatory axis of democracy now became a grave concern to the city's economic elite.[17] At the core of these fears was the desire of upper-class New Yorkers to safeguard their political power, a goal that had become at once more important and more elusive in an age of increasing inequality, strikes, and labor-backed political campaigns.

The efforts by New York's economic elite to restrict democratic participation expressed themselves on three levels during the Gilded Age. First, upper-class New Yorkers built a movement to scale down the suffrage rights of workers and the poor in city politics. Second, they sought to constrict popular power by limiting the scale and scope of the state. And third, they retreated from a prior willingness to back the federal government in protecting African-American citizenship rights in the postbellum South and eventually not only accepted the disenfranchisement of freedmen but at times argued for it in positive terms.

The articulation of such a vision, and especially the political mobilization behind it, was a distinct departure from the past. While there had been a weak current of antidemocratic thought among New York's upper class or, more generally, northern elites before the Gilded Age, it had been marginal and had remained unorganized.[18] As early as the 1780s, of course, Alexander Hamilton and James Madison, influenced by Burkean conservatism, had expressed unease about democracy and anticipated with concern the advent of a large number of propertyless voters.[19] Yet by the 1820s, the nation's economic elites had acceded to the enfranchisement of all adult white men. In 1833, indeed, Alexis de Tocqueville was able to report that those who oppose democracy "hide their heads."[20] By the 1870s, however, efforts to restrict the meaning and content of democracy forcefully reemerged among upper-class Americans—in the North as well as in the South. An explanation for this change can be found only by looking at two developments that unfolded simultaneously: the emergence of bourgeois class identities and the sharpening social conflicts of the Gilded Age. The lesson of the 1877 mobilizations in New York was that even in the world's premier democratic state, the meaning of democracy was continually negotiated, with economic elites at times showing great ambivalence about popular political power.

The struggle to disenfranchise New York's lower classes had begun innocuously in 1875, when the Democratic governor of New York State, Samuel Tilden, created a bipartisan commission to propose reforms in the structure of municipal government in the state.[21] The creation of this commission had been one of his promises during the prior election campaign. It also had been one of the most powerfully advanced demands of a reform movement that had spread among the city's economic elite during the decade. The commission Governor Tilden created consisted of twelve men, all of them members of the state's business and legal elites. Best known among them were Wall Street lawyer William M. Evarts, editors E. L. Godkin and Oswald Ottendorfer, iron manufacturer Edward Cooper, and railroad lawyer Simon Sterne. They deliberated for nearly two years. When they issued their report in early 1877, they presented a strikingly antidemocratic document, asserting "the fruitlessness of any effort for improvement through the regular instrumentality of popular election" and demanding "that the excesses of democracy be corrected."[22]

The commission expressed dissatisfaction with the traditional system of urban rule. More specifically, they located its problems in allowing for high debts, excessive expenditures, and high taxes, which had risen from 1.69 percent of the assessed value of their real and personal property in 1860 to 2.65 percent in 1877.[23] While this was still a minuscule rate of taxation compared to modern times and while tax evasion among upperclass New Yorkers was rampant, for the city these payments were by far the most important source of revenue, funding more than 90 percent of the core budget.[24] The city's economic elite, however, believed this to be an unacceptably high level of taxation and municipal spending, partly because of the squeeze on profits that they experienced during the crisis years of the mid-1870s, but more significantly for ideological and political reasons. The origins of these ills, they concluded, lay in the election of "[i]ncompetent and unfaithful" municipal officials and the prevalence of parties in municipal politics.[25] Cities, they argued, needed to become the chief battleground for reform because it was there that taxes redistributed significant resources, ordinary citizens enjoyed considerable influence, and a majority of voters were propertyless.

But how to improve municipal rule? After dismissing a whole range of reform ideas that had been traditionally articulated—the prosecution of corrupt officials, the strengthening of the position of the mayor, civil service reform—the commission concluded that only an attack on the roots of the problem would do.[26] The work, they asserted, "must begin at the very foundation of the structure."[27] The question was "whether the election by universal suffrage of the local guardians of the financial concerns of cities can be safely retained."[28] The commission resolved that this was not the case and therefore advised that "the choice of the local guardians and trustees of the financial concerns of cities should be lodged with the taxpayers."[29]

In order to secure such an outcome, the commission recommended the passage of a constitutional amendment.[30] At the heart of this proposed amendment was the creation of a board of finance, its members elected by those residents of the city who "have paid an annual tax on property owned by them, and officially assessed for taxation in such city [New York], of the assessed value of not less than five hundred dollars," or those who paid yearly rent of at least $250. These were substantial sums in a city in which workers, including skilled workers, could hope to take home only between $400 and $600 annually, of which they would not spend more than 20 percent on rent.[31] The board of finance was to be endowed with all powers regarding taxation, expenditures, and debt—including the allocation of city expenditures to specific projects.[32] The amendment would also have made the borrowing of money by cities unconstitutional except for tightly regulated emergencies.[33] As a result, the mayor and the board of aldermen, though still elected by popular suffrage, would have lost most of their powers. An estimate by the *New York Times* found that of a total electorate of about 140,000 New Yorkers, 60,000 to 65,000 would retain the right to vote as taxpayers, with another 35,000 to 40,000 as rent payers.[34] These numbers suggest that about 29 percent of the city's voters would have lost their right to participate in the choosing of the "financial guardians of the city." This is a conservative estimate, however, since the 100,000 New Yorkers who would still have been allowed to vote constituted only 31 percent of the total number of men aged twenty-one years or older who lived in Manhattan in 1880.[35] As many as 69 percent of all potential voters might have lost their right to vote, gained more than half a century earlier, in 1821. Among those to be disenfranchised, according to the *Sun*, were "ten thousand clerks and salesmen of the city who live in boarding houses . . . thousands of professional men who are neither property owners nor rent payers . . . thousands of small shopkeepers . . . tens of thousands of honest, industrious and patriotic mechanics and labouring men . . . the thousands of voters who live in hotels . . . the sons of wealthy citizens who live with their parents at home; and . . . many of the talented young men whose minds give life to the newspapers."[36]

The commission's plan was nothing less than a fundamental, even revolutionary reconceptualization of how New York City should be ruled, albeit one that harked back to the venerable ideas of propertied republicanism. Nevertheless, it received broad support from the city's merchants, industrialists, bankers, and elite professionals, who were struggling to retain their control and influence over a rapidly growing city. The *Commercial and Financial Chronicle*, a prominent voice of the city's merchants and bankers, editorialized, "If we really want relief, we must bestir ourselves vigorously and at once."[37] And indeed, they did. In public meetings, through editorials, and in numerous resolutions, upper-class New Yorkers, both Democrats and Republicans, lobbied for the adoption of the amendment. The Chamber of Commerce, which counted virtually all of the city's important merchants and bankers and many of its manufacturers among its more than seven hundred members, went as far as to call a special meeting in March 1877 (with an "unusually large number of members assembled") to consider the issue, and unanimously expressed its backing.[38] One of the chamber's members, the lawyer William Allen Butler, praised the plan because it excluded "the irresponsible, floating and shiftless vote, which never has any but a mischievous and indefensible relation to the exercise of the right of suffrage."[39] Joining him at the podium, Simon Sterne predicted that as a result of the reforms, "[m]erchants will no longer find themselves in contest with the loafer element, which would eventually outnumber and beat them."[40] More control, the merchant George T. Hope argued at the same meeting, would mean lower taxes.[41] Not only the Chamber of Commerce but also the New York Stock Exchange, the Produce Exchange, the Importers' and Grocers' Board of Trade, the Council of Reform, the Union League Club, the Municipal Society, the New York Board of Trade, and the Cotton Exchange passed resolutions in support of the amendment.[42] Indeed, all major business groups of New York City endorsed the constitutional change, the *New York Times* noting that it "is warmly supported by the entire commercial and tax-paying interests of the City."[43] When it came to the constitutional amendment, New York's economic elite spoke with one voice.

Upper-class concerns about universal male suffrage grew directly out of the changing nature of American capitalism.[44] Sharpening social conflicts were an important part of this change, as the years since the Civil War saw workers organize as never before in trade unions and engage in an unprecedented number of strikes. Bourgeois New Yorkers articulated their fears of such upheavals when they reacted in horror to the specter of the Paris Commune in 1871, which gave "an air of practicalness to what all the rest of the world sneered at as unpractical": that "a great crowd of persons" could seize the "government of a great capital, and administer it. . . . "[45] Such social upheaval was all the more threatening as the number of wage workers increased rapidly, undermining claims that the unique qualities of American society would prevent the emergence of a permanent proletariat of the kind that populated London, Paris, and the textile towns of Saxony. Indeed, the industrialization of Manhattan proceeded with unprecedented speed, and by 1880 one in twelve wage workers employed in the United States labored on the island.[46] Each year, thousands of new workers streamed into New York City from Europe or the American countryside to find employment in the city's burgeoning apparel, iron, and print shops. By 1880, there were two and a half times as many toilers in Manhattan as there had been twenty years earlier.[47] Even more important, an ever larger number of bourgeois New Yorkers built their businesses by employing these wage workers—in sharp contrast to the city's antebellum merchants, who had profited from trade, not manufacturing. With thousands of workers arriving in New York City to fuel the city's burgeoning metropolitan industries, and with the emergence of large enterprises, steered from afar, universal male suffrage became more threatening in the eyes of the city's economic elite than it had been in earlier times, when shops were small, proletarians usually only temporary wage earners, and employers in constant and personal contact with their employees. With this older world destroyed, the power of workers on the shop floor and in politics suddenly moved to the center of the political discourse of the city's economic elite.

These challenges were further amplified by the depression of the 1870s. During the second half of the 1860s, social conflicts had gone hand in hand with prosperity and enormous opportunities for profit, but after 1873 profits fell precipitously. Yet workers' activism continued. In the winter of 1873–1874, when unemployment skyrocketed in New York, thousands demonstrated in the streets of Manhattan. Those workers who managed to hold on to their positions saw their wages decline, in turn radicalizing a small but important minority into embracing the new ideas of socialism.[48] Adding to this sense of social upheaval were the thousands of homeless and jobless Americans who traveled around the countryside in a desperate search for work, leading to upper-class calls for containing "the tramp menace." And as if to show that the worst fears of the city's economic elite were justified, in the summer of 1877 the Great Uprising, a strike of the nation's railroad men, closed the nation's rail system and led to pitched battles between workers and the militia. These conflicts, along with the increasingly violent social relations in the states of the former Confederacy, resulted in a sense of acute social crisis among merchants, industrialists, bankers, and elite professionals. During the 1870s they wondered openly how well capitalism and democracy would be able to coexist or, for that matter, how stable capitalist economic arrangements would turn out to be. By 1877 a banker such as Junius S. Morgan saw the construction of armories for National Guard troops in central Manhattan as "a sure guarantee for the future"—a notion that would have been all but incomprehensible to antebellum merchants, bankers, and industrialists.[49]

The depression sharpened conflicts not only in the workplace but also in politics. It fundamentally undermined the optimism that bourgeois New Yorkers had come to embrace in the immediate postbellum years. Before 1873, this optimism had enabled them to accept a measure of working-class political power in the city and even Boss Tweed, since the resulting politics of urban growth also benefited large segments of the city's economic elite—because they sold municipal bonds, built the urban infrastructure itself, or profited indirectly from infrastructure improvements.[50] With the depression's squeeze on profits, however, the politics of urban growth came to an abrupt halt. In effect, the depression amplified the fear of bourgeois New Yorkers that local political power was slipping out of their hands. They watched with particular concern the emergence of strong political machines such as Tammany Hall, machines that increasingly were able to mobilize the resources and votes necessary to succeed in a competitive urban politics without the financial backing of the city's economic elite—a system of government, combined with spectacular corruption, that had been the hallmark of Boss Tweed's rule a few years earlier. Yet despite this ascendancy of machine politics, upper-class New Yorkers had not lost all influence over municipal politics. Instead, what they experienced was a slow but persistent waning of their power: "It is in the cities," concluded the liberal reformer Francis Parkman, "that the diseases of the body politic are gathered to a head, and it is here that the need of attacking them is most urgent."[51]

The problem could be "attacked" in many different ways, and retrenchment was one of them. Reducing the scale and scope of the state, the city's economic elite hoped, would not only relieve their purses but also limit the power of elected representatives while elevating the power of those who controlled markets.[52] Throughout the 1870s, upper-class New Yorkers demanded tax cuts and reduced spending by the municipal government, both of which had increased considerably since the 1850s.[53] Expressing the deep-seated hostility against an activist state, sugar manufacturer and New York mayor William F. Havemeyer told the *New York Times* in November 1873 that "[h]e could not see why the property of those who, by thrift and industry, had built up their houses, should be confiscated [by] men who had . . . by strikes or the like, contributed to the present state of things themselves."[54] Demands for retrenchment in state and national politics also became louder. In New York State, Samuel Tilden himself, as governor, was an avid advocate of retrenchment and weak regulation. During his tenure, for example, he cut state taxes in half.[55] In national politics, New York's economic elite closed ranks on monetary politics, demanding a return to the gold standard, effectively handing monetary politics to the Bank of England, and thus insulating monetary politics from popular political pressure. As *Iron Age*, the journal and voice of the iron, steel, and machinery entrepreneurs, emphasized, "[w]e must have a monetary system which will not be threatened by every biennial election of a House of Representatives."[56] Retrenchment thus stood at the core of bourgeois politics: it motivated the economic elite's struggle for greater political control while at the same time evolving into a strategy to reduce the political power of those New Yorkers who controlled insufficient amounts of capital to enjoy much influence on markets.[57]

By 1877, then, the world in which upper-class New Yorkers lived had changed decisively and by their own making. However, this changed world also transformed the city's economic elite themselves, giving them the inclination and capacity to engage in collective action. For a long time, of course, bourgeois New Yorkers had many things in common: they all owned and invested capital, employed wage workers (at the very least servants), did not work for wages, and did not work manually. But the jelling of shared identities and their transformation into political mobilizations was a departure, since throughout most of the century their diverse economic interests, their divergent religious and political views, and their ethnic heterogeneity had divided them deeply. Most important, by the 1870s bourgeois New Yorkers had left behind the political and ideological cleavages of the antebellum era. Before the Civil War, merchants on the one side and industrialists on the other side had embraced sharply divergent political economies—most merchants were deeply rooted in the political economy of Atlantic trade, while industrialists embraced with increasing vengeance the conflicting political economy of domestic industrialization. These disagreements had expressed themselves in relationship to the South and slavery, which in turn had influenced the way economic elites saw the emergence of a large working class in the North.

With these deep political and ideological cleavages overcome, bourgeois New Yorkers fashioned an increasingly powerful shared identity. By the 1870s, they had distanced themselves geographically, socially, and ideologically from other social groups. Mounting residential segregation drove the city's merchants, manufacturers, and bankers away from areas of the city in which they once had lived in close proximity to the people in their employ. Upper-class homes of sometimes enormous proportions went up in rapidly shifting sets of fashionable neighborhoods, and already by 1870, nearly half of all bourgeois New Yorkers lived on or just east of Fifth Avenue between Fourteenth Street and Central Park. At the same time, bourgeois New Yorkers built a number of new cultural institutions that solidified their social networks: J. Pierpont Morgan, Alexander T. Stewart, James Brown, William E. Dodge, Theodore Roosevelt, and others established the Museum of Natural History in 1871, the Metropolitan Museum of Art in 1880, and the Metropolitan Opera in 1883, and took control of the Philharmonic Society of New York.[58] Even more exclusive were the social clubs that now sprung up in upper-class neighborhoods, and by the 1870s the Union Club, the Union League, the Manhattan Club, the Knickerbocker Club, the Calumet, the Metropolitan, the Tuxedo, and the New York Yacht Club, among others, self-consciously strengthened networks among the city's economic elite. Less dramatically, but nonetheless important, marriages tied different segments of the city's bourgeoisie together. Manners and habits, ways of eating, socializing, and interior decorating forged further common cultural bonds. As New York's economic elite organized and distanced themselves from other social groups, they saw themselves increasingly as a separate class.

This greater self-awareness as a distinct social group went hand in hand with a dramatic ideological reorientation. Moving away from their universalist antebellum traditions of stewardship and free labor—worldviews that were very much rooted in the particular kinds of capital they controlled—bourgeois New Yorkers instead embraced the unfettered rights of property as well as notions of the social or even racial superiority of the holders of wealth. As Antonio Gramsci has argued, elites have almost always seen subordinate groups as displaying "barbaric and pathological" features, and it was thus not surprising that the city's upper class "naturalized" inequality by referring to different physical and mental endowments.[59] The president of the New York Central Railroad, Chauncey Depew, for example, asserted that the social elite of New York represented "the survival of the fittest." They had won in the struggle for dominance because they were endowed with "superior ability, foresight and adaptability."[60] The Manufacturer and Builder, a journal read mostly by small-scale industrialists, concurred, concluding that the applicability of Darwin's theory of the survival of the fittest to an understanding of society was "self-evident."[61] In consequence, workers were no longer perceived as the temporary proletarians of free-labor times but as the "dangerous classes" who threatened the rights of property holders. The upper-class Union League Club, for example, reported in 1875 on the "antagonism between capital and labor," a notion that would have been alien to the antebellum mercantile elite and manufacturers.[62] While free-labor ideology had allowed for the essential equality of employers and temporary proletarians, the new acceptance of an "antagonism" had dramatic ideological and political implications.

Ideological reorientation, rapid proletarianization, sharpening social inequality, and conflicts at the workplace and in politics as well as economic crisis all came together in 1877. It was in the context of these changes that the problem of political rule under the conditions of popular suffrage and extreme social inequality had arisen and the critique of democracy had taken the shape of a proposed constitutional amendment limiting voting rights in the state's cities.

Though the amendment was a clear break with the past, its underlying ideas were not without precedent. Already in the late 1860s and early 1870s, antidemocratic ideas and policy proposals had appeared with increasing frequency in bourgeois discourse. During the 1860s, the elite Citizens' Association, for example, had advocated restrictions upon the franchise, and in the wake of the downfall of Boss Tweed's regime in 1871, the political power of workers in local politics had become an issue of grave concern in upper-class circles. In effect, the 1870s became a turning point in American democratic thought.[63] The idea that the city was a corporation that only its stockholders should control now spread like wildfire among the economic elite. "Thirty or forty years ago it was considered the rankest heresy to doubt that a government based on universal suffrage was the wisest and best that could be devised," observed the reformer Jonathan B. Harrison in 1879. "Such is not now the case. Expressions of doubt and distrust in regard to universal suffrage are heard constantly, . . . [beginning] at the top of our society, among some of the most intelligent, the most thoughtful, and the most patriotic men. . . . "[64] Expressing this sentiment most succinctly, the *New York Times* editorialized that "[i]t would be a great gain if our people could be made to understand distinctly that the right to life, liberty, and the pursuit of happiness involves, to be sure, the right to good government, but not the right to take part, either immediately or indirectly, in the management of the State."[65]

In this ideological reorientation, bourgeois New Yorkers could also draw on a body of ideas that a small but influential group of intellectuals had formulated since the mid-1860s. Indeed, the debates on democracy that unfolded in the summer of 1877 among New York's economic elite, in institutions such as the Chamber of Commerce, were part of a broader set of ideas that had hardened among reformers writing in such elite journals as the *North American Review,* the *Journal of Social Science, The Nation,* and *Harper's Weekly.* These intellectuals had become increasingly wary of American democracy and now provided justifications for undermining democracy substantively and procedurally.[66] They pointedly argued that expansive notions of democracy threatened property rights, an argument to which their bourgeois audiences were receptive.

Two key members of the commission drafting the constitutional amendment, Simon Sterne and E. L. Godkin, indeed directly connected the world of reform discourse with the world of bourgeois New Yorkers. Conceptualizing the city as a "corporative administration of property interests," Simon Sterne claimed throughout the 1860s and 1870s that just as in a bank the depositors have no right to "take part in the election of the officers of the bank," propertyless citizens, "the paupers and criminals," should have no right to vote for municipal officials. The ballot, in effect, had become an "element of aggression" of the poorer classes against the well-off.[67] For these reasons, he declared, there should not be any "representation without taxation."[68]

Godkin, like Sterne, also became ever more concerned about the injurious effects of universal male suffrage on the social order of the United States. While in 1865 he had defended the participatory axis of American democracy against its European critics (albeit by arguing that suffrage was a privilege, not a right), by the early 1870s Godkin found enormous dangers in universal male suffrage, even advocating a literacy test for national elections.[69] He now compared the state of the modern world with that "in which Rome found herself in the closing days of the Empire." Rome failed, according to Godkin, because it was assailed by the "portion of the human race [that] lagged behind"—a situation that reminded him of his own city, in which the "body of persons known as the upper or educated classes of society . . . find that . . . the barbarians can no longer be kept out." As a result of what Godkin called the emergence of "industrial enterprise," the modern world had come into contact with "the poor and despised and ignorant of all other races." But while Rome had confronted these people in considerable distance from the center of power, in the modern world the "frontiers . . . are not territorial, but social; its barbarians are found within its own borders, in the streets and lanes of its own cities."[70] The only defense against these "barbarians," Godkin concluded, was to limit their political power.[71]

At first, things looked good for the city's merchants, industrialists, bankers, and elite professionals as the constitutional amendment passed the state legislature in the spring of 1877.[72] It did not go into effect, however, because constitutional amendments had to be passed by two subsequent assemblies before being put to a vote before the people as a whole. Therefore, the electoral campaign in the fall of 1877 turned into a referendum on the antidemocratic policies of bourgeois New Yorkers. Throughout the spring and summer, upper-class New Yorkers together with elite publications such as the *New York Times*, *Harper's Weekly*, and *The Nation* agitated for the amendment and tried to persuade New Yorkers to vote for candidates supporting it. In a highly unusual step, upper-class New Yorkers themselves actively campaigned, creating what they termed a movement of "tax-payers."[73] The support they received from the city's propertied voters was so great that even the amendment's initiators were surprised, finding that "a much greater interest had been developed in the movement than had been anticipated by the most sanguine of gentlemen. . . ."[74] In October, merchants William E. Dodge, John Jacob Astor, Royal Phelps, and Theodore Roosevelt, among many others, summoned a "mass meeting" at Steinway Hall (which seated 2,500) to agitate for the amendment.[75] The speakers called upon property owners to "unite" to regain political control of the city.[76] "[I]f property did not get power," thundered one of them, "power would take property."[77]

Yet the significance of the amendment did not escape other New Yorkers. Indeed, because large numbers of New York's citizens rightly saw the amendment as a threat to their political rights, they mobilized against candidates supporting the amendment, even founding a "Universal Suffrage Club."[78] Their mobilization gained its strength from its broad base of supporters among lower-middle-class and working-class New Yorkers. The October meeting in support of the amendment, for example, had also attracted a group of workers who protested the proceedings until the police ejected them. Unsurprisingly, Tammany Hall, one of the local Democratic party organizations that had been the most important target of these efforts and that included a large number of lower-middle-class activists among its ranks, waged a determined campaign for universal male suffrage.[79] On October 29, Tammany organized a huge rally to defend the franchise, with "Disenfranchisement Set Before the People in all its Deformity."[80] Irish immigrants, another favorite target of elite reformers, also spoke out against disenfranchisement, fearing that the amendment was "the thin end of the wedge to disfranchise the great body of citizens."[81]

Most articulate and most consistent in its defense of democratic politics, however, was the city's labor movement in general, and the nascent Workingmen's Party in particular.[82] In its paper, the *Labor Standard*, the party defined resistance against disenfranchisement "a duty which we owe to ourselves and to posterity not to allow the wealthy schemers of society to steal from us one of the most important political rights which the people possess."[83] A "Workingmen's Mass Meeting," called by the party a few weeks after the businessmen's April 7 meeting in Chickering Hall, mobilized against the amendments, whose measures it called "infamous in character, revolutionary in principle and an insult to every honest citizen."[84] By the summer, in the wake of the Great Uprising of railroad workers that had been contained by state militias, working-class New Yorkers' concern with the measure increased even further, as they gained a fresh appreciation for the need to retain continued access to state power. "The elective franchise," thundered the radical journalist George McNeill, "is a privilege and power that must be retained by the wage labor class even at the cost of bloody revolution."[85] Safeguarding access to the ballot box also led to calls for a further expansion of the suffrage, with *Irish World*, for example, publishing a letter by "R.W.H." who argued for women's suffrage, and the *Labor Standard* demanding continued access to the polls by African-Americans in the South.[86]

In early 1878 the amendment failed to pass the New York State legisla-ture. That it failed, and hence that universal male suffrage was sustained in New York State, was not because upper-class New Yorkers had not tried hard enough but because other social groups rose to the support of one of the most fundamental rights of liberal democracy. These defenders of suffrage could put up powerful resistance because they enjoyed access to resources and institutions such as political parties, trade unions, and newspapers. In fact, once broad-based democratic rule had been estab-lished in New York City, the institutional and political forces available to maintain it were too strong to allow for a limitation of suffrage rights through a constitutional process. It was rather unlikely, as the *Sun* re-marked, for "universal suffrage to commit suicide by destroying universal suffrage."[87] This was the lesson the city's economic elite learned in 1877. Lacking the inclination and power to step entirely out of the bounds of the political-constitutional framework, a step that Southern elites would take later in the nineteenth century, they accepted their defeat. It was an insight that even the singularly driven Simon Sterne eventually came to accept: "[P]olitical power, once granted, cannot be modified. . . ."[88]

But in a surprising and indirect way, Sterne was proved wrong. While mu-nicipal democratic institutions survived in the North, the former Confeder-ate states saw an eventual destruction of their fledgling democratic experi-ment. This is not the place to review the strategies that southern elites employed in this campaign, except to note that they, like elite northerners, employed the language of taxpayers' rights to advocate the disenfranchise-ment of the poor.[89] This was much easier, as southerners could formulate their program of disenfranchisement in terms of race and not of class.[90] In addition, they were more successful because they resorted to extralegal violence and because they encountered opponents who did not enjoy access to many of the usual prerequisites of successful collective action. Southern elites, in effect, attacked not only the participatory axis of democracy, namely universal male suffrage (as their counterparts did in the North), but also the procedural axis of democracy, for instance the rule of law, the functional separation of the state from civil society, and citizenship rights such as the freedom of speech and assembly. Despite these differences, however, it is noteworthy that elite southerners' destruction of democracy encountered very little opposition from upper-class New Yorkers. Here, northern tolerance for southern disenfranchisement relates directly to the disenchantment with democracy among bourgeois New Yorkers.

Indeed, the experience of Reconstruction itself had helped fuel the growing ambivalence among bourgeois New Yorkers about an activist state legitimized and controlled by nonpropertied voters. Although during the war and immediately afterward they had mostly supported federal intervention in the South, even black enfranchisement, they had demanded an end to Reconstruction much earlier than most northerners. They believed that political uncertainty along with social upheaval interfered with their economic interests in cotton production and with an economic climate suitable to investments in railroads and extractive industries.[91] Reconstruction governments, in their eyes, proved especially unable to create a stable system of labor relations so crucial to the production of agricultural commodities for world markets. By the early 1870s, New York's economic elite responded to this continued uncertainty in the South by formulating an ever more aggressive critique of Reconstruction. Republican lawyer George T. Strong angrily noted in his diary in September 1874 that "[t]he governments of South Carolina and Louisiana are, I fear, mere nests of corrupt carpet-baggers upheld by a brute nigger constituency."[92] A year later, the *Commercial and Financial Chronicle* explained to its well-heeled readers that "Southern States have been fearfully robbed by their ruler."[93] So dismal was the record of Reconstruction in the eyes of the city's economic elite that by 1877 the *Commercial and Financial Chronicle* concluded that it had "totally failed" and that it was best "to leave every Southern State to its own people."[94]

This critique of the activist state in the South was further strengthened by bourgeois New Yorkers' growing dissatisfaction with the shape of northern politics. In effect, critiques of Reconstruction and of northern politics fed into one another. This connection was most powerfully expressed by the 1872 rise of the Liberal Republicans, who, with important support from bourgeois New Yorkers, deserted the Republican party of Ulysses Grant to embrace a politics of governmental retreat.[95] Expressing a liberal censure of the activist state, fears of newly mobilized social groups, and a desire to move away from the ideological politics of the Civil War years, these activists believed that the key to the political future of the nation lay in turning the federal government's attention away from the South.[96]

Thus by the early 1870s upper-class New Yorkers, the "best men" of the North, increasingly came to view Reconstruction in terms of their own political problems, making them sympathize with the "best men" of the South. The discourse on Reconstruction among New York's economic elite, in effect, took on the same vocabulary as their discourse on the problems of political rule in northern cities. What bourgeois New Yorkers did was to formulate a "taxpayers' " view on political rule, a view that eventually merged their inclinations and interests with those of propertied white southerners. Even Horace Greeley's old free-labor and antislavery *New-York Daily Tribune* began to sympathize with the southern elite, stating that "[t]he intelligent people of the State have no voice in public affairs . . . and are obliged to submit to the rule of a class just released from slavery," a class of "ignorant, superstitious, semi-barbarians."[97] It was only a small step from such an argument to more explicit links between North and South. Emphasizing this connection most forcefully, the elite weekly *The Nation* came to speak of a "cancerous disease" that had infected the American body politic, a disease that in the North as well as in the South was robbing the propertied of their assets. Arguing that African-Americans (whose intelligence, they asserted, was only "slightly above the level of animals") were using their power in South Carolina to rob the well-off, they found that "socialism" had crept into the American political system, making it that much more urgent to support white redemptionists in the South.[98] The journal directly linked the power of workers in the North to that of freedpeople in the South, fearing that the political power of freedmen could serve as a bad example for workers in the North: "Stimulated by the example [of] black laborers elevated to the condition of legislators . . . it will not be long before the white workmen of the North will aspire to the same privileges."[99] It was then hardly surprising that in 1877, when bourgeois New Yorkers fought for suffrage restrictions in their own city, they explicitly linked their struggle to that of southern redeemers, with the *Commercial and Financial Chronicle* concluding that "[t]hey have there an ignorant class to deal with, as we have here."[100]

This rapprochement was encouraged and furthered by elite southerners' appropriation of the language of northern reformers, the most important being their shared critique of rising levels of taxation.[101] When in the late 1860s and early 1870s reconstructed states passed higher taxes, southern elites formed so-called taxpayers' associations that resisted these measures and pushed for an end to Reconstruction. Upper-class northerners, among them those from New York City, related well to these movements because they also opposed the rising taxes passed by northern municipalities and states. Indeed, northern and southern elites increasingly agreed on the notion that taxation was confiscation and that, therefore, the vote was a tool to expropriate the rich. Disenfranchisement came to be seen as an attractive way to limit such "confiscations." The ideological themes of the southern taxpayers' revolt were the same as those in the North, among them the "tyranny of a majority," "rights of property," "retrenchment," "taxation without representation," "fraud," and "extravagant spending."[102] "Taxes," in effect, turned into a code word for concerns about the political power of the propertyless, symbolizing the perceived threats to property rights that also seemed to emerge ever more frequently during strikes and working-class riots.

The similarities between the movements in the North and South are not surprising, considering that both elites faced a comparable problem: the majority of voters were propertyless proletarians of one kind and another.

Or, as Strong put it in his diary, while New York City had its "Celtocracy," the South was burdened by its "niggerocracy."[103] It was the fear of the lower classes that increasingly suggested to elite southerners and northerners that they shared a political agenda, an agenda that decisively transcended the animosities of the Civil War and Reconstruction.

Uniting around this northern taxpayers' viewpoint, the city's merchants, industrialists, and bankers employed their considerable political influence to mobilize against Reconstruction. This mobilization was part of a general rise of political assertiveness that they exhibited during the 1870s and included in its ranks such august businessmen as bankers August Belmont and James M. Brown, iron manufacturers Edward Cooper and Abram S. Hewitt, lawyer Simon Sterne, and merchants Robert B. Minturn and William E. Dodge.[104] They were supported in their endeavor to bring an end to federal intervention in the South by powerful institutions such as the Chamber of Commerce, the Stock Exchange, the Produce Exchange, the Corn Exchange, the Gold Board, the Cotton Exchange, the Maritime Exchange, and the "various clubs."[105] Even William E. Dodge, one of the few upper-class Lincoln supporters in 1860, came to decry federal efforts to reconstruct the South: "Ten years have now passed since the close of the war," he argued in 1875, "and there is a very general feeling that the time has come when we should all . . . say 'Let us have peace.' "[106] Dodge saw Reconstruction's main mission as accomplished. Despite a "radical change in the social system of the South," freedpeople worked and produced large crops of cotton. "Now," he concluded, "let the South alone. . . ."[107]

The disenchantment of upper-class New Yorkers with Reconstruction, then, helps to account for their ever louder critique of an activist and democratically legitimized state, which, in turn, helps to explain the destruction of democracy in the states of the former Confederacy. New York drug manufacturer and merchant Samuel B. Schieffelin made this point explicit when he warned of the dangerous connection between democracy in the North and the rights of freedmen in the South.[108] He advised southern states to write constitutions that would limit suffrage rights, thus saving themselves from "future danger and evil."[109] Universal suffrage, he bluntly asserted, "is a curse to any community, whether white or black, until fitted for it."[110] Views like these eased the acceptance of the eventual destruction of democracy in the South, as the antisuffrage policy in New York fed into the federal government's retreat from a commitment to reconstruct southern states and vice versa.

Sterne and Schieffelin, like many others, expressed the deep anxiety that prevailed among upper-class New Yorkers during the 1870s over the question of whether extreme social inequality and political equality could coexist. Such ambivalence found support not only among the white elites of the South but also among upper-class citizens in other northern cities. Indeed, while the campaign in New York might have been the most far-reaching and best organized of its kind, it found champions elsewhere. The *St. Louis Dispatch* declared that "the people of New York have the sympathy of all honest taxpayers, who will be glad to hear of their success."[111] The elite *Boston Evening Transcript* seconded this notion, asserting that "New York State or New York city or Boston can no more be 'run bottom upwards' than South Carolina or Louisiana."[112] And the *Cincinnati Commercial Tribune* "hoped there will be the courage to do that which is so obviously needed."[113]

Upper-class Americans in other northern cities indeed welcomed the efforts at disenfranchisement in New York not least because they also were concerned with the political power of lower-class citizens. While it seems that New York City was the only northern city that saw such a powerful effort at reintroducing property qualifications, discussions on suffrage spread throughout the North, and efforts to reform municipal politics were often motivated by the desire to limit the political power of workers and the poor.[114] Most dramatically, Rhode Island, the only state in the nation that had never removed its property qualifications for suffrage, resisted agitation against them until 1928.[115]

While the political power of the propertyless thus became a contentious issue throughout the nation, in New York City the 1877 movement was the last of its kind. It was not that upper-class New Yorkers had assuaged their fears about the threats posed by the broad political participation of nonpropertied voters; indeed, attacks on universal male suffrage continued. Simon Sterne, E. L. Godkin, William A. Butler, and others persistently argued for suffrage restrictions, and during the 1894 New York State constitutional convention various members of the "committee on suffrage" again suggested educational qualifications.[116] The motif of "taxpayers" as the only legitimate rulers of the city remained high on the agenda.[117] But the failure of the 1877 constitutional amendment in effect allowed for the emergence of new political strategies—political strategies that were more successful because they included a much wider variety of constituents than the antisuffrage struggle had ever been able to muster. Throughout the 1880s and 1890s, elite reform organizations such as the New York City Reform Club, the City Club, the Citizens' Union, the New York Tax Reform Association, and the Committee of Seventy mobilized bourgeois New Yorkers, along with a select group of intellectuals, around a program of government efficiency, low taxes, and limitation of the role of parties in local politics.[118] Their most important goal was to weaken the institutional underpinnings of political mobilizations independent of elite support. The political machine stood as the symbol of this ability, and bourgeois New Yorkers set out with singular determination to undermine it in order to create a "non-partisan city government."[119] As Simon Sterne argued, "[t]he next revolt must be against this political class."[120]

In many ways, these upper-class demands for structural changes were informed by the same critique of democracy that had earlier in the Gilded Age taken the form of assaults against universal male suffrage. This link became clearest in the South, where Progressive reforms indeed included the disenfranchisement of the region's African-American men. Yet in the North as well, where attacks against suffrage itself had moved to the margins, upper-class efforts to isolate municipal politics from voters stood in the tradition of their earlier reform efforts. These new reform movements, with their stress on "efficiency" and "professionalism," were the more successful as some lower-middle-class and even working-class citizens now joined into the bourgeois critique of existing political arrangements, though their motives for doing so were often quite different.[121] While the manifold political reforms that eventually came out of these impulses had varied effects on the possibilities for democratic participation, important strands of Progressivism emerged from the antidemocratic discourse of the 1870s. After all, for many upper-class Progressive activists, one of the most promising goals was to lessen the influence of working-class voters, especially those of immigrant background. This was an even more important objective as an increasing number of them began to embrace an expansion of the scale and scope of the state.[122]

Disenchantment with democracy thus became a hallmark of the late-nineteenth-century economic elite. This may surprise those who assume that the unfolding of capitalism, the rise of the bourgeoisie, and democracy are unproblematically correlated or those who hold the United States to be a truly "exceptional" society. Yet if there is no simple correlation between the emergence of capitalist social relations, the rise of the bourgeoisie, and democracy, what then is their relationship? This case study has suggested a complicated answer. On the one hand, it has confirmed that capitalism is historically quite conducive to creating democratic outcomes. After all, despite the enormous social conflicts of the Gilded Age, democracy did flourish in the United States, at least in the North and West. Once democratic institutions are deeply entrenched, they tend to be relatively sturdy, even if the most powerful social groups desire to alter them. Both defenders and critics of suffrage rights organized their political struggles within existing constitutional institutions and ideological traditions, speaking to their deep roots in American society.

We should be cautious, however, about giving too central a role to the bourgeoisie in the story of democratization. Despite Barrington Moore's claims to the contrary, the history of the 1877 constitutional amendment has demonstrated that the bourgeoisie is not the decisive social group responsible for creating democratic outcomes. In New York City during the 1870s, and also in many other places at other times, the bourgeoisie instead has shown profound ambivalence about democracy. Indeed, in 1877 it was workers and lower-middle-class citizens, not the city's economic elite, who fought for suffrage rights. Ironically, the bourgeoisie was often (but not always) at the forefront of opposition to key aspects of "bourgeois society."[123] This was particularly true in the United States, where universal white male suffrage preceded the emergence of a self-conscious and politically mobilized upper class. While the European bourgeoisie had frequently developed class identities in their struggle against the aristocracy and had couched their demands for power in terms of democracy, American merchants, bankers, industrialists, and elite professionals developed collective identities only in the social, conflicts of the 1870s, when the nature of capitalism itself had changed and had resulted in unprecedented spatial, social, and ideological distance between employers and employees. At this point, however, it was primarily their fear of the political power of the propertyless that drove the city's upper-class citizens into the political arena, unlike their European counterparts, whose efforts at securing access to political power for themselves often included demands for a widening of the franchise. And at this point they found in suffrage restrictions a new answer to the old Madisonian question of how political equality and economic inequality could be reconciled. Alexis de Tocqueville had suggested the possibility of such an outcome nearly five decades earlier, when he noted that "the manufacturing aristocracy which is growing up under our eyes is one of the harshest that ever existed in the world" and warned that "friends of democracy should keep their eyes anxiously fixed in this direction"[124]

The retreat from the expansive notions of democracy that followed the Civil War hence needs to be understood in the context of the changing identities, beliefs, and political capacities of the American bourgeoisie. At the same time, the emergence of shared identities among bourgeois New Yorkers can be understood only in the context of the political conflicts of Gilded Age America. Such a perspective allows also for an alternative to whiggish and exceptionalist discourses on the rise of American democracy. And in more general terms, the strange career of Gilded Age democracy suggests that the correspondence between the emergence of capitalist social relations and democratization is located in a more complicated relationship than either modernization theory or some strands of Marxism have allowed for: capitalism helped create the modern nation state, which, in turn, contributed to the formation of a vibrant civil society that encouraged the mobilization and organization of all social groups.[125] The spread of capitalist social relations, in the United States and elsewhere, fashioned huge new groups of people with claims to political power and the political capacity to act upon these claims, namely the lower middle and working classes. In 1877, it was they who continued to favor an expansive democracy. And their determination to protect suffrage rights shows that the meaning of democracy, just like that of freedom, is the result of struggles and conflicts.[126]

NOTES

This is an abbreviated version of an article by Sven Beckert, "Democracy and Its Discontents," *Past and Present* 174 (February 2002): 116–57, and is reprinted by permission of Oxford University Press. David Blackbourn, Lizabeth Cohen, Leon Fink, Brad Flehinger, Eric Foner, Charles Forcey, Robert Johnston, Devesh Kapur, James Kloppenberg, Lisa McGirr, Rebecca McLennan, Charles Tilly, and the contributors to this volume have provided valuable comments on earlier drafts of this article. The author thanks Nancy Elam, John-Paul Giugliano, JuNelle Harris, Rachel Hindin, and Daniel Mosteller for their superb research assistance. Audiences at Bilkent University, Harvard University's Charles Warren Center for Studies in American History, and the annual meeting of the Organization of American Historians provided helpful comments. Grants from Harvard University's C. Boyden Gray Fund in American History and the Clark Fund supported the research.

1. *Labor Standard*, April 14, 1877, p. 1.

2. *New York Times* (hereafter *NYT*), April 8, 1877, p. 1.

3. The speaker was New York lawyer and Secretary of State William Evarts. *New York Herald*, April 8, 1877, p. 7.

4. *New York Daily Tribune* (hereafter *NYDT*), April 9, 1877, p. 3.

5. Miscellaneous Letters, *Irish World*, April 28, 1877, p. 6.

6. For discussions of the amendment, see especially Michael McGerr, *The Decline of Popular Politics: The American North, 1865–1928* (New York: Oxford University Press, 1986), 49–52; Seymour J. Mandelbaum, *Boss Tweed's New York* (New York: J. Wiley, 1965), 168–72; John G. Sproat, *The Best Men: Liberal Reformers in the Gilded Age* (New York: Oxford University Press, 1968), 253–57. In a different context see also the suggestive discussion on the Tilden Commission in Roy Rosenzweig and Elizabeth Blackmar, *The Park and the People: A History of Central Park* (Ithaca, N.Y.: Cornell University Press, 1992), 278–79; Eric Foner, *The Story of American Freedom* (New York: Norton, 1998), 119–20; Edwin G. Burrows and Mike Wallace, *Gotham: A History of New York City to 1898* (New York: Oxford University Press, 1999), 1032–33; Joseph Logsden, *Horace White: Nineteenth-Century Liberal* (Westport, Conn.: Greenwood, 1971), 266–67; 310–11.

7. For discussions of the retreat from expansive notions of democracy in the post–Civil War years, see among others McGerr, *Decline of Popular Politics*; David Montgomery, *Beyond Equality: Labor and the Radical Republicans, 1862–1872* (New York: Knopf, 1967); Eric Foner, *Reconstruction: America's Unfinished Revolution, 1863–1877* (New York: Harper and Row, 1988).

8. The bourgeoisie is here defined as a group of people who own and invest capital, employ wage workers (at the very least servants), do not work for wages themselves, and do not work manually. Most unambiguously, this group includes the city's substantial merchants, industrialists, and bankers, along with rentiers (people who lived off investments they did not manage themselves), real estate speculators, owners of service enterprises, and many of its professionals. In this essay, I use the term bourgeoisie synonymously with "upper class" and "economic elite."

9. The only exception here is Alexander Keyssar's recently published and path-breaking *The Right to Vote: The Contested History of Democracy in the United States* (New York: Basic, 2000).

10. For an introduction to this debate, see Eva Etzioni-Halevy, *Classes and Elites in Democracy and Democratization* (New York: Garland, 1997). Among the important texts are Seymour Martin Lipset, "Some Social Requisites of Democracy," in *American Political Science Review* 53 (1959): 71–85, esp. 75; Barrington Moore, *Social Origins of Dictatorship and Democracy: Lord and Peasant in the Making of the Modern World* (Boston: Beacon Press, 1966), 413–32; Vladimir I. Lenin, *The Proletarian Revolution and the Renegade Kautsky* (Moscow: Foreign Languages Publication House, 1952), 132. For powerful critiques of these assumptions, see especially David Blackbourn and Geoff Eley, *The Peculiarities of German History: Bourgeois Society and Politics in Nineteenth-Century Germany* (New York: Oxford University Press, 1984), 80, and Dietrich Rueschemeyer, Evelyn Huber Stephens, and John D. Stephens, *Capitalist Development and Democracy* (Chicago: University of Chicago Press, 1992).

11. Moore, *Social Origins of Dictatorship and Democracy*, 418.

12. Seymour Martin Lipset, *Continental Divide: The Values and Institutions of the United States and Canada* (London: Routledge, 1990), 25.

13. See Louis Hartz, *The Liberal Tradition in America: An Interpretation of American Political Thought since the Revolution* (New York: Harcourt, Brace, 1955), 7, 51, 52.

14. See, among many others, Alan Dawley, *Class and Community: The Industrial Revolution in Lynn* (Cambridge, Mass.: Harvard University Press, 1976); Sean Wilentz, *Chants Democratic: New York City and the Rise of the American Working-Class, 1788–1850* (New York: Oxford University Press, 1984); Steven Hahn, *The Roots of Southern Populism: Yeoman Farmers and the Transformation of the Georgia Upcountry, 1850–1890* (New York: Oxford University Press, 1983); Eugene Genovese, *The World the Slaveholders Made: Two Essays in Interpretation* (New York: Pantheon Books, 1969).

15. *The Nation*, September 7, 1871, p. 159.

16. Citizens' Association of New-York, *The Constitutional Convention, the Basis or General Plan for the Government of the City of New-York* (New York: George F. Nesbitt, 1867), 10, 26.

17. For the distinction between the participatory and institutional axes of democracy, see Eileen L. McDonagh, "Race, Class, and Gender in the Progressive Era," in *Progressivism and the New Democracy*, ed. Sidney M. Milkis and Jerome M. Mileur (Amherst: University of Massachusetts Press, 1999), 146.

18. See Chilton Williamson, *American Suffrage: From Property to Democracy, 1760–1860* (Princeton, N.J.: Princeton University Press, 1960), 282

19. James Madison, "The Same Subject Continued: The Union as a Safeguard against Domestic Faction and Insurrection," in *New York Packet*, November 23, 1787.

20. Alexis de Tocqueville, *Memoir, Letters, and Remains*, 2 vols. (London: Macmillan and Co., 1861), 1:309.

21. Samuel Tilden, "Municipal Reform Message" (Address to the legislature), Albany, May 11, 1875, reprinted in *The Writings and Speeches of Samuel J. Tilden*, vol. 2, ed. John Bigelow (New York: Harper and Brothers, 1885), 119–37.

22. *Report of the Commission to Devise a Plan for the Government of Cities in the State of New York: Presented to the Legislature, March 6th, 1877* (New York: Evening Post Steam Press, 1877), 3.

23. Ibid., 4–10; Edward Dana Durand, *The Finances of New York City* (New York: Macmillan, 1898), 373.

24. Durand, *Finances of New York City*, 187–200.

25. *Report of the Commission to Devise a Plan*, 10, 13, 15.

26. Ibid., 21–27.

27. Ibid., 27

28. Ibid., 28.

29. Ibid. Since there was no income tax of any kind in 1877, all "taxpayers" owned real property—a small segment of the urban population.

30. The commission favored a constitutional change because, as they argued, only such an amendment would guarantee "stability." Ibid., 43. On the relationship between the state government and New York City, see Henrik Hartog, *Public Property and Private Power: The Corporation of the City of New York in American Law, 1730–1870* (Chapel Hill: University of North Carolina Press, 1983).

31. *Report of the Commission to Devise a Plan*, 48. The wage data are from Clarence D. Long, *Wages and Earnings in the United States, 1860–1890* (Princeton, N.J.: Princeton University Press, 1960), esp. 27, 28, 41, 150. On rents as a percentage of income, see Long, *Wages and Earnings in the United States*, 51–59. These are very rough estimates, and their only purpose here is to allow us to see that the property qualification was a significant hurdle that few, if any, New York workers could have passed.

32. *Report of the Commission to Devise a Plan*, 42.

33. Ibid.

34. *NYT*, October 21, 1877, p. 7.

35. For the number of males age twenty-one or older, see United States, Department of the Interior, Census Office, *Statistics of the Population of the United States at the Tenth Census, June 1, 1880* (Washington, D.C.: GPO, 1883).

36. *Sun*, October 22, 1877, p. 2.

37. *Commercial and Financial Chronicle* (hereafter CFC), March 31, 1877, p. 285.

38. *NYT*, March 30, 1877, p. 2.

39. *Nineteenth Annual Report of the Corporation of the Chamber of Commerce of the State of New York For the Year 1876–'77* (New York: Press of Chamber of Commerce, 1877), 99.

40. Ibid., p. 100.

41. Ibid., p. 104.

42. *NYDT*, April 5, 1877, p. 2; *NYDT*, April 13, 1877, p. 8; *NYT*, April 25, 1877, p. 8; *NYT*, November 30, 1876, p. 7; *NYT*, April 25, 1877, p. 8; *NYT*, March 30, 1877, p. 2.

43. The quote is from *NYT*, April 17, 1877, p. 10. See also Mandelbaum, *Boss Tweed's New York*, 171.

44. For a history of New York City's bourgeoisie, see Sven Beckert, *The Monied Metropolis: New York City and the Consolidation of American Bourgeoisie* (New York: Cambridge University Press, 2001).

45. *The Nation*, May 18, 1871, p. 334.

46. In 1880, there were 227,352 wage workers employed on the island of Manhattan and 2,732,595 in all of the United States.

47. "Manufactures, by Counties, 1860," in United States, Department of the Interior, *Manufactures of the United States in 1860; Compiled from the Original Returns of the Eight Census* (Washington, D.C.: GPO, 1865), 379–85; "Manufactures of 100 Principal Cities, By Totals, 1880," in Department of the Interior, Census Office, *Report of the Manufactures of the United States at the Tenth Census* (Washington, D.C.: GPO, 1883), 380.

48. Wages fell between 1873 and 1879 by approximately 4 percent (in real terms). See "Average Annual and Daily Earnings of Nonfarm Employees: 1860 to 1900," in *Historical Statistics of the United States, Colonial Times to 1970*, vol. 1 (Washington, D.C.: U.S. Department of Commerce, 1975), 165.

49. *NYT*, November 22, 1877, p. 8.

50. For an excellent analysis of the rise and fall of Tweed, see Iver Bernstein, *The New York City Draft Riots, Their Significance for American Society and Politics in the Age of the Civil War* (New York: Oxford University Press, 1990), 195–236.

51. Francis Parkman, "The Failure of Universal Suffrage," *North American Review* 127 (1878): 20.

52. On bourgeois demands for retrenchment, see *Writings and Speeches of Samuel J. Tilden*, ed. John Bigelow, 2: 172–73; Simon Sterne, *Representative Government: Its Evils and their Reform* (New York, 1869), p. 23; *Commercial and Financial Chronicle* (hereafter *CFC*), February 14, 1874, p. 157; *New York Commercial Advertiser*, October 22, 1873, p. 2.

53. *Nineteenth Annual Report of the Corporation of the Chamber of Commerce*, 13; *Eighteenth Annual Report of the Corporation of the Chamber of Commerce of the State of New York For the Year 1875–'76* (New York: Press of the Chamber of Commerce, 1876), 18, 33; *NYT*, June 9, 1875, p. 4; *NYT*, November 30, 1876, p. 7; *NYT*, January 31, 1877, p. 8; *NYT*, February 28, 1877, p. 5. *Real Estate Record and Builders' Guide*, January 1, 1876, p. 2. See also John C. Teaford, *The Unheralded Triumph: City Government in America, 1870–1900* (Baltimore: Johns Hopkins University Press, 1984), 188, 288, 293; Jerome Mushkat, *The Reconstruction of New York Democracy, 1861–1874* (Rutherford, N.J.: Fairleigh Dickinson University Press, 1981), 215; *Sixteenth Annual Report of the Commissioner of Public Charities and Correction, New York, For the Year 1875* (New York: Bellevue Press, 1876); Barry J. Kaplan, "Reformers and Charity: The Abolition of Public Outdoor Relief in New York City, 1870–1898," *Social Service*

Review 52 (June 1978): 202–3, 207; Jeffrey Sklansky, "The War on Pauperism: Responses to Poverty in New York City during the Depression, 1873–1878" (M.A. thesis, Columbia University, 1990), 13; Herbert G. Gutman, "The Tompkins Square 'Riot' in New York City on January 13, 1874: A Re-examination of Its Causes and Its Aftermath," *Labor History* 6 (winter 1965): 45, 67.

54. *NYT*, November 22, 1873, p. 2.

55. *Writings and Speeches of Samuel J. Tilden*, ed. John Bigelow, 2:172.

56. *Iron Age*, November 12, 1896, p. 915. Similarly, bourgeois New Yorkers supported the rapid ascendancy of courts in the regulation of the relationship between workers and employers, preferring to leave this important field of policy making to an institution removed from the immediate political pressure of voters.

57. For a discussion of retrenchment, see also William E. Forbath, "The Ambitions of Free Labor: Labor and the Law in the Gilded Age," *Wisconsin Law Review* (1985): 787.

58. For a detailed history of the institution building of New York's upper class, see Beckert, *Monied Metropolis*, 267–69.

59. Antonio Gramsci, *Il Risorgimento* (Turin: Einaudi, 1950), 199–200; Sproat, *Best Men*, p. 206.

60. Chauncey Depew, *My Memories of Eighty Years* (New York: Charles Scribner's Sons, 1922), 384.

61. *The Manufacturer and Builder* 8 (March 1875): 99; James J. Hill, *Highways of Progress* (New York: Doubleday, Page and Co., 1910), 126.

62. Henry W. Bellows, *Historical Sketch of the Union League Club of New York* (New York: G. P. Putnam's Sons, 1879), 132.

63. Robert Green McCloskey, *American Conservatism in the Age of Enterprise, 1865–1910* (New York: Harper and Row, 1964), 3, 15, 18.

64. Jonathan Baxter Harrison, "Limited Sovereignty in the United States," *Atlantic Monthly* 43 (February 1879): 186.

65. *NYT*, August 4, 1878, p. 6.

66. The antidemocratic beliefs of these reformers are also discussed in McGerr, *Decline of Popular Politics*, 45–52; Sproat, *Best Men*, 253–57.

67. Sterne, "The Administration of American Cities," *International Review* 4 (1877): 635, 637. Sterne diagnosed "tumors," "cancers," and "dangerous abscesses" in the body politic. Simon Sterne, *Representative Government*, 5, 20. In December 1877, he argued that suffrage could be both a tool of protection as well as aggression but found that since the 1830s, when large numbers of propertyless had streamed into American cities, the vote had largely become a tool of aggression. Simon Sterne, *Suffrage in Cities* (New York: G. P. Putnam's Sons, 1878), 11.

68. Sterne, *Suffrage in Cities*, 36.

69. See E. L. Godkin, "Aristocratic Opinions of Democracy," *North American Review* 100 (January 1865): 194–232. Also E. L. Godkin, "The Democratic View of Democracy," *North American Review* 101 (July 1865): 119–20; Sproat, *Best Men*, 253.

70. E. L. Godkin, "The Prospects of the Political Art," *North American Review* 110 (April 1870): 418–19.

71. This was a lesson that also led Godkin to argue that "it would in my judgement too have been far better . . . to have kept the Irish absolutely disenfran-

chised." E. L. Godkin to John P. Spencer, New Rochelle, September 5, 1886, Godkin Papers, Houghton Library, Harvard University.

72. McGerr, *Decline of Popular Politics*, 50.

73. *NYT*, October 11, 1877, p. 8.

74. *NYT*, October 13, 1877, p. 2.

75. *NYT*, October 9, 1877, p. 5. For the names see *Sun*, October 23, 1877, p. 1.

76. *NYDT*, October 23, 1877, p. 2.

77. *NYT*, October 23, 1877, p. 1.

78. *Irish–American*, November 3, 1877, p. 1; *Sun*, October 13, 1877, p. 2.; *NYDT*, October 23, 1877, p. 2; *Labor Standard*, October 28, 1877, p. 4.

79. *Irish–American*, November 10, 1877, p. 1; October 20, 1877, p. 4.

80. *Sun*, October 30, 1877, p. 1.

81. The quote is from the *Irish World*, October 20, 1877, p. 4. See also *Irish World*, April 7, 1877, p. 5; April 21, 1877, p. 2; April 28, 1877, 1, 6;

82. On the importance of the labor movement to the defeat of the amendment see also John Swinton, *A Momentous Question: The Respective Attitudes of Labor and Capital* (New York: Burt Franklin, 1895), 237.

83. *Labor Standard*, April 14, 1877, p. 1. See also *Labor Standard*, April 21, 1877, p. 1; May 19, 1877, p. 1; May 26, 1877, p. 1; October 7, 1877, p. 1; October 28, 1877, p. 5; November 4, 1877, p. 2.

84. *Labor Standard*, April 28, 1877, p. 3.

85. *Labor Standard*, November 4, 1877, p. 2. For working-class opposition, see also the speech by J. W. Maddox at the Cosmopolitan Conference on April 22, 1877. See *NYT*, April 23, 1877, p. 8.

86. *Irish World*, May 12, 1877, p. 6; *Labor Standard*, October 28, 1877, p. 4.

87. *Sun*, October 22, 1877, p. 2.

88. Speech by Simon Sterne in front of the German-American Citizens' Association, 1887, quoted in John Foord, *The Life and Public Services of Simon Sterne* (London and New York: MacMillan, 1903), 289.

89. See, for example, Charleston *News and Courier*, April 21, 1877, p. 2.

90. It is important to note, though, that even in the South appeals for disenfranchisement were at times formulated in terms of class. In Texas, for example, a group of urban businesspeople advocated ever since the 1870s limiting suffrage rights to property owners, arguing explicitly that white workers should be deprived of political influence just as much as their African-American counterparts. For an incisive discussion of this moment in Texas politics, see Patrick G. Williams, "Suffrage Restriction in Post-Reconstruction Texas: Urban Politics and the Specter of the Commune," *Journal of Southern History* 68 (February 2002): 31–64.

91. For a detailed account of the shifting attitudes toward Reconstruction, see Beckert, *Monied Metropolis*, 157–71.

92. Allan Nevins and Milton Thomas, eds., *The Diary of George Templeton Strong* (New York: Macmillan, 1952), 4:538, entry of September 16, 1874.

93. *CFC*, January 2, 1875, p. 3.

94. *CFC*, April 18, 1877, p. 383.

95. Foner, *Reconstruction*, 500–11.

96. Ibid., 460–511.

97. *NYDT*, May 1, 1871, p. 1.

98. See *The Nation*, April 16, 1874, 247–48.

99. *Dry Goods Economist*, September 5, 1868, p. 4.

100. *CFC*, April 28, 1877, p. 383.

101. See also Foner, *Reconstruction*, 460–511.

102. See, among many examples, the speech by Richard Lathers, *South Carolina: Her Wrongs and the Remedy, Remarks of Col. Richard Lathers, Delivered at the Opening of the Taxpayers' Convention, in Columbia, S.C., Tuesday, February 17, 1874* (Charleston: n.p., 1874).

103. Nevins and Thomas, eds., *Diary of George Templeton Strong*, 4:538, entry of September 16, 1874. Interestingly, it was again the labor press that made the connection between the policies of southern elites and the fate of democratic rights in the North. See esp. *Labor Standard*, October 28, 1877, p. 4.

104. Foner, *Reconstruction*, 554; *NYT*, January 8, 1875, p. 1.

105. *NYT*, January 8, 1875, p. 1; *NYT*, January 9, 1875, p. 5.

106. *NYT*, January 12, 1875, p. 2.

107. Ibid.

108. *NYT*, November 14, 1866, p. 2.

109. *NYT*, January 25, 1867, p. 2.

110. Ibid.

111. *St. Louis Dispatch*, October 30, 1877, p. 2.

112. *Boston Evening Transcript*, October 5, 1877, p. 4.

113. *Cincinnati Commercial Tribune*, April 6, 1877, p. 4.

114. As Samuel Hays has argued, one of the principal goals of urban reformers was to limit lower-class political power. Samuel Hays, "The Politics of Reform in Municipal Government in the Progressive Era," *Pacific Northwest Quarterly* 17 (October 1964): 157–69, in particular 164. Others have argued that the principal goal of the reformers was "to diminish lower-class electoral influence" and to weaken "political parties, the basis of organization of the poor." Susan Welch and Timothy Bledsoe, *Urban Reform and Its Consequences* (Chicago: University of Chicago Press, 1988), 6.

115. As one of the first states to industrialize, and as a state with an unusually large proportion of immigrant workers among its people, Rhode Island had a business elite that feared the political power of propertyless voters. Until 1888, any immigrant wishing to vote in Rhode Island needed to own $134 in real property, while voting in municipal elections in the city of Providence took $134 in real or personal property even for the native-born. See the excellent work by Eve Sterne, "Politics after Populism: The Working Class in Providence, Rhode Island, 1896–1936," paper presented at the Annual Conference of the American Historical Association, Seattle, 1998, p. 3.

116. Charles Z. Lincoln, *The Constitutional History of New York*, 5 vols. (Rochester, N.Y.: The Lawyers Co-operative Publishing Co., 1905–1906), 3:79.

117. *Campaign Book of the Citizens' Union (September–October)* (New York: Citizens' Union, 1897), 28–29.

118. The New York Tax Reform Association agitated against taxation based on "abilities [to pay]." See Bolton Hall, ed., *Who Pays Your Taxes? A Consideration on the Question of Taxation* (New York: G. P. Putnam's Sons, 1892), 4; Clifton K. Yearly, *The Money Machines: The Breakdown and Reform of Govern-*

mental and Party Finance in the North, 1860–1920 (Albany: State University of New York Press, 1970), 173.

119. For their ideas, see *Speeches by Ex-Judge Joseph F. Daly, Governor Theodore Roosevelt and Reverend Thomas R. Slicer, Delivered at the Dinner of the Citizens' Union Club of the 27th & 29th Assembly Districts at Tuxedo Hall, New York, March 24, 1899* (New York: n.p., 1899). CFC, November 10, 1894, p. 813.

120. Simon Sterne, *Address Before the German-American Citizens' Association on the Proposed Constitutional Convention and the Work Before It* (New York: n.p., 1887), 38.

121. McCormick, *From Realignment to Reform: Political Change in New York State, 1893–1910* (Ithaca, N.Y.: Cornell University Press, 1981): 264, Theda Skocpol, *Protecting Soldiers and Mothers: The Political Origins of Social Policy in the United States* (Cambridge, Mass.: The Belknap Press of Harvard University Press, 1992).

122. Foner, *Story of American Freedom*, 141, 154.

123. Blackbourn and Eley, *Peculiarities of German History*, 80–90. See also Gareth Stedman Jones, "Society and Politics at the Beginning of the World Economy," *Cambridge Journal of Economics* 1 (March 1977): 77–92.

124. Alexis de Tocqueville, *Democracy in America*, vol. 2, chap. 20.

125. This argument is inspired by Charles Tilly, "Democracy Is a Lake," in *The Social Construction of Democracy, 1870–1990*, ed. George Read Andrews and Herrick Chapman (New York: New York University Press, 1995), esp. 383–84.

126. For the contested history of freedom, see Foner, *Story of American Freedom*.

Chapter Seven

DOMESTICITY VERSUS MANHOOD RIGHTS

REPUBLICANS, DEMOCRATS, AND "FAMILY VALUES"

POLITICS, 1856–1896

Rebecca Edwards

Let us then go beyond the political party to the relationship
between society and politics, make forays from the
world of each party system back into the social order
from which it sprang.
—*Samuel P. Hay*

THOUGH CONFLICTS over "family values" are all too visible
in the American political landscape today, historians have not yet
appreciated the significance of such conflicts to party politics in the
nineteenth century.[1] On the one hand, historians of women have redefined
the political, emphasizing relations within the family, economic roles, and
activities ranging from literary clubs to suffrage activism. They have studied women's interactions with the state, asking questions about law, citizenship, and identity. But in thinking about parties and elections most
historians of women reinscribe the notion of separate spheres: they describe women's political values and organizations as separate from men's,
with convergence occurring only in the twentieth century. Since historians
can rarely analyze the choices of female voters before 1920, most con-
clude that the electoral system excluded women, and they look elsewhere
for "women's politics."[2]

Meanwhile, among political historians, controversy rages over the significance of nineteenth-century parties, the factors that drove voter participation, and the links (or lack thereof) between popular campaigns and
government policy. While voters' religious, racial, and ethnic loyalties
have received close attention, the maleness of the electorate has seemed
perhaps too obvious to warrant analysis. Historians now recognize their
subject as gendered, calling electoral politics "all-male territory" and noting that the major parties "of course were not open to women." Some
note in passing that nineteenth-century women took an active interest in
partisan campaigns.[3] Yet little attention has been given to ways in which

gender values might have shaped conflicts *between* the parties, rather than reinforcing male bonds.

This essay proposes that an epic battle over men's and women's places in the family, and government's role in supporting or enforcing those roles, was a critical dimension of major-party conflict between 1856 and 1896. The defense of proper family order, according to each party's definition of that ideal, was central to an array of policy objectives on each side. Aspects of this fight can be traced to Whigs and Democrats in the antebellum era and perhaps even further back in American history, but it emerged most fully with the arrival of the Republicans, a militantly sectional party whose economic and religious interests were inseparable from their domestic ideal.[4] Nineteenth-century Republicans and Democrats agreed on two key points: they saw the family as the basic unit of society, and by *family* they meant a male breadwinner, his wife, and their children. Beyond these agreements lay a bitter dispute, especially over the respective roles of wives and husbands. Republicans proposed multiple forms of government intervention to restrain deviance and address unmet needs within the family. They introduced policies to support husbands and fathers as breadwinners, and they used state payments as a substitute for certain absent or incapacitated men. They sought to control both male and female sexuality, reflecting their desire to "protect" good Christian women and discipline male irresponsibility. Democrats responded by denouncing what they tellingly called "state paternalism," which they depicted as a direct attack on individual men's liberties and a dangerous intrusion into the home.

My claim here is not that the parties battled over the family *instead* of slavery, industrialization, or other crucial issues. Rather, it is that all these concerns were intertwined, and a particular model of family life was central to each party's larger worldview. Republicans and Democrats pursued their first four decades of conflict amid the enormous social and economic transformations of industrialization, while also engaging in an armed struggle that ended slavery. It is hardly surprising that, as Michael Vorenberg argues elsewhere in these pages, the years surrounding the Civil War were among the most politically and legally creative in United States history. Politics reflected all the classic tensions between rural and urban concerns, social classes, different religious faiths, and the economic core and periphery. As William Novak observes, industrialism brought the end of apprenticeship and indentured servitude as well as slavery; all adult men were now assumed to be free agents capable of contracting their labor. In this context defenders of "manhood rights"—often speaking on behalf of working-class or white men—confronted the professional and "striving" classes, among whom male responsibility and female domesticity became urgent concerns. In politics these positions were represented by, respectively, the Democratic and Republican parties.[5]

Republican goals were based in what historians have termed *domestic ideology*, a complex of ideas that arose among the northeastern middle classes in the 1830s and 1840s and spread from there to other sectors of society. According to this view the duty of husbands and fathers was to strive in the world of work, enabling wives and mothers to devote themselves to nonwage-earning activities as "angels of the home." Good husbands and fathers were not tyrants demanding obedience: they practiced self-control and deferred to women where appropriate, since the latter were thought to be better Christians, more nurturing parents, and morally and sexually purer beings than were men. Domestic ideology placed a premium on sexual restraint and male duty; true respect and love for a good woman made a man work hard and restrain his passions, while a womanly woman devoted herself to homemaking, motherhood, and Christian benevolence in her community. The domestic family was, in short, the key to higher civilization, as well as a marker of America's unique strengths.[6]

Democrats consistently resisted this ideology, seeking to protect individual citizens' "manhood rights" from dangerous Republican meddling. In essence Democrats defended the prerogatives of male household heads, which included men's control over their wages, their property, and their dependents: wives, children, and before the Civil War, slaves. Democratic arguments tended to be highly racialized and class-conscious, focusing on the rights of white workingmen and depicting men of "lower races" as incapable of exercising such rights. But as we shall see, some Democrats extended their defense to nomadic Indian hunters, Mormon polygamists, and other men who deviated from the presumed norms of settled labor and monogamous domesticity. Government, such Democrats argued, had no right to impose any particular family model on American men.

Neither of the major parties was, of course, fully united on any question, and regional differences remained significant throughout the era. Based on the preliminary research presented here, I suspect that northeastern Republicans and southern Democrats held the most starkly opposing "family values" agendas. But their allies in other regions articulated similar views, and similar patterns of conflict surfaced in many parts of the country on an array of issues. Since some readers may suspect that family-based appeals were simply a "cover story" for "real" economic or other interests, my goal here is to demonstrate that specific policy objectives were linked to domesticity and manhood rights, and that these values played a substantive role in party platforms and agendas. Concentrating on Republicans, who were the innovators, the following pages consider five key initiatives grounded in domestic ideology. These exploratory paragraphs derive from my research into national electoral campaigns. They also draw upon an extensive and growing literature that considers the connections between law and family in the nineteenth-century United States. Most of that scholarship ignores electoral politics as the era's key mechanism for translating social agendas into policy; I take responsibility, here, for the speculative context in which this work is used. While the overall pattern seems clear, the points below are at least as much a call for research as a report of findings.

MORMON PLURAL MARRIAGE

Though the Constitution reserves family law to the states, Republicans made vigorous use of federal power to eradicate plural marriage in the Church of Jesus Christ of Latter Day Saints. Republicans' 1856 national platform denounced "those twin relics of barbarism, polygamy and slavery," and thirty years later GOP congressmen were still trying to purge Utah of its "harems." The significance of this issue in the rise of the Republican party has, I think, been understated. Utah was not the only source of outrage: in the late 1850s, scandals involving breakaway Mormon groups made polygamy a pressing local issue in Arkansas, Michigan, and other states. There is some evidence that when Democratic president James Buchanan sent United States troops to Mormon country in 1857, he sought to preempt one rising Republican issue while deflecting attention from another one—slavery. Many commentators, in fact, linked the two questions. Republican-leaning editors compared the plight of Mormon wives to that of slave women, while a southern Democrat argued that "we do not wish to see the Federal government legislating on the marriages or morals of domestic life." On the eve of the Mormon conflict one man warned, "we call slavery a domestic institution [and] our General Government has no power over it. Polygamy is certainly a domestic institution and is equally beyond its power. . . . We are contemplating a civil war [in Utah]; . . . let us not plunge into it thoughtlessly."[7]

Polygamy continued to preoccupy Republicans all the way to 1890, when Mormon leaders officially ended plural marriage. In almost every session of Congress until that date, Republicans introduced bills for stronger penalties or more effective enforcement of antipolygamy laws. The persistence of these efforts suggests an ongoing commitment to regulating marital relations. It also demonstrates the mixed implications of domestic ideology for women's rights. The Utah Territory enfranchised women in 1870, after which Mormon women overwhelmingly voted with their men. In the name of protecting such women Congress first disfranchised all polygamists, male and female, in 1882 (the Supreme Court upheld its right to do so) and then revoked all Utah women's voting rights in 1887. Clearly, Republicans' defense of domestic ideology did not necessarily translate into a women's rights agenda.[8]

EMANCIPATION AND THE FREEDMEN'S BUREAU

Both defenders and critics of slavery asserted that that institution was a way of ordering family life. Southern statute books treated the relations of master and slave, husband and wife, and parent and child all in the category "domestic relations." As Nancy Cott observes, the most important parallel between slavery and marriage was "the master-husband's power to command the dependent," and both northern and southern Democrats saw abolitionism as a threat to that patriarchal order. Apologists claimed that antislavery would lead directly to women's rights by sanctioning "Free Women and Free Negroes." Abolition came, of course, as a punitive war measure against the seceded states. But in explaining for decades afterward why they had ended slavery, Republicans stressed the protection of women, restraint of male tyranny in the household, and creation of "Happy Homes." The crucial role of domestic ideology in the abolitionist movement has long been recognized, and historians such as Stephanie McCurry are now tracing counterideologies among southern secessionists. Such analyses could fruitfully be extended to electoral politics in the 1850s and beyond.[9]

In shaping postwar civil rights legislation, Republicans were forced to distinguish between the "domestic relations" of slavery and marriage in order to secure freedmen's rights without liberating married women entirely. The impact of civil rights legislation on marriage was a serious concern in Congress, and neither Democrats nor the vast majority of Republicans sought to grant married women full autonomy. But Republican agents in the field, in contrast to Democrats, sought to promote domesticity among freedmen and women and took measures that suggest a strong commitment to regulating freedmen's marriages. Protecting and reshaping the black family was a central concern of the Freedmen's Bureau, for example, which issued a set of "marriage rules" that listed the "duties of husbands" and the "rights of wives and children" (significantly, *not* vice versa). Bureau officials took a strong stance against wife beating and family violence. In most cases they fought southern conservatives (overwhelmingly Democrats) on the issue of forced apprenticeship, returning black children to their natural parents. While bureau officials urged black women to do work they would not have endorsed for white middle-class mothers, overall the bureau was the chief government ally for blacks seeking to protect their marital and parental relations. Bureau officials denied

aid to able-bodied men but offered it to women, whom they acknowledged as "dependents" or "wards" of the Union. As bureau funds for
Virginia were cut off, final payments went to "women who have no husbands, living or present, to provide for them, who have large families of
children."[10]

The bureau sought to inculcate domestic ideology in both women and
men. In Tennessee, General Clinton Fisk exhorted black women to learn
to read, sew, and keep a clean house. He told husbands that "your wives
will not love you if you do not provide bread and clothes for them. They
cannot be happy and greet you with a kiss, when you come home, if they
are hungry, ragged, and cold." Fisk's description of contented
freedwomen, waiting at the door to greet their breadwinner husbands,
says a great deal about Republicans' vision of civilization. Many freedmen
and women did embrace aspects of domestic ideology: thousands of families withdrew women from field labor, while black politicians and editors
urged husbands to be responsible and temperate and wives to be good
housekeepers. Such ideals foundered, not only on the rocks of poverty
and discrimination, but on the independence of black women. Those who
worked for wages, voted at mass meetings, and defended themselves with
pitchforks often saw domesticity as a backward step.[11]

The case of the Freedmen's Bureau highlights the role of bureaucratic
agencies in promoting Republicans' family agenda. It also shows how domestic ideology could both liberate and control women, depending on the
circumstances and one's point of view, and it suggests the ways in which
the Republican policy makers sought to foster domesticity across racial
lines. Bureau officials contrasted their ideal of family life with that of southern (Democratic) white men, whom they deemed violent, uncontrolled,
and tyrannical. The latter's responses carried forward into the era of segregation and lynching, both of which were, in different ways, attempts to
reassert white men's control over white women as well as over the African-
Americans who had once been classified as dependents in the household.

UNION PENSIONS

Theda Skocpol has argued that the Civil War pension system, America's
first federal welfare program, was designed to benefit male veterans. But
the system evolved in stages, and until the post-Reconstruction years it
directed a large percentage of its benefits to widows and their minor children. As late as 1875 more than half of the $28 million spent annually on
pensions went to war widows and their dependents, as well as to widowed
mothers who had lost the support of a son, and even to "orphan sisters."
Thus the early breadwinner state, if such it was, made a high proportion

of its payments to women. Those payments became a staple of Republican platforms and rhetoric for thirty years. In a typical argument one party leader stated that "the widows and orphans of the gallant dead are the wards of the people—a sacred legacy bequeathed to the nation's protecting care."[12]

As Megan McClintock has shown, pensions for disabled men and especially for widows became enormously controversial in the 1880s. At this point congressional Republicans granted pensions to widows and injured veterans on a case-by-case basis, passing thousands of bills in all-night sessions that the Democratic minority did not even bother to attend. To Democrats such payments were offensively paternalist. As President Grover Cleveland vetoed stacks of pension bills, he and other party leaders charged that Republicans were supporting promiscuous widows, whose benefits would be cut off if they remarried and who thus chose to live in sin. More broadly, Democrats suggested that direct payments to women usurped men's power in the home. Pensions became one of the hottest issues of the decade, with each party denouncing the other's alleged effort to undermine the family.[13]

While pensions substituted government payments for dead and disabled breadwinners, Republicans also created a federal surrogate for the domestic labor of veterans' wives. The National Home for Disabled Volunteer Soldiers, a network of institutions created during Reconstruction, provided tens of thousands of injured veterans with a facsimile of "homelike" care. Patrick Kelly argues that the National Home was far less controversial than pension payments were. If so, this suggests that resistance to government paternalism did not preclude state benefits to men. My own research suggests that the National Home did meet criticism from Democrats, who rejected both paternal *and* maternal roles for the state. As one western Democrat colorfully expressed it, Republicans wanted to institute "High Daddy" policies that enlisted government "to rock the cradle and drive the hearse, weep over the grave and sit up with the widow, and pay every man for cracking his own lice."[14]

THE PROTECTIVE TARIFF

Economic issues came to dominate politics in the post-Reconstruction years, and much of the debate centered around Republican protective tariffs on imported manufactures. Republicans championed "tariff protection" as the centerpiece of their economic program and their chief industrial policy, while Democrats assailed high tariffs as an illegitimate tax on American wage earners and consumers.[15] Central to these debates was the question of whether and how government should assist male breadwinners. Republicans depicted their tariffs as "protecting the home," enabling American men to earn a family wage and women to refrain from paid labor and devote themselves to motherhood and domesticity. Republican investigators sent back warnings from their tours of "free-trade" England and Ireland, where women allegedly donned trousers to toil in field, mine, and forge, sometimes stripped to the waist. In a typical statement to an Irish-American audience, presidential candidate Benjamin Harrison contrasted "the American mother and wife, burdened only with the cares of motherhood and of the household, with the condition of women in many of the countries of the old world where she is loaded also with the drudgery of toil in the field. . . . Who, if not Irish-Americans, versed in the sad story of the commercial ruin of the island they love [i.e., under British 'free trade'], should be instructed in the beneficent influence of a protective tariff . . . upon their individual and upon their home lives?"[16]

Republican speakers and editors made such arguments all over the country to all kinds of audiences. Parade floats included large signs with the exhortation, "Fathers, protect your daughters by your vote." "Every woman should be a protectionist," argued a campaign pamphlet, because the tariff "makes a more self-respecting and womanly life possible." Republican speakers frequently linked protective tariffs to other policies that assisted breadwinners and helped ensure female domesticity. "It is my pride," announced Harrison, "that the Republican Party has always been a promoter and protector of the home. By the Homestead Act it created half a million homes, and by the Emancipation it turned one half a million cattle pens into homes." Through the tariff, he claimed, Republicans also helped husbands and wives, fathers and mothers fulfill their proper roles.[17]

Democrats, predictably, denounced high tariffs as a form of paternalism that interfered with manhood rights, in this case by effectively taxing consumer goods and hampering men's ability to support their families. Democrats pitched these appeals to farmers and white workingmen on the basis of regional interest, class, and gender; tariff debates were thus fought over a constellation of related concerns. The underlying gender ideologies had concrete implications for women's involvement on each side. Republican leaders organized a National Republican Women's Association, recruiting female writers and stump speakers to draw links between high tariffs and the "protection" of non-wage-earning women. Democratic leaders, on the other hand, squelched a movement by loyal women to create a league for their own party.[18] Clearly, women's partisan activism was more welcomed by supporters of domesticity than by defenders of manhood rights.

Observers noted, of course, that protective tariffs did not enable all American men to earn a family wage. Many early critics came from the progressive wing of the Republican party; they endorsed state intervention in the economy and supported a high-tariff policy but believed it was not enough. In the early 1870s the pioneering Massachusetts Bureau of Labor investigated workmen's wages, taking as the basic definition of a living wage the "ability of a man to support his family." Bureau officials found that thousands of men earned less than that amount, and their reports began to propose minimum-wage legislation, to ensure a living wage for men and thus provide the basis for female domesticity in the working class. In national hearings on labor conditions, held in 1883, congressmen repeatedly asked witnesses whether workingmen's wages enabled them to marry and support wives and children.[19]

But the Republican party as a whole rejected measures such as minimum-wage legislation, which—like full suffrage for women and other proposals that arose from the most progressive interpretations of domestic ideology—most viewed as far too radical. Agitation for such legislation became the province of labor leaders and third-party movements. By the 1880s, then, Republicans' insistence on the benefits of the tariff for Americans' "home lives" can be viewed in part as a defense of a statist industrial policy, which was under attack by advocates of smaller government. But viewed from the left, by those who sought more vigorous measures to mitigate the hardships of industrialization, Republican tariff arguments largely served to defend the status quo. Flowery rhetoric about "protection to American women" helped stave off more radical proposals for government intervention in the economy that would have helped male workers earn a living wage.

INDIAN POLICY

Federal Indian policy in the postwar years, like many Republican initiatives, was influenced by a zealous constituency of northern middle-class Protestants. President Grant made much-celebrated appointments of Quaker Indian agents in 1869; more significantly, an influential group of United States senators led by Henry Dawes shepherded through legislation in the 1880s to bring domesticity, "civilization," and citizenship to native peoples. Above all they worked to abolish collective landholding under the reservation system, which Dawes likened to "Henry George's system"—that is, socialism. As a central part of their mission Republicans sought to enforce the proper roles of Indian men and women in relation to each other, to labor, and to land. There is no better example of Republicans' combination of domestic ideology with race uplift and the Protestant work ethic than the campaign for Indian assimilation.[20]

"Each head of a family should be encouraged to select and improve a homestead," recommended a (Republican-appointed) federal Peace Commission in 1868. "Let the women be taught to weave, to sew, and to knit. Let polygamy be punished." In debates over the Dawes Act, United States senators repeatedly referred to the need to promote domesticity and what one called "this trinity upon which all civilization depends—family, and home, and property." An advisory letter from John Wesley Powell, read into the *Congressional Record*, undertook a lengthy explanation of the connections among these ideas. The basic problem with Indian kinship, Powell argued, was its extended, complex nature: under traditional clan systems "husband and wife continue to belong to different families," weakening the marriage tie and preventing husbands and fathers from serving as proper breadwinners. What was needed, Powell and many senators claimed, was "the simplicity of family organization under monogamic marriage and inheritance." Thus, Republicans sought simultaneously to promote the domestic family as an economic unit and reconstruct Indian manhood and womanhood.[21]

Reformers were especially keen to stamp out Indian customs of arranged marriage, easy separation, and polygyny, the latter a concern that mirrored their obsession with Mormon plural marriage. Chester Arthur's Secretary of the interior, Henry Teller, created special Indian courts that placed the punishment of male polygamists at the top of their agenda. Closely related to this goal was the insistence that Indian men fulfill a proper breadwinner role, usually through farming. Over and over, supporters of the Dawes Act argued that domesticity was the spur to male labor and successful ownership of private property. As a member of the Board of Indian Commissioners wrote, their goal was to develop "the sanctities of family life and an allegiance to the laws which grow naturally out of the family." Those laws included, first and foremost, "the desire for property"; "family life"—including female dependency—was what "ennobled that desire."[22]

Republicans who sought to raise Indian men to a "higher manhood" took a parallel approach to Indian womanhood. "The condition of women is the test of progress," declared Hampton Institute principal S. C. Armstrong. "What girls are, mothers are, and mothers make the home." Indian girls at government-funded boarding schools invariably learned sewing, cooking, and housekeeping skills while their male counterparts took up farming, animal husbandry, and construction. In a similar vein Senator Dawes proposed sending "families of young married people" among the Indians to "teach them how to set up housekeeping and be men and women." The specificity of this agenda could be astounding: one teacher measured progress in the regularity with which Indian women served meals at specific hours of the day, as well as their proper "use of crockery." In 1890 the Office of Indian Affairs set up a field matron program to inculcate domestic values.[23]

Republican constituents and policy makers were invariably behind these projects. "As I look around me here I feel lonesome," joked a Cleveland administration official at the 1885 Conference of the Friends of the Indian. "You are nearly all Republicans." (The remark drew a laugh and an earnest attempt by the chairman to point out Democrats in the audience. He found three.) Republican presidential administrations provided the strongest support for assimilationist legislation; all of Dawes's allies in the Senate were Republicans, most from the Northeast. In response, as on an array of other issues, Democrats ridiculed Republican "theories and fancies" and suggested that it was not the federal government's business whether Indian men kept more than one wife, or how those wives used crockery. Some such arguments were bluntly racist; one Democratic congressman doubted whether the government could "take a people after centuries of barbarism and hurl them into the terrible struggle with civilization." "To tell them to work or die," he asserted, "is simply to say die." But on occasion Democrats sounded tolerant—even multicultural—in their defense of Indians' right to do as they pleased. A Texas congressman proposed that nomadic groups "be situated with reference to their own convenience, their own hopes and interests . . . out upon the plains where their wild habits would not be interrupted." "The government of the United States includes people who speak five hundred different languages," declared Senator John Morgan of Alabama. He argued that the federal government could impose no universal system of family or labor on such a diverse population and that Indian ways should be respected. "I would take," Morgan said tartly, "the Indian's experience in reference to the support of his family on the land or by herd grazing or hunting before I would take the experience of any white man who does not understand the subject." Such Democrats defended Indians' manhood rights as parallel to those of white men. However self-interested their arguments (especially when constituents wanted local Indians shipped somewhere else) they contrasted starkly with the goals of Republican reformers, who emphasized government's "moral obligation" to foster civilization.[24]

This brief case study of Indian policy suggests that Republican domesticity was not mere rhetoric, promulgated on the stump in tough campaign years. Reforming the Indian family was a central goal of Republican citizens who lobbied for policy change; of a powerful cadre of the party's senators and congressmen; of cabinet officials in Republican administrations; and of Republican appointees in such bureaucratic agencies as the Office of Indian Affairs and government-funded boarding schools. Domestic ideology, then, was not lip service but an integral part of what Republicans hoped to achieve and how they understood themselves. The majority of Democrats, by contrast, rejected the idea that government should enforce or encourage any particular model of marriage or family life. Debates over domestic ideology and manhood rights had, of course, broad regional, social, and cultural dimensions beyond the electoral system, many of which historians have explored. But they had a sharp partisan dimension as well, and that is what historians have missed.

REPUBLICAN INITIATIVES IN THE STATES

The centrality of gender in national policy debates suggests that domestic ideology might also have played a crucial role at the state level, where many aspects of citizenship and almost all family laws were determined. A cursory review suggests that this is the case. Domestic ideology carried powerful impulses toward the control of sexuality, and James Mohr has shown that the first great wave of United States antiabortion legislation passed between 1860 and 1880, peaking during Reconstruction. A law passed by Connecticut's 1860 legislature (overwhelmingly Republican in both branches) served as the model for most other states after the war. Republican Reconstruction governments were the first to address the issue in the South. In the same years some northern states passed new measures to stamp out prostitution—a development that takes us back to the federal level. There, efforts at sex regulation were capped by the Comstock Act of 1873, which banned from the mail any devices or information intended for "obscene purposes," including contraception and abortion. Two years later the Page Act banned the importation of "immoral" women, by implication a move to exclude female Chinese immigrants but in fact addressing the entire trade in international prostitution. The Page Act was a significant step in the regulation of both immigration and sex, and it might also be considered in light of trade policy. Republicans, who championed high tariffs for "protection to the home," also protected American morality by banning the importation of sex workers.[25]

While the Comstock Act sought to place severe limits on reproductive choice, in other instances Republicans invoked domestic ideology to advance the cause of women's rights. The party's emphasis on male self-control and female moral influence translated into breakthrough legislation that shifted certain powers away from male household heads and recognized new rights for married women. The first such law passed in Massachusetts under an American (Know-Nothing) administration in 1855; in addition to wives' property rights it established the power of the state to garnish divorced men's wages for child support. New York's famous Earnings Act of 1860 asserted married women's right to run businesses, own property they acquired by trade or labor, and claim custody of their children. It was passed by a legislature with enormous Republican majorities in both houses; in 1861 Ohio adopted a similar package, sponsored by none other than Salmon P. Chase. On the eve of the Civil War, a southern writer in *DeBow's Review* observed with alarm that northern Republicans were beginning to "divide the household into separate interests," and a proslavery Democrat warned that "the principle of Republicanism" was "to meddle with the domestic institutions of other States, and to meddle with family arrangements in their own."[26]

During the heyday of Reconstruction two-thirds of the states passed married women's earnings acts, and some began to recognize other forms of female autonomy, such as women's voting rights in school elections. Reconstruction also brought the first state-level legislative support for women's higher education. Following a sensational Illinois case in which a minister had his wife committed to an insane asylum because she disagreed with his religious views, states began to recognize a wife's right to keep her own conscience. Enhancement of women's rights—however limited in retrospect—was also a marked feature of Reconstruction governments in the South. New married women's property acts brought state laws in closer alignment with innovations in the North, and southern women, married or not, gained substantial powers to charge men with rape and sexual abuse. The partisan configuration of these legislative initiatives is clear. During the extraordinary legislative surge of the 1870s, very little legislation passed that was not Republican-inspired and Republican-sponsored; a decade later, Redeemer Democrats overrode many of the southern laws.[27]

The women's rights component of Republican domesticity was most overt, then, in the crisis of secession, war, and Reconstruction; it faded in the 1880s, a trend Morton Keller noted two decades ago. Only in 1872 and 1876 did the party's national platforms call for "respectful consideration" of women's "honest demands . . . for additional rights," a vague statement, but more than the party granted later on. By the late 1880s both women's rights advocates and reformers who sought new government initiatives expressed frustration with the party, which continued to promote domesticity but did so in ways that looked increasingly hidebound. Thousands of progressive voters and activists abandoned Republicanism to take up third-party crusades. While a full analysis of such movements is beyond the scope of this essay, certain commonalties between two of them, Prohibitionism and western Populism, are worth noting briefly. Both groups were made up largely of former Republicans who entered politics in opposition to the GOP; both invoked domestic ideology as the justification for new extensions of government power; both included women in highly visible positions as speakers, delegates, and even candidates for office.[28]

For Prohibitionists antiliquor work was the key to women's empowerment within the family, addressing the related problems of male alcoholism, domestic violence, and the liberty of male breadwinners to spend their paychecks without reference to their dependents' needs. By ending the liquor trade and enfranchising women Prohibitionists hoped to use the state to set new limits on men's power. Some Republicans agreed, and in states such as Iowa, Kansas, and Wisconsin they led the fight for Prohibition. (Some of the same Republicans pushed through municipal and school suffrage for women and strengthened laws against statutory rape.) But other party leaders argued that Prohibitionists were meddling with male prerogatives. Along with Democrats they denounced female suffrage and Prohibitionism, distinguishing between voluntary temperance—men exercising their right to choose—and the efforts of a so-called women's party to interfere with male prerogatives. In other words, faced with an upstart party that proposed new extensions of government power, Republicans began to sound distinctly like Democrats in their defense of manhood rights.[29]

Populist extensions of the old Republican domestic ideology were more complicated. The party's southern wing consisted largely of former Democrats. Even outside the South Populists drew less purely on Republican constituencies than Prohibitionists had, and fusion deals with Democrats further muddied the waters. (Significantly, it was in the wake of Populism that the national Democratic party began to advocate measures such as the progressive income tax, becoming for the first time a state-building party and starting oh-so-tentatively down the path toward the New Deal.) Nonetheless a key issue for Populists, as for Prohibitionists, was whether government powers should expand to "protect the home." For Populists the chief threat to male breadwinners and their female dependents was poverty. Calling for an income tax on the wealthy, state ownership of railroads and telegraphs, and other interventions in the economy, they drew powerfully on the rhetoric of domesticity, with significant attention to women's rights. Populist conventions in almost every state outside the South endorsed women's suffrage; the only successful suffrage campaigns of the 1890s, in Colorado and Idaho, succeeded through Populist sponsorship and support. In these states, especially, Populists put on the old Republican mantle, though they went further in the direction of both state building and women's rights than the GOP had been willing to do. Faced with this challenge, Republicans characterized Populists as a party of "hysterical men and unsexed women." They began to make overt calls for the defense of political manhood and argued that Populist measures would undermine men's prerogatives as voters, property owners, and household heads. Fixing on Colorado, where Populists had enfranchised women, Republicans linked that measure to other "socialistic, communistic" schemes. Such Republicans retreated from their position as the state-building party and as champions of domestic ideology at the same time.[30]

The tangled history of partisan conflict over domesticity and manhood rights sheds light on several key questions. Richard McCormick has suggested that historians of nineteenth-century politics face a crisis in that we do not clearly understand the relationships between voter decisions, partisanship, and policy. Some historians have gone so far as to suggest that elections and policymaking were entirely unrelated activities. If this were true, Paula Baker might be correct in arguing that the era's partisan women were "either stupidly willing to waste their time or the dupes of men who extracted free political labor."[31] Did party loyalists participate in a "golden age" of democracy, or were they suckers and fools? As historians mediate between these claims, attention to domestic ideology may help reconnect the separate threads of voting, campaigning, and policymaking. The fact that Republicans and Democrats fought over the distribution of power within families and the relationship of families to the state suggests a reason why major-party politics had substantive appeal to a broad array of citizens, women as well as men.

Understanding the partisan dimensions of domestic ideology might also help link the vast and growing literature on law, the family, and social movements to events and agendas in the electoral sphere. The proper size and scope of government was *the* chief issue over which United States parties fought in the second half of the nineteenth century, and the prospect of a more activist state was both attacked and defended in terms of its alleged impact on the home. It is important to stress, again, that Republican advocates of domesticity sometimes supported women's rights (by our modern definition) and sometimes did not. While they passed an array of laws that empowered women—especially at the state level—they also introduced the Comstock Act, stripped the vote from women in Utah, and supported dubious gender reeducation programs at Indian boarding schools.

The ambiguous legacy of Republican policies helps explain why feminist historians have largely missed the partisan dimensions of domesticity. Such historians have searched the electoral arena for clear support of women's equal rights, and that vision had as yet no partisan champion. Even at the time, certain questions divided ardent supporters of domestic ideology who disagreed over how women's interests should be advanced. Many Republicans argued for the liberalization of divorce laws, for example, and by the end of Reconstruction almost every state had set up a judicial divorce process to make it easier for women to escape miserable marriages. But other Republicans argued that loose statutes abetted male adultery and allowed promiscuous husbands to shirk their responsibilities. (The position of woman "has risen with Christian marriage," wrote one divorce critic. "It has been her strongest defense, her greatest safeguard.") Republicans' efforts to "protect the home" left a conflicted legacy, clearly visible in early-twentieth-century debates between supporters of the Equal Rights Amendment and labor activists who sought to protect female workers with gender-specific legislation. Today's antiabortion and pro–welfare rights movements—both of which want to use government powers to protect the family, but in dramatically different ways—are heirs to disparate parts of the same late-nineteenth-century Republican agenda. Of course domestic ideology also carried racial and class biases, privileging the interests of nonwage-earning women and reinforcing a male breadwinner model of the family. Today's feminists have had difficulty recognizing such a legacy, much less making effective use of it.

Yet a limited enhancement of women's rights—as defined by the tenets of domestic ideology—*did* characterize the early Republican party, especially in its state-building phase. During the Civil War and Reconstruction, when Republicans sought substantial increases in government power, they emphasized women's protection and empowerment. As they ceased to take on new projects, party leaders placed greater emphasis on assisting breadwinners through pensions and tariffs. By the late 1880s and 1890s, confronted by parties that proposed new expansions of federal power, Republicans took a hostile stance on both women's rights and government activism, becoming more conservative in relation to government activism and simultaneously defending manhood rights. Both statists and conservatives, then—the latter including Democrats throughout the era and Republicans toward the end—drew persistent links between state building and the promotion of women's rights. Advocates of women's suffrage found themselves stuck with the party most vigorously engaged in state building, or sometimes the one least engaged in state dismantling. In periods when the latter was the case, women's rights initiatives tended to stall.

Understanding the role of "family values" in nineteenth-century partisan politics may thus help us better understand some of the impulses behind American state building, as well as the various forms of antistatism that have been, as Julian Zelizer shows elsewhere in this volume, a persistent theme in American political thought. Manhood rights—ultimately a defense of patriarchal power—began to lose ground at the very moment Americans began building a modern bureaucratic state. The party that ushered in that revolution was fiercely devoted to a new definition of family relations; while Republicans issued no clarion call for women's liberation, they denied that the state and male household heads were locked in a zero-sum game, in which increased powers for the former threatened the autonomy of the latter. Instead, Republicans (and more radically, their Prohibitionist and Populist successors) believed that an activist government should support and protect families. That idea offered policy makers a rationale not only to discipline men and women into their proper roles but also, perhaps more significantly in the long run, to liberate women. The latter possibility was even more disturbing to the era's antistatists than the former, as shown by panicked warnings about the prospect of unruly "unsexed women," issued whenever policy makers proposed new measures for the public welfare. Evidence from the nineteenth century suggests that even today would-be state builders, whatever their priorities, are likely to be attacked for interfering with manhood rights and upsetting traditional power relationships within the family. Such state builders may often be forced, then, to confront the fact that they can.

NOTES

1. The epigraph quotation appears in Samuel P. Hays, *American Political History As Social Analysis* (Knoxville, Tenn.: University of Tennessee Press, 1980), 248. For indispensable advice I am grateful to the organizers of the "Democracy in America" conference and to all of the participants, as well as to Reuel Schiller, Miriam Cohen, Clyde Griffen, participants in the Women's Studies First Fridays series at Vassar College, and Mark Seidl. In addition, Ron Formisano provided especially helpful advice on antebellum politics. Mistakes and reckless speculations remain my own responsibility.

2. Recent treatments include Nancy F. Cott, *Public Vows: A History of Marriage and the Nation* (Cambridge, Mass.: Harvard University Press, 2000); Lori D. Ginzberg, *Women and the Work of Benevolence: Morality, Politics, and Class in the Nineteenth-Century United States* (New Haven, Conn.: Yale University Press, 1990); Nancy Isenberg, *Sex and Citizenship in Antebellum America* (Chapel Hill, N.C.: University of North Carolina Press, 1998); Linda K. Kerber, *No Constitutional Right to Be Ladies: Women and the Obligations of Citizenship* (New York: Hill and Wang, 1998); Alison M. Parker and Stephanie Cole, eds., *Women and the Unstable State in Nineteenth-Century America* (College Station, Tex.: Texas A&M University Press, 2000); Mary P. Ryan, *Women in Public: Between Banners and Ballots, 1825–1880* (Baltimore: Johns Hopkins University Press, 1990); and Kathryn Kish Sklar, "The Historical Foundations of Women's Power in the Creation of the American Welfare State, 1830–1930," in *Mothers of a New World: Maternalist Politics and the Origins of Welfare States*, ed. Seth Koven and Sonya Michel (New York: Routledge, 1993). Overviews of the field include Suzanne Lebsock, "Women and American Politics, 1880–1920," in *Women, Politics, and Change*, ed. Louise A. Tilly and Patricia Gurin (New York: Russell Sage

Foundation, 1990), 35–32; and Jane Sherron de Hart, "Women's History and Political History: Bridging Old Divides," in *American Political History: Essays on the State of the Discipline*, ed. John F. Marszalek and Wilson D. Miscamble (Notre Dame, Ind.: University of Notre Dame Press, 1997), 25–53. Historians such as Ellen Carol DuBois, who emphasize "formal" politics, have long been in the minority: see "Politics and Culture in Women's History," *Feminist Studies* 6 (1980): 26–64. The argument that women were anti- or apartisan before the 1900s draws on the work of Paula Baker, "The Domestication of Politics: Women and American Political Society, 1780–1920," *American Historical Review* (hereafter *AHR*) 89 (1984): 620–47, and Baker, *The Moral Frameworks of Public Life: Gender, Politics, and the State in Rural New York, 1830–1930* (New York: Oxford University Press, 1991). See also Michael McGerr, "Political Style and Women's Power, 1830–1930," *Journal of American History* (hereafter *JAH*) 77 (1990): 864–85. Recent reconsiderations include Norma Basch, "Marriage, Morals, and Politics in the Election of 1828," *JAH* 80 (1993): 890–913; Melanie Gustafson, Kristie Miller, and Elisabeth Israels Perry, eds., *We Have Come to Stay: American Women and Political Parties, 1880–1960* (Albuquerque, N.Mex.: University of New Mexico Press, 1999); Elizabeth R. Varon, *We Mean to Be Counted: White Women and Politics in Antebellum Virginia* (Chapel Hill, N.C.: University of North Carolina Press, 1998); Melanie S. Gustafson, *Women and the Republican Party, 1854–1924* (Urbana, Ill.: University of Illinois Press, 2001); Jo Freeman, *A Room at a Time: How Women Entered Party Politics* (Lanham, Md.: Rowman and Littlefield, 2000); and Rebecca Edwards, *Angels in the Machinery: Gender in American Party Politics from the Civil War to the Progressive Era* (New York: Oxford University Press, 1997).

3. See recent debates and surveys of the field in Ronald P. Formisano, "The Invention of the Enthnocultural Interpretation," *AHR* 99 (1994): 453–77; Ronald P. Formisano, Mark Voss-Hubbard, Michael F. Holt, and Paula Baker, "Round Table: Alternatives to the Party System in the 'Party Period,' 1830–1890," *JAH* 86 (1999): 93–166; Joel H. Silbey, "The State and Practice of American Political History at the Millennium: The Nineteenth Century as a Test Case," *Journal of Policy History* 11 (1999): 1–30; and Elisabeth Israels Perry, "Men Are from the Gilded Age, Women Are from the Progressive Era," *Journal of the Gilded Age and Progressive Era* 1.1 (January 2002): 25–48. Glenn C. Altschuler and Stuart M. Blumin question the significance of politics for ordinary Americans in *Rude Republic: Americans and Their Politics in the Nineteenth Century* (Princeton, N.J.: Princeton University Press, 2000). Quotations from Baker, "Domestication," 628, and McGerr, "Political Style," 866–67.

4. Formisano et al., "Round Table." As Formisano notes, the parties were not competitive at the state level in large swaths of the postbellum United States, as key national questions were fought on regional lines. See Richard Franklin Bensei's provocative formulation in *The Political Economy of American Industrialization, 1877–1900* (Cambridge: Cambridge University Press, 2000).

5. On developments before the rise of the Republican party see Daniel Walker Howe, "The Evangelical Movement and Political Culture in the North during the Second Party System," *JAH* 77 (1991): 1216–39; Basch, "Marriage, Morals, and Politics;" Varon, *We Mean to Be Counted*.

6. Barbara Welter, "The Cult of True Womanhood," in *Dimity Convictions: The American Woman in the Nineteenth Century* (Athens, Ohio: Ohio University Press, 1976); Mary P. Ryan, *Cradle of the Middle Class: The Family in Oneida County, New York, 1790–1865* (Cambridge: Cambridge University Press, 1981); Nancy Hewitt, *Women's Activism and Social Change: Rochester, New York, 1822–1872* (Ithaca, N.Y.: Cornell University Press, 1984); and Stephen Mintz and Susan Kellogg, *Domestic Revolutions: A Social History of American Family Life* (New York: Free Press, 1988), chap. 3. My arguments here are influenced also by Paul Johnson, *A Shopkeeper's Millennium: Society and Revivals in Rochester, New York: Hill and Wang, 1815–1837* (New York, Hill and Wang, 1978); Cindy Sondik Aron, "The Evolution of the Middle Class," in *The Companion to Nineteenth-Century America*, ed. William L. Barney (New York, 2001); Linda K. Kerber, "Separate Spheres, Female Worlds, Woman's Place: The Rhetoric of Women's History," *JAH* 75 (1988): 9–39; Nancy F. Cott, "On Men's History and Women's History," in *Meanings for Manhood: Constructions of Masculinity in Victorian America*, ed. Mark C. Carnes and Clyde Griffen (Chicago: University of Chicago Press, 1990), 205–11.

7. Joan Smyth Iversen, "A Debate on the American Home: The Antipolygamy Controversy, 1880–1890," in *American Sexual Politics: Sex, Gender, and Race since the Civil War*, ed. John C. Fout and Maura Shaw Tantillo (Chicago: University Chicago Press, 1990), 123–40; Sarah Barringer Gordon, " 'The Liberty of Self-Degradation': Polygamy, Woman Suffrage and Consent in Nineteenth-Century America," *JAH* 83 (1996): 815–47; Cott, *Public Vows*, 73–75, 111–20; Michael Grossberg, *Governing the Hearth: Law and the Family in Nineteenth-Century America* (Chapel Hill, N.C.: University of North Carolina Press, 1985), 123–26; Ronald P. Formisano, *The Birth of Mass Political Parties* (Princeton, N.J.: Princeton University Press, 1971), 158–60; quotations from Joel Silbey, "The Surge of Republican Power: Partisan Antipathy, American Social Conflict, and the Coming of the Civil War," in *Essays on American Antebellum Politics, 1840–1860*, ed. Stephen E. Maizlish and John J. Kushma (Arlington, Tex.: Texas A&M Press, 1982), 220; *New York Times*, January 19, 1857. See also *New York Times*, May 5, 1855, and *New York Herald*, May 4, 1855, May 3, 1857. Southern Democrat Robert Taylor advised Buchanan, "I believe that we can supersede the Negro-Mania with the almost universal excitements of an Anti-Mormon Crusade." Norman F. Furniss, *The Mormon Conflict, 1850–1859* (New Haven, Conn.: Yale University Press, 1960), 62–94.

8. In 1856 and 1857 Justin Morrill of Vermont introduced a Senate bill outlawing polygamy in United States territories; amid laughter, Democrats proposed sending it to the Committee on Naval Affairs, since sailors had a woman in every port. Morrill got revenge when Lincoln signed the law in 1862. George Edmunds (R-Vt.) sponsored much subsequent legislation. *Congressional Globe*, 34th Cong., 1st and 2d sess., 1491, 1501, and 35th Cong. 1st sess., 184–85, 2114; Grossberg, *Governing the Hearth*, 120–26; Iversen, "Debate on the American Home."

9. Cott, *Public Vows*, 62–63; Stephanie McCurry, *Masters of Small Worlds: Yeoman Farmers, Gender Relations, and the Political Culture of the Antebellum South* (New York: Oxford University Press, 1995); Lee Ann Whites, "The Civil

War as a Crisis in Gender," in *Divided Houses: Gender and the Civil War*, ed. Catherine Clinton and Nina Silber (New York: Oxford University Press, 1992), 3–21; Victoria E. Bynum, *Unruly Women: The Politics of Social and Sexual Control in the Old South* (Chapel Hill, N.C.: University of North Carolina Press, 1992); Peter W. Bardaglio, *Reconstructing the Household: Families, Sex, and the Law in the Nineteenth-Century South* (Chapel Hill, N.C.: University of North Carolina Press, 1995). Quotations from George Fitzhugh, *Cannibals All! Or, Slaves Without Masters*, ed. C. Vann Woodward (1857; Cambridge, Mass.: Belknap Press, 1961), 212–14; "Happy Homes" in *New York Press*, July 19, 1888. On the political culture of slave masters, see Kenneth S. Greenberg, *Masters and Statesmen: The Political Culture of American Slavery* (Baltimore: Johns Hopkins University Press, 1985).

10. Amy Dru Stanley, *From Bondage to Contract: Wage Labor, Marriage, and the Market in the Age of Slave Emancipation* (Cambridge: Cambridge University Press, 1998), 55–59, though my view of Republican motives is more positive than Stanley's; Cott, *Public Vows*, 85–96; Barry A. Crouch, *The Freedmen's Bureau and Black Texans* (Austin, Tex.: University of Texas Press, 1992), 58–59; Sara Rapport, "The Freedmen's Bureau as a Legal Agent for Black Men and Women in Georgia, 1865–1868," *Georgia Historical Quarterly* 73 (spring 1989): 37–43; Laura F. Edwards, *Gendered Strife and Confusion: The Political Culture of Reconstruction* (Urbana, Ill.: University of Illinois Press, 1997); Mary J. Farmer, " 'Because They Are Women': Gender and the Virginia Freedmen's Bureau's 'War on Dependency,' " in *The Freedmen's Bureau and Reconstruction: Reconsiderations*, ed. Paul A. Cimbala and Randall M. Miller (New York: Fordham University Press, 1999), 161–92.

11. Fisk quoted in Dorothy Sterling, ed., *We Are Your Sisters: Black Women in the Nineteenth Century* (New York: W. W. Norton, 1984), 319–20; Rapport, "The Freedmen's Bureau," 38. On black women's resistance to northern white Republicans' domestic ideals, see Elsa Barkley Brown, "Negotiating and Transforming the Public Sphere: African-American Political Life in the Transition from Slavery to Freedom," *Public Culture* 7 (1994): 116–38.

12. Theda Skocpol, *Protecting Soldiers and Mothers: The Political Origins of Social Policy in the United States* (Cambridge, Mass.: Belknap Press, 1992); William H. Glasson, *Federal Military Pensions in the United States* (New York: Oxford University Press, 1918), 128, 144; *Proceedings of the National Union Republican Convention, 20–21 May 1868* (Chicago: National Republican Committee, 1868), 67.

13. Megan McClintock, "Civil War Pensions and the Reconstruction of Union Families," *JAH* 83 (1996): 456–80.

14. Patrick J. Kelly, *Creating a National Home: Building the Veterans' Welfare State, 1860–1900* (Cambridge, Mass.: Harvard University Press, 1997); John P. Irish quoted in R. Hal Williams, "Dry Bones and Dead Language: The Democratic Party in the Gilded Age," in *The Gilded Age*, 2d ed., ed. H. Wayne Morgan (Syracuse, N.Y.: Syracuse University Press, 1963), 141.

15. On the political significance of the tariff, see Joanne Reitano, *The Tariff Question in the Gilded Age: The Great Debate of 1888* (University Park, Pa.: Pennsylvania University Press, 1994); Bensel, *Political Economy*; and H. Wayne

Morgan, *From Hayes to McKinley: National Party Politics, 1877–1896* (Syracuse, N.Y.: Syracuse University Press, 1969).

16. Reitano, *Tariff Question*; Giles B. Stebbins, *The American Protectionist's Manual* (Detroit: T. Nourse, 1883); Harrison in *Indianapolis Journal*, September 16, 1888 (reprinted nationwide); investigative reports, also widely reprinted, include William P. Frye, *What Senator Frye Saw in Europe* (Boston: Home Market Club, 1888), and Nathaniel McKay, *Free Trade Toilers* (New York: Gildersleeve, 1892); see *Minneapolis Tribune*, October 5, 1892; *Los Angeles Times*, October 11, 1892; campaign poster in Robert W. Cherny, *American Politics in the Gilded Age, 1868–1900* (Wheeling, Ill.: Harlan Davidson, 1997), 84–85.

17. Harrison in *New York Press*, July 19, 1888; Rebecca Edwards, *Angels*, 68–82. As I argue in *Angels*, Democrats began for the first time in the tariff debates to acknowledge women's influence as consumers; Kristi Andersen suggests that male voters in the 1920s supported high tariffs more than did women. On consumer influence, see Meg Jacobs's chapter 10 in this volume, and Kristi Andersen, *After Suffrage: Women in Partisan and Electoral Politics before the New Deal* (Chicago: University of Chicago Press, 1996), 159–60.

18. Gustafson, *Women and the Republican Party*.

19. Stanley, *From Bondage to Contract*, 148–74.

20. Frederick E. Hoxie, *A Final Promise: The Campaign to Assimilate the Indians, 1880–1920* (Lincoln, Nebr.: University of Nebraska Press, 1984); Dawes quoted in *Proceedings of the Third Annual Meeting of the Lake Mohonk Conference of Friends of the Indian, October 7–9 1885* (Philadelphia: Indian Rights Association, 1886), 43.

21. Congressional debates in Wilcomb E. Washburn, ed., *The American Indian and the United States* (Westport, Conn.: Greenwood Press, 1979), quotations from 1730, 1751–53; see also Hoxie, *Final Promise*; David Wallace Adams, *Education for Extinction: American Indians and the Boarding School Experience* (Lawrence, Kans.: University of Kansas Press, 1995), 173–81.

22. Merrill Gates quoted in Francis Paul Prucha, *The Great Father: The United States Government and the American Indians* (Lincoln, Nebr.: University of Nebraska Press, 1984), 621–23.

23. Hoxie, *Final Promise*, 33–36, 57–60; Adams, *Education for Extinction*, 173–81; Carol Devins, " 'If We Get the Girls, We Get the Race': Missionary Education of Native American Girls," and Lisa E. Emmerich, " 'Right in the Midst of My Own People': Native American Women and the Field Matron Program," both in *American Nations: Encounters in Indian Country, 1850 to the Present*, ed. Frederick E. Hoxie, Peter C. Mancall, and James H. Merrell (New York: Routledge, 2001), 156–71 and 142–55.

24. John H. Oberly quoted in *Proceedings of the Third Annual Meeting*, 59; Charles Hooker (D-Miss.), George Vest (D-Mo.), John Reagan (D-Tex.), and John Morgan (D-Ala.) quoted in Washburn, ed., *American Indian*, 1673, 1829, 1647, 1709–12; John Kasson (R-Iowa) quoted in Hoxie, *Final Promise*, 37. Hoxie demonstrates the shifts in Indian policy as western Republicans took the lead between 1900 and 1910, followed by Democrats in the Wilson years. On Indian assimilation, as on every other issue discussed in this essay, policy makers divided along regional as well as party lines. Some of these divisions were *intra*party: Teller's

agenda for Indian policy differed from Dawes's, and a vocal group of Kansas Republicans held views closer to those I characterize here as Democratic. The larger pattern of partisan conflict was, I believe, fairly consistent despite such exceptions.

25. James C. Mohr, *Abortion in America: The Origins and Evolution of National Policy 1800–1900* (New York: Oxford University Press, 1978), esp. 200–225; Philip D. Swenson, "Illinois," in *Radical Republicans in the North: State Politics during Reconstruction*, ed. James C. Mohr (Baltimore: Johns Hopkins University Press, 1976), 106; Nicola Beisel, *Imperiled Innocents: Anthony Comstock and Family Reproduction in Victorian America* (Princeton, N.J.: Princeton University Press, 1997); Heywood Brown and Margaret Leech, *Anthony Comstock: Roundsman of the Lord* (New York: A. & C. Boni, 1927), 130–34.

26. Norma Basch, *In the Eyes of the Law: Women, Marriage, and Property in Nineteenth-Century New York* (Ithaca, N.Y.: Cornell University Press, 1982); Elizabeth Bowles Warbasse, *The Changing Legal Rights of Married Women, 1800–1861* (New York: Garland, 1987); John R. Mulkern, *The Know-Nothing Party in Massachusetts: The Rise and Fall of a People's Movement* (Boston: Northeastern University Press, 1990), 111; Elizabeth Cady Stanton, Susan B. Anthony, and Matilda Jocelyn Gage, *History of Woman Suffrage*, vol. 3 (Rochester, N.Y.: Susan B. Anthony, 1886), state-by-state review of legislation, esp. 379, 483, 543–48, 636–39, 964. Southerners quoted in Silbey, "Surge of Republican Power," 217, 226, and Bardaglio, *Reconstructing the Household*; 117–18. Data on partisan control of state legislatures are from *New York Tribune Almanac* (New York, 1860–1875). On nativism, sexuality, and women's rights, see also the suggestive chapter 5, "Population, Culture, and Ideology," in Paul Bourke and Donald DeBats, *Washington County: Politics and Community in Antebellum America* (Baltimore: Johns Hopkins University Press, 1995).

27. Stanley, *From Bondage to Contract*, 198–217; Richard H. Abbott, "Massachusetts," George W. Blackburn, "Michigan," and Robert J. Dykstra, "Iowa," in Mohr, *Radical Republicans*, 6, 126–28, 187; Stanton, Anthony, and Gage, *History of Woman Suffrage*, as in n. 26 above; Grossberg, *Governing the Hearth*, chap. 7; Laura Edwards, *Gendered Strife and Confusion*; Bardaglio, *Reconstructing the Household*; Joan Hoff, *Law, Gender, and Injustice: A Legal History of U.S. Women* (New York: New York University Press, 1990), chaps. 4–5. On the Civil War and Reconstruction as United States history's "leading exhibit of a [legislative] surge driven by one party" see David R. Mayhew, "Parties, Elections, Moods, and Lawmaking Surges," in *Encyclopedia of the American Legislative System*, ed. Joel Silbey (New York: Charles Scribner, 1994), 890. Lawmakers were unwilling to grant wives control of their own bodies: marital rape was not a crime until the late twentieth century. Nonetheless, after the Civil War new standards began to emerge in the courts. Reconstruction judges dismissed divorce petitions from husbands whose wives refused sex, arguing that such refusal did not constitute cruelty or desertion; a husband's excessive sexual demands *did* begin to count as cruelty when they endangered a wife's health. Reconstruction judges intervened more vigorously in cases of incest, while Redeemers in the South permitted maximum autonomy to male household heads (even those clearly guilty of incest). Similar patterns emerged in recognition of cruelty to children. Connections among

social movements, legislators, judges, and state agencies need further exploration. Jill Elaine Hasday, "Contest and Consent: A Legal History of Marital Rape," *California Law Review* 88 (October 2000): 1375–1505; Bardaglio, *Reconstructing the Household*; Elizabeth Pleck, *Domestic Tyranny: The Making of Social Policy against Family Violence from Colonial Times to the Present* (New York: Oxford University Press, 1987), 49–96; Linda Gordon, *Heroes of Their Own Lives: The Politics and History of Family Violence: Boston, 1880–1960* (New York: Viking, 1988), chaps. 1 and 2.

28. Morton Keller, *Affairs of State: Public Life in Late-Nineteenth-Century America* (Cambridge, Mass.: Belknap Press, 1977), 158–61; Edwards, *Angels*, chaps. 2, 5–6.

29. Pleck, *Domestic Tyranny*; Ballard C. Campbell, *Representative Democracy: Public Policy and Midwestern Legislatures in the Late Nineteenth Century* (Cambridge, Mass.: Harvard University Press, 1980), 92–121; Ruth Bordin, *Woman and Temperance: The Quest for Power and Liberty* (Philadelphia: Temple University Press, 1981), and Bordin, *Frances Willard: A Biography* (Chapel Hill, N.C.: University of North Carolina Press, 1986). See also Rebecca Edwards, *Angels*, chap. 2. There may have been unifying gender themes among progressive third parties that emerged in the wake of Republicanism, including the Greenback-Labor coalition and others I do not consider here.

30. Rebecca Edwards, *Angels*, chap. 5; Michael Lewis Goldberg, *An Army of Women: Gender and Politics in Gilded Age Kansas* (Baltimore: Johns Hopkins University Press, 1997); Robert C. McMath, Jr., *American Populism: A Social History, 1877–1898* (New York: Hill and Wang, 1993) 169–71; Mari Jo Buhle, *Women and American Socialism, 1870–1920* (Urbana, Ill.: University of Illinois Press, 1981). On the Knights of Labor origins of Populist women's activism, see Susan Levine, "Labor's True Woman: Domesticity and Equal Rights in the Knights of Labor," *JAH* 70 (1983): 323–49.

31. Richard McCormick, *The Party Period and Public Policy* (New York: Oxford University Press, 1986), 197–98; Formisano on the voting-policy split and Baker on women, both in Formisano et al., "Round Table," 106–7, 164.

Chapter Eight

THE CASE FOR COURTS

LAW AND POLITICAL DEVELOPMENT IN THE

PROGRESSIVE ERA

Michael Willrich

What the past left to the home and to the church, we are compelled more and more to commit to the law and to the courts. The circumstances of city life and the modern feeling that law is a product of conscious and determinate human will put a larger burden upon the law, and hence upon the agencies that administer the law, than either has been prepared to bear.
—*Roscoe Pound, 1913*

ACCORDING TO THE conventional historical wisdom, America's modern administrative and welfare state grew up in spite of the courts. The dominant narrative of law and political development in the Progressive Era (1890–1919) portrays "the courts" as a monolith: a singularly conservative obstacle to progressive legislation enacted to bring industrial capitalism under the heel of a socially responsive interventionist state. This essay argues that to a large extent the modern administrative and welfare state arose *within* the courts—but not the high-level state and federal appellate courts that historians typically study. In the three decades before the New Deal, the criminal courts of America's industrial cities were a fertile seedbed for progressive social policies and ambitious new forms of administrative social intervention. The national model was the Municipal Court of Chicago, a massive judicial bureaucracy founded in 1906 to handle the hundreds of thousands of civil disputes and criminal cases that arose each year in the second-largest city of the world's leading industrial nation. The incipient welfare state that emerged within such local judicial bodies did much more than we expect a welfare state to do—regulate working conditions and provide material aid to the poor. City courts with their enormous caseloads served as local laboratories for a more far-reaching effort to govern everyday life in a new urban-industrial society. The court-centered regime of urban social governance joined the ancient coercive power of the criminal law to modern administrative strategies of population management, expert social intervention, and therapeutic treatment of individuals. The result was a new relationship between law and administrative statecraft and an unprecedented, sometimes violent expansion of governmental power into the lives of city people.[1]

Between the collapse of Reconstruction and the height of the New Deal, the role of law in American life underwent a halting but decisive transformation. The common-law polity of nineteenth-century America—organized around core principles of local self-government, individual liberty and responsibility, and the supremacy of law—gave way to the increasingly centralized, pluralistic, and administrative political framework of the modern liberal state. The turn of the twentieth century witnessed extraordinary social and political upheaval in America and other Western industrial nations. Amidst industrial strife, rapid urbanization, and (especially in the United States) unprecedented waves of immigration, political reformers, intellectuals, and cross-class social movements staged a lasting revolt against the classical liberal doctrine of laissez-faire. A new interventionist rhetoric of "social facts" and "social interests" gradually displaced the autonomous individual from the center of American liberal ideology and jurisprudence. At the same time, Americans remade their governmental institutions in order to more effectively regulate their complex corporate-industrial economy and interdependent urban-industrial society. Increasingly, modern social and economic problems were handled by the expert authorities of a rising administrative state. New administrative agencies at the local, state, and federal levels took on much of the regulatory business hitherto handled by common-law courts and carried "executive justice" into new fields of social and economic governance—from setting electricity rates to insuring workingmen and their families against industrial accidents.[2]

Contrary to the predictions of many progressive politicians and commentators, however, the common-law courts did not grow brittle and crumble in significance as the administrative state grew up around them. From the lowliest city criminal tribunal to the federal judiciary, the courts themselves assumed a more flexible administrative style and a broader social purpose. No longer content to play the role of neutral umpires who adjudicated private suits, criminal cases, or constitutional issues, judges self-consciously weighed the social policy implications of their cases. In many areas of the law, from probation in criminal cases to equity receivership in bankruptcy, judges even crafted distinctly administrative remedies that, unlike the traditional judicial verdict or ruling, required ongoing supervision by the court. Americans would not see the full effect of these historic changes until well into the New Deal. But the tipping point was the Progressive Era.[3]

The myth of judicial obstructionism dates back to that era. Theodore Roosevelt, gearing up for his 1912 presidential run at the head of the Progressive party ticket, led the charge against what some progressives called America's "judicial oligarchy." Theodore Roosevelt himself appropriated much of his antijudicial rhetoric from the labor movement, which had all too often seen its efforts to organize industrial workers and demand an equal role in industrial governance thwarted by judicial intervention. The progressive Republican senator Robert LaFollette of Wisconsin distilled the narrative of judicial usurpation to its pure populist plotline: "The people in their struggle to destroy special privilege and to open the way for human rights through truly representative government, found barrier after barrier placed across the way of progress by the courts."[4]

Whatever its merits as political rhetoric, however, the narrative of judicial obstructionism distorts historical analysis. The thesis is debatable even on its own narrow terms. For Progressive Era critics and historians alike, the case against the courts centers on the abuse of a single dramatic but relatively exotic form of judicial power—judicial review—while discounting the workaday business of the trial courts. Of course, there were infamous cases of "laissez-faire constitutionalism" such as *Ritchie v. People* (1895), *Lochner v. New York* (1905), and *Ives v. South Buffalo Railway Co.* (1911), which struck down state laws intended to protect wage earners or their families from industrial hazards. But state and federal appellate courts actually *upheld* most of the social legislation that crossed their desks. And more than just clearing the constitutional way for new forms of governmental power, the courts themselves took on new regulatory functions. Progressive reformers reorganized and, in their language, "socialized" many American courts—particularly "inferior" trial courts at the municipal, county, and federal levels—in order to make them more efficient, powerful, and quasi-administrative instruments of social and economic governance.[5]

In 1905 a loose alliance of lawyers, businessmen, Republican politicians, municipal home-rule advocates, and social activists won a decades-long constitutional struggle to abolish Chicago's justice-of-the-peace system and establish in its place America's first modern centralized municipal court. The Municipal Court of Chicago stood at the cutting edge of a national trend, driven by the legal pressures produced by urbanization and industrialization, middle-class demands for professionalization in law and government, and a broader political effort to restore the vitality and legitimacy of the courts. Some forty cities reorganized their court systems on the Chicago model. The American Bar Association and the American Judicature Society touted it as the paragon of judicial modernization. By the 1920s, it had inspired managerial reforms in the state and federal courts. As the Harvard administrative law experts Felix Frankfurter and James M. Landis observed in 1927, "The reorganization of the local courts of Chicago into a unified municipal court was a concrete demonstration of the part to be played by organization and administration in securing competence, dispatch and economy from courts."[6]

The Chicago model may not have spread so widely without the outspoken support of Roscoe Pound, a Harvard Law School professor and progressive legal theorist whose influence ultimately surpassed that of most Supreme Court justices. If Chicago gave the municipal court movement a model, Professor Pound gave it an entire language that made court reform seem not only desirable but inevitable. Reformers, social scientists, and judges cribbed shamelessly from Pound's writings and speeches. For Pound, court reform involved three imperatives. First, trial courts must be "organized": the existing decentralized court systems must be consolidated and professionalized to function like bureaucracies. Second, civil and criminal procedure—the cumbersome rules governing the trial process—must be reformed to enable courts to act with greater speed and flexibility. Third and most provocatively, Pound followed Continental legal theorists such as Rudolph von Jhering by insisting that the law itself must be "socialized": rather than merely protect abstract individual rights such as liberty of contract, judges must take notice of the concrete "social facts" of urban-industrial life and address actual "human needs" and "social interests." All of this was necessary, said Pound, for courts to compete with emerging administrative agencies in a "modern" society, where urbanization severed local community ties, ethnic and racial heterogeneity replaced Anglo-Saxon homogeneity, economic inequality reduced formal individual liberty to a hollow fiction, and the pressure of litigation and criminal complaints forced courts to broaden their scope of administration. Significantly, it was the Municipal Court of Chicago, not some appellate court or administrative tribunal in Washington, that Pound hailed as the way of the future: "the pioneer modern judicial organization in the United States."[7]

The municipal court movement was a consummate "progressive" reform. It embodied progressivism's twin impulses toward administrative statecraft and sweeping social intervention. The progressive reconstruction of urban courts set the agenda for a major overhaul of common-law adjudication, introducing simplified forms of pleading and record keeping, specialized courts for specific classes of civil and criminal cases, and other procedural innovations that served as a model for the sweeping federal reforms of civil procedure in 1938. And during the 1910s and 1920s, the formative era of the American welfare state, this judicial reform created the institutional framework and administrative capacities for a new ideology and practice of court-based social governance. Merging criminal legal authority with the novel disciplinary techniques of social work, welfare administration, probation, psychiatric testing, and eugenics, the new municipal courts produced authoritative social knowledge and used it to govern everyday life in its most intimate details. "Under metropolitan conditions a court has necessarily a profound social duty," Chief Justice Harry Olson of the Municipal Court of Chicago explained in 1913. "Without in any way impairing the nature of the obligation that the court must be essentially the judicial branch of government, it must give a larger meaning to the word 'judicial' in an age when society is bent upon remedial action, when it is necessary to throw light into the dark corners of our civilization and procure data essential to the constructive treatment of social ills."[8]

The history of urban judicial administration offers two opportunities to political historians: a fresh angle from which to rediscover and reconceptualize the central role of legal change in American political development, and a fertile, eminently institutional terrain upon which to engage some of the main themes of social and cultural history, which have in recent years pushed political analysis to the margins of the historical discipline. But in order to seize those opportunities we must set aside old myths. The time has come to put law back at the vital center of modern political history, deflate the myth of "the courts" as a monolithic antistatist force, and view the changing American legal order, as Pound and many other progressives did, from the bottom up.

The Municipal Court of Chicago—America's first centralized urban court system—was invented during a pivotal period in the social history of the Second City. Perched at the nexus of the nation's transportation and communications networks, Chicago epitomized to the world the wonders and dangers of the industrial city. After visiting Chicago in 1904, the German sociologist Max Weber wrote that "the whole gigantic city . . . is like a man whose skin has been peeled off and whose entrails one sees at work." Between 1880 and 1900, Chicago had exploded in size from 23,000 to 122,000 acres and in population from 0.5 million to 1.7 million people— more than three-quarters of them of foreign birth or parentage. (This stunningly cosmopolitan population doubled again by 1930; by then, African-Americans, first drawn to the city in large numbers during World War I, constituted nearly 7 percent of the populace.) While the stone mansions of the lakefront Gold Coast attested to the sturdy fortunes amassed in dry-goods retailing, steel manufacturing, futures trading, and corporate lawyering, the city's notorious Nineteenth Ward—crowding the south branch of the Chicago River with congested tenements, unpaved streets, and reeking privies—vividly revealed to the public the unequal yields of capitalist enterprise. As early as 1894 the United States commissioner of labor reported that 162,000 Chicagoans lived under the conditions of a "slum," which he defined as an "area of dirty back streets, especially when inhabited by a squalid and criminal population." The everyday criminality that plagued some working-class neighborhoods—public drunkenness, theft, prostitution, domestic violence, wife and child abandonment—was upstaged by the violence of Chicago's labor conflicts: from the massive national railroad strike of 1877 to the Haymarket bombing of 1886 to the Pullman strike of 1894 to the Teamsters' strike of 1905. For many immigrants from southern and eastern Europe, the hardest-fought political battles were not over work but leisure. They organized the United Societies for Local Self-Government and defended their "personal liberties"—especially the Continental tradition of public drinking on Sundays—against sporadic efforts to enforce state liquor regulations in the city.[9]

To the eyes of court reformer Robert McMurdy, a local lawyer who had experience representing African-American litigants in civil rights cases, the cultural complexity of the Second City tested the limits of the law. Addressing elite lawyers and judges at a meeting of the Illinois State Bar Association, McMurdy declared, "The population of Chicago is so heterogeneous, so restless, so virile, so diversified in the matter of previous condition, customs, manner and thought that it becomes in any case difficult to make a law to fit the whole." Until 1906, that colossal task—applying the law to the diverse and contentious social whole of Chicago—was entrusted to the justice-of-the-peace (JP) system.[10]

American JPs at the turn of the twentieth century presided over a decentralized system of judicial administration long hailed by domestic and foreign commentators as the linchpin of civil liberty and local self-government. An institution whose origins extended back to medieval England, the office of JP, as legal historian J. Willard Hurst once observed, was "the arch symbol" of the American "emphasis on local autonomy in the organization of courts." The typical justice had little or no legal training, enjoyed a quasi-proprietary control over his office, and collected most, if not all, of his pay in the fees that state statutes authorized him to levy against litigants and criminal defendants. JPs occupied the bottom rung of the legal order. They had no power of judicial review. They heard no appeals. They tried no big-ticket civil cases or felony crimes. They simply handled the vast majority of America's legal business. In the cities, they delivered their rough justice in a ceaseless deluge of routine civil and criminal cases, which a committee of eminent progressive lawyers, including Roscoe Pound and Louis Brandeis, aptly described in a 1914 report as "the everyday rights and wrongs of the great majority of an urban community." From the country hamlet to the great city, these so-called people's courts or poor man's courts traded in the everyday judicial business of the working people. In Chicago, where the high-volume judicial market enabled enterprising justices to rake in fees unimaginable in the hinterland, the working people had their own nickname for these public offices: "the justice shops." The sobriquet mocked the JPs' pretensions of judicial rectitude in a court where justice was literally for sale. But the nickname also nicely captured the frankly entrepreneurial quality of an institution deeply embedded in the rough-and-tumble practices of everyday life in an urban market economy.[11]

In 1900 Chicago, fifty-two justices of the peace, appointed by the governor, did a robust local "justitial business" out of private offices concentrated along busy, low-rent commercial strips. JPs' set up shop in the Loop and other convenient locations, favoring the 100s block of Clark Street, known for its saloons, gambling rooms, and dance halls. The typical Chicago JP disposed of nearly two thousand civil cases and a smattering of criminal cases each year, exacting a fee, set by statute, for every judicial service he provided—from performing a marriage to issuing a guilty verdict. From this pool of justices, the mayor selected eighteen men for a simultaneous appointment as police magistrate. In this capacity, the justices spent part of each work day trying minor criminal cases in seedy, smoke-filled police station courtrooms around the city. Only in their role as police magistrates did the justices receive a public salary; that did not stop them from collecting fees of various sorts in criminal cases. The justices' criminal jurisdiction included local ordinance violations, such as the routine public-order-maintaining charge of disorderly conduct; state misdemeanors in which the punishment was by fine only (not to exceed $200); cases of assault and battery; and vagrancy cases. Their civil jurisdiction covered cases in which the plaintiff claimed less than $200, such as actions to recover wages unpaid and debts overdue or to settle the so-called clothesline quarrels that arose between neighbors in crowded tenement districts.[12]

The circuit and superior courts of Cook County had jurisdiction over Chicago's more serious misdemeanors, felonies, and civil cases in which more than $200 was involved. But the so-called inferior jurisdiction of the JP system actually gave the justices the lion's share of the city's judicial business, including nearly all of the civil business of wage earners and poor people. For workers, $200 was a princely sum. According to a report of the United States commissioner of labor, the typical male laborer in Chicago earned roughly $570 in 1900; a skilled bricklayer earned about twice that. Together, Chicago's justice courts tried roughly five times as many civil cases as the higher county courts. In 1890, Chicago police magistrates handled a total of 62,230 cases—96 percent of the city's criminal caseload. The caseload of the justice courts graphically illustrated the social tensions produced by a generation of breakneck industrialization, urbanization, and mass immigration. The police hauled in strikers and union "sluggers." Workers sued employers for wage theft. Collection agency lawyers sued unrepresented working-class debtors. Wives had their husbands prosecuted for desertion. Immigrant parents filed complaints against their own children for being "idle" and "unruly" or just failing to bring home their wages. No wonder McMurdy chided lawyers who shunned the justice courts for the more dignified halls (and higher fees) of the superior and circuit courts. Police court cases, McMurdy said, "involve the liberty of our humble citizens" and "constitute the really difficult puzzle of such a metropolis."[13]

By legislative design and local custom, the men who presided over the justice courts were laymen well connected to ward politics, which meant they were unschooled in the technical niceties of common-law procedure and, their critics claimed, unversed in the ethical standards of the city's increasingly self-conscious and self-policing professional bar. The paucity of professional training, formal procedure, and centralized discipline lamented by legal professionals at the turn of the twentieth century had been lauded by earlier generations as essential to the effectiveness of the JP system. The eighteenth-century English legal commentator Sir William Blackstone observed that statutes entrusted the local JP with "an infinite variety of business" and his work was of "so great importance to the public" that higher courts were obliged to greet "any undesigned slip in his practice" with "great lenity and indulgence." In nineteenth-century America, the JP's informality and autonomy was vital to an office that, in the old cliché, "brought justice to every man's door." As the Illinois Supreme Court opined in 1873, "Justices of the Peace are established in every township in the State, to enable parties not acquainted with the formal requirements of law to obtain speedy trials, without pleadings, and without being compelled to employ counsel skilled in the law to assist." Trials in Chicago JP courts tended to be highly informal and often proceeded without interference from lawyers. Justices ran their police courts with a similarly personal style. Some justices also let their local aldermen use their courts as instruments of political discipline for the local machine; in the most notorious example, aldermen in the Levee redlight district allegedly used the threat of prosecution or the promise of protection in the police courts to keep brothel keepers and their customers in line. Despite the taint of political corruption, the justice courts did provide forums where ordinary people could file their own civil suits and criminal complaints and argue their own cases. Recent immigrants relied on the untrained counsel of more established fellow countrymen, who were better versed than themselves in the language and folkways of the justice courts—if not of the written law.[14]

The fact that America's urban JPs tended to the legal business of the common people gave them a heightened public visibility in an era of social struggle and reform. As early as 1888, New York mayor Abram Hewitt observed that "the position of police justice is more important to the community than that of judge of the court of appeals; the latter finally settles the law, but the former applies it in the first instance, in nearly all cases affecting the life, liberty, and property of the citizens." By every measure, the social importance of the justice courts had been growing for years, as the law acquired ever greater responsibilities for dealing with everyday rights and wrongs in urban-industrial society. Consider the increasing heft of Elijah M. Haines's volume, *A Practical Treatise on the Powers and Duties of Justices of the Peace and Constables, in the State of Illinois.* When it first appeared in 1855, the manual already filled 459 pages. By the time the fifteenth edition lumbered off the press in 1896, the page count had more than tripled to nearly 1,500 hundred pages. As McMurdy observed, Chicago's police courts had become "the eyes of the municipality." In fact, for ordinary Chicagoans, the police courts *were* the municipality. "Those who are drawn into these courts . . . hardly come into physical contact with any branch of Government in any other way. . . . It would seem near-sighted for us not to give the great number of people assembling here day after day a better idea of our institutions than they must now carry away with them to their homes and their neighbors."[15]

At the turn of the twentieth century, this ancient system of local governance fell under political attack. Particularly in the great cities such as New York, Chicago, Philadelphia, and Boston, the JP system seemed outmoded and corrupt. If the law was, as sociologist Edward A. Ross put it in 1901, "the most specialized and highly finished engine of control employed by society," the men in whose hands cities had entrusted this precious mechanism seemed utterly unfit for the task. Ross himself mourned "the undignified and demoralizing conduct of many of our police courts, presided over by burly, vulgar-minded political henchmen, without personal prestige, professional traditions, or good manners." Critics everywhere faulted the JP system for qualities that had long been heralded as its chief virtues: its decentralized structure, its administration by lay officials, and its swift and informal style of justice.[16]

In Chicago, the cause of judicial reform united a cast of businessmen, lawyers, and elite civic reformers, as well as social activists who assisted immigrants and working people in private legal aid organizations and settlement houses. Although most of these court reformers were men, and most voted Republican, their interests and motives varied. Lawyers who provided free legal aid to poor women and children protested that the police court justices culled profits from the misfortune of prostitutes. Businessmen protested that the justice shops were an uncertain and inefficient mechanism for collecting debts and resolving commercial disputes. Conservative lawyers and progressive social settlement activists alike worried that the JP system eroded the working people's faith in the rule of law, turning them toward more radical means of seeking justice. Appearing before the United States Industrial Commission on the Chicago Labor Disputes of 1900, the social settlement leader Graham Taylor testified that "even among the more intelligent workingmen of irreproachable character" he had observed a "deep disappointment and discouragement" in the relief provided by the justice courts. All of these reformers condemned the "iniquitous fee system." In an age of professionalization and heightened concerns about political corruption, a method of compensation once associated with fiscal economy signified an inherently corrupting contract between perennial plaintiffs such as collection agencies and entrepreneurial justices. As the German-born Cook County judge and prolabor Democratic governor John Peter Altgeld put it, the fee system "leads everywhere to the same results, viz., injustice, oppression, extortion and frivolous law-suits, ruinous in the expense and in the loss of time which they entail. The courts become clogged with business, while the poor and ignorant suffer."[17]

But despite the growing groundswell of support, getting rid of the justice shops was no easy task. The Illinois Constitution of 1870 barred the state legislature from enacting special legislation for local communities. In order to abolish the JP system in Chicago, it seemed, reformers would have to abolish it everywhere in the state, a plan that legislators from socalled downstate communities outside Chicago had no interest in supporting. Their support was crucial because the state constitution also dictated that the General Assembly could consider amendment to only one article of the constitution per session. Supporters of court reform in Chicago had to persuade their downstate peers to make their problem the number one constitutional priority of the session. The tide finally turned after 1900, when the cause of court reform won the support of "home rule" advocates, who were fighting for a new municipal charter from the state that would give Chicago greater powers to tax, spend, and govern itself. New charter advocates, whose ranks included labor leaders as well as businessmen and professionals, saw justice court reform as integral to a larger plan to make the municipal administration more efficient and democratic. In 1904, charter reformers secured a constitutional amendment that allowed the Chicago electorate to vote on a new court plan for the Second City.[18]

Lawyers and prominent businessmen from the Chicago New Charter Convention drafted the municipal court bill. In the Illinois General Assembly, Cook County lawmakers revised the measure to ensure that the new court's hundreds of new clerical and bailiff positions would not be governed by civil service rules (thus replacing one system of patronage with another). The final bill went before the Chicago electorate in a city-wide election. On November 7, 1905, the enfranchised men of the Second City voted to abolish the city's justice-of-the-peace system, establishing the nation's first modern centralized municipal court. A fixture of local government in the Anglo-American world since the late Middle Ages, the office of JP had survived revolutions and civil wars, constitution-making and codification campaigns, only to be cast aside by progressive reformers as an "antiquated" and corrupt institution, ill suited to the complex task of administering justice in a "modern city."[19]

Contemporary observers divined a legal revolution in the Municipal Court Act of 1905. In abolishing the entrepreneurial model of the justice shops, the court reformers embraced the managerial model of the modern business corporation. In place of autonomous justices who were allowed to freely appropriate their political offices as long as they satisfied their political sponsors, the act created twenty-seven salaried judges, elected in citywide contests, who convened regularly as a board of directors and answered to an elected chief justice. In place of a sprawling archipelago of offices, the statute created a centralized bureaucracy. The municipal court's jurisdiction was much larger than the JPs': it included the full range of civil complaints, ordinance violations, and misdemeanors, as well as preliminary jurisdiction over felonies. (If a judge found probable cause that a felony had occurred, he had to transfer the case to Cook County Criminal Court.) The act empowered the chief justice, modeled after a corporate chief executive, to craft court procedure, establish specialized branch courts, assign the associate judges to criminal or civil branches, and require them to submit monthly reports—sufficient powers to keep unruly judges in line.[20]

By the time the municipal court opened in 1906, there was considerable interest in court reform in great cities across America. The municipal court movement had diverse origins and served multiple purposes. The most important were institutional, procedural, and political. Institutionally, there was widespread consensus that the old decentralized, fee-driven JP system had to go; Chicago's 1905 Municipal Court Act supplied a model for how to replace it. The procedural agenda arose originally in relation to the "regular courts," the higher local courts such as the Cook County circuit and superior courts, where backlogs were so deep that an ordinary suit might take years to come to trial. Critics expressed an inchoate sense that the "uncertainty, delay and expense" of justice in the regular courts had something to do with the complexity and contentiousness of modern economic life. But the more proximate cause was "archaic" judicial machinery: the technical formalism of common-law procedure, the procedural restraints that state legislators placed upon trial judges, and the unruly structure of the courts. These, too, had to go. The Chicago solution was to give a municipal court unified jurisdiction over civil and criminal cases and to arm judges with authority to create new rules of procedure to meet new circumstances. Finally, the American judiciary had become an explosive political issue; thanks to such appellate decisions as the 1905 *Lochner* ruling, the courts in general were widely criticized as the most regressive of the nation's political institutions. As Roscoe Pound announced in a famous speech to the American Bar Association in 1906, the institutional disarray, procedural inefficiency, and apparent political conservatism of the courts created great "popular dissatisfaction with the administration of justice." Some champions of direct democracy were demanding that the public be given power to remove judges and "recall" court decisions. Perhaps the clearest evidence of the declining faith in the courts was the fact that state and federal lawmakers were handing over pressing regulatory matters of traditionally judicial purview—such as industrial accidents, immigration law enforcement, and public health—to new administrative agencies.[21]

Urban court reformers saw the centralized municipal court, based on the corporate model, as the one institution capable of solving all these problems. "Business management for the courts"—a slogan of the municipal court movement—promised to streamline civil procedure, an attractive prospect to business interests demanding a more predictable system of debt collection and commercial litigation. It promised to make courts more socially responsive, restoring popular faith in American institutions against the claims of socialism and radicalism. Above all, the managerial model seemed well equipped to carry out the double-edged disciplinary project of urban court reform: to provide a more efficient and penetrating machinery of social regulation in America's great cities and, not least, to police the behavior of judicial officials themselves.[22]

Historians have forgotten that progressive critics of "the courts" came in two very different sets of rhetorical clothing with two quite different agendas. The best-remembered critics are those such as Roosevelt, LaFollette, and the political scientist Charles Beard, who insisted that the judiciary had become a reactionary and antidemocratic bulwark against progressive social change, ruthlessly striking down social legislation to protect property rights and using labor injunctions to criminalize peaceful strikes. Roosevelt accused the Supreme Court of handing down decisions that were "flagrant and direct contradictions of the spirit and needs of the times." As books with titles like *Our Judicial Oligarchy* rolled off the presses, Rooseveltian court critics pushed for two kinds of solutions. The first were efforts to give administrative agencies jurisdiction over matters of vital public concern, such as antitrust. (The Federal Trade Commission, established in 1914, is one example.) The second were measures to bring judicial power under the control of direct democracy: popular recall of judges, recall of judicial decisions, and reforms that would make the position of federal judge an elective, term office.[23]

But there was another, ultimately more successful, set of progressive court critics. They included President William Howard Taft, Roscoe Pound, and the members of the American Judicature Society, a national clearinghouse for court reform that Pound and Harry Olson helped to found in Chicago in 1913. Some of these reformers also took a sharply critical view of the formal individualism of decisions such as *Lochner*. Indeed, Pound's famous 1909 essay "Liberty of Contract" remains one of the most powerful sociological critiques of judicial conservatism in the annals of modern jurisprudence. But for Pound, the paramount goal was to *save* the common law and the courts by reforming them, not to rein in their authority. The court-savers proposed measures to strengthen judicial power, including giving judges more power to create their own procedural rules and more discretion in the handling of cases. In his speeches to state bar associations and prescriptive essays on judicial administration published during the early 1910s, Pound argued that America's highly decentralized system of courts, designed for an agrarian society, was no match for the administrative demands made upon it by a population exploding in numbers and diversity. Touting the Municipal Court of Chicago as a model, Pound proposed that state court systems be unified on a bureaucratic model with specialized branch courts for particular classes of cases, so that judges might become experts. Pound insisted it was imperative to "meet the movement away from law by modernizing the legal and judicial machinery[,] which will enable it to meet more effectively the demands of the present." For all of Pound's modernist criticisms of the legal system, he still clung to the notion that the courts provided real protections for liberty, and that the buildup of governmental power in administrative agencies rather than courts would in the long run increase arbitrary power over the individual.[24]

Pound was hardly alone in worrying about a future in which discretionary executive actions by an administrative leviathan would replace the rule of law. By the early twentieth century, administrative agencies, commissions, and boards were regulating railroads, setting rates for public utilities, handling industrial accident claims, adjudicating water rights disputes, administering antitrust law, enforcing public health ordinances, implementing federal immigration policy—the list seemed to grow longer each year. Even in criminal justice, which Pound called "par excellence the domain of the common law," state parole boards had usurped an important element of sentencing discretion from judges. John Dickinson, who published one of the first American treatises on administrative law in 1927, called the "penetration" of the common law's old domain "an institutional change of very great magnitude." "That government officials should assume the traditional function of courts of law, and be permitted to determine the rights of individuals, is a development so out of line with the supposed path of our legal growth as to challenge renewed attention to certain underlying principles of our jurisprudence." American Judicature Society secretary Herbert Harley warned about the proliferation of administrative agencies to "adjudicate the living issues of modern law." "[W]e might easily forecast a day not far distant when our courts still dignified and ritualistic, would be holding an empty bag," he wrote. Much of Pound's prodigious output can be read in precisely this spirit: as an attempt to save common-law courts from the jurisdictional imperialism of the modern administrative state. To achieve this, the courts themselves had to become better organized, cast off the deadweight of old procedures, and learn to function more like administrative agencies—without discarding the basic legal safeguards of the common law.[25]

Of course, common-law courts always had administrative functions. But in the discourse of Progressive Era reformers, "administration" and "law" referred to entirely different sets of institutions and processes. As Dickinson suggested, common-law courts were supposed to be independent from "government." Common-law courts "adjudicated." This meant they did not initiate cases; they heard cases initiated by a private citizen or an officer of the state. Clear procedural rules limited judges' power and governed the judicial process. In the adversarial courtroom, lawyers or prosecutors presented their facts to the court. Evidentiary rules regulated what facts were relevant and how they must be introduced. Judges acted as neutral referees, determining the rights of individuals before the bar according to "fixed and general rules" rather than by considerations of government policy. The outcome of the case—the decree or penalty—was a final, imposed decision. It occurred in a specific temporal moment (or, in a criminal case, two specific moments: the verdict and the sentence).

Administrative bodies, on the other hand, were agencies of executive power. Administrators made their own regulatory codes and rules of procedure. They had the power to initiate cases and conduct their own fact-finding investigations. Some administrative officers had power to take direct action, as when a local health inspector ordered the destruction of diseased animals. Administrative agencies paid little heed to the separation of powers: they merged powers of rule making (legislative), application of standards (executive), and determining facts and individual rights (judicial). Administrative tribunals were not bound by the procedural safeguards of the common law. As Dickinson put it, agencies decided cases "not by fixed rules of law, but by the application of governmental discretion or policy." And unlike temporally bounded judicial remedies, administrative remedies involved "ongoing" or "thoroughgoing" intervention by the agency.[26]

This is, of course, an ideal-typical description of the distinction between common-law adjudication and administration—a distinction that was probably never pure at any level of government. But municipal court reformers set out to blur it deliberately in order to make courts more efficient instruments for the administration of justice in the modern city. In the eyes of Chicago's court reformers, the city would master its social problems not by rejecting law for the allure of administrative power but by combining the two in ways that would, as Harry Olson promised, give the word "judicial" a new social meaning.

The new municipal court and Chief Justice Olson, a former prosecutor, quickly won national acclaim as a center of procedural innovation. When President Taft declared in 1909 that the reform of civil and criminal procedure constituted "the greatest need in American institutions," he voiced a concern shared by many within the legal profession. Olson and his associate judges sent a fact-finding mission to England to collect ideas for streamlining organization and civil procedure. The judges devised a system of abbreviated record keeping that would have impressed scientific management expert Frederick Winslow Taylor. They also established specialized branches in which judges could become "expert" administrators over specific classes of cases, such as small claims cases or landlord-tenant disputes.[27]

The public response in America's great cities was overwhelming. Newspapers bathed the Municipal Court of Chicago in the sort of praise they usually reserved for bare-knuckle boxers. In 1910 the *New York Tribune* praised the court as a paragon of corporate efficiency.

> A judicial system that is organized and operated on the lines of a business corporation, with board of directors, executive officer, administrative staff and superintendents; presumably a minor bench, but exercising in reality far greater powers than courts having similar jurisdiction; whose order is law unto every policeman of the city, his chief willing or unwilling; an institution that has decreased crime through the terror its swift trials have inspired among evildoers; that has knocked verbiage out of legal forms and records; that makes its own rules of practice and procedure, and that is recommended by the American Bar Association as a model for the reconstruction of the judicial systems of all the states of the Union—such is the Municipal Court of Chicago, at the beginning of its fourth year of existence.

Between 1905 and 1935, the municipal court movement radiated outward from Chicago like so many railroad lines to urban centers across America, until progressive reformers and bar association lawyers in some forty cities persuaded lawmakers to abolish their JP systems and centralize local judicial authority into quasi-corporate bureaucracies.[28]

The Chicago Municipal Court made its name as a "businessman's court." But it soon came to represent the ideals and techniques of more socially progressive reformers, especially members of women's groups such as the Chicago Woman's Club and the Juvenile Protective Association (JPA), an offshoot of Jane Addams's Hull House social settlement. Like most social scientists of the day, these women understood crime as the product of "social" causes beyond the individual's control, including bad heredity, family poverty, low wages, and long working hours. The reformers favored "socialized" criminal justice, a quasi-administrative approach that emphasized "social responsibility" for crime and "individual treatment" for criminals. They saw in the new municipal court an institution equipped to address a host of social and moral concerns much broader than lawbreaking. They also saw an opportunity for professional social workers, including female members of their own organizations, to secure government jobs in the male-dominated world of law and the courts. Olson responded to the prodding of reform associations by creating specialized criminal branches focused on specific areas of social life. The Domestic Relations Court, founded in 1911 at the urging of the JPA, handled desertion and non-support. The Morals Court, opened in 1913 at the recommendation of the famous Chicago Vice Commission, specialized in prostitution. And the Boys' Court, which Olson created in 1914, again at the JPA's urging, handled adolescent male offenders. That same year, Olson secured city council funding for the Psychopathic Laboratory, a criminological clinic where defendants from the criminal branches could be tested for "mental defects." To head the laboratory, he hired a European-trained psychiatrist who shared Olson's own belief that the overwhelming majority of criminals were the products of hereditary defects such as feeblemindedness. The new branches and the eugenics laboratory would have been inconceivable under the JP system. They required the centralized structure of an "organized court" to classify cases and legitimate their discretionary power.[29]

The Progressive Era witnessed a proliferation of private associations and professional experts who acquired cultural authority and public power by defining urban social problems such as feeblemindedness, single motherhood, and sexual inversion, and then claiming expertise in managing the populations they labeled deviant. Michel Foucault has argued that the rise of such experts in modern liberal states coincided with a declining importance of legal power; powerful new "disciplines" such as medicine and psychiatry displaced the law as the principal mechanisms of modern social control. In America, however, legal institutions served as *preeminent* sites for the production of urban social knowledge and social governance well into the twentieth century. Indeed what made the new city courts "modern," in addition to their bureaucratic structures, was that they aimed not merely to punish offenders but to assist and discipline entire urban populations: to police public health and morals, to reduce child neglect and family poverty, to correct deviant personalities and teach immigrants good citizenship, and to prevent "the unfit" from reproducing. Urban court systems grew more powerful than ever during these years. They did so by incorporating psychiatry, medicine, social work, and other disciplinary techniques into routine judicial practice.[30]

The reform of criminal procedure in the Municipal Court of Chicago, especially in the so-called socialized branch courts, built upon the court's earlier innovations in the administration of economic disputes in civil cases. Judges specialized in a distinct field of cases. Whether their jurisdiction consisted of small claims or prostitution cases, this specialization emboldened judges to think of themselves as experts and makers of social policy rather than as impartial umpires. Formal strictures of common-law procedure were loosened to allow for a more direct, "inquisitorial" style of judging that contemporary observers described as more in line with continental traditions of judging than the conventional practice of American courts. In both civil and criminal cases, parties typically waived their rights to jury trials—exercised at a cost of six dollars in the municipal court—leaving all questions of fact and law to judges. The municipal court collected and published statistics that totaled up, for the interested public, the caseload of each branch court, fines levied and sentences served, and demographic profiles of criminal defendants. Olson provided space in the court's annual reports for judges presiding in the specialized criminal branches to describe their work; the judges composed miniature treatises on socialized law in action. The judges took pride in the fact that they were not handling criminal complaints on a case-by-case basis, as common-law courts had done for centuries. They were making social policy.[31]

All of the municipal court's thirty civil and criminal branches handled cases that originated outside the court itself, in the troubled social and economic relations of everyday life in the industrial city. Criminal proceedings were initiated by relatives, neighbors, and social activists in addition to the police, probation officers, and other public officials. In that sense, the institutions still functioned like traditional courts. But especially in the specialized criminal courts, which had their own staffs of social workers, the case itself was only the starting point, the point of entry for a broader range of ongoing administrative interventions that included probing personal interviews with defendants and complainants; visits to defendants' homes; referrals to private charities; and compulsory psychiatric and medical examinations. Across urban America, the rising class of professional social experts found in socialized courts a means of expanding their cultural authority and public power in a society that increasingly prized expertise. Rather than clearing the way for a new administrative state, the municipal courts made themselves into centers of expert social administration.[32]

There is no mistaking the powerful cultural effect that these socialized legal institutions had as they mapped for the public gaze the social landscapes of the modern city. Judges and social personnel in the Municipal Court of Chicago worked, often with great earnestness and compassion, to understand scientifically the social environment, psychological dimensions, and racial origins of criminality. But they had a much larger hand than they acknowledged in inventing—through the kinds of social data they deemed relevant and the varieties of policy arguments they distilled from that data—the facts of social life in the modern city. Court officers applied their own moral views and cultural assumptions to the populations they were charged to manage in the name of an objectified, scientific conception of social order. Judge Charles Goodnow of the Morals Court, for example, cited the Psychopathic Laboratory's eugenics data in his personal campaign for stricter marriage laws, telling the Woman's City Club in 1916 that "the marriage license window is an open way to the destruction of the national health and morals, with the ultimate certainty of irreparable race degeneracy." The municipal court was a living social laboratory that shaped how contemporary observers understood urban society. Sociologists pored over the court's reports. Newspapers found in the court's daily deluge of humanity a ready supply of narrative subjects for their public stories of moral danger and social reform. To the social workers of the United States Children's Bureau, a federal agency created in 1912 and staffed with many veterans of Chicago women's reform organizations, the courts were a rich source of data and experience as they developed welfare policy ideas for the nation.[33]

Viewing the Progressive Era legal order from the perspective of its urban underbelly sheds new light on the origins of modern welfare policies. Many of those policies first appeared in local courts. Until the creation of a welfare state with enlarged state and national governmental capacities during the New Deal, progressive social reformers, women's activists, and policymakers assumed that local governments—local judiciaries in particular—would have to shoulder most of the burden of welfare governance in America. Reformers called upon local juvenile and municipal courts to make productive citizens of juvenile delinquents, administer public assistance for single mothers, facilitate the eugenic sterilization of "mental defectives," and compel "home slacker" husbands to support their families. Groups such as the JPA found in local criminal courts powerful instruments for addressing the multiple ends of modern welfare governance. Welfare governance was not concerned exclusively with providing for or insuring working families against the risks of industrial accidents. It also involved using the criminal courts to regulate morals, sexual behavior, and domestic relations among working-class city people. Indeed, the aspect of the modern welfare state that left-liberal critics have found most objectionable—policies that make public aid contingent upon recipients' keeping "suitable homes" for their children—has origins in the progressive effort to use institutions of criminal justice as instruments of social welfare. Social provision and social policing were intertwined from the start.[34]

A 1928 Children's Bureau report summed up the procedural revolution that had taken place in city courts during the past two decades:

> The distinction between the new procedure and the old common-law ways cannot be overemphasized. The old courts relied upon the learning of lawyers; the new courts depend more upon psychiatrists and social workers. The evidence before the old courts was brought by the parties; most of the evidence before the new courts is obtained by the courts themselves. The old courts relied upon precedents; the new courts have few to follow. . . . The judgments of the old courts were final, save for appeal; in the new courts, appeals are infrequent, and the judgment of the court is often only the beginning of the treatment of the case. In the old courts the jury was a vital factor; in the new courts, in practice, the jury is discarded. The system of the old courts was based upon checks and balances; the actual power of the new courts is practically unlimited. Justice in the old courts was based on legal science; in the new courts it is based on social engineering.

The authors did warn, in an afterthoughtish manner, that the new "socialized" procedure carried within it the "danger of all magisterial justice." But they insisted that "the theory of the new procedure is sound because it is adapted to modern conditions."[35]

That was the same assumption that Roscoe Pound and other progressive court-savers made: socialized law was sound because it adapted judicial practices to scientific knowledge of urban social conditions. Pound also assumed there was something inherent in a court that safeguarded human liberty against arbitrary governmental power. In practice, though, socializing criminal justice weakened the old protections of due process and civil liberties. Women hauled before the Morals Court were routinely examined for venereal disease, with or without their permission; if they tested positive for disease, they were incarcerated for weeks in a public hospital for medical treatment. This exercise of state power, which violates post-1960s notions of civil liberties, occurred without the inconvenience of a trial. In the case of the municipal court's eugenics program, Pound's optimism about judicial safeguards seems tragically misplaced. On the recommendation of the Psychopathic Laboratory, judges committed some one thousand criminal defendants each year to sexually segregated state institutions for the insane or feebleminded—regardless of whether the court had found them guilty of breaking any law. "It cannot be doubted," Olson declared, "that this practice . . . has been a very effective means for the preventing of crimes." Progressive court reformers cited the origins of criminality in the social conditions of the industrial city. But in local judicial practice, the progressives' social conception of crime entailed an intensified scrutiny of defendants and their families, rather than the structural attack on social inequality that progressive rhetoric seemed to demand.[36]

Familiar images of the early-twentieth-century courts as a monolithic obstacle to a modern regulatory and welfare state no longer make much sense when we recognize the sweeping transformations in court-based governance taking place in America's great cities. Progressive court reformers did away with an ancient system of local justice and created a new form of centralized municipal court, whose innovations in administration and social governance help explain how American courts in the twentieth century became such powerful instruments of economic and social governance. The national crisis of the Great Depression exposed the practical limits of local court-based social governance as well as other local traditions of welfare administration. But Progressive Era court reform remained a fund of experience as New Deal policymakers, jurists, and judges dealt anew with the complex relationship of law and administration in modern America. And even then, the courts did not fade away. Both administrative agencies and the courts emerged from the New Deal era's political battles stronger than ever: uneasy institutional partners in a modern liberal state that is distinctive in the world for its marriage of law, rights, and administrative power.

NOTES

1. See Michael Willrich, *City of Courts: Socializing Justice in Progressive Era Chicago* (New York: Cambridge University Press, 2003). For a critique of the literature on judicial obstructionism, see William J. Novak, "The Legal Origins of the Modern American State," American Bar Foundation Working Paper #9925 (1999). For their useful comments on this essay, the author wishes to thank Bill Novak, Julian Zelizer, Elizabeth Sanders, and especially Sid Milkis and Meg Jacobs.

2. On the intellectual, legal, and political contexts invoked here, see esp. Daniel R. Ernst, "Law and American Political Development, 1877–1938," *Reviews in American History* 26 (1998): 205–19; James T. Kloppenberg, *Uncertain Victory: Social Democracy and Progressivism in European and American*

Thought, 1870–1920 (New York: Oxford University Press, 1986); Daniel T. Rodgers, *Atlantic Crossings: Social Politics in a Progressive Age* (Cambridge, Mass.: Belknap Press, 1998); Lucy E. Salyer, *Laws Harsh as Tigers: Chinese Immigrants and the Shaping of Modern Immigration Law* (Chapel Hill, N.C.: University of North Carolina Press, 1995); Theda Skocpol, *Protecting Soldiers and Mothers: The Political Origins of Social Policy in the United States* (Cambridge, Mass.: Belknap Press, 1992); Stephen Skowronek, *Building a New American State: The Expansion of National Administrative Capacities, 1877–1920* (New York: Cambridge University Press, 1982).

3. See David S. Clark, "Adjudication to Administration: A Statistical Analysis of Federal District Courts in the Twentieth Century," *Southern California Law Review* 55 (1981): 65–145; Morton J. Horwitz, *The Transformation of American Law, 1870–1960* (New York: Oxford University Press, 1992); James Willard Hurst, *The Growth of American Law: The Law Makers* (Boston: Little Brown, 1950).

4. LaFollette quoted in Gilbert E. Roe, *Our Judicial Oligarchy* (New York: B.W. Huebsch, 1912), v. See William E. Forbath, *Law and the Shaping of the American Labor Movement* (Cambridge, Mass.: Harvard University Press, 1991).

5. *Ritchie v. People*, 155 Ill. 98 (1895). *Lochner v. New York*, 198 U.S. 45 (1905). *Ives v. South Buffalo Railway Co.*, 201 N.Y. 271 (1911). See Melvin I. Urofsky, "State Courts and Protective Legislation during the Progressive Era: A Reevaluation," *Journal of American History* 72 (1985), 63–91.

6. Felix Frankfurter and James M. Landis, *The Business of the Supreme Court: A Study in the Federal Judicial System* (New York: Macmillan, 1927), 226. See "Harry Olson, Former Chief Justice, Dies," *Chicago Tribune*, August 2, 1935; Herbert Harley, "Business Management for the Courts: As Exemplified by the Municipal Court of Chicago," *Virginia Law Review* 5 (1917): 1–26; [Herbert Harley], "Success of Organized Courts," *Journal of the American Judicature Society* 1 (1918): 133–51; "To Reform Courts of Inferior Jurisdiction," *Survey* 4 (1910): 177–79. See also Michael R. Belknap, *To Improve the Administration of Justice: A History of the American Judicature Society* (Chicago: American Judicature Society, 1992); Hurst, *Growth of American Law*, 113–14; Eric H. Steele, "The Historical Context of Small Claims Courts," *American Bar Foundation Research Journal* 6 (1981): 313–29.

7. Roscoe Pound, "Organization of Courts," 1914, reprinted in *Journal of the American Judicature Society* 11 (1927): 80. See Roscoe Pound, "The Administration of Justice in the Modern City," *Harvard Law Review* 26 (1913): 302–28.

8. City of Chicago, Municipal Court, *Seventh Annual Report of the Municipal Court of Chicago: For the Year December 2, A.D. 1912 to November 30, A.D. 1913, Inclusive* (Chicago: City of Chicago, n.d.), 87.

9. "Introduction: The Man and His Work," in Max Weber, *From Max Weber: Essays in Sociology*, trans. and ed. H. H. Gerth and C. Wright Mills (New York: Oxford University Press, 1946), 15. Edith Abbott, *The Tenements of Chicago, 1908–1935* (Chicago: University of Chicago Press, 1936), 16, 30, esp. 31. See, esp., Martin Bulmer, *The Chicago School of Sociology: Institutionalization, Diversity, and the Rise of Sociological Research* (Chicago: University of Chicago Press, 1984), 12–27; Lizabeth Cohen, *Making a New Deal: Industrial Workers in*

Chicago, 1919–1939 (New York: Cambridge University Press, 1990); James R. Grossman, *Land of Hope: Chicago, Black Southerners, and the Great Migration* (Chicago: University of Chicago Press, 1989); Joanne Meyerowitz, *Women Adrift: Independent Wage Earners in Chicago, 1880–1930* (Chicago: University of Chicago Press, 1988); Harold Barton Myers, "The Policing of Labor Disputes in Chicago," (Ph.D. dissertation, University of Chicago, 1929); Harvey Warren Zorbaugh, *The Gold Coast and the Slum: A Sociological Study of Chicago's Near North Side* (1929; Chicago: University of Chicago Press, 1976), 17–68.

10. Robert McMurdy, "The Law Providing for a Municipal Court of Chicago," in Illinois State Bar Association, *Proceedings of the Illinois State Bar Association: Thirtieth Annual Meeting, Chicago, July 12 and 13, 1906* (Springfield, Ill.: Illinois State Bar Association, 1906), 2: 81–82.

11. Hurst, *Growth of American Law*, 147–52, esp. 148; Charles W. Eliot et al., *Preliminary Report on Efficiency in the Administration of Justice* (Boston: [Caustis-Clafin, 1914]), 29; "For People's Courts of Justice," Chicago *Record-Herald*, November 2, 1905; "Rescuing the Poor Man's Court," *Chicago Times-Herald*, January 28, 1897. Essential sources on the JP system include *Chicago Revised Municipal Code*, 1905, ch. 50, secs. 1785–87; "Constitution of 1870," *Illinois Revised Statutes*, 1911, art. vi, secs. 21, 28; Hiram T. Gilbert, *The Municipal Court of Chicago* (Chicago: [the author], 1928), 9–10; Elijah M. Haines, *A Practical Treatise on the Powers and Duties of Justices of the Peace and Police Magistrates; with a Summary of the Law Relating to the Duties of Constables, Coroners, and Notaries Public in the State of Illinois*, 15th rev. ed. (Chicago: E. B. Myers, 1896); "Law in relation to justices of the peace," approved June 26, 1895, *Illinois Revised Statutes*, 1905, ch. 79, art. i, secs. 2–5; art. ii, sec. 16; art. xviii, sec. 164; Albert Lepawsky, *The Judicial System of Metropolitan Chicago* (Chicago: University of Chicago Press, 1932); Harry Olson, "Conditions in Chicago Which Led to the Institution of the Municipal Court," draft speech, Judge Harry Olson Papers, University Archives, Northwestern University, box 3.

12. If a justice found probable cause that a more serious crime had occurred—a felony or misdemeanor punishable by imprisonment—he had to "bind over" the case to Cook County Criminal Court.

13. McMurdy, "Law Providing for a Municipal Court," 82. Wage figures cited in Chicago Public Library, "Chicago in 1900—A Millennium Biography: Family Economics," www.chipubliclibrary.org/004Chicago/1900/fam.html. See City of Chicago, Department of Police, *Report of the General Superintendent of Police of the City of Chicago for the Fiscal Year Ending December 31, 1890* (Chicago: [Police Dept.], 1891), 53; City of Chicago, Municipal Court, *First Annual Report: The Municipal Court of Chicago: For the Year December 3rd, A.D. 1906, to November 30th, A.D. 1907, Inclusive* (Chicago: City of Chicago, n.d.), 50–51.

14. Blackstone quoted in Haines, *Practical Treatise*, 38; *Bliss v. Harris*, 70 Ill. 343, 345 (1873); McMurdy, "Law Providing for a Municipal Court," 96.

15. Hewitt quoted in Mary Roberts Smith, "The Social Aspect of New York Police Courts," *American Journal of Sociology* 5 (September 1899), 150; McMurdy, "Law Providing for a Municipal Court," 83. Elijah M. Haines, *A Practical Treatise on the Powers and Duties of Justices of the Peace and Constables,*

in the State of Illinois (Chicago: Keen & Lee, 1855); Haines, *Practical Treatise*, 15th rev. ed., 1896.

16. Edward Alsworth Ross, *Social Control: A Survey of the Foundations of Order* (New York: Macmillan, 1901), 106, 113–14. See Charles A. Beard, *American City Government: A Survey of Newer Tendencies* (New York: Century, 1912), 173–84.

17. U.S. Industrial Commission on the Chicago Labor Disputes of 1900, *Report of the Industrial Commission on the Chicago Labor Disputes of 1900* (Washington, D.C.: Government Printing Office, 1901), 3: 539; John P. Altgeld, *Live Questions: Including Our Penal Machinery and Its Victims* (Chicago: Donohue and Henneberry, 1890), 63. See Edward F. Dunne, "Against Justice Court Fees," in *Dunne: Judge, Mayor, Governor*, ed. William L. Sullivan (Chicago: Windermere Press, 1916), 83; "The Waste of Time at Court," *Nation*, March 25, 1886, 253–54.

18. "Constitution of 1870," art. iv, sec. 22; New Charter Campaign Committee, *The Chicago New Charter Movement: Why the Pending Constitutional Amendment Should Be Adopted* (Chicago, 1904). See Maureen A. Flanagan, *Charter Reform in Chicago* (Carbondale, Ill.: Southern Illinois University Press, 1987); Thomas R. Pegram, *Partisans and Progressives: Private Interest and Public Policy in Illinois, 1870–1920* (Urbana, Ill.: University of Illinois Press, 1992), 87–120.

19. "An Act in relation to a municipal court in the city of Chicago," approved May 18, 1905, *Illinois Revised Statutes*, 1911, ch. 37, secs. 264–330. Citizens' Association of Chicago, *Annual Report of the Citizens' Association of Chicago*, 1892 (Chicago: Citizens' Association of Chicago, 1892), 11.

20. "Act in relation to a municipal court."

21. Roscoe Pound, "The Causes of Popular Dissatisfaction with the Administration of Justice," 1906, reprinted in *Journal of the American Judicature Society* 20 (1927): 178–87. See Steele, "Historical Context."

22. Harley, "Business Management."

23. Roosevelt quoted in Roe, *Our Judicial Oligarchy*, 6. See William L. Ransom, *Majority Rule and the Judiciary: An Examination of Current Proposals for Constitutional Change Affecting the Relation of Courts to Legislation* (New York: C. Scribner's Sons, 1912).

24. Pound, "Organization of Courts," 73. See Roscoe Pound, "Liberty of Contract," *Yale Law Journal* 18 (May 1909): 454–87.

25. Pound, "Organization of Courts," 71. John Dickinson, *Administrative Justice and the Supremacy of Law in the United States* (Cambridge, Mass.: Harvard University Press, 1927), 6, 3; Harley, "Business Management," 24–25. See Roscoe Pound, *Administrative Law: Its Growth, Procedure, and Significance* (Pittsburgh: University of Pittsburgh Press, 1942).

26. Dickinson, *Administrative Justice*, 36. See Clark, "Adjudication to Administration"; Pound, *Administrative Law*.

27. Taft quoted in William Bayard Hale, "A Court That Does Its Job," *World's Work*, March 1910, 12695.

28. "A Court That Runs Like a Business Corporation," *New York Tribune*, January 16, 1910.

29. See Harry Olson, "The Municipal Court of Chicago: A Tribunal of Procedural Reform and Social Service," *San Francisco Recorder*, May 12, 1916.

30. Michel Foucault, *The History of Sexuality*, vol. 1: *An Introduction*, trans. Robert Hurley (New York: Pantheon, 1990), esp. 81–91, 144–45. See Laura Engelstein, "Combined Underdevelopment: Discipline and the Law in Imperial and Soviet Russia," *American Historical Review* 98 (1993): 338–53; Jan Goldstein, "Framing Discipline with Law: Problems and Promises of the Liberal State," ibid., 364–75; Engelstein, "Reply," ibid., 376–81.

31. On "inquisitorial" judging, see Judge Willis B. Perkins, "Family Courts," *Journal of the American Judicature Society* 3 (1919): 19–21.

32. Andrew Abbott, *The System of Professions: An Essay on the Division of Expert Labor* (Chicago: University of Chicago Press, 1988), 280–314. See V. V. Anderson, "The Immoral Woman as Seen in Court: A Preliminary Report," *Journal of the American Institute of Criminal Law and Criminology* 8 (1918): 902–10.

33. "Goodnow Urges Eugenics Law to Save Race," *Chicago Examiner*, June 23, 1916; "Goodnow Tells Why Girls Fall," *Chicago Tribune*, November 9, 1916. On the constitutive power of law, see Pierre Bourdieu, "The Force of Law: Toward a Sociology of the Juridical Field," trans. Richard Terdiman, *Hastings Law Journal* 38 (1987): 838; Christopher L. Tomlins, *Law, Labor, and Ideology in the Early American Republic* (New York: Cambridge University Press, 1993), esp. 16. On the Children's Bureau, see U.S. Children's Bureau, *Youth and Crime: A Study of the Prevalence and Treatment of Delinquency among Boys over Juvenile-Court Age in Chicago*, by Dorothy Williams Burke (Washington, D.C.: U.S. Government Printing Office, 1930); Robyn Muncy, *Creating a Female Dominion in American Reform, 1890–1935* (New York: Oxford University Press, 1991).

34. Joanne L. Goodwin, *Gender and the Politics of Welfare Reform: Mothers' Pensions in Chicago, 1911–1929* (Chicago: University of Chicago Press, 1997); David Spinoza Tanenhaus, "Policing the Child: Juvenile Justice in Chicago, 1870–1925," 2 vols. (Ph.D. dissertation, University of Chicago, 1997); Michael Willrich, "The Two Percent Solution: Eugenic Jurisprudence and the Socialization of American Law, 1900–1930," *Law and History Review* 16 (spring 1998): 63–111; Michael Willrich, "Home Slackers: Men, the State, and Welfare in Modern America," *Journal of American History*, 87 (September 2000), 460–89.

35. U.S. Children's Bureau, *The Child, the Family, and the Court: A Study of the Administration of Justice in the Field of Domestic Relations*, part 1: *General Findings and Recommendations* (Washington, D.C.: Government Printing Office, 1929), 21–22.

36. City of Chicago, Municipal Court, *Sixteenth, Seventeenth, and Eighteenth Annual Reports of the Municipal Court of Chicago: For the Years December 4, 1921, to November 30, 1924, Inclusive* (Chicago: City of Chicago, n.d.), 13; Willrich, "Two Percent Solution"; George E. Worthington and Ruth Topping, *Specialized Courts Dealing with Sex Delinquency* (1925; Montclair, N.J.: Patterson Smith, 1969).

Chapter Nine

"MIRRORS OF DESIRES"

INTEREST GROUPS, ELECTIONS, AND THE TARGETED STYLE

IN TWENTIETH-CENTURY AMERICA

Brian Balogh

THE TEMPLATE USED by elected officials to discern the preferences of their constituents is fundamental to democratic governance. This template shifted in the first third of the twentieth century. The way in which elected officials conceptualized voters evolved
from one that employed reliable partisan cues about voters' wishes to one
that relied upon far more specialized profiles of voters and that delivered
policy-prone information to elected officials. The dynamic relationship
between interest groups, rapidly changing conceptions of consumers, and
electoral politics, combined with the declining ability of political parties
to convey voter preferences, accounts for this fundamental shift. Conceptualizing the electorate as a congeries of group preferences best discerned
through the platforms and policy agendas of interest groups constituted
a distinct period in the American political development that shaped the
political system from roughly 1900 through 1970.

Interest groups played a key role in linking voters to public officials in
the first half of the twentieth century. A pronounced feature of the political landscape since the founding, they began to replace political parties
as the most reliable media for both ascertaining and responding to the
views of segments of voters by the twentieth century. In that regard, they
anticipated the daily tracking polls that emerged by the 1970s as the most
reliable link between public officials and key constituencies. Indeed, the
emergence of regularized and reliable public opinion polling signaled the
end of a distinct period in American democracy that ranged roughly from
1900 through 1970 during which interest groups served as crucial con-
duits of the democratic will.

During this period, political parties, the nineteenth-century mechanism
used by public officials to take the pulse of the electorate, proved less
adept at fulfilling this task. The reasons for this are varied. Voter participa-

tion fell off dramatically. While some scholars have argued that this was the result of elite reforms that self-consciously sought to restrict poor and uneducated citizens from voting, others have suggested that broader social trends contributed to activities that, in effect, competed for voters' attention in a world filled with mass-produced entertainment. With the rise of civil service requirements and professional administration at the state and local level, parties lost control of some of the tangible benefits they had once had at their disposal to reward voters.[1]

In response to the declining electoral hold of political parties, presidential candidates beginning with William McKinley in 1896 experimented with new techniques of campaigning and with "going public" as a strategy for governing. Public officials, by the 1920s, operated in a broader social and cultural environment characterized by the emergence of mass marketing and the celebration of consumer choice. This market model of mass consumption also explained why public officials turned to interest groups for political intelligence.[2]

The shift in the medium through which day-to-day exchanges between citizens and their representatives took place was not dramatic or sudden. Nor did the proliferation of interest groups eliminate political parties. But it did reshape the connection between democratic choice and policy outcomes. Recognizing a shift in the nineteenth-century party system, scholars have focused much of their attention on the relationship between presidents and the mass public, emphasizing the growing role played by an independent news media and the emergence of personality as an important factor. The role of interest groups in the electoral process, however, has largely been neglected in this literature.

This chapter examines one campaign for the presidency—Herbert Hoover's in 1928. Hoover did not invent a new role for interest groups. As Gerald Gamm and Renee M. Smith demonstrate, McKinley delivered policy-related speeches to groups such as the National Association of Manufacturers as early as 1898. Hoover, however, did integrate interest groups into his campaign more fully than had previously been the case. He was the first modern president who rose to power outside of the party structure and who was more beholden to interest group cues than partisan intelligence for his connection to the voters. This essay also focuses on the 1928 campaign because of the extraordinary documentation contained in the Hoover Presidential Library. These rich sources have allowed me to capture the role played by interest groups at a level of detail rarely glimpsed by historians. Hoover sought to tap the votes of a variety of interests by adapting some of the same techniques used by savvy marketers who appealed to a variety of consumer communities.[3]

Understanding the way in which consumer choice drove electoral politics provides a framework through which scholars can reexamine the links between electoral behavior and public policy outcomes. Hoover, like General Motors, appealed to diverse "markets" by targeting specific messages toward discrete groups of "consumers," seeking their votes rather than their money. A rapidly nationalizing communications system made it more difficult to do this along sectional and regional lines—the most basic fault lines reinforced by partisan competition. Nevertheless, the powerful networks established by interest groups and their mastery of communications made it easier for candidates to distinguish between voters by class, occupation, and policy preference, and for voters to reflect their wishes back through these same channels.

The portrait of the political system that emerges from this case study is one in which elected officials and administrators alike differentiated between voters in far greater detail, just as marketers in the 1920s and 1930s began to distinguish the subtle differences in communities of consumption. The ability to distinguish between one's constituents in a more selective fashion than Republican or Democrat, Pole, or German, southerner or northerner, laid the groundwork for crafting public policies that expanded the scope of government to serve select (and powerful) constituencies while avoiding the always dangerous charge in America of contributing to the growth of "big government." Because the business sector and professionals were often "first movers" in this pattern of politics and often maintained a healthy advantage when it came to organizational resources, many of the areas in which the government expanded in the first half of the century served the needs of these interests.[4]

Interest groups broke down the heterogeneous mass electorate along class, business, occupational, professional, and eventually gender lines, complementing the long-standing racial, ethnic, and regional ties that supported partisan conceptions of the electorate. As the federal government expanded, interests that were organized around beneficiaries of public "entitlements" (as contrasted to partisan patronage) played an even greater role.

Often left out of scholarly discussions of interest groups, however, is the electoral connection. Since the days of Mark Hanna and the growing reliance of political parties on contributions from corporations and interest groups, it has been assumed that interest groups influence electoral politics through campaign contributions. While the recurring efforts to reform campaign finance law over the twentieth century pay ample tribute to this straightforward means of influencing electoral outcomes and the policies pursued by winning candidates, it ignores a far more important role played by organized interests during the first two-thirds of the twentieth century. Interest groups traded valuable electoral intelligence for commitments to public policies ostensibly endorsed by their members. Politicians could increase their "market share" of the vote by listening to these cues and delivering the policy goods.

In bringing the state back in, we have left elections, and the democratic politics that elections represent, out. Recent gendered interpretations of social provision in the early twentieth century epitomize the "disconnect" that has transpired between scholars' treatment of interest politics and electoral clout. The reigning paradigm in this field has reinvigorated interest in interest groups by painstaking and pathbreaking studies of the ways in which women organized and the public policies that these interests crafted. However, the paradigm emphasizes the advantages that accrued to middle-class women *because* they were denied the vote, arguing that the vote made women less politically effective. Hoover, my evidence suggests, took the votes of women quite seriously, and his campaign went to great efforts to treat independent and Democratic women as a nascent interest group.[5]

Like many of the authors in this collection, I consider my topic through the lens of institutions, broadly defined to include values and patterns of behavior and, most significantly, historical context. The interest group is the central institution that I examine in this essay. I employ David Truman's classic definition of interest group to mean groups that share attitudes and make claims upon society based upon those attitudes. The ways in which interest groups mobilize range from small group initiatives by economically or professionally integrated associations to coalitions that emerge out of broad social movements.[6]

The conceptual model that frames my evidence was crafted by political scientist John Mark Hansen. Interest groups, Hansen argues, interpreted voter demand for politicians. Ultimately, they were able to do this, in some instances, even more effectively than political parties. Hansen's work has been augmented recently by the scholarship of political sociologist Elisabeth Clemens who, like Hansen, grounds the emergence of interest group politics in the first two decades of the twentieth century. Like Clemens, I hope to show the significance of interest groups without assuming that their triumph was foreordained. This distinguishes my perspective from the organizational synthesis, which assumes that modern institutions required the kind of "continuous management" provided by interest groups, and from advocates of corporate liberalism, whose model assumes that interest group politics would inevitably have served corporate America. Like Clemens, I hope to construct a framework that encompasses "the people" without overdetermining their eventual triumph or oppression. Interest group politics did not automatically appear as an alternative to partisan politics. Rather, it was nurtured and developed by innovators who often had tried a number of alternatives first—some quite radical by American standards. Americans learned, and eventually natu-

ralized, the language of group interest. Although prominent political scientists found the nation awash in it by the 1920s, its roots lay in state
and local activities reaching back three or four decades, Clemens argues.
Over that period, popular movements learned how to narrow their
claims. While falling short of the social democracy envisioned by some
populists, the organizational repertoire from which activists drew broadened the range of options available to interest groups. Thus women's
groups, though using some of the same techniques as business lobbies,
turned far more readily to state intervention than business did.[7]

Besides seeking to restore the electoral basis for interest group clout,
this chapter also poses an important—and underappreciated—corollary
to the interest-groups-shape-public-policy model. Hoover, the administrator, crafted techniques based upon his experience as secretary of commerce that energized, mobilized, and in some cases organized interests in
the hope of shoring up firmer bases of electoral support. This aspect of
"policy feedback" directly affected the electoral base from which public
officials sought cues about voter preferences. As the federal government
increased its range of day-to-day dealings with organized interests, politicians seized upon the pattern of transactions that occurred in the administrative realm to shape not only policy outcomes but electoral preferences
as well. Public policy, in other words, reconfigured the key medium for
influencing elections.[8]

Interest groups, like political parties, proved to be less than perfect en-
gines for transmitting the will of the people. But like political parties, they
managed to get the job done some of the time and, indeed, far more often
than the scathing attacks on interest groups launched in the mid-1960s,
and glorified in today's headlines, might suggest. With the emergence of
reliable public opinion polling data, public officials began to explore a
third mechanism for intuiting the will of the people (along with political
parties and interest groups). By the 1970s the daily tracking poll had
begun to gain the kind of allegiance among public officials that information about voters conveyed through political parties in the nineteenth century, then interest groups in the twentieth century, had once enjoyed. With
this ability to target voter preference more specifically and more regularly,
another era in the evolving relationship between democratic choice and
public policy emerged. And just as political parties were maligned by progressive reformers for their corrupt distortion of the people's will, today's
reformers rail against the vested interests for their failure to represent
accurately the opinion of all Americans. Indeed, with the information-
transmitting function of interest groups dwarfed by public opinion polling, the constructive role once played by interest groups was eclipsed,
leaving behind only a residue of financial influence in increasingly expensive campaigns driven by interest group contributions.[9]

FROM SODA POP TO TARGETING INDEPENDENT VOTERS

The political basis for targeting voters was built upon pervasive trends in the emerging mass-consumption economy. In business, the original thrust toward national markets tended to homogenize consumers into a one-size-fits-all mentality epitomized by the rise of brand names. Both mass production and the national scope of markets encouraged the kind of standardization and homogenization epitomized by Henry Ford's Model T automobile. However, homogeneous consumers were soon replaced by segmented consumption communities. Marketing strategies that imbued products such as Coca-Cola and the Model T Ford with a "changeless quality" were soon displaced by the strategy pioneered by General Motors in the 1920s. GM viewed its consumers through a far more specialized lens than Ford. Its slogan—a "car for every purse and purpose"—helped inaugurate market segmentation.[10]

The trajectory was identical in politics. Nationalizing trends quickly gave way to segmentation. As with corporate consolidation and mass-produced standardized goods, the twentieth century gave birth to a distinctly national polity. A national citizenry that transcended party and regional boundaries was one of the progressives' core beliefs.[11]

Standing between individuals and their potential contribution to a national electorate in the nineteenth century were political parties. Progressives prepared to fill the role served by political parties by reaching "independent" voters through new techniques. The New Republic, for instance, praised the political introduction of radio: "It has found a way to dispense with political middlemen," this progressive mouthpiece swooned. Just as business moguls had originally hoped to sell one brand of biscuit or soda to a homogeneous national market, progressives envisioned a newly nationalized citizenry, reachable through national communication networks, ready to break the bonds of section, ethnicity, and party.[12]

Like the commercial techniques it was modeled on, commodified politics was perceived to be homogenizing and standardizing. The earliest and most incisive commentator on the trend was Walter Lippmann. In Public Opinion (1922), Lippmann recognized that with communications carried on at greater distances and at a faster pace, citizens—even well-informed citizens—were forced to rely on stereotypes and images to arrive at decisions. Lippmann pointed explicitly to politicians as the most sophisticated observers and practitioners of this process. Politicians relied on vague symbols to bring disparate groups together. The apparent consensus that elections created was not a product of rational agreement. Instead, it reflected the ability of successful politicians to use effective symbols to disguise disagreement. The "politics of personality" forged a bond that appeared to be intimate but that in fact was ephemeral. It leveled and consolidated constituencies, reducing the masses to the lowest common denominator, mesmerized by personality and celebrity.[13]

While homogenization certainly took place, in politics as in business, standardization was only part of the story. Interest groups in the twentieth century learned how to harness mass communications so as to build support among constituencies. The old-style interest group lobbying turned inward toward the political center and was usually linked to one political party; the new style continued to mount political pressure along traditional lines but was far more adept at molding public opinion to support legislative ends. It cut against the grain of partisan attachment. It sought broad-based support for policies by appealing directly to the electorate. It identified and mobilized segments of a given politician's constituency around specific policy ends. From the interest groups' perspective, this created a more permanent base, ensuring continued legislative and administrative support. Interest groups and politicians seeking their members' votes used the new techniques of publicity including advertising. They beamed their message at a narrower spectrum, thereby crafting the "targeted style."

As advertisers scrambled to understand newly segmented markets, politicians sought any assistance they could find in reconceptualizing constituencies. No savvy politician would turn down support from his or her party or miss an opportunity to pick off votes through the politics of personality. But most politicians also embraced ubiquitous interest groups as sources of information. Harwood Childs, a leading student of interest group politics in the twenties, summed up his detailed study of the chamber of commerce and American Federation of Labor this way:

> The Chamber and the Federation . . . play an important role in the policy-determining activities of the state. They are at the same time reservoirs of ideas, mirrors of desires, sifters of major from minor policies, agencies for leading and directing the legislative activities of the government.[14]

The discovery of political transformations wrought by interest groups was a growth industry for political scientists in the twentieth century. Arthur Bentley's *Process of Government* (1908) led the way. Bentley wanted political scientists to dig beneath the calm surface of politics constructed of rhetoric, formal rules, constitutional division of power, and party platforms. There they would discover that most citizens were members of a number of crosscutting groups. Public opinion was driven by group preference, according to Bentley. "There is no public opinion that is not activity reflecting or representing the activity of a group or of a set of groups," Bentley wrote in his chapter on public opinion and leadership. Political success required the reading of group interests.[15]

The tendencies toward a new kind of segmentation observed by Bentley in 1908 became increasingly apparent to a generation of political scientists writing in the first two decades of the twentieth century. Summing up the major developments of the past thirty years in *Recent Social Trends* (1933), Charles Merriam, arguably the nation's preeminent political scientist, declared: "The upward thrust of organized social groupings and their intimate and often dominating relation to traditional government are one of the most striking of all governmental trends, and perhaps the most profoundly significant." Merriam readily acknowledged that the pressure of organized interests was as old as the state. But the greater size and power of many groups now active, and their ability to engage the modern techniques of "propaganda," made their activities a formidable new development. While estimates of the actual number of interest groups at work during the first third of the twentieth century vary, it is clear that Bentley and Merriam were reacting to significant growth. One estimate placed the number of lobbyists in Washington, D.C., at the end of the Civil War at about 50. By 1929, E. Pendleton Herring estimated the number at 500.[16]

Beneath the progressive vision of national opinion, a far more variegated picture emerged. In their rhetoric, progressives stood by "the people" in opposition to "the interests." In the world of practical politics, however, progressives, as well as their opponents, turned to interest groups to divine illusive public opinion. Politicians, like marketers in the first two decades of the twentieth century, thrilled to the possibility of national constituencies, only to discover that these national markets could often be reached most successfully by identifying and targeting fragments of the whole—whether defined by gradations in income, functional group representation, or gender. By 1920 progressives such as Herbert Hoover subscribed to the belief that the only way to make the national government democratic was to insert group participation directly into the policymaking process.[17]

POLISHING THE MIRRORS OF DESIRES: HOOVER AS SECRETARY OF COMMERCE

When war broke out in 1914, Hoover acted on his commitment to public service, creating the Commission for Belgian Relief. After the United States entered the First World War, Hoover returned from Europe to accept the position of federal food administrator. Hoover's wartime experience taught him a great deal about reaching mass markets. Public relations and advertising were key factors in the success of his public ventures. As United States food administrator, Hoover mastered the techniques of well-publicized slogans and stunts such as pledge cards or "meatless" and "wheatless" days. As a result, in the 1920s Secretary of Commerce Hoover was able to call upon a network of influential newspapermen, publicists, and public relations experts unequaled by any cabinet member or, for that matter, president.[18]

Hoover understood that although markets were national in scope, a one-size-fits-all approach would not suffice. At the Department of Commerce, he spearheaded an effort to conduct a census of distribution. It would provide the kind detailed information on consumption that the Bureau of the Census had for some time been collecting on production. The endeavor, stimulated by government, cofunded by the chamber of commerce, and promoted by trade associations, epitomized the cooperative approach to planning embodied in Hoover's vision of the "associative state." The "associative state" would not rely on government coercion. Rather, it would depend on voluntary cooperation. This vision could function only if trade associations and interest groups accurately conveyed the preferences of each sector of the economy to the Department of Commerce, collected data for national distribution, and disseminated policy directives back to the grass roots. The crucial vessel for uniting disparate individuals toward associative ends was the interest group.[19]

The Department of Commerce under Hoover was a veritable incubator and magnet for business, functional, occupational, consumer, and charitable interests. Frederick Feiker, who ran the Associated Business Papers after consulting for Hoover at the department seemed almost to caricature the associative state when he reported that "Camp Co-operation, [the] annual conference of the electrical leagues sponsored by this Society, has been in session all week at Association Island, New York. . . ." Addressing businessmen on November 25, 1928, about what to expect from the president-elect, Feiker predicted that "business may expect to see plans and methods further set up whereby all groups in our community may take collective action in their relationships to the Federal government." At the Commerce Department, Hoover had established over 350 advisory committees staffed with representatives from business. "Once appointed the members or their successors form a connecting link with the work of the Government and make collaboration easy and constant," Feiker concluded.[20]

Herbert Hoover thus entered the presidential race of 1928 after having spent the previous fifteen years of his life grappling with markets and encouraging the articulation of interest groups. Hoover understood that America's electoral markets were as segmented as they were vast. Fearful of both state control and the waste of competition, Hoover built his vision of America's future on the bedrock of interest group politics. He was a novice at electoral politics and had weak ties to his political party. He detested the "politics of personality." The situation was ripe for a campaign that balanced the chimera of personality with appeals made through channels of ubiquitous interests.[21]

MASTER OF REFLECTIONS: HOOVER AND THE ELECTION OF 1928

The standard political histories of the 1928 campaign suggest that politics proceeded as usual. There is ample evidence in the campaign files to support this standard interpretation. The independent Hoover for President organization indulged in the kind of appeals that had been the staple of Republican campaigns for well over half a century: appeals to ethnicity, race, and patronage. There is even reason to believe that Hoover served as the bagman for cash contributions funneled to the New York headquarters of Hoover for President.[22]

Examples of the campaign's determination to use Hoover's personality to its advantage also abound. Indeed, at times it appears that finding a personality to display was the greatest challenge faced by Hoover's handlers. Hoover viewed public displays of his family life and publicity about his past accomplishments as unprincipled appeals to base emotions. When Will Irwin turned his flattering biography of Hoover into an even more emotionally charged campaign film titled *Master of Emergencies*, Hoover bristled. "I remember that the night you saw it," Irwin wrote Hoover in September 1928, "you said that it would get votes only from the morons." Hoover's qualms aside, the film was political gold. "We had to repeat it and re-repeat it," Irwin reported. The crowd went wild over it. "By the end," Irwin told Hoover, "they were sobbing all over the house. And when they cry, you've got em. Those tears mean votes." As for Hoover's misgivings? "[A]t least three-fourths of the voters, in my opinion," Irwin assured Hoover, "are moronic enough to be persuaded by their eyes and their emotions."[23]

Over the course of the campaign, Hoover succumbed to more intrusive forays into his personal life. Although he refused to part with his collection of mining photographs, he could do little but throw a tantrum when campaign aide George Barr Baker "lifted" them—frames and all—from Hoover's house and put them to use in the campaign. The campaign could easily purchase photos of Hoover from the wire service, another staffer noted. But "the ones we were after were more personal."[24]

Historians, however, have failed to grasp the way in which human interest stories and the elaboration of Hoover's personality were targeted at specific constituencies. Hoover also deployed past policy achievements in the service of these policy and electoral appeals. Although scholars have taken it as axiomatic that women did not vote as a bloc in the 1920s, the Hoover campaign made women the centerpiece of its targeted efforts. Recently enfranchised, women exemplified the potential vote that Republicans hoped to garner through the elaboration of personality. In an appeal that urged women to display their support for Hoover publicly, Marie M. Maloney telegrammed the essence of the Hoover campaign's strategy vis-à-vis women. "If Mr. Hoover is to be elected against Tammany Organization . . . it will be largely due to the votes of great numbers of women who have never taken part in politics. Political counselors agree on this. Possible to get votes of home women if they can be reached in time and in right way. Churches and women's magazines are most direct contact."[25]

Hardened political professionals such as Kansas senator Arthur Capper agreed that women would be a crucial factor in the election. Capper predicted that the percentage of women in the midwestern farm states voting for Hoover would top 80 percent. When asked to assess the key factors in Hoover's victory, William H. Hill, the head of the campaign for the state of New York and editor of the *Binghamton Sun*, was unambiguous: "The women were the big factor to my way of thinking." Republican state headquarters in Texas came to a similar conclusion. In an analysis of national election returns published in the *New York Times*, Yale economist Irving Fisher named increased registration and the women's vote as the top two entries in his list of factors that had led to Hoover's victory.[26]

After the election, transition adviser Lawrence Richey employed the Republican National Committee's Research Bureau to poll knowledgeable party operatives about the nature of Hoover's victory. Richey wanted to know "just how the various voters did align themselves—whether into racial, religious or just what sort of groups." Undoubtedly, Richey's December 15 deadline reflected his desire to incorporate the detailed analysis of voting patterns into the Hoover administration's program planning. The national committee was particularly eager to learn how Hoover had fared among women. J. Bennet Gordon summed up the answer in a report back to Richey:

> Most conspicuous and important was the tremendous support given President-elect Hoover by the women. No matter how variant were other influences, or how the support from other groups of voters fluctuated, according to local conditions and political cross-currents, the militant support of Mr. Hoover by America's womenhood was constant in every state.[27]

Public policy played a crucial role in attracting the female vote. Hoover's support of prohibition undoubtedly excited women and motivated them to participate actively in the campaign. Gordon's report notes, "The general testimony of the reports is to the effect that the prohibition issue more than any other *issue* accounted for the outpouring of women and their activity in support of Hoover." Building upon this appeal, Republicans made kitchens the focal point of their appeal to women. The "kitchen" campaign capitalized upon Hoover's record as food administrator. The campaign also publicized the fact that Hoover was the first secretary of commerce to list "homemaking" as an occupation in the census.[28]

Important as they remained, traditional partisan techniques and the linking of the politics of personality to policy did not begin to exhaust the ways in which the Hoover campaign mobilized voters. A framework that takes seriously Hoover's conception of government, considers the mechanisms he employed to govern, and examines the ways in which these influenced his campaign reveals impressive evidence documenting the campaign's acute awareness of the role to be played by independent voters. It demonstrates the promise that the "targeted" style held for campaigners wishing to capture voters who had been loosened from the grip of partisan ties.[29]

Tension over how best to pursue the independent vote and allegiance to Hoover (as opposed to allegiance to the party) at times threatened to tear the campaign apart. The Hoover for President organization was often at odds with the Republican National Committee. Frustrated by the internecine fighting that continued as patronage was handed out after the election, Hoover dashed off a brusque note to national committee leader Hubert Work. "I greatly regret your attitude toward practically every one of my loyal friends. . . . They all want to work with you but they have so many rebuffs that it is a matter of common gossip." The problem was structural, not just a question of personalities. It was particularly acute in the South, where white voters, eager to support Hoover, were not keen about sharing resources with African-Americans who had long since established a beachhead in the Republican party.[30]

Political parties had always been the central mechanism for determining which way the wind was blowing. Strongest at the local level, the organizations could report up the chain of command just how "their" voters were thinking. As the link between party and voter loosened, candidates resorted to alternative techniques to determine voter preference. Freed from the organizational base of parties when it came to surveying voter attitudes, campaigns began to perceive segments that had not been transparent during the heyday of partisan politics.

Hoover was in an ideal position to do this, having worked extensively with both interest and trade groups during his tenure as secretary of commerce. Hoover, by 1928, was knowledgeable about the growing body of social science that had begun to encourage product differentiation. He supported further development of that knowledge and threw the government's data-gathering facilities behind it. If producers, wholesalers, retailers, and consumers could pool data, and if the Department of Commerce could collect and publicize that data, inefficiencies could be wrung out of the system, reducing costs and increasing profits for all parties involved. The "associative state" would not rely on government coercion. Rather it touted voluntary cooperation.[31]

Hoover's vision of interest groups was clearest when directed toward his own profession, engineering. Hoover believed that acting as a profession, engineers could draw upon science to negotiate between the individual and society. As he told The American Engineering Council in 1924, "There is somewhere to be found a plan of individualism and associational activities that will preserve the initiative, the inventiveness, the individual, the character of man and yet will enable us to socially and economically synchronize this gigantic machine that we have built out of applied sciences. Now, there is no one who could make a better contribution to this than the engineer. . . ." One did not have to be a professional to participate in this vision. As Hoover told the American Wholesale Grocers' Convention in 1923, "We have come to appreciate a new value in trade associations. There may be some acts which may seem contrary to the public welfare but the great majority of associations and their work are distinctly helpful and in the public interest."[32]

In the absence of reliable sampling techniques, Hoover's aides developed a targeted style built around some of the very interest groups and trade associations that had worked with the Hoover administration while he was at the Commerce Department. The point man for this strategy was Nathan MacChesney. MacChesney presided over an empire of Hoover organizations that claimed to have captured five million voters. The Hoover organization was best distinguished by the degree to which it eschewed partisan rhetoric and thrived in sectors of the electorate where party ties were weakest. A graduate of Stanford, Hoover's alma mater, in the early 1920s, MacChesney served as general counsel to the National Association Real Estate Board and was appointed by Hoover to chair the Committee on Uniform Law and Regulation of Hoover's National Conference of Street and Highway Safety. As head of the Hoover-Curtis Organization Bureau, MacChesney viewed it as his mission to attach wayward independents to the Hoover slate. He summed up this approach in a final report on his campaign activities to the Republican National Committee:

> In a campaign like the present one, when party lines are broken down and hundreds of thousands of voters are dropping old partisan ties, they can make the change to another politcal party through the medium of a volunteer organization with less violence to their former partisan prejudices than would be the case if they were approached by the regular Republican organization.

A volunteer campaign that was in harmony with the state party apparatus, MacChesney wrote Hubert Work, "can lay hold of voters who are breaking away from former party ties; or who are without party affiliations; and bring them into the Republican party."[33]

MacChesney's Organization Bureau spearheaded the targeted style. In some cases, the bureau simply added a touch of coherence to groups that were already well entrenched and highly mobilized. But the bureau also reached all the way down to the grass roots, bringing together voters who had little in common except their gender, or the college they had attended, or the fact that they were first-time voters. Those reached at the amorphous end of the continuum hardly constituted organized interests. The framework through which the Hoover campaign approached these individuals, however, was forged through the "Chief's" vast experience with highly organized interests.

MacChesney swung into action in mid-July. He was highly sensitive to the potential threat to party functionaries that this new style of organization represented. Although it was time-consuming, MacChesney's bureau cleared the names of state and congressional district chairs through state Republican National Committee channels. Drawing upon a technique used by Hoover during the war, all of the volunteer organizations collected signed pledge cards, accumulating millions of names. This undoubtedly unnerved Republican regulars. To facilitate the election day get-out-the-vote drive and assuage the fears of party loyalists, the cards were handed over to party workers. "This produced the results election day," MacChesney reported, and also avoided the fear in some quarters of a continuing rival organization."[34]

MacChesney established three broad categories of volunteer organizations at the state and county levels. Hoover-Curtis business and professional leagues paralleled the associative relationships already established by Hoover's service at the Department of Commerce and drew upon the strength of well-established economic interests. For these business and professional groups, past policy positions and future policy opportunities loomed largest. A second order of groups, built around the Hoover-Curtis civic volunteers, sought to mobilize support through existing channels of fraternal, charitable, and educational organizations. Although less tied to specific policies, these groups were attuned to Hoover's general vision of an associative state. Like the economically based groups, these interests predated the Hoover campaign. Last, there were the broad-based Hoover-Curtis volunteer groups that encompassed voters previously unattached or only loosely attached to business or voluntary organizations. Included in this category were the Hoover-Curtis Women's Activities Division, Hostesses for Hoover, college campus volunteer clubs, First Voters for Hoover, and the most generic, Volunteers for Hoover.

A brief review of groups at either end of the organizational spectrum illustrates the way in which Hoover's targeted style earmarked segments of the population. The more highly organized the group, the greater the role of policy in the campaign's appeal. The Hoover Waterways Clubs, for instance, distributed a pamphlet titled *What One Man's Vision and Efforts Have Accomplished for the Northwest.* At the other end of the spectrum, Hoover-Curtis volunteer clubs sought the least common denominator at the grass roots, urging members to arrange radio parties to listen to Republican National Committee broadcasts, to hand out literature, to display posters in their homes, wear buttons, and post Hoover stickers on auto windshields.[35]

Many of these groups appealed directly to their members' self-interest, reminding them that Hoover's past policies had proved beneficial and noting that a spirited campaign on their part could hardly fail to pay policy dividends should Hoover win. Realtors were the most outspoken in this regard. Harry Culver, president of the National Realtors' Association, organized Hoover clubs in five hundred cities, personally paying the expense of setting them up. "He went a little farther than I suggested," a sheepish Hoover wrote Hubert Work, "but I do not believe these informal organizations can do any harm." W. I. Hollingsworth, the national vice chair of the Real Estate Men's League for Hoover, left little room for imagination when he wrote realtors, urging them to set up clubs. "Get the boys together so that we can put you on record as not only being for Hoover, but having a live organization for him. We want your City recorded as having a League for Hoover. There is no telling—later on this work on your part may become invaluable to the National administration and we pledge you in advance Secretary Hoover's appreciation." As Hollingsworth reminded the boys, "If any organization in the United States needs a direct representation in Washington, it is the real estate fraternity."[36]

The Hoover Waterways Club pursued a similar angle. The Minneapolis branch of the club called upon the citizens of the Mississippi Valley, "No matter to what parties they belong, to unite on Mr. Hoover in the coming election as the one man in all of this country who understands best the economic needs of the Mississippi Valley and the one man in the United States who can bring to us real and genuine measures of relief. After all, the thing in which we are most interested is our economic pocketbook. The maximum development of inland waterways transportation in the Mississippi Valley will go a long ways toward filling our economic pocketbooks."[37]

Phil Brockman, writing on behalf of the Hoover-Curtis Automobile Dealers Sales League, urged his fellow car dealers to join up because Hoover had supported them in the past, organizing the Hoover conference—which Brockman claimed was held "for our sole benefit, so to speak, as we are the ones who will profit in a way by having good laws governing the operation of automobiles. . . . Also, the safer the streets and highways, the more automobiles we will sell." Not to be outdone, the director of the Western Division, Hoover-Curtis Fruit and Vegetable League—a potato distributor—wrote fellow distributors urging them to join up. "I have often heard the thought expressed," he concluded, "that our industry was not given the consideration which it should receive. Perhaps this has not been our fault in the past, but if we neglect to bend every effort to elect the first President whom, I may say has had any understanding of the functions and importance of our industry the fault will certainly not lie with us."[38]

Many of the business and professional leagues went out of their way to state their appeals in nonpartisan terms. "Not knowing your politics, I am somewhat hesitant in calling upon you," a letter from the president of the De Luxe automobile company began. Fred Voiland, writing on a letterhead that advised recipients to "DRESS WELL AND SUCCEED," urged fellow clothiers to "lay aside party affiliation, and do this great work for the United States of America. We are, after all," Voiland philosophized, "Americans first, and after that, retailers."[39]

At the other end of the spectrum lay blocs of voters who did not necessarily share business or professional ties. From the perspective of the Hoover campaign, they formed a bloc precisely because their members were more likely than other voters to cross party lines in support of Hoover. If these individuals could be identified, targeted, and cultivated—if they themselves came to perceive a shared interest—they might make the difference in a close election. No group better matched these criteria than women. Both political parties had cultivated women as a distinct voting group since the late 1910s. Political scientist Anna Harvey has documented the extensive campaign to enroll women by establishing women's committees in both parties and by campaign organizations such as "parlor meetings" and Home and Harding groups, or the Democractic Victory Clubs of women. The National League of Women Voters took the lead in forming the Women's Joint Congressional Commitee in November 1920 that represented the legislative proposals of a number of other women's groups as well. About the same time, the American Federation of Labor spearheaded a campaign to attract working women to the Democratic party. No doubt the clear divide between Hoover and Smith's positions on prohibition in 1928, and Smith's association with Tammany Hall politics, motivated women more than other issues. What is impressive nonetheless is the degree to which the Hoover campaign reconceptualized the electorate, identifying the "women's vote" as a crucial factor. Hoover forged an organizational path to capture this segment of his constituency.[40]

Like the savvy political aide she was, Mrs. Martin Kent Northam, assistant director of Women's Activities at the Hoover-Curtis Organization Bureau, attributed the strong interest of women to the candidate. The body of the report that she submitted outlined the ways in which the campaign had been organized to tap this resource. The Women's Activities Division sprang to life on July 26 when it established Hoover-Curtis Women's Volunteer Clubs at the precinct and township level. The clubs secured the written pledges of women to vote for Hoover. To do this, they handed out literature, buttons, and automobile stickers. In all, more than one million pledge cards were received. These cards were in turn used to get out the vote on election day.[41]

One of the clubs' most significant activities entailed voter education. Here, the object was not the usual instruction in how to vote the straight party ticket: quite the opposite. As Mrs. Northam reported, the clubs "conducted lessons in correct voting in order that those women of opposite party affiliations could learn how to split their ballot without disqualifying it." Indeed, the value of the organization, as Northam saw it, was to give "women with no definite party affiliations and also Democratic women, who did not wish to be considered as Republicans, an opportunity to unite with the Hoover-Curtis Organization for the head of the ticket, as the organization was understood to be only for the duration of the campaign." Splitting votes like this allowed women to vote with their party for the local candidate and Hoover for president. This approach, Northam argued, aroused the "civic consciousness" of women.[42]

In the final weeks of the campaign the Organization Bureau intensified its activities, establishing the Hoover Hostesses. Mrs. Silas H. Strawn directed the program. The objective of this program was "to have interested groups in every home in the country listening in to Republican campaign speakers over the radio." Contacted through a gigantic chain letter operation, hostesses created a nationwide network. At the high point, these meetings produced three thousand new pledges a day, according to Strawn's report. As the program grew in size, the campaign targeted radio broadcasts specifically at this specialized audience. As Strawn put it, "It is the first time that women who cannot leave their homes, who cannot give money, —old and young, rich and poor, shut-in, incapacitated, in any walk of life—can become active workers in a political campaign. In many cases, where a woman did not own a radio, she went to her neighbor, interested her and made her a radio hostess."[43]

Samples of hostess correspondence reveal the breadth of the program. There was, for instance, a special mailing aimed at recruiting "Colored" hostesses. The program also signed up Billy Sunday's wife and Mrs. Thomas Edison. Mrs. Strawn considered her program to be nothing short of a contribution to the "civic intelligence" of the nation. In revealing her plans for the future, Strawn embraced the associative spirit spawned by the Hoover campaign. "With more time and sufficient funds in subsequent campaigns," Mrs. Strawn concluded in her final report, "the plan could be enlarged upon by emphasizing the organization of industrial workers, welfare groups, churches, hospitals, business women's and social clubs, farmers' organizations and fraternal bodies. This would be in addition to the radio parties in private homes. An organization embracing *every activity in life*, both men and women, can be developed."[44]

Hoover Hostesses made great use of *Master of Emergencies*. MacChesney broadcast the results of the first public showing in New York, quoting the president of the local Hoover League, Mrs. Clarence Hancock: "Picture tremendous success. Made wonderful impression on our women." MacChesney also quoted the woman who was vice chair of the Massachusetts committee. "Throughout the last fifteen or twenty minutes of the showing a great many people were in tears and the applause in each case was emotional, spontaneous and very heartfelt. [A]s a vote-getter," she continued, "it was far superior to any speaker whom we had heard and could undoubtedly be made very effective in reaching many voters who would never come to a regular Republican gathering." Some of the attributes most associated with the rise of personality in twentieth-century campaigning were evident in the reactions to this film. Yet in thousands of meetings "hosted" by women, the Organization Bureau targeted its message at the very voters thought to be most receptive to its message and sought to connect Hoover the humanitarian portrayed in the film to the public policies of Hoover the secretary of commerce and candidate for president.[45]

Hoover won the election handily. He racked up 444 electoral votes to Smith's 87. He outpaced Smith in the popular vote by almost 6.5 million of the 36.5 million votes cast. Hoover made deep inroads into the border South, carrying North Carolina, Virginia, Tennessee, Texas, and Florida. He won every nonsouthern state with the exception of Massachusetts. Although scholars continue to debate the nature of the female vote in 1928, Alan Lichtman has argued persuasively that women constituted a disproportionate number of the newly registered voters, swelling the electorate in 1928.[46]

CONCLUSION

Placing the Hoover campaign of 1928 in the context of market segmentation and examining the election through the lens of interest group politics revises the prevailing framework used to understand politics during this period. Issue-oriented politics was deployed interchangeably with the politics of personality. The image that Hoover projected to the electorate was one drawn from his accomplishments and his stance on the issues. Alongside the politics of personality, the campaign waged a war for business and professional groups almost exclusively designed to appeal to their self-interest. Even when it came to the politics of personality, the campaign sought to target specific groups that it felt would be more receptive to its message. Women were the most prominent of these, and they were singled out because they were thought to be the most likely to confound party loyalty. Although it is beyond the scope of this study to examine the ways in which electoral clout translated into policy influence, it is clear that policy making prior to the campaign influenced the shape of that campaign. Hoover's vision of the associative state was replicated in MacChesney's Organization Bureau. Even a cursory review of correspondence following the election reveals a strong expectation of policy rewards by the organized groups that lined up behind Hoover in the campaign. As W. I. Hollingsworth reminded his buddies, "There is nothing of more importance to the realtor than taxation and legislation and we need an intelligent, unbiased sympathetic friend in Washington." Electoral mobilization might ensure that an "unbiased" president would be both friendly and sympathetic.[47]

As some women found out in 1929, when Hoover failed to endorse legislation that would have restored women and children's health programs to the Children's Bureau, electoral influence did not automatically translate into policy victory. For advocates of gendered interpretations of politics, this failure is often seen as evidence that women were more influential before they had the vote than after. Anna Harvey, who examines the ways in which past gender bias influenced the structural barriers to female political participation in the 1920s, argues that "the severely diminished efficacy of women's organizations after 1925 was to last for approximately forty-five years, until 1970." For Lichtman, "Women became neither an independent force in American politics nor an interest group within the parties whose loyalty had to be preserved."[48]

If I am correct in asserting that the most fundamental shift in the political system between 1900 and 1970 was the emergence of interest groups as indicators of voter preference—and if we accept Childs' characterization of them as "mirrors of desires"—then gender, rather than forming a fault line around which all politics revolved, should be viewed as just another interest around which groups could and did organize. As such, women, like funeral directors, realtors, and osteopaths, would win their share of battles and lose their share of battles as they tried to convert their electoral clout into public policy. The degree to which the Hoover campaign sought to capitalize on the votes of women, however, should leave little doubt that practical politicians took the connection between elections and public policy seriously. This is not to say that women constituted an interest group. Women, however, did share certain broad sets of preferences that both politicians and corporate marketers sought to discern and cater to. Nor is it to argue that the influence of gender was limited to the interest group model. However, to ignore the ways in which women's votes were sought through mechanisms that discerned policy cues from groups that shared attitudes and advanced claims based upon those shared attitudes, to paraphrase David Truman's words, is to deny a large part of the history of politics and gender in the first two-thirds of the twentieth century.

By the 1930s Franklin D. Roosevelt had mastered the use of radio, perfecting the "politics of personality." The election of 1932 witnessed a dramatic shift in partisan alignment—a realignment that continues to shape politics even today. Both of these developments have been examined by political historians in great detail. More subtle, less conspicuous, but perhaps of equal significance, by 1928 candidates were targeting campaign appeals to interest groups in an effort to reach newly segmented political markets. This too was part of a much larger trend that shaped the twentieth-century polity.

Given the vibrant scholarship on the culture of consumption, now is the time for scholars to revise their conception of how market models informed political development. Had markets remained the homogeneous aggregates that Ford hoped to reach with the Model T, there would be little reason to look for the roots of our complex and variegated public policies in political equivalents of the market. Electoral politics would continue to occlude, not illuminate. Had segments of that market remained exclusively the ethnic, cultural, and sectional groups that dominated nineteenth-century politics, there would be little cause to seek in them the origins of the complex policies of the twentieth-century state. That politicians identified markets, using interest groups and voting blocs as markers, and that policy was seen as the equivalent to merchandising— a way to attach interest groups to political coalitions—connects the study of elections to the evolution of governance. It also explains, in part, how the central government expanded in a political culture wary of big government. The targeted style laid a democratic framework for public policies that favored incremental growth powered by interest group pressure.

Filling out the framework that I have sketched in this chapter will revise political history in several ways. First, it reperiodizes political history, eschewing "cycles of history" and regimes defined by the degree to which they advance liberalism. Rather, periods should be defined by the mechanisms used by public officials to discern the public will. From Reconstruction through the end of the nineteenth century, partisan intelligence remained the staple of voter–public official relations. From 1900 through the early 1970s, public officials used interest groups as surrogates for specialized intelligence about the electorate. This was eclipsed by the use of daily tracking polls, which remain the staple of today's public official–constituent relationship. A framework built upon the mechanisms for interpreting voter preferences would illuminate the connection between election campaigns, the public policies that emerged from those campaigns, and the way in which those public policies in turn reshaped the new electoral landscape. This approach restores agency to the world of politics by focusing on key actors, such as Herbert Hoover, who adapted the political system to their electoral needs and policy ends.

Most significantly, concentrating on the ways in which public officials conceptualize their constituencies offers political historians the opportunity to integrate their work into the broader contours of their profession. Ultimately, it was long-term structural changes in the economy, in the relationship between marketers and consumers, and in the cultural construction of public opinion and consumer choice that underlay the symbiotic relationship forged between public officials and interest groups in the twentieth century. It is up to historians of politics, culture, business, and communications to fill out a framework that, to date, is but partially glimpsed. I hope that they will take as their central question the ways in which public officials conceptualized their constituency, for it is by answering, more definitively, this question that scholars can tackle some of the most fundamental issues that undergird the problems and promise of democracy in twentieth-century America.

NOTES

I would like to thank Ed Ayers, Lou Galambos, Mark Hansen, Shelly Kaplan, Ira Katznelson, Mike Lacey, Chuck McCurdy, Peter Onuf, Lori Gates Schuyler, Gil Troy, Hal Wells, and McGee Young for their comments and suggestions. I would also like to thank the staff at the Hoover Presidential Library for their archival assistance. Participants at seminars at The Johns Hopkins University and the University of Virginia and OAH and Policy History Conference panels made valuable comments. The editors of this volume offered a number of useful criticisms and comments, as did the invited readers, Sid Milkis, Jim Morone, and Elizabeth Sanders. I am also grateful for the support of the Woodrow Wilson Center for International Affairs, the Hoover Presidential Library Foundation, and the University of Virginia School of Arts and Sciences.

1. Alex Keyssar, *The Right to Vote: The Contested History of Democracy in the United States* (New York: Basic Books, 2000); Michael McGerr, *The Decline of Popular Politics: The American North, 1865–1928* (New York: Oxford University Press, 1986); Mark Lawrence Kornbluh, *Why America Stopped Voting: The*

Decline of Participatory Democracy and the Emergence of Modern American Politics (New York: New York University Press, 2000).

2. Gil Troy, *See How They Ran: The Changing Role of the Presidential Candidate* (New York: Free Press, 1991). Richard Jensen, *The Winning of the Midwest: Social and Political Conflict, 1888–1896* (Chicago: University of Chicago Press, 1971), 165; McGerr, *Decline of Popular Politics*, chap. 6, "Advertised Politics"; and Robert Westbrook, "Politics as Consumption: Managing the Modern American Election," in *Culture of Consumption*, ed. Richard Wightman Fox and T. J. Jackson Lears (New York: Pantheon Books, 1983), 143–74; John A. Morello, *Selling the President, 1920: Albert D. Lasker, Advertising, and the Election of Warren G. Harding* (Westport, Conn.: Praeger Publishers, 2001). On "going public, see Samuel Kernell, *Going Public: New Strategies of Presidential Leadership*, 2d ed. (Washington D.C.: Congressional Quarterly Press, 1993).

On the decline of the party system and the rise of alternatives, see Richard L. McCormick, "The Party Period and Public Policy: An Exploratory Hypothesis, *Journal of American History* 66 (1979): 279–98; Sidney M. Milkis, *Political Parties and Constitutional Government: Remaking American Democracy* (Baltimore: Johns Hopkins University Press, 1999), 4–8; Gerald Gamm and Renee M. Smith, "Presidents, Parties, and the Public: Evolving Patters of Interaction, 1877–1929," in *Speaking to the People: The Rhetroical Presdiency in Historical Perspective*, ed. Richard J. Ellis (Amherst: University of Massachusetts Press, 1998), 90–93; Jeffrey K. Tulis, *The Rhetorical Presidency* (Princeton, N.J.: Princeton University Press, 1987); Sidney M. Milkis and Daniel J. Tichenor, " 'Direct Democracy' and Social Justice: The Progressive Campaign of 1912" *Studies in American Political Development* 8, no. 2 (fall 1994): 282–340.

3. Gamm and Smith, "Presidents, Parties, and the Public," 104–8.

4. Exploring the ways in which the reconceptualization of interest groups contributed to the rise of big government is beyond the scope of this essay. It is, however, one of the central questions addressed in the manuscript that I am currently working on, titled, "Selling Big Government: The Political Culture of State Building in Twentieth-Century America." On "consumption communities," compare Daniel J. Boorstin, *The Americans: The Democratic Experience* (1973; New York: Vintage, 1974), 89–164, and Olivier Zunz, *Why the American Century?* (Chicago: University of Chicago Press, 1998), chap. 4. See also the examples of consumption transcending geographical boundaries in Edward L. Ayers, *The Promise of the New South: Life after Reconstruction* (New York: Oxford University Press, 1992), 81–103, and Lizbeth Cohen, *Making a New Deal: Industrial Workers in Chicago, 1919–1939* (New York: Cambridge University Press, 1990), chap. 3. On the prevalence of business and professional groups, see Jack L. Walker, Jr., *Mobilizing Interest Groups in America: Patrons, Professions, and Social Movements* (Ann Arbor: University of Michigan Press, 1991), 12.

5. Brian Balogh, "The State of the State among Historians," *Social Science History* (2003); Louis Galambos, *America at Middle Age* (New York: McGraw-Hill, 1983), and *Competition and Cooperation: The Emergence of a National Trade Association* (Baltimore: Johns Hopkins University Press, 1966); Robert Wiebe, *Businessmen and Reform: A Study of the Progressive Movement* (Cambridge, Mass.: Harvard University Press, 1962), and *The Search for Order, 1877–*

1920 (New York: Hill and Wang, 1967); and Samuel P. Hays, *The Response of Industrialism, 1885–1914* (Chicago: University of Chicago Press, 1957).

For an explanation and critique of the "organizational synthesis," see Brian Balogh, "Reorganizing the Organizational Synthesis: Federal-Professional Relations in Modern America," *Studies in American Political Development* 5, no. 1 (1991): 119–72. Stephen Skowronek relies heavily on the "organizational" approach in *Building a New American State: The Expansion of National Administrative Capacities, 1877–1920* (New York: Cambridge University Press, 1982). In *The Politics That Presidents Make: Leadership from John Adams to Bill Clinton* (Cambridge, Mass.: The Belknap Press of Harvard University Press, 1997), Skowronek carves out a far greater role for ideas, replacing some of the organizational baggage of his earlier work with the concept of policy regimes. As in my own work, and that of most scholars who focus on policy, the electoral basis for these policy regimes is not as well grounded.

Although Theda Skocpol conceptualizes an electorate integrally connected to the policy-making system in *Protecting Soldiers and Mothers: The Political Origins of Social Policy in the United States* (Cambridge, Mass.: Harvard University Press, 1992) and notes the politically convenient way in which veterans' benefits were funneled to Republican constituents after the Civil War, this is not the case for part 3 of *Protecting*, where women are effective politically before gaining the right to vote. Thus, progressive women could set agendas in terms of their own ideals as long as they did *not* have the vote. "Ironically," Skocpol writes, "this situation prevailed only as long as women were collectively mobilized for styles of politics that did not depend primarily on voting. . . . [A]fter the franchise was fully won, politically active American women faced the same choices and obstacles 'within the system' as other U.S. citizens." Skocpol, *Protecting*, 319. What Skocpol neglects to say is that they also now had the same clout when it came to voting.

Anna L. Harvey, in *Votes without Leverage: Women in American Electoral Politics, 1920–1970* (New York: Cambridge University Press, 1998), also sees a marked decline in the influence of women by the mid-1920s. In a recent synthesis of the role played by women in politics during the 1920s, Kristi Andersen documents (as do Skocpol and Harvey) the ways in which the political system adapted to women, redefining the boundary that distinguished men and women in public life in *After Suffrage: Women in Partisan and Electoral Politics before the New Deal* (Chicago: University of Chicago Press, 1996). But Andersen too concludes that suffrage resulted in declining clout for women by the late 1920s in *After Suffrage*, 102–9. For a good discussion of the long-standing presumption among scholars that women's influence declined after gaining the vote, see Andersen, *After Suffrage*, 5–9. For its origins, see William Henry Chafe, *The American Woman: Her Changing Social, Economic, and Political Roles, 1920–1970* (New York: Oxford University Press, 1972), 299–300.

Nancy Cott, in *The Grounding of Modern Feminism* (New Haven, Conn.: Yale University Press, 1987), sees more continuity with "voluntarist" politics continuing from the Progressive Era through the 1920s. Because Cott frames the question as whether a "woman bloc" would emerge and whether it would elect women to office—something that clearly did not happen—rather than whether the power of the vote would make those lobbying for issues disproportionately supported by women more effective, she concludes that acquiring the vote mattered little. Voluntarist politics "continued as women's principal political mode." Cott, Grounding, 114 and chap. 3. The most striking of these continuities is "women's favoring the pursuit of politics through voluntary associations over the electoral arena." Cott, Grounding, 85. This bifurcation of associations and the electoral arena is characteristic of the more general tendency within political history to separate policy from the electoral sphere.

Cott and Robin Muncy also distinguish women's voluntary groups—even after women obtained the vote—from traditional interest groups because the women's groups did not have the capacity to make huge monetary contributions to political campaigns. See Cott, Grounding, 99, and Robin Muncy, Creating a Female Dominion in American Reform, 1890–1935 (New York: Oxford University Press, 1991), 128. Paula Baker, in "The Domestication of Politics: Women and American Political Society, 1780–1920," American Historical Review 89 (June 1984): 639, argues that because women created a separate sphere in politics, they were the first to craft "interest-group tactics, providing a model that men would follow as partisan politics declined in the twentieth century." I take issue with this argument on two grounds. First, it ignores the rich history of male interest groups that proliferated in the late nineteenth century, alongside the dominant party system. Second, and more relevant to this article, it neglects the crucial connection between votes and interest group effectiveness.

Even the more recent revisionist literature, which seeks to restore some agency to women after they gained suffrage, implicitly suggests that women settled for the politics of symbolism. Andersen sums this up succinctly, writing that by the late 1920s, "Male leaders responded to women's concerns on a primarily symbolic basis. . . ." Andersen, After Suffrage, 105. This fits squarely within the traditional politics of consumption, which views candidates in Lippmannesque terms as manipulators of symbols, adept at appealing to homogeneous audiences. For impressive evidence that the votes of women did matter during the 1920s, see Lori Gates Schuyler, "The Weight of Their Votes: Southern Women and Politics in the 1920s" (Ph.D. dissertation, University of Virginia, 2001).

David Truman refers to "widely held attitudes that are not expressed in interaction" as "potential interest groups." The Hoover campaign provided the organizational catalyst to forge behavior and action, ideally resulting in a vote for Hoover. David B. Truman, The Governmental Process: Political Interests and Public Opnion (1951; Berkeley, Calif.: Institute of Governmental Studies, 1993), 35.

6. Truman, Governmental Process, 33; Walker, Mobilizing Interest Groups, 12–13.

7. John Mark Hansen, Gaining Access: Congress and the Farm Lobby, 1919–1981 (Chicago: University of Chicago Press, 1991), 228–29. Wiebe, Search for Order; Gabriel Kolko, The Triumph of Conservatism: A Reinterpretation of American History (New York: Free Press, 1977). Elisabeth S. Clemens, The People's Lobby: Organizational Innovation and the Rise of Interest Group Politics in the United States, 1890–1925 (Chicago: University of Chicago Press, 1997), 6–7, 207.

8. On policy feedback, see Skocpol, Protecting, 57–60.

9. Jean M. Converse, *Survey Research in the United States: Roots and Emergence, 1890–1960* (Berkeley: University of California Press, 1987); Susan Herbst, *Numbered Voices: How Opinion Polling Has Shaped American Politics* (Chicago: University of Chicago Press, 1993).

10. Susan Strasser, *Satisfaction Guaranteed: The Making of the American Mass Market* (New York: Pantheon Books, 1989), 161 and chap. 5.; see also a review of Strasser by Lizbeth Cohen, "The Mass in Mass Consumption," *Reviews in American History* (December 1990): 549–55; Hal Wells, "Remapping America: Market Research and American Society, 1900–1940," (Ph.D. dissertation, University of Virginia, 1999); Richard Tedlow, *New and Improved: The Story of Mass Marketing in America* (New York: Basic Books, 1990), 6; Roland Marchand, *Advertising the American Dream: Making Way for Modernity, 1920–1940* (Berkeley: University of California Press, 1985); The President's Research Committee on Social Trends, *Recent Social Trends in the United States*, vol. 2 (New York: McGraw-Hill, 1933), 866; Cohen, *Making a New Deal*, chap. 3.

11. On rationalization, see Herbert Croly, *The Promise of American Life* (1909; Cambridge, Mass.: Harvard University Press, 1965), 270. Eldon Eisenach, *The Lost Promise of Progressivism* (Lawrence: University Press of Kansas, 1994), chap. 1.

12. Eisenach, *Lost Promise*, chaps. 1, 4; Harwood Lawrence Childs, *Labor and Capital in National Politics* (1930; New York: Arno Press, 1974), 243; E. Pendleton Herring, *Group Representation before Congress* (Baltimore: Johns Hopkins University Press, 1929), 2. "Electioneering on the Air," *New Republic* 40 (September 3, 1924): 9, quoted in Clayton R. Koppes, "The Social Destiny of the Radio: Hope and Disillusionment in the 1920s," *The South Atlantic Quarterly* 68, no. 3 (summer, 1969): 366.

13. Walter Lippmann, *Public Opinion* (1922; New York: Free Press, 1965), Part 3, chap. 15. Robert Westbrook, *John Dewey and American Democracy* (Ithaca, N.Y.: Cornell University Press, 1991) 294–96. Richard Jensen, *The Winning of the Midwest: Social and Political Conflict, 1888–1896* (Chicago: University of Chicago Press, 1971), 165; McGerr, *Decline of Popular Politics*, chap. 6; Troy, *See How They Ran*, 133. Robert Westbrook, "Politics as Consumption: Managing the Modern American Election," in *Culture of Consumption*, ed. Fox and Lears, 143–74.

14. Childs, *Labor and Capital*, 247.

15. Arthur F. Bentley, *The Process of Government* (1908; Cambridge, Mass.: Harvard University Press, 1967), 204, 209–10, 223.

16. Michael J. Lacey and Mary O. Furner, eds., *The State and Social Investigation in Britain and the United States* (New York: Woodrow Wilson Center Press and Cambridge University Press, 1993), 40–49; Herring, *Group Representation*, 60;Edward Bernays, *Crsytallizing Public Opinion* (New York: Boni, Liveright, 1923), 146, cited in Wells, "Remapping America," 338; for Merriam, see President's Research Committee, *Recent Social Trends*, 1515; Barry D. Karl, *Charles E. Merriam and the Study of Politics* (Chicago: University of Chicago Press, 1974), 201. Estimates cited in Mark P. Petracca, "The Rediscovery of Interest Group Politics," in *The Politics of Interests: Interest Groups Transformed*, ed. Mark P. Petracca (Boulder, Colo.: Westview Press, 1992), 13.

17. Peri Ethan Arnold, "Herbert Hoover and the Continuity of American Public Policy," *Public Policy* 20 (fall 1972): 525–44.

18. Joan Hoff Wilson *Herbert Hoover: Forgotten Progressive* (1975: Prospect Heights, Ill., 1992), 46; Craig Lloyd, *Aggressive Introvert: A Study of Herbert Hoover and Public Relations Management, 1912–1932* (Columbus: Ohio State University Press, 1972), 37, 45–52; Frederick M. Feiker, "Washington as a date line is news," and "What Business May Expect from the Next President," Speeches and Articles, 1928 folder, box 16, Feiker Papers, Herbert Hoover Presidential Papers, Herbert Hoover Presidential Library, West Branch, Iowa (hereafter HHPL).

19. Wells, "Remapping America," chaps. 3 and 5, and William Leach, *Land of Desire: Merchants, Power, and the Rise of a New American Culture* (New York: Pantheon Books, 1993), 364–65. Ellis Hawley, "Herbert Hoover, the Commerce Secretariat, and the Vision of an 'Associative State,' 1921–1928," *Journal of American History* 61, no. 1 (1974): 116–40; David E. Hamilton, "Building the Associative State: The Department of Agriculture and American State-Building," *Agricultural History* 64, no. 2 (spring 1990): 207–18; and Colin Gordon, *New Deals: Business, Labor, and Politics in America, 1920–1935* (New York: Cambridge University Press, 1994).

20. Correspondence between Arthur Rule and Lewis Strauss, general manager of the Federated Fruit and Vegetable Growers, box 67, and Aaron Sapiro and Lewis Strauss, box 68 and Subject File I—Accretions, Herbert Hoover, 1927, box 68, Papers of Lewis L. Strauss, HHPL. Monahan to Matthews, April 30, 1925, Department of Commerce Files, box 2, Advertising 1925 folder. Assistant to Feiker to Tay, reporting on "Camp Cooperation," September 11, 1925, Advisory Committee on Statistics (2), 1924–25 box 1; Feiker, "What Business May Expect," HHPL. "Associations" correspondence, Department of Commerce Files, HHPL. April 12, 1921, Associations Information, 1921, box 38, Commerce Collection, HHPL. May 5, 1921, Associations Information, 1921, box 38, Commerce Collection, HHPL. MacChesney to Dear Sir, October 25, 1928, Republican Party—1928, Final Report of National Committee, box 38, MacChesney Papers, HHPL. Hoover to Bradfute, February 14, 1923, American Farm Bureau Federation, 1922–1927 folder, Department of Commerce Collection, box 24, HHPL.

21. Gary Dean Best, "The Hoover-for President Boom of 1920," *MidAmerica* 53, no. 4 (Oct 1971): 227.

22. Roy V. Peel and Thomas C. Donnelly, *The 1928 Campaign: An Analysis* (New York: Richard R. Smith, 1931), 87; David Burner, *Politics of Provincialism: The Democratic Party in Transition, 1918–1932* (1968; Cambridge, Mass.: Harvard University Press, 1986), 179–80; for an opposing view on the possibility of a Smith victory, see Allan J. Lichtman, *Prejudice and Old Politics: The Election of 1928* (Chapel Hill: University of North Carolina Press, 1979), 245. Paul A. Carter, "Déja Vu; or Back to the Drawing Board with Alfred E. Smith," *Reviews in American History* 8, no. 2 (1980): 272–76.

St. Louis Globe-Democrat, September 25, 1928; Edward Flesh to George Barr Baker, October 1, 1928, Baker folder, box 7, Campaign and Transition Files (hereafter C & T), HHPL. Unattributed note, September 27, 1928, Hubert Work, file, box 72, C & T, HHPL. Colored People 1928 files, box 7, Akerson Papers, HHPL, particularly A. L. Holsey, secretary to the principal, Tuskegee Normal and Industrial Institute, to Akerson, March 29, 1928. Akerson to Richey telegram, January 26, 1929, Akerson folder, box 2, C & T, HHPL. Akerson to Richey, February 7, 1929, Strauss folder, box 66, C & T, HHPL. Akerson to Mr. Graves, March 27, [1928], Fox folder, box 8, Akerson Papers, HHPL. Fox to Akerson, March 26, 1928, Fox folder, box 8, Akerson Papers, HHPL; and Akerson to Fox, March 28, 1928, Fox folder, box 8, Akerson Papers, HHPL. "Fort Memo," undated, Fort file, box 27, C & T, HHPL. Rickard Diaries, memo, August 1, 1928, HHPL. "My general impression," Edgar Rickard, Hoover's close personal friend, confided to his diary, is "that HH is so completely absorbed in winning nomination that absolutely nothing else at the moment counts and I am sorry to see how completely this dominates his every action." As if to confirm Rickard's worst fears, Hoover wrote Republican National Committee chair Hubert Work in July 1928, "you must get some more political people here." Having come this far with his friend, Rickard could hardly object when Hoover handed him $5,000 in cash that had been given to the chief for "campaign purposes." On Rickard's concern regarding Hoover's political operatives, see Rickard Diaries, February 12, 1928; and on Hoover's funds for "campaign purposes," see Rickard Diaries, June 7, 1928; Hoover to Work, July 14, 1928, Work folder, box 73, C & T, HHPL.

23. Rickard Diaries, August 24, 1928; Irwin to Hoover, September 13, 1928, Irwin folder, box 38, C & T, HHPL; "Me and the Movies," 3, *Baloney Knife* folder, box 1, Akerson Papers, HHPL. Bruce Barton to Hoover, February 23, 1929, Barton folder, box 8, HHPL.

24. Edward Anthony, *Oral History*, 25–27, 74, HHPL; "Back Stage in Washington," January 2, 1929, no citation, Akerson folder, box 1, Akerson Papers, HHPL; Henry C. Morris to Hunt, September 28, 1928; Henry C. Morris to Hunt, September 28, 1928, Hunt folder, box 9, Strother Papers, HHPL.

25. Keyssar, *Right to Vote*, 218; Baker, "Domestication," 643–47; Muncy, *Female Dominion*, 128. "Women's Page Service" in Anthony to Akerson, March 10, 1928, Anthony folder, box 5, Akerson Papers, HHPL. Victoria French Allen, "Some Pages from Hoover History," Edward Anthony Papers, Women's Page Service folder, box 1, HHPL; Maloney to Rosenwald, July 31, 1928, misc. M folder, box 14, Strauss Papers, Campaign of 1928 Collection, HHPL.

26. Capper statement, August 20, 1928, Capper folder, box 8, C & T, HHPL. Hill to Alan Fox, November 24, Rickard folder, box 58, C & T, HHPL. *New York Times*, November 25, 1928; Akerson to Anthony, April 9, 1928, Anthony folder, box 5, Akerson Papers, HHPL. Harvey, *Votes without Leverage*, chap. 4.

27. Lawrence Richey to unstated [most likely J. Bennett Gordon], undated [November 1928], box 157, C & T, HHPL; J. Bennett Gordon to Lawrence Richey, January 3, 1929, p. 5, box 157, C & T, HHPL. Harvey, *Votes without Leverage*, chap. 4.

28. Gordon to Richey, January 3, 1929, p. 7; Harvey, *Votes without Leverage*, 130.

29. Nathan William McChesney to Work, November 12, 1928, Work folder, box 73, C & T, HHPL; McChesney to Hoover, October 19, 1928, McChesney folder, box 45, C & T, HHPL; Goodrich to Hoover and attached, February 9,

1929, Goodrich folder, box 29, C & T, HHPL; Nagel to Hoover, November 12, 1928, Nagel folder, C & T, HHPL.

30. Anthony, *Oral History*, 41–47, HHPL; Goodrich to Hoover, August 24, 1928, Goodrich folder, box 29, C & T, HHPL; Hoover to Work, February 7, [1929], Work folder, box 73, C & T, HHPL. Kruesi to J.R.R. Nutt, RNC, October 8, 1928, Negroes folder, box 14, Straus Campaign 1928 Collection, HHPL; Wellford to Kruesi, October 5, 1928, Negroes folder, box 14, Strauss Campaign 1928 Collection, HHPL; Kirchoffer to Hoover, August 24, 1928, Kirchoffer folder, box 41, C & T, HHPL.

31. Hawley, "Herbert Hoover."

32. Herbert Hoover, "The Engineer's Place in the World," January 10, 1924, p. 3, HHPL; Herbert Hoover, May 24, 1923, p. 1, HHPL.

33. MacChesney to James W. Good, November 7, 1928, "Final Report," Hoover-Curtis Organization Bureau, MacChesney Papers, HHPL; MacChesney to Hoover, July 5, 1921, and Jackson to Hoover, October 29, 1925, MacChesney 1921–1925 folder, Commerce Collection, HHPL. MacChesney to Good, November 7, 1928, "Final Report"; MacChesney to Work, November 12, 1928, Work folder, box 72, C & T, HHPL.

34. MacChesney, "Final Report," 8.

35. MacChesney, "Special Bulletin," MacChesney Papers, HHPL.

36. Harry H. Culver to Hoover, August 29, 1928, Culver folder, C & T, HHPL; Hoover to Work, August 31, 1928, Work folder, box 72, C & T, HHPL; undated form letter from Hollingsworth in MacChesney, "Special Bulletin."

37. S. G. Rubinow to Akerson, September 14, 1928, and Attachment B, Hoover Waterways Club folder, box 35, C & T, HHPL; Rand to Grocers, October 16, 1928, in MacChesney, "Special Bulletin."

38. Brockman to Dear Sir, in MacChesney, "Special Bulletin;" E. Percy Miller to Dear Friends, undated, in MacChesney, "Special Bulletin."

39. Brockman to Dear Sir in MacChesney, "Special Bulletin"; Voiland to Mr. L.C. Biglowe, September 15, 1928, in MacChesney, "Special Bulletin."

40. Harvey, *Votes without Leverage*, 107, 115, 119, 122; Rebecca Edwards, *Angels in the Machinery: Gender in American Party Politics from the Civil War to the Progressive Era* (New York: Oxford University Press, 1997). MacChesney, "Final Report."

41. Hoover-Curtis Organization Bureau, "Women's Activities," Final Report, HHPL.

42. Ibid.

43. "Hoover-Curtis Organization Bureau," Hoover Hostesses, Final Report, HHPL.

44. Ibid., my italics.

45. Strawn, "Final Report"; MacChesney, "The Master of Emergencies Film," Herbert Hoover 1920–1921 folder, box 15, MacChesney Papers, HHPL.

46. *New York Times*, November 8, 1928, p. 2; Peel and Donnelly, *1928 Campaign*, 170. Lichtman, *Prejudice*, 160–62.

47. Hollingsworth, in MacChesney, "Special Bulletin."

48. Skocpol, *Protecting*, 519–22. Harvey, *Votes without Leverage*, 7–12, quotation from 7; Lichtman, quoted from *Prejudice*, 165.

Chapter Ten

POCKETBOOK POLITICS

DEMOCRACY AND THE MARKET IN

TWENTIETH-CENTURY AMERICA

Meg Jacobs

IN THE TWENTIETH CENTURY, pocketbook issues rose to prominence in American politics. In 1914, the young Progressive journalist Walter Lippmann declared, "the real power emerging to-day in democratic politics is just the mass of people who are crying out against the 'high cost of living.' That is a consumer's cry."[1] That phrase, the "high cost of living," gained currency at the turn of the century, when more Americans became urban consumers and when prices began an upward trend, reversing a century of deflation. As Americans became increasingly dependent on basic goods purchased in the market rather than produced at home, they started to pay more attention to costs. For those living on limited means, a jump in prices, even if small, could make the difference between having and going without. A new era of inflation affected everyone, including the rapidly expanding group of white-collar workers on fixed salaries. Throughout the twentieth century, even in times of deflation or relative price stability, politicians have tapped into pocketbook concerns to mobilize voters.

Why have historians overlooked the influence of pocketbook politics in the twentieth century? The conventional wisdom holds that consumers are notoriously apathetic and politically weak. As Lippmann acknowledged, many "pretend to regard the consumer's interest as a rather mythical one. 'All the people' sounds so sentimental, so far removed from the clash of actual events." Indeed, it is a staple of American political science that consumers are difficult to organize into coherent political movements. Precisely because all citizens are potential consumers, their interests are diffuse and often changing. As New Deal historian Ellis Hawley concludes, "In many respects, then, the consumer remained the 'forgotten man' of the New Deal, the most prominent gap in the new organizational economy. Inarticulate, indifferent, and unorganized, he could wield little economic or political power."[2]

In fact, consumers have played a key role in the expansion and retraction of the modern regulatory state. Like the middle class itself, "the consumer" has been a shifting category with changing meanings and political allegiances. As generations of social historians have demonstrated, class and group identities are always subjective, constructed categories. They result not just from social construction, but they are also politically constructed. At key moments, politicians have sought to win elections and influence public policy by politicizing pocketbook issues and appealing to citizens, especially housewives, as consumers. A clear, unified consumer interest never emerged. But politicized debates over consumer purchasing power—what income would buy at the market—often provided the medium through which competing factions battled for public support. Consumers always have opinions about their pocketbooks. Depending on political circumstances, at times that meant lending and at other times withdrawing their support for a strong New Deal state and its labor allies. We can appreciate consumers' significance only by combining the insights of social and political history. That combination enables us to understand the dynamic interaction between policy making and popular political culture. States craft constituencies who, in turn, condition the development of the state.

There were three great moments of government-assisted consumer mobilization that were central to modern state formation and American politics. In World War I, President Wilson portrayed large corporations as profiteers who charged exorbitant prices, and he solicited the consuming public's help in checking inflation. Next, during the Great Depression, a group of influential New Dealers blamed large American businesses for charging high prices and paying low wages. Franklin Roosevelt recruited middle-class voters to police prices and asked for support of the organized labor movement as the best way to increase wages and bring about economic recovery. Finally, in World War II, government policies again mobilized consumers to check prices, this time endowing them with state authority. These institutional arrangements to regulate the market, from volunteer price checkers to industrial labor unions, were pervasive and intrusive in private enterprise, but they gained acceptance by relying on grassroots participation—what contemporaries termed democracy in action and I call state building from the bottom up. The result was the creation of a New Deal state with collective bargaining and politicized consumption at its center.

Consumer rhetoric united many interest groups and gave the New Deal a certain amount of political strength until consumers turned on the government and labor in the postwar period. By boosting consumption and encouraging a sense of entitlement to higher living standards, the New Deal at once gained legitimacy and also created tensions that became impossible to manage. Without a broader social movement, a philosophy, or institutionalized government representation, consumers' backing of the state and organized labor was fragile and contingent. In the context of postwar inflation, the New Deal alliance fractured. As unions' ability to achieve high wages became increasingly institutionalized and as corporations passed on those higher costs by raising prices, middle-class consumers tempered their support of organized labor.

Pocketbook issues thus have served as a pivot issue for twentieth-century America politics and state building. The masses of unorganized voters and their concerns about their purchasing power conditioned the regnant but brittle liberal order. That phenomenon became clearer during the stagflation of the 1970s, with President Nixon's successful appeals to what he called the silent majority. But tensions had existed throughout. This chapter begins by showing the politicization of prices in the early twentieth century. Next it examines the institutionalization of low-price, high-wage policies in the New Deal and World War II that appealed to both organized labor and unorganized middle-class consumers. It concludes by exploring the fragmenting of the New Deal order as a result of political battles over postwar inflation.

POLITICIZING PRICES IN THE EARLY TWENTIETH CENTURY

The early twentieth century marked a significant departure in how Americans understood, and therefore tried to improve, their standards of living. Amid agricultural hardship and declining commodity prices of the nineteenth century, farmers supported inflationary policies as a way of easing their debt and increasing the value of their land. These agrarian producers understood purchasing power in terms of the quantity of money, a question determined in large part by the gold supply and currency debates. That way of thinking about the so-called money question reached a crescendo with William Jennings Bryan's 1896 presidential campaign for free coinage of silver.[3] As new sources of gold were discovered, as inflation replaced deflation, and as Americans became more integrated into a national economy and thus more dependent on purchased goods, their mind-set gradually shifted. When twentieth-century Americans thought about purchasing power, they thought less about the money supply and more about the market basket, about what their dollars would buy. Once people had to shop for more things, they became more cost conscious, especially if the prices they paid seemed to be constantly inching upward.

By World War I, the High Cost of Living, as contemporaries termed it, became a central political issue.[4]

Americans have a long history of political activism at the point of consumption.[5] The moment of greatest activism across the social spectrum came when consumers had to pay for everything from milk to meat to mass transit. Precipitous price increases destabilized wage-earner family budgets and led to food riots, consumer boycotts, and rent strikes. Working-class housewives fought for more in the market basket, while organized labor pushed for bigger paychecks, arguing that they deserved a "living wage." The demand for higher pay was not new, but now wage earners justified their demands as consumers entitled to an "American standard of living." From bargain basements to bargaining tables, a new mass consumption economy brought with it a new price consciousness and a new kind of social protest.[6]

White-collar workers on fixed salaries felt particularly put upon by price increases. Between 1880 and 1930 the number of salaried employees increased eightfold as clerical positions in new corporations and government bureaucracies grew.[7] On the one hand these jobs gave real opportunities to the sons and daughters of immigrants and farmers for advancement into a rapidly expanding new middle class. But on the other hand inflation placed real limitations in a world where few were self-sufficient. The 1 to 2 percent annual inflation between 1896 and 1914 jarred a generation of older middle-class professionals and elites whose historical memory knew only deflation.[8] As corporate trusts and labor unions grew in number and influence, many white-collar workers believed that prices were unnaturally high. Newspaper accounts of trusts fueled suspicions about a high-price conspiracy. Muckraking journalist Ray Stannard Baker grasped this sense of victimization: "The unorganized public, where will it come in? . . . Is there any doubt that the income of organized labor and the profits of organized capital have gone up enormously, while the man-on-a-salary and most of the great middle class, paying much more for the necessaries of life, have had no adequate increase in earnings?"[9]

Striking workers gained white-collar support when they included lower prices as part of their demands. The potential conflict between the high wages that labor sought and the low prices consumers desired was real. But in this pre–World War I era, when neither consumers nor labor were effectively organized, such tensions were largely latent. At times a mutual antipathy toward the overweening power of trusts could provide a basis for a broader alliance. In cities across the country, urban residents supported municipal strikes against public franchise corporations, which they believed, had breached a "civic contract." Members of the Street Railway Employee Union of St. Louis, for example, defended their actions on behalf of the consuming public. They struck, they claimed, to prevent "the great organized power of tyrannical trusts . . . from crushing down wages and pauperizing the great masses of people, thereby destroying the purchasing power of our customers and injuring our business."[10]

From streetcars to storefronts, new sites of consumption could easily become transformed into places of protest. Once basic goods and services became commodified, changes in prices wreaked havoc. In 1900, the average wage-earning or clerical family spent 40 percent of its annual income on food. That percentage remained as high as 35 percent in 1940. Rent amounted to roughly 25 percent, and clothes another 15 percent. Given those economic realities, making ends meet was no easy accomplishment. As the main provisioners, women found price increases especially challenging. Walter Lippmann argued that once women got the vote, consumer issues would increase in significance. "The mass of women do not look at the world as workers; in America, at least their prime interest is as consumers. It is they who go to the market and do the shopping; it is they who have to make the family budget go around; it is they who feel shabbiness and fraud and high prices most directly. . . . [T]heir influence will make the consumer the real master of the political situation." Another commentator, Dr. Henry Leffmann, explained in 1910: "The cry against the high prices of the necessaries of life is heard all over the land. The housekeeper does not need to consult statistics nor to read the discussions of Congress. She finds out the condition whenever she visits the grocery store or market."[11] In an era that predated home refrigeration, daily trips to the market allowed for regular price comparisons and, at particular moments, could easily become politicized.

Protests against the high cost of living came to a head in World War I. Prices more than doubled, and President Wilson made the attack on profiteering part and parcel of his war program. In morally charged language, Wilson explained that a newly created Food Administration could prevent prices "from being unreasonably and oppressively high."[12] The Wilson administration condemned such high prices, which bred instability from New York's Lower East Side to Seattle's shipyards. Intended to diffuse tension, the administration's denunciations of manufacturers, middlemen, and merchants as war profiteers only validated and encouraged grassroots activism. By attacking "unfair or unreasonable profits," United States Food Administrator Herbert Hoover replaced a market standard for profits with a patriotic political understanding.[13] Castigating high prices as unpatriotic, the administration legitimized the stresses and struggles of the nation's working classes and made them hopeful about government redress. The administration's National War Labor Board linked democracy in the workplace to the maintenance of living wages for the industrial masses.

Under the leadership of Herbert Hoover, the Food Administration initiated a vast mobilization of the nation's housewives. In October 1917 Hoover led a pledge campaign to recruit women into voluntary government service: "I accept membership in the United States Food Administration, and pledge myself to carry out the suggestions of the Food Administrator, so far as I am able." In exchange for signing, each housewife received an official membership card for her window. She also received "The War Creed of the Kitchen," urging patriotic conservation and elimination of waste.[14] What Hoover called a "voluntary mobilization" signaled a new kind of federal power. Along with the War Industries Board, the National War Labor Board, and countless other wartime agencies, the Food Administration mobilized economic resources and engaged in national planning.[15] But whereas industrial mobilization relied on the business elite and drew them to Washington, consumer mobilization appealed to all the nation's housewives in their own localities. Women not only conserved food, but they also compared local prices to the administration's Fair Price lists printed biweekly in the nation's newspapers. In an organizational form that would reoccur in the next war, the Food Administration employed 3,000 in Washington and recruited 800,000 volunteers. Though asking for consumer sacrifice, the Food Administration reinforced notions of profiteering and unreasonable prices that had animated earlier sporadic protests.

Wartime inflation put consumer purchasing power at the top of the nation's political agenda and moved to the fore a policy network of labor-oriented intellectuals and policy planners. Attention to the nation's pocketbooks during the war and especially in the economic boom and bust that followed gave way to a lasting critique of the American economy. When the economy collapsed in 1921, a group of labor reformers blamed high prices that had exceeded consumers' purchasing power, especially when businesses launched a massive wage-cutting program. Reformers aimed to discredit and marginalize a nineteenth-century moral sensibility in which family and individual prosperity stemmed from virtuous personal character. In a modern capitalist economy, they argued, consumers had little control over the larger structural forces that shaped their economic destiny. Not only were prices too high, they claimed, but wages were too low. In the wake of the economic catastrophe of 1921, labor seized on the problem of consumer purchasing power and connected it to questions of income distribution and national prosperity. American Federation of Labor president William Green explained, "The Nation cannot destroy its purchasing power through the creation of an army of unemployed and expect to maintain increased commodity production." As he put it, "buying power [is] at stake."[16]

Throughout the 1920s, a new consumer ideology coalesced around the idea of mass purchasing power. That phrase, "mass purchasing power," would stand at the center of American liberalism for the next half century. A group of purchasing-power progressives in and around the labor movement developed their critique of high prices and low wages into an economic theory of underconsumption. They argued that for the economy to continue to grow and prosper workers had to be able to consume. Mostly trained in economics at Columbia, Wisconsin, and Chicago, they worked at institutions such as the Twentieth Century Fund, the Russell Sage Foundation, the Labor Bureau Inc., Brookwood Labor College, the Amalgamated Clothing Workers, the American Federation of Labor, the United States Bureau of Labor Statistics, the United States Bureau of Home Economics, the American Association of University Women, the American Home Economics Association, and the National Consumers' League. This community included intellectuals, social scientists, and other prominent reformers such as Robert F. Wagner, Edward Filene, George Soule, Leon Henderson, Stuart Chase, Gardiner Means, Robert Lynd, Paul Douglas, Caroline Ware, William T. Foster, and Waddill Catchings.[17] Still marginal in the 1920s, they would become central to political reform in the 1930s. A commitment to high wages, low prices, and a high volume of production shaped their agenda. At a time when many Americans lived at or below subsistence levels, these progressives saw mass consumption as a great liberating force that would enhance quality of life and forestall destabilizing economic cycles.

The purchasing-power argument aligned the interests of the worker with those of the rest of society. Department store magnate and leading reformer Edward Filene explained, "Mass production can live only through mass distribution, and mass distribution means a mass of people who have buying power."[18] "The real answer" to postwar prosperity, he argued, is "to increase the buying power of the masses."[19] George Soule of the Labor Bureau chided the businessman who mistakenly "thinks of the wage-earner merely as a factor in production costs and forgets that he also makes up one of the most numerous classes of consumers."[20] The Amalgamated Clothing Workers' Sidney Hillman warned that "[T]he question of a high living standard for the American workers is a matter of vital importance to the entire nation. . . . Any attempt to lower the living standards is certain to bring industrial depression."[21] Echoing that sentiment, Garet Garrett of the *Saturday Evening Post* cautioned that "[w]hen you dispense with the worker as a producer you dispense with him also as a consumer. And as a consumer he is indispensable. Unemployment, once the anxiety of the worker alone, now becomes the anxiety of business."[22]

The idea of mass purchasing power gained a following not only in labor halls but also at academic conferences, in government agencies, in mass-circulation magazines, and in corporate boardrooms. In 1926, the *New York Times* editorial staff announced, "it is today widely recognized that the purchasing power of the masses is one of the prime determinants of general business prosperity."[23] As secretary of commerce and then as president, Herbert Hoover endorsed labor's purchasing-power program of high wages. Purchasing-power arguments received legitimacy outside the labor movement when in the 1920s an unprecedented increase in productivity sent business looking for consumers. Executives found that the rise of installment selling in the 1920s and slick new advertisements could expand markets but not indefinitely. "Our country can have an adequate market," Filene argued, "only by having properly paid wage-earners."[24] Many businessmen in mass-production industries appreciated the significance of mass purchasing power, especially as employment slowed in 1927. As president of Bethlehem Steel Company Eugene G. Grace put it, "Unemployed textile workers cannot buy automobiles."[25] Grace articulated a new understanding of the connection between workers' income and national prosperity. "In the old days we looked on the annual pay roll with horror, as something subtracted from the profit and surplus account. More recently we have learned that the national pay roll is the source of profit and surplus, and the only source." On the eve of the stock market crash in 1929, Charles F. Abbott, the executive director of the American Institute of Steel Construction, expressed an increasingly common view. "We must take on the responsibility of providing a larger income . . . in order to increase consumption." "The principal difficulty will never be over-production. The trouble is under-consumption."[26]

Though American manufacturers turned out more consumer goods at better prices and paid higher wages than in other industrialized nations, American liberals feared that corporations had not gone far enough. Amid the fantastic wealth of the 1920s, purchasing-power progressives fretted over the lurking evils of nominal wages, monopoly prices, and consumer powerlessness. They argued that the monopolistic structure of the economy allowed a small number of large firms to impose high prices, low wages, and stylized consumer goods designed to become obsolete. In 1927 Stuart Chase and F. J. Schlink released their best-selling book, *Your Money's Worth*, a phrase that entered popular discourse and found a ready audience among consumers who sought more control over their purchases.[27] In 1928, amid growing numbers of unemployed, Senator Robert Wagner (D-N.Y.) warned: "With bread lines and idleness come diminution in purchasing power, a gradual slackening of business and industry and great unemployment. Behind this curtain stalk misery, want, hunger, and discontent in all our cities."[28] When the economy began its decade-long descent into the Great Depression of the 1930s, a lack of purchasing power was a ready-made explanation for labor reformers. The Labor Bureau explained, "What America needs now is higher wages without higher prices. . . . [A]ny slackening of production recently felt in American manufacture is due to inadequate purchasing power of the consuming public for the greatly enlarged quantities of goods which industry is capable of turning out."[29] Edward Filene cautioned, "Mass production can live only if there is mass consumption—that is, only if the masses are able to buy all the goods produced."[30]

INSTITUTIONALIZING HIGH WAGES AND LOW PRICES IN THE NEW DEAL AND WORLD WAR II

The Great Depression solidified the link between middle- and working-class interests by seemingly exposing "underconsumption" as the country's major problem.[31] With millions out of work, from unskilled factory workers to white-collar managers, underconsumption appeared to be everywhere. Even for those fortunate enough to have a job, income seemed to fall faster than prices. In that context, labor's argument for increasing wages and attacking high prices gained appeal and provided necessary justification for workers' political gains. In 1932, Adolph Berle and Gardiner Means published *The Modern Corporation and Private Property*. In this landmark work, they argued that, in spite of antitrust laws, the two hundred largest corporations controlled about half of corporate wealth and nearly one-quarter of the nation's wealth. These purchasing-power progressives believed that monopoly power subverted the flexible adjustment of prices. When faced with an economic downturn, large corporations elected to cut production, employment, and wages rather than reduce prices to meet market demand. That type of restrictive behavior became known as "administered prices," a phenomenon that undermined the nation's purchasing power. Though capital investment had actually fallen far more than consumption, underconsumptionist theories provided a popular explanation for the Depression to a general public unschooled in economics.[32]

Conflicting agendas marked the New Deal, but purchasing-power theories informed much of the administration's rhetoric. President Roosevelt and his advisers decried the lack of purchasing power among America's consuming public, including the nation's farmers. In announcing the National Recovery Act (NRA) of 1933 to resuscitate industry, Roosevelt explained, "The aim of this whole effort is to restore our rich domestic market by raising its vast consuming capacity."[33] The idea behind this act was to raise purchasing power by giving workers the right to organize and bargain for higher wages and by priming the pump through government spending on public works. Simultaneously, the NRA allowed businesses to collaborate in setting prices high enough to revive production but not so high as to undercut newly created purchasing power. Following a strategy filled with risks, Roosevelt mobilized public opinion to assure compliance and warned businessmen against "taking profiteering advantage of the consuming public." At the same time, to lift farmers out of a decade of depression, the Agricultural Adjustment Act (AAA) sought to increase commodity prices through a domestic allotment plan that restricted agricultural production. That plan, like the NRA's suspension of antitrust laws, was, by design, inflationary. But here too administration rhetoric promised price increases high enough to help farmers but not so high as to raise prices beyond what urban consumers could afford. Both the NRA and the AAA established consumer bodies to protect "the interests of the consuming public." In using the language of consumers, President Roosevelt sought to win middle-class support to make the New Deal more than just a vehicle for labor and farm reform and to assure its survival beyond the crisis of the Depression.

The New Deal brought the purchasing-power program to the fore and mobilized citizens in support of it. Reformers staffed the National Recovery Administration Consumer Advisory Board (CAB) and the Agricultural Adjustment Agency's Consumer Counsel. Yet in spite of consumer rhetoric and representation, corporate-dominated NRA codes led to restricted output, higher prices, and reduced purchasing power. Working in conjunction with Leon Henderson of the NRA's Research and Planning Division and Isador Lubin of the Bureau of Labor Statistics, Gardiner Means, now at the CAB, argued that NRA codes had exacerbated a tendency toward administered prices above what consumers could afford. Other New Dealers such as Mordecai Ezekiel, Jerome Frank, Rexford Tugwell, Henry Wallace, Thomas Blaisdell, Thurman Arnold, and Corwin Edwards shared that view.[34] As consumer advocate Thomas Blaisdell argued, "The consumer's interest requires that goods be turned out in large and increasing volume . . . [with] prices kept low." He continued: "Thousands are improperly fed, badly housed, inadequately clothed. . . . In such a situation it would be fantastic to talk of over-production." The CAB sought to protect the consumers' interest by opposing price-fixing, by lobbying for grade labeling, and by organizing county councils as local agencies to monitor prices.[35] The last point was most significant. By mobilizing this consuming public, the CAB effectively transformed underconsumption from an abstract theory that denounced high prices into the basis of political activism.[36]

Under the New Deal consumers regarded the government as the proper authority to assess what constituted a "fair price." Because NRA and

AAA supporters had adopted a purchasing-power rationale, working- and middle-class Americans came to expect justice, or at least price relief, in the marketplace. It was not long before the public railed against the inflationary aspects of the programs themselves, directing their animus not at the New Deal but rather at producers who, New Dealers claimed, charged unfair prices. In the summer and fall of 1933, the rise in bread prices as a result of the AAA wheat program led to a public backlash and was front-page news. When bakers raised their prices above what the public deemed fair, consumers across the country sent thousands of bread wrappers to their new allies in Washington to demonstrate what they perceived to be unfair price increases. "We are glad to see you are after the profiteers," explained a woman who signed her name, "A Consumer." A distraught citizen from York, Pennsylvania, who sent in a newspaper clipping announcing the end to the nickel loaf, inquired, "Is it justifiable or is it profiteering?" An Ohio woman demanded: "Is this a fair increase? . . . It appears that improved machinery and mass production have made things worse for the consumer."[37] With substantial government support and encouragement, housewives took to the streets to demonstrate against high prices. In the summer of 1935, protesters across the country led campaigns against meat packers for raising their prices, ignoring the packers' defense that the drought of 1934 had left them little choice.[38] The potency of consumer protest drew its strength from a reciprocal rela- tionship between consumers and the state. Government officials fed con- sumers product and pricing information that consumers then used as am- munition in their activism.

Consumerism shaped the way labor's wage demands resonated with the larger public. Labor liberals viewed the organization of workers under the National Labor Relations Act (1935) as a key institutional remedy to the Great Depression.[39] With unemployment as high as 25 percent, neither labor nor its supporters worried about the inflationary impact higher wages could have. Instead, enlarging labor's income seemed critical to national recovery. Leon Keyserling, aide to Senator Wagner, chief sponsor of the bill, explained, "The failure of the total volume of wage payments to advance as fast as production and corporate surpluses has resulted in inadequate purchasing power, which has accentuated periodic depres- sions and disrupted the interstate flow of commerce." Many echoed that formulation, including workers themselves. Writing in support of the Wagner Act, a grocery-chain-store worker asserted, "We of the laboring class want this bill passed. . . . Give the 2/3 buyers of all national produc- tion a break by passing the Wagner Bill."[40] Labor unions sold themselves and won public support as agents of recovery and prosperity by boosting the nation's purchasing-power through higher wages.

The purchasing-power argument helped to legitimize the growth of the New Deal state, winning support from and linking the interests of both the working and middle classes in a new Democratic majority. In the context of severe depression, wage increases and collective bargaining became synonymous with an increase in purchasing power for all consumers. This expansive definition of a consuming public was also at the heart of a demand-based Keynesian fiscal policy that rendered the consumption function of all citizens vital to economic health. The need to increase consumption helped to justify other New Deal programs. The Fair Labor Standards Act of 1938 promised to extend the benefits of the Wagner Act to unorganized workers, particularly those in the South.[41] Agencies such as the Tennessee Valley Authority, the Electric Home and Farm Authority, and the Rural Electrification Agency also sought to enrich the consuming capacity of the South and other underdeveloped areas. These were popular programs informed by a broader purchasing-power ideology that, in part, predicated loyalty to the New Deal state on politicized consumption.[42]

Throughout the New Deal and World War II, this policy community maintained that mass purchasing power through high wages and low prices would bring economic growth. When the economy declined again in 1937, after a short-lived recovery, many New Dealers such as Leon Henderson, Gardiner Means, Thomas Blaisdell, Harold Ickes, and Harry Hopkins pointed to "outrageous" administered price increases as the culprit.[43] "Were monopolies responsible for this price rise . . . by reducing the general public's capacity to consume?" asked Henderson. "My answer is emphatically yes. I believe the unbalance in prices was touched off by the monopolistic prices."[44] In April 1938, President Roosevelt called for a major government-spending program to stimulate the economy; two weeks later he delivered an antimonopoly speech, and Congress established the Temporary National Economic Committee (TNEC) to investigate the concentration of economic control. The appointments of Leon Henderson as the executive director of the TNEC along with the Department of Justice Antitrust Division's Thurman Arnold, the Securities and Exchange Commission's Jerome Frank, and the Department of Labor's Isador Lubin reflected a continued commitment to attacking monopoly prices.[45] In an appeal to middle-class consumers, Thurman Arnold promised to lower "the price of pork chops, bread, spectacles, drugs, and plumbing."[46] Despite Democratic losses in the 1938 elections, Arnold's Antitrust Division doubled its appropriations between 1939 and 1943. Only war mobilization forced him to call off investigations into the steel, shipbuilding, and aircraft industries.

World War II led to an expansion of the administration's redistributive purchasing-power agenda. The Office of Price Administration (OPA) implemented an economywide system of price controls and rationing to check inflation. Roosevelt appointed Leon Henderson as OPA's first administrator, and he brought with him his commitment to protecting consumers' pocketbooks. By 1944, OPA affected over 3 million business establishments and issued regulations controlling 8 million prices, stabilizing rents in 14 million dwellings occupied by 45 million tenants, and rationing food to more than 30 million shoppers. From gathering ration tokens and stamps to checking price lists to saving extra fat for recycling, consumers felt the government's presence at each step in the consumption cycle. OPA regulations reached into the kitchen and closet of every home, influencing eating habits and fashion. Wartime propaganda sold sacrifice as the price to be paid for a prosperous postwar life.[47]

Central to its effectiveness, OPA undertook the organization of a broad, cross-class coalition of consumers as shock troops in enforcing price regulations in local markets. With a staff numbering over 250,000, OPA was indeed an enormous bureaucracy. Like the Food Administration in World War I, its strength came from its decentralization. By appealing to and relying on thousands of middle- and working-class shoppers to police prices as government agents, OPA extended state supervision to private market transactions. Volunteer price inspectors worked with "Little OPAs," the 5,525 local War and Price Rationing Boards. In March 1944 alone, 41,000 volunteers checked prices at 430,000 food stores. OPA also launched a massive home front pledge for the nation's housewives to obey ceiling prices.[48] Under the direction of Caroline Ware, leading consumer activist and spouse of Gardiner Means, OPA's Consumer Advisory Board initiated the distribution of price ceiling charts directly to individual consumers. As the war progressed, OPA propaganda grew increasingly militant, culminating with its image of a snarling housewife, gritting her teeth, fist clenched, proclaiming, "I'm out to lick Runaway Prices." OPA validated citizens' understanding of themselves as consumers with enforceable rights.

The end of the war did not automatically demobilize this consuming public. Though long lines and shortages had caused aggravation, many saw OPA as their ally and their best hope for cheap prices. Facing tough producer opposition, OPA won a temporary extension through popular support. Nearly one year after the end of the war, Gallup polls revealed that three-quarters of the public favored a continuation of controls. The public also supported unions in their efforts to preserve labor's substantial wartime gains. Unions, now representing one-third of nonagricultural workers, justified their actions on the grounds that higher wages would benefit all. In the most celebrated strike of the postwar era, which pitched the United Auto Workers against General Motors, the UAW's Walter Reuther used the purchasing-power argument once again. In the winter of

1946, the UAW adopted "Purchasing Power for Prosperity" as its strike slogan. Taking their cue from the OPA, these workers argued that only their formula of high wages and low prices would prevent a return to depression and sustain postwar prosperity. They demanded that GM "open the books" to demonstrate that it could afford to pay higher wages without raising prices. Walter Reuther insisted, "We fight to make progress with the community and not at the expense of the community." "We will not be a party to sand-bagging the American consumer." And indeed, for months, many Americans—white-collar, middle-class—accepted the UAW's assertion that GM could afford to increase wages by as much as 30 percent.[49]

THE END OF A LABOR-CONSUMER ALLIANCE IN THE POSTWAR PERIOD

The alliance between consumers and organized labor had held firm in the Depression and remained intact during the war. This New Deal coalition put into place a powerful engine of economic redistribution, the national collective bargaining regime. But as economic and political circumstances changed and as Congress dismantled the wartime state, this coalition fractured. Mild levels of inflation in the postwar era served as the issue upon which the New Deal alliance split apart. In the postwar years, the "problem of inflation" became a key battleground between corporations and unions and their political representatives, who sought to capture the loyalty of the middle classes in hopes of influencing public policy. Business capitalized on unions' growing strength to foment tensions between organized workers and the unorganized middle classes. Without a consumer agency or an effective consumer movement concerned about prices, consumers felt alienated from interest group politics, particularly their labor allies.

The first major signs of fissure became visible in the fight over extending price controls. In a dramatic show of concentrated market manipulation, meat packers withheld meat from butcher shops in 1946 rather than sell under OPA guidelines. Headlines warned of "famine," and black market prices more than doubled. In this crisis OPA appeared ineffectual, and consumers rapidly abandoned it. This sudden shift brought to the fore inherent instabilities of the purchasing-power program that had existed all along: that it rested on a precarious cross-class consensus and was subject to short-term consumer gratification. Fed up with OPA's inability to face down its enemies and force meat from hoof to table, the public's support turned to anger and apathy. As one enraged mother put it, "I am just one of the many thousands of harassed housewives trying to feed a family and keep them healthy during these days of 'no Meat.' "[50] Unable to deliver the goods, OPA alienated the consumers whose expectations it had raised and on whose support it depended, while its labor allies worried first about securing wage increases regardless of the overall stabilization program. As soon as the war had ended, the National Association of Manufacturers (NAM) led a direct attack on OPA, blaming price controls for the scarcity of consumer goods. In newspapers across the country, it ran ads asking, "Would You Like Some Butter or a Roast of Beef?" The result was the political defeat of OPA in the November 1946 elections, appropriately dubbed the "beefsteak" elections.[51]

Conservatives played to the fears of a consuming public. NAM explained inflation as the product of the "wage-price spiral" forced on the nation by what they labeled "monopoly unionism." That phrase was a linguistic inversion of the New Deal attack on monopoly capitalism. In nationwide newspaper advertisements, NAM blamed "labor monopoly" and industrywide bargaining for "rais[ing] the prices of things you need." A full-page ad declared, "The price of MONOPOLY comes out of your pocket." Another insisted, "Industry-wide bargaining is no bargain for you." "How about some Pro-Public legislation?" another asked.[52] The disruptive set of strikes that unions waged in this inflationary era enhanced antilabor sentiment. Holding organized labor accountable for the high cost of living culminated in the passage of the Taft-Hartley Act of 1947, the first major attempt to undo labor's gains under the Wagner Act. Taft-Hartley, known best for its anticommunist restrictions on union members, was a product of consumer-driven backlash against organized labor. By conflating inflation with labor's power, conservatives in Congress and industry leaders aimed to drive a wedge through the New Deal alliance of middle-class consumers and organized labor.[53]

Americans consistently lamented the continuous, albeit relatively small, increases in the consumer price index of the 1950s. The emerging Keynesian consensus on the left mistakenly maintained that mild inflation would alleviate distributional conflict by enabling economic growth and full employment. As it turned out, the "creeping inflation" of the 1950s fueled tensions between social groups and thus led to the very conflict this technocratic elite sought to avoid. When annual inflation averaged less than 3 percent, public opinion polls revealed that Americans considered inflation the most important domestic problem in eight of ten years.[54] As historian Charles Maier correctly notes, creeping inflation typically reflects a successful alliance of corporations and unions against middle-class proprietors, pensioners, and savers.[55] The demographic fact that more and more workers were obtaining employment in professional and service-sector jobs during this period did create a real split between blue-collar workers and their white-collar middle-class counterparts. By all accounts, fixed-income workers fared worst from the wage-price spiral.

Collectively teachers, public servants, other white-collar workers, and pensioners constituted roughly one-third of the workforce. In his 1952 classic work, *The Future of American Politics*, journalist Samuel Lubell predicted that inflation would remain an insurmountable problem for the labor left. Contemporaries feared that mild inflation would erode the aspirations for a prosperous postwar life that the Roosevelt administration had done so much to cultivate. In that context, wage-generated inflation threatened to tear apart the Democratic alliance. As Lubell explained, "No new economic gains can be promised any group of Democrats today without threatening the gains of other Democrats." He concluded, "Inflation has clearly become the breaking point of the Roosevelt coalition."[56]

Republicans embraced the fight against inflation as a key electoral issue in 1952. Of the forty-two freshmen Republican candidates running for Congress, nearly all mentioned inflation in their campaigns. Attributing it to New Deal–Fair Deal irresponsibility, they discussed inflation more than any other issue including taxes, "creeping socialism," and the Korean War.[57] Middle-class consumers resented not only labor's strength but also President Truman's willingness, at particular moments, to support their demands as demonstrated by his seizure of steel mills in 1952 when steel executives refused to grant government-sanctioned wage increases.[58] The Republican platform blamed Democratic policies for the high cost of living: "The wanton extravagance and inflationary policies of the Administration in power have cut the value of the dollar in half. . . . If this Administration is left in power, it will further cheapen the dollar, rob the wage earner, impoverish the farmer and reduce the true value of the savings, pensions, insurance and investment of millions of our people."[59]

Republican presidential candidate Dwight Eisenhower dramatized the evils of inflation in a series of political commercials. With approximately three-quarters of American households now owning televisions, these commercials revealed the salient issues of the day.[60] In one, a middle-aged woman holding her groceries declared, "I paid twenty-four dollars for these groceries—look, for this little." Eisenhower responded, "A few years ago, those same groceries cost you ten dollars, now twenty-four, next year thirty—that's what will happen unless we have a change." Another elderly woman lamented, "You know what things cost today. High prices are just driving me crazy." Eisenhower soothed, "Yes, my Mamie gets after me about the high cost of living. It's another reason why I say, it's time for a change. Time to get back to an honest dollar and an honest dollar's work." In another, when a man asked which party would lick inflation, Eisenhower replied, "Well, instead of asking which party will bring prices down, why not ask which party has put prices up?" In many spots, the general broke a presawed piece of wood in half to demonstrate the decrease in the nation's purchasing power since 1945.[61]

The idea of a "wage-price spiral" was cemented in the public imagination. Not strong enough to secure a general incomes policy, unions protected their own workers. Union gains in securing wage increases, coupled with frequent strikes, made labor susceptible to charges of acting as a "special interest" and causing what many perceived as "ruinous inflation." It weakened labor's case that by the late 1950s over half of all union contracts included cost-of-living adjustments that protected labor from price increases while loading the burden on nonunionized sectors. The 1955 merger between the American Federation of Labor and the Congress of Industrial Organizations further secured the idea of big labor as a monolithic force capable of subverting the economic well-being of the nation.[62] The popular press translated abstract economic phenomena into concrete numbers. Business reports explained the United Steelworkers' 1956 demand for a sixty-cent hourly raise would increase the cost of a refrigerator by fifteen dollars.[63] U.S. Steel president Roger Blough charged that higher wages led to "phantom profits." "As a result of postwar inflation, it is possible for a company to earn what appears to be a most substantial profit, and still wither away."[64] John Kenneth Galbraith, a former OPA deputy administrator and prominent liberal economist, explained that, in the competition to assign blame, "The public will always attribute the whole of the price increases at such a time to the presumed rapacity of the unions."[65]

The campaign against wage-push inflation reinforced a renewed legislative assault on organized labor. Business leaders and a reinvigorated conservative movement launched a major effort to nationalize "right to work" restrictions that banned the union shop and heretofore had been confined to the South and the Mountain West. Within companies, corporations engaged in extensive public relations efforts to persuade union members of their faulty policies. NAM pamphlets routinely warned workers of disastrous consequences from their wage demands and denounced labor's "purchasing power fallacy."[66] Although labor successfully flexed its political muscles in the 1958 and 1960 elections, leading to substantial Democratic gains, it reaped no political dividends. It did not help organized labor that two-thirds of union workers were concentrated in ten states. The passage of the Landrum-Griffin Act in 1959 allowed for more government regulation of union affairs and further restricting of union actions.[67] Those challenges to labor's power led to a downward cycle. Even as labor waxed in numerical strength, its political defeat constricted its vision and undermined its purchasing-power program. In that context, the middle classes, including many highly skilled blue-collar workers who suffered from wage compression, came to see union power and the New Deal that had spawned it as illegitimate.

The waning influence of a purchasing-power program became clear in the 1960s. Labor was politically successful in the mid-1960s, winning among other things its fight for Medicare. But it was no longer spokesman for a larger coalition. Attempts to blame corporations for inflation gained no political traction. Gardiner Means's writings in the 1950s, with the same rallying cry of two hundred corporations controlling over half of all corporate assets, prompted renewed interest in administered prices. Beginning in 1957, New Deal Democrat senator Estes Kefauver (D-Tenn.) pushed for an investigation into administered prices in the steel and auto industries as the chair of the Anti-Trust and Monopoly Subcommittee of the Senate Judiciary Committee. Between 1957 and 1963 Kefauver interrogated the steel, auto, bread, drug, and other industries. He called before him U.S. Steel president Roger Blough and challenged his pricing practices. As a young attorney, Blough had defended U.S. Steel before the TNEC.[68] Kefauver appealed to a broadly conceived consuming public. He explained: "Every day in our lives monopoly takes its toll. Stealthily it reaches down into our pockets and takes a part of our earnings. . . . [T]he deed is done so smoothly, so deftly, that we are not even conscious of it."[69] In the end these hearings went nowhere. As Richard Hofstadter concluded in 1964, "once the United States had an antitrust movement without antitrust prosecutions; in our time there have been antitrust prosecutions without an antitrust movement."[70]

The consumer movement that sprang to life under Ralph Nader's leadership signaled a departure from rather than a continuity in New Deal–style consumer politics. Though not an antitrust movement, Nader's efforts led to aggressive antitrust measures and regulation of corporations.[71] But the consumer movement of the 1970s was indifferent if not avowedly hostile to labor unions. For regulation these activists relied on bureaucracies and courts rather than elections. While in favor of quality of life issues, they were hostile to the New Deal regulatory apparatus and appeared uninterested in the pocketbook issues dear to consumers' hearts.

The inflation of the 1970s sealed the fate of a labor-consumer purchasing-power alliance. On August 15, 1971, President Nixon boldly proclaimed a New Economic Policy and imposed a ninety-day wage and price freeze. The past several years had witnessed rising inflation as a result of large budget deficits from the Vietnam War and an accompanying increase in the money supply. Although disdainful of the OPA, President Nixon put in place a program originally designed by OPA liberals. But now these radical tools represented only a tepid liberalism at best. Facing reelection in 1972 and fearing accelerating inflation, Nixon put aside his ideological aversions and announced his wage-price program. Though the idea of wage-price-profit policies had grown from the hopeful days of New Deal planning, Nixon's implementation of these same tools signaled their death. Unlike the policies implemented during World War II, this time controls came without local price checkers, without labor support, and without any redistributive ideology. Instead the freeze now served as a remedy to what policy makers and the public saw as the problem of excessive wage settlements.[72] By the end of the 1970s all the government tools of the postwar period, including unions, regulation, New Deal macroeconomic policy, and controls, had been discredited, making way for the return of a pre–New Deal skepticism of government and a renewed confidence in promarket policies.

This story of twentieth-century pocketbook politics suggests that consumers can be mobilized in particular political circumstances. At specific moments and given certain configurations of state power, politicians successfully appealed to middle-class consumers to strengthen government regulation of the market. During the Great Depression and World War II, reformers argued that the nation could prosper only if business met labor demands for mass purchasing power and redistribution. Yet after the war, unable to escape blame for the wage-price spiral, labor alienated other members of the middle-class community who felt that even a mild inflation threatened their standard of living. In this sea of shifting alliances, pocketbook concerns served as a crucial conditioning element. To appreciate that phenomenon, we must pay more attention to the intersection of popular and institutional politics.

NOTES

1. Walter Lippmann, *Drift and Mastery: An Attempt to Explain the Current Unrest* (Madison: University of Wisconsin Press, 1985), 54.

2. Ellis Hawley, *The New Deal and the Problem of Monopoly* (New York: Fordham University Press, 1995), 204–5. For the rise of interest group politics and the decline in voter participation, see Sidney Milkis, *The President and the Parties: The Transformation of the American Party System since the New Deal* (New York: Oxford University Press, 1993). There are a few exceptions showing how diffuse interests can prevail over well-defined narrow interests. See, for example, Martha Derthick and Paul J. Quirk, *The Politics of Deregulation* (Washington, D.C.: Brookings Institution Press, 1985).

3. For an overview of these farmer politics, see Michael Kazin, *The Populist Persuasion: An American History* (New York: Basic Books, 1995); Gretchen Ritter, *Goldbugs and Greenbacks: The Antimonopoly Tradition and the Politics of Finance in America, 1865–1896* (New York: Cambridge University Press, 1997); Elizabeth Sanders, *Roots of Reform: Farmers, Workers, and the American State, 1877–1917* (Chicago: University of Chicago Press, 1999).

4. David Hacket Fisher, *The Great Wave: Price Revolutions and the Rhythm of History* (New York: Oxford University Press, 1996), 179–234; Daniel Horowitz, *The Morality of Spending: Attitudes toward Consumer Society in America, 1875–1940* (Baltimore: Johns Hopkins University Press, 1985). See also Eric Rauchway, "The High Cost of Living in the Progressives' Economy," *Journal of American History* 88, no. 3 (December 2001): 898–924.

5. From the colonists' tea boycotts in the American Revolution to the sit-ins at Woolworth's counters in the civil rights era, Americans have fought for political rights in the marketplace. For examples, see T. H. Breen, " 'Baubles of Britain': The American and Consumer Revolutions of the Eighteenth Century," *Past and Present* 119 (May 1988): 73–104; Breen, "The Meanings of Things: Interpreting the Consumer Economy in the Eighteenth Century," in *Consumption and the World of Goods*, ed. John Brewer and Roy Porter (London: Routledge, 1993), 249–60; Robert E. Weems, Jr., *Desegregating the Dollar: African-American Consumerism in the Twentieth Century* (New York: New York University Press, 1998), 56–69.

6. Elizabeth Ewen, *Immigrant Women in the Land of Dollars: Life and Culture on the Lower East Side* (New York: Monthly Review Press, 1985), 176–83; Paula Hyman, "Immigrant Women and Consumer Protest: The New York City Kosher Meat Boycott of 1902," *American Jewish History* 70 (September 1980): 91–105; Herbert G. Gutman, *Work, Culture, and Society in Industrializing America: Essays in American Working-Class and Social History* (New York: Vintage, 1977), 61–62; Ronald Lawson, "The Rent Strike in New York City, 1904–1980: The Evolution of a Social Movement," *Journal of Urban History* 10, no. 3 (May 1984): 235–58; Steven L. Piott, *The Anti-monopoly Persuasion: Popular Resistance to the Rise of Big Business in the Midwest* (Westport, Conn.: Greenwood Press, 1985); Dana Frank, "Housewives, Socialists, and the Politics of Food: The 1917 New York Cost-of-Living Protests," *Feminist Studies* 11 (summer 1985): 255–85; Jenna Joselit Weissman, "The Landlord as Czar: Pre–World War I Tenant Activity," in *The Tenant Movement in New York City, 1904–1984*, ed. Ronald Lawson (New Brunswick, N.J.: Rutgers University Press, 1986), 39–50; Morton J. Friedman, "American Consumer Boycotts in Response to Rising Food Prices: Housewives' Protests at the Grassroots Level," *Journal of Consumer Policy* 18 (1995): 55–72; and Annelise Orelick, *Common Sense and a Little Fire: Women and Working-Class Politics in the United States, 1900–1965* (Chapel Hill: University of North Carolina Press, 1995), 220–25. For labor, see Lawrence B. Glickman, *A Living Wage: American Workers and the Making of Consumer Society* (Ithaca, N.Y.: Cornell University Press, 1997); Leon Fink, *Progressive Intellectuals and the Dilemmas of Democratic Commitment* (Cambridge, Mass.: Harvard University Press, 1997), 214–41.

7. Oliver Zunz, *Making America Corporate, 1870–1920* (Chicago: University of Chicago Press, 1990); Susan Porter Benson, *Counter Cultures: Saleswomen, Managers, and Customers in American Department Stores, 1890–1940* (Urbana: University of Illinois Press, 1986); Seymour Martin Lipset and Reinhard Bendix, *Social Mobility in Industrial Society* (Berkeley: University of California Press, 1959), 48–56.

8. Horowitz, *Morality of Spending*, 67–84.

9. Ray Stannard Baker, "Capital and Labor Hunt Together," *McClure's*, 21 (September 1908): 463, as quoted in Richard Hofstadter, *The Age of Reform: From Bryan to F.D.R.* (New York: Alfred A. Knopf, 1955), 214.

10. Piott, *Anti-monopoly Persuasion*, 64, 76, 79, 99.

11. Lippmann, *Drift and Mastery*, 54; Henry Leffmann, "Who Is to Blame for the High Prices? Why the Trusts Are to Blame," *Ladies' Home Journal*, November 1, 1910, p. 21. See also Temma Kaplan, "Female Consciousness and Collective Action: The Case of Barcelona, 1910–1918," *Signs* 7 (spring 1982): 545–66.

12. "Wilson Warns Foes of Food Bill of Nation's Blame," *New York Times*, June 19, 1917, pp. 1, 2.

13. "Control of Food by Government to Begin On November 1," *New York Times*, October 10, 1917, pp. 1, 22; "Proclaims Food License System," *New York Times*, October 11, 1917, p. 1; "To Control Retail Prices Now," *New York Times*, October 12, 1917, p. 10; "Hoover Assumes Control of Prices," *New York Times*, November 4, 1917, p. 17.

14. "Retailers of Sugar Agree to Cut Price," *New York Times*, October 27, 1917, p. 12; "Food Canvass This Week," *New York Times*, October 28, 1917, p. 18. For the role of women in World War I, see Christopher Capozzola, "Uncle Sam Wants You: Political Obligations in World War I America" (Ph.D. dissertation, Columbia University, 2002), 124–78.

15. "Must Save to Win War, Hoover Warns Public," *New York Times*, July 4, 1917, p. 4. For an overview of wartime mobilization, see David M. Kennedy, *Over Here: The First World War and American Society* (New York: Oxford University Press, 1980), 93–143; Robert D. Cuff, *The War Industries Board: Business-Government Relations during World War I* (Baltimore: Johns Hopkins University Press, 1973); Paul A. C. Koistinen, *Mobilizing for Modern War: The Political Economy of American Warfare, 1865–1919* (Lawrence: University Press of Kansas, 1997). For the Food Administration, see Frank M. Surface and R. L. Bland, *American Food in the World War and Reconstruction Period* (Stanford, Calif.: Stanford University Press, 1931); William C. Mullendore, *History of the United States Food Administration, 1917–1919* (Stanford, Calif.: Stanford University Press, 1941); and Maxcy R. Dickson, *The Food Front in World War I* (Washington, D.C.: American Council on Public Affairs, 1944).

16. William Green, "Buying Power at Stake," *Forbes*, n.d., in Edward A. Filene Papers, Credit Union National Association, Madison, Wisconsin (hereafter EAF Papers).

17. For a representative point of view, see William Trufant Foster and Waddill Catchings, "Business under the Curse of Sisyphus: A New Theory on Causes of Depressions," *World's Work*, September 1926, pp. 503–11.

18. H. S. Person to Edward A. Filene, June 23, 1925, box 7, EAF Papers; Edward A. Filene, "Distribution of the Future," Address to the Taylor Society, October 29, 1925, p. 16.

19. "Finds Europe Improved," *New York Times*, October 15, 1925, p. 10.

20. "287 Wage Advances in May Reported," *New York Times*, June 11, 1923, p. 14.

21. Steve Fraser, *Labor Will Rule: Sidney Hillman and the Rise of American Labor* (New York: Free Press, 1991), 194–96.

22. Garet Garrett, "The American Book of Wonder," *Saturday Evening Post*, December 24, 1927, pp. 16–17, 64, 66, 69.

23. "Money for the Masses," *New York Times*, January 18, 1926, p. 20.

24. Edward Filene, "Minimum Wage and Maximum Efficiency," *American Economic Review* 13, no. 3 (September 1923): 411–15. See also Robert H. Zieger, "Herbert Hoover, the Wage-earner, and the 'New Economic System,' 1919–1929," *Business History Review* 51, no. 2 (summer 1977): 161–89.

25. Eugene G. Grace, "Distributed Prosperity," *Saturday Evening Post*, September 4, 1926, pp. 3–4, 57–58.

26. Charles F. Abbott, "Creative Spending," *Magazine of Business*, August 1929, pp. 164, 166.

27. Stuart Chase and F. J. Schlink, *Your Money's Worth: A Study in the Waste of the Consumer's Dollar* (New York: Macmillan, 1927). See also Paul H. Douglas, *Real Wages in the United States, 1890–1926* (Boston: Houghton Mifflin, 1930); Adolph Berle and Gardiner C. Means, *The Modern Corporation and Private Property* (New York: Macmillan, 1932); Robert S. Lynd, "The People as Consumers," in United States President's Research Committee on Social Trends, *Recent Social Trends in the United States* (New York: McGraw Hill, 1933), 857–911.

28. Unemployment Speech of Hon. Robert F. Wagner of New York in the U.S. Senate, March 5, 1928, box 2, Leon H. Keyserling Papers, Littauer Library, Georgetown University, Washington, D.C.

29. "Labor Bureau Sees Lower Wage Trend," *New York Times*, February 9, 1930, p. 16.

30. Edward A. Filene, "Mass Production Must Have Mass Consumption," *Magazine of Wall Street*, January 5, 1930.

31. On the prevalence of underconsumptionist ideas, see Alan Brinkley, *The End of Reform: New Deal Liberalism in Depression and War* (New York: Alfred A. Knopf, 1995), 67–72. See also Fraser, *Labor Will Rule*, and Theodore Rosenof, *Economics in the Long Run: New Deal Theorists and Their Legacies, 1933–1939* (Chapel Hill: University of North Carolina Press, 1997), 28–43.

32. Frederic S. Lee, "*The Modern Corporation* and Gardiner Means's Critique of Neoclassical Economics," *Journal of Economic Issues* 23, no. 2 (September 1990): 673–93. Charles Geisst, *Monopolies in America: Empire Builders and Their Enemies from Jay Gould to Bill Gates* (New York: Oxford University Press, 2000), 121–25.

33. Franklin D. Roosevelt, quoted in Dexter M. Keezer, "The Consumer under the National Recovery Administration," *Annals of the American Academy of Political and Social Sciences* 171 (1934): 89. For an overview of the New Deal, see Hawley, *New Deal*; Anthony J. Badger, *The New Deal: The Depression Years, 1933–1940* (New York: Hill and Wang, 1989); and Jordan Schwarz, *The New Dealers: Power Politics in the Age of Roosevelt* (New York: Alfred A. Knopf, 1993). See also Persia Campbell, *Consumer Representation in the New Deal* (New York: Columbia University Press, 1940).

34. Frederic C. Lee, "A New Dealer in Agriculture: G. C. Means and the Writing of Industrial Prices," *Review of Social Economy* 46 (October 1988): 180–202.

35. "Suggestions for Code Revision," Consumer Advisory Report to General Hugh S. Johnson, February 19, 1934; and Bulletin No. 2, Activities of the Con-

sumers' Advisory Board of the NRA and the Consumers Counsel of the AAA, in folder C.A.B. Reports and Speeches (General), box 2 (February–November 1935), Office Files of Emily Newell Blair, Records of the Consumer Advisory Board, Records of the National Recovery Administration, Entry 363 (PI-44), RG 9, National Archives, Washington, D.C.

36. This discussion of the New Deal draws on my article: Meg Jacobs, " 'Democracy's Third Estate': New Deal Politics and the Construction of a 'Consuming Public,' " *International Labor and Working-Class History* 55 (spring 1999): 27–51.

37. Ibid., 42–43. These bread wrappers are preserved in the Records of the Agricultural Adjustment Administration, RG 145, National Archives, College Park, Md.

38. Orelick, *Common Sense*, 229–40; Orelick, " 'We Are That Mystical Thing Called the Public': Militant Housewives during the Great Depression," *Feminist Studies* 19, no. 1 (spring 1993): 147–72; Darlene Clark Hine, "The Housewives League of Detroit: Black Women and Economic Nationalism," in *Visible Women: New Essays on American Activism*, eds. Nancy A. Hewitt and Suzanne Lebsock (Urbana: University of Illinois Press, 1993); Beth S. Wenger, *New York Jews and the Great Depression: Uncertain Promise* (New Haven, Conn.: Yale University Press, 1996), 103–35; Cheryl Greenberg, *Or Does It Explode? Black Harlem in the Great Depression* (New York: Oxford University Press, 1997); Mark Naison, *Communists in Harlem during the Great Depression* (New York: Grove, 1983), 149–50; Naison, "From Eviction Resistance to Rent Control: Tenant Activism in the Great Depression," in Lawson, ed., *Tenant Movement in New York City*, 94–133; and Elizabeth Faue, *Community of Suffering and Struggle: Women, Men, and the Labor Movement in Minneapolis, 1915–1945* (Chapel Hill: University of North Carolina Press, 1991).

39. Christopher Tomlins, *The State and the Unions: Labor Relations, Law, and the Organized Labor Movement in America, 1880–1960* (New York: Cambridge University Press, 1985); Fraser, *Labor Will Rule*; and Colin Gordon, *New Deals: Business, Labor, and Politics in America, 1920–1935* (Cambridge: Cambridge University Press, 1994). The Wagner Act also stemmed from the pressing need to restore industrial peace and Roosevelt's 1936 electoral maneuvering.

40. Kenneth Casebeer, "Drafting Wagner's Act: Leon Keyserling and the Precommittee Drafts of the Labor Disputes Act and the National Labor Relations Act," *Industrial Relations Law Journal* 11 (1989): 88; Casebeer, "Clashing Views of the Wagner Act: the Files of Leon Keyserling," *Labor's Heritage* (April 1990): 50.

41. Landon R. Y. Storrs, *Civilizing Capitalism: The National Consumers' League, Women's Activism, and Labor Standards in the New Deal Era* (Chapel Hill: University of North Carolina Press, 2000), 177–205; Fraser, *Labor Will Rule*, 391–94.

42. Ronald C. Tobey, *Technology as Freedom: The New Deal and the Electrical Modernization of the American Home* (Berkeley: University of California Press, 1996); Badger, *New Deal*, 169–86; Schwarz, *New Dealers*.

43. Geisst, *Monopolies in America*, p. 161; Brinkley, *End of Reform*, 55–58, 62–64.

44. "Message Interests," *New York Times*, January 1, 1938, p. 1. See also Frederic S. Lee, "From Multi-industry Planning to Keynesian Planning: Gardiner

Means, the American Keynesians, and National Economic Planning at the National Resources Committee," *Journal of Policy History* 2, no. 2 (1990): 186–212; Helen Sorenson, *The Consumer Movement: What It Is and What It Means* (New York: Harper, 1941), 23.

45. Hawley, *New Deal*, 389–90, 409, 416, 453, 458; Brinkley, *End of Reform*, 48–49; Rosenof, *Economics in the Long Run*, 82. In contrast to much of the literature, I argue that the late New Deal did not signal a dramatic and irreversible shift to Keynesianism. Though Roosevelt embraced deficit spending as a conscious strategy, few in Washington wanted a permanent run-up of government expenditure as the solution to economic ills, and fiscal conservatism still characterized the political culture of the American public and the New Deal. See, for example, Julian Zelizer, "The Forgotten Legacy of the New Deal: Fiscal Conservatism and the Roosevelt Administration, 1933–1938," *Presidential Studies Quarterly* 30, no. 2 (June 2000): 331–58.

46. Hawley, *New Deal*, 427, 438.

47. Unless otherwise noted, the discussion of OPA draws on my article: Meg Jacobs, " 'How about Some Meat?' The Office of Price Administration, Consumption Politics, and State-Building from the Bottom-Up, 1941–1946," *Journal of American History* 84 (December 1997): 910–41. I reconstruct the history of OPA from the Records of the Office of Price Administration, RG 188, National Archives, College Park, Md. For wartime sacrifice, see Mark H. Leff, "The Politics of Sacrifice on the American Home Front in World War II," *Journal of American History* 77 (March 1991): 1296–1318; Robert B. Westbrook, "Fighting for the American Family: Private Interests and Political Obligation in World War II," in *The Power of Culture: Critical Essays in American History*, ed. Richard Wightman Fox and T. J. Jackson Lears (Chicago: University of Chicago Press, 1993), 195–221.

48. On propaganda aimed at women, see also Amy Bentley, *Eating for Victory: Food Rationing and the Politics of Domesticity* (Urbana: University of Illinois Press, 1998).

49. Walter Reuther, "GM versus the Rest of Us," *New Republic*, January 14, 1946, p. 42; George Soule, "Wages, Prices, and Employment," *New Republic*, November 5, 1945, 592–94; Nelson Lichtenstein, *The Most Dangerous Man in Detroit: Walter Reuther and the Fate of American Labor* (New York: Basic Books, 1995), 231–34. Gallop polls report that in the middle of the 113-day-long strike, 60 percent of the public supported the UAW's demands for higher wages. See Hugh Rockoff, *Drastic Measures: A History of Wage and Price Controls in the United States* (New York: Cambridge University Press, 1984), 101–2.

50. Jacobs, " 'How about Some Meat?' " 939–40.

51. Ibid., 935.

52. All ads were found in the Records of the National Association of Manufactures, Pamphlets Collection, Hagley Museum, Wilmington, Del.

53. See "President's Statement on Taft and Prices," *New York Times*, June 6, 1947, 1, 18; "Taft Says Truman Is Man to Blame for Higher Prices," *New York Times*, June 7, 1947, 1, 18; "Truman Calls Special Session Nov. 17 on High Prices and Relief in Europe," *New York Times*, October 24, 1947, 1, 2; "High Prices: Should We Restore Price Control?" *New Republic*, October 20, 1947, 19–26;

"High Prices: They Will Be One of Congress' Biggest Headaches as It Meets Nov. 17," *Life*, November 10, 1947, 31–35. I explore inflationary fears in Meg Jacobs, "Inflation: 'The Permanent Dilemma' of the American Middle Classes," in *Social Contracts under Stress: The Middle Classes of America, Europe, and Japan at the Turn of the Century*, ed. Olivier Zunz, Leonard Schoppa, and Nohuhiro Hiwatari (New York: Russell Sage Foundation, 2002), 130–53. On antiunion campaigns, see Howell John Harris, *The Right to Manage: Industrial Relations Policies of American Business in the 1940s* (Madison: University of Wisconsin Press, 1982); Elizabeth A. Fones-Wolfe, *Selling Free Enterprise: The Business Assault on Labor and Liberalism, 1945–60* (Urbana: University of Illinois Press, 1994); and David Plotke, *Building a Democratic Political Order: Reshaping American Liberalism in the 1930s and 1940s* (New York: Cambridge University Press, 1996). For postwar labor, see Lichtenstein, *Most Dangerous Man*; Kevin Boyle, *The UAW and the Heyday of American Liberalism, 1945–1968* (Ithaca, N.Y.: Cornell University Press, 1995); Robert H. Zieger, *American Workers, American Unions, 1920–1985* (Baltimore: Johns Hopkins University, 1986).

54. For public opinion data, see George H. Gallup, *The Gallup Poll: Public Opinion 1935–1971* (Wilmington, Del.: Scholarly Resources, 1972); Louis Harris, *The Harris Survey Yearbook of Public Opinion, 1970–1973* (New York: Louis Harris and Associates, 1971–1974).

55. Charles Maier, "The Politics of Inflation in the Twentieth Century," in *The Political Economy of Inflation*, ed. Fred Hirsch and John Goldthorpe (Cambridge, Mass.: Harvard University Press, 1978), 37–72. See other essays in that volume and Robert J. Gordon, "The Demand for and Supply of Inflation," *Journal of Law and Economics* 18 (1975): 807–36.

56. Samuel Lubell, *The Future of American Politics* (New York: Harper, 1952), 75, 218–19.

57. Gary R. Reichard, *The Reaffirmation of Republicanism: Eisenhower and the Eighty-third Congress* (Knoxville: University of Tennessee Press, 1975), 13, 16–17, 24.

58. Craufurd D. Goodwin and R. Stanley Herren, "The Truman Administration: Problems and Policies Unfold," in *Exhortation and Controls: The Search for a Wage-Price Policy, 1945–1971*, ed. Craufurd D. Goodwin (Washington, D.C.: Brookings Institution Press, 1975), 84–86.

59. Kirk Porter and Donald Bruce Johnson, comps. *National Party Platforms*, vol. 1 (Urbana: University of Illinois Press, 1978), 480–81, 500–501.

60. Edwin Diamond and Stephen Bates, *The Spot: The Rise of Political Advertising on Television* (Cambridge, Mass.: MIT Press, 1992), 38, 41; James T. Patterson, *Grand Expectations: The United States, 1945–1974* (New York: Oxford University Press, 1996), 348.

61. Diamond and Bates, *Spot*, 56–57; Paul F. Boller, Jr., *Presidential Campaigns* (New York: Oxford University Press, 1996), 282. See also Kathleen Hall Jamieson, *Packaging the Presidency: A History and Criticism of Presidential Campaign Advertising* (New York: Oxford University Press, 1984), 38–89; Patterson, *Grand Expectations*, 258–59.

62. "Who's Making the Big Money," *U.S. News*, August 31, 1956, pp. 111–12; "Latest Argument for Pay Raises," *U.S. News*, August 31, 1956, pp. 112–13;

Benjamin L. Masse, "Joe Smith's 50-cent Dollar," *America*, November 24, 1956, pp. 227–29.

63. "Steel—Why the Inflation Threat," *Newsweek*, June 4, 1956, p. 72; "Inching Inflation," *Fortune*, August 1956, p. 40; "Inflation Race—Who's Ahead, Who's Behind," *U.S. News*, August 3, 1956, 95–97; "Why Our Dollars Won't Go as Far," *Newsweek*, August 6, 1956, pp. 19–20; "It Now Costs More Than Ever to Live," *U.S. News*, August 31, 1956, pp. 44–45; "This Inflation Is Serious," *America*, September 8, 1956, p. 520; "Why Prices Are Rising," *U.S. News*, September 28, 1956, pp. 27–29; "Beefsteak: $1.49 a Pound and Still Going Up," *U.S. News*, September 28, 1956, p. 30; "Cost of Living: What's Happening to It," *Business Week*, October 27, 1956, p. 169; "Why Inflation Is Threatening," *U.S. News*, May 18, 1956, pp. 118–22; "Inflation Checked?" *New Republic*, September 10, 1956, p. 6; "Inflation or Deflation? Burns Says Both Must Be Avoided," *U.S. News*, June 1, 1956, p. 126–29.

64. Henry Hazlitt, "Built-in Inflation," *Newsweek*, May 28, 1956, p. 86; Roger M. Blough, Annual Address to U.S. Steel Stockholders, May 7, 1956, as printed in "A Picture of the Wage-Spiral at Work," *U.S. News*, May 18, 1956, pp. 64–66; "Steel—Why the Inflation Threat," *Newsweek*, June 4, 1956, p. 71.

65. John Kenneth Galbraith, "Are Living Costs Out of Control?" *Atlantic*, February 1957, pp. 37–41.

66. "Purchasing Power: Fact versus Fallacy," April 1956; "A New Force for Inflation," May 1956; and "The American Triangle of Plenty: Joe the Umbrella Maker," September 1951, in NAM Pamphlets, Hagley Museum. More generally, see Fones-Wolfe, *Selling Free Enterprise*, 272–74.

67. Judith Stein, *Running Steel, Running America: Race, Economic Policy, and the Decline of Liberalism* (Chapel Hill: University of North Carolina Press, 1998), 17, 22–25.

68. Geisst, *Monopolies in America*, 212–16; Stein, *Running Steel*, 18–22.

69. Estes Kefauver, *In a Few Hands: Monopoly Power in America* (New York: Pantheon, 1965), 3.

70. As quoted in Brinkley, *End of Reform*, 122.

71. A useful treatment of consumer politics is David Vogel, *Fluctuating Fortunes* (New York: Basic Books, 1987).

72. Rockoff, *Drastic Measures*, 200–234; Allen J. Matusow, *Nixon's Economy: Booms, Busts, Dollars, and Votes* (Lawrence: University Press of Kansas, 1998); Neil de Marchi, "The First Nixon Administration: Prelude to Controls," in Goodwin, ed., *Exhortation and Controls*, 295–353.

Chapter Eleven

THE UNEASY RELATIONSHIP

DEMOCRACY, TAXATION, AND STATE BUILDING SINCE

THE NEW DEAL

Julian E. Zelizer

MOST POLITICIANS SENSE that Americans hate taxes. We are a nation with a long tradition of tax revolts. Yet despite an abundance of historical studies about state building in the twentieth century, few have confronted the reality of tax resistance and fiscal constraint. Even research on American antistatism has emphasized the intellectual history of liberalism and republicanism rather than opposition to federal taxes, the most concrete manifestation of antistatism. Hostility toward federal taxation has remained extremely strong in all income brackets, ranging from blue-collar workers who were central beneficiaries of New Deal programs to elite financial investors. Resistance to local taxation has ebbed and flowed to a greater extent, since the benefits of taxation have been more apparent to constituents; those taxes have also conformed to the localist ethos that Thomas Sugrue examines in the following chapter.

As a result of tax resistance, and the perception among policy makers that tax resistance is and was strong, state builders have been handcuffed by fiscal constraint. The Founding Fathers virtually guaranteed that the task of modern state building would be extremely difficult by locating the power to levy federal taxes in the House of Representatives, where it would be most susceptible to democratic pressure. Revealingly, much of the Progressive Era state growth occurred before the nation had a federal income tax in place; tariffs were the principle source of federal revenue, and the federal income tax touched only a small portion of the population after it became permanent in 1913.[1] The next major expansion of the federal government, the New Deal, preceded the creation of a mass income tax. Therefore, the problem of revenue extraction has loomed large throughout the twentieth century. In the nineteenth century, federal fiscal capacity was not as important, since the principal form of government intervention revolved around less costly court decisions as well as state and local government.[2] What made fiscal restraint so central after 1933 was the persistence of strong antitax sentiment among most segments of society in an era when the federal government achieved more of a presence in society than ever before. Citizens came to expect a large number of federal government services and resisted retrenchment after the Great Depression.[3] Through interest groups—which, as Brian Balogh shows, became the intermediary institution through which most citizens conveyed their demands outside the ballot box—Americans pressured Congress to provide more and more services. The irony was that some of the strongest opposition to federal taxes came from populations who were most dependent on government.[4] Yet this irony was of more interest to academic scholars than politicians, who still needed to extract money for programs from a population that was not comfortable with its own dependencies. The awkward juxtaposition of an antipathy toward taxes with stronger demands for federal services resulted in a deficit-based state. As much as deficits were a product of Keynesian macroeconomic policy, they were likewise a symptom of a democratic dilemma: Americans wanted more federal benefits but did not want to pay for them.

One reason that historians have failed to incorporate popular resentment of taxation into their meta-narratives is because it contradicts a basic tenet of postwar historiography, namely, the harmony between state building and democracy. In the following pages, I make two arguments. The first is that a fundamental tension has existed between state building and national resistance to federal taxation. In this respect, democracy has sometimes been at odds with state building as it comes into conflict with strong antitax sentiment. Given that the United States is a democracy, elected officials have had considerable trouble avoiding the opposition to taxes that exists across economic classes. To highlight this tension in the post–New Deal period, my chapter examines how politicians have operated under fiscal restraint since the 1930s. My second argument, however, is that fiscal restraint has not been an insurmountable barrier. This is evident with the emergence of the mass income tax and social-insurance tax systems as well as the substantial state presence achieved in all areas of life, ranging from welfare to highway construction.

The construction and maintenance of a viable federal tax system remains an underappreciated development in twentieth-century political history. State builders were able to overcome the challenges of antitax sentiment and fiscal restraint by four principal strategies: building democratic support for taxation in times of war, using earmarked taxes and trust funds, relying on automatic revenue generated by economic growth, and accepting federal deficits. One strategy that policy makers used to raise taxes was to mobilize support to expand the tax system during national crises. Even when there was not a direct military conflict, politicians relied on military rhetoric to overcome antistatism, as is evident with President Lyndon Johnson's "War" on Poverty.[5] The most striking moment came during World War II, when policy makers sold the mass income tax through a national public relations campaign that promoted taxpaying as the patriotic duty of citizens who were not fighting abroad. Another method involved trust funds and earmarked taxes. These devices were used to create the appearance that taxes would be linked to specific benefits and that programs being funded would be protected from wasteful spending. The next strategy for obtaining funds was to maintain a tax system that raised higher revenues due to economic growth. Between 1945 and 1973, government revenue increased rapidly as a result of economic growth rather than legislated tax increases. Finally, state builders were forced to accept temporary deficits, which was difficult in a nation that continued to revere balanced budgets.[6] While scholars have considered budgetary deficits as a type of conscious economic policy promoted by Keynesians or supply-siders, it must be recognized that deficits offered the only viable solution for political actors who wanted to build a state with limited federal revenue. What is most notable about the conservative revolution of the 1980s is not just that conservatives mobilized support around tax resistance but that the fiscal infrastructure did not disintegrate amidst this onslaught. The durability of the fiscal system that state builders put into place, in response to popular resistance to taxation, continued a pattern in American political history in which federal politicians created a state that did not necessarily resemble European models but was nonetheless effective and powerful on its own terms.[7]

My interpretation makes four historiographical claims. First, the challenge of raising revenue must be put at the forefront of the new political history. While fiscal restraint has been one of the most powerful forces in national politics, historians have downplayed its importance among the pressures facing politicians. Second, my interpretation suggests that the history of taxation offers insights into the areas in which public policy, institutional development, and political culture intersected. Third, I raise questions about prevailing interpretations of American political history. My interpretation is critical of historians who have usually linked democratic politics to state building while minimizing the persistent tensions that just as often existed between them. It simultaneously challenges New Left and race-centered scholars who exclusively blame corporate interests or conservative southern congressmen for subverting state building while ignoring the role of a mass electorate that detested taxes. Finally, I argue that historians must pay closer attention to what has been achieved in American political history rather than alternatives that were rejected. Too often, political history has focused on the failures of state building rather than on what was actually accomplished (consider, for example, the extensive literature on our lack of national health insurance, compared with the rather limited work on Medicare and Medicaid). The operating assumption has been that politicians stifled democratic pressure from the left, rather than that they faced equivalent, if not greater, pressure from the right.[8] When scholars take into account the formidable obstacles that state builders faced, the importance of understanding American state building on its own terms rather than only comparing it with European systems becomes evident.

HISTORIANS, DEMOCRACY, AND THE STATE

United States historians have generally postulated a harmonious relationship between democracy and state building in the twentieth century. During the 1950s and 1960s, the leading interpretation of political history was termed the liberal synthesis. The scholars who developed this synthesis, including Arthur Schlesinger, Jr., and William Leuchtenburg, argued that the expansion of the state corresponded with growing democratic demands.[9] Adopting a progressive teleology that pitted "selfish" economic interests against the virtuous "people," they described a series of liberal presidents (including Republican Dwight Eisenhower) who built federal programs as a countervailing force against big business. The New Deal, in this analysis, reflected the triumph of democratic politics. As Leuchtenburg wrote, "Roosevelt and his aides fashioned a government which consciously sought to make the industrial system more humane and to protect workers and their families from exploitation."[10]

In the 1960s, the liberal scholars were challenged by the "corporate liberal" synthesis.[11] Born of the domestic conflicts of the era, this synthesis claimed that the federal government had been expanded to protect the modern corporation, not to tame it. Corporate liberal scholars did not deny that most citizens wanted an expansive domestic state but instead argued that the institutions that emerged served the interests of big business. The state, in this view, aimed to quell destructive competition and social unrest. Taking populists and progressive labor unions as representative of the democratic impulse, historian Gabriel Kolko wrote that business leaders concluded "the best way to thwart change was to channelize it."[12] These historians implied that popular state-building alternatives were rejected to fulfill the interests of corporate capitalism. Even social historians in the 1980s, whose outlook differed from that of this earlier generation of scholars, were primarily interested in tracing social support of the New Deal rather than the factors behind persistent citizen opposition.[13] Their focus reflected a professional lack of interest in the history of conservatism, which has become a source of serious intellectual concern only in the 1990s.[14]

There was a less conspiratorial variant of the corporate liberal interpretation, called the "organizational synthesis," whose practitioners focused on the interdependence of corporations, the federal government, and the new professional class that emerged with the industrial economy. The organizational synthesis posited that at the turn of the century large-scale national institutions eclipsed the nineteenth-century society of "island communities."[15] This school abandoned the progressive teleology of liberal historians, examining instead how the nation's political and economic systems achieved equilibrium.[16] In depicting the inevitable growth of large-scale institutions, organizational historians paid minimal attention to the resistance that state builders encountered, such as fiscal constraint or popular anxiety with large-scale institutions.[17] When these historians looked at failure, they focused on institutional weaknesses or conflicting visions of state building that had hampered policy.

The most recent incarnation of political history has been developed by historical social scientists. These scholars have been extremely interested in why the development of the American state lagged behind those of Europe.[18] Everyone and everything has been suspect for limiting state growth, except for the majoritarian interests of voters themselves. In many versions of this scholarship, the power of southern Democrats has been featured as the major obstacle to expansive government, as they fought against state intervention to protect regional racist institutions.[19] Others working in this vein have blamed perceptions that politicians held about gender roles in economic life.[20] America's underdeveloped bureaucracy and federalism have also been prominent culprits. Still others have highlighted "political discourses" that restricted the scope of policy.[21] The common assumption is that without these obstacles, a sizable majority of citizens would have supported a larger state. Those who have acknowledged voter resistance to the federal government, particularly that of blue-collar workers who at one time championed the New Deal, have tended to present this opposition as centering on racial concerns rather than a broader distrust of government.[22] While all of this work points to important sources of resistance to government expansion, the work tends to downplay questions of taxation and broad-based antistatism that have continually shaped America's political culture.[23]

Nonetheless, there are alternative schools that have moved historians closer to the problem of antistatism. This chapter builds on the work of a handful of scholars who have identified antistatism as a central problem in American state building.[24] One group of scholars has focused on political culture.[25] Emanating from the field of intellectual history, this approach has tended to focus on the abstract realm of Lockean individualism. These scholars argue that shared national values caused Americans to oppose centralized political power. However, this work has been vulnerable to attack; other scholars have pointed to shared national values that actually supported government. By not grappling with resistance to taxation—the most concrete manifestation of antistatism—many of the scholars who have focused on antistatism have often omitted the most striking evidence that supports their claims. Nonetheless, their works have played a pivotal role in channeling research into a new direction.[26] Another important body of research has come from neoconservatives who have approached the state more skeptically by highlighting grassroots resistance to government expansion.[27] From a different perspective, liberal scholars have shown how white voters were often extremely hostile to federal government programs as a result of racial tension.[28] Their research has raised important questions by placing antistatism at the center, rather than periphery, of its analysis.

Recently, there has been renewed interest in the history of taxation. While most political historians have treated taxation as a technical matter that is not central to national politics, over the past few years a number of scholars have recognized the importance of taxation to political history.[29] In doing so, they have discovered the intense struggle that was required to construct the nation's existing, albeit limited, income tax system and to contain the proliferation of tax loopholes.[30]

Finally, some political scientists and economists have contributed pertinent research by examining business, professional, and investor opposition to the state.[31] Among most business leaders, David Vogel wrote, "a sense of suspicion toward the state has managed to survive the most impressive and decisive political triumphs."[32] Although these scholars have modified their argument to account for corporate liberalism, their work has explored how most capitalist leaders fought to keep taxes low. These scholars have discussed how businessmen limited taxation, partially because they encountered little public opposition in their efforts to do so. Even businessmen who supported a role for the federal government tended to champion Keynesian tax reductions.[33]

This historiographic analysis reveals that until recently political historians have tended to downplay the strong strain of antitax sentiment that has been an important component of the nation's political culture, and they have downplayed as well the problem of fiscal restraint. Most interpretations have posited that democracy and state building have usually worked in tandem while overlooking public opposition to taxes that was given a strong voice through the democratic process. To undermine this premise would raise troubling questions for the teleology of these narratives. This chapter does not claim democracy is *always* at odds with state expansion. Indeed, many federal programs in the twentieth century had strong grassroots support, without which they most likely would never have been enacted.[34]

Yet democratic pressure has also imposed a brake on government expansion. The most powerful evidence of this strand of democratic pressure has been the fact that most federal politicians have feared supporting direct and visible tax increases. State builders have rarely identified a single source of tax opposition; the sentiment was blamed on business, the middle class, blue-collar workers, home owners, wealthy families, and others. While different politicians targeted different coalitions, no social group escaped blame. This made it difficult to mobilize countercoalitions in favor of tax hikes.

Therefore, federal politicians of all parties, regions, and ideologies have been forced to grapple with the question, Where is the money coming from? But what has been obvious to politicians remains obscure in the historical literature. As a result, one of the largest obstacles that has faced politicians is a ghost in many scholarly accounts of state building. Since the 1950s, historians have pointed to many forces working against the growth of government, from racism to weak institutions. But they have not looked at democratic pressure from voters to maintain low rates of taxation.

STATE BUILDING WITH EMPTY POCKETS

Since the 1930s, state builders have had to grapple with the problem of fiscal constraint. The American electorate has never moved toward an agenda of high taxes and high spending. During the biggest economic crisis in the nation's history, the Great Depression, resentment toward federal taxation remained strong. At the local level, intense opposition to rising property taxation produced organized tax revolts in parts of the country. In those revolts, voters passed measures that limited local and state taxes as over one thousand taxpayer organizations formed by 1932.[35] Even in moderate states, constituents continued to elect state government officials who were unsympathetic to many New Deal programs and progressive government in general, including higher income taxes.[36]

At an institutional level, the nation did not have a federal mass income tax in the 1930s. Less than 5 percent of the population encountered income tax returns in those years.[37] The Roosevelt administration never pushed to broaden the tax base to the size needed to fund the New Deal. Instead, the government relied on hidden regressive taxes (including alcohol and tobacco taxes, the Social Security tax, and the agricultural-processing tax) and one increase, albeit watered down, on corporations. But even the famous tax on corporation profits, the centerpiece of Roosevelt's notorious shift to the left, was "more bluff than bludgeon" that affected only a small number of elite capitalists.[38] Except for programs with earmarked taxes, Roosevelt relied heavily on state and local spending while rejecting proposals that required significant increases in the federal income tax. Even with a strong liberal majority in Congress, Roosevelt's 1936 budget rejected a general tax increase and did not include permanent spending for public assistance.[39] The most significant new tax was the Social Security tax in 1935, which remained small until 1950. This earmarked tax was promoted by the Social Security Board as a "premium."[40]

The New Deal tax agenda left the federal government with a limited and inflexible revenue source. Deficits of the 1930s were largely a result of the increased need for public spending, combined with limited revenue sources. While Roosevelt used Keynesian rhetoric to justify a deficit in 1938, this was not the driving force behind his policies. Rather, the deficit resulted from having to enact programs without sufficient revenue.[41] This was problematic for liberals since Roosevelt and congressional leaders remained committed to fiscal conservatism, which severely restricted how much federal officials were able to spend.[42] Although he did not balance a budget, Roosevelt continued to strive for that objective, promoting expenditure reduction as soon as the economy improved. Progressive ideology, moreover, sometimes worked against the imposition of federal taxation. During the 1930s, influential congressional liberals and the Roosevelt administration would actively oppose popular congressional proposals for a national sales tax on the grounds that it would be regressive (and that implementation would be impossible).[43]

It was not until World War II that the American state adopted a mass federal income tax. Policy makers mobilized during the war to expand the fiscal infrastructure of the state. Strikingly, even during the war, federal officials felt the need to market this idea to the wage-earning public. The government launched a public relations campaign to sell the idea of taxpaying to average citizens. The Department of Treasury used all sorts of messages that told Americans it was patriotic to pay their taxes. To promote the tax, the Office of War Information placed ads in magazines such as *Ladies' Home Journal, House Beautiful*, and *True Detective*. The treasury broadcast radio jingles by Danny Kaye and Irving Berlin and released Disney animations in which Donald Duck taught citizens why they should pay taxes.[44] The campaign worked as the government successfully expanded the income tax base to include over 40 million wage earners and implemented withholding at the source.

The wartime experience revealed how new policies could reconfigure politics.[45] By time the war ended, there was no strong pressure to eliminate the mass income tax altogether. Conservatives accepted a permanent mass income tax, just as liberals had accepted the regressive system of the New Deal era as a permanent feature in American politics. A majority of citizens and politicians had developed new conceptions of what types of government intervention were legitimate and essential. The tax system would never return to its prewar condition. Tax reductions after the Korean War meant lowering rates within the existing, progressive income tax system rather than retrenching the entire code. This was a significant change in a nation where most citizens had not been subject to this federal income tax until World War II. Once the mass tax was in place and the Cold War required high revenue permanently, the assumption about what constituted minimum taxation changed.

Just as World War II tax policies reconfigured notions about what was legitimate for the federal government to ask of its citizens, social policy in this era expanded popular conceptions of entitlement. A larger number of citizens came to expect certain types of programs ranging from Social Security retirement payments to farm subsidies. The most famous of these interest groups was the American Farm Bureau Federation, which made it virtually impossible for politicians to cut farm subsidies without facing severe economic risks, as the Eisenhower administration learned when it attempted to take on this challenge. When the influence of the Farm Bureau waned, it was replaced by organizations representing particular commodities.[46] Interest groups were also willing to protect any particular tax mechanisms that were attached to their program. The elderly, for instance, would mobilize through the American Association of Retired Persons (AARP) several decades after Congress had created Social Security. This organization was founded in 1958 as a small vehicle for insurance and turned into an interest group by the 1980s and 1990s that aggressively lobbied legislators in support of Social Security. Interest groups such as the AARP represented the voices of different segments of the population, as Herbert Hoover had discerned back in 1928, and they helped protect federal programs such as contributory social insurance from retrenchment. When politicians attempted to reform Social Security or Medicare, they encountered fierce electoral resistance from working- and middle-class constituents.

Despite the rising number of interest groups that formed to protect federal programs, after World War II public opposition to current federal tax rates rose as well. Whereas only 15 percent of those polled by Gallup said federal income taxes were unfair in February 1943, that figure jumped to 38 percent by February 1946 and kept rising steadily.[47] Congress moved to reduce income taxes within the new institutional framework. In 1948, Congress passed a sizable tax reduction. When President Truman vetoed the bill, claiming that it would lead to inflation and be fiscally irresponsible, Congress succeeded in overriding him. Although the mass tax system was needed to pay for the Korean War in the early 1950s, Congress continued its incremental expansion of loopholes for all income brackets to help ease the tax burden. The tax recodification of 1954, which legitimated the progressive rate structure in effect during the Korean War, provided a wide array of loopholes for all classes of citizens. After the recodification, an extremely large number of citizens had a vested interest in the loophole system of the federal tax code. As Aaron Wildavsky and Carolyn Webber concluded, "The truth is out: As Pogo might have put it, we—the broad middle and lower classes—have met the special interests, and 'they is us.' "[48] It was clear to most politicians by the 1950s that large federal tax increases, other than those involving earmarked taxes, were off the table. Indeed, the horrors of German fascism, discoveries about the brutalities of the Soviet Union, and the domestic politics of the Cold War all heightened antistatist sentiment within the public, thereby placing federal programs and proposals at risk of being tagged as Communist.[49] This reality governed policy decisions.

Throughout the 1950s, public opinion data continued to show support for lower taxes. When polled, a majority of Americans said consistently that they felt their taxes were too high (even when the question was worded in different ways) and that they supported proposals for tax reductions. In 1947, Gallup polls found that 54 percent of those polled thought that taxes were too high; that number peaked in 1952 when 71 percent of those polled felt that their taxes were too high. While this number would drop by 1961, it steadily climbed back up to 69 percent by 1969. Between 1943 and 1997, the proportion of Americans who said they were satisfied with federal income tax rates was never more than 3 percent.[50] Although there were obvious discrepancies between these opinion polls and the reality that most citizens accepted a sizable overall tax burden (local, state, federal) in practice, opinion polls sent clear signals that raising nonearmarked federal taxes could have high electoral costs. Importantly, polls did not identify any single component of society as being the source of this opposition.

Nevertheless, few Americans actually paid the statutory income tax rates. Congress institutionalized tax reduction through a generous system of loopholes. Through this system, called "tax expenditures" by some experts, tax reductions were automatically granted even if Congress did not take action. The tax code subsidized the growth of private welfare benefits that employers at private companies offered their workers. Through indirect spending, legislators found a short-term solution to America's chronic fiscal dilemma. By international standards, the United States distributed generous tax loopholes, exemptions, and deductions. Although top tax rates reached 94 percent by the late 1950s, the system never yielded more than 10.6 percent of the GNP.[51] A variety of loopholes available to citizens and organizations during much of the twentieth century. Technical errors in the tax code and vague statutory language, for instance, enabled lawyers to hide their clients' income. Furthermore, Congress enacted specific provisions with the intent of providing tax relief to certain industries; the most famous of these was the depletion allowance through which the oil industry avoided its tax obligations. Additionally, credits, exemptions, and exceptions were designed to encourage categories of citizens and industries to invest money in special ways, ranging from providing health care coverage for workers, to home ownership, to investment in new industrial machinery. Political scientist John Witte concluded: "Unless faced with a dire alternative, people favor lower rather than higher taxes, and politicians have accommodated them. Although favoring base-broadening tax reform in theory, when details are presented they strongly support existing tax reduction provisions and seem eager to expand the tax expenditure system to include new and increased benefits."[52]

Since most policy makers never abandoned the precepts of fiscal conservatism, believing that deficits were economically harmful and a sign of political corruption and instability,[53] there was a constant tension between limited federal revenue and increased demand for government services. The impact of a limited tax base was relevant not just to domestic welfare policies in the 1950s but also to the Cold War. If there was any area of policy that commanded widespread popular support, it was the fight against international communism. But even here, revenue concerns loomed large. When the Truman administration attempted to expand the national security state, the president had to settle for a more modest plan than he had initially hoped for, due to fiscal constraint.[54] Military planners unsuccessfully proposed that the military budget be increased by 100 to 300 percent. Aaron Friedberg found that if military planners had achieved their objectives, the United States would have dedicated 15 percent of its national output to defense in the 1960s rather than 10 percent.[55] When Congress established a civil defense program to protect citizens in case of a nuclear attack, the program relied heavily on state and local government as well as voluntarism, so that Congress had to allocate only limited funds for the program, almost 50 percent less than President Eisenhower requested between 1954 and 1958.[56] Fiscal restraint worked both ways. Eisenhower, for example, opposed tax cut proposals during his second term, realizing that the combination of the entrenched federal state with the existing tax structure curtailed policy makers' budget flexibility.[57] He sensed that if taxes were cut too much, it would be extremely difficult to raise them in the future. Given that international and domestic commitments that were not likely to disappear, excessive tax cuts seemed imprudent since inadequate taxes would lead to higher deficits, which would hamper investment and growth.

In addition to wartime crises, state builders relied on accounting devices and earmarked taxes in the 1950s. Americans proved willing to pay specific types of taxes if they were distinguished by trust funds or packaged as earmarked contributions. As a result, politicians linked taxes with specific benefits that the contributor would receive in the future and created the appearance that such funds were to be protected from irresponsible spending. After fifteen years of uncertainty, Congress decided in 1950 that contributory old age insurance, financed through the earmarked payroll tax, would be the centerpiece of social provision for the elderly rather than means-tested public assistance, which was funded through general revenue.[58] The strategy proved to be successful. Unlike corporate and income taxes, which steadily declined during the postwar period, Social Security taxes would continue to rise. In 1950, the combined Social Security tax rate was 3.0 percent; by 1990, the combined rate reached 15.3 percent.[59] During this same period, federal income taxes were cut more than twelve times. At the creation of Social Security, policy makers equated the promised benefits with private insurance. Under this rhetoric, the Social Security "tax" was really a "contribution" or "premium," which entitled taxpayers to receive a benefit during their retirement years. Even after politicians downplayed the insurance rhetoric, the Social Security tax proved durable as citizens continued to believe their money was paying for a contributory, non-welfare program.

The extensive use of earmarked taxes and trust funds in American budgeting has been a testament to the fact that policy makers have felt pressure to deal with fiscal restraint while crafting durable policy commitments. The fact that Social Security and Medicare—the nation's two largest domestic programs—have been financed through these devices reveals the persistence of both tax resistance and policy makers' success in devising strategies around that problem. Earmarked taxes provided policy makers the latitude to build viable programs. By the 1990s, almost 40 percent of federal revenues were committed to trust funds, mainly for the Social Security and Medicare programs, but also for domestic programs such as highway construction, airport development, nature conservation, and the environmental Superfund.[60] In the end, the programs that relied on dedicated revenue sources have proved to be much more resistant against political retrenchment than those that relied on general revenue.

Another strategy through which state builders were able to raise taxes in peacetime was automatic revenue. The income tax system was not indexed for inflation. As a result, an important method of tax collection in the 1950s and 1960s was the automatic increase in revenue generated by economic growth, not federal tax hikes. In the first two decades after

World War II, economic growth pushed taxpayers into higher income brackets so that the federal government received increased levels of revenue. Because low inflation sustained the value of their dollars as incomes rose, citizens seemed tolerant of moving up to higher brackets. This phenomenon also benefited Social Security as Congress found itself with extra revenue to distribute as cash benefits without raising taxes. Economic growth, together with earmarked taxes, made revenue raising possible despite an electorate that fiercely protected its money.

The burst of state building in the 1960s, like those of the New Deal and World War II, also took place in a context of limited fiscal capacity. In economic policy, liberals embraced tax reduction as an effective means of helping wage earners and stimulating the economy, a stark alternative to increasing defense and welfare spending.[61] Congress never discussed increasing taxes dramatically when the new programs were being planned. From the start of the decade, President Kennedy and then Johnson set the tone of the policy agenda in 1963 and 1964 with the campaign for and passage of a $10-billion-dollar, across-the-board tax cut. The reduction was sold on the grounds that it would stimulate the economy and minimize "fiscal drag." Johnson explained that through the tax cut "the federal government will not have to do for the economy what the economy should do for itself."[62] According to the president's close adviser on domestic issues, Joseph Califano, "Johnson's extravagant rhetoric announcing new programs belied the modest funds he requested to begin them. Conservative members of Congress distrusted him because they believed that he was hiding his real intentions just to get a foot in the door. The Great Society's liberal advocates were frustrated because he wasn't asking for enough to smash the door open. And Congress was providing even less."[63] The guiding assumption of the period was that increased revenue would be produced automatically from economic growth. As a result of tax cuts and incentives passed in the 1960s, corporate taxes declined as well. After Congress passed a major investment credit to stimulate corporate investment in 1962, the top corporate tax rate declined from 70 percent in 1964 to 36 percent in 1986.[64] Tax breaks continued to erode the nation's tax base. By 1967, for example, the federal government spent almost $2.3 billion in tax breaks for the elderly through provisions that included a tax exemption, a tax credit for retirement income, and the exclusion of Social Security benefits from income taxation. Congress reported that in 1967 federal tax breaks cost $37 billion (21 percent of federal expenditures).[65]

The commitment to low taxes constrained state-building efforts in the 1960s, both in defense and domestic programs. Fiscal pressure remained evident in 1962 when President Kennedy abandoned his goal of building a national network of underground bomb shelters because of insufficient revenue, and he angered defense advisers when he cut spending requests for the armed forces by $13 billion.[66] From the start, the War on Poverty received meager appropriations. President Johnson balanced his desire to help the poor with his perception that the federal budget needed to remain below $100 billion and that taxes could not be raised.[67] "The War on Poverty," Michael Brown explained, was "mortgaged to the tax cut." Johnson advisers Charles Schultze and Walter Heller embraced a targeted poverty program, abandoning proposals for liberalized cash transfers, job training, and social services, largely because of budgetary constraints.[68] The results of this budgetary decision were clear. The War on Poverty received $500 million, while Medicare received $6.5 billion upon its creation. The largest social program, Medicare, was paid for with increased Social Security taxes, not revenue derived from income taxes. Unlike other national health care programs that had previously been proposed in the United States, Medicare passed by substantial margins in 1965 in large part because proponents sold the program within the Social Security system and tied benefits to an earmarked payroll tax.[69] Medicare proponents believed from the start of their campaign that, unlike income taxes, citizens would be willing to accept higher Social Security taxes in exchange for new benefits. According to one Gallup poll, 67 percent of those polled supported increasing Social Security taxes to pay for health care for the elderly.[70] But in other areas, those in charge of creating the War on Poverty never had the type of financial resources that they felt were necessary to succeed. Johnson embraced a course that reallocated existing federal funds rather than seeking new revenue. He explained his outlook when he warned his administration: "The Great Society will require substantial investment. This means: that as a nation we cannot afford to waste a single dollar of our resources on outmoded programs . . . [and] that as a government we must get the most out of every dollar of scarce budget resources, reforming old programs and using the savings for the new programs of the Great Society."[71] Johnson repeatedly frustrated his closest advisers by rejecting requests for more spending.

When the Vietnam War consumed federal funding, the War on Poverty suffered. Between 1966 and 1968, Johnson and his congressional allies fought for a $10 billion tax surcharge to finance the war in Vietnam while maintaining the War on Poverty. His administration also justified the measure as antiinflationary. But, sticking to the policy agenda of the early 1960s, Congress forced the administration to accept steep spending cuts of more than $6 billion.[72] The president was told by the tax-writing committees that he could have either guns *or* butter, but he could not have both. When Johnson sacrificed the War on Poverty on the altar of Vietnam, he learned quickly about the impact of fiscal restraint on the possibilities of state building. "That bitch of a war," Johnson lamented, "killed the lady I really loved—the Great Society."[73] Even though social welfare spending continued to rise in the next decade, the enthusiasm for expanding social programs had been quelled. "What was left," concludes the historian Robert Collins, "was not the powerful reform surge of mid-decade but only its inertia."[74]

By the 1960s, blue-collar workers—an integral part of the New Deal coalition—were becoming less tolerant of existing income tax rates as well. Beginning in World War II the union movement, policy makers looking for alternatives to direct government intervention, and welfare capitalists had constructed generous systems of private benefits within their institutions, ranging from health insurance to workers' pensions (all of which were subsidized by federal tax breaks). These benefits constituted an integral and sizable supplement to America's public welfare state. As Jacob Hacker has explained: "The United States, we have seen, ranks last according to the traditional measure of social welfare effort. But once we adjust for relative tax burdens, tax expenditures, and publicly subsidized private benefits . . . the United States rises to the middle of the pack." In none of the eleven nations that were the subject of a recent Organization for Economic Co-operation and Development report on this issue that used the most sophisticated measures, "does private social welfare spending comprise even half as large a share of total social spending as it does in the United States."[75] Combined with Social Security taxation, workers had less reason to support income taxation, since general welfare programs did not seem to benefit them. Many workers felt as if paying union dues and higher income taxes amounted to a "double tax." The private welfare state weaned blue-collar support away from the welfare state, thereby transforming this key constituency in the New Deal coalition into a prime opponent of taxation.[76] Republican presidents from Richard Nixon to Ronald Reagan capitalized on the resentment of the new middle class as they attempted to create a conservative majority.

Many successful state building initiatives starting in the 1970s took place in the form of federal regulations that did not require direct tax increases. This became yet another way through which state builders worked around the problem of fiscal restraint. "Governments short on money but desiring to have an impact," one scholar noted, "are likely to be drawn to regulatory mechanisms."[77] Indeed, many important policy breakthroughs in this decade emerged through the courts and bureaucracies rather than the legislative branch. The most dramatic extensions of government came through regulations to protect minorities, consumers, the environment, and individuals in the workplace.[78] One of the biggest domestic policy breakthroughs of the decade was deregulation, which of course consisted of the government diminishing its responsibilities.[79]

While antitax sentiment constrained state builders since the 1930s, it bolstered the conservative movement that overtook domestic politics in the 1970s and 1980s. With the notable exception of the Cold War, nothing unified conservatives as much as resistance to taxation. In the 1970s, the animosity toward taxes did not emanate just from corporate quarters. It was particularly acute with wage earners, who felt squeezed as inflation pushed them into higher tax brackets while weakening the value of their dollars. This dynamic was called "bracket creep." Conservative politicians played to this anger. At the grassroots level, conservatives mobilized around referendums to reduce property taxes.[80] The property tax revolt in California brought national attention to the problem of taxation. Some observers argued that rising antitax sentiment was a disguise for racial tensions.[81] While the argument had validity, it downplayed the deep-rooted resistance to taxation in the United States that extended beyond race and centered on a basic antipathy in funding the federal government.

The California tax revolt that resulted in the passage of Proposition 13 in 1978, which greatly reduced property taxes—and the debate that ensued in the media about all types of taxation—did not create broad opposition to taxation, as it is commonly portrayed in the scholarly and popular literature. The political drive to lower federal taxes was not a backlash against a "liberal" era when citizens had accepted high taxation. No such era ever existed: the New Deal did not endorse a mass tax, while Presidents Kennedy and Johnson launched the Great Society after cutting taxes. This is why policy makers in those times felt the need to rely on all sorts of complex mechanisms to raise revenue while building the government. As this chapter attempts to show, state builders constantly fretted about strong antitax sentiment. Raising money to pay for federal programs was always a problem. The conservative movement that coalesced at the national level in the 1970s was the first to articulate many antigovernment themes but hostility toward high taxation was an age-old tradition.

While the conservative movement failed to retrench the nation's biggest federal policies, such as Social Security, it was able to weaken the federal tax system. President Ronald Reagan's administration passed the largest tax cut in history through Congress, the Economic Recovery Tax Act of 1981, and indexed the tax code to eliminate "bracket creep." Some of the 1981 tax cut was soon reversed in the coming years when fiscal conservatives raised taxes to lower the deficit. However, fiscal conservatives were unable to offset the 1981 reduction.[82] Indexation of the tax code deprived the American state of automatic revenue. It was costing the government approximately $180 billion a year by 1990. The top tenth of income earners received the greatest benefit, since by that time the primary tax burden of wage earners in the lower income brackets was Social Security and energy taxes.[83]

Changes in the budget process made things even more difficult for policy makers. In 1990, the Budget Enforcement Act created stringent rules. Discretionary spending would be subject to annual budget caps. Any legislated expenditure increases in entitlement programs had to be offset by reductions in other parts of the program, in another program, or by raising taxes. Until economic growth generated higher revenues, Congress had the choice of raising taxes or cutting spending to compensate for revenue shortfalls. Moreover, when Congress passed a sweeping tax-loophole-closing measure in 1986, it also agreed to a trade-off of steep rate cuts.[84] Income taxes as a share of all federal taxes fell to 57 percent in 1990 after reaching 63 percent in 1980.[85] By the 1990s, moreover, many of the loophole-closing tax reforms were reversed by the emergence of new breaks for industry and the middle class. So popular was opposition to taxation that the Earned Income Tax Credit, a tax benefit for the working poor, proved to be enormously strong in the 1980s, unlike other forms of welfare.[86] Federal tax breaks had increased to 35 percent of federal spending by 1984. In 1995, the federal tax breaks for social welfare alone cost $400 million.[87]

The most important outcome of the conservative era was that tax increases became more difficult politically because the system no longer generated sufficient revenue automatically. Increasing spending commitments combined with a stagnant revenue base. By 1986, Paul Pierson concluded, "the easiest roads to higher taxes were effectively blocked."[88] The impact of conservative tax cuts, combined with the success of postwar policy makers in using earmarked taxes and trust funds, became evident in the last decade of the century. By the 1990s, skyrocketing deficits and precommitted spending, particularly for entitlements for senior citizens, resulted in reduced levels of discretionary funds. A precommitted federal budget, large deficits and debt, and diminished income tax revenue left the government in what one fiscal expert called a "fiscal straitjacket."[89] As a result, domestic politics became "fiscalized" as debates were subsumed under the rubric of deficit reduction.[90] Lack of revenue constrained the types of policies that were even proposed. Upon taking office in 1993, President Clinton hoped to offer a welfare reform package that would end the existing welfare system but provide necessary services to help the poor find jobs. This involved a substantial expenditure, as became apparent in state-based initiatives such as those in Wisconsin. The administration realized that Congress would not redirect funds from another program toward this objective. Nor did the administration want to propose higher taxes even when Democrats controlled both chambers of Congress. Liberal Democrats opposed proposals to reduce spending in other entitlement programs to pay for reform. Therefore, insufficient money was the "biggest hurdle," according to the leading account of welfare reform, that stifled the administration's initial welfare proposal.[91] As a result, the issue was left to the Republican majority elected in 1994. The final result was more stringent than Clinton's original plan, providing virtually no assistance to former welfare beneficiaries.

Even when budget surpluses returned in the late 1990s, politicians discovered that the projected long-term costs of Social Security and Medicare were so large that there was little room to discuss the creation of new initiatives. Rather, excess funds were geared to the protection of the long-term stability of entitlement programs. The first significant change in this pattern came as a result of the war against terrorism, launched after the devastating attacks on the United States on September 11, 2001. Despite starting his administration with a massive tax cut and promising to curtail spending, President George W. Bush's administration found, as had many presidents before him, that it is nearly impossible to hold down spending in times of war.[92] The result was a quick return to deficit government. Yet much of the defecit spending has shored up preexisting programs, including farm supports, and the amount of slack that is available to create fundamentally new initiatives remains limited.

While fiscal restraints did reign in government expansion, yet it is just as crucial that in the so-called conservative era politicians did not overturn the existing federal tax structure. Social insurance taxes continued to rise in the 1980s and 1990s. By 2001, 80 percent of working Americans were paying more in payroll taxes than in income taxes.[93] Meanwhile, conservatives cut the overall income tax burden only slightly from 1981 levels. Deficit reduction actually forced significant income tax *increases* in 1990, a decision that cost President George H. Bush substantial Republican support. The fact that the tax system remained intact meant that more automatic revenue would be generated once economic growth returned in the 1990s. Once again, conservative success at mobilizing tax opposition confronted the institutional inheritance of those who had built the federal tax system.

THE UNEASY RELATIONSHIP

Antitax sentiment has required that state builders operate with limited fiscal capacity. Throughout the era of most intense state building, limited revenue has simply been a fact of life as politicians feared the electoral impact of raising taxes on wage earners or business. The reality of strong antitax sentiment raises normative questions about state building. At a fundamental level, state building has often been at odds with crucial aspects of public opinion and the popular will as they were conveyed through the democratic process. While opinions of government vary depending on what policies are being discussed, public pressure has been relatively steadfast in its opposition to federal taxation. Ultimately, this reality has been the clearest manifestation of antistatism.

The dissonance between democratic impulses and state building challenges the teleology of several generations of historical narratives. Acknowledging fiscal restraint throws new light on the process of American state building. Most important, it helps us appreciate those politicians who succeeded in building an American state despite limited resources and constituent hostility. This story of tax resistance should not be surprising, since it is a basic fact of life in domestic politics. Indeed, it is a dilemma that politicians have faced since the emergence of the modern state.[94] However, historians have not integrated tax resistance and fiscal constraint into their narratives of recent political history. Taking this step will challenge the analytic frameworks that have been used to examine the history of twentieth-century state building.

Coming to terms with antistatism in modern America, as expressed through resistance to taxation and in other incarnations, is an important challenge facing the new generation of political historians. The project will take scholars into the heart of American democracy, where citizens and politicians retained old cultural fears even while accepting the need for new political institutions. The result of this dilemma was not always pristine. New institutions were constructed around all sorts of restraints, lack of revenue being one of the most powerful. In the end, American state builders were able to construct an impressive government infrastructure given the opposition they faced. The story of how state builders overcame their own constituencies must be a defining question for historians who now seek to reshape narratives of our political past.

NOTES

1. Steven R. Weisman, *The Great Tax Wars: Lincoln to Wilson—The Fierce Battles over Money and Power That Transformed the Nation* (New York: Simon and Schuster, 2002).

2. On the legal state of the nineteenth century, see Stephen Skowronek, *Building a New American State: The Expansion of National Administrative Capacities, 1877–1920* (Cambridge: Cambridge University Press, 1982), and William Novak, *The People's Welfare: Law and Regulation in Nineteenth-Century America* (Chapel Hill: University of North Carolina Press, 1996).

3. Paul Pierson, *Dismantling the Welfare State? Reagan, Thatcher, and the Politics of Retrenchment* (Cambridge: Cambridge University Press, 1994).

4. Anthony J. Badger, "The Limits of Federal Power and Social Politics, 1910–1955," in *Contesting Democracy: Substance and Structure in American Political History, 1775–2000*, ed. Byron E. Shafer and Anthony J. Badger (Lawrence: Uni-

versity Press of Kansas, 2001), 194–95; Lisa McGirr, *Suburban Warriors: The Origins of the New American Right* (Princeton, N.J.: Princeton University Press, 2001); Patricia Nelson Limerick, *The Legacy of Conquest: The Unbroken Past of the American West* (New York: Norton, 1988).

5. Michael S. Sherry, *In the Shadow of War: The United States since the 1930s* (New Haven, Conn.: Yale University Press, 1995), 261–62.

6. James Savage, *Balanced Budgets and American Politics* (Ithaca, N.Y.: Cornell University Press, 1988), 161–286.

7. Although focusing on an earlier era, Ira Katznelson has shrewdly urged scholars of American political history to avoid using European models of state building to understand this country and to abandon the "weak state" versus "strong state" dichotomy. See Katznelson, "Flexible Capacity: The Military and Early American Statebuilding," in *Shaped by War and Trade: International Influences on American Political Development*, ed., Ira Katznelson and Martin Shefter (Princeton, N.J.: Princeton University Press, 2002), 82–86.

8. For alternative narratives that take the threat of the right more seriously, see David Plotke, *Building a Democratic Political Order: Reshaping American Liberalism in the 1930s and 1940s* (Cambridge: Cambridge University Press, 1996); Elizabeth Fones-Wolf, *Selling Free Enterprise: The Business Assault on Labor and Liberalism, 1945–1960* (Urbana: University of Illinois Press, 1994); Robert Griffith, "Forging America's Postwar Order: Domestic Politics and Political Economy in the Age of Truman," in *The Truman Presidency*, ed. Michael J. Lacey (Cambridge and Washington, D.C.: Cambridge University Press and Woodrow Wilson International Center for Scholars, 1989), 57–88.

9. Arthur Schlesinger, Jr., *The Age of Roosevelt*, 3 vols. (Boston: Houghton Mifflin, 1957–1960); William E. Leuchtenburg, *Franklin D. Roosevelt and the New Deal, 1932–1940* (New York: Harper Torchbooks, 1963).

10. Leuchtenburg, *Franklin D. Roosevelt*, 332–33.

11. See, for example, Martin J. Sklar, *The Corporate Reconstruction of American Capitalism, 1890–1916: The Market, the Law, and Politics* (Cambridge: Cambridge University Press, 1988); David F. Noble, *America by Design: Science, Technology, and the Rise of Corporate Capitalism* (New York: Knopf, 1977); James Weinstein, *The Corporate Ideal and the Liberal State, 1900–1918* (Boston: Beacon Press, 1968); Gabriel Kolko, *Triumph of Conservatism* (New York: Free Press, 1963).

12. Kolko, *Triumph of Conservatism*, 58.

13. Lizabeth Cohen, *Making a New Deal* (Cambridge: Cambridge University Press, 1990).

14. "AHR Forum: The Problem of American Conservatism," *American Historical Review* 99 (April 1994): 409–52.

15. Louis Galambos, "The Emerging Organizational Synthesis in Modern American History," *Business History Review* 44 (August 1970): 279–90; Samuel P. Hays, *The Response to Industrialism, 1885–1914* (Chicago: University of Chicago Press, 1957); Robert Wiebe, *The Search for Order, 1877–1920* (New York: Hill and Wang, 1967).

16. Louis Galambos, "Parsonian Sociology and Post-Progressive History," *Social Science Quarterly* 50 (June 1969): 25–45.

17. For two insightful critiques of the organizational synthesis that stress inevitability and lack of attention to opposition, see Brian Balogh, "Reorganizing the Organizational Synthesis: Federal-Professional Relations in Modern America," *Studies in American Political Development* 5 (spring 1991): 119–72, and Alan Brinkley, "Writing the History of Contemporary America: Dilemmas and Challenges," *Deadalus* 113 (summer 1984): 121–41.

18. For an excellent review of this literature, see Theda Skocpol, *Protecting Soldiers and Mothers: The Political Origins of Social Policy in the United States* (Cambridge, Mass.: The Belknap Press of Harvard University Press, 1992), 1–62.

19. Robert Lieberman, *Shifting the Color Line: Race and the American Welfare State* (Cambridge, Mass.: Harvard University Press, 1998); Jill Quadagno, *The Color of Welfare: How Racism Undermined the War on Poverty* (New York: Oxford University Press, 1994); Ira Katznelson, Kim Geiger, and Daniel Kryder, "Limiting Liberalism: The Southern Veto in Congress, 1935–1950," *Political Science Quarterly* 108 (1993): 283–302; Quadagno, *The Transformation of Old Age Security: Class and Politics in the American Welfare State* (Chicago: University of Chicago Press, 1988).

20. Linda Gordon, *Pitied but Not Entitled: Single Mothers and the History of Welfare, 1890–1935* (New York: Free Press, 1994); Eileen Boris, *Home to Work: Motherhood and the Politics of Industrial Homework in the United States* (Cambridge: Cambridge University Press, 1994).

21. Michael B. Katz, *The Undeserving Poor: From Poverty to the War on Welfare* (New York: Pantheon, 1989).

22. Thomas Byrne Edsall and Mary D. Edsall, *Chain Reaction: The Impact of Race, Rights, and Taxes on American Politics* (New York: Norton, 1991); Thomas J. Sugrue, *The Origins of the Urban Crisis* (Princeton, N.J.: Princeton University Press, 1998). My point is not to deny that racial animosity fueled resistance to government expansion at key points in American history, since it clearly did. Rather, I argue that these claims are too narrow as explanatory models. I believe that antistatism, and particularly antitax sentiment, was not always about race. It involved a broader distrust of federal government intervention and, more important, an unwillingness to pay money for its services.

23. Gareth Davies and Martha Derthick, "Race and Social Welfare Policy: The Social Security Act of 1935," *Political Science Quarterly* 112 (summer 1997): 217–35.

24. James Morone, *The Democratic Wish: Popular Participation and the Limits of American Government*, rev. ed. (New Haven, Conn.: Yale University Press, 1998); Morton Keller, *Affairs of State: Public Life in Late-Nineteenth-Century America* (Cambridge, Mass.: The Belknap Press of Harvard University Press, 1977); Ellis W. Hawley, "Social Policy and the Liberal State in Twentieth-Century America," in *Federal Social Policy: The Historical Dimension*, ed. Donald T. Critchlow and Ellis W. Hawley (University Park: Pennsylvania State University Press, 1988), 117–39; Ellis W. Hawley, *The New Deal and the Problem of Monopoly: A Study in Economic Ambivalence* (Princeton, N.J.: Princeton University Press, 1966).

25. See, for example, Anthony King, "Ideas, Institutions, and the Policies of Governments: A Comparative Analysis," part 3, *British Journal of Political Sci-*

ence 3 (October 1973): 409–23; Charles Lockhart, *Gaining Ground: Tailoring Social Programs to American Values* (Berkeley: University of California Press, 1989); Alan Brinkley, *Voices of Protest: Huey Long, Father Coughlin, and the Great Depression* (New York: Vintage, 1982); John W. Kingdon, *America the Unusual* (New York: Worth Publishers, 1998).

26. Recently, political scientists have also started to develop a more nuanced understanding of antistatism by showing how different groups of Americans opposed particular types of government rather than federal intervention altogether. See Elizabeth Sanders, *Roots of Reform: Farmers, Workers, and the American State, 1877–1917* (Chicago: University of Chicago Press, 1999).

27. Robert Higgs, *Crisis and Leviathan: Critical Episodes in the Growth of American Government* (New York: Oxford University Press, 1987); David Beito, *Taxpayers in Revolt: Tax Resistance during the Great Depression* (Chapel Hill: University of North Carolina Press, 1989); Mark Thornton and Chetley Weise, "The Great Depression Tax Revolts Revisited," *Journal of Libertarian Studies* 15 (summer 2001): 95–105.

28. Sugrue, *Origins of the Urban Crisis.*

29. W. Elliot Brownlee, ed., *Funding the Modern American State, 1941–1995: The Rise and Fall of the Era of Easy Finance* (Cambridge and Washington, D.C.: Cambridge University Press and Woodrow Wilson Center Press, 1996); Julian E. Zelizer, *Taxing America: Wilbur D. Mills, Congress, and the State, 1945–1975* (Cambridge: Cambridge University Press, 1998); Christopher Howard, *The Hidden Welfare State* (Princeton, N.J.: Princeton University Press, 1997).

30. Robin Einhorn has documented how slavery hindered the construction of a national tax system during the founding period. See Robin L. Einhorn, "Slavery and the Politics of Taxation in the Early United States," *Studies in American Political Development* 14 (fall 2000): 156–83.

31. See, for example, Michael Brown, *Race, Money, and the American Welfare State* (Ithaca, N.Y.: Cornell University Press, 1999); Cathie J. Martin, *Shifting the Burden: The Struggle over Growth and Corporate Taxation* (Chicago: University of Chicago Press, 1991); Ronald F. King, *Money, Time, and Politics: Investment Tax Subsidies and American Democracy* (New Haven, Conn.: Yale University Press, 1993); James R. O'Connor, *The Fiscal Crisis of the State* (New York: St. Martin's Press, 1973).

32. David Vogel, *Kindred Strangers: The Uneasy Relationship between Politics and Business in America* (Princeton, N.J.: Princeton University Press, 1996), 30.

33. Robert M. Collins, *The Business Response to Keynes* (New York: Columbia University Press, 1981).

34. See, for example, Sanders, *Roots of Reform.*

35. Beito, *Taxpayers in Revolt,* 161.

36. James T. Patterson, *The New Deal and the States: Federalism in Transition* (Princeton, N.J.: Princeton University Press, 1969), 168–93.

37. Mark Leff, *The Limits of Symbolic Reform: The New Deal and Taxation, 1933–1939* (Cambridge: Cambridge University Press, 1984), 287.

38. David M. Kennedy, *Freedom from Fear: The American People in Depression and War, 1929–1945* (New York: Oxford University Press, 1999), 284. Leff

provides an excellent account of the "symbolic" nature of Roosevelt's taxes on the rich in *Limits of Symbolic Reform*.

39. Brown, *Race, Money, and the American Welfare State*, 32.

40. Jerry R. Cates, *Insuring Inequality: Administrative Leadership in Social Security, 1935–1954* (Ann Arbor: University of Michigan Press, 1983); Brian Balogh, "Securing Support: The Emergence of the Social Security Board as a Political Actor, 1935–1939," in *Federal Social Policy*, ed. Critchlow and Hawley, 55–78.

41. Herbert Stein, *The Fiscal Revolution in America: Policy in Pursuit of Reality*, 2nd ed. (Washington, D.C.: The AEI Press, 1996), 122.

42. Julian E. Zelizer, "The Forgotten Legacy of the New Deal: Fiscal Conservatism and the Roosevelt Administration, 1933–1938," *Presidential Studies Quarterly* 30 (June 2000): 331–58.

43. W. Elliot Brownlee, *Federal Taxation in America: A Short History* (Cambridge and Washington, D.C.: Cambridge University Press and Woodrow Wilson Center Press, 1996), 67–72.

44. Carolyn C. Jones, "Mass-Based Income Taxation: Creating a Taxpaying Culture, 1940–1952," in *Funding the Modern American State*, ed. Brownlee, 121–25.

45. Theodore J. Lowi, "Four Systems of Policy, Politics, and Choice," *Public Administration Review* 32 (July/August 1972): 299.

46. John Mark Hansen, *Gaining Access: Congress and the Farm Lobby, 1919–1981* (Chicago: University of Chicago Press, 1991), 176–77.

47. Karlyn Bowman, "The History of Taxing Questions in America," *Roll Call*, March 26, 1998. To be sure, polls are an imperfect gauge of public opinion, yet they remain one of the best measures we have of how representative groups of citizens felt on issues in the past, and they have been considered crucial by policy makers (along with interest groups, the media, and elections) as a sign of the "public will."

48. Carolyn Webber and Aaron Wildavsky, *A History of Taxation and Expenditure in the Western World* (New York: Simon and Shuster, 1986), 531.

49. Jill Quadagno, "Culture as Politics in Action: How the 'Red Menace' Derailed National Health Insurance," paper presented at New York University, 2001; Aaron L. Friedberg, "American Antistatism and the Founding of the Cold War State," in *Shaped by War and Trade: International Influences on American Political Development*, ed. Ira Katznelson and Martin Shefter (Princeton, N.J.: Princeton University Press, 2002), 246–47.

50. Bowman, "History of Taxing Questions."

51. Sven Steinmo, *Taxation and Democracy: Swedish, British, and American Approaches to Financing the Modern State* (New Haven, Conn.: Yale University Press, 1993), 39.

52. John F. Witte, *The Politics and Development of the Federal Income Tax* (Madison: University of Wisconsin Press, 1985), 364. For excellent data on polls, see pp. 339–63.

53. Savage, *Balanced Budgets and American Politics*, 1–8.

54. Michael J. Hogan, *A Cross of Iron: Harry S. Truman and the Origins of the National Security State* (Cambridge: Cambridge University Press, 1998).

55. Aaron L. Friedberg, *In the Shadow of the Garrison State: America's Anti-Statism and Its Cold War Grand Strategy* (Princeton, N.J.: Princeton University Press, 2000), 82.

56. Laura McEnaney, *Civil Defense Begins at Home: Militarization Meets Everyday Life in the Fifties* (Princeton, N.J.: Princeton University Press, 2000), 25–26.

57. Iwan W. Morgan, *Deficit Government: Taxing and Spending in Modern America* (Chicago: Ivan R. Dee, 1995), 83–84. See also Morgan, *Eisenhower versus "The Spenders": The Eisenhower Administration, the Democrats, and the Budget, 1953–1960* (New York: St. Martin's Press, 1990).

58. Julian E. Zelizer, " 'Where Is the Money Coming From?' The Reconstruction of Social Security Finance, 1939–1950," *Journal of Policy History* 9 (fall 1997): 339–424.

59. C. Eugene Steuerle, "Financing the American State at the Turn of the Century," in *Funding the Modern American State*, ed. Brownlee, 420.

60. Eric M. Patashnik, *Putting Trust in the US Budget: Federal Trust Funds and the Politics of Commitment* (Cambridge: Cambridge University Press, 2000), 2.

61. Robert M. Collins, *More: The Politics of Economic Growth in Postwar America* (New York: Oxford University Press, 2000).

62. Robert Dallek, *Flawed Giant: Lyndon Johnson and His Times, 1961–1973* (New York: Oxford University Press, 1998), 74.

63. Joseph A. Califano, Jr., *The Triumph and Tragedy of Lyndon Johnson: The White House Years* (New York: Simon and Schuster, 1991), 148.

64. Martin, *Shifting the Burden*, 19.

65. Brownlee, "Tax Regimes, National Crisis, and State Building," in *Funding the Modern American State*, ed. Brownlee, 100.

66. Friedberg, *In the Shadow of the Garrison State*, 141–42.

67. Gareth Davies, *From Opportunity to Entitlement: The Transformation and Decline of Great Society Liberalism* (Lawrence: University Press of Kansas, 1996), 52–53.

68. Brown, *Race, Money, and the American Welfare State*, 227–30.

69. Julian Zelizer and Eric Patashnik, "Paying for Medicare: Benefits, Budgets, and Wilbur Mills's Policy Legacy," *Journal of Health Policy, Politics, and Law* 26 (February 2001): 7–36.

70. Lawrence Jacobs, *The Health of Nations* (Ithaca, N.Y.: Cornell University Press, 1993), 140.

71. Cited in Brown, *Race, Money, and the American Welfare State*, 241.

72. Zelizer, *Taxing America*, 255–82.

73. Cited in Bruce J. Schulman, *Lyndon B. Johnson and American Liberalism: A Brief Biography with Documents* (Boston: Bedford Books, 1995), 101.

74. Robert M. Collins, "The Economic Crisis of 1968 and the Waning of the 'American Century,' " *American Historical Review* 101 (April 1996): 422.

75. Jacob S. Hacker, *The Divided Welfare State: The Battle over Public and Private Social Benefits in the United States* (Cambridge: Cambridge University Press, 2002), 13–16.

76. Nelson Lichtenstein, "Labor in the Truman Era: Origins of the 'Private Welfare State,' " in *The Truman Presidency*, ed. Lacey, 128–55; Sanford M. Jacoby, *Modern Manors: Welfare Capitalism since the New Deal* (Princeton, N.J.:

Princeton University Press, 1997); Michael B. Katz, *The Price of Citizenship: Redefining the American Welfare State* (New York: Metropolitan Books, 2001), 177.

77. Paul Pierson, "From Expansion to Austerity: The New Politics of Taxing and Spending," in *Seeking the Center: Politics and Policymaking at the New Century*, ed., Martin A. Levin, Marc K. Landy, and Martin Shapiro (Washington, D.C.: Georgetown University Press, 2001), 73.

78. Gareth Davies, "The Great Society after Johnson: The Case of Bilingual Education," *The Journal of American History* 88 (March 2002): 1405–29; Sidney M. Milkis, *Political Parties and Constitutional Government: Remaking American Democracy* (Baltimore: Johns Hopkins University Press, 1999), 103–73; Hugh Davis Graham, "Since 1964: The Paradox of American Civil Rights Regulation," in *Taking Stock: American Government in the Twentieth Century*, ed. Morton Keller and R. Shep Melnick (Cambridge and Washington, D.C.: Cambridge University Press and Woodrow Wilson Center Press, 1999), 187–218; Marc K. Landy and Martin A. Levin, eds. *The New Politics of Public Policy* (Baltimore: Johns Hopkins University Press, 1995); Hugh Davis Graham, *The Civil Rights Era: Origins and Development of National Policy, 1960–1972* (Oxford: Oxford University Press, 1990); Samuel P. Hays, *Beauty, Health, and Permanence: Environmental Politics in the United States, 1955–1985* (Cambridge: Cambridge University Press, 1987).

79. Martha Derthick and Paul J. Quirk, *The Politics of Deregulation* (Washington, D.C.: Brookings Institution Press, 1985).

80. Godfrey Hodgson, *The World Turned Right Side Up: A History of the Conservative Ascendancy in America* (Boston: Houghton Mifflin, 1996), 205.

81. Edsall and Edsall, *Chain Reaction*.

82. Pierson, *Dismantling the Welfare State?* 154–55.

83. Morgan, *Deficit Government*, 156.

84. Jeffrey H. Birnbaum and Alan S. Murray, *Showdown at Gucci Gulch: Lawmakers, Lobbyists, and the Unlikely Triumph of Tax Reform* (New York: Random House, 1987).

85. Brownlee, "Tax Regimes, National Crisis, and State Building," 101.

86. Christopher Howard, "Protean Lure for the Working Poor: Party Competition and the Earned Income Tax Credit," *Studies in American Political Development* 9 (fall 1995): 404–36.

87. Howard, *Hidden Welfare State*, 25.

88. Pierson, *Dismantling the Welfare State?* 154.

89. Steuerle, "Financing the American State," 430.

90. Paul Pierson, "The Deficit and the Politics of Domestic Reform," in *The Social Divide: Political Parties and the Future of Activist Government*, ed. Margaret Weir (New York and Washington, D.C.: Russell Sage Foundation and Brookings Institution Press, 1998), 127.

91. R. Kent Weaver, *Ending Welfare as We Know It* (Washington, D.C.: The Brookings Institution, 2000), 240–41.

92. Editorial, "Guns and Butter," *Wall Street Journal*, May 17, 2002.

93. Glenn Kessler, "Payroll Tax: The Burden Untouched," *Washington Post*, February 6, 2001.

94. Margaret Levi, *Of Rule and Revenue* (Berkeley: University of California Press, 1988).

Chapter Twelve

ALL POLITICS IS LOCAL

THE PERSISTENCE OF LOCALISM IN

TWENTIETH-CENTURY AMERICA

Thomas J. Sugrue

T HE TWENTIETH CENTURY witnessed a remarkable expansion
of the power of the federal government. An increasingly powerful
executive branch supplanted the state of "courts and parties." Imperial ventures, two world wars, and a cold war dramatically extended
the power of the military and the state's influence over key sectors of the
economy. After World War II, a new "prominstrative state" consolidated
power in the hands of bureaucrats and experts. Witness the profusion of
new government agencies, the alphabet soup of federal social and economic programs, and the staggering growth of public-sector employment.[1] Despite the irrefutable expansion of central government power,
particularly in the executive branch, one of the most distinctive features of
the twentieth-century American state remains the persistence of localism.

In the early twentieth century, it seemed that localism would soon be a
vestige of the past. In a complex, interconnected society, linked by rail,
automobile, telephone, and telegraph, local identities were increasingly
attenuated. The face-to-face contacts that dominated commerce and politics were profoundly disrupted by modernity.[2] Political parties, long tied
to the local world of ritual and participation, waned as new forms of
advertised politics took their place.[3] It is something of a historian's cliché
to note that already by the late nineteenth century, the singular "United
States" had supplanted the plural "these United States." But explanations
of government growth that rest explicitly or implicitly on modernization
theory are belied by a far more complicated reality. Despite the pulls of
modernity, the dramatic growth in the federal government's power and
administrative apparatus, and the decline of local political parties, localism remained surprisingly resilient. As Eric Monkkonen has forcefully
argued, the American state stands apart for its "system of local govern-

ments uniquely dispersed across the political and geographic landscape, especially when compared with those of other Western nations."[4]

Twentieth-century American state building rested on an uneasy tension between center and locality. The fates of the New Deal and the Great Society were to a great extent determined by local public officials and their constituents. To understand the peculiarities of America's liberal state requires that we bring the local back in. The politics of liberalism was ineluctably a politics of place. States and localities became battlegrounds over the meaning and implementation of federal policies. By exploring the interplay of top-down policy making and grassroots political activity, we can best explain the limitations and possibilities of American social policy.

It is striking how few social scientists and historians have grappled with the implications of localism for the history of the modern American state. Over the last twenty years, "new institutionalists" in political science and their counterparts in history have produced a vast literature explaining the distinctive patterns of state capacity and social policy in the United States. But, with a few exceptions, scholars of American political development have directed their attention to Congress and to federal agencies, with little attention to local political institutions.[5]

Even political scientists who have been attentive to the history and development of state and local political institutions have downplayed the resilience of localism. As Martha Derthick has argued, "localism lacks vitality in modern America," because it has been "directly attacked" by national government, particularly in the Supreme Court's voting rights and school desegregation rulings. This unidirectional interpretation of federal government power emphasizes the impact of jurisprudence and regulation on the states and municipalities, with little attention to the ways in which subnational political institutions and actors have continued to shape and constrain policy outcomes.[6]

Political historians—particularly those interested in questions of political culture—have offered alternative explanations of America's "uneasy state." They suggest that a deep tradition of individualism militated against the creation and legitimization of a powerful central government.[7] Others, skeptical of the emphasis on liberal individualism, chronicle the persistence of a republican political language that contrasted independence and mutualism with dependency and tyranny.[8] Both schools of thought treat localism as a transhistorical constant, rather than considering the ways that localism was contingent and contested over the course of the twentieth century. Embracing structural and cultural explanations, participants in the vast and hoary debate on American exceptionalism also have little to say about local political institutions. Exceptionalists point to the relative weakness of labor as a political force in the United

States but generally ignore the ways that local struggles over both labor and business power impacted the implementation of regulation, labor law, and economic development policies over the course of the twentieth century. The fact that most twentieth-century trade unions adopted their own version of federalism, organizing locally but often acting in confederation, has passed largely without comment in analyses of labor's political fortunes.[9]

If the historical and social scientific literature on politics and state formation has little to say about localism, social history contributes scarcely more. Despite the proliferation of community studies over the last thirty years, historians of race, labor, ethnicity, and popular culture have seldom concerned themselves with questions of political development and state building. Even local studies that trace the development of political ideologies seldom consider the national and local political institutions and rules that impacted everyday life.

Given the paucity of work that brings together local and national, political and social histories, I will suggest three synthetic themes. First, federal power reached into virtually every aspect of daily life in mid- and late-twentieth-century America. To an extent unimaginable in the nineteenth century, ordinary Americans lived life in the shadow of the state. Second, local officials and ordinary constituents played a role in shaping and constraining federal policy in ways that have only begun to be examined. New Deal and post–New Deal social policies bounded and shaped local political action; but at the same time, local actors influenced government policy to a greater extent than has been recognized. Third, the relationship between the local and the national was not static. On the local level, different groups struggled for control of federal programs and federal funding. Many local groups who benefited from the New Deal fought to maintain their hold on power and resources during the Great Society, while those who were disadvantaged by federal policies demanded rights and entitlements that had been denied them in the past. In response to grassroots activism and political pressure, Congress and federal agencies changed their agendas and altered the balance of power in state and local governments and among local interest groups. At the same time, local political institutions adapted in response to the fiscal incentives and regulatory structures of the state.[10]

LOCAL POLITICAL INSTITUTIONS AND THE POWER OF PLACE

For most Americans in the twentieth century, locality has been the touchstone of both power and identity. On a daily basis, most Americans' primary encounter with government was local. Many government-provided goods and services (such as welfare, unemployment benefits, education, housing, and economic development) have been administered locally, financed at least in part locally, consumed locally, and, in legal scholar Richard Briffault's words, "controlled locally, with the interests of local residents as the exclusive desideratum of local decision makers."[11] Over the course of the twentieth century, federal policy makers have left crucial areas of local prerogative (such as educational policy, land use regulation, and taxation) largely untouched. Even when the federal government influenced local policy makers, it left local institutions largely intact.

The persistence of local government autonomy, even amidst the expansion of national government power, has had profound social consequences. Local politics were imbricated in larger patterns of racial and economic inequality because of deeply entrenched patterns of racial and economic segregation. The local isolation of minorities, in particular, deeply affected federal social policy and determined its beneficiaries. In addition, federal social programs set into motion a feedback loop that reinforced patterns of place-based racial and economic inequality.[12]

For most historians (and other social scientists), local and state governments remain a terra incognita.[13] Cities and other incorporated areas, whose powers are granted under state laws, have long enjoyed a fair degree of autonomy in the American political system. Often coterminous with city boundaries, sometimes overlapping municipalities, are school districts. Over the course of the twentieth century, a wide variety of other geographically defined governmental and quasi-governmental districts have been created, including housing agencies, transportation authorities, water and sewer districts, planning districts, soil conservation areas, business improvement districts (BIDS), enterprise and empowerment zones, and model cities neighborhoods, not to mention private or "shadow governments" that provide goods and services to property owners in addition to (or in place of) those provided by the public sector.[14]

Amidst the bureaucratization and centralization of power in Washington, D.C. over the last half century, local governments and authorities have proliferated. In the late 1950s, political scientist Robert Wood found more than 1,400 governments in the metropolitan New York area alone.[15] By the late twentieth century, the state of Illinois had 102 counties, 1,282 municipalities, 1,433 townships, 997 independent school districts, and 2,995 special governmental districts. Altogether, the United States had 86,692 local governments in 1992. The scale and complexity of subnational governments in the United States created—ironically, given the deep antibureaucratic rhetoric in American political discourse—a metastasis of bureaucracies, fragmented and overlapping, competitive and, at the same time, duplicative.[16]

Each of these place-specific governmental institutions served a mediating function, on one hand responsible to citizens and community groups, on the other hand accountable to federal regulations and to varying degrees dependent on federal expenditures. In the post–New Deal era, local governments found themselves in an ambiguous position, delimited by their concern for local interests but increasingly affected by national-level policies. As a result, local political institutions implemented and contested federal politics from the New Deal on.

The proliferation of local governments and authorities resulted in a profusion of locally oriented constituent and interest groups. Often small but well organized, these extragovernmental organizations have played a significant role in state and local debates about such issues as taxation, public education, zoning and land use, civil rights, and housing. The history of grassroots mobilization around public policy is still in its infancy, but it already suggests a rich and largely untold process of state building and dismantling from the bottom up.[17]

THE NEW DEAL COMPROMISE

The tensions between localism and centralization have played out throughout American political history, but they were particularly acute in periods when the federal government expanded its power and reach. The New Deal was the formative moment in the twentieth-century struggle over the proper scope, scale, and locus of government. Historian Robert Wiebe has memorably described the New Deal as "one of the major political compromises in American history."[18] The Roosevelt administration labored mightily to balance visions of an expansive federal government with demands for local control over public policy. In addition, New Deal social programs built on Progressive Era precedents in local social reform and welfare provision without wholly rejecting reformers' abiding concern with local intervention and local control. Local experiments in social reform and welfare during the Progressive Era provided New Dealers with models for their own social policies. However imaginative, these progressive experiments were small in scale and fragile. As the Depression deepened, the hodgepodge of local efforts to provide social welfare—both public and private—proved to be woefully inadequate. Private charities, which had borne the burden of social provision prior to the 1930s—from charitable aid to medical care to housing provision—collapsed under the crushing weight of mass impoverishment. Self-help organizations such as ethnic and fraternal organizations, churches, and mutual aid societies lacked the resources to confront the magnitude of social dislocations unleashed by the Depression. And corporate welfare programs, never particularly robust, withered in face of the financial crises and mass unemployment of the 1930s. City governments teetered on the brink of insolvency, unable to provide more than a modicum of services, employment, and relief to their needy citizens. Local officials and their constituents cried out for federal assistance to fill the gap left by failing local institutions.[19]

During the first several years of the Roosevelt administration, the federal government innovated. It created jobs through the Works Progress Administration and the Civilian Conservation Corps. Through the Social Security Act of 1935, it took over some financial responsibility for aid to the elderly, children, the unemployed, and the disabled. Through labor regulations, it expanded the federal reach over work standards and wages that had formerly been the bailiwick of states and localities. New Deal housing programs promised Americans the "right to a decent home," while creating new construction jobs. Many New Dealers, inspired by the social democratic experiments of early-twentieth-century Europe, hoped to create a strong central state.[20]

To accomplish his domestic policy goals, Roosevelt consolidated power in the executive branch and dramatically expanded the scale and scope of federal agencies. Centralization, however, had its limits. At every step of the way, calls for the expansion of executive power were met by strong counter demands for state and local control. The New Dealers' aspirations were cut short by five forces arrayed against them.

First was the congressional power of the South. Southern Democrats, beneficiaries of their party's long monopoly of power in the region, had amassed the seniority that allowed them to control key congressional committees and put checks on expansive liberal policies that threatened to disrupt the region's racialized political economy. Southern members of Congress were especially vigilant about threats to "states' rights," particularly legislation that challenged the racial division of labor. For example, southerners adamantly defended the payment of the local prevailing wage, rather than a national standard, for Works Progress Administration projects.[21]

Second, urban mayors in the north resisted centrally administered social programs that would weaken their control over the distribution of public goods and services. Democratic policy makers were reluctant to siphon power away from local elected officials who served as the field soldiers for the party. Roosevelt, himself the product of the fragmented, localist political culture of New York, was comfortable creating programs that respected local boundaries and local political autonomy. As a result, in many northern cities, government spending and patronage were the glue that held together the diverse constituents of the potentially fractious New Deal order.[22]

Third, Republicans and their business allies vigorously opposed national government expansion, particularly in defense of managerial prerogative in the workplace. Anti–New Dealers couched their opposition in the venerable political language of individualism, freedom, and rights, all of which they believed would be abrogated by a too-powerful central government. From the late 1930s onward, many Republicans forged a powerful alliance with southern Democrats that stymied liberal legislative efforts on labor relations, public housing, social welfare, and regulation. The deeply entrenched suspicion of "big government" gained traction in the Cold War, as policy makers warned of the dangers of Soviet-style centralization. Even liberals, sensitive to criticisms of their programs, displayed respect for local political institutions as a bulwark against socialistic government.[23]

Fourth, local social workers and reformers retained much control over the administration of New Deal social programs. The progressive experiments in social welfare that became the blueprint for New Deal were their creation. Local relief and reform programs provided the personnel and the infrastructure for federal policy implementation. Short of a wholesale reorganization of government structures, New Dealers had to work within the constraints of deeply rooted institutional forms.[24]

Fifth, Roosevelt administration officials were reluctant to rely solely or primarily on the unpopular federal income tax to fund social programs. Many liberal social and economic programs relied at least to some extent on local and state funding. As a consequence, federal programs were vulnerable to the vicissitudes of local economies and the anger of local constituents who felt pinched by spending on unpopular programs. Already by the late 1940s, for example, public housing and welfare programs were coming under siege in many cities by local antitax activists who tapped both fiscal and racial resentments.[25]

The New Deal was a hybrid of centralization and local control. New Deal policy delicately balanced an expansion of federal spending and power with a resolute effort to leave local political structures intact and local political control unchallenged. Three New Deal programs illustrate the persistence of local interests during the mid–twentieth century: federal housing policy, economic development policy, and social welfare policy. The consequences of the New Deal compromise would shape the contours of American politics for the remainder of the century.

HOUSING POLICY

One of the largest and most successful New Deal policy initiatives was intervention in the private housing market. In 1930, less than one-third of Americans owned their own homes. Mortgages were available to a very small share of potential home buyers; their terms were short and interest rates high. Although the institutional mortgage market had expanded dramatically in the 1920s, it favored the rich. Those working-class Americans who aspired to build or buy their own homes had to rely on self-financing or, in some cases, the assistance of mutual aid societies, churches, and savings and loan associations.[26]

Three federal housing programs profoundly reconfigured the American real estate, banking, and housing construction industries, with dramatic social consequences. The Home Owners' Loan Corporation and the Federal Housing Administration brought the government into what had been a fragmented and deregulated real estate market. In 1944, the newly created Veterans Administration provided housing subsidies for GIs and their families. The results reshaped metropolitan housing markets and reorganized patterns of metropolitan growth. Between the 1930 and 1960, rates of home ownership doubled in the United States. High rates of home ownership slowed the residential mobility that had long been characteristic of American life and deepened residents' attachment to place.[27] Housing and mortgage programs created regional and national construction and banking industries. Most important, federal housing programs hardened patterns of residential segregation by race and class. Actuarial policies that forbade the introduction of "nonconforming uses" and ethnic diversity into neighborhoods reinforced restrictive zoning laws and officially sanctioned private policies of racial discrimination.[28]

The three federal programs that intervened in the private housing market intensified patterns of local fragmentation and separation. Federal appraisers relied on local brokers and bankers to determine the eligibility of neighborhoods for loans and mortgage guarantees. By redlining mixed-use and ethnically and racially diverse communities, they privileged white, middle-class localities at the expense of the poor and minorities. In addition, loan and mortgage programs rewarded communities with exclusionary zoning policies and in the process hardened municipal boundaries.

The lower tier of New Deal housing policy, public housing for workers and the poor, also represented an unprecedented expansion of state activity into the private sector. Earlier in the century, progressive housing reformers had targeted deteriorating slum housing as part of their efforts to uplift the poor. Reformers, philanthropists, and settlement-house workers had long demanded slum eradication and lobbied for municipal laws to regulate housing conditions. Before the New Deal, their efforts met with limited success. The culmination of decades of housing reform efforts, the 1937 Housing Act channeled federal dollars to efforts to eradicate slum housing and create modern, publicly supported housing for the poor. [29]

Federal housing policies, however, enshrined local practices and prejudices into law. Public housing authorities were locally appointed and locally controlled. Local activists organized in favor and in opposition to housing projects and demanded participation in decisions about the sites and scale of subsidized housing developments.[30] Attempts to shift control from the localities to the federal government met with fierce congressional resistance. During World War II, when the United States Housing Authority attempted to centralize the planning and development of public housing for defense workers, it faced a hostile investigation by the House of Representatives and a barrage of attacks from local officials and real estate groups. Roosevelt, fearful of a congressional revolt, restructured the defense housing effort and appointed a new administrator who believed that "housing was fundamentally a community responsibility."[31] In the aftermath of the war, the federal government gave even more power over housing policy to local officials. Localities issued bonds, acquired land for demolition and construction, and brokered deals with private building contractors. Federal spending on public housing directly benefited local interests. Representatives of the real estate industry, major construction firms, and building-trades unions sat on many public housing authority boards and lobbied local elected officials for contracts. Public housing also became a vehicle for political patronage, bolstering the influence of urban elected officials and party leaders.[32]

Most importantly, federal housing policy left locational decisions entirely in the hands of local elected officials, who, responsive to their constituents' fears of racial and class heterogeneity, largely concentrated housing projects on uncontroversial central city sites, usually in minority neighborhoods. Grassroots opposition to scattered-site public housing was powerful and effective. Chicago's infamous Richard Taylor and State Street homes created a "vertical ghetto" in a black neighborhood cut off from the rest of the city by a major expressway, rail yards, and a lake. Detroit's meager public housing efforts were stymied by intense white opposition and built on marginal land in predominantly minority neighborhoods. Boston's Columbia Point project was constructed on a dump site on a peninsula cut off from nearby white working-class neighborhoods. Philadelphia's Passyunk Homes sat on a former wetland bounded by oil refineries. The federal goal of creating decent, affordable housing for workers and the poor was compromised by local administration.[33]

WELFARE POLITICS

The Social Security Act of 1935 was at once an unprecedented expansion of the welfare state and at the same time a vehicle for the replication of many social inequalities. The Social Security Act created a divided system of welfare that implicitly or explicitly sorted the population by work status, race, and gender. The most generous assistance was linked to workforce participation, disproportionately benefiting men; the least generous programs targeted those outside of the labor force, mainly women and children.[34] Initially African-Americans were largely excluded from old age insurance, which included most working people with the exception of domestic and agricultural workers—the most significant job niches for blacks. Other programs created by the Social Security Act were potentially open to African-Americans but were largely administered by state and local officials. As Robert Lieberman has argued, when "African-Americans were potentially included among a policy's beneficiaries, Southerners demanded institutional structures that preserved a maximum of local control." The Social Security Act left the South's political economy of racial exclusion largely intact.[35]

Of the programs created by the Social Security Act, only old age insurance was administered centrally. Other programs, including Unemployment Insurance (UI), Old Age Assistance (OAA), and, most important, Aid to Dependent Children (ADC), were funded by federal matching grants and administered locally.[36] The Social Security Act also left general relief, or general assistance, cash payments to the nonworking poor (predominantly men) wholly funded and administered on the state level.

Welfare localism had three consequences. First, it ensured that access to poor relief did not vitiate local norms. State "suitable homes" restrictions allowed local officials to determine eligibility for ADC. The vagueness of the category "suitable" allowed local officials to exclude unmarried mothers, women who were insufficiently deferential to local welfare authorities, and, particularly in the South, African-Americans. Second, it ensured wide local variations in relief expenditures since a large chunk of funding for UI, OAA, and ADC came from state and local taxes. Southern states paid significantly less in benefits than their northern counterparts. Third, welfare aroused significant taxpayer resentment. In states where minorities, particularly urban African-Americans, were disproportionately represented on welfare rolls, antitax sentiment combined with racial resentment to create a poisonous reaction against relief programs.[37] Finally, the relief program left out of the Social Security Act—general assistance—remained by far the most impoverished. In 1940, many states did not offer general relief, and those that did put stringent barriers on the condition and length of receipt. None offered benefits comparable in value to even the stingiest federal program, ADC.[38]

CIVIL RIGHTS POLITICS

Localism—as in the case of housing and social welfare policies—often reinforced structural patterns of inequality by enshrining local prejudices into practice. But not all localities were alike. Decentralization gave subnational governments some discretion to experiment, to push at the boundaries of the law, to enact local ordinances and regulations with little input from the federal government. In the matter of civil rights, local discretion was almost completely untouched by the New Deal. Before the late 1950s, Congress thwarted antilynching legislation and even the most tepid attempts at civil rights reform.[39] It is noteworthy that during the most important period of state expansion in American history—the New Deal and World War II—Congress passed no significant civil rights legislation and the executive branch created only two small, underfunded units to deal with racial inequality, arguably the nation's most pressing and intractable domestic problem. Of the 111 federal agencies created or restructured between 1933 and 1952—agencies that oversaw matters major and minor, including petroleum and soil conservation, the minimum wage, coal mine safety, civil aeronautics, labor relations, the training of apprentices, and much, much, more—only one temporary agency, the Fair Employment Practices Committee, dealt centrally with civil rights. The FEPC was dissolved in 1946, and efforts to legislate a permanent FEPC were rebuffed again and again in the 1940s and 1950s. In 1939, the Department of Justice created a small civil liberties unit to handle race discrimination cases, among others. But it faced both financial constraints and, during the Cold War, challenges to its mission and legitimacy. The only significant civil rights regulations in the period were the result of executive orders, such as Truman's order to desegregate the military and Eisenhower's weak nondiscrimination order for government contractors. When it came to the question of race relations, the United States was still a nation of courts and parties. The lack of administrative capacity on the matter of civil rights left questions of racial inequality to the localities and—in ways that would have far-reaching implications for the path that civil rights politics would take—to the judicial branch.[40]

Left to their own devices, most subnational governments simply perpetuated racial segregation. In the South, Jim Crow was built on an elaborate edifice of state laws and local ordinances that regulated interracial contact and governed nearly every realm of economic and political participation from employment to jury duty to voting. In the North, local school districts gerrymandered student catchment areas to correspond to racial patterns, limited the opportunity for black participation in local political organizations, and failed to intervene in discriminatory practices in workplaces and public accommodations such as hotels, restaurants, and hospitals.

The lack of federal intervention in local racial practices led to a hardening of Jim Crow in the South but a gradual softening of racial restrictions in much of the rest of the United States. Localism allowed for the creative development of antidiscrimination policy at the subnational level, particularly in the North and West. As a result, states and localities were at the cutting edge of civil rights policy making before the Civil Rights Act of 1964. The most important impetus to innovation in civil rights legislation was the rapid increase of the urban black population, particularly during and after World War II. In politically competitive states such as Michigan, Illinois, and New York, the Democratic party needed black support. Civil rights activists, discouraged by congressional hostility, turned their attention to local struggles for fair employment with hopes that their efforts would lead to a centralization and standardization of antidiscrimination laws at the federal level. Beginning in the early 1940s, a number of major cities, such as Detroit, Chicago, and Philadelphia, created civil rights commissions to investigate racial inequality and to advocate for pro-integration public policies. Between 1945 and 1964, dozens of cities and twenty-seven states passed fair employment practices laws that forbade workplace discrimination and provided some redress for those denied a job on grounds of race or religion. Even if many of these laws were tepid (often the result of compromises between probusiness Republicans and conservative Democrats), they became the blueprint for federal civil rights legislation in the 1960s. In the face of presidential inaction or congressional indifference, cities and states became the incubators of civil rights policy.[41]

Civil rights legislation emerged from the crucible of local innovation, but local institutions also remained the greatest barriers to racial equality throughout the United States, even in the North. In the South, public officials, elected and unelected, led the battle to defend Jim Crow. They were joined by an army of whites engaged in "massive resistance" and abetted by moderates who embraced token, gradualistic local changes in their desire to keep a lid on black unrest. In the North, where the most serious problems facing blacks were the result of de facto rather than de jure segregation in housing and schools, local bureaucratic and institutional inertia served as a barrier to racial integration. Into the breach left by the federal government and only inadequately filled by subnational governments stepped the federal courts.[42]

As early as the 1920s, civil rights activists, led by the National Association for the Advancement of Colored People (NAACP), turned to the courts for a remedy to racial inequality. In a carefully planned litigation strategy, NAACP attorneys targeted nearly every facet of Jim Crow, from all-white primaries to racially restrictive covenants to segregated schools. In a period where the president and Congress were reluctant to interfere with local prerogative on matters of civil rights, the courts became a decisive player. The Warren Court, in particular, greatly winnowed away local and state laws that permitted segregation in public accommodations, electoral politics, and, most controversially, education. Two sets of cases, those involving education and voting rights, most decisively challenged localism. Beginning with *Brown v. Board of Education*, the landmark case involving the Topeka, Kansas, public schools, the Warren Court threatened the most cherished of local prerogatives by banning local school districts from creating separate and fictively equal schools for African-American students. The herculean task of implementing school desegregation largely fell to the appellate courts; local educational practices came under federal judicial scrutiny; and courts devised plans to accomplish school integration that they imposed on local school districts. Likewise, a series of federal voting rights decisions, beginning with *Baker v. Carr*, brought judicial power to bear on the drawing of electoral boundaries, from city wards to congressional districts, in the service of minority electoral representation.[43]

Judicial intervention in school desegregation and in voting rights cases recast localism. In these two crucial arenas, localities were less autonomous than they had been earlier in the twentieth century. But localism was by no means dead. The court orders affected only selected localities. The vast majority of racially homogeneous educational and electoral districts remained wholly untouched by the courts. There were several limitations to court intervention. For one, cases were difficult to mount; it was not always easy to find plaintiffs, lawyers, and the financial resources to litigate complex cases. Even when cases were successful, the resources of the courts were limited, especially when judges attempted to implement grand visions of social restructuring. Local officials often resisted desegregation and creatively gerrymandered electoral districts. And the multiple, reinforcing processes of residential segregation, local zoning, and jurisdictional fragmentation usually proved too complex for the judicial system to handle.[44]

Local control of education was challenged in the most far-reaching way by court-ordered desegregation, but here, local interests ultimately triumphed. The Supreme Court's ruling against mandatory interdistrict busing in *Milliken v. Bradley* left local school district boundaries and administrative fragmentation wholly untouched. In a controversial five to four decision, the court overturned a federal court order that had mandated the desegregation of the predominantly black Detroit public schools and fifty-three surrounding overwhelmingly white school districts. In his opinion, Chief Justice Warren Burger adamantly defended the principle of localism. "No single tradition in public education," he wrote, "is more deeply rooted than local control over the operation of schools; local autonomy has long been thought essential both to the maintenance of community concern and support for public schools and to the quality of the educational process."[45] Opponents of school desegregation could withdraw behind the still-intact boundaries of school districts, unaffected by court desegregation orders. In addition, persistent housing segregation ensured that the vast majority of whites would never be substantively affected by school integration orders. De jure localism took a beating in the courts, but de facto localism remained alive and well.

REORGANIZING LOCALISM: THE GREAT SOCIETY

Outside the courtroom, the delicate New Deal compromise was challenged, but not undermined, by the expansion of federal power during the 1950s and the 1960s. A series of policy initiatives threatened to alter the balance of power between the federal government and states and localities. Under the Taft-Ellender-Wagner Housing Act of 1949, the federal government significantly increased grants-in-aid to cities for the purposes of urban renewal. But local officials continued to drive the "federal bulldozer." Local housing and planning agencies chose sites for redevelopment and responded to local concerns. In welfare, local control eroded more as federal regulations shifted power away from local welfare authorities toward state welfare agencies, which regulated the distribution of federal grants-in-aid to the poor and elderly. But even as local welfare authorities began to lose some of their autonomy, the trend toward centralization left welfare administration firmly in the hands of state governments.[46]

Lyndon Johnson's Great Society is often portrayed as a moment of a dramatic expansion of federal power. But the War on Poverty and Great Society reorganized localism without fundamentally undermining its place in the American political tradition. The Great Society's place-based programs did not augment federal government largesse at the expense of localism. Instead they challenged local and regional balances of power, while leaving the administration of key public policies decidedly at the subnational level.

Two contradictory impulses undergirded Johnson's vision of the Great Society. At once, his far-reaching legislative agenda rested on an optimistic statism, confident in the federal government's capacity to solve the pressing problems of racial and economic inequality. At the same time, the Great Society empowered localities to carry out the bulk of social reforms. Like the New Deal, the Great Society reconfigured the balance of power between federal and local while leaving intact local governments' independence, narrow place-based orientation, and overarching concern with place-specific interests.

During the Johnson years, grassroots activists reinforced the ambivalent view of the relationship between the federal government and localities. On one hand, civil rights groups demanded the intervention of the

Justice Department and the federal courts in such arenas as voting rights, school desegregation, and workplace antidiscrimination efforts. On the other hand, organizations as diverse as the Students for a Democratic Society (SDS), the Student Nonviolent Coordinating Committee, the National Welfare Rights Organization, Mobilization for Youth, and the Black Panthers demanded community control over economic development spending, urban planning, welfare, education, and health. The War on Poverty's Community Action Program (CAP) enshrined demands for citizen participation in its very structure. Demands for citizen involvement in welfare and public health programs and demands in minority communities for local control of schools echoed the CAP's emphasis on "maximum feasible participation." Likewise, "participatory democracy," the SDS slogan, was fundamentally localist in its orientation. Each grassroots insurgency rested on a distrust of centralized government and the assumption that community organizations could better respond to the needs of the poor and the disenfranchised than could Washington's remote and self-interested bureaucrats.[47]

The local-national balance did shift in two important ways during the Great Society. First was an explosion of federal grants-in-aid to localities for social services, education, and public works. Cities and towns relied to a far greater extent on federal funds than ever before. Federal grants came with strings attached; funding became contingent on compliance with federal rules and regulations. Localities lost some of the discretion—particularly on matters of education and welfare—that had long been indisputably local. Their loss of discretion did not, however, fundamentally undermine local control and autonomy. The local boundaries that determined jurisdictions for education, public services, and social welfare remained largely intact. In addition, local officials exercised considerable discretion about whether to apply for federal grants and how to use those grants once obtained. Great Society programs reshaped but did not ultimately undermine localism.[48]

Second, the Great Society altered the balance of power in subnational governments. In particular, it reshuffled the deck of state and local political power, especially in urban areas. Direct grants to cities, for example, undermined the role that state governments had played in the distribution of federal resources during the New Deal.[49] In addition, the provision of grants-in-aid to community action agencies and local social service agencies angered urban mayors who feared that the War on Poverty would weaken their control over patronage and social services. The demand for "maximum feasible participation" of the poor in antipoverty programs put some control in the hands of local activists, particularly minorities, and threatened the long-sacrosanct local administration of federal urban programs by mayors and political machines. Both states and urban machines fought back, with a fair degree of success. In Chicago and Philadelphia, for example, urban machines gained control over community action agencies, ensuring that they did not disrupt patronage politics. But even amidst these changes, the Great Society left the fragmented governmental structures at the state and local level entirely unscathed.[50]

Perhaps the most far-reaching change in the local-national balance came with welfare policy. New regulations governing Aid to Families with Dependent Children (AFDC) undermined local control by taking discretionary power from local welfare authorities. The ranks of welfare recipients grew significantly over the course of the 1960s, as eligibility requirements were relaxed. But AFDC benefit levels were still determined on a state-by-state basis, preserving part of the New Deal compromise intact. Cities and state governments also continued to pay for social services. Despite the infusion of federal grants, such payments proved increasingly burdensome to localities, which faced declining property and income tax revenues. Finally, localities continued to provide the lion's share of funds for general assistance and public health expenditures.[51]

The Great Society also threatened local control over education, a policy realm where local prerogative had remained almost wholly untouched during the New Deal. The Elementary and Secondary Education Act (ESEA) of 1964, particularly Title I (which targeted students from impoverished families), dramatically expanded federal involvement in public education throughout the country. Critics of the ESEA worried about an unprecedented federal incursion into local education. Introducing his education agenda, Lyndon Johnson promised that "federal assistance does not mean federal control." But by channeling federal funds to local school districts, the ESEA could not help but influence the priorities of local school districts. Still, the critics' fears proved to be largely unwarranted. The ESEA did not mandate a one-size-fits-all educational reform agenda. Rather, ESEA was implemented by thirty thousand local education agencies, which retained a great deal of discretion.[52] Bureaucratic inertia further protected local autonomy, for federal officials had great difficulties overseeing and evaluating local spending practices.[53] ESEA funds for vocational education, textbooks and educational technology, library materials, and the like were also allocated on a district-by-district basis, thus leaving intact the place-based inequalities that pervaded American public education.[54] Despite bipartisan outcry about growing federal control of public education, funding and curricular decisions remained deeply, resolutely local. As a result, racial disparities, shaped by patterns of residential segregation, were reinforced rather than undermined.

Devolution and the New Politics of Place

The balance of power between localities and the federal government shifted toward the latter during the 1960s, even if localism remained surprisingly robust. But during the 1970s and beyond, a shift in political culture led to an even greater reassertion of local control. From Nixon through Clinton, the federal government restructured federalism by devolving power to the states and localities. Nixon's "new federalism" called for a strengthening of the power of the states and grants to localities that would allow them "wide administrative leeway." William Safire, writing for Nixon and his domestic policy advisers, advocated the creation of a "national localism" that "says to communities, 'Do it your way.' " Nixon dismantled much of the Great Society but did not jettison its emphasis on funding local community development organizations. Nixon's "revenue sharing" policy provided grants to local governments with relatively few strings attached. In place of the community action and model cities programs, the Nixon administration created the community development block grant program, an effort to channel smaller federal grants to local self-help and community development corporations.[55]

The growing emphasis on public-private partnerships was by no means a solely Republican initiative. Jimmy Carter, elected in 1976, was also suspicious of the New Deal/Great Society welfare state and embraced an alternative vision of community empowerment and local self-help. Carter administration officials argued that centrally administered government programs were often wasteful and undemocratic. Like the Republicans, they believed that local problems were best solved by state and local officials, with a minimum of interference from the federal government. National policy makers drew from the rhetoric of decentralization that enjoyed support from both free-marketeers on the right and community-based activists on the left. A wide range of grassroots social movements in the 1970s—from environmentalists to antibusing activists—emphasized the importance of citizen participation in politics and expressed deep suspicion of experts and bureaucrats inside the Beltway. In place of "big government," they advocated the "empowerment" of local "mediating institutions" that would, it was believed, provide an antidote to impersonal, distant bureaucracy.[56]

Nixon and Carter revised urban policy. Their successors in the Reagan, Bush, and Clinton administrations pushed even more aggressively to decentralize. Reagan reduced federal funding to cities to a trickle, winnowed public housing programs, and reduced community development block grants and aid to mass transit. Between 1980 and 1990, the federal share of local government expenditures fell dramatically, from nearly 12 percent to just over 3 percent. In addition, Republican officials pushed policies that would give even more discretion to state- and local-governments. In the 1980s and 1990s, state governors and urban mayors, less reliant on federal funds than they had been earlier, turned localities into laboratories for experimentation on the weakened body of the welfare state. Led by the governors of Michigan, Wisconsin, and Massachusetts, states began to reduce welfare assistance and experiment with work requirements and strictures on parental behavior. Many states eliminated general assistance altogether. All drew from a provision in the 1962 welfare law that allowed states to obtain "waivers" from federal welfare regulations to experiment with social service delivery.[57]

The popularity of these state- and local-level reforms, particularly among Republicans and some conservative Democrats, became the basis for demands for greater devolution of federal social programs. When Republicans, committed to enhancing the power of states, gained control of Congress and the Senate in 1994, they made local experiments the basis for the dismantling of AFDC in the 1996 Welfare Reform Act. In the latest contest between federal power and localism, a new, increasingly assertive localism got the upper hand. Social welfare policy had always tensely balanced local, state, and federal power. But in the aftermath of 1996, the scales tipped away from the federal government once again. That said, local control—as it had since the Great Society—came with restrictions. Even as the responsibility for welfare and work devolved to the states and localities, the architects of welfare reform established eligibility rules, work requirements, and other national standards that delimited local programmatic flexibility. The process of "ending welfare as we know it" did not entail a return to the pre–New Deal system of unstandardized, locally administered poor laws.[58]

In the realm of education policy as well, localism and centralization remained in tension. Congressional Republicans and President Reagan and the two Presidents Bush continued to profess their commitment to local control over schools, while simultaneously pushing for federally mandated educational standards, school safety regulations, and strictures on controversial curricular offerings such as sex education. However centralizing these educational impulses might be, they have left unchallenged the fragmentation of local school districts. Structural localism, even as local control over curriculums was up for grabs, reinforced the administrative balkanization and decentralization of education. Most important, the persistence of residential segregation meant that school district boundaries firmly reinforced racial distinctions. To take one example, in metropolitan Detroit, twenty years after the *Milliken* decision, over four-fifths of African-American students attended school in just three of eighty-three area school districts. All but a handful of the remaining districts were overwhelmingly white. In the 1990s, patterns of school segregation hardened as courts rolled back the last vestiges of court-ordered desegregation plans from the 1960s and 1970s.[59] The mutually reinforcing boundaries of race and privilege became the most visible legacy of persistent localism.

THE LEGACY OF PERSISTENT LOCALISM

Over the course of the twentieth century, much in American government changed. It is incontestable that the influence of Washington over everyday life grew vastly, from the power of federal regulatory agencies, to the reach of the courts into school districts and state and local elections, to the rapid growth of federal employment, to the award of federal grants-in-aid to localities. But the dramatic expansion of the state need not blind historians and other social scientists to the ways that the persistence of localism fundamentally shaped the process of state formation in the United States. The twentieth century witnessed a struggle to define the limits of federal power and a shift in the balance of power between federal, state, and local governments. Nothing was static in the relationship between these governmental units. But rarely did federal initiatives dismantle local institutions and wholly undermine jurisdictional autonomy. Federal assistance and federal social programs did not flow smoothly to localities; instead local jurisdictional boundaries directed the stream of governmental assistance, channeling it to some places and away from others. Although late-twentieth-century America scarcely resembled the bygone world of "island communities" memorably described by historian Robert Wiebe, the persistence of fragmented and autonomous local governments and authorities preserved a fair degree of local insularity—particularly with regard to race, education, land use, and social welfare. As we grapple with questions of democracy and the state in modern America, it pays to remember the adage of one of the great state builders of recent American history, late Speaker of the House Thomas P. "Tip" O'Neill. Never at a loss for an apt quip, schooled in the art of pragmatic liberalism, O'Neill reminded us that "all politics is local."[60]

NOTES

Thanks to Brian Balogh, Dana Barron, Stephanie Foster, Ira Katznelson, David King, Julian Zelizer, and the other editors and various contributors to this volume for their assistance.

1. Brian Balogh, "Reorganizing the Organizational Synthesis," *Studies in American Political Development* 5, no. 1 (1991): 119–72.

2. For the definitive statement of this perspective, see Robert Wiebe, *The Search for Order* (New York: Hill and Wang, 1967).

3. Michael McGerr, *The Decline of Popular Politics* (New York: Oxford University Press, 1987); for an evocative description of local politics in the nineteenth century, see Paul Bourke and Donald A. DeBats, *Washington County: Politics and Community in Antebellum America* (Baltimore: Johns Hopkins University Press, 1998).

4. Eric Monkkonen, *The Local State: Public Money and American Cities* (Stanford, Calif.: Stanford University Press, 1995), 105.

5. Stephen Skowronek, *Building a New American State: The Expansion of National Administrative Capacities, 1877–1920* (New York: Cambridge University Press, 1982); Theda Skocpol, *Protecting Soldiers and Mothers: The Political Origins of Social Policy in the United States* (Cambridge, Mass.: Harvard University Press, 1992); Theda Skocpol, *Social Policy in the United States: Future Possibilities in Historical Perspective* (Princeton, N.J.: Princeton University Press, 1995); Margaret Weir, Ann Shola Orloff, and Theda Skocpol, eds., *The Politics of Social Policy* (Princeton, N.J.: Princeton University Press, 1988); Robert C. Lieberman, *Shifting the Color Line: Race and the American Welfare State* (Cambridge, Mass.: Harvard University Press, 1998); Edwin Amenta, *Bold Relief* (New York: Cambridge University Press, 1998); Margaret Weir, *Politics and Jobs: The Boundaries of Employment Policy in the United States* (Princeton, N.J.: Princeton University Press, 1992). For a critical overview of the field, see Phil Ethington, "Mapping the Local State," *Journal of Urban History* 27 (2001): 686–702.

6. Martha Derthick, "How Many Communities? The Evolution of American Federalism," in *Dilemmas of Scale in America's Federal Democracy*, ed. Derthick (Cambridge: Woodrow Wilson Center Press and Cambridge University Press, 1999), 150.

7. Ellis Hawley, "Social Policy and the Liberal State in Twentieth-Century America," in *Federal Social Policy: The Historical Dimension*, ed. Donald Critchlow and Ellis Hawley (University Park: Pennsylvania State University Press, 1988); Barry Karl, *The Uneasy State* (Chicago: University of Chicago Press, 1983); James Holt, "The New Deal and the American Anti-Statist Tradition," in *The New Deal: The National Level*, ed. John Braeman, Robert H. Bremner, and David Brody (Columbus: Ohio State University Press, 1975), 27–49; Gareth Davies, *From Opportunity to Entitlement: The Transformation and Decline of Great Society Liberalism* (Lawrence: University Press of Kansas, 1998), esp. chap. 1.

8. See for example, James Morone, *The Democratic Wish: Popular Participation and the Limits of American Government* (New York: Basic Books, 1990); Gary Gerstle, *Working-Class Americanism: The Politics of Labor in a Textile City, 1914–1960* (New York: Cambridge University Press, 1989), 183–95, 331–36.

9. The most comprehensive introduction to the debate about American exceptionalism is Seymour Martin Lipset and Gary Marks, *It Didn't Happen Here: Why Socialism Failed in the United States* (New York: Norton, 2000); for another recent overview, see Rick Halpern and Jonathan Morris, eds., *American Exceptionalism?* (London: Macmillan, 1997). One of the few books that grapples with the question of exceptionalism in a local context is Ira Katznelson, *City Trenches: Urban Politics and the Patterning of Class in the United States* (New York: Pan-

theon, 1981). Labor historian Kevin Boyle has offered a brief but enlightening discussion of the local-federal structure of unions in his analysis of civil rights politics in the United Auto Workers. See Boyle, " 'There Are No Union Sorrows the Union Can't Heal': The Struggle for Racial Equality in the United Automobile Workers, 1940–1960," *Labor History* 36 (1995): 3–32.

10. I take my cue here from William Leuchtenburg's still-timely argument that "groups that have not been part of the elite have often been affected by the state, and have affected it, in ways that have only begun to be appreciated." William Leuchtenburg, "The Pertinence of Political History: Reflections on the Significance of the State in America," *Journal of American History* 74 (1987): 596. See also Alan Brinkley, "Writing the History of Contemporary America: Dilemmas and Challenges," *Daedalus* 113 (1984): 121–42.

11. Richard Briffault, "Our Localism," part 2, "Localism and Legal Theory," *Columbia Law Review* 90 (1990): 444.

12. Martha Derthick offers a pithy description of what she calls the "social functions of federalism" that pertains here: "By sustaining subnational communities with some residual degree of governmental independence and distinctiveness, federalism gives individuals choices about where to live. This gives inequality a spatial form, because of course the better off use their freedom to congregate in communities that suit their tastes, and use the power of local governments to protect their property values and lifestyles. Thus federalism in its social form, helping to give definition to distinct communities, is a leading ground of the continuing American battle between liberty and equality." Martha Derthick, "The 1992 John Gaus Lecture: Up to Date in Kansas City: Reflections on American Federalism," *PS: Political Science and Politics* 25 (December 1992): 675.

13. Other disciplines have provided little guidance. American political scientists, who focus heavily on Congress and the presidency, treat state and local governments as an inconsequential byway. One important exception is Nancy Burns, *The Formation of American Local Governments: Private Values in Public Institutions* (New York: Oxford University Press, 1994). In most law schools, local government law is a marginal topic but one that has recently generated a growing body of cutting-edge scholarship. See, for example, Briffault, "Our Localism"; Gerald Frug, *City Making* (Princeton, N.J.: Princeton University Press, 1999); and Richard Thompson Ford, "The Boundaries of Race: Political Geography in Legal Analysis," in *Critical Race Theory: The Key Writings That Formed the Movement*, ed. Kimberle Crenshaw (New York: The New Press, 1995), 449–64.

14. For a lucid discussion of local governments in the United States, see Kathryn M. Doherty and Clarence N. Stone, "Local Practice in Transition," in *Dilemmas of Scale*, ed. Derthick, 157–60.

15. Robert Wood, *1400 Governments: The Political Economy of the New York Metropolitan Region* (Cambridge, Mass.: Harvard University Press, 1961).

16. David Rusk, *Cities without Suburbs*, 2d ed. (Washington, D.C.: Woodrow Wilson Center Press, 1995), 95; Doherty and Stone, "Local Practice," table 6.1, 158.

17. I have explored these issues in Thomas J. Sugrue, *The Origins of the Urban Crisis: Race and Inequality in Postwar Detroit* (Princeton, N.J.: Princeton University Press, 1996), esp. chap. 3 and 8. Other important work in this vein includes

Peter Siskind, "Growth and Its Discontents: Localism, Protest, and Politics on the Postwar Northeast Corridor" (Ph.D. dissertation, University of Pennsylvania, 2002); Robert Self, *American Babylon: Race, Class, and Power in Oakland and the East Bay, 1945–1977* (Princeton, N.J.: Princeton University Press, forthcoming); Lisa McGirr, *Suburban Warriors: Grassroots Conservatives in the 1960s and the Making of the New Right* (Princeton, N.J.: Princeton University Press, 2001).

18. Robert Wiebe, *Self Rule: A Cultural History of American Democracy* (Chicago: University of Chicago Press, 1995), 211.

19. Lizabeth Cohen, *Making a New Deal: Industrial Workers in Chicago, 1919–1939* (New York: Cambridge University Press, 1991); Kenneth Scherzer, "The Politics of Default: Financial Restructuring and Reform in Depression Era Fall River, Massachusetts," *Urban Studies* 26 (1989): 164–76; Eric Monkonnen, *America Becomes Urban: The Development of US Cities and Towns, 1780–1980* (Berkeley: University of California Press, 1988), 222–23.

20. No overview of the New Deal has yet supplanted William Leuchtenburg, *Franklin D. Roosevelt and the New Deal, 1932–1940* (New York: Harper and Row, 1963). A very useful historiographic synthesis is Anthony Badger, *The New Deal: The Depression Years, 1933–1940* (New York: Hill and Wang, 1989).

21. Ira Katznelson, Kim Geiger, and Daniel Kryder, "Limiting Liberalism: The Southern Veto in Congress, 1933–1950," *Political Science Quarterly* 108 (September 1993): 283–306; Jill Quadagno, "From Old Age Assistance to Supplemental Security Income: The Political Economy of Relief in the South, 1935–1972," in *Politics of Social Policy*, ed. Weir, Orloff, and Skocpol, 235–63; Bruce Schulman, *From Cotton Belt to Sunbelt: Federal Policy and the Economic Development of the South, 1938–1980* (New York: Oxford University Press, 1991); Alan Brinkley, "The New Deal and Southern Politics," in *The New Deal and the South*, ed. James C. Cobb and Michael Namorato (Jackson: University Press of Mississippi, 1984), 97–117.

22. There is a large and useful literature on the New Deal and urban politics, but much of it is quite old and uninterested in the social history of politics. See Lyle W. Dorsett, *Franklin D. Roosevelt and the Big City Bosses* (Port Washington, N.Y.: Kennikat Press, 1977); Bruce Stave, *The New Deal and the Last Hurrah: Pittsburgh Machine Politics* (Pittsburgh: University of Pittsburgh Press, 1970); Charles H. Trout, *Boston, the Great Depression, and the New Deal* (New York: Oxford University Press, 1977) and "The New Deal and the Cities," in *Fifty Years Later: The New Deal Evaluated*, ed. Harvard Sitkoff (New York: Knopf, 1985); Roger Biles, *Big City Boss in Depression and War: Mayor Edward J. Kelley of Chicago* (DeKalb: Northern Illinois University Press, 1984). The most influential local study of the New Deal's constituents, Cohen, *Making a New Deal*, pays almost no attention to local political institutions despite its setting in the ground zero of machine politics, Chicago.

23. James T. Patterson, *Congressional Conservatism and the New Deal: The Growth of the Conservative Coalition in Congress, 1933–1939* (Lexington: University of Kentucky Press, 1967); for an analysis of labor and the Dixie-GOP alliance, see Melvyn Dubofsky, *The State and Labor in Modern America* (Chapel Hill: University of North Carolina Press, 1994); Robert Booth Fowler, *Believing*

Skeptics: American Political Intellectuals, 1945–1960 (Westport, Conn.: Greenwood Press, 1978).

24. Progressive reformers attempted grassroots experiments in a wide range of policies, including housing and slum clearance, poor relief, and mothers' pensions. See Gail Radford, *Modern Housing for America: Policy Struggles in the New Deal Era* (Chicago: University of Chicago Press, 1996); Robert Fairbanks, *Making Better Citizens: Housing Reform and the Community Development Strategy in Cincinnati, 1890–1960* (Urbana: University of Illinois Press, 1988); Robert Halpern, *Rebuilding the Inner City: A History of Neighborhood Initiatives to Address Poverty in the United States* (New York: Columbia University Press, 1995); Michael B. Katz, *In the Shadow of the Poorhouse*, 2d ed. (New York: Basic Books, 1996); Skocpol, *Protecting Soldiers and Mothers*; and Joanne Goodwin, *Gender and the Politics of Welfare Reform: Mother's Pensions in Chicago, 1911–1929* (Chicago: University of Chicago Press, 1997). The connections between local social welfare agencies and New Deal programs have yet to be fully examined, but a useful starting point is William R. Brock, *Welfare, Democracy, and the New Deal* (Cambridge: Cambridge University Press, 1988).

25. This topic has yet to be explored fully by historians. For a useful starting point, see Julian Zelizer's chapter in this volume, "The Uneasy Relationship: Democracy, Taxation, and State Building since the New Deal." One scholar who has considered the consequences of taxes on social policy is Michael C. Brown, in his *Race, Money, and the American Welfare State* (Ithaca, N.Y.: Cornell University Press, 1998). On local antitax movements, see Self, *American Babylon*, chaps. 3 and 8, and Becky Nicolaides, *My Blue Heaven: Life and Politics in the Working-Class Suburbs of Los Angeles, 1920–1965* (Chicago: University of Chicago Press, 2002), 135–82, 302–3.

26. Radford, *Modern Housing*, 12–14, 19–27. A good description of working-class home building and home buying practices is Olivier Zunz, *The Changing Face of Inequality: Urbanization, Industrial Development, and Immigrants in Detroit, 1880–1920* (Chicago: University of Chicago Press, 1982), 129–76.

27. Ronald Tobey, Charles Wetherell, and Jay Brigham, "Moving out and Settling In: Residential Mobility, Homeowning, and the Public Enframing of Citizenship, 1921–1950," *American Historical Review* 95 (1990): 1395–1422, esp. 1415–20.

28. Kenneth T. Jackson, *Crabgrass Frontier: The Suburbanization of the United States* (New York: Oxford University Press, 1985), 190–218; Michael Danielson, *The Politics of Exclusion* (New York: Columbia University Press, 1976).

29. Radford, *Modern Housing*; Fairbanks, *Making Better Citizens*.

30. For two case studies of grassroots activism around public housing, see Sugrue, *Origins of the Urban Crisis*, 57–88, and Jo Ann E. Argersinger, *Toward a New Deal in Baltimore: People and Government in the Great Depression* (Chapel Hill: University of North Carolina Press, 1988), 93–112.

31. Philip J. Funigiello, *The Challenge to Urban Liberalism: Federal-City Relations during World War II* (Knoxville: University of Tennessee Press, 1978), 80–119, quote 109.

32. Richard Davies, *Housing Reform during the Truman Administration* (Columbia: University of Missouri Press, 1966); Roger Biles, "Public Housing Policy in the Eisenhower Administration," *Mid-America: An Historical Review* 81 (1999): 5–25.

33. Thomas J. Sugrue, "Crabgrass-Roots Politics: Race, Rights, and the Reaction against Liberalism in the Urban North, 1940–1964," *Journal of American History* 82 (1995): 551–78; Arnold Hirsch, *Making the Second Ghetto: Race and Housing in Chicago, 1940–1960* (New York: Cambridge University Press, 1983); Thomas O'Connor, *Building a New Boston: Politics and Urban Renewal, 1950 to 1970* (Boston: Northeastern University Press, 1993), 123–24; John Bauman, *Public Housing, Race, and Renewal: Urban Planning in Philadelphia, 1920–1974* (Philadelphia: Temple University Press, 1987).

34. Linda Gordon, *Pitied but Not Entitled: Single Mothers and the History of Welfare* (New York: The Free Press, 1994); Barbara J. Nelson, "The Origins of the Two-Channel Welfare State: Workmen's Compensation and Mothers' Aid," in *Women, the State, and Welfare*, ed. Linda Gordon (Madison: University of Wisconsin Press, 1990), 123–51.

35. Lieberman, *Shifting the Color Line*, 7. On race and welfare, see also Jill Quadagno, *The Color of Welfare: How Racism Undermined the War on Poverty* (New York: Oxford University Press, 1994); Brown, *Race, Money, and the Welfare State*; for a skeptical analysis, see Gareth Davies and Martha Derthick, "Race and Social Welfare Policy: The Social Security Act of 1935," *Political Science Quarterly* 112 (1997): 217–35.

36. Weir, *Politics and Jobs*; Jill Quadagno, *The Transformation of Old Age Security: Class and Politics in the American Welfare State* (Chicago: University of Chicago Press, 1988).

37. See, for example, Lisa Levenstein, "From Innocent Children to Unwanted Migrants and Unwed Moms: Two Chapters in the Public Discourse on Welfare in the United States, 1960–1961," *Journal of Women's History* 11 (2000): 10–33.

38. On general relief, another underexplored topic in the history of welfare, see Brown, *Race, Money, and the Welfare State*, 74–76. The best overview of ADC remains Winifred Bell, *Aid to Dependent Children* (New York: Columbia University Press, 1965). See also Lieberman, *Shifting the Color Line*, chap. 4.

39. On the New Deal and race, see especially Harvard Sitkoff, *A New Deal for Blacks: The Emergence of Civil Rights as a National Issue* (New York: Oxford University Press, 1978), and Nancy J. Weiss, *Farewell to the Party of Lincoln: Black Politics in the Age of FDR* (Princeton, N.J.: Princeton University Press, 1983).

40. Skowronek, *Building a New American State*, 39–46. For a comprehensive list of governmental agencies, see Brian Balogh, Joanna Grisinger, and Philip Zelikow, "Making Democracy Work: A Brief History of Twentieth-Century Federal Executive Reorganization," Miller Center Working Paper in American Political Development, University of Virginia, July 22, 2002, chart 2. See also Robert Frederick Burk, *The Eisenhower Administration and Black Civil Rights* (Knoxville: University of Tennessee Press, 1984), and Brian Landsberg, *Enforcing Civil Rights: Race Discrimination and the Department of Justice* (Lawrence: University Press of Kansas, 1997).

41. See the brilliant dissertation by Anthony S. Chen, "From Fair Employment to Equal Opportunity Employment and Beyond: Affirmative Action and the Politics of Civil Rights in the New Deal Order, 1941–1972" (Ph.D. dissertation, University of California, Berkeley, 2002). For case studies of state and local antidiscrimination efforts, see Sidney Fine, *"Expanding the Frontiers of Civil Rights": Michigan, 1948–1968* (Detroit: Wayne State University Press, 2000); Paul Moreno, *From Direct Action to Affirmative Action: Fair Employment Law and Policy in America, 1933–1972* (Baton Rouge: Louisiana State University Press, 1997); Thomas J. Sugrue, "Breaking Through: The Troubled Origins of Affirmative Action in the Workplace," in *Color Lines: Affirmative Action, Discrimination, and Civil Rights Options for America*, ed. John D. Skrentny (Chicago: University of Chicago Press, 2001), 31–52.

42. Works on massive resistance and liberal capitulation in the South are too extensive to cite comprehensively here. Particularly useful are Numan Bartley, *The Rise of Massive Resistance* (Baton Rouge: Louisiana State University Press, 1970); William Chafe, *Civilities and Civil Rights* (New York: Oxford University Press, 1980); and Tony Badger, "Fatalism Not Gradualism: The Crisis of Southern Liberalism, 1945–65," in *The Making of Martin Luther King and the Civil Rights Movement*, ed. Badger and Brian Ward (New York: NYU Press, 1996), 67–95. The history of civil rights in the North remains almost entirely unwritten.

43. Mark Tushnet, *The NAACP's Strategy against Segregated Education, 1925–1950* (Chapel Hill: University of North Carolina Press, 1987); Jack Greenberg, *Crusaders in the Courts: How a Dedicated Band of Lawyers Fought for the Civil Rights Revolution* (New York: Basic Books, 1994); *Brown v. Board of Education of Topeka, Kansas* 347 U.S. 483 (1954); Steven F. Lawson, *Black Ballots: Voting Rights in the South, 1944–1969* (New York: Columbia University Press, 1976); *Baker v. Carr* 369 U.S. 16 (1962).

44. Jennifer L. Hochschild, *The New American Dilemma: Liberal Democracy and School Desegregation* (New Haven, Conn.: Yale University Press, 1984); Robert L. Herbst, "The Legal Struggle to Integrate Schools in the North," *Annals of the American Academy of Political and Social Science* 407 (May 1973): 43–62; J. Morgan Kousser, *Colorblind Injustice: Minority Voting Rights and the Undoing of the Second Reconstruction* (Chapel Hill: University of North Carolina Press, 1999).

45. *Milliken v. Bradley* 418 U.S. 717 (1974), at 741–42. More generally, see Paul R. Dimond, *Beyond Busing: Inside the Challenge to Urban Segregation* (Ann Arbor: University of Michigan Press, 1985).

46. On welfare, see Martha Derthick, *The Influence of Federal Grants: Public Assistance in Massachusetts* (Cambridge, Mass.: Harvard University Press, 1970); on urban renewal, see Hirsch, *Making the Second Ghetto*; and more generally Jon Teaford, *The Rough Road to Renaissance: Urban Revitalization in America, 1940–1985* (Baltimore: Johns Hopkins University Press, 1990).

47. Thomas F. Jackson, "The State, the Movement, and the Urban Poor: The War on Poverty and Political Mobilization in the 1960s," in *The "Underclass" Debate: Views from History*, ed. Michael B. Katz (Princeton, N.J.: Princeton University Press, 1993), 403–39; Allen J. Matusow, *The Unraveling of America: A History of Liberalism in the 1960s* (New York: Harper and Row, 1984); for the

emphasis on "community" in a wide range of social movements during the 1960s, see Howard Brick, *Age of Contradiction: American Thought and Culture in the 1960s* (Ithaca, N.Y.: Cornell University Press, 2000), 98–123.

48. James T. Patterson, *America's Struggle against Poverty, 1900–1994* (Cambridge, Mass.: Harvard University Press, 1995), 146–48.

49. Robert Reischauer, "Fiscal Federalism in the 1980s: Dismantling or Rationalizing the Great Society?" in *The Great Society and Its Legacy: Twenty Years of U.S. Social Policy*, ed. Marshall Kaplan and Peggy Cuciti (Durham: Duke University Press, 179–84.

50. Dennis R. Judd, *The Politics of American Cities: Private Power and Public Policy* (Boston: Little Brown, 1979), 329–42.

51. See Michael B. Katz, *The Price of Citizenship: Redefining the American Welfare State* (New York: Metropolitan Books, 2001), 79–80.

52. James L. Sundquist, *Politics and Policy: The Eisenhower, Kennedy, and Johnson Years* (Washington, D.C.: Brookings Institution Press, 1968), 216–20.

53. Milbrey Wallin McLaughlin, *Evaluation and Reform: The Elementary and Secondary Education Act of 1965, Title I* (Cambridge, Mass.: Ballinger, 1975).

54. Hugh Davis Graham, "The Transformation of Federal Education Policy," in *The Johnson Years: Volume 1: Foreign Policy, the Great Society, and the White House*, ed. Robert A. Divine (Austin: University of Texas Press, 1981), 155–84.

55. A. James Reichley, *Conservatives in an Age of Change: The Nixon and Ford Administrations* (Washington, D.C.: Brookings Institution Press, 1981), 154–73, quote 166.

56. Alice O'Connor, "Swimming against the Tide: A Brief History of Federal Policy in Poor Communities," in *Urban Problems and Community Development*, ed. Ronald F. Ferguson and William T. Dickens (Washington, D.C.: Brookings Institution Press, 1999), 108–13; Thomas J. Sugrue, "Carter's Urban Policy Crisis," in *The Carter Presidency: Policy Choices in the Post–New Deal Era*, ed. Gary M. Fink and Hugh Davis Graham (Lawrence: University Press of Kansas, 1998), 137–57.

57. John Mollenkopf, "Urban Policy at the Crossroads," in *The Social Divide: Political Parties and the Future of Activist Government*, ed. Margaret Weir (Washington, D.C.: Brookings Institution Press and the Russell Sage Foundation, 1998), 464–505.

58. Katz, *Price of Citizenship*, 77–136.

59. Thomas J. Sugrue, "Expert Report of Thomas J. Sugrue," *University of Michigan Journal of Race and the Law* 5 (fall 1999): 289; Gary Orfield, Susan Eaton, and the Harvard Project on School Desegregation, *Dismantling Desegregation: The Quiet Reversal of* Brown v. Board of Education (New York: The New Press, 1996).

60. Tip O'Neill with Gary Hymel, *All Politics Is Local and Other Rules of the Game* (New York: Times Books, 1994).

Chapter Thirteen

SUBURBAN STRATEGIES

THE VOLATILE CENTER IN POSTWAR AMERICAN POLITICS

Matthew D. Lassiter

The Politics of Middle-Class Consciousness

D URING THE LATE 1960S and early 1970s, a populist revolt of the Silent Majority rippled upward into national politics and established powerful constraints on Great Society liberalism and civil rights reform. In an opening phase, suburban parents in the Sunbelt South launched grassroots uprisings to defend their children's neighborhood schools against the legal challenge of court-ordered busing. White-collar home owners who claimed membership in the Silent Majority invented a potent "color-blind" discourse that portrayed residential segregation as the product of economic stratification rather than historical racism. This political formula eventually gained national traction as a bipartisan defense of middle-class consumer privileges and suburban residential boundaries. The rise of the Silent Majority reflected broader trends spreading throughout metropolitan America, a politics of middle-class consciousness based in subdivision associations, shopping malls, church congregations, PTA branches, and voting booths. The political culture of suburban populism—from taxpayer revolts and antibusing crusades to home owner movements and antisprawl campaigns—galvanized a top-down response marked by the persistent refusal of all three branches of the federal government to address the historical legacies of residential segregation through collective remedies for metropolitan inequality. From the "conservative" subdivisions of southern California to the "liberal" townships of New England, the suburbanization of American society and politics has empowered a bipartisan ethos of private-property values, individual taxpayer rights, children's educational privileges, family residential security, consumer freedom of choice, and middle-class racial innocence.[1]

The growth policies of New Deal liberalism and the rise of the Cold War military-industrial complex shaped the patterns of postwar residential expansion and transformed the South and West into the booming

Sunbelt. The Federal Housing Administration and the GI Bill subsidized the "American Dream" of middle-class home ownership for millions of white families who moved from rural regions and urban centers to the sprawling suburbs. By excluding racial minorities from new suburban developments and "redlining" racially mixed urban neighborhoods, federal mortgage policies during the initial postwar decades systematically enforced residential segregation and reinforced marketplace discrimination. The 1956 Interstate Highway Act facilitated automobile-based commuting and corporate mobility in the outlying suburbs and simultaneously enabled municipal governments to concentrate racial minorities within inner-city ghettos. Cold War spending priorities propelled a population shift to the South and West, where middle-class migrants settled in residentially segregated suburbs clustered around military bases, defense industries, and regional branch offices. The white-collar character of Sunbelt expansion also depended on the explosive growth of the technology-driven and service-oriented sectors of corporate capitalism. After the Rust Belt recession of the 1970s, industrial centers in the Midwest and Northeast increasingly emulated the Sunbelt model of high-tech innovation, capital mobility, corporate deregulation, flexible labor markets, and residential sprawl.[2]

Suburban decentralization and Sunbelt development ultimately produced a volatile political climate in which neither the Democrats nor the Republicans could maintain a stable electoral majority. The upward mobility subsidized by the middle-class entitlement programs of the federal government undermined the working-class base of New Deal liberalism and turned suburban voters into a vital demographic that came to drive the electoral strategies of both parties. When the civil rights movement launched a direct assault on residential and educational segregation in suburban jurisdictions, the Silent Majority responded with a localist politics of home owner rights and middle-class warfare. In the affluent white-collar suburbs that have commanded the attention of national politicians, the celebratory ideology of the free market and the "color-blind" ethos of meritocratic individualism effectively concealed the role of the state in forging metropolitan patterns of residential segregation and structural inequality. Although the Republican party initially benefited from the grassroots surge of middle-class consciousness, the populist revolt of the center transcended the conservative mobilization of the New Right. The reinvention of the "New Democrats" as the champions of quality-of-life issues in suburban swing districts and the fiscally responsible managers of the "new economy" has revitalized the competitiveness of the center in a postliberal political order.[3]

Historians have only begun to examine the local political culture of white-collar voters and the grassroots movements of upper-middle-class home owners in the suburban neighborhoods of postwar America. In recent years, the new urban history has explored the racial contradiction at the heart of postwar liberalism, as the promise of equal opportunity for black citizens clashed with a grassroots white backlash that defined segregated housing and secure neighborhoods as an essential feature of the New Deal social contract. Narratives of "reactionary populism" have revealed that in the working-class precincts of the urban North, the counterattack against race-conscious liberalism began with the Great Migration and not the Great Society, and then exploded during the busing and housing integration controversies of the 1960s and 1970s. But most of the new urban history has been written from the inside out, largely confined to episodes of direct racial friction within the city limits of the urban North and lacking a consciously suburban approach to the postwar metropolis.[4] Students of grassroots conservatism have significantly expanded the narrative of political realignment through close attention to the "suburban warriors" of the Sunbelt, from the Goldwater troops of the 1960s, to the tax revolts of the 1970s, to the Religious Right in the 1980s and 1990s. But the emphasis of the Sunbelt literature on the origins of the New Right fails to incorporate the vast majority of suburban home owners who were not right-wing activists or conservative ideologues.[5] The populist revolt of the Silent Majority fused racial and class politics into a centrist ideology that created an underlying suburban consensus in the electoral arena. Understanding the political culture of middle-class entitlement requires analysis of the suburban strategies that simultaneously reshaped the metropolitan landscape and the electoral map.[6]

THE FAILURE OF THE "SOUTHERN STRATEGY"

The suburban strategies developed in the Sunbelt South, not a top-down "southern strategy" inspired by the Deep South, provided the blueprint for the reconfiguration of the political center in American politics. Many pundits and scholars have embraced a reductionist narrative of political realignment in the modern South, building on GOP strategist Kevin Phillips's book *The Emerging Republican Majority* (1969). In this account of the New Right, presidential candidates Barry Goldwater and George Wallace emerge as the two most influential losers in American political history, the progenitors of a racialized conservatism that subsequently shaped the coded appeals of the Republican party and united working-class and middle-class white voters in an alliance of reactionary populism. To explain the national collapse of the New Deal order, the "southern strategy" school offers a corollary called the "southernization of American politics"—a schematic portrait that highlights Nixon's "law and order" platform, Reagan's "states' rights" rhetoric, Bush's "Willie Horton" television advertisements, and Gingrich's invective against "welfare mothers."[7] At the grassroots level, however, the "southern strategy" conspicuously backfired in each of its four genuine incarnations: the Dixiecrat revolt of 1948, the Goldwater debacle in 1964, the third-party Wallace movement in 1968, and the Republican disaster in the 1970 midterm elections. Each of these campaigns failed to carry the high-growth states of the peripheral South and instead achieved Pyrrhic victories in the Deep South strongholds that supported the losing candidate in all but one presidential election between 1948 and 1968. During the same era, the suburban residents of the metropolitan regions and the white-collar migrants to the New South increasingly diverged from the racial politics of the Black Belt and converged with the class-based voting patterns in the rest of the nation. As a top-down and race-driven account of regional transformation, the "southern strategy" framework obscures a more compelling narrative that revolves around the class-stratified politics produced by the postwar suburbanization of southern society and the population shift to the metropolitan Sunbelt.[8]

The southern base of the Republican party always depended more on the middle-class corporate economy than on the top-down politics of racial backlash, and the region's pioneering contribution to national political realignment came primarily from the suburban ethos of New South metropolises such as Atlanta and Charlotte, North Carolina, not the exportation of the working-class racial politics of the Black Belt. In 1968, Richard Nixon triumphed through a de facto "suburban strategy" that, by calculation and by default, positioned the Republican party as the moderate alternative to the reactionary racial platform of George Wallace and the discredited Great Society liberalism of Hubert Humphrey. Recognizing that an overt appeal for the segregationist vote would alienate white moderates everywhere else, the Nixon campaign essentially conceded the Goldwater base in the Deep South to the Wallace insurgency and instead aimed directly at the middle-class voters who lived in the suburban South and had voted for Eisenhower during the 1950s. Through populist appeals to the political center and a consciously "color-blind" stance on controversial racial issues, Nixon forged an electoral coalition between the dynamic states of the Sunbelt South and West and the upwardly mobile voters of the Midwest and Northeast. The Republican candidate expressly adopted racially inclusive imagery in his convention speech, subsequently repackaged in a series of evocative television advertisements that contrasted burning cities and campus upheaval with happy nuclear families engaged in activities such as raking their leaves and making homemade ice cream. "Let us listen now to . . . the voice of the great majority of Americans, the forgotten Americans, the non-shouters, the non-demonstrators," implored Nixon. "They are black and they are white. . . . They work in America's factories. . . . They run America's businesses. . . . They give lift to the American dream. . . . They work, they save, they pay their taxes, they care." At a shopping mall in Charlotte, the future president launched his southeastern campaign swing with similar "color-blind" praise for the "people who pay their taxes and go to work and support their churches, white people and black people, people [who] are not rioters." The New South represented a progressive place to live, Nixon told the enthusiastic audience of middle-class suburbanites and grassroots Republican activists, a region that had become "a lot like the rest of the country."[9]

Rather than illustrating the "southernization of American politics," the Republican victory in 1968 signaled the increasing suburbanization of both southern and national politics. Although Nixon quietly ratified backroom deals to appease the Goldwater-Reagan wing of the party, including a pledge to minimize federal enforcement of school desegregation and open-housing legislation, the candidate's public comments reflected the emerging suburban blueprint on civil rights issues, a nominally "color-blind" and frankly class-conscious ideology that revolved around the twin pillars of neighborhood schools and residential exclusivity. In his well-publicized Charlotte appearance, Nixon expressed support for the moral principle of racial integration, but he also charged that "busing for racial balance" would backfire because of the wide socioeconomic gap in academic aptitude between wealthy schools in the suburbs and poor students in the ghettos. In the three-way campaign of 1968, the first national election in which suburban residents constituted a plurality of the electorate, opinion surveys clearly identified Nixon as the status quo candidate regarding race relations, the overwhelming choice of white voters who endorsed equal opportunity in the abstract but opposed most of the specific remedial policies necessary to tackle historical structures of racial discrimination. Nixon's temperate rhetoric on civil rights became a crucial element in securing a narrow plurality of what political scientists called the "tripartite southern electorate," divided almost evenly among the GOP base in the middle-class suburbs, the Wallace supporters in the rural and working-class precincts, and the Humphrey coalition of white liberals and almost all black voters. Nixon carried the critical states of the Upper South with a much more substantial 45 percent plurality, powered by wide margins of victory in the new white-collar subdivisions of metropolitan regions such as Charlotte and Richmond.[10]

The midterm elections of 1970 demonstrated the political independence of the middle-class suburbs and the intellectual bankruptcy of the "southern strategy" in the electoral climate of the Sunbelt South. Following the calculus of Kevin Phillips, who argued that the backlash against racial liberalism created a unique opportunity to unite the Wallace and Nixon voters in a cohesive conservative majority, White House strategists turned the off-year elections into a top-down experiment to determine whether the exploitation of racial passions could overcome the class and geographic divisions of the white southern electorate. The Nixon administration abandoned its previous suburban strategy and embraced a genuine "southern strategy" as both a defensive maneuver to neutralize George Wallace and an ill-fated offensive to expand the presidential base into a GOP majority in southern state politics. Between 1968 and 1970, as the pace and scope of court-ordered school desegregation accelerated dramatically throughout the South, the administration responded by aligning the Republican party with reactionary politicians who resurrected the rhetoric of massive resistance and preached defiance of the federal judiciary. The White House aggressively recruited and financed candidates across the region, rejecting moderate Republicans for segregationist former Democrats, many of whom had switched parties as "Goldwater Republicans." In Virginia, Nixon operatives destroyed the grassroots coalition of black voters and suburban moderates assembled by Linwood Holton, the liberal Republican governor, and channeled party support to the independent candidacy of right-wing Senator Harry F. Byrd, Jr. In Florida, the administration embraced Claude Kirk, a GOP governor who tried to prevent court-ordered busing by reprising Wallace's infamous stand in the schoolhouse door, and the president appeared personally to tell voters that "it is time to stop kicking the South around." And in South Carolina, in response to segregationist movements in the countryside, the White House championed gubernatorial candidate Albert Watson, a racial demagogue who called on citizens to fight integration with "every means at your disposal."[11]

The 1970 election turned out to be the last stand for massive resistance, the epitaph for explicit race baiting in the regional climate of the New South. The "southern strategy will not work," the longtime liberal activist Charles Morgan warned the White House. "The only way to outflank George Wallace is to go into the Gulf of Mexico." Instead of expanding the party's southern wing, the administration's tactics turned off middle-class voters in the recently developed and normally Republican suburbs, especially white moderates who interpreted racial extremism as a greater threat than court-ordered desegregation to the New South priorities of economic development and quality public schools. The "southern strategy" also galvanized a massive turnout by black voters and opened the door for a modern breed of Democrats known as the "New South Governors." In Florida, Reuben Askew easily defeated the GOP incumbent by rallying black voters and white moderates behind the issues of legal compliance, equal opportunity, and quality education. In South Carolina, John

West won the governorship by denouncing Republican demagoguery, openly courting the black electorate, and reaching out to suburban swing voters with a platform of economic development, quality public schools, and "color-blind" nondiscrimination. "The silent majority said loud and clear that South Carolina will take the high road to progress," West proclaimed after his victory. The reincarnation of southern Democrats as the interracial party of the center held throughout the region, including the elections of Dale Bumpers in Arkansas, Jimmy Carter in Georgia, Lawton Chiles in Florida, and the subsequent emergence of moderate Democratic governors in the Deep South states of Louisiana and Mississippi. The White House had nothing to show for its hard shift to the right in the 1970 election, except for an idiosyncratic success in a heavily financed campaign to unseat liberal Senator Al Gore in Tennessee. The Gallup organization reported that the administration chased "after the wrong group," repelling white-collar professionals and Sunbelt migrants who usually voted Republican without attracting enough Wallace partisans to make up the difference. The Ripon Society, a progressive Republican think tank, observed that the Democrats "stole the center from Nixon" because the Kevin Phillips strategy had "alienated progressive suburbanites from the GOP." "The party must cultivate the moderate parts of the South," Ripon concluded. "Racism will fail, as it has in the past."[12]

The white electorate's rejection of Great Society liberalism during the late 1960s never translated into a conservative governing majority or an enduring Republican realignment. The key lesson of the underappreciated 1970 election cycle is the persistent competitiveness of the two-party system in the American South, not simply during an era of political realignment, but during any era when the center is legitimately contested. The futility of the Nixon administration's "southern strategy" reveals a political truth that New Right strategists have discovered again and again: rural white residents, working-class voters, and affluent suburban professionals do not fit comfortably into a stable political coalition. In the 1972 campaign, a few weeks before he carried forty-nine states, President Nixon told an audience in the Sunbelt metropolis of Atlanta that "it has been suggested that . . . I have a so-called southern strategy. It is not a southern strategy. It is an American strategy. . . . That is what the South believes in and that is what America believes in. . . . We seek what I call a new American majority." The power of this populist vocabulary arose from its ability to transcend divisions between middle-class and working-class white voters—but never more than temporarily. During the three decades following the national disintegration of the New Deal order, both parties have grappled with an unstable class dynamic at the center of their electoral strategies. The Republicans have depended upon the upward mobility facilitated by suburban expansion and Sunbelt development, and they have capitalized on the populist revolts against rights-based liberalism evident in the McGovern disaster of 1972, the Reagan ascendance in the 1980s, and the Gingrich surprise of 1994. The Democratic party has won back working-class defectors during periods of economic turmoil—most notably the Carter election in 1976, the Reagan recession of 1982, and the Clinton victory in 1992—and has also become increasingly attractive to white-collar professionals and suburban swing voters who dislike the social conservatism of the New Right. Neither political party has proved capable of maintaining the allegiance of the broad and elusive group that Richard Nixon labeled the forgotten voters of Middle America. But in the volatile grassroots arena of the 1970s, in the vast realm of political culture that exists beyond the control of top-down strategists, a powerful uprising of the Silent Majority reframed racial policies and subsumed regional differences beneath a national politics of middle-class consciousness.[13]

The Silent Majority

During the 1970s, a grassroots suburban strategy that revolved around a "color-blind" defense of the middle-class rights and residential privileges of the Silent Majority succeeded where the overtly racialized tactics of the top-down "southern strategy" had failed. In the 1968 campaign, Richard Nixon appealed to the white suburban electorate through a combination of racially inclusive imagery and residentially exclusive policies, framed by a populist outreach to the "forgotten Americans" who worked hard and played by the rules. Over the course of the next decade, in response to the civil rights movement's concerted attack on metropolitan patterns of residential segregation and educational inequality, a series of grassroots uprisings in the white-collar suburbs appropriated the populist discourse of the Silent Majority and forced a new class-driven version of "color-blind" politics into the national arena. The collective debut of the Silent Majority came during the summer of 1970, when representatives from antibusing movements throughout the New South suburbs gathered in Atlanta to forge a political alliance called the National Coalition of Concerned Citizens. The leaders of the grassroots revolt included physicians, dentists, attorneys, and other upper-middle-class professionals—the most affluent tier of the white parents and home owners mobilizing under the national banner of the Silent Majority. Claiming a membership of one million supporters of "neighborhood schools" in twenty-seven states, the confederation adopted a "color-blind" stance that demanded political protection for the socioeconomic and residential privileges of the middle-class suburbs. Two weeks later, more than one hundred local activists reconvened in Norfolk to launch a national membership drive, revolving around the constitutional claim that federal courts could not address the "de facto" segregation that allegedly prevailed throughout metropolitan America. The alliance warned that "government tyranny" threatened the tradition of neighborhood schools, denounced President Nixon for failing to keep his campaign promise to prevent "forced busing," and urged supporters to flood the White House and the United States Congress with letters of protest. "We are going on the offensive," promised a Miami Beach attorney named Ellis Rubin. "We are going to organize the largest, most effective lobby this country has ever seen."[14]

The rise of the Silent Majority demonstrates the dynamic interplay between the local and the national in postwar political culture. By the mid-1970s, the grassroots protests of the white-collar suburbs and the top-down reaction of the federal government produced a new public policy framework that reshaped desegregation case law and circumscribed civil rights reform on the metropolitan landscape. The neighborhood-based outbreak of suburban populism also provides a revealing example of the unintended consequences of the growth policies of an activist state filtered through the volatile topography of representative democracy. During the 1970s, the bitter battles over court-ordered busing transcended the traditional struggle over Jim Crow to grapple with a new version of the American Dilemma: the spatial fusion of class and racial inequality embodied in the urban-suburban divide. Millions of white home owners who had achieved a residentially segregated embodiment of the suburban dream, with the assistance of federal subsidies, forcefully rejected the race-conscious agenda of redistributive liberalism as an unconstitutional exercise in social engineering and an un-American violation of free-market principles. The grassroots antibusing movement recast a historical debate over the legal burdens of state-sponsored racial discrimination into an ahistorical defense of meritocratic individualism and family autonomy. This novel refashioning of "color-blind" ideology naturalized pervasive patterns of residential segregation by refusing even to acknowledge the centrality of public policies in the construction of the metropolitan landscape. The collective politics of middle-class consciousness defined "freedom of choice" and "neighborhood schools" as the core privileges of home owner rights and consumer liberties, and rejected as "reverse discrimination" any collective integration remedies or affirmative action mandates designed to provide redress for historical structures of inequality. The mobilization of the Silent Majority ultimately pushed the White House and the Supreme Court to adopt explicit policies of suburban protection that rejected metropolitan remedies for metropolitan inequities and effectively placed residential segregation beyond the reach of constitutional law. The transparent responsiveness of political and judicial institutions to the organized protests of upper-middle-class voters ultimately exempted most affluent suburban neighborhoods from any collective responsibility for the public policies that had simultaneously developed the postwar metropolis and contained the inner-city ghettos.

The New South metropolis of Charlotte, North Carolina, a white-collar banking center with a reputation for racial moderation, became the national test case for large-scale busing between the sprawling suburbs and the crowded ghettos. In the spring of 1969, the National Association for the Advancement of Colored People (NAACP) reopened desegregation litigation based on the pathbreaking contention that the prevailing distinction between "de jure" and "de facto" segregation was artificial, and therefore the Constitution required the school system to take affirmative action to overcome residential patterns shaped by government policies and reinforced by private discrimination. During the Cold War boom, municipal leaders and corporate executives in Charlotte had implemented the national model of residential segregation with the systematic efficiency of the Sunbelt economic blueprint, leveraging federal funds to construct a landscape of spatial apartheid achieved through the twin processes of suburban expansion and urban redevelopment. Between 1950 and 1970, when the metropolitan population doubled to include more than 350,000 residents, almost all white-collar families drawn into the corporate economy moved into newly developed subdivisions located to the south and east of the downtown business district. During the same period, the municipal government displaced more than 10,000 black residents through federal urban renewal and highway construction programs and relocated almost all of these families in public housing projects invariably located in the opposite quadrant of the city. Official planning policies meticulously separated the middle-class white suburbs of southeast Charlotte from the overwhelmingly black neighborhoods of northwest Charlotte through industrial zoning buffers and interstate highway placement. By the time of the busing litigation, about 96 percent of the African-American population lived in the highly segregated northwest sector, and more than 14,000 black students attended completely isolated public schools. In April 1969, in *Swann v. Charlotte-Mecklenburg*, district judge James McMillan issued an unprecedented and explosive remedy: the two-way exchange of students from the black neighborhoods of the central city and the white subdivisions on the metropolitan fringe, a comprehensive busing formula designed to integrate every facility throughout the consolidated metropolitan school system.[15]

Tens of thousands of middle-class white families immediately joined forces in the Concerned Parents Association (CPA), a powerful grassroots organization based in the outer-ring suburbs of southeast Charlotte. From the beginning, the CPA rallied around a "color-blind" platform of middle-class respectability and insisted that opposition to busing had nothing to do with racial prejudice or segregationist preference. The accidental activists in this suburban social movement consisted of young professional couples and white-collar home owners who had moved to Charlotte from across the nation, settled in recently developed subdivisions marked by racial exclusivity and upward mobility, and cast more than 70 percent of their ballots for Richard Nixon in the 1968 presidential election. Tom Harris, an insurance executive who headed the CPA, explained that the membership did not represent either right-wing ideologues or the "upper crust" of the city but rather "essentially the middle class, and we have every intention of maintaining the proper dignity and respect." The petitions circulated by the group defended the rights of hardworking families who had purchased homes based on "proximity to schools and churches of their choice" and condemned busing as a violation of the equal protection clause of the Fourteenth Amendment and the original spirit of the *Brown* decision. "I am not opposed to integration in any way," claimed one suburban father during a CPA demonstration. "But I was 'affluent' enough to buy a home near the school where I wanted my children to go. And I pay taxes to pay for it. They can bring in anybody they like to that school, but I don't want my children taken away." Another member of the group warned that the "moderate majority . . . has civil rights too . . . and has tried to be very understanding, but we don't like having our feet stepped on repeatedly and we can't be expected to keep turning the other cheek forever." Identifying themselves as parents and taxpayers from the middle-class mainstream, the suburban populists in the CPA co-opted the rhetoric of the civil rights movement in their promises to take the political offensive in order to secure the defense of their homes and families. "The people of Charlotte have had it with Judge McMillan and liberal federal courts," warned Dr. Don Roberson, a physician who served as vice chairman of the organization. "The unorganized silent majority is about ready to take to the streets with tactics that have seemed to work so effectively for the vocal minority groups."[16]

The antibusing movement in Charlotte represented a populist revolt of the center, as white-collar parents from secure suburban neighborhoods responded to the racial crisis of metropolitan desegregation through a "color-blind" politics of middle-class consciousness. "I couldn't believe such a thing could happen in America," Don Roberson explained. "So many of us made the biggest investment of our lives—our homes—primarily on the basis of their location with regard to schools. It seemed like an absurdity that anyone could tell us where to send our children." In a way, *Swann* plaintiff James Polk agreed with this class analysis of Charlotte's racial showdown: "We were smacking against the whole American dream. To whites, that meant pull yourself up by your bootstraps, buy a nice home and two cars, live in a nice neighborhood and go to a nice church, send your kids to the appropriate school. . . . We understood that a lot of white people would raise holy hell." During Charlotte's protracted busing crisis, the CPA platform never acknowledged the judicial finding that federal and municipal policies had shaped the methodical patterns of residential segregation that produced school segregation. The white parents who joined the antibusing movement thought of the location of their homes and the proximity of quality schools as nothing more and nothing less than the individual rewards for their willingness to work hard and make sacrifices for their children's future. This philosophy of middle-class accomplishment obscured the centrality of the state in the process of suburbanization and finessed the internal contradictions in the meritocratic ethos through an unapologetic defense of the rights of children to enjoy the fruits of their parents' success. The futuristic ethos of the white suburbs simply did not address the question of whether the black families systematically relocated by city planners to the northwest quadrant enjoyed "freedom of choice" to live in the upscale neighborhoods and attend the excellent schools of southeast Charlotte. The CPA's "anti-bus hysteria [seems] more mistaken than racist," observed one civil rights activist, in the context of fifteen years of municipal development and federal policy based on the "hypocrisy of blinding itself to the 'de jure' nature of most 'de facto' segregation." The federal government had permitted "leaders in a place like Charlotte to convince themselves or kid themselves into thinking that, even as they continued the process of building a ghetto and a system of segregated schools, they were in compliance with the law against segregation."[17]

During the winter and spring of 1970, as antibusing movements spread from the suburban South to metropolitan centers such as Denver and Los Angeles, the Concerned Parents Association pioneered the emergence of the Silent Majority on the national political landscape. After taking control of the local board of education, the antibusing movement in Charlotte embraced a compromise position that reluctantly accepted one-way busing of black students to suburban facilities but fiercely rejected the transportation of white students away from their neighborhood schools. When the district court set a firm deadline for two-way busing, the CPA immediately demanded White House intervention in the judicial process. CPA leaders promptly secured private audiences with senior members of the executive branch, and the foot soldiers of the movement sent thousands of letters and telegrams to President Nixon. One suburban physician, identifying himself as a "concerned member of the silent majority which has possibly remained silent too long," asked the president why prosperous communities should be punished simply because their residents worked hard and bought respectable homes in safe neighborhoods near quality public schools. After clarifying that his views had "nothing to do with race or integration," this father insisted that the "thought that this course is un-American is simply untenable." A married couple from an upper-middle-class subdivision informed the president that they supported racial integration and believed that high-achieving black students deserved to attend the best white schools, but warned that two-way busing would drive away affluent families and destroy public education. Another resident of southeast Charlotte, explaining that he was neither a crackpot nor a segregationist, denounced busing as reverse discrimination and asked Nixon "to come to the rescue of the silent majority who . . . has been pushed about as far as it will tolerate." "As a member of the silent majority," yet another Charlotte parent declared, "I have never asked what anyone in government or this country could do for me; but rather have kept my mouth shut, paid my taxes and basically asked to be left alone. . . . I think it is time the law abiding, tax paying white middle class started looking to the federal government for something besides oppression."[18]

The suburban uprising of the Silent Majority established the busing controversy as an urgent and unavoidable crisis in national politics. The White House quickly responded to the pleas and demands of upper-middle-class voters with a major policy statement on school desegregation, released under President Nixon's signature in March 1970. The address attempted to stake out the middle ground by implicitly rejecting the recent Supreme Court mandate to eliminate racial segregation "root and branch," but offering no escape hatch for the segregationist movements based in the rural South. Instead, in a direct appeal to suburban voters throughout the nation, the president adopted the "color-blind" framework of the grassroots antibusing movement and defended an inviolable right to attend neighborhood schools even if they reflected residential segregation. In accord with his vocal constituents, Nixon argued that most school segregation in both the metropolitan South and the urban North resulted from "de facto" market forces beyond the jurisdiction of the federal courts. While civil rights groups expressed outrage, the White House promised to intervene against the comprehensive busing precedent in the Charlotte litigation, which clearly represented the primary target of the president's address. The administration position effectively endorsed a national antibusing standard that revolved around a laissez-faire approach to residential segregation and an overt defense of the spatial and socioeconomic privileges of middle-class suburbs throughout the country. A political agenda presented in constitutional wrapping, this policy represented a calculated effort to shift the heat for desegregation enforcement from the executive branch to the federal judiciary, and a prescient recognition that suburban hostility toward racial busing transcended partisan, class, and regional boundaries.[19]

Court-ordered busing in Charlotte became a conspicuous exception to the national rule, because the prior existence of a metropolitan school system provided the leverage for a suburban remedy that achieved stable racial desegregation through a social-class-based integration resolution. In the case of *Swann v. Charlotte-Mecklenburg* (1971), the United States Supreme Court rejected the "color-blind" defense and approved busing as a legitimate remedy for state-sponsored racial discrimination. While the CPA soon faded as a grassroots force, the antibusing leaders on the school board adopted an unstable formula that exempted the affluent suburbs of southeast Charlotte from two-way integration and assigned working-class white students from residentially transitional neighborhoods to the historically black schools. After several years of "white flight" caused by the foreseeable flaws in this plan, Judge McMillan ordered the school district to prevent racial resegregation through an affirmative action commitment to "socioeconomic integration." In the most significant feature of the new approach, the board reluctantly agreed to reassign white students from the upper-middle-class suburbs to stabilize school enrollment in the black residential areas of northwest Charlotte. By including every section of the school district in the comprehensive integration formula, the emphasis on class and geographic fairness defused the controversy over the preferential treatment of southeast Charlotte and removed the incentive for white families to relocate to the suburban neighborhoods that had previously escaped two-way busing. The favorable conditions created by the class-based busing compromise eventually turned Charlotte-Mecklenburg into a national success story, a New South showcase that boasted a greater degree of racial integration and a lower percentage of "white flight" than most other large cities in the nation. Although the Charlotte example illustrates that an expansive metropolitan remedy could overcome the organized resistance of suburban home owners, by the end of the 1970s a powerful mythology had emerged that court-ordered busing caused the decline of urban school systems. This political consensus ignores the necessity of metropolitan strategies to stabilize racial integration and misapplies the lessons of cities such as Boston, where secure suburban spectators watched struggling white communities fight reassignment to poor black neighborhoods. "To understand reactionary populism," Ronald Formisano has concluded, "we must recognize the role of class and its consequences in the formation of public policy, particularly policies designed to alleviate racial injustice. If class is ignored, as it was in Boston and consistently tends to be in dealing with desegregation, then those policies have little chance of success."[20]

The antibusing movement in Charlotte lost the local battle but won the national war. In the wake of *Swann*, the NAACP launched a campaign to overcome urban school segregation through city-suburban integration formulas and metropolitan consolidation remedies. During the same period, President Nixon appointed four justices to the Supreme Court, and the grassroots resistance of the Silent Majority converged with the top-down defense of suburban autonomy. In 1972, as an organized antibusing movement roiled the Virginia capital of Richmond, the Fourth Circuit Court of Appeals overturned a metropolitan integration plan that combined the black-majority city schools with two overwhelmingly white suburban districts. A deadlocked Supreme Court affirmed the appellate ruling that the "last vestiges of state-imposed segregation have been wiped out," and the striking conclusion that the "root causes of the concentration of blacks in the inner cities of America are simply not known." In 1974, in the landmark case of *Milliken v. Bradley*, a narrow majority on the Burger Court invalidated a three-county busing formula designed to stem "white flight" from the city schools of Detroit by including the entire metropolitan region in the quest for stable integration and equal opportunity. The majority opinion in *Milliken* immunized most suburbs throughout the nation from the burdens and opportunities of meaningful integration and foreshadowed the hypersegregation by race and income in large urban school districts across the United States. In a scathing dissent, Thurgood Marshall highlighted the uncomfortable truth that the judicial accommodation of political resistance had transformed residential segregation into a historical wrong without a constitutional remedy. Alluding to the broad antibusing movement in metropolitan Detroit, which ranged from the blue-collar subdivisions of Macomb County to the wealthy island suburbs of Grosse Pointe, Marshall portrayed the majority decision as "a reflection of a perceived public mood that we have gone far enough in enforcing the Constitution's guarantee of equal justice. . . . In the short run, it may seem to be the easier course to allow our great metropolitan areas to be divided up each into two cities—one white, the other black—but it is a course, I predict, our people will ultimately reject."[21]

The New Metropolitan Dilemma

The grassroots revolt of the Silent Majority accelerated the reconfiguration of national politics around programs to protect the rights and privileges of the affluent suburbs and policies to reproduce the postindustrial economy of the corporate Sunbelt. Since the 1970s, the bipartisan battle for the volatile center has increasingly pursued shifting groups of middle-class swing voters in the sprawling metropolises of an increasingly suburban nation. The Reagan coalition in the 1980s included the white-collar home owners who launched the tax revolts in southern California, the corporate Republicans in wealthy Northeast counties such as Westchester and Fairfield and Bergen, the blue-collar populists in the Rust Belt suburbs of the Midwest, and the evangelical Protestants whose organizational base rests in Sunbelt "edge cities" such as Colorado Springs and Virginia Beach. The resurrection of the "New Democrats" during the 1990s revolved around an operational suburban strategy of social and fiscal moderation that included targeted entitlement programs for "soccer moms" and working women, cultural tolerance for suburban moderates alienated by the New Right, probusiness management of the "new economy" shaped by the Sunbelt boom, and Democratic Leadership Council policies selected for their acceptability in middle-class focus groups. In the 1992 election, the first in which suburban voters represented an outright majority, Bill Clinton launched his populist "third way" with an unattributed homage to the Nixon era and the Silent Majority: a "campaign for the future, for the forgotten hard-working middle class families of America." The new century ushers in an "emerging Democratic majority" in American politics, according to the leading strategists of the New Democratic movement, because while the Republicans "scour the coal pits of West Virginia or the boarded up steel mills of Youngstown for converts, [the Democrats understand that] America's future lies in places like Silicon Valley and North Carolina's Research Triangle."[22]

The United States became politically and geographically a definitively suburban nation during the final decades of the twentieth century, increasingly dominated by the priorities and anxieties of voters in the broad middle-class spectrum, persistently unreceptive to policy initiatives designed to address the structural disadvantages facing central cities and impoverished communities. In 1968, the Kerner Report, issued by the National Advisory Commission on Civil Disorders, asked the residents of the booming suburbs to rethink the "color-blind" ideology of middle-class innocence and ponder a controversial interpretation of their own history: "What white Americans have never fully understood—but what the Negro can never forget—is that white society is deeply implicated in the ghetto. White institutions created it, white institutions maintain it, and white society condones it." The Kerner Report issued a stark warning: "To continue present policies is to make permanent the division of our country into two societies; one, largely Negro and poor, located in the central cities; the other, predominantly white and affluent, located in the suburbs and outlying areas." Court-ordered busing soon emerged as the most hotly contested remedy for this new metropolitan dilemma: the fusion of residential segregation, suburban political autonomy, and geographic stratification by race and class. But ultimately, the default reliance on the NAACP and the judicial branch to devise and implement the nation's desegregation policies illustrated the absence of a political coalition willing to address the suburban synthesis of racial inequality and class segregation, or even to acknowledge that the spatial landscape of metro-politan fragmentation and the middle-class ideology of meritocratic individualism constituted a "New American Dilemma" at all. If the Kerner Report represented the last gasp of the progressive imagination during the era of the Great Society, the ensuing decades have demonstrated the inability and the unwillingness of both political parties to confront the metropolitan boundaries and class constraints placed on the reach of race-conscious liberalism by the grassroots revolt of the Silent Majority.[23]

The federal government never launched a sustained assault on the structural forces undergirding residential segregation, and the persistent suburban resistance to collective remedies for educational and housing inequality has spanned regional boundaries and partisan affiliations. Despite the explosive impact of court-ordered busing, the transportation remedy addressed only the symptoms and not the causes of school segregation in metropolitan regions: the public policies that simultaneously constructed the middle-class suburbs and contained the urban ghettos. For a brief moment in the late 1960s and early 1970s, the United States Congress contemplated an open-housing policy that moved beyond individual-based remedies, and the Department of Housing and Urban Development (HUD) considered a plan to withhold federal highway funds from suburbs that employed zoning policies to ban low-income housing. Organized protests erupted throughout metropolitan Detroit, rumored to be the target of a residential integration pilot program, and pundit Kevin Phillips issued a shrill warning that federal bureaucrats planned to "produce a racial balance in America's suburbs." The White House promptly curtailed the HUD initiative, and President Nixon personally reassured voters that "forced integration in the suburbs is not in the national interest." In June 1971, the administration released a major policy statement on "equal housing opportunity" that extended the same protection to suburban neighborhoods that the previous antibusing manifesto had extended to suburban neighborhood schools. Although he promised prosecution of individual violations of open-housing law, Nixon drew a distinction between (illegal) racial discrimination and (legal) class segregation, and guaranteed that the federal government would not "seek to impose economic integration" or destabilize suburban neighborhoods "with a flood of low-income families." The NAACP responded with a legal assault on suburban zoning policies, but a series of Supreme Court decisions effectively eliminated the ability of civil rights plaintiffs to bring class-action litigation against residential segregation in suburban municipalities. The Burger Court formalized the doctrine that the Constitution permitted state-sponsored "economic discrimination" in *San Antonio v. Rodriguez* (1973), which overturned a district panel ruling that massive funding disparities in adjacent school districts violated equal protection guarantees.[24]

In the absence of a federal commitment to tackle metropolitan structures of "economic segregation" and residential inequality, civil rights
organizations and low-income plaintiffs have increasingly turned to state
courts to challenge discriminatory features such as suburban zoning policies and school funding formulas. In the *Mount Laurel* cases of the 1970s,
the New Jersey Supreme Court agreed that exclusionary zoning violated
the equal protection clause of the state constitution and ordered suburban
municipalities to provide a "fair share" affordable housing remedy. The
political backlash began immediately—grassroots resistance by affluent
neighborhoods, obstructionist tactics by the legislature—and a powerful
wedge issue emerged for the suburban Republicans who gained control
of the state government. While developers in New Jersey have built numerous affordable housing units, the litigation has lasted for more than
three decades and yet has barely dented the prevailing patterns of residential segregation. A concurrent class-action lawsuit securing court-ordered
equalization of school financing galvanized a fierce "color-blind" revolt
by upper-middle-class residents of New Jersey's wealthy suburbs, which
systematically delayed legal compliance and denied any good-faith obligation to achieve equal opportunity. The chastened Democrats in New Jersey regained power only through reinvention as a culturally liberal, fiscally responsible party that will hold the line on property taxes and defend
suburban quality of life at all costs. While the political bellwethers of New
Jersey and Connecticut, which also resisted court-ordered school funding
equalization, began trending away from the GOP during the 1990s, it is
not incidental but intrinsic to the electoral strategy of the "New Democrats" that they represent the two most racially segregated, income-stra-
tified, corporate-clustered, and demographically suburbanized states in
the nation.[25]

In an era that demonstrates both the vitality and the limitations of the
political center, the two most ambitious proposals to address the lingering
inequities of the metropolitan landscape both revolve around explicit
class-over-race appeals to the self-interest of the suburban majority. The
"Hidden Agenda" developed by William Julius Wilson distinguishes between the historical racial discrimination that created the urban underclass and the primacy of economic structures such as deindustrializa-
tion and a "spatial mismatch" between employment and residence in the
contemporary perpetuation of cycles of poverty. In the context of rapid
suburbanization by millions of minority Americans, and the collapse of
moral authority in the liberal discourse surrounding racial inequality, Wilson advocates superseding race-specific individualist remedies with a macroeconomic agenda that appeals to a broad alliance of working-class and
middle-class citizens through universal programs such as a full employment policy, federal child care, guaranteed health insurance, and af-

fordable housing subsidies. The "metropolitanist" platform advanced by the Brookings Institution and other regionalist policy makers revolves around capitalizing on the current sprawl crisis to rethink the traditional urban-suburban dichotomy and mobilize a new political coalition behind public policies that provide mutual benefits to all metropolitan residents and forge new structural links between the core and the fringe. As traffic and school crowding have replaced crime and taxes as the primary anxieties in the sprawling exurbs, and as the racial and socioeconomic challenges of central cities have penetrated the inner-ring suburbs, metropolitanism seeks to connect smart growth and social justice in a spatial agenda of mass transit, mixed-income housing, fiscal equity, and land-use reform. If middle-class citizens accept the need for metropolitan institutions to address the quality-of-life crisis caused by suburban sprawl, then perhaps policy makers can use regional structures as leverage to overcome fragmented political governance and ameliorate persistent patterns of employment discrimination, housing segregation, and educational inequality.[26]

A comprehensive assessment of the grassroots ferment of the political center and the metropolitan dilemmas of the contemporary landscape requires attention to the population shift to the middle-class suburbs and the power shift to the Sunbelt economy. For more than three decades, from the collective revolt of the Silent Majority in the 1970s to the bipartisan accommodation of middle-class consciousness in the 1990s, suburban home owners and their political and judicial champions have naturalized residential segregation and defended metropolitan inequality through an explicit discourse of socioeconomic privilege and free-market meritocracy. For just as long, civil rights activists and progressive scholars have challenged the foundational mythology of suburban racial innocence and the "color-blind" ethos of middle-class individualism by exposing the de jure roots of almost all cases of allegedly "de facto" residential segregation—a historical verdict based on overwhelming evidence that has proved to be singularly unpersuasive in the political and legal spheres. The dominant ethos of American suburbia has always idealized the present and celebrated the future at the expense of any critical reflection on the past. The search for new directions in political history and new approaches in public policy should begin by expanding traditional models of analysis through a metropolitan framework that confronts instead of obscures the pervasive politics of class in the suburban strategies of the volatile center.

Notes

1. Matthew D. Lassiter, *The Silent Majority: Suburban Politics in the Sunbelt South* (Princeton, N.J.: Princeton University Press, forthcoming).

2. Kenneth T. Jackson, *Crabgrass Frontier: The Suburbanization of the United States* (New York: Oxford University Press, 1985); Alan Brinkley, *The End of Reform: New Deal Liberalism in Recession and War* (New York: Alfred A. Knopf, 1995); Robert M. Collins, *More: The Politics of Economic Growth in Postwar America* (New York: Oxford University Press, 2000); Bruce J. Schulman, *From Cotton Belt to Sunbelt: Federal Policy, Economic Development, and the Transformation of the South, 1938–1980* (New York: Oxford University Press, 1991); Joel Garreau, *Edge City: Life on the New Frontier* (New York: Doubleday, 1991).

3. Carl Abbott, *The New Urban America: Growth and Politics in Sunbelt Cities* (Chapel Hill: University of North Carolina Press, 1981); Peter Schrag, *Paradise Lost: California's Experience, America's Future* (Berkeley: University of California Press, 1998); Bruce J. Schulman, *The Seventies: The Great Shift in American Culture, Society, and Politics* (New York: Free Press, 2001).

4. Arnold R. Hirsch, *Making the Second Ghetto: Race and Housing in Chicago, 1940–1960* (Cambridge: Cambridge University Press, 1983); J. Anthony Lukas, *Common Ground: A Turbulent Decade in the Lives of Three American Families* (New York: Alfred A. Knopf, 1985); Jonathan Rieder, *Canarsie: The Jews and Italians of Brooklyn against Liberalism* (Cambridge, Mass.: Harvard University Press, 1985); Ronald P. Formisano, *Boston against Busing: Race, Class, and Ethnicity in the 1960s and 1970s* (Chapel Hill: University of North Carolina Press, 1991); Thomas J. Sugrue, *The Origins of the Urban Crisis: Race and Inequality in Postwar Detroit* (Princeton, N.J.: Princeton University Press, 1996).

5. Lisa McGirr, *Suburban Warriors: The Origins of the New American Right* (Princeton, N.J.: Princeton University Press, 2001); John A. Andrew III, *The Other Side of the Sixties: Young Americans for Freedom and the Rise of Conservative Politics* (New Brunswick, N.J.: Rutgers University Press, 1997); Mary C. Brennan, *Turning Right in the Sixties: The Conservative Capture of the GOP* (Chapel Hill: University of North Carolina Press, 1995); Rick Perlstein, *Before the Storm: Barry Goldwater and the Unmaking of the American Consensus* (New York: Hill and Wang, 2001).

6. For scholarship that examines the political center and investigates the evolution of class politics in contemporary America, see Mike Davis, *City of Quartz: Excavating the Future in Los Angeles* (London: Verso, 1990); Alan Wolfe, *One Nation, after All: What Middle-Class Americans Really Think About: God, Country, Family, Racism, Welfare, Immigration, Homosexuality, Work, the Right, the Left, and Each Other* (New York: Viking Press, 1998); Michael Kazin, *The Populist Persuasion: An American History* (New York: Basic Books, 1995).

7. Dan T. Carter, *The Politics of Rage: George Wallace, the New Conservatism, and the Transformation of American Politics* (New York: Simon and Schuster, 1995); Carter, *From George Wallace to Newt Gingrich: Race in the Conservative Counterrevolution, 1963–1994* (Baton Rouge: Louisiana State University Press, 1996); Peter Applebome, *Dixie Rising: How the South Is Shaping American Values, Politics, and Culture* (New York: Harcourt Brace and Co., 1996); Thomas Byrne Edsall with Mary D. Edsall, *Chain Reaction: The Impact of Race, Rights, and Taxes on American Politics* (New York: W. W. Norton, 1992). Kevin P. Phillips accurately recognized the economic significance of the Sunbelt but misinterpreted

the dynamics of political realignment in his first and still widely accepted book, *The Emerging Republican Majority* (New Rochelle: Arlington House, 1969).

8. Earl Black and Merle Black, *Politics and Society in the South* (Cambridge, Mass.: Harvard University Press, 1987); Black and Black, *The Vital South: How Presidents Are Elected* (Cambridge, Mass.: Harvard University Press, 1992); Numan V. Bartley, *The New South: 1945–1980* (Baton Rouge: Louisiana State University Press, 1995); Dewey W. Grantham, *The Life and Death of the Solid South: A Political History* (Lexington: University Press of Kentucky, 1988); Jack Bass and Walter De Vries, *The Transformation of Southern Politics: Social Change and Political Consequence since 1945*, 2d ed. (Athens: University of Georgia Press, 1995); Schulman, *Cotton Belt to Sunbelt.*

9. Richard M. Nixon, "Acceptance Speech," August 8, 1968, in *Campaign Speeches of American Presidential Candidates, 1948–1984*, ed. Gregory Bush (New York: Frederick Ungar, 1985), 153–63; *Nixon/Wallace 1968 TV Election Spots* (International Historic Films, 1985); *Charlotte Observer*, September 12–13, 1968.

10. *Charlotte Observer*, September 12–13, 1968; Richard M. Scammon and Ben J. Wattenberg, *The Real Majority* (New York: Coward-McCann, 1970); Numan V. Bartley and Hugh D. Graham, *Southern Elections: County and Precinct Data, 1950–1972* (Baton Rouge: Louisiana State University Press, 1978); Numan V. Bartley and Hugh D. Graham, *Southern Politics and the Second Reconstruction* (Baltimore: Johns Hopkins University Press, 1975), 126–35.

11. Lassiter, *Silent Majority*, chap. 10.

12. "New Day A'Coming in the South," *Time* (May 31, 1971): 14–20; *New York Times*, February 15, 1970; *Washington Post*, November 6–8, 1970; *Richmond Times-Dispatch*, July 23, 1970; Bartley and Graham, *Southern Politics and the Second Reconstruction*, 136–63.

13. Jonathan Rieder, "The Rise of the 'Silent Majority,' " in *The Rise and Fall of the New Deal Order, 1930–1980*, eds. Steve Fraser and Gary Gerstle (Princeton, N.J.: Princeton University Press, 1989), 243–68; Earl Black and Merle Black, *The Rise of Southern Republicans* (Cambridge, Mass.: Harvard University Press, 2002). Nixon speech reprinted in Harry S. Dent, *The Prodigal South Returns to Power* (New York: John Wiley and Sons, 1978), 171–74.

14. *Atlanta Constitution*, August 31, 1970; *Charlotte Observer*, August 31, 1970; *Norfolk Virginian-Pilot*, September 13, 1970.

15. "Opinion and Order," April 23, 1969, pp. 285a–323a, "Transcript of Hearing," March 10, 13, 1969, pp. 1a–64a, 173a–219a, U.S. Supreme Court Records and Briefs, *Swann v. Charlotte-Mecklenburg*, 402 U.S. 1; Paul Leonard, "Research Report," March 1970, box 9, Julius L. Chambers Papers, University of North Carolina at Charlotte Library.

16. CPA, "A Struggle for Freedom Is Coming" (1970), CPA, "Beverly Woods Bulletin," February 26, 1970, box 14, Fred Alexander Papers, University of North Carolina at Charlotte Library; *Charlotte Observer*, November 6, 1968, May 3, 19, July 8, December 10, 1969; *Charlotte News*, May 3, 10, 1969; William Overhultz interview, August 20, 1997, Charlotte, N.C.; Sharon McGinn interview, August 20, 1997, Charlotte, N.C.

17. *Charlotte Observer,* July 12, 1975; Pat Watters, "Charlotte, North Carolina: 'A Little Child Shall Lead Them,' " in *The South and Her Children: School Desegregation, 1970–1971* (Atlanta: Southern Regional Council, 1971), 29–33.

18. Robert M. Diggs to Richard Nixon, January 31, 1970, Thomas E. Condor to Nixon, February 5, 1970, Mr. and Mrs. Isaac L. Falkner to Nixon, February 2, 1970, James E. McDavid, Jr., to Charles Jonas, February 5, 1970, series 1.1, folder 494, Charles Raper Jonas Papers, Southern History Collection, University of North Carolina at Chapel Hill.

19. *New York Times,* March 25–26, 1970; Stanley M. Elan, ed. *A Decade of Gallup Polls of Attitudes toward Education, 1969–1978* (Bloomington, Ind.: Phi Delta Kappa, 1978).

20. *Swann v. Charlotte-Mecklenburg Board of Education,* 402 U.S. 1 (1971); Lassiter, *Silent Majority,* chap. 7–8; Gary Orfield, *Must We Bus? Segregated Schools and National Policy* (Washington, D.C.: Brookings Institution Press, 1978); Jennifer L. Hochschild, *The New American Dilemma: Liberal Democracy and School Desegregation* (New Haven, Conn.: Yale University Press, 1984); Formisano, *Boston against Busing,* 237–38.

21. *Bradley v. School Board of City of Richmond et al.,* 462 F. 2d 1058 (1972); *School Board of City of Richmond v. State Board of Education of Virginia,* 412 U.S. 92 (1973); *Milliken v. Bradley,* 41 L Ed 2d 1069 (1974); Eleanor P. Wolf, *Trial and Error: The Detroit School Segregation Case* (Detroit: Wayne State University Press, 1981); Gary Orfield and Susan E. Eaton, eds., *Dismantling Desegregation: The Quiet Reversal of* Brown v. Board of Education (New York: New Press, 1996).

22. "Suburbs Rule: How the Suburban Majority Is Changing America," *New York Times Magazine* (April 9, 2000); Nicholas Lemann, "The New American Consensus: Government of, by, and for the Comfortable," *New York Times Magazine* (November 1, 1998): 37–42; Thomas Marc Cooper, "God and Man in Colorado Springs," *The Nation* (January 2, 1995): 9–12; William Schneider, "The Suburban Century Begins," *Atlantic Monthly* (July 1992): 33–44; Stanley B. Greenberg, *Middle-Class Dreams: The Politics and Power of the New American Majority,* rev. ed. (New Haven, Conn.: Yale University Press, 1996), 182 (first quotation); John B. Judis and Ruy Teixeira, "Majority Rules: The Coming Democratic Dominance," *The New Republic* (August 5 and 12, 2002), 18–23 (second quotation).

23. *Report of the National Advisory Commission on Civil Disorders* (New York: New York Times Co., 1968), 1–2; John Charles Boger and Judith Welch Wegner, eds., *Race, Poverty, and American Cities* (Chapel Hill: University of North Carolina Press, 1996); Douglas S. Massey and Nancy A. Denton, *American Apartheid: Segregation and the Making of the Underclass* (Cambridge, Mass.: Harvard University Press, 1993).

24. "Battle to Open the Suburbs: New Attack on Zoning Laws," *U.S. News & World Report* (June 22, 1970): 39–40; "Furor over a Drive to Integrate the Suburbs," *U.S. News & World Report* (August 10, 1970), 23–24; *New York Times,* June 3, November 11, 1970, June 12, 1971; *Washington Post,* November 6, 1970; *Warth v. Seldin,* 422 U.S. 490 (1975); *San Antonio v. Rodriguez,* 411 U.S. 1 (1973).

25. David L. Kirp, John P. Dwyer, and Larry A. Rosenthal, *Our Town: Race, Housing, and the Soul of Suburbia* (New Brunswick, N.J.: Rutgers University Press, 1995); Jonathan Kozol, *Savage Inequalities: Children in America's Schools* (New York: HarperPerennial, 1992); *New York Times*, August 19, November 8, 2001; *Newark Star-Ledger*, November 7, 2001.

26. William Julius Wilson, *The Truly Disadvantaged: The Inner City, the Underclass, and Public Policy* (Chicago: University of Chicago Press, 1997); Bruce Katz and Jennifer Bradley, "Divided We Sprawl," *Atlantic Monthly* (December 1999): 26–42; Myron Orfield, *American Metropolitics: The New Suburban Reality* (Washington, D.C.: Brookings Institution Press, 2002).

Chapter Fourteen

FROM HARTZ TO TOCQUEVILLE

SHIFTING THE FOCUS FROM LIBERALISM TO

DEMOCRACY IN AMERICA

James T. Kloppenberg

EMOCRACY IN AMERICA has been a contest among diverse groups of people sharing neither common convictions nor common aspirations. Disagreements over issues as basic as salvation, slavery, and sovereignty date from the arrival of English settlers in North America. Although the impulse to identify an essential and enduring American ethos has persisted ever since, the evidence of struggle has become irresistible. Designating any specific set of commitments as genuinely or distinctively "American" no longer seems convincing. The chapters in this volume emphasize both the depth of the battles that have shaped our national political culture and the contingency of the outcomes. They demonstrate why students of American political history should renounce efforts to characterize as definitive a particular unchanging set of animating substantive values.

In the context of these chapters, which illustrate the uncertain, open-ended, and provisional nature of the apparent triumphs (and defeats) in American public life, I undertake here a ground-clearing exercise. By examining in some detail the arguments that the political scientist Louis Hartz advanced in his influential volume *The Liberal Tradition in America* (1955), I want to show why scholars who study American political history should trade in the tarnished notion of an American liberal tradition for the richer insights available from a focus on struggles over democracy in America.

I do not intend to minimize the importance of such liberal ideals as individual autonomy, representative government, and toleration of diversity. To the contrary, taking such ideals seriously is indispensable to the historical study of American culture. I want only to insist that liberalism historically has included such ideals (the "virtues of liberalism," as I have called them elsewhere). Liberalism should not be understood merely as the self-interested assertion of the right to own property. Moreover, in American history such liberal ideals have coexisted and interacted with others drawn from quite different religious, ethnic, and political traditions. In other words, liberalism has been one among a number of strands in American public life.[1]

Nor do I propose to replace a one-dimensional conception of liberalism with an equally unsatisfying one-dimensional conception of democracy; to the contrary, democracy provides an attractive analytical framework precisely because it highlights the ceaseless wrangling—the deep disagreements over procedures as well as principles—that has marked American history. Focusing on democracy need not imply any particular teleology. Although it is true that early-twentieth-century progressive historians tended to lionize "the people" and demonize "the interests," such a simple Manichean model distorts the more complex historical reality these chapters illuminate. Neither the masses nor the moneyed have played the parts written for them in such simple-minded morality tales. Instead the combatants discussed in these chapters fought, and continue to fight, sometimes in quite unexpected ways and sometimes by forging odd alliances, as bitterly over rules as over results. The most radical and profound truth of popular sovereignty—one of the core principles of democracy— is that it puts everything up for grabs. This volume illustrates that the temporary outcomes of political struggles have generated not only endless challenges from the defeated but sometimes preemptive strikes from winners who feared the outcome of the next battle. Although I insist on the inadequacy of the idea of a "liberal consensus," I do not seek to put in its place an equally creaky notion of "democratic conflict" premised on assumptions about class, race, or gender antagonisms. The historical record is more complicated—and more fascinating.

In part from dissatisfaction with a fractured narrative and in part from a yearning to understand those on the right or the left who have been dismissed as "un-American" by scholars or by popular perception, American historians are returning to the study of politics. In part from dissatisfaction with behaviorism and rational choice theory and in part from a yearning to understand the relation between institutions and individuals, political scientists likewise are returning to the historical study of American politics.

The contributors to this volume make clear how much historians owe the political scientists engaged in studying American political development. All of us hope these essays will contribute to the continuing cross-fertilization between history and political science. Historians need not, and most do not, resist theory as antithetical to our work. Many of these chapters implicitly or explicitly draw on theoretical frameworks derived from social science; historical study surely need not be antitheoretical.

But the human sciences are empirical disciplines, and only by continuing to test our theories against evidence can we keep them supple. The ideas Hartz advanced in *The Liberal Tradition in America* have become too brittle to be of further use.

Almost half a century after its publication, *The Liberal Tradition in America* continues to influence the way many Americans think about their nation and its history. Conservatives and radicals alike still invoke Hartz to support the claim that devotion to individualism and defense of property rights have defined American culture. Ira Katznelson's chapter in this volume exemplifies that tendency. In this chapter I advance two arguments. First, despite its importance as a historical document, *The Liberal Tradition in America* provides an inadequate account of America because its analysis is too flat and too static. Hartz focused exclusively on issues of economics and psychology and missed the constitutive and changing roles played by democracy, religion, race, ethnicity, and gender in American history. He therefore misunderstood (as thoroughly as did his predecessors and progressive bêtes noires Charles Beard, Frederick Jackson Turner, and Vernon Louis Parrington, whose work he sought to replace) the complicated and changing dynamics of the democratic struggles that have driven American social and political conflict since the seventeenth century. We should understand Hartz's analysis in the context of the early post–World War II era rather than treating it as a source of timeless truths about America. Second, acknowledging the inaccuracies of *The Liberal Tradition* is important for us, because the widespread acceptance of its argument has had consequences unfortunate for the study of American political culture and poisonous for political debate. The time has come to refocus our attention away from Cold War–era controversies over liberalism and socialism, and away from more recent scholarly controversies over liberalism and republicanism, and toward the multidimensional and essentially contested concept of democracy.

Hartz's thesis, advanced by means of a rhetorical strategy calculated to dazzle his readers, was simple and elegant. He conceded that his approach could be characterized as a " 'single factor' analysis" with two dimensions: "the absence of feudalism and the presence of the liberal idea."[2] America lacked both a "genuine revolutionary tradition" and a "tradition of reaction" and contained instead only "a kind of self-completing mechanism, which insures the universality of the liberal idea" (5–6). In order to grasp the contours of this all-encompassing liberal tradition, Hartz argued, we must compare America with Europe. Only then can we understand not only the absence of socialism and conservatism but the stultifying presence and "moral unanimity" imposed by "this fixed, dogmatic liberalism of a liberal way of life." Moreover, the "deep and unwritten tyrannical compulsion" of American liberalism "transforms eccentricity into sin," an alchemy that explains the periodic eruption of red scares (9–12). In short, "the master assumption of American political thought" is "the reality of atomistic social freedom. It is instinctive in the American mind" (62).

Hartz advanced his interpretation by contrasting, in a series of chronologically arranged chapters, the nation's continuous history with the convulsions of European revolutions and restorations. He insisted that Americans' shared commitment to Lockean (or, as he spelled it, "Lockian") liberalism had enabled them to avoid upheavals at the cost of enforcing conformity. He used "Locke" as a shorthand for the self-interested, profit-maximizing values and behaviors of liberal capitalism, against which he counterposed, on the one hand, the revolutionary egalitarian fervor of Jacobins and Marxian socialists and, on the other, the traditional hierarchical values of church elites and aristocrats under various European ancien régimes. Unfortunately, however, because Hartz never paused to explain exactly how he understood feudalism or precisely what he meant by Locke or liberalism, the meaning of his terms remained vague and his central claims fuzzy.[3]

It was an arresting argument, though, especially coming so soon after Senator Joseph McCarthy's anticommunist crusade and during a time of widespread national self-congratulation. Hartz's reviewers, historians as well as political scientists, hailed the book for its ambition and its originality. But unlike those who continue to revere the book, some commentators challenged its accuracy. Others counterposed Wilhelm Dilthey's densely textured hermeneutics to Hartz's ascent to the heights of theory. Still others dissented from the use Hartz made of Tocqueville. They pointed out correctly that whereas Tocqueville did indeed stress the absence of feudalism in America, he also emphasized the importance of religion, the legacy of English law and liberty, the fact of slavery, the uniquely elevated status of women, the distinctive pattern of decentralized settlement in North America, a set of sturdy political institutions and wise founding documents, and other sociocultural, geographical, and demographic factors—all of which together constitute the history of democracy in America.[4]

The genre distinction between history and political theory helps to account for the divergence in assessments of *The Liberal Tradition*. Some historians thought Hartz was flying too high to see clearly the details necessary for understanding the American historical record. Political theorists, as Hartz's student Paul Roazen has observed, instead saw that "Hartz had little interest in the study of political ideas as a scholastic exercise but rather wanted to use Locke as a symbol for a brand of political thought that could illuminate political reality."[5] Hartz himself, responding to his historian critics, ascended for refuge to the sanctuary of theorizing: "Comparative analysis," he instructed his slow-witted historian-critics, "is destined to produce disturbing results. In the American case it seems suddenly to shrink our domestic struggles to insignificance, robbing them of their glamour, challenging even the worth of their historical study." Moreover, and here Hartz cut to the heart of the difference between the historian's interest in the particular and the social scientist's quest for the universal, "the comparative approach to American history is bound in the end to raise the question of a general theory of historical development."[6] Perhaps so, for some social scientists, but not necessarily for those who evaluate such claims against empirical evidence. Leonard Krieger pointed out that historians tend to "qualify" and "pluralize" the grander claims of social science. Hartz's fundamental comparison between the United States and Europe, Krieger argued, was misconceived. Had he compared apples with apples, Hartz could have seen that liberty, equality, and democracy have mattered rather less the further east one goes in Europe. National differences within Europe would then loom as large as those Hartz had identified. Every national tradition is distinctive.[7] Because I share Ira Katznelson's judgment about the importance of comparative study for deepening our understanding of American history, I will return to this question of American exceptionalism in my conclusion.

Almost two decades after the publication of *The Liberal Tradition in America*, writing in response to yet another historian's critique of his cavalier treatment of evidence and failure to recognize the deep conflicts in American history, Hartz skirted the issue of evidence and reiterated his earlier proclamation of American uniqueness: "the United States is distinctive as against Europe, and its distinctiveness derives from the fact that the *Mayflower* left behind in Europe the experiences of class, revolution, and collectivism out of which the European socialist movement arose."[8] The facts of history should be seen to flow from the framework Hartz provided, not vice versa. In his spirited defense of *The Liberal Tradition*, Roazen too invokes the genre distinction. He concedes the inaccuracies that critics have identified in Hartz's treatment of individual thinkers and historical incidents, then explains that "Hartz was all along basically using history for the sake of eliciting answers to some theoretical queries in connection with the nature of a free society; and those fundamental issues remain with us today."[9]

Those issues do indeed remain with us, which is why an accurate understanding of the history of American political thought and experience remains so important. Before examining the particular arguments of *The Liberal Tradition*, I want to note the almost complete absence from Hartz's analysis of four issues that now seem to us American historians essential to understanding our nation's past, race, ethnicity, gender, and religion. To indict Hartz for overlooking issues that escaped the attention of most historians until recently seems unfair; such blindness surely typified most scholarly writing until the 1960s and still typified much—including my own—until even more recently. Even so, if one is trying to assess the persuasiveness and lasting value of Hartz's analysis from the perspective of 2002, acknowledging that American public life has revolved around crucial battles over race, ethnicity, and gender has become inescapable.[10]

The same is true of religion, which Hartz examined briefly in *The Liberal Tradition* but dismissed for reasons that merit discussion because they illustrate the distance that separates Hartz's arguments from those advanced by the contributors to this volume. Hartz contended that because religion in eighteenth-century America generated neither iconoclasm nor anticlericalism, it was of only minor significance. Colonial religious diversity "meant that the revolution would be led in part by fierce Dissenting ministers." In Europe, "where reactionary church establishments had made the Christian concept of sin and salvation into an explicit pillar of the status quo, liberals were forced to develop a political religion—as Rousseau saw it—if only in answer to it." But American liberals, "instead of being forced to pull the Christian heaven down to earth, were glad to let it remain where it was. They did not need to make a religion out of the revolution because religion was already revolutionary" (40–41).

These passages reveal two important characteristics of Hartz's analysis. First, because the standard continental European—or, more properly, French and Italian—division between an anticlerical republican left and an entrenched Church hierarchy generated cultural and political warfare that American religious divisions did not, Hartz concluded that religion in America could safely be fitted within the liberal consensus. Second, Hartz did not realize how corrosive to his argument was his concession that American "religion was already revolutionary." Like many secular Jewish intellectuals in the middle of the twentieth century, Hartz either failed to see or refused to acknowledge the pivotal role of Christianity in shaping early American public life.[11]

Hartz did not understand that in America religious identity (like racial and ethnic identity and gender identity) has not been merely epiphenomenal, simply an analytical category separable from the *real* class identity at the core of all social life, but has instead been a central, constitutive component of American culture from the seventeenth century to the present. Almost all Americans' "structures of meaning," to use a phrase of David Hall's, have derived from an unsteady blend of religious and secular, elite and popular, male and female, white and nonwhite cultures. For that reason religion does not shrink to insignificance but exerts a powerful force shaping individual decisions, interpretations of experience, and social interactions. The diversity of Americans' religious commitments prevented the emergence of a state church, as Hartz noted, but the depth and persistence of those commitments likewise undermined the simple, straightforward Lockean attachment to self-interested property seeking that Hartz defined as the essence of America. Locke himself was no Lockean, at least in Hartz's sense of the word, because of the depth of his Calvinist convictions. Similarly Americans from the seventeenth century onward have struggled—as Tocqueville and Max Weber saw much more clearly than Hartz did—not merely for riches but also for salvation as they understood it. That quest has carried them toward a variety of goals not reducible to the simple maximizing of self-interest that drove and defined Hartz's liberal tradition. Unlike the subtler, and consequently more enduring, work by Hartz's contemporaries ranging from Reinhold Niebuhr to John Courtney Murray, who emphasized the complex relation between America's Christian roots and the nation's sense of its moral and political failures, *The Liberal Tradition* simplifies this crucial issue.[12]

The opening page of *The Liberal Tradition in America* contained a minor but telling error that makes clear why we must broaden our analytical focus from liberalism to democracy. Seeking to replace the progressive historians' focus on conflict with a focus on unanimity, Hartz adorned his book's title page with an epigraph taken from Tocqueville's *Democracy in America*: "The great advantage of the Americans is, that they have arrived at a state of democracy without having to endure a democratic revolution; and that they are born free, instead of becoming so." Unfortunately for Hartz, and for his readers' understanding of American culture, Tocqueville had written that Americans were born *equal* rather than free. The mistake, noted initially by errata slips and corrected in later editions, is less trivial than Hartz's defenders have claimed. The misquoted passage appears at the end of a chapter preceded by Tocqueville's profound insight into the differences between the ancient vice of egoism and the modern, democratic tendency toward individualism. The passage was followed by Tocqueville's even more arresting claim that Americans "have used liberty to combat the individualism born of equality, and they have won."

Although Hartz invoked Tocqueville repeatedly and criticized historians for neglecting the implications of his analysis, his own argument rests not on a simple, understandable error of transcription but on a deeper misunderstanding of Tocqueville's point. Tocqueville certainly understood the consequences of the absence of feudal traditions and corporate institutions. He warned that in a democracy "each man is forever thrown back on himself alone, and there is danger that he may be shut up in the solitude of his own heart." But he then pointed out—immediately after the passage Hartz misquoted for his epigraph—that participation in the "free institutions" of American democracy actually mitigates these potentially anomic consequences. "Local liberties, then, which induce a great number of citizens to value the affection of their kindred and neighbors, bring men constantly into contact, despite the instincts which separate them, and force them to help one another."

Whereas one might expect Tocqueville to have concluded—as Hartz did—that self-interest leads democratic citizens away from the public interest, and to have lamented the ways in which freedom (or, as the corrected versions of *The Liberal Tradition* properly have it, equality) erodes concern for others, Tocqueville made exactly the opposite point: "I have often seen Americans make really great sacrifices for the common good, and I have noticed a hundred cases in which, when help was needed, they hardly ever failed to give each other trusty support." Because the penultimate paragraph of that crucial chapter so directly challenges the heart of Hartz's argument and points toward the alternative interpretation I advance in this chapter, an interpretation consistent with many of the chapters in this volume, I will quote it at length:

> The free institutions of the United States and the political rights enjoyed there provide a thousand continual reminders to every citizen that he lives in society. At every moment they bring his mind back to this idea, that it is the duty as well as the interest of men to be useful to their fellows. Having no particular reason to hate others, since he is neither their slave nor their master, the American's heart easily inclines toward benevolence.[13]

As that passage makes clear, Hartz flattened Tocqueville's rich conception of American democracy by eliminating the crucial significance of participation in civic life. Such participation, Tocqueville insisted, prevented Americans from ignoring each other and nourished in them the animating and distinctive ethic of reciprocity that manifested itself prototypically in jury deliberations and implicitly in the broader culture of democracy. Although Tocqueville—like the culture he was describing—did find it problematic that democratic citizenship was limited to white male property holders, he had identified the logic that eventually drove the United States to extend the privileges and duties of citizenship to all adults. That logic, like the ethic of reciprocity and the culture of participation, eluded Hartz entirely.

From the perspective of 2002, the historical errors of *The Liberal Tradition* only begin with the title page. Hartz's focus on a unitary liberal tradition prevented him from seeing the depth and complexity of the disagreements in American democracy. As I examine the principal arguments Hartz advanced, I will very briefly compare his characterizations of (1) the American Revolution, (2) antebellum American politics, (3) the Progressive Era, (4) the New Deal, and (5) the culture of the post–World War II United States with the findings of more recent historical scholarship. It would be pointless to criticize Hartz for failing to see what it has taken half a century of historical scholarship to make clear. But it is equally pointless to claim, as some of Hartz's bolder champions continue to do, that *The Liberal Tradition* nevertheless remains a uniquely valuable guide to the history of American public life. For reasons I will outline in my conclusion, the stubborn persistence of belief in an American liberal tradition of the sort Hartz described obscures both our understanding of our nation's past and our ability to envision strategies toward a more egalitarian future.[14]

Hartz laid out the heart of his analysis in his provocative opening chapter, "The Concept of a Liberal Society." Although he admitted the presence of some conflict in America, its shallowness prevented the development of political theory. "America represents the liberal mechanism of Europe functioning without the European social antagonisms" (16). That claim reveals his blinkered vision. Because American social antagonisms operated on fault lines different from those of European revolutionaries confronting landed and titled aristocracies, or from those of later European socialists confronting an entrenched, antidemocratic bourgeoisie, Hartz denied the existence of significant conflict and significant political thought in the United States. More recent students of American political development, including the contributors to this volume, have paid more attention to the depth and persistence of disagreements over the fate and place of, say, Indians, blacks, Asians, Jews, Slavs, and Hispanics. They have been more alert to the gender wars that have divided generations, families, and coworkers, and they have examined the implications for political and social life of other fundamental cultural or religious differences. As a result, they have put the problem in a different framework. In the combative words of Richard J. Ellis, one of the political scientists who dissents from the view of liberalism that has attracted many in his profession since the publication of *The Liberal Tradition*, "Political conflict in the United States has been and continues to be animated by fundamentally different visions of the good life. . . . That all sides appeal to terms such as equality or democracy or liberty should not conceal from us the fundamentally different meanings these terms have in different political cultures." Even the most casual glance at scholarship from the last three decades dealing with race, ethnicity, gender, or religion would suffice to confirm Ellis's judgment.[15]

The American Revolution, to begin where Hartz did, was from his perspective no revolution at all. Compared with the French Revolution, which served as his standard of measurement, what happened in the War for Independence merely codified what had previously been taken for granted in English North America. If Americans disestablished the Anglican Church, abolished primogeniture, and confiscated Tory estates, they were merely bringing to fruition processes already under way.[16] If they separated the powers of government, further divided authority by establishing a federal republic, and provided for judicial review of legislative and executive decisions, those mechanisms merely testified to their deep, preexisting agreement on fundamentals. The scholarship of the last three decades has obliterated this aspect of Hartz's argument, not only—to cite the most obvious challenges—by demonstrating the centrality and force of republican and religious rhetoric and ideals, but even more centrally by showing the creativity of the democratic mechanisms adopted to deal with the genuine conflicts invisible to Hartz.

The significance of the American Revolution lay not so much in the founders' liberalism, which was complicated by its mixture with republican and religious values, as in their commitment to nourishing the seeds of a democratic culture. They constructed or altered institutions that made possible continuous mediation, the endless production of compromises, a system deliberately calculated to satisfy some of the aspirations of all citizens and all of the aspirations of none. From the declarations of independence adopted by towns, counties, and states in the spring of 1776 through the ratification of the United States Constitution and the Bill of Rights, Americans authorized their representatives to gather together and deliberate on the form they wanted their government to take. Precisely because they could not agree once and for all on their common principles, they agreed to make all their agreements provisional and to provide, for one of the few times in human history, a range of escape hatches for dissent, ranging from a free press to the separation of church and state, from judicial review to provisions for amending the Constitution. It is true that such comfort with compromise did indeed distinguish the American founders from later Jacobins and Bolsheviks. But it is crucial to see that the American founders emphatically did not agree to codify atomistic individualism, because that idea appealed to practically no one—neither Federalists nor Anti-Federalists—in late-eighteenth-century America. Although the sobersided John Adams has recently attracted more attention than most of his like-minded contemporaries, both his doubt that republican virtue would eradicate sin and his disdain for profiteering resonated widely in the new republic. He and his contemporaries were not trying to make a world safe for bankers—whose work Adams described acidly in a letter to Jefferson as "an infinity of successive felonious larcenies"—but were seeking instead to create a liberal republic safe for honor as well as worldly asceticism, a "Christian Sparta" in the phrase of Samuel Adams, where even those who failed to reach that lofty ethical ideal might not only survive but thrive. As Joanne Freeman has shown, in the founders' world honor trumped rights.[17] Codifying the procedures and stabilizing the institutions of democracy, even as they sought to contain it within strict boundaries, was their means to that end.

Hartz's conviction that property holding and profit making exhausted the ambitions of eighteenth- and nineteenth-century Americans guided even his explicit analysis of state involvement in the economy in his first book, *Economic Policy and Democratic Thought: Pennsylvania, 1776–1860*. There Hartz argued that even though laissez-faire did not exist in early America, the activity of state governments served only to facilitate economic activity. The same assumption also drove his interpretation of antebellum America in *The Liberal Tradition*. Among the most explicit and convincing recent challenges to that analysis are the distinct but complementary writings of William J. Novak and Elizabeth B. Clark. Novak has demonstrated both the pervasive regulation, in myriad domains, of economic activity in antebellum America and, even more directly challenging Hartz, the equally pervasive reliance of courts on the principle *"salus populi,"* the welfare of the people, as the rationale used to justify that regulation.[18] Clark has shown the presence and explosive power of a different set of ideas missing from Hartz's account, ideas of sympathetic identification with slaves and other oppressed Americans, derived from diverse religious and secular sources, that motivated antebellum reformers and eventually coalesced in a sensibility that helped generate passionate loyalty to the Union cause. Such values cannot be shoehorned into Hartz's liberal tradition.[19]

From Hartz's perspective, the quarrels between Whigs and Democrats betrayed "a massive confusion in political thought" that stemmed from both sides' refusal to concede their shared commitment to liberal capitalism. Whereas Whigs really should have become Tories, and Jacksonians really should have become socialists, instead they all mutated into the "American democrat," a "pathetic" figure "torn by an inner doubt," "not quite a Hercules but a Hercules with the brain of a Hamlet" (117–19). To Hartz's champions such writing is brilliant, but it masks a strategy that Hartz himself lampooned when he saw it in others. For example, Orestes Brownson was, in Hartz's words "a classic intellectual"; in his disenchantment with America he "did not blame his theory: he blamed the world" (139). Likewise Hartz, when confronting Whigs who advocated reform in a language of self-discipline and harmony and Jacksonians who spoke in terms of equality and democracy, refused to admit that antebellum Americans saw themselves, each other, and their culture in terms quite different from his. Rather than modifying or abandoning his theory, Hartz "blamed the world" of American history. He lamented the "veritable jig-saw puzzle of theoretical confusion" generated by Americans who might have pretended to disagree over slavery, temperance, education, Indian removal, and a hundred other issues when, viewed from his vantage point, "the liberal temper of American political theory is vividly apparent" beneath all their disputes (140). The confusion, though, is

Hartz's rather than theirs. As the chapters in this volume by William Novak and Richard John make clear, Americans in the antebellum period refused to play their scripted roles as aristocrats and proletarians. Instead they enacted an altogether different drama, with subtly nuanced and strangely amalgamated characters impossible to reduce to European types. The richness and complexity of the American historical record reveals the poverty of one-dimensional theory when it confronts that world.[20]

Hartz conceded the anomalous quality of some southerners' defense of slavery, but he presented it as the exception that proved his liberal rule. Careful analysis of nineteenth-century America shows instead that within as well as between North and South, Americans differed on many fundamental issues. Only the culture and institutions of democracy (as Jefferson, Madison, and Tocqueville all saw) provided ways to mediate their deep disagreements over issues as diverse as free speech, slavery, Sabbatarianism, temperance, polygamy, and the legitimacy of using the authority of government—local, state, and national—to regulate the behavior of individuals. John Stuart Mill looked to the United States for examples of government regulation antithetical to the conception of liberal freedom he articulated in *On Liberty*.[21] Only the election of Abraham Lincoln, who insisted that the principle of popular sovereignty must be yoked to the principle of autonomy for all Americans, made manifest that on one issue compromise had at last become impossible. Lincoln's election did not augur "the triumph of a theory of democratic capitalism" (199), as Hartz contended. Instead it signaled, as Lincoln's second inaugural address made plain, the finally irresistible power of the alliance between Augustinian Christianity and republican ideals, which ultimately inspired the North to uproot the evil of slavery, the deepest of all the divisions within the "liberal tradition" that Hartz imagined marching uninterrupted through American history.[22]

If Andrew Carnegie and Horatio Alger were indeed the only legitimate "children of Lincoln's achievement" (199), as Hartz argued to explain Americans' purportedly unanimous embrace of laissez-faire after the Civil War, it would be impossible to explain the appearance of the populists and the Knights of Labor, Jane Addams and Lillian Wald, John Dewey and Herbert Croly, Richard Ely and Walter Rauschenbusch, and Charlotte Perkins Gilman and W.E.B. DuBois. For that matter, it would be impossible to explain both Theodore and Franklin Roosevelt. Hartz understood progressivism, as did many of his contemporaries, including of course Richard Hofstadter, as Woodrow Wilson's futile harking back to a lost world of small towns and small businesses, an exercise in nostalgia with no political or economic consequences. Historians fifty years later must disagree.

Diverse and incompatible as their strategies were, progressives nevertheless constructed from the materials they had inherited a new order in
governance, law, business, social organization, and culture. Louis Brandeis lost his battle against bigness, yet the government regulation of private enterprise and the use of courts for what Michael Willrich terms
"social policing" became permanent facts of life.[23] The National Association for the Advancement of Colored People failed to enact all of the
program announced when it formed in 1909–1910, yet the civil rights
movement, launched as *The Liberal Tradition* appeared, employed not
only rights-talk but images of deliverance and salvation from Exodus and
Matthew rather than Hartz's language of the main chance. The crusade
for women's rights reached only a limited fulfillment in the franchise, yet
feminists have invoked a variety of ideals concerning moral autonomy,
civic responsibility, and more egalitarian households equally incompatible
with Hartz's framework. Finally, the social democrats among American
progressives failed to achieve their goals of a more egalitarian structure
for work or wages, yet, from the platforms of the Populist party in 1892
and the Progressive party in 1912 through the agendas of the New Deal
and the Fair Deal, such ambitious plans were at the heart, rather than on
the margins, of political debate. To underscore the point, all were utterly
inconsistent with Hartz's notion of an American liberal tradition. The
opponents of the Civil War amendments examined by Michael Vorenberg
and the members of the New York bourgeoisie examined by Sven Beckert
did defend the prerogatives of wealthy white males in terms that would
fit within Hartz's framework. It is important to remember that they failed
to hold back the tides of democracy they feared.[24]

Hartz, writing in the shadow of McCarthyism, expected that all the
moderate reforms of the twentieth century would meet the same fate:
"Where capitalism is an essential principle of life," he wrote, "the man
who seeks to regulate it is peculiarly vulnerable to the waving of the red
flag." Just as Hartz could concede the presence of regulation in antebellum America and dismiss its significance (209–10), so his magic wand
made Addams, Dewey, Ely, Croly, Gilman, and DuBois—and all they
stood for—disappear. Where, he asked, were the American analogues of
the British collectivist philosopher T. H. Green and the "new liberal" pub-
licist L. T. Hobhouse, and of the French and German moderate social
democrats Jean Jaurès and Edward Bernstein? Whereas such Europeans
shared a "frank recognition of the need for collective action to solve the
class problem," Americans missed the point. Wages and hours legislation
and workmen's compensation he judged but the "loose marginalia" of
the progressive movement. Croly's democratic nationalism dissolved into
"practically unintelligible rhetoric" (230, 233). Progressives, in Hartz's
words, wanted only "to smash trusts and begin running the Lockian race

all over again. But even the pathetic hope of Brandeis was blasted with an outpouring of liberal irrationalism" that made any notion of organization likely to be "denounced as 'unamerican' " (223). In *The Liberal Tradition* the religious or ethical impulses that drove the champions of the social gospel, the founders of social settlements, the creators of municipal courts, and the architects of social security and government planning vanish beneath a fog of liberal individualism. The progressives' enduring achievements, from the graduated income tax through regulation of the economy to the transformation of law and governance, not surprisingly never surface.

Hartz insisted that European progressive reformers such as David Lloyd George and Léon Bourgeois could flirt with, and even ally with, socialists such as the Webbs or Jaurès, but that path, he insisted, remained closed in America. As I have tried to make clear elsewhere, this analysis relies on a widespread but faulty understanding of the dynamics of reform in England, France, and Germany as well as in the United States during these crucial years. Moderate social democracy (sometimes designated revisionism or Fabianism to indicate its divergence from Marxism) in these European nations emerged for many of the same reasons, and made possible the appearance of quite similar coalitions, as those behind the more social democratic of American progressive reform measures. The disappearance of those coalitions, which Hartz attributes in the American case to the red scare orchestrated by A. Mitchell Palmer after World War I, had consequences just as dramatic in England and France as in the United States. The consequences in Germany, of course, were far deadlier.[25]

Why did Hartz miss the substantial similarities and the dramatic difference? The answer reveals another reason why his analysis is no longer convincing more than a decade after 1989. "The attitude toward socialism remains, however, the final test of Progressive 'Americanism' " (243). That standard of judgment, reasonable as it might have been at the time, is no longer compelling. How many decades should historians wait before inverting Werner Sombart's question and asking "why was there socialism in Europe?" Given his Eurocentric framework, Hartz understandably placed the piecemeal, pragmatic New Deal, limited as it was by Roosevelt's ability to forge a consensus from the fractured pieces of his party's coalition, comfortably within the liberal tradition. "What emerges then in the case of the New Deal is a liberal self that is lost from sight: a faith in property, a belief in class unity, a suspicion of state power, hostility to the utopian mood, all of which were blacked out by the weakness of the socialist challenge in the American liberal community" (270). This interpretation of the limits of the New Deal has since become standard; only varying degrees of admiration (from the center) or contempt (from left and right) for FDR's moderation have distinguished the major studies written in recent decades.

Historians have paid surprisingly little attention to the New Deal's unfulfilled social democratic agenda. Roosevelt's 1944 state of the union address called for a "second bill of rights" assuring all Americans access to education, a job with a living wage, adequate housing, medical care, and insurance against old age, sickness, accident, and unemployment. Such ideas had been percolating in FDR's administration since his Commonwealth Club speech in 1932. Roosevelt thought the ambitious proposals for social provision contained in England's Beveridge Report had derived so directly from the plans of his own administration that it should have been called "the Roosevelt Report." Roosevelt campaigned—and was reelected—on just such a platform in 1944. Truman made such proposals the centerpiece of his Fair Deal; such ideas were at the heart of the universally hailed GI Bill. The components of this far-reaching legislative program, caught in the cross fire between an incipient Cold War aversion to anything resembling government activity and southern Democrats' intensified animosity toward anything resembling or contributing to equal treatment of African-Americans, went down to defeats so decisive in Congress that historians refuse to believe that either FDR or Truman could have been serious about them. More consistent with Hartz's concept of a liberal individualist, antigovernment straitjacket than with the historical evidence, such treatments confirm—indeed, seem to rest on—Hartz's judgment: since the New Deal did not try to bring socialism to America, its reformism must have been tepid at best.[26]

Perhaps American historians should stop using socialism as the litmus test of reform in the United States. When Hartz was writing, the social democratic governments sweeping into power across northern Europe had only recently traded in their comprehensive socialist economic programs for more limited agendas featuring mixed economies supplemented with more or less extensive welfare states. Although the Social Democratic Party of Germany continued to speak the language of Marxism until the Bad Godesberg program of 1959, it was already getting lonely for those on the left who insisted on ideological purity. Elsewhere in Western Europe the coalitions of urban professionals, farmers, and industrial workers that supported postwar social democratic governments had already surrendered the apocalyptic rhetoric of revolution. As Claus Offe and, more recently, Herrick Chapman and George Reid Andrews have pointed out, the post–World War II welfare states of northern Europe depended more on a democratic consensus than American democracy ever did. The intensified pressure of unprecedented immigration and the subsequent diversification of population have led to increasingly wary and ungenerous electorates everywhere; only in America did progressives ever dare to proclaim that they were building their coalitions, as FDR and Truman (and later Lyndon Johnson) did, on celebrations of such diversity. In Scandinavia, as in Britain and throughout northwestern Europe, voters backed social democratic parties that promised economic growth for their nations and members of their constituencies as enthusiastically as they promised greater security and increasing equality.[27]

From the perspective of the twenty-first century, it is easy for us to discern the steady transformation of European labor parties from revolutionary Marxism to varieties of reformist social democracy, a political position far less distant from the left wing of the twentieth-century American Democratic party than were nineteenth-century European socialist parties. Not only the styles but more importantly the policies of Prime Minister Tony Blair of the British Labour Party, Chancellor Gerhard Schröder of the German Social Democratic Party, and (despite his shrill protests) Prime Minister Lionel Jospin of the French Socialist Party bear striking similarities to those of progressives in the U.S. Democratic party. Hartz, writing in the wake of right-wing repression at home, confronting a hostile communist presence in Eastern Europe and Asia, and pondering the prospect of anticolonial revolutions looming elsewhere, could not have anticipated that development. Writing two decades after 1989, however, we should not continue to ignore it.

Despite that process of development, that emergence of a "third way" in fact prior to its announcement as an ideology in the 1990s, it would be an obvious error to exaggerate the appeal of social democratic agendas. In Europe as in the United States, forces with deep cultural roots opposed every aspect of that program; on both sides of the Atlantic they have succeeded in tapping into widespread and passionate commitments. As the chapters in this volume by Meg Jacobs, Julian Zelizer, and Thomas Sugrue demonstrate, Americans' long-standing fears of inflation and aversion to taxation, and their attachments to localism and various social, religious, and cultural traditions, combined to propel the conservative political movement that has dominated public life in recent decades. Although acknowledging the legitimacy of their opponents' claims to embody authentic American traditions has been difficult for social democrats, just as seeing egalitarianism as an aspiration with deep roots in American history has been difficult for the New Right, the chapters in this volume show why we should abandon shopworn stories about "the people" battling heroically against "the interests." Preferences for the local over the national, the familiar over the novel, and authority and hierarchy against racial, class, and gender equality are as old as the United States. Pretending that such commitments betray rather than perpetuate American traditions obstructs our understanding of our nation's past and its present.[28]

Assuming that we scholars know Americans' deeper or more authentic aspirations has inspired a generation of scolding or wishful thinking masquerading as history, political science, or cultural studies—on both ends of the political spectrum. Individuals have different ideas about human motivation: Marx's concept of false consciousness, Gramsci's concept of hegemony, and Foucault's concept of power/knowledge remind some analysts of consent and consensus. Rather than presuming to identify genuine preferences beneath Americans' choices as voters or consumers and to discern deeper longings buried beneath behavior we dislike, the contributors to this volume examine the struggles that have shaped our nation from a different point of view: the perspectives of those who fought them. Many scholars have unwittingly adopted Noah Webster's creed: "for God's sake, let not falsehood circulate without disproof," seeking, in his words, "to *keep public opinion correct*" by showing the perfidy of power.[29] Historians of American politics should exchange that arrogance for the more modest task of coming to grips with the complex evidence we face.

Hartz worried about Americans' smug assumption that they had solved their own problems and that other nations, both emerging and established, should simply follow the American lead toward a paradise of consumption and complacency. From his uneasiness about the Cold War to the wrenching national debate over Vietnam is a very short distance; indeed, the terms of that debate helped confirm Hartz's book as a classic and helped establish him as a sage. Given the current discrepancy between, on the one hand, the enthusiasm toward the United States expressed by the elites of many other nations and, on the other, the distrust often sliding into contempt toward the United States expressed by many of the world's dispossessed peoples, Hartz's insight into the problematic nature of America's tendency toward self-satisfied provincialism remains perhaps the most incisive part of *The Liberal Tradition*, as valuable today as it was in 1955.

During the two decades between the publication of *The Liberal Tradition in America* and Hartz's resignation from Harvard in 1974, admiration for the book and its author mushroomed. The oracular quality of Hartz's writing, which elicited awe during a period when European émigrés such as Karl Popper, Eric Auerbach, Hannah Arendt, Max Horkheimer and Theodor Adorno, and Leo Strauss were producing their masterworks, now seems less convincing. Few historians or political theorists in our hyperhistoricist culture of irony adopt a similar tone of voice. Consider a typical example of Hartz's rhetorical style:

American pragmatism has always been deceptive because, glacierlike, it has rested on miles of submerged conviction, and the conformitarian ethos which that conviction generates has always been infuriating because it has refused to pay its critics the compliment of an argument. Here is where the joy of a Dewey meets the anguish of a Fenimore Cooper; for if the American deals with concrete cases because he never doubts his general principles, this is also the reason he is able to dismiss his critics with a fine and crushing ease. . . . History was on a lark, out to tease men, not by shattering their dreams, but by fulfilling them with a sort of satiric accuracy (59–60).

Although this is writing of rare eloquence, historians usually want clarity and evidence served alongside such rich turns of phrase. Yet Hartz repeatedly relied on allusions and epigrams when he needed to develop arguments. His style demands that readers know what he meant not only when he dropped relatively familiar names such as Filmer and Locke, Rousseau and Maistre, Marx and Comte, or Dewey and Cooper; they must also know, because Hartz provided no clues to their identity, many more obscure thinkers on whose significance the persuasiveness of his particular arguments rests. To choose only a small random sample—French figures whose last name begins with the letter B—how many readers could identify Gracchus Babeuf, Pierre Simon Ballance, Pierre Nicolas Berryer, Louis Blanc, Vicomte Louis Gabriel Bonald, Jacques Bénigne Bossuet, Louis Boudin, and Aristide Briand? Few American readers, today or fifty years ago, know the questions to which those names provide the answers. Although Hartz engaged in a sophisticated form of intimidation, it was intimidation nonetheless: readers who fail to grasp the force of a comparison are left doubting their judgment in the face of Hartz's apparent erudition.

Yet many of Hartz's allusions and comparisons—as in the case of eighteenth-century American revolutionaries and French philosophes, in the case of the early-twentieth-century European progressives and social democrats for whom no American analogues are said to exist, or in the case of his comments on American pragmatism—fall flat when one is familiar with the individuals or incidents involved. Given Hartz's soaring flights of rhetoric, applying standard rules of evidence to *The Liberal Tradition* can seem pointless. Aphorisms and witticisms are perhaps better judged on cleverness than verifiability. It is meaningless to ask whether the sentences in, say, Friedrich Nietzsche's *Beyond Good and Evil* are "true." Yet, unlike Nietzsche, Hartz made empirical claims, which, when tested against the evidence, fail more often than they succeed.

Equally unsettling from our perspective is Hartz's breezy implication that the writings of notoriously complex thinkers such as Locke, Rousseau, Marx, Jefferson, Madison, or Lincoln have a unitary meaning. Since Hartz wrote, the scholarship on all these thinkers has developed to the point that such one-dimensional interpretations seem not only unconvincing but simpleminded. Yet even a half century ago most political theorists and intellectual historians exhibited greater care when characterizing the ideas of complicated thinkers. In short, even when Hartz wrote the book his bold style stood out, but his dazzling displays of erudition and his equally sparkling prose bought him credibility. These days, hanging arguments on personal authority is out of fashion; we prefer the hermeneutics of suspicion. When we see Hartz offering an epigram or sliding over an inconvenient fact or discrepancy, we want to examine the evidence and reconsider the analysis. His writing asks us to genuflect; we raise an eyebrow instead.[30]

After the publication of *The Liberal Tradition* Hartz devoted himself to defending and elaborating his "fragment theory" of comparative cultural development and then, in the final years of his life, to rambling ruminations on the meaning of world history. In an essay published in 1960, Hartz undertook to expand his argument in *The Liberal Tradition* to encompass contemporary debates over democracy. This essay shows his characteristic imagination and insight, but in the end it merely reframes his argument about American exceptionalism and again subordinates the untidy evidence of history to the spare elegance of Hartz's analytical scheme. In other words, it illustrates why even historians who value social science will remain wary of it.[31] As in *The Liberal Tradition*, Hartz presented a deviant American case spinning away from a Western European norm. He was now contrasting America against an even more wildly divergent communist world, but the logic of his exceptionalist model remained intact. With Thomas L. Haskell I believe we should dispense with such conceptions of America—whether exceptionalist or antiexceptionalist—and adopt a "postexceptionalist" perspective that might enable us to follow the historical evidence without claiming, in Haskell's words, "to have discovered in the uniqueness of national experience an explanatory key that unlocks all doors." Liberated from debates between exceptionalists and antiexceptionalists, we can "admit that sweeping claims and counterclaims about the similarity or difference of entire nations will forever elude empirical resolution." As historians, we might find that a postexceptionalist perspective liberates us from the necessity of freezing our evidence into the static typologies that prevented Hartz, even at his best, from dealing with the particularities of different times and different nations. As political historians act on Ira Katznelson's wise recommendation to undertake more comparative studies, we must proceed with greater care than will be possible if we continue to embrace the no longer useful concept of American exceptionalism.[32]

Why does Hartz's analysis of America's liberal tradition matter now? Why can't we historians simply acknowledge the book's significance as a product of the 1950s and leave it at that? Hartz's argument has proved so powerful and so resistant to critics' charges that its legacy has had serious consequences of two sorts in America since the 1950s.

First, Hartz persuaded almost an entire generation of political theorists that there is no reason to study American political thought. Because America had no social conflicts, he argued, Americans contributed "relatively little political thought at all." Given moral consensus, "political philosophy did not have to get going in the first place."[33] American undergraduates and graduate students interested in political theory learn to grapple with the writings of Rousseau or Hegel or Marx, but most of them learn little or nothing about the American intellectual tradition. Hartz himself seems to have focused most of his energies as a teacher on European thinkers, and his profession has tended to follow his lead. Not only is it possible to earn a Ph.D. in first-rate graduate programs of political science without having studied American political thought; few courses in the field exist. Few political scientists consider it worth studying. Until its recent resurgence,[34] the field attracted relatively little interest.

At least four distinct reasons can be offered to explain this odd phenomenon. First, political theorists usually concentrate on philosophers in the tradition of Plato and Aristotle, Hegel and Marx, who derived their politics from elaborate systems ranging from ontology to metaphysics. The American tradition has indeed produced few such thinkers. Second, the style of linguistic analysis that has dominated Anglo-American philosophy since the middle of the twentieth century has been inhospitable to issues of the sort discussed by earlier American political theorists. Although recent theorists, following the lead of John Rawls, have returned to issues such as justice, rights, and equality, most of them have also followed the methodology of the early Rawls, concentrating on thought experiments and eschewing a historical or empirical approach. Third, the discipline of political science continues its curious obsession with what Donald P. Green and Ian Shapiro have fittingly termed the "pathologies of rational choice theory," an approach to politics that can be antagonistic to the classic concerns of political theory. In the words of William Riker, a founding father of rational choice theory, political scientists should dispense with "traditional methods—i.e., history writing, the description of institutions, and legal analysis," because such work can produce at best only wisdom, not science. Fourth and finally, many of those who teach political theory in American universities are the students (or the students of students) of two influential scholars who agreed on little except the insignificance of American thought, Leo Strauss and Louis Hartz.[35]

Hartz's devaluing of American political thought has thus helped justify the failure, for too long, of too many American political theorists to take seriously their own heritage, poor as it is in Aristotles and Hegels but rich in debates about what democracy is and what it should be. Ideas have been at the center of American popular political debates since the seventeenth century. Because citizenship in the English North American colonies was relatively widespread from the outset, writers of compacts, covenants, constitutions, laws, and (at least until fairly recently) court decisions in America have sought to communicate with a broad public in terms ordinary people could understand and endorse. For that reason, as Donald S. Lutz has demonstrated, students of American political theory should examine the meanings of public texts rather than limiting their attention to a canon of abstract political philosophy.[36] From Plato onward, most of the writers of "great books" of political philosophy either never had to deal with such practical matters as persuading the public, never had the chance to implement their ideas, or, when the opportunity presented itself, came up with schemes quite different from those suggested in their theoretical treatises. Locke, for example, dreamed up a semifeudal never-never land in response to his friend Shaftesbury's invitation to write a constitution for the colony of Carolina. Rousseau prescribed for Poland a constitution allowing room for aristocrats, serfs, and forms of representative democracy inimical to the republican forms he envisioned for his native Geneva or for unspoiled Corsica.

America's most enduring theorists, by contrast, have been actively involved in the complexities of the political process. For that reason their writings show not only a distinctive engagement with the practical questions of democratic governance but an equally distinctive tensile strength that too many American professors and students of political theory, hurrying to get from Locke and Rousseau to Mill and Marx and then on to Rawls and Habermas, fail to grasp in their quick readings of *Federalist* number 10 and Calhoun's *Disquisition on Government*. Hartz's portrait of America's "liberal tradition," by denying the depth and seriousness of the issues addressed by those who have shaped America's political and legal traditions, helped authorize such unfortunate disregard, and the enduring respect of many scholars for *The Liberal Tradition* perpetuates it.

A second consequence of the widespread acceptance of Hartz's argument has been the tendency to assume that the only authentic, legitimate questions of American politics are those concerning self-interest, individual rights, and the sanctity of personal property. This astonishing assumption is shared across the political spectrum. As John Diggins has pointed out, there is a surprising congruence between Hartz's *Liberal Tradition* and Herbert Marcuse's *One Dimensional Man*. Both books reduce Americans to a band of single- and simpleminded consumers who lack the personal or cultural resources to see beyond the appeals of corporate and/or mainstream political advertisements. Whereas free-market capitalists and conservative cultural commentators unanimously dismissed Marcuse's diagnosis as simplistic and his prescriptions for reform as proto-totalitarian, they have tended implicitly to endorse Hartz's analysis, perhaps because it led, as he admitted himself (33), only to a shoulder-shrugging acceptance of unthinking individualism and market "imperatives."[37]

The ready embrace by radical scholars of Hartz's portrait of a one-dimensional American tradition, which depends on ignoring or denying the significance of a continuing series of democratic reform efforts stretching from the seventeenth century to the present, ironically reinforces the assumptions such scholars intend to criticize and transform. For if property holding alone mattered to Americans in the past and matters in the present, and if frontal (i.e., socialist) challenges to the institution of private property alone can be judged genuinely radical, then perhaps America ought to be defined as nothing more than a culture of consumer capitalism—so too, of course, should nations such as Great Britain, Germany, France, and Sweden. That way of thinking seems better suited to the interests of free-marketeers than to those calling for America to become more egalitarian, but a surprising number of leftist scholars in the fields of law, philosophy, political theory, cultural studies, and history have embraced it. Criticizing Hartz thus ruffles feathers across the contemporary political spectrum. Too many people, right and left, have too much invested in the idea of an American liberal tradition to surrender it without a fight.

By diminishing the significance of dissenting thinkers, activists, and movements in American history, those who continue to endorse Hartz's notion of a liberal tradition—whether from the right or the left—consciously or unwittingly reinforce the claims of those who define as un-American any conception of radical democracy. Challenging hierarchies, reasoning from the logic of the principle "one citizen, one vote" to the conclusion that economic and social power should not extend into political power, has been a recurring theme in American history. As the chapters in this volume demonstrate, opposition to such initiatives likewise has persisted from the nation's beginnings to the present. Such battles never end. Differences of experience, perception, and values lead to disagreement, deliberation, and provisional compromises, which in turn generate new disagreements. That is the ineluctable dynamic of democracy, the proper subject of American political history. Unfortunately, the shorthand term "conflict" can flatten that complex and ever changing cultural process into caricature just as surely as does the term "consensus." Democracy, as Tocqueville saw in the nineteenth century and John Dewey in the twentieth, is a much more fluid and multidimensional cultural phenomenon.

Hartz's *Liberal Tradition* came to prominence just as Dewey's ideas went into eclipse. Perhaps the recent renaissance of American pragmatism will help to refocus attention on the potential harmonies that Dewey envisioned between our culture's commitments to open-ended empirical inquiry and his ideal of an open-ended, experimental, pluralist democracy. Only when viewed through the backward telescope of Hartz's liberal tradition do the struggles for a democratic culture that Dewey saw at the heart of American history—struggles of various kinds, such as those documented by the chapters in this volume—shrink to insignificance. For the sake of historical accuracy as well as democratic renewal, we should widen our focus as scholars to the projects that Tocqueville identified, the sometimes successful efforts to build a democratic culture on an ethic of reciprocity, efforts blurred beyond recognition by Hartz's distorting lens.

Hartz was worried about America's relevance to a world of nations shaking themselves free from the bonds of colonialism. At the dawn of a new millennium the United States seems not only relevant but, to the surprise of those Americans accustomed to thinking of their nation as an imperial bully and oppressive capitalist power, in certain respects even a model. Developed and developing nations alike are drawn toward our sturdy democratic political institutions and our troubled but still relatively vibrant state-regulated market economy. The enthusiasm of the early 1990s for unchecked market economies in the formerly communist nations of Eastern Europe has faded into a renewed appreciation of the fundamental importance of popular sovereignty and the rule of law. The business scandals of 2002 have shown Americans the perils of the cowboy capitalism that has been preached by many in the Republican party since 1980. Skepticism about business lends renewed luster to the progressives' idea of a mixed economy overseen by a vigilant state. In the wake of September 11, 2001, public authority has demonstrated again not only its indispensability but its potential effectiveness when exerted with resolve in behalf of the common good. Especially when mobilized from the ground up rather than from the top down, popular government has enormous potential. Since the eighteenth century it has been less the absence of feudalism than the presence of democracy—albeit imperfect, contested, and constricted but nevertheless slowly expanding—that has distinguished the United States from other nations, and that difference has shrunk as democracy has spread. It is democracy that now makes America attractive to nations shaking themselves free from bonds of other kinds.[38] During the last fifty years varieties of liberal democratic polities and mixed economies have become the rule rather than the exception in the developed world and prototypes for developing nations eager to enjoy more stable politics and to share the richer nations' prosperity. "Democracy will come into its own," Dewey predicted, "for democracy is a name for a life of free and enriching communion. It had its seer in Walt Whitman."[39]

We know too much now, both about the stubborn persistence of inequality in America and about America's unsettling tendency to assert its will globally, to share entirely Whitman's indomitable optimism. Nevertheless, as we turn from the flattened analytical model of Hartz's liberalism to the richer problem of studying American democracy, we can at least attempt to recover the shrewd insight and vibrant sense of possibility that infused Whitman's *Democratic Vistas*, written in the bleak days after the Civil War:

> America, filling the present with greatest deeds and problems, cheerfully accepting the past, including feudalism, (as, indeed, the present is but the legitimate birth of the past, including feudalism,) counts, as I reckon, for her justification and success, (for who, as yet, dare claim success?) almost entirely on the future. Nor is that hope unwarranted. To-day, ahead, though dimly yet, we see, in vistas, a copious, sane, gigantic offspring. For our New World I consider far less important for what it has done, or what it is, than for results to come. Sole among nationalities, these States have assumed the task to put in forms of lasting power and practicality, on areas of amplitude rivaling the operations of the physical kosmos, the moral political speculations of ages, long, long deferr'd, the democratic republican principle, and the theory of development and perfection by voluntary standards, and self-reliance.[40]

From the perspective of the year 2002, it is not the sober-minded Hartz but the democratic "seer" Whitman who appears the more reliable guide to and the more incisive analyst of American culture. Those who seek to understand the dynamics of liberal democracy in American history would do well to keep both of their perspectives in view.

NOTES

Portions of this chapter have appeared in James T. Kloppenberg, "In Retrospect: Louis Hartz, The Liberal Tradition in America," *Reviews in American History* 29 (2001): 460–78. © The Johns Hopkins University Press. Reprinted with permission of the Johns Hopkins University Press.

1. See James T. Kloppenberg, *The Virtues of Liberalism* (New York: Oxford University Press, 1998).

2. Louis Hartz, *The Liberal Tradition in America* (New York: Harcourt, Brace and World, Inc., Harvest, 1955), 20. All further page references, noted in parentheses in the text, are to this edition.

3. For fine recent discussions of Locke's ideas, including an especially helpful account of Locke's "worldly asceticism," which enabled him to take seriously both his commitment to Protestantism and his commitment to property, which enabled Americans such as Jefferson and Adams to take Locke seriously, and which distinguishes the historical Locke decisively from the one-dimensional, liberty-and-property-obsessed Locke of Hartz's account, see Joshua Foa Dienstag, "Serving God and Mammon: The Lockean Sympathy in Early American

Thought," *American Political Science Review* 90 (1996): 497–511, and Dienstag, "Between History and Nature: Social Contract Theory in Locke and the Founders," *The Journal of Politics* 58 (1996): 985–1009.

4. See, for example, the reviews of Hartz's *Liberal Tradition* by George Mowry in *The American Historical Review* 61 (1955): 140–41; by Arthur Mann in *William and Mary Quarterly*, 3d ser. 12 (1955): 653–55; by Ralph Henry Gabriel in *Journal of the History of Ideas* 17 (1956): 136–38; and the review essay by Marvin Meyers, "Louis Hartz: *The Liberal Tradition in America*: An Appraisal," *Comparative Studies in Society and History* 5 (1963–1964): 261–68. For further discussion of the issues raised by these reviews and Hartz's response to them, and for a more detailed critique of other aspects of Hartz's analysis than is possible here, see James T. Kloppenberg, "In Retrospect: Louis Hartz's *Liberal Tradition in America*," *Reviews in American History* 29 (2001): 460–78. For an informative analysis of a recent study by the German political scientist Hans Vorländer, *Hegemonialer Liberalismus: Politisches Denken und politische Kultur in den USA, 1776–1920*, which revises some of Hartz's arguments and reasserts others, see Klaus J. Hansen, "The Liberal Tradition in America: A German View," *The Journal of American History* 87 (2001): 1397–1408.

5. Paul Roazen, introduction to Louis Hartz, *The Necessity of Choice: Nineteenth-Century Political Thought* (New Brunswick, N.J.: Transaction Books, 1990), 8.

6. Louis Hartz, "Comment," *Comparative Studies in Society and History* 5 (1963–1964): 279–84.

7. Leonard Krieger, "A View from the Farther Shore," *Comparative Studies in Society and History* 5 (1963–1964): 269–73. Hartz had attempted to preempt this criticism in *The Liberal Tradition* (26–27) by pointing out how little intra-European comparative history had been done. Krieger was not persuaded. Adrienne Koch put the same point more bluntly: Hartz's method "produces no substantial documentation or analysis, but proceeds rather to pick up one name after another and freeze its arbitrarily selected essence to support the author's historical intuition. Individuality, chance, and the complex, specific coloration of a thinker's outlook are rudely sacrificed." Far from making "history 'scientific,' " Hartz's method of comparison merely reaffirms assumptions he was "obligated to establish in the first place." Adrienne Koch, review of Hartz, *The Liberal Tradition*, in *The Mississippi Valley Historical Review* 43 (1955): 550–52.

8. Louis Hartz, "Reply," in John H. M. Laslett and Seymour Martin Lipset, eds., *Failure of a Dream? Essays in the History of American Socialism*, rev. ed. (1974; Berkeley: University of California Press, 1984), 357–61. For Kenneth McNaught's critique of *The Liberal Tradition*, which emphasizes the significance of class divisions and democratic reform movements in American history, see 345–56.

9. Roazen, introduction, 20.

10. For evidence of the centrality of race and gender in contemporary scholarship, see, for example, three of the most widely read and celebrated works of the last several years, Rogers M. Smith, *Civic Ideals: Conflicting Visions of Citizenship in U.S. History* (New Haven, Conn.: Yale University Press, 1997); Eric Foner,

The Story of American Freedom (New York: Norton, 1998); and Linda K. Kerber, *No Constitutional Right to Be Ladies: Women and the Obligations of Citizenship* (New York: Hill and Wang, 1998).

11. The role of secular Jewish intellectuals in mid-twentieth-century American cultural criticism has not attracted the attention it deserves. On the paradoxical consequences of this dynamic for our post–World War II understanding of America's "liberal tradition" as a cultural phenomenon distinct from its Christian origins, see David A. Hollinger, *Science, Jews, and Secular Culture: Studies in Mid-Twentieth-Century American Intellectual History* (Princeton, N.J.: Princeton University Press, 1996), esp. chaps. 2, 3, and 8. Hartz could be an acute analyst of religion and its critics. In *The Necessity of Choice*, chapter 2, he examined brilliantly the eighteenth-century French *philosophes'* reliance on a standard of "nature" rather than "science" once they realized that a thoroughgoing empiricism would require them to take seriously the religious experience of French Catholics. Whereas a similar insight drove William James, committed to a radical empiricism, to examine in detail the varieties of religious experience, Hartz, for reasons not altogether clear, chose instead simply to dismiss the political significance of religion in America.

12. David D. Hall, *Worlds of Wonder, Days of Judgment: Popular Religious Belief in Early New England* (Cambridge, Mass.: Harvard University Press, 1990), 245. See more generally David D. Hall, "Narrating Puritanism," in *New Directions in American Religious History*, ed. Harry Stout and D. G. Hart (New York: Oxford University Press, 1997), 51–83, and Stephen Innes, *Creating the Commonwealth: The Economic Culture of Puritan New England* (New York: Norton, 1995). On Niebuhr, see Richard Wightman Fox, *Reinhold Niebuhr: A Biography*, with a new introduction and afterword (Ithaca, N.Y.: Cornell University Press, 1996); and on Murray, Patrick Allitt, *Catholic Intellectuals and Conservative Politics in America, 1950–1985* (Ithaca, N.Y.: Cornell University Press, 1993). For a fuller exposition of my argument concerning the role of religion in American political culture, see James T. Kloppenberg, "Knowledge and Belief in American Public Life," in Kloppenberg, *Virtues of Liberalism*, 38–58.

13. Alexis de Tocqueville, *Democracy in America*, ed. J. P. Mayer, trans. George Lawrence (Garden City, N.Y.: Doubleday and Co., Anchor Books, 1969), 506–13. For my understanding of Tocqueville and discussion of the various uses American scholars and politicians have made of his work, see James T. Kloppenberg, "Life Everlasting: Tocqueville in America," in Kloppenberg, *Virtues of Liberalism*, 71–81.

14. In other words, although Ira Katznelson's chapter in this volume serves to illustrate how influential Hartz's thesis remains, I dissent from Katznelson's contention that liberalism, "both as doctrine and as a set of institutions," has been "fundamental" "to the American experience as a boundary condition." That claim, which Katznelson adapts from the work of J. David Greenstone, seems to me overstated because it takes for granted that Americans agreed on "the central values of the liberal tradition." I believe that deep disagreements over the meaning of precisely the values Katznelson identifies—concepts such as individualism, rights, pluralism, the public versus the private sphere, market capitalism, and de-

mocracy—have shaped the American historical experience. For more detailed discussion of these controversial issues, see Kloppenberg, *Virtues of Liberalism*, 3–20, and especially the discussion of Greenstone on 181–82n16. But Katznelson is surely right that sophisticated historical investigations of democracy require equally sophisticated analyses of political ideas, and that historians should be reading the work of political theorists to sharpen their understanding. They should also remain alert to the ways in which the meanings and significance of political ideas—especially of such essentially contested concepts as democracy and liberalism—change over time and across cultures.

15. Richard J. Ellis, *American Political Cultures* (New York: Oxford University Press, 1993), 151. This spirited book can be read as an extended essay devoted to demonstrating, in considerable detail, the inadequacy of Hartz's argument in *The Liberal Tradition*. Readers still persuaded by Hartz's interpretation should read *American Political Cultures*, which examines more fully many of the shortcomings in *The Liberal Tradition* that I can only highlight briefly here. Another convincing rebuttal of Hartz's argument is the outstanding book by Daniel T. Rodgers, *Contested Truths: Keywords in American Politics since Independence* (New York: Basic Books, 1987). On the issues of race, ethnicity, and gender, see especially Smith, *Civic Ideals*; and Kerber, *No Constitutional Right to Be Ladies*.

16. For a strikingly different interpretation emphasizing the genuinely democratic and revolutionary achievements of the American Revolution, likewise examined in a comparative framework, see the still rewarding masterpiece by R. R. Palmer, *The Age of the Democratic Revolution*, 2 vols. (Princeton, N.J.: Princeton University Press, 1959, 1964), 1:185–235.

17. John Adams quoted in Joseph J. Ellis, *Passionate Sage: The Character and Legacy of John Adams* (New York: Norton, 1993), 136; Samuel Adams quoted in Gordon Wood, *The Creation of the American Republic, 1776–1787* (New York: Norton, 1969), 407. On the distance separating John Adams in particular from Hartz's notion of a liberal tradition, see the penetrating essay by John P. Diggins, "Knowledge and Sorrow: Louis Hartz's Quarrel with American History," *Political Theory* 16 (1988): 355–76. The book most responsible for John Adams's surprising recent popularity is David McCullough, *John Adams* (New York: Simon and Schuster, 2001); on Adams's ideas, a more valuable study is C. Bradley Thompson, *John Adams and the Spirit of Liberty* (Lawrence: University Press of Kansas, 1998). For recent studies establishing the founders' commitment to democratic procedures and challenging the idea that they should be seen as champions either of atomistic liberalism or of classical republicanism, see especially Lance Banning, *The Sacred Fire of Liberty* (Ithaca, N.Y.: Cornell University Press, 1995); Bernard Bailyn, *Faces of Revolution: Personalities and Themes in the Struggle for American Independence* (New York: Knopf, 1990); and Robert E. Shalhope, *The Roots of Democracy: American Thought and Culture, 1760–1800* (Boston: Twayne, 1990). On the question of honor and rights, see Joanne Freeman's chapter in this volume.

18. Cf. Louis Hartz, *Economic Policy and Democratic Thought: Pennsylvania, 1776–1860* (Cambridge, Mass.: Harvard University Press, 1948), and Oscar Handlin and Mary Flug Handlin, *Commonwealth: A Study of the Role of Government*

in the American Economy: Massachusetts, 1774–1861 (New York: New York University Press, 1947; rev. ed. Cambridge, Mass.: The Belknap Press of Harvard University Press, 1969), with William J. Novak, *The People's Welfare: Law and Regulation in Nineteenth-Century America* (Chapel Hill: University of North Carolina Press, 1996), esp. 1–18, 84–88, and 284–85. A common response to Novak's head-on challenge to the prevailing wisdom of American economic and legal historians is simple incredulity. Like the mountain of evidence for the language of republicanism that Gordon Wood presented in *The Creation of the American Republic*, however, Novak's evidence cannot be dismissed or explained away so easily; only extensive further research will confirm or challenge his interpretation. For a wealth of evidence further disputing Hartz's portrait of an uncomplicated, triumphant liberal ethos, presented within an explicitly comparative framework, see the fine essays in James Henretta and Jürgen Heideking, eds., *Republicanism and Liberalism in America and the German States, 1750–1850* (New York: Cambridge University Press, 2002).

19. Elizabeth B. Clark, "The Sacred Rights of the Weak: Pain, Sympathy, and the Culture of Individual Rights in Antebellum America," *Journal of American History* 82 (1995): 463–93. For other portraits of antebellum American culture irreconcilable with Hartz's, see Thomas L. Haskell's contributions to Thomas J. Bender, ed., *The Antislavery Debate: Capitalism and Abolitionism as a Problem in Historical Interpretation* (Berkeley: University of California Press, 1992), and Daniel Walker Howe, *Making the American Self: Jonathan Edwards to Abraham Lincoln* (Cambridge, Mass.: Harvard University Press, 1997).

20. See the chapters in this volume by William Novak and Richard John.

21. In John Stuart Mill, *On Liberty* (1859); see esp. chap. 4. I am grateful to William Novak for reminding me of this point.

22. Recent works investigating these issues include William Lee Miller, *Lincoln's Virtues: An Ethical Biography* (New York: Knopf, 2002), and Ronald C. White, Jr., *Lincoln's Greatest Speech: The Second Inaugural* (New York: Simon and Schuster, 2002). Hartz's undeniable power as teacher and interpreter is apparent in the work of J. David Greenstone, whose *analysis* in *The Lincoln Persuasion: Remaking American Liberalism* (Princeton, N.J.: Princeton University Press, 1993) inadvertently shows the inadequacy of Hartz's "liberal tradition." Greenstone's admiration for his teacher Hartz prevented him from seeing that his own compelling analysis of the "bipolarity" of American political thought, which he thought was overcome only by Lincoln and a few later progressive reformers, was incompatible with Hartz's argument in *The Liberal Tradition* for a unitary liberalism.

23. See the chapter by Michael Willrich in this volume.

24. On these issues, see the chapters in this volume by Michael Vorenberg and Sven Beckert.

25. I have tried to make clear the similarities as well as the differences between these American and European theorists and reformers in *Uncertain Victory: Social Democracy and Progressivism in European and American Thought, 1870–1920* (New York: Oxford University Press, 1986). More recent interpretations that place progressivism in a transatlantic context are Daniel T. Rodgers, *Atlantic*

Crossings: Social Politics in a Progressive Age (Cambridge, Mass.: Harvard University Press, 1998), and Axel R. Schäfer, *American Progressives and German Social Reform, 1875–1920* (Stuttgart: Franz Steiner Verlag, 2000). An excellent study of progressive thought that emphasizes its ethical and religious dimensions is Eldon Eisenach, *The Lost Promise of Progressivism* (Lawrence: University Press of Kansas, 1994).

26. On the origin, development, and fate of these ideas, the light they cast on American politics, and historians' dismissal of their importance, see James T. Kloppenberg, "American Democracy and the Welfare State: The Problem of Its Publics," in *The American Century in Europe*, ed. R. Laurence Moore and Maurizio Vaudagna (Ithaca, N.Y.: Cornell University Press, forthcoming in 2003), and Patrick D. Reagan, *Designing a New America: The Origins of New Deal Planning, 1890–1943* (Amherst: University of Massachusetts Press, 1999).

27. Claus Offe, *Contradictions of the Welfare State* (Cambridge, Mass.: MIT Press, 1984); George Reid Andrews and Herrick Chapman, eds., *The Social Construction of Democracy, 1870–1990* (New York: New York University Press, 1995). See also Stein Ringen, *The Possibility of Politics: A Study in the Political Economy of the Welfare State* (Oxford: Clarendon Press of Oxford University Press, 1987), and Abram de Swaan, *In Care of the State: Health Care, Education and Welfare in Europe and the USA in the Modern Era* (New York: Oxford University Press, 1988).

28. See the chapters in this volume by Meg Jacobs, Julian Zelizer, and Thomas Sugrue for illuminating explorations of the reasons behind opposition to the agendas of the New Deal and the Great Society.

29. For the source of the quotation from Noah Webster, see Joanne B. Freeman's chapter in this volume, p. 44, n. 23.

30. What can Hartz have meant, for example, by "the joy of a Dewey" or "the anguish of a Fenimore Cooper" in the passage quoted above? Given Dewey's deep dissatisfaction about the distance between his own radical democratic politics and his own educational theory versus the more limited achievements of twentieth-century American reformers and so-called progressive educators, and given Cooper's indomitable, triumphalist nationalism, one might as easily (and perhaps just as accurately) invoke "the anguish of a Dewey" and the "joy of a Fenimore Cooper." But in either case elegance plays Charlemagne to meaning, doing all the analytical work and leaving readers out of the circuit, puzzled. All of us call attention to our writing sometimes, depending on shorthand or imagery to do our work for us (as I did in the preceding sentence). *The Liberal Tradition* depends heavily on such sleights.

To continue this exercise, if "miles of submerged conviction" lie beneath pragmatism and if that conviction generates a "conformitarian ethos" that "has refused to pay its critics the compliment of an argument," why did Charles Sanders Peirce, William James, George Herbert Mead, and Dewey have to explain and defend themselves against critics (and each other) from the moment Peirce tried to explain how we make our ideas clear? Scrutinizing the pragmatists' writings would have forced Hartz to confront their challenge to the assumptions about Americans' thoroughgoing, unexamined individualism undergirding his argu-

ment. Like the religious language of eighteenth-century America or the more social democratic wing of American progressivism, pragmatism remained absent
from *The Liberal Tradition*. For a discussion of pragmatism in its older and newer
versions, see James T. Kloppenberg, "Pragmatism: An Old Name for Some New
Ways of Thinking?" *The Journal of American History* 83 (1996): 100–38; reprinted in John Pettegrew, ed., *A Pragmatist's Progress? Richard Rorty and American Intellectual History* (Lanham, Md.: Rowan and Littlefield, 2000), 19–60.

31. Louis Hartz, "Democracy: Image and Reality," in *Democracy Today*, ed.
William N. Chambers and Robert H. Salisbury (St. Louis: Washington University
Press, 1960), 13–29.

32. Thomas L. Haskell, "Taking Exception to Exceptionalism," *Reviews in
American History* 28 (2000): 151–66. For a recent set of instructive articles placing American history in comparative perspective, see *Rethinking American History in a Global Age*, ed. Thomas Bender (Berkeley: University of California Press,
2002).

33. Hartz, *Necessity of Choice*, 178; see also Roazen's discussion of this issue
in the introduction to that volume: "If, as Hartz believed, philosophizing exists
only where there is fundamental social conflict, it is no wonder that American
political thought, compared to what happened in Europe, never succeeded in getting off the ground" (5).

34. Valuable studies of the history American political theory have been written
recently by scholars such as Eldon Eisenach, Richard J. Ellis, J. David Greenstone,
George Kateb, Ira Katznelson, Donald S. Lutz, Nancy Rosenblum, Michael San-
del, Rogers Smith, and Shannon Stimson—to name only a few of the more prominent practitioners among political scientists who have sparked a return of interest
in the field. An alliance between such historically minded political theorists and
politically minded intellectual historians could do for American political thought
what scholars such as Quentin Skinner and Reinhard Koselleck have been doing
to place the study of early modern European thought in its historical context.

35. Donald P. Green and Ian Shapiro, *Pathologies of Rational Choice Theory:
A Critique of Applications in Political Science* (New Haven, Conn.: Yale University Press, 1994); *The Rational Choice Controversy: Economic Models of Politics
Reconsidered*, ed. Jeffrey Friedman (New Haven, Conn.: Yale University Press,
1996), includes voices on all sides of the debate over rational choice. William H.
Riker, *The Theory of Political Coalitions* (New Haven, Conn.: Yale University
Press, 1962), viii. For a wide-ranging and thoughtful discussion of these issues,
see Rogers Smith, "Science, Non-Science, and Politics," in *The Historic Turn in
the Human Sciences*, ed. Terrence J. McDonald (Ann Arbor: University of Michigan Press, 1996), 119–59. Two comprehensive histories of the profession of political science are David M. Ricci, *The Tragedy of Political Science: Politics, Scholarship, and Democracy* (New Haven, Conn.: Yale University Press, 1984); and
Raymond Seidelman and Edward J. Harpham, *Disenchanted Realists: Political
Science and the American Crisis, 1884–1984* (Albany: State University of New
York Press, 1985).

36. Donald S. Lutz, *A Preface to American Political Theory* (Lawrence: University Press of Kansas, 1992).

37. John Patrick Diggins, *The Proud Decades: America in War and Peace, 1941–1960* (New York: Norton, 1988), 255–56.

38. This is of course not the first time the United States has played such a paradoxical role, to the disgust and dismay of American dissenters who have understandably questioned whether the nation should be seen as a symbol of democratic promise. To cite just one example, Woodrow Wilson, although himself a racist and an imperialist, inspired democratic or anticolonialist movements in Egypt, India, China, Korea, and Indochina by proclaiming the principle of self-determination of peoples. See Erez Manela, "The Wilsonian Moment and the Rise of Anticolonial Nationalism" (Ph.D. dissertation, Yale University, 2003).

39. John Dewey, *The Public and Its Problems* (1927), in Dewey, *The Later Works*, ed. Jo Ann Boydston et al., vol. 2: 1925–1927 (Carbondale: Southern Illinois University Press, 1984), 350. See also Robert B. Westbrook, *John Dewey and American Democracy* (Ithaca, N.Y.: Cornell University Press, 1991), 552.

40. Walt Whitman, *Democratic Vistas* (1867, 1871), in Whitman, *Complete Poetry and Collected Prose*, ed. Justin Kaplan (New York: Library of America, 1982), 929.

Chapter Fifteen

THE POSSIBILITIES OF ANALYTICAL POLITICAL HISTORY

Ira Katznelson

WRITING IN 1956 with the authority conferred by three path-breaking books, Richard Hofstadter, the most important political historian of the United States in his generation, bemoaned the unfilled cavernous space between historical narratives and focused monographs. "Authors of narrative histories," he observed, "rarely hesitate to retell a story that is already substantially known, adding perhaps some new information but seldom in systematic fashion or with a clear analytical purpose," while "many a monograph . . . leaves its readers, and perhaps even its author, with misgivings as to whether that part of it which is new is truly significant." Seeking an alternative, he counseled more attention to the insights and creative possibilities proffered by the social sciences, whose use "promises to the historian . . . a special kind of opportunity to join these two parts of his tradition in a more effective way." By disturbing fixed historiographical routines and tendering a fresh stock of ideas, the social sciences, he believed, could offer historians access to concerns in the wider culture, a larger stock of methods, more rigor in argumentation, and, most important, the "ability to open new problems which the historian usually has ignored."[1]

It is worthy of note that Hofstadter did not endorse a literal-minded application of social science theory or technique, nor did he restrict his attention to the quantitative side of the ledger. He hardly wished that historians would either ascend to the region of grand theory or retreat to the zone of relatively focused, even small, questions where such techniques might best apply.[2] Entreating historians, rather, to address insistently large and relatively comprehensive questions—"eventually," he wrote, "the historian must deal in such categories as the Reformation, the Renaissance, the Industrial Revolution, with wars and social upheavals, with the great turning points in human experience, still tantalizingly unexplained or half-explained, still controversial"[3]—Hofstadter appealed to his colleagues to renew history as a vocation by developing a somewhat new historical genre, which will be a mixture of traditional history and the social sciences. It will differ from the narrative history of the past in that its primary purpose will be analytical. It will differ from the typical historical monograph of the past in that it will be more consciously designed as a literary form and will focus on types of problems that the monograph has all too often failed to raise. It will be informed by the insights of the social sciences and at some points will make use of methods they have originated. Without pretending to be scientific, it may well command more reciprocal interest and provide more stimulation for social scientists than a great deal of the history that is now being written.[4]

Hofstadter's call for a new analytical history at home in the disciplines of both history and the social sciences proved premature.[5] To be sure, there were efforts by various (then) "new" political historians to import tools of analysis from political science, sociology, and psychology into historical studies of political behavior, but these were more narrowly focused and literal-minded in their terms of trade, and less attentive to institutional practices, than Hofstadter had counseled or had practiced in his own scholarship. More broadly, moreover, political history, the main site of his own work, soon was displaced from its lead position at the top of the discipline's hierarchy of prestige by the generation of his students who sought to capture mobilization and resistance while stretching history beyond political storytelling limited to elite political behavior within mainstream institutions. These historians subjected political history to wide-ranging substantive, epistemological, and ideological critiques—many of which were on the mark—that increasingly marginalized political studies while favoring social and cultural inquiries that looked more to the humanities than to the social sciences for intellectual sustenance and that, at their most far-reaching, called into question some of the most basic practices that had guided the discipline since its founding as a modern profession.[6]

Curiously, insurgent sociologists and political scientists of the same generation, recoiling from and responding to the same stimuli of civil rights struggles at home and a colonial war abroad, turned to, not from, an engagement with political history.[7] Linked by a rallying cry to "bring the state back in" and the broader tandem effort to fashion a "historical institutionalism" emphasizing both how institutions originate and develop over time and how they shape human identities, preferences, and purposive action, a growing body of social scientists in the 1980s and 1990s began to address systematically the history of state building and state formation in the United States, and to rethink issues of American exceptionalism under the umbrella of American Political Development (APD).[8] The fresh and interesting scholarship they produced possesses a closer kinship with Hofstadter's analytical agenda geared to highlight the merits of a catholic and eclectic deployment of social scientific approaches to political subjects than work written by most historians, including political historians, of the United States. Positioned mainly on the "soft," qualitative side of political science and political sociology, APD's founding scholars—including J. David Greenstone, Amy Bridges, Karen Orren, and Stephen Skowronek—were particularly keen to understand what has been distinctive about the American regime and about transformations to political authority and capacity in the United States by treating the country's political arrangements, ideas, and behavior within a growing emphasis in various disciplines on institutions and within the ambit of comparative political studies about states and regimes.[9] Thus just when political history inside the history profession was losing its panache, risking dislocation and displacement, this new venture in a sister discipline was starting to ask big questions about the American polity and its past.[10]

Political history as a project for historians is beginning to make a strong comeback. Providing a happy challenge to Joel Silbey's recent judgment that "the subject itself is holding on by its fingertips,"[11] the collection of chapters in this volume signifies how some of the best younger American historians have begun to revivify the genre. Thankfully, this renewal is more a revitalization than a reprise. Breathing new life into such traditional subjects as law, federalism, and public administration, its practitioners are stocking, thus gaining, intellectual provisions on terms that advance their own agendas from quite distinct scholarly impulses. These include work on gender, race, and postcoloniality, as well as identity and the diffusion of sites of power approached within a way of working keenly influenced by Michel Foucault and by subsequent work focusing on discourse and power. They also have begun to draw from main currents in APD, including its state-oriented themes and concern for the status of liberalism in American political development. With the advancement of APD as a genuinely historical social science, boundary crossing between history and the social sciences has become easier and more frequent (though not, we will see, entirely simple or regular), and it is about this relationship that I primarily wish to comment.

Fortified by these currents, a new group of political historians has begun to produce problem-oriented, wide-scope studies much like those Hofstadter's program proposed. We can see this ambitious agenda at work in the chapters in this volume that often draw on social scientific questions, propositions, theories, and methods without any sacrifice of their grounding in the particularities of time and place. They traverse across boundaries within history and between history and the social sciences, especially APD, by focusing on the linguistic and symbolic meaning of honor in the early republic (Freeman); coming to terms with antebellum state formation and the putatively democratic character of Jacksonianism (John); utilizing citizenship as a tool to better integrate political and social history (Novak); linking constitutionalism with political culture (Vorenberg); informing the history of voting and illuminating issues of class by way of social history from below and above (Beckert); showing how gender helped (re)constitute zones of public and private even in such an unlikely arena as tariff policy (Edwards); examining the imbrication of the local and the national (Willrich); attending closely to mechanisms of linkage between elites and masses (Balogh); apprehending close ties between culture and political economy via politics (Jacobs); developing a historicist political economy (Zelizer); identifying signification and practices in localist ideology and policy (Sugrue); noting connections between microscopic and relational experiences and large-scale movements for change (Lassiter); and defining a place for intellectual history within political studies (Kloppenberg). By showing in their practice how analytical political history might proceed, these contributions constitute and suggest a kaleidoscope of appealing options and possibilities.

How might the current opportunity to develop robust political history best move ahead in tandem with the brisk expansion of historical approaches within the social sciences, especially in political science? Which issues, prospects, and openings offer opportunities and demand attention if Hofstadter's appealing goals as well as the key objectives underpinning this volume's collective effort are to be advanced (including its quest for syntheses, the pursuit of fresh approaches to temporality, considerations of such capacious concepts as state, democracy, and liberalism, and a better balance between consensus and conflict in American history)?

I proceed by briefly reviewing the benefits and the perimeters defining the limits of the current relationship connecting political history and APD. I then identify insufficiently attended empirical sites, treating Congress and international relations as examples. I also single out some underutilized intellectual resources, including aspects of recent scholarship on institutions in the social sciences and current work in political theory. Finally, I close by counseling against two overly sharp pendulum swings discernible in the new analytical political history at work in this book: from contested discussions about the regime's liberal character to an emphasis on the qualities of American democracy, and from consensus back to conflict. These, in my view, represent overcorrections.

POLITICAL HISTORY AND APD

In retrospect, we can see why Hofstadter's advocacy of a new analytical political history proved ill timed. With scant exception, social scientists at midcentury evidenced little interest in the past, often seeking to transcend history by discovering patterns and mechanisms that prevail irrespective of historical time or a given situation. Looking back, it is not difficult to comprehend why most historians found such social and behavioral sciences forbidding, even alien; or why they asserted the value and primacy of their mainly narrative orientation that focused on discrete situations and their complex concatenation of elements as distinct from ventures that seemed to quest for lawlike propositions that could be transported from time to time and place to place. Empirical work in political sociology and political science was marked, the sociologist Robert Merton observed in the late 1940s, by a "small vision" addressing "trivial matters in an empirically rigorous fashion," while theoretical work, his colleague C. Wright Mills discerned a decade later, tended to be pitched at "a level of thinking so general that its practitioners cannot logically get down to observation."[12] Political historians looking across the divide at the social sciences thus could find many reasons to retreat to familiar ground. When Hofstadter issued his appeal to engage with the social sciences in order to better compose analytical political histories, the doggedly ahistorical social sciences were not well equipped for the productive engagement he advocated to be sufficiently enticing to historians (except in such spheres as demographic or electoral studies). Interestingly, Hofstadter found more stimulation in psychology, both social and Freudian, than in political science or political sociology, but apart from generating a controversial focus on such mechanisms as status anxiety this orientation did not prove particularly felicitous or secure many adherents.[13]

Conditions for producing analytical political history in tandem with the social sciences now are vastly better. Today, the APD school warmly beckons historians to form a partnership for the subject's revival. As political history's closest cousin in the social sciences, APD's encounters with historical material resonate sufficiently with historians to make such an engagement both comfortable and productive. Itself indebted to historical scholarship and no longer just an insurgent, marginal enterprise in political science (APD sits alongside rational choice, grounded in microeconomics and game theory, and behavioral studies, an extension of psychology, as one of three main players in the discipline's studies of American politics), this orientation to political history makes available vigorous intellectual and organizational support for political historians who wish to work in a more analytical vein.

But it is not primarily the similarities but the differences that make the complementarities of APD and political history especially promising. APD political scientists rarely produce articles and books with the same richness of empirical material or command of primary sources as historians. In turn, historians tend to be theoretically modest and cautious, even reclusive, about defining problems or identifying causal mechanisms outside relatively enclosed spatial, temporal, and empirical boxes.[14] Political historians, a recent contributor to a political science roundtable on the future of political history observed, "possess what most historically-minded political scientists presently lack: namely, the professional training, incentives, and hands-on expertise to engage the primary empirical sources upon which the historical works of both disciplines ultimately rest." By contrast, political scientists "possess what American political historians presently lack: namely, an expanding corps of individuals interested in raising old and new questions of American political history and the theoretical and methodological expertise to construct intelligible, publicly relevant, and often novel answers to these questions."[15] Not just this diversity of research skills and orientations but a more fundamental divergence in proclivities divides most historians from most social scientists, even those with the strongest historical bent. Historians heeding particularity and contingency often are suspicious of efforts by social scientists to build causal analyses of social reality that deliberately highlight, even exaggerate, certain key features of their subjects to help us see the importance of these factors in shaping outcomes we wish to understand.[16] This tension is inescapable; the question is how to make it intellectually productive.

APD scholars produce model-like stories that shadow actual history at a higher level of abstraction and with more portable goals than can be found in most writing by historians. These deliberately simplified accounts that characterize actors, designate situations, and portray mechanisms linking agents to structures in ways that often privilege categories and variables over people and places with proper names offer suggestive helpmates to historians who are more enclosed in the peculiarities and exclusivities of their distinct periods and locations.[17] Such intentionally lean representations selectively portray the attributes of actors (what they want and why, what they know, and how they can act) and structures (the circumstances actors are in, including the distributional properties of the populations to which they belong and the networks to which they are linked, and the probabilistic implications of those states) in order to specify the configuration of mechanisms that shape both these actors and structures and define the terms of their interconnection. For practitioners of APD and the larger field of historical institutionalism within which it is embedded, this linkage is provided mainly by institutions, both formal and informal, and best grasped by analysis of institutions.

Based on this mix of charged familiarity and difference, the collaboration of political history and APD already has borne fruit in areas where APD has been particularly strong: studies of state formation and the history of political thought. Seeking to bring American history within the ambit of large-scale comparative historical accounts of the creation of "modern" centralized warfare states and welfare states in the West, and focusing, among other issues, on law and constitutionalism, center and periphery, and bureaucratic capacity and administrative adaptability, APD scholars have unmasked the "stateless" qualities of the American regime as a partial, chimerical, and ideological construct.[18] They also have advanced understanding of the role of political ideas, especially liberal thought, in American political development.[19] In this regard, Louis Hartz's *Liberal Tradition in America* continues to loom very large, having sparked a still-lively discussion about the sufficiency of its consideration of race, region, and gender, and its failure to attend to other strands of republican, democratic, racist, patriarchal, and protestant ideas that have been vibrant players in the country's political thought and discourse.[20] Manifestly, as the chapters in this volume demonstrate, these two substantive poles of work in APD already have enriched the new political history.

The productive association of political history and APD, in some respects now almost a joint venture, also is characterized by potential pitfalls. These tend to be both methodological and substantive. The deeper its engagement with qualitative political history, for example, the more APD's relationship with the rest of political science becomes harder to navigate, especially when its practitioners are reluctant to engage with or utilize the formal and statistical tools that now are common currency for their colleagues, even when these instruments could advance the agendas of APD.[21] Further, though APD scholars almost always are careful to deploy unbiased concepts and measures they define carefully and take care to assess their arguments and results against other possibilities, thus playing by the dominant positivist standards of the discipline, their "literary" mode of presentation often obscures this scaffolding and reinforces their isolation, limiting the impact of their work on that of other scholars in their discipline.

But here, I am mainly interested in the problems that cut the other way, that is, those distortions introduced when political historians risk reproducing APD's present habits and limits without sufficient reflection. These problems come in two bundles—methodological and substantive—that at times go together. Because APD tends to utilize a limited kit bag of methods, historians nourished by its offerings sometimes can find themselves constrained from utilizing the full range of tools they might usefully appropriate from the social sciences, ranging from studies of culture to model-building exercises. We can see this latter restriction at work, for example, in scholarship on Congress, where even outstanding work in the APD tradition has tended to refrain from utilizing statistical and mathematical techniques that might have been deployed to answer the authors' own questions.[22] Substantively, political history risks a mimetic approach to topics and theory that can produce a very close correspondence between the preoccupations and omissions in APD and the preoccupations and omissions by political historians as they look to APD, thus unduly restricting the range and scope of current historical scholarship.

This homologous intellectual geography is not misplaced or wrong-headed—quite the contrary, in my view, as we can see in this volume's chapters that consider the developmental, constitutional, and spatial complexity and plasticity of the American state, the state's transactions with the economy and civil society, and the relationship of liberalism and democracy in American political thought, each of which is a prototypical APD theme—but it is too narrowly constrained. More substantive, theoretical, and methodological locations are needed to serve as border crossings between history and the social sciences if research and writing by political historians and APD scholars is not to become too confined within a repertoire of issues and questions too limited in scope. What we need are more self-conscious considerations of the terms and limits of exchange between APD and political history of the kind Richard John provides in his revisionist treatment of the antebellum state, a subject where APD has been led astray by its imported centralized notion of stateness to think that one of the globe's most effective states, a state that could secure and extend its sovereignty and geographic scope, deploy a stable and effective ensemble of institutions, and tell a powerful integrative normative story, somehow was "weak."[23] More profitably, practitioners of American political studies need to assess the country's national state without deploying a too-simple foil of developed centralized authority as the exclusive hallmark of stateness. Rather, both historians and political scientists should be clearer about the various dimensions of stateness, about the special character of a liberal state, and about how the political regime has changed over time, especially at critical junctures when the character and content of the state have been contested most robustly.

Some silences are more consequential than others. I think two have been particularly baleful. In their emerging close relationship, both APD and political history have been paying insufficient attention to international influences on American political development, and both have accorded inadequate notice to Congress, the country's most important site of political representation (arguably, the legislature is the most important institutional location in any liberal democracy).

The vast majority of work in APD and most political history, including the chapters written for this book, is concerned in the main with politics enclosed within American borders. To be sure, diplomatic and geopolitical matters enter into consideration from time to time as appropriate, but these subjects rarely compose primary objects for theoretical or historical scrutiny.[24] High walls separate studies of American politics at home from "foreign" affairs, as if these were entirely autonomous domains. This division makes it difficult to probe how such international factors as war, military pressure, trade, and the country's position in the global economic order operate both as constant causes operating in broadly similar ways across time and as historical causes shaping outcomes at specific formative moments.[25]

There is a massive missed chance here. If we treat the international arena as a regular source of pressure-producing sets of expectations about how given causes shape outcomes, it would be reasonable, for example, to hypothesize that central state claims to sovereignty would be heightened by military pressure, that executive power would be enhanced by war, that the regulative and redistributive activities of the state would expand under the impact of both trade and military pressure, and that a sense of stateness would become more pronounced as military pressures increased but would diminish with the interdependence of trade. Each of these propositions is familiar to students of international relations and comparative politics, but they have not been investigated systematically or regularly on either side of the political science–history divide for their effects on American political development. International causes also can be studied for the way they shape outcomes at specific historical junctures, even while recognizing that the resulting pattern may persist without the continuing presence of the initial formative causes. Whether caused by "shocks" such as depressions and wars or by endogenous processes, at relatively indeterminate moments new configurations of stateness and ideas about the state may be fashioned under the impact of international effects.[26]

In Congress, liberal and democratic theory is made flesh. It is hard to see how the American national state can be understood, or how such issues as legislative enactments, citizenship, bureaucratic organization, constitutional innovation, voting rights, gender and the party system, federalism and courts, styles of interest group politics, the rules of political economy, patterns of taxation, the federal qualities of public policy, the rise of antigovernment social movements, or the status of liberal and democratic values—that is, the core themes in this book—can be reckoned and combined into larger syntheses without placing Congress at the center of historical investigation. Yet, with the exception of Julian Zelizer's recent major book on taxation and the House of Representatives and Michael Holt's magisterial study of the Whig party, political historians are producing much less work on this institution now than before the rise of APD.[27] Books like David Rothman's fine study in the 1960s of the United States Senate or the considerable literature chronicled in review essays written by Silbey in the early 1980s no longer are being produced.[28] Speculatively, I think this intellectual stillness is in part a result of disappointment with earlier studies of roll call behavior by historians and in part a result of how APD has been appropriated by political historians who have matched its interest in the executive branch and the powers of the bureaucratic state and its neglect of Congress.[29] As a result, both groups of scholars now wear reinforcing blinders.

By contrast, congressional studies in mainstream political science of the high positivist kind usually resisted by historians have more to offer. In the past half dozen years, influenced in part by APD's turn to history, these students of Congress have been exploiting variations in legislative institutions and historical contexts to test hypotheses they previously applied only to the contemporary (post-1945) Congress. Approached with appropriate historical, substantive, and methodological sensibilities and caution, it should be possible to open up political history (and APD) to this vast body of scholarship.[30] To be sure, acts of translation and adjustment will be required. For if part of the appeal of the new historical research to congressional scholars in political science is its application of "modern" methods such as formal theory and statistical modeling to the large data set of past events and behavior, a key puzzle is how to apply these methods in a way that is sensitive to the nuances of historical analysis. In shaping answers to these questions, political historians might come to play a role that is formative. But this challenge remains to be addressed, let alone accomplished.

INSTITUTIONALISM AND POLITICAL THEORY

International and congressional affairs hardly exhaust the list of subjects to which insufficient attention has been paid. A longer list would have to include subjects that have been sequestered inside specialist historical literatures rather than integrated into political history. It would take in the military, the main institutional hinge between international and domestic politics, and studies of sectionalism, as distinct from federalism, which often are stuck inside regional histories, especially of the South and West, in a history profession that remains very fragmented.[31] But it is easier to shift empirical focus to incorporate these subjects than to extend analytical horizons. In looking to, and beyond, APD for sustenance, political historians might want to consider two important bodies of work that provide a substructure for APD: historical-institutional analysis and contemporary political theory.

A recent overview of historical institutionalism in contemporary political science by Paul Pierson and Theda Skocpol stresses that there is no essentialist definition to turn to. Unlike classical Marxism, for example, historical institutionalism is not integrated by one full-size theoretical framework. Rather, its practitioners tend to share ways of asking questions sufficiently to understand key political outcomes that they meaningfully can be said to compose a discernible "school." Its defining elements, Pierson and Skocpol suggest, include three main elements. First, there is a propensity to address such "big, substantive questions" as the circumstances under which ethnic identities become politicized, revolutions occur, democracies become stable, and welfare states develop along divergent paths. "The focus is on explaining variations in important or surprising patterns, events, or arrangements—rather than accounting for human behavior without regard to context or modeling very general processes presumed to apply at all times and places." Second, and quite unusual in the social sciences, this orientation takes "time seriously, specifying sequences and tracing transformations and processes of varying scale and temporality." In so doing, historical institutionalists are particularly sensitive to the temporal sequencing of causal factors and to the combination of distinct causal processes that become conjoined at distinct periods, especially at critical branching junctures. Third, this "school" often analyzes constellations or configurations of elements, rather than taking factors or variables one at a time, to show how institutions and processes develop over the long term and how they combine at distinct moments and are remade over time.[32]

I know of no political historian reading this list who would not nod, then affirm that this surely is what good historians actually do when they characterize situations rather than merely describe them. Except as broad guiding orientations, however, historians rarely take these three features of historical institutionalism fully to heart. Within American political history, it is rare for the problems chosen for study to be defined in terms of the more general substantive and theoretical challenges identified by Pierson and Skocpol as central to historical institutionalism. Neither are questions of temporality and periodicity tackled with the kind of theoretical acuity they pinpoint; nor are causal stories developed in configurative hierarchies resembling causal models. Historians, even historians most open to APD, tend to abjure such detailed engagement with the analytics of history. This is a pity, I think, because without overtly grappling with these themes and utilizing them to structure historical inquiries, Hofstadter's goal of a genuinely analytical history will remain beyond our ken.

There is another advantage in attending to the broader body of work by historical institutionalists rather than exclusively to the APD subset of work in this genre. Notoriously, both history and political science segregate American political studies from systematic comparative research, reinforcing both the absence of attention to the impact of international influences and the conceit that politics in the United States is entirely sui generis, thus making it difficult to look beyond country-specific actors and conditions within the United States.[33] A host of comparative possibilities are ignored, not least with other postrevolutionary and formerly slave societies in the Americas,[34] with other "new nations" undergoing separation from colonial rulers, with other states that effectively functioned as empires, and with other states that have constructed confederations, federations, and empires.[35]

Historical institutionalism's deep affinity with comparative scholarship thus can prod American political history to escape its provincial temptations. But here, too, not without watchfulness and care. For despite support for tolerant methodological pluralism as a value, there is a tendency to methodological closure among many historical institutionalists, who at times bluntly oppose what they do to other "new" institutionalisms, thus prematurely closing opportunities for synergism. Kenneth Finegold and Theda Skocpol's fine comparative-historical study of the New Deal's National Recovery Administration and Agricultural Adjustment Administration, as an example, invites readers to measure the abilities of historical institutionalism against rational choice institutionalism (as well as pluralism, elitism, and Marxism) rather than ask how this intellectual tableau might be put to work concurrently.[36] I prefer more modesty and greater assertiveness. More modesty because the power of a given theory can vary not just from case to case or from one object of analysis to another but even inside the moments of the cases under investigation. Challenging substantive puzzles, moreover, always are complex; no one set of analytical tools should claim exclusive purchase. But also greater assertiveness. There is nothing wrong with wagering strongly on a particular approach, provided it remains open and self-reflective, willing to engage other theoretical and analytic approaches on its own terms, assuredly making selections disciplined by its own purposes.[37]

One could well have expected that the investment APD has made in laying emphasis on political liberalism in the United States, and especially on debates about the adequacy of the Hartzian tradition, might have led to the door of analytic liberal political thought. But it has not. Though APD has taken a vibrant interest in jurisprudence, it has been far less engaged with the problems, literature, and projects political theorists have been producing even though these bear directly on one of its central questions, the place of liberalism in the country's regime. Since John Rawls led the revival of political theory some three decades ago,[38] there has been an explosion of work by philosophers, legal scholars, and political scientists to consider the tension-ridden linkage joining political liberalism (based on such values as consent, freedom, representation, toleration, and secure political rights) to democracy (based on participation, deliberation, and transparent decision-rules and procedures). Among other issues, they have considered and illuminated questions concerning qualities of citizenship, rules and barriers to membership, bases of legitimacy, the relationship of liberalism to nationalism and other potentially illiberal and nondemocratic constructs, social policy and distributive justice, the role of political associations, incommensurable values and deep cultural pluralism, and public morality.[39] It makes little sense for either APD or political history to sidestep this rich and suggestive body of scholarship, for its themes intersect so directly with many of their most pressing concerns. Each of these subjects, after all, has an institutional as well as a philosophical component. Each provides a plentiful list of questions with empirical possibilities. Each can help us understand what is at stake at key moments of large-scale historical inflection.

LIBERALISM AND DEMOCRACY, CONSENSUS AND CONFLICT

Most important, work in political theory can help guide us as we think historically and empirically about the core challenge of apprehending the character and significance of the braiding of liberalism and democracy in American history. We know that Hartz and the postwar consensus historians overstated the uncontested quality of America's "nationalist articulation of Locke,"[40] failing to give adequate recognition to the country's multiple political traditions, especially to the deep illiberalism of race.[41] We know that Hartz made insufficient provision for deep conflict about the substance of American liberalism or the degree of its democratization, preferring to underscore continuities and consensus with regard to the basic features of the regime. And we know that his and other consensus scholarship does not sufficiently understand that liberalism, as an institutional boundary condition in American life embodying norms of speech and action, has been disputed with regard to its democratic qualities, especially at such pivotal moments as the Civil War and Reconstruction or the New Deal. A boundary condition, David Greenstone has observed, is "a set of relatively permanent features of a particular context that affect causal relationships within it" even as it remains subject to dispute.[42] As just such a condition, liberalism in America has been dominant but not unchanging or unchallenged. The content of its grammar of rules—its bundle of institutions and norms—was not settled once and for all; hence the consensus view of American liberalism is misleading to the extent that it suggests a static set of limits rather than diverse possibilities.

And yet, we should not forget that Hartz was quite correct to underscore how liberalism has been fundamental—both as doctrine and as a set of institutions—to the American experience as a boundary condition. The central values of the liberal tradition, including equal respect of persons as citizens (coupled with an irreducible individualism and a doctrine of rights), consent, toleration of a plurality of beliefs and ways of life, and a demarcation of separate public and private spheres, as well as the central institutional arrangements of Western liberalism, including representative democracy and markets,[43] have been far more continuous features in the United States than elsewhere. Further, Hartz and consensus history more broadly had what Hofstadter called the "transitional merit" of providing a useful corrective to the exaggerations about conflict and democracy by the progressive historians. In so doing, these scholars, some of whom have been dismissed too hastily as status quo conservatives,[44] forced attention to tacit power and hegemonic assumptions (thus anticipating Foucault).[45]

What Hartz and the consensus school undervalued, however, was the extent to which these durable regime features themselves have defined vigorous disagreement in constitutional jurisprudence, the politics of social movements, electoral mobilizations, and recurring discord about language and culture—that is, in debates about America as a democracy. After all, the most basic conflicts about liberalism as a boundary condition in American life have been concerned with issues vital not only to its liberalism but to its democracy: the institutional structure of the American state (including its territorial extensiveness, the character of its federalism, and the powers it can exercise); the nature of the body of citizens in civil society eligible to participate in American political life (relevant issues include barriers of property, race, nationality, and gender); and the rules and institutions that govern the ties between this state and these citizens. Once we seek to grasp the moments when struggles about norms, institutions, and practices have been most robust and thus introduce indeterminacy into the story of American political development, the contradiction between the claim that the United States is the West's most durably liberal regime and the view stressing cacophony and conflict about democracy is revealed as artificial.

Hofstadter serves as a trustworthy guide. As "an essentially negative proposition," he cautioned, consensus is "a counter-assertion more than an empirical tool. . . . It sets the boundaries of the scene and enables us to see where the picture breaks off and the alien environment begins; but it does not provide the foreground or the action." Questioning whether the canons of consensus "can explain or give an adequate account of those conflicts which did take place," he underscored "the genuinely revolutionary aspects of the American Revolution," which built a liberal regime of "living institutions" while democratizing the distribution of power among social classes and introducing a healthy disrespect for vested interests; the issues related to the Civil War, "the racial, ethnic, and religious conflict with which our history is saturated" and the litany of American violence, including "the long ruthless struggle with the Indian; our filibustering expeditions; our slave insurrections; our burned convents and mobbed abolitionists and lynched Wobblies; our sporadic, furiously militant Homesteads, Pullmans, and Pattersons; our race lynchings, race riots, and ghetto riots; our organized gangsterism; our needless wars . . . with England, Mexico, Spain, and North Vietnam."

Notwithstanding, Hofstadter wrote, by "forcing us to think about the importance of those things Americans did not have to argue about" (at least most Americans much of the time), consensus can function analytically much as "an appropriate frame . . . to a painting." As "a matter of behavior as well as thought, of institutions as well as theories," it never comes in a single package. Constitutional consensus differs from policy consensus, and both are distinct from moral consensus. Moreover, the concept is best deployed "not as a satisfactory general theory or as an answer but as a whole set of new questions about the extent to which agreement prevails in a society, who in fact takes part in it, and how it is arrived at." Characteristically, he counseled against overextending the idea of conflict or consensus, however true, refusing the choice of frame or picture. Instead, Hofstadter urged historians to turn the rather abstract debate about liberal consensus and democratic conflict into an opportunity to create analytical histories nourished but not unduly constrained by scholarship in the social sciences.[46]

But with a humanistic distinction. "In an age when so much of our literature is infused with nihilism," the last sentence of *The Progressive Historians* reads, "and other social disciplines are driven toward narrow positivistic inquiry, history may remain the most humanizing among the arts."[47] As political history regains its élan, we could do worse than build analytical studies in this generous and open spirit.

Notes

For their extended and thoughtful comments on an earlier draft, I am indebted to Richard John, Julian Zelizer, and the two reviewers for this volume.

1. Richard Hofstadter, "History and the Social Sciences," in *The Varieties of History*, ed. Fritz Stern (Cleveland and New York: World Publishing Co., 1956), 359, 362, 364. Reciprocally, he thought history had much to offer the social sciences, which must learn, he believed, to transcend their penchant for transhistorical generalization in their search for explanations of variation.

2. His own work, of course, was deeply interested in issues of culture and the human psyche, among other subjects, and its span took in the study of political parties, social movements, violence, political thought, and issues of leadership, among other subjects.

3. Hofstadter, "History," 369–70.

4. Ibid., 363.

5. I do not mean to imply that Hofstadter's broader substantive legacy was not taken up by many historians. In particular, an important strand of work, including that of his own students (among them Stanley Elkins, Eric McKitrick, Eric Foner, Linda Kerber, and Paula Fass) has produced what many rightly see as a distinct Hofstadterian tradition that includes close attention to the interplay of politics and culture. My point, rather, is that his call for a particular kind of analytical history based on particular terms of engagement between history and the social sciences remains to be realized but now has uncommonly good chances to be achieved for reasons I consider below. For discussions of Hofstadter's work and legacy, see Daniel Walker Howe and Peter Elliot Finn, "Richard Hofstadter: The Ironies of an American Historian," *Pacific Historical Review* 43 (February 1974); Daniel Joseph Singal, "Beyond Consensus: Richard Hofstadter and American Historiography," *American Historical Review* 89 (October 1984); Eric Foner, "The Education of Richard Hofstadter," *The Nation*, May 4, 1992; and Alan Brinkley, "Richard Hofstadter's *The Age of Reform*: A Reconsideration," in *American Retrospectives: Historians on Historians*, ed. Stanley I. Kutler. (Baltimore: Johns Hopkins University Press, 1995).

6. See Peter Novick, *That Noble Dream: The "Objectivity Question" and the American Historical Profession* (New York: Cambridge University Press, 1988).

7. For a discussion of this turn and this contrast, see Theda Skocpol, "Social History and Historical Sociology: Contrasts and Complementarities," *Social Science History* 11 (spring 1987).

8. Peter Evans, Dietrich Rueschemeyer, and Theda Skocpol, eds., *Bringing the State Back In* (Cambridge: Cambridge University Press, 1985); Sven Steinmo, Kathleen Thelen, and Frank Longstreth, eds., *Structuring Politics: Historical Institutionalism in Comparative Perspective* (Cambridge: Cambridge University Press, 1992); Kathleen Thelen, "Historical Institutionalism in Comparative Politics," *Annual Review of Political Science* 2 (1999). There was a good deal of historical and institutionalist work in political science at the start of the twentieth century, but it would be a forced claim to represent current work as a return to an older, lost tradition. For an overview of the history of political science, see Ira Katznelson and Helen V. Milner, "American Political Science: The Discipline's State and the State of the Discipline," in *Political Science: State of the Discipline*, ed. Katznelson and Milner (New York and Washington, D.C.: Norton and The American Political Science Association, 2002).

9. A key moment in the development of the APD subfield came in 1986 with the founding of a new journal, *Studies in American Political Development*, edited by the political scientists Karen Orren of UCLA and Stephen Skowronek of Yale.

10. I have reviewed this disciplinary history at greater length in "The State to the Rescue? Political Science and History Reconnect," *Social Research* 59 (winter 1993).

11. Joel Silbey, "The State and Practice of American Political History at the Millennium: The Nineteenth Century as a Test Case," *Journal of Policy History* 11 (March 1999): 1. One strand of "the new political history" focusing on political parties and behavioral regularities, to which Silbey, in major work on political parties and elections, has been a significant contributor, has been quite close to parts of the social sciences and now is in a middle age characterized by Paula

Baker as a "midlife crisis." Paula Baker, "The Midlife Crisis of the New Political History," *The Journal of American History* 86 (June 1999).

12. Robert K. Merton, *Social Theory and Social Structure* (New York: Harper and Row, 1947), 443–44; C. Wright Mills, *The Sociological Imagination* (New York: Oxford University Press, 1959), 33.

13. Historians influenced by Hofstadter have drawn on Geertzian cultural theory and linguistic analysis to pursue aims Hofstadter sought to advance via Freudian importations.

14. I discuss, as an example, the fine synthetic volume by James T. Patterson, *Grand Expectations: The United States, 1945–1974* (New York: Oxford University Press, 1997), in "Patterson's Umbrella: Does It Keep Us Too Dry?" (a review essay) and in "Description, Interpretation, and Explanation: An Addendum in Response to James Patterson," *Journal of Policy History* 10, no. 3 (1998).

15. Charles A. Krumkowski, "The Future of Political History: An Introduction," unpublished contribution to the Roundtable on the Future of American Political History, American Political Science Association Annual Meeting, September 2000.

16. In turn, social scientists too often treat the work of the history profession as something of a service industry, providing information and data for analysis.

17. Gudmund Hernes, "Real Virtuality," in *Social Mechanisms: An Analytical Approach to Social Theory*, ed. Peter Hedström and Richard Swedberg (New York: Cambridge University Press, 1998).

18. Key works in this vein include Stephen Skowronek, *Building a New American State: The Expansion of National Administrative Capacities, 1877–1920* (New York: Cambridge University Press, 1982); Richard Franklin Bensel, *Yankee Leviathan: The Origins of Central State Authority in America, 1859–1877* (New York: Cambridge University Press, 1990); and Theda Skocpol, *Protecting Soldiers and Mothers: The Political Origins of Social Policy in the United States* (Cambridge, Mass.: Harvard University Press, 1992). Alas, these excellent works, and the state-oriented impulse of APD more generally, have tended to neglect or misrepresent the qualities of stateness of the antebellum period. I return to this subject below.

19. For a representative collection of APD essays along these lines, see David F. Ericson and Louisa Bertch Green, *The Liberal Tradition in American Politics: Consensus, Polarity, or Multiple Traditions?* (Boston: Routledge, 1999).

20. Louis Hartz, *The Liberal Tradition in America: An Interpretation of American Political Thought since the Revolution* (New York: Harcourt Brace, 1955); Rogers M. Smith, *Civic Ideals: Conflicting Visions of Citizenship in U.S. History* (New Haven, Conn.: Yale University Press, 1997).

21. For a discussion of this issue, see Ira Katznelson, "Reflections on History, Method, and Political Science," *The Political Methodologist* 8 (fall 1997), and Rogers M. Smith, "Politics, History, and Bush v. Gore," *Clio: Newsletter of Politics and History* 12 (spring/summer 2002): 1.

22. Here I have in mind the excellent scholarship by Richard Bensel and Elizabeth Sanders. Richard Franklin Bensel, *Sectionalism and American Political Development, 1880–1980* (Madison: University of Wisconsin Press, 1984); Bensel, *Yankee Leviathan*; Richard Franklin Bensel, *The Political Economy of American*

Industrialization, 1877–1900 (New York: Cambridge University Press, 2000; Elizabeth Sanders, *Roots of Reform: Farmers, Workers, and the American State, 1877–1917* (Chicago: University of Chicago Press, 1999).

23. I have in mind not only Richard John's contribution to this volume but also his "Governmental Institutions as Agents of Change: Rethinking American Political Development in the Early Republic, 1787–1835," *Studies in American Political Development* 11 (fall 1997): 347–80.

24. In part, this situation reflects the marginalization of diplomatic history within the history profession, even more so than the fate of political history. There are important exceptions to my lament about neglect, especially in work by historians on the early republic. See Robert H. Wiebe, *The Opening of American Society: From the Adoption of the Constitution to the Eve of Disunion* (New York: Knopf, 1984); William W. Freehling, *The Road to Disunion: Secessionists at Bay, 1776–1854* (New York: Oxford University Press, 1990); Andrew R. L. Cayton, " 'Separate Interests' and the Nation-State: The Washington Administration and the Origins of Regionalism in the Trans-Appalachian West," *Journal of American History* 79 (June 1992); Stanley M. Elkins and Eric L. McKitrick, *The Age of Federalism* (New York: Oxford University Press, 1993); and Nicholas Greenwood Onuf and Peter S. Onuf, *Federal Union, Modern World: The Law of Nations in an Age of Revolutions, 1776–1814* (Madison, Wis.: Madison House, 1993).

25. For discussions of these two types of causality, see Arthur L. Stinchcombe, *Constructing Social Theories* (New York: Harcourt Brace, 1968), 101–29, and Ruth Beirns Collier and David Collier, *Shaping the Political Arena* (Princeton, N.J.: Princeton University Press, 1991).

26. These themes are the subjects of Ira Katznelson and Martin Shefter, eds., *Shaped by War and Trade: International Influences on American Political Development* (Princeton, N.J.: Princeton University Press, 2002).

27. Julian E. Zelizer, *Taxing America: Wilbur D. Mills, Congress, and the State, 1945–1975* (New York: Cambridge University Press, 1998); Michael Holt, *Rise and Fall of the American Whig Party: Jacksonian Politics and the Outset of the Civil War* (New York: Oxford University Press, 1999). Another emerging exception to this rule is the series of volumes on the early history of Congress that are being published by the Capitol Historical Society. See Kenneth R. Bowling and Donald R. Kennon, eds., *The House and Senate in the 1790s: Petitioning, Lobbying, and Institutional Development* (Athens: Ohio University Press, 2002).

28. David Rothman, *Politics and Power: The United States Senate, 1869–1901* (Cambridge, Mass.: Harvard University Press, 1966); Joel H. Silbey, "Congressional and State Legislative Roll-Call Studies by U.S. Historians," *Legislative Studies Quarterly* 4 (1981): 597–697; Margaret Susan Thompson and Joel H. Silbey, "Historical Research on Nineteenth-Century Legislatures," *Legislative Studies Quarterly* 7 (1984): 319–50. For a discussion of the current state of the literature, see Joel H. Silbey, "Current Historiographic Trends in the Study of the Twentieth-Century Congress," *Social Science History* 24, no. 2 (2000): 317–31.

29. Within APD, the work of Bensel and Sanders, referenced above, offers the most important exception to this generalization. Also see Elaine K. Swift, *The Making of an American Senate: Reconstitutive Change in Congress, 1787–1841* (Ann Arbor: University of Michigan Press, 1996).

30. A helpful guide to the massive literature on Congress in political science is Nelson W. Polsby and Eric Schickler, "Landmarks in the Study of Congress Since 1945," *Annual Review of Political Science* 5 (2002).

31. This generalization is only partly true in the work of Freehling, *Road to Disunion*. Also see Andrew R. L. Cayton and Peter S. Onuf, *The Midwest and the Nation: Rethinking the History of an American Region* (Bloomington: Indiana University Press, 1990).

32. Paul Pierson and Theda Skocpol, "Historical Institutionalism in Contemporary Political Science," in *Political Science*, ed. Katznelson and Milner.

33. Here I echo Peter Kolchin, "Comparing American History," *Reviews in American History* 10 (December 1982).

34. There has been, by contrast, important comparative work in the history of slavery. See David Brion Davis, *The Problem of Slavery in Western Culture* (New York: Oxford University Press, 1966), and Peter Kolchin, *Unfree Labor: American Slavery and Russian Serfdom* (Cambridge, Mass.: Harvard University Press, 1987).

35. An effort to work more comparatively and internationally still worth attending to is C. Vann Woodward, ed., *The Comparative Approach to American History* (New York: Basic Books, 1968).

36. Kenneth Finegold and Theda Skocpol, *State and Party in America's New Deal* (Madison: University of Wisconsin Press, 1995). This treatment draws on Ira Katznelson, "The Doleful Dance of Politics and Policy: Can Historical Institutionalism Make a Difference?" (a review essay), *American Political Science Review* 92 (March 1998).

37. For an illuminating overview of institutional analysis guided by rational choice drawn mainly form microeconomics and by problem-solving approaches drawn primarily from cognitive psychology that, alas, has no historical dimension, see C. Mantzavinos, *Individuals, Institutions, and Markets* (Cambridge: Cambridge University Press, 2001). For an attempt to combine the institutional perspectives of economists and sociologists, see James E. Rauch and Alessandra Casella, eds., *Networks and Markets* (New York: Russell Sage Foundation, 2001), and Mauro F. Guillén, Randall Collins, Paula England, and Marshall Meyer, eds., *The New Economic Sociology: Developments in an Emerging Field* (New York: Russell Sage Foundation, 2002).

38. John Rawls, *A Theory of Justice* (Cambridge, Mass.: Harvard University Press, 1973).

39. The relevant literature is immense. Three recent representative examples, perhaps not as well known as those by such leading figures as John Rawls, Ronald Dworkin, Will Kymlicka, and Iris Marion Young, are Raymond Geuss, *History and Illusion in Politics* (Cambridge: Cambridge University Press, 2001); Anne Phillips, *The Politics of Presence* (Oxford: Clarendon Press, 1995); and Samuel Scheffler, *Boundaries and Allegiances: Problems of Justice and Responsibility in Liberal Thought* (New York: Oxford University Press, 2001).

40. Hartz, *Liberal Tradition*, 10–11.

41. For a recent critique along these lines, see Rogers M. Smith, "Beyond Tocqueville, Myrdal, and Hartz: The Multiple Traditions in America," *American Political Science Review* 87 (September 1993).

42. J. David Greenstone, *The Lincoln Persuasion: Remaking American Liberalism* (Princeton, N.J.: Princeton University Press, 1993), 42, 45.

43. For discussions of the core features of liberal doctrine, see Ronald Dworkin, "Liberalism," and "Why Liberals Should Care about Equality," in Dworkin, *A Matter of Principle* (Cambridge, Mass.: Harvard University Press, 1985); Charles Larmore, "Political Liberalism," *Political Theory* 18 (August 1990); and Jeremy Waldron, "Theoretical Foundations of Liberalism," *The Philosophical Quarterly* 37 (April 1987).

44. The charge does fit Daniel Boorstin but certainly not Hartz.

45. Richard Hofstadter, *The Progressive Historians: Turner, Beard, Parrington* (New York: Alfred A. Knopf, 1968), 452.

46. Ibid., 437–66.

47. Ibid., 466.

Free Soil approach to, 126; and judicial review of state constitutions, 124–25; literal vs. historical reading of, 136; living, 139–40n.4; permanence of, 121, 125–26, 128–30, 134–35, 137, 145n.63 (*see also* secession); and popular democracy, 137; Progressive Era views of, 123; Reconstruction amendments, generally, 121–23, 137 (*see also* Fifteenth Amendment; Fourteenth Amendment; Thirteenth Amendment); Thirteenth Amendment, 11, 106, 133, 134–37 (*see also* Constitution, and the antislavery movement *above*); Twelfth Amendment, 121; and women's suffrage, 139–40n.4
Consumer Advisory Board (CAB), 259, 262
Consumer Counsel, 259
contract, 85, 94
Cook, Daniel P., 69, 71, 83n.92
Cook County courts (Illinois), 204, 208, 219n.12
Cooley, Thomas, 90
Cooper, Edward, 150, 163
Cooper, Fenimore, 378–79n.30
Cooper, Peter, 146
Cooper, Thomas, 32–39, 46nn.40 and 43, 47nn.54 and 57
Corfield v. Coryell, 92, 107, 114–15n.28
Cornell, John B., 146
Corn Exchange (New York City), 163
corporate liberal synthesis, 279–80, 281
corporations, legal status of, 95–96
Cott, Nancy, 96–97, 179, 244–45n.5
Cotton Exchange (New York City), 152, 163
Council of Reform (New York City), 152
country party tradition (whig tradition; classical republican tradition), 55, 65–66
courts, 198–217; vs. administrative law, 210–12; *Baker v. Carr,* 313; as blocking state development, 12, 198, 217; boys' court, 213; *Brown v. Board of Education,* 313, 337; common-law, 199–200, 208–9, 210–11; courts and parties thesis, 53–54, 301; and crime/criminals, 213, 217; criminal, 214; criticism/reform of, 208–10; domestic relations court, 213; judicial obstructionism, 200; judicial power, strengthening of, 210; judicial review, 200; managerial model of, 209; *Milliken v. Bradley,* 313, 341; mor-

als court, 213, 216; municipal, as administrative tribunals, 13; Municipal Court of Chicago, 198, 200–201, 202, 207–9, 210, 212–15; and private associations/professional experts, 213–15; progressiveness of, 201–2; social administration/governance by, 201–2, 214–17; urban court systems' power, 213–14; the welfare state as emerging in, 198, 201–2, 215–16. *See also* justice-of-the-peace system
Cox, Samuel ("Sunset"), 135
Crawford, William H., 53, 57–58, 59
Crenson, Matthew, 52–53, 75nn.11 and 12, 76n.17
Critchlow, Donald, 4
Croly, Herbert, 361, 362
cultural vs. social historians, 7
Culver, Harry, 236
Cunningham, Noble E., Jr., 77n.24

Dallas, Alexander, 36
Darwinism, 156
Dauer, Manning, 22, 43n.5, 45n.37
Dawes, Henry, 183, 184–85, 195–96n.24
Dawes Act, 184
DeBow's Review, 187
decentralization, 9. *See also* antistatism; federal government
deficits, 277, 293
democracy: and bourgeoisie, 147–48, 157, 165–66; and capitalism, 147–48, 157, 165–67; as civic disorder/unrest, 20; and conflict, 351, 371, 393–95; decline in the South, 160, 165, 172n.90; distinctiveness of, 372; and liberalism, 393–95; vs. republicanism, 20; and state building, 277, 279–82
Democracy in America (Tocqueville), 77n.27, 90, 356–57, 371
Democratic Victory Clubs, 237
Democratic Vistas (Whitman), 372–73
Democrats: antiabolitionism of, 179; on the antislavery amendment, 132–33; on Civil War pensions, 181; democracy championed by, 51; early names of party, 75n.7; emergence of, and rise of executive departments, 51, 55, 65, 72; factionalism of, 130, 132; on "family values" politics, 176–77, 181, 182, 187, 189; and labor, 7; on market expansion, 51–52; as a mass party, 51, 65; and the